Evolutionary Psychology

An Introduction

THIRD EDITION

LANCE WORKMAN AND WILL READER

University of South Wales and Sheffield Hallam University

CAMBRIDGE
UNIVERSITY PRESS

CAMBRIDGE
UNIVERSITY PRESS

University Printing House, Cambridge CB2 8BS, United Kingdom

Published in the United States of America by Cambridge University Press, New York

Cambridge University Press is part of the University of Cambridge.

It furthers the University's mission by disseminating knowledge in the pursuit of education, learning and research at the highest international levels of excellence.

www.cambridge.org
Information on this title: www.cambridge.org/9781107622739

First published 2004
Second edition 2008
Third edition 2014

Printed in Spain by Grafos SA, Arte sobre papel

A catalogue record for this publication is available from the British Library

Library of Congress Cataloguing in Publication data
Workman, Lance.
Evolutionary psychology : an introduction / Lance Workman and Will Reader. – Third edition.
    pages   cm
Includes bibliographical references and index.
ISBN 978-1-107-04464-7 (hardback)
1. Evolutionary psychology.   I. Reader, Will.   II. Title.
BF698.95.W67   2014
155.7 – dc23   2013032788

ISBN 978-1-107-04464-7 Hardback
ISBN 978-1-107-62273-9 Paperback

Additional resources for this publication at www.cambridge.org/workman-reader

For Sandie

To Anna and Georgia. Thank you for all the
love you give. I love you both.

Contents

Boxes

Figures

Tables

Preface to the third edition

Evolutionary psychology: past, present and future

If we use the 1992 publication date of *The Adapted Mind* as the birth date of evolutionary psychology then, at the time of writing, it is now 21 years old, traditionally the age at which children become adults and are expected to make their way in the big, wide world. It therefore seems to be an appropriate time to ask whether evolutionary psychology has, as it were, become a respectable member of the scientific community, or whether it is still metaphorically tied to the apron strings of its progenitors at the University of California, Santa Barbara: loved by its parents but ignored or even despised by its peers?

Part of an answer to this question can be seen in some subtle changes to this book compared to previous editions. When we wrote the first edition way back in the late 1990s and early 2000s the Santa Barbara version of evolution psychology was pre-eminent. The manifesto that was enshrined in *The Adapted Mind* proposed domain specific mental modules that evolved in some mythical time and place referred to as the Environment of Evolutionary Adaptedness, or the EEA. We were enthralled by tales of hunter-gatherers in the Upper Pleistocene, of images of minds festooned with tools like Swiss Army knives, and of the principle that minds adapted for ancestral tasks might be less than successful in the twentieth (as it then was) century. This precocious child gained many vocal supporters in the scientific community, philosopher Daniel Dennett and psycholinguist Steven Pinker to name just two prominent members. But there were many critics and many points of criticism. Developmentalist Annette Karmiloff-Smith, for example, questioned the notion of innate mental modules, evolutionary anthropologists such as Eric Alden Smith pointed at problems with the concept of the EEA and David Buller, well, David Buller seemed to dislike all of it. Not to be outdone by his erstwhile colleague, philosopher Jerry Fodor – who started the whole modularity movement in the first place – wrote a book with Massimo Piattelli-Palmarini which attempted to show that the whole concept of evolution by natural selection was philosophically untenable (an argument that was dismantled by two other philosophers, Ned Block and Philip Kitcher, who managed to keep their faces admirably straight throughout).

This third edition sees a subtle change in emphasis. Rather than presenting the Santa Barbara school as the definitive version of evolutionary psychology, we discuss other versions – some more influenced by behavioural ecology – that make no appeal to modularity, domain specificity and the EEA. This should not be seen as us distancing ourselves from the Santa Barbara school, but more our recognising what the core principles of an evolutionary psychology are and pointing out that a version of evolutionary psychology can survive even if the aforementioned assumptions are proved to be incorrect. As the philosopher of science Imre Lakatos might say, these assumptions are part of the protective belt rather than the hard core of evolutionary psychology. These changes appear in many chapters, but particularly chapter 1.

As well as these scientific and philosophical objections there are those who see evolutionary psychology to be politically distasteful, particularly the research on sex differences in mate choice which is seen as merely reinforcing patriarchal stereotypes of men and women. Such a point seems to imply that evolutionary psychology is some kind of political dogma which provides us with rules as to how we should live rather than a field of scientific enquiry. We hope we have addressed this issue in revisions to chapter 1.

Some adopters of our text have requested more primate comparative material in order to help illuminate our understanding of the evolution of human reproductive strategies. In chapter 4 (mate choice) we have greatly expanded our coverage of the social and reproductive behaviour of primates by incorporating new material on gorillas, bonobos and baboons. In particular we feel that the discussion of female coalitional behaviour adds balance to the male-centred common chimpanzee material presented in earlier editions.

Chapter 6 on social development includes more recent research on the fascinating notion that children base their future reproductive strategy on the environment in which they develop, a hypothesis that gives the lie to those who think that evolutionary psychology is nothing more than a blind and mechanical unfurling of a rigid developmental manifesto. Evolution has not only made us sensitive to environmental conditions, but it may also have given us a plan to help us deal with it.

If proof were needed that the Santa Barbara school is alive and kicking chapter 9 on cognition presents research that our memories might be sensitive to something called s-value, or survival value. Items that are presented under a context relevant to conditions in the EEA seem to be more memorable than those presented in a non-EEA relevant context, even when the latter context is more familiar to participants than the former. The fact that these results have been replicated by a team led by long-standing memory researcher Henry Roediger III, who has no evolutionary axe to grind, make these somewhat startling results all the more compelling. Later in the chapter research by Tooby and Cosmides on deontic problem solving reinvigorates the notion of cheater detection as a means for understanding why some problems are difficult and others easy. A proposition that had previously been given something of a pummelling by some of the big names in logical reasoning research.

The 'social chapters' (7 and 8) both have new material that reflects current areas of debate. Chapter 7 now considers the 'Cinderella Effect' (the notion that parents invest more in 'biological' than in 'non-biological' offspring), while chapter 8 has added a new pre-industrial culture – the Aché to add balance to debates concerning how levels of reciprocation vary between different human societies. The changes to chapter 9 on language are rather more modest. Here we include more on the apparent ability of prairie dogs to generate novel, mutually comprehensible 'words' for things they have never encountered before, a re-evaluation of Chomsky and more on FOXP2 and Specific Language Impairment. We have included some new material on the evolution of schizophrenia in chapter 12 alongside a recent evolutionary based explanation for the eating disorder anorexia nervosa. We anticipate that these explanations will appeal and disturb in equal measure.

Chapter 13 contains new material on the hunt for 'candidate genes' that are considered to play a role in individual differences. We are less positive about the findings here than we were in previous editions, since these proposed single gene effects have not stood up well to scrutiny or where they appear to do so the amount of variation they account for between people appears to be really quite small. Finally chapter 14 on culture re-evaluates the status of memes in cultural transmission and has a new section on the importance of cultural specialisation to our rapid cultural development. In many ways it is the topic of culture which sees evolutionary psychology at its most inter-disciplinary, with contributions from historians, anthropologists, economists, biologists and philosophers as well as psychologists, and at its most ambitious: the attempt is to use evolution to partially explain how we got where we are now as twenty-first century hominins, the ape that tweeted, we might say.

So where are we now? The above should make it clear that to us evolutionary psychology is not an only child. The offspring of Santa Barbara is still doing well and if it is not universally loved, well that is a result of its reluctance to adhere to the status quo. But its siblings (or half-siblings) that are perhaps not so strident in their pronouncements, not so fundamentalist in their commitment to particular assumptions such as modularity or the EEA, are finding a voice too.

Who should read this book?

We have designed this book for those with a background in psychology. Unlike many books on the same topic we do not require readers to have prior knowledge of the intricacies of natural selection, genetics or inclusive fitness theory. We have also tried to relate evolutionary theory, where relevant, to some of the classic studies and theories familiar to readers with a psychological background – the 'Robber's Cave' study, Piaget's developmental theory, Bartlett's research on memory to name but three. We have also, where possible, organised the chapters in this way: developmental psychology, social psychology, individual differences, cognitive psychology and so on.

This said, we also explain the traditional psychological concepts too, so the book will be accessible to anybody with an interest in evolutionary psychology whatever their background.

Pedagogical features

We hope that the book's greatest pedagogical feature is the book itself. We have tried to explain the relevant concepts and research as clearly as we can. We also hope that we have tried to convey our enthusiasm for evolutionary psychology tempered with a critical eye when we think things don't quite add up. In addition to this we have included extra **critical thinking** questions at the end of each chapter which can be used – for example – for seminar discussion points. Perhaps the biggest change from previous editions is that we have written 240 **multiple-choice questions** (twenty per chapter) for either formative or summative assessment.

Acknowledgements

Finally, once again we would like to take this opportunity to thank all of the instructors and students who have made use of the first and second editions of our book and in particular to those who have provided useful feedback. In particular we would like to thank Richard Andrew, Gordon Bear, Jannes Eshuis and Fred Toates. At Cambridge University Press we would especially like to thank Valerie Appleby, Martin Barr, Joanna Breeze, Charles Howell, Hetty Marx and Carrie Parkinson.

1 Introduction to evolutionary psychology

KEY CONCEPTS

the Environment of Evolutionary Adaptedness (EEA) • proximate and ultimate levels of explanation • the inheritance of acquired characteristics • particulate inheritance • eugenics • the Great Chain of Being (*scala naturae*) • sociobiology • modularity

Evolutionary psychology is a relatively new discipline that applies the principles of Darwinian natural selection to the study of the human mind. The principal assumption of evolutionary psychology is that the human mind should be considered to be an organ that was designed by natural selection to guide the individual in making decisions that aid survival and reproduction. This may be done though by species-specific 'instincts' that enabled our ancestors to survive and reproduce and which give rise to a universal human nature. But equally the mind is an organ which is designed to learn, so – contrary to what many people think – evolutionary psychology does not suggest that everything is innate. In this chapter we trace the origins of evolutionary psychology, and present some of the arguments between those who hold that the mind is a blank slate and those who believe that human behaviour, like that of other animals, is the product of a long history of evolution.

The origins of evolutionary psychology

The fundamental assumption of evolutionary psychology is that the human mind is the product of evolution just like any other bodily organ, and that we gain a better understanding of the mind by examining evolutionary pressures that shaped it. Why should this be the case? What can an understanding of evolution bring to psychology? After all, scientists were able to learn a great deal about bodily organs such as the heart and the hand long before Darwin formulated the theory of natural selection. Unfortunately, not all body parts are as easy to understand as heart and hand. A classic example is the peacock's tail. This huge structure encumbers the animal to the extent that it makes it difficult to escape from predators and requires a considerable amount of energy to sustain it – energy that might otherwise be used for reproduction. Darwin was similarly troubled by this and in a letter to his colleague Asa Gray remarked that 'The sight of a feather in a peacock's tail, whenever I gaze at it, makes me sick' (Darwin, 1859). Or to take another even more perverse example, the male Australian redback widow spider (*Latrodectus hasseltii*) who sacrifices himself to the female following copulation: why would you design an animal to do *that*? These types of questions are known as **ultimate** questions as they ask why a particular behaviour exists at all. These are usually contrasted with **proximate** questions which ask about, for example, how a particular behaviour develops, what are its neural or cognitive underpinnings or whether it is acquired or innate.

The answers to these questions highlights a deep-rooted problem in the foundations of traditional psychological thinking. To the extent that psychologists ever consider why we perform particular behaviours – and this, admittedly doesn't happen very often – they usually concern themselves with the benefit to the individual who performs the behaviour. But current Darwinian theory turns this thinking on its head. We are not necessarily the beneficiaries of our own behaviour: the beneficiaries of behaviour are, in many cases, our genes.

It is worth pausing for a second to reflect upon this point and considering its implications. The peacock dragging his tail behind him might well prefer – should he be able to consider such things – to be rid of it. The male redback widow spider might choose, on reflection, to forgo indulging the cannibalistic urges of his erstwhile squeeze. But placing the individual at the centre of the action in this way doesn't always give us the complete picture. Modern evolutionary theory sees the individual as merely an ephemeral and transient bit-player in the theatre of existence, acting out a script that was not of his or her writing, a script written in the language of the genes. Richard Dawkins probably best summarised this when he made the famous replicator–vehicle distinction (see chapter 2). 'We are survival machines – robot vehicles blindly programmed to preserve the selfish molecules known as genes' (Dawkins 1976, p. xxi). If you think about it this has to be the case. Life originated from replicating chemicals – precursors of DNA – and only after many millions of years did these chemicals start to build structures around them to form the precursors of cells: unicellular organisms became multicellular, tissue became organs until we eventually ended up with animals with brains and behaviour. So bodies and brains clearly benefited DNA otherwise they wouldn't have been produced; they would have been outcompeted by the brainless and the bodiless. So our genes aren't for our benefit, we are for their benefit. Dawkins goes on to say '[t]his is a truth which still fills me with astonishment'. If you aren't astonished, you haven't understood it, but don't worry, we discuss this further and in greater depth in chapter 2.

It is worth adding a caveat to all of this: the above only applies to evolved behaviour (or organs); any behaviour which has not evolved, such as a purely learned behaviour, may not benefit genes at all. Deciding exactly which behaviours are evolved and which are not (and which are a bit of both) is a difficult task and one to which we return many times throughout the subsequent chapters.

In terms of psychology, we have only scratched the surface in trying to apply evolutionary thinking to understanding behaviour. Many of the ideas expressed in this book will doubtless be proved wrong in the fullness of time, but if we are to properly understand humanity in all its shapes and sizes, loves and hates in sanity and madness, then we need an understanding of basic evolutionary principles and, in particular, the gene-centred view of life.

It is said that science has presented humans with three hammer blows to its sense of self-importance. Copernicus taught us that the Earth was not at the centre of the universe; Freud showed us that our instincts are emotional and sexual rather than rational and godly; and Darwin demonstrated that we were descended not from angels but from apes. To this we might add the gene-centred view of life which shows that in many cases we are not the final beneficiaries of our own behaviour; the buck stops not with us but our genes.

A history of evolutionary thinking

Evolution before Darwin

For millennia humans have been fascinated by the natural world, not just the complexities of the organisms that constitute it, but the interdependencies that exist between different species. Flowers provide food for insects that are eaten by birds that are consumed by small mammals that are preyed upon by larger animals that eventually die and provide food for the plants that produce flowers and so the cycle continues. Surely such a complex system could not have arisen by accident? Surely this must have somehow been designed, created by some all-powerful being? The idea that nature in all its complexity was created all at once held sway for a long time, not just as religious doctrine but as a true account of the origin of Everything. It still does hold sway in the minds of many today. Debates about the scientific status of creationism and intelligent design have recently approached boiling point and, in the United States, entered the courtroom. In December 2005 Judge John Jones ruled that intelligent design was not science and therefore it is not permissible to teach it as science in the classroom. More recently the so-called 'new atheist' movement, headed by Daniel Dennett, Richard Dawkins, Sam Harris and the late Christopher Hitchens (sometimes referred to as the Four Horsemen) have written provocative and, in some cases, inflammatory anti-religious texts. However, the purpose of bringing up religion in this chapter is not to ultimately bury it, but to show how many religions were grappling with the same problems as many scientists: to understand where life came from, and what it means.

Not every ancient belief system proposed steady states and immutability. The Ancient Greek philosopher Thales (c.624–545 BC) tried to explain the origins of life in terms of natural as opposed to supernatural terms. He also proposed that life 'evolved' out of simpler elements with the most basic element – from which all else ultimately derived – being water. Later another Ancient Greek, Empedocles (495–435 BC), suggested that in the beginning the world was full of bodily organs which occasionally came together and joined up, driven by the impelling force of Love. The results of most of these unions were 'monstrosities' and died out, but a minority were successful and went on to reproduce, producing copies of themselves. Although we can clearly recognise this as being fanciful in that we now see love as a human emotion rather than as an impelling force of nature, Empedocles' mechanism has conspicuous similarities to natural selection (see chapter 2). In particular, the idea that change occurs over time by a gradual winnowing of less successful forms. Aristotle (384–322 BC) seemingly killed off evolutionary thinking for some time by proposing that each species occupied a particular space in a hierarchical structure known as the *Great Chain of Being* or *scala naturae*. In this scheme, which was later adopted by the Christian religion, God occupied the topmost rung of the ladder followed by angels, then the nobility (males *then* females), then ordinary men, ordinary women, animals, plants and finally inanimate objects. Moving from one rung to another was not permitted which meant that there was a natural order of things. Aristotle's view was not merely descriptive (describing the way the world is) but was also *prescriptive* (this was deemed to be the way the world *should* be) so any change to the established hierarchy would lead to chaos until the order was re-established. By fixing the hierarchy in this way Aristotle's view effectively closed down debate about evolutionary change, not only would such an approach be considered theoretically incoherent, it was also considered morally wrong to question the way things should be.

Much more recently in 1798 the German philosopher Immanuel Kant wrote in his work *Anthropology* that:

[A]n orang-utan or a chimpanzee may develop the organs which serve for walking, grasping objects, and speaking – in short, that he may evolve the structure of man, with an organ for the use of reason... (Kant, 1798)

In direct contradiction of Aristotle, Kant imagines how one organism can change over time, perhaps acquiring the characteristics of other organisms. Notice also that Kant does not merely refer to physical change: 'an organ for the use of reason' is a psychological faculty. In this way Kant presaged evolutionary psychology by two centuries.

Figure 1.1 Erasmus Darwin

Darwin's own grandfather, Erasmus Darwin (1731–1802), wrote that all living things could have emerged from a common ancestor (what he called 'one living filament'). He also suggested that competition might be the driving force behind evolution. He saw this competition occurring between different species and within a species between members of the same sex (presaging the theory of sexual selection proposed in 1871 by his grandson). In *The Laws of Organic Life*, he states:

The final course of this contest among males seems to be, that the strongest and most active animal should propagate the species which should thus be improved. (Darwin, cited in King-Hele, 1968, p. 5)

Although we can see close similarities between these ideas and Darwin junior's theory of evolution, Erasmus failed to produce a plausible mechanism for evolutionary change.

A contemporary of Erasmus Darwin, Jean-Baptiste Lamarck (1744–1829), proposed just such a mechanism to account for change. Lamarck's first law suggested that changes in the environment could lead to changes in an animal's behaviour which, in turn, might lead to an organ being used more or less. The second law was that such changes are heritable. Taken together these laws prescribe an organism's continuous gradual change as the result of the interaction between the organism's needs and the environment. Most evolutionary biologists agree that **the inheritance of acquired characteristics,** as Lamarck's theory has since been called, is incorrect. Although the environment can indeed affect bodily organs, for example increased exercise can increase the capacity of the heart and lungs, such changes cannot be passed on to the organism's offspring. Although Lamarck's theory has fallen from favour, Charles Darwin did cite Lamarck as a great influence in the development of his theory of evolution: natural selection.

Darwin and natural selection

Natural selection depends on two components: **heritable variation** (individuals within a population tend to differ from each other in ways that are passed on to their offspring) and **differential reproductive success** (as a result of these differences some individuals leave more surviving offspring than others). You can see this process laid bare in asexual species where an individual reproduces simply by producing an identical copy of itself. In such cases, the overwhelming majority of offspring will be identical to the parent, but a few will be different in some way due to errors in the copying process. Should these different offspring survive and reproduce, then the majority of *their* offspring will be identical to them and the process repeats itself. However, copying errors seldom have positive consequences. To see this, imagine that you make an error copying down a recipe: there is a good chance that this error will make no noticeable difference to the end product (for instance you might add two grinds of pepper rather than one). On the other hand, it may make the end product substantially worse (adding a tablespoon rather than a teaspoon of salt); only very rarely will an error actually improve the recipe. Similarly, in the natural world, copying errors would probably have no effect or would lead to the individual failing to pass on its genes. On very rare occasions, however, an error might produce an organism that is actually better fitted to the environment than its parents or it might be able to exploit some property of the environment that its ancestors could not. In such cases, barring unfortunate random accidents, this individual will tend to produce more offspring and the 'error' will soon become the norm. In some cases the new lineage might outcompete the old, and come to replace it. In other cases, particularly if the two variants become geographically separated, both versions might coexist and ultimately form two different species.

As we shall see in chapter 3, the state of affairs is somewhat more complicated for organisms that reproduce sexually. For asexual species, variation only comes from copying errors (or mutations). Sexually reproducing species combine the genes of two individuals during reproduction, meaning that offspring will always be different from either parent. The increased variation produced by sexual reproduction is thought to be one of the reasons why sex evolved in the first place.

Mendel and the birth of genetics

Darwin knew nothing about genetics, and for good reason: at the time of Darwin's death, no one on earth knew about genetics except the Austrian monk Gregor Mendel.

Figure 1.2 Gregor Mendel

Between 1858 and 1875 Mendel conducted a series of breeding experiments on hybrid pea plants in the garden of his monastery in Brunn.

One of Mendel's greatest insights was that inheritance was **particulate**. Darwin presumed that the traits of an individual were some sort of blend of the traits of the mother and father, as might happen when mixing paint. Some observations seem to support this belief. In many species, the result of a mating between a comparatively large female and a small male will tend to produce offspring whose size is somewhere in between the two: a fact that animal breeders had known for some time. Mendel demonstrated that the blend model is incorrect. He found that if two pea plants were crossed, one having white flowers and one having red flowers, the offspring would be either red or white, never pink, as might be expected if the two traits blended. The reason why some traits, such as height or skin colour, seem to blend is because they are controlled by a number of genes, for traits controlled by single genes, inheritance is always particulate.

In truth, it probably didn't need Mendel's data to highlight the inadequacies of the blend model. Any child who has mixed the colours in a paint set will soon realise that after a few mixes you always end up with the same dirty brown colour. Likewise if sex merely blended traits, after a sufficiently large number of generations everyone would end up being the same, reducing variation. Since natural selection depends on variation to work, evolution would soon grind to a halt. Darwin was certainly aware of the shortcomings of the blend model (Dawkins, 2003), but did not produce a better theory to replace it, although he did come close; in a letter to his friend Alfred Wallace (and co-discoverer of the theory of natural selection) in 1866 he wrote that:

I crossed the Painted Lady and Purple sweetpeas, which are very differently coloured varieties, and got, even out of the same pod, both varieties perfect but none intermediate [...] [T]ho' these cases are in appearance so wonderful, I do not know that they are really more so than every female in the world producing distinct male and female offspring.

Unfortunately Darwin never made the next step that would have enabled him to understand the true mechanism of inheritance, nor, it seems, was he aware of Mendel's work. There were rumours that Darwin possessed a copy of the journal containing Mendel's article 'Versuche über Pflanzenhybriden' ('Experiments in plant hybridisation') but no copy was found in Darwin's extensive library now housed at Cambridge University. Generally, the scientific community was rather slow to realise the significance of Mendel's ideas and biology had to wait until the twentieth century before Mendel's work was rediscovered. The subsequent fusion of genetics and evolutionary theory led to what in biology has become known as 'the modern synthesis' (see chapter 2).

From evolution to evolutionary psychology

Although most of Darwin's examples in *The Origin of Species* concerned physical traits, he also believed that natural selection had a role to play in the evolution of behaviour. Darwin appeared to see the human mind as being explainable by the same fundamental physical laws as other bodily organs, in terms of mechanistic principles. In one of his early notebooks, written in 1838, he speculated that:

Experience shows the problem of the mind cannot be solved by attacking the citadel itself – the mind is function of body – we must bring some *stable* foundation to argue from.

That stable foundation was **materialism**, the approach adopted by modern cognitive psychology that sees the mind as being ultimately reducible to the activity of the brain, or as Steven Pinker puts it, 'the mind is the information processing activity of the brain' (Pinker, 1997). This materialism is important to evolutionary psychology because if the mind is just the activity of the brain, then the brain, being a physical organ, is subject to the pressures of natural selection. Therefore the mind and hence behaviour is also, at some level, the product of evolution by natural selection (see chapter 9).

Darwin did make some forays into psychology. In *The Expression of the Emotions in Man and Animals* (1872; see chapter 11 in this book), Darwin theorises on the evolutionary origins of emotions and their expressions. In 1877 Darwin wrote *A Biographical Sketch of an Infant* based on his observations of his infant son. This last work, however, is largely descriptive and although it speculates on the instinctual basis of early crying and sucking behaviours, it makes no mention of the role of evolution and natural selection in shaping such behaviours.

Early attempts at an evolutionary psychology

Francis Galton

Figure 1.3 Sir Francis Galton

Darwin's cousin (also a grandson of Erasmus Darwin) Francis Galton (1822–1911) (see figure 1.3) was much influenced by the theory of natural selection:

The publication in 1859 of the *Origin of Species* by Charles Darwin made a marked epoch in my own mental development, as it did in that of human thought generally. Its effect was to demolish a multitude of dogmatic barriers by a single stroke, and to arouse a spirit of rebellion against all ancient authorities whose positive and unauthenticated statements were contradicted by modern science. (Galton, 1908, p. 287)

Galton was a very important figure in the history of psychology; he proposed that character and intelligence were inherited traits and developed some of the first intelligence tests to explore these issues. He was, in many respects, the father of what is now known as psychometrics. He also anticipated the method of experimental psychology by emphasising the need to use quantitative data from large samples of individuals. Galton also proposed that traits that may have been useful in ancestral times might be less useful in contemporary (in this case, Victorian) society. For instance, he suggested that during ancestral times evolution had favoured humans who were group-minded or gregarious. Humans live in groups, he reasoned, so those who thrived under such circumstances would leave more surviving offspring than their less gregarious counterparts. However, in Galton's time, when greater emphasis was placed upon self-reliance and personal industry, gregariousness might be a less desirable trait (see chapter 13).

The argument that traits that were important in hunter-gatherer communities might be suboptimal in contemporary society is a familiar one in modern evolutionary psychology. Such an observation is comparatively uncontroversial and should be judged as a scientific theory that stands or fails on the basis of the evidence. More controversial was Galton's attempt to apply his scientific findings to help the greater good of society. He suggested that one way that society might be improved would be to engage in a little selective breeding. He suggested that those individuals whose traits might benefit society (the innovators, the highly intelligent, etc.) be encouraged to produce many offspring, and those whose traits are seen as less desirable (the less intelligent, the indolent, etc.) be discouraged from reproducing, a controversial programme that he called **eugenics** (see box 1.1).

William James and the concept of instinct

William James (1842–1910) is one of the most influential psychologists of all time. He made the distinction between short- and long-term memory used to this day by modern cognitive psychologists, studied attention and perception, had a keen interest in the nature of consciousness and was also very much interested in applying Darwin's ideas to human psychology. In particular he outlined instincts such as fear, love and curiosity as driving forces of human behaviour and proposed that:

Box 1.1 Eugenics

The word 'eugenics' coined by Francis Galton comes from the Greek word *eugenes* meaning 'well born'. The idea was also Greek. In *The Republic* Plato proposed that although friendships between the sexes should be permitted, procreation should be controlled by the government with the aim of breeding a better society. In a sense, all sexual beings participate in a form of eugenics, albeit unconsciously. There is evidence to suggest (see chapters 3 and 4) that when an animal (including a human animal) selects a sexual partner it does so, among other things, on the basis of characteristics that are indicative of good genes. Good looks, it appears, are not arbitrary. But eugenics is rather more than that; it was developed as a method of trying to dictate who breeds with whom and, in extreme cases, who doesn't breed at all.

There are two forms of eugenics, often called positive and negative. Positive eugenics operates by encouraging people with high fitness to mate together and produce many offspring. The word 'fitness' here is used in a quasi-Darwinian sense, and can be treated as meaning 'possessing characteristics which are thought to be good for society'. This is probably the most benign form of eugenics although it has to be said that even this form of eugenics is anathema to most people. Negative eugenics, on the other hand, attempts to curtail or prohibit reproduction among those who are considered unfit. When Galton founded the Eugenics Education Society in 1907 (later the Eugenics Society and finally the Galton Society in 1989) the goal was to improve the human species by positive means:

> If a twentieth part of the cost and pains were spent in measures for the improvement of the human race that is spent on the improvement of the breed of horses and cattle, what a galaxy of genius might we not create! We might introduce prophets and high priests of civilization into the world, as surely as we can propagate idiots by mating *cretins*. Men and women of the present day are, to those we might hope to bring into existence, what the pariah dogs of the streets of an Eastern town are to our own highly bred varieties. (1864, pp. 165–6)

Charles Darwin's son Major Leonard Darwin took over the eugenics society from Galton and instigated the transition from positive to negative eugenics. He proposed that a policy of segregation should be implemented whereby the fit were separated from the unfit. 'Compulsion is now permitted if applying to criminals, lunatics, and mental defectives; and this principle must be extended to all who, by having offspring, would seriously damage future generations' (L. Darwin, 1925).

In the early part of the twentieth century, hundreds of thousands of people were sterilised worldwide on the grounds that they were deemed psychologically unfit. In the United States alone it was reported that by 1960 almost 60,000 individuals had undergone involuntary sterilisation (Reilly, 1991). Undoubtedly the largest and most systematic programme of eugenics occurred in Nazi Germany. Beginning with segregation and sterilisation and finishing with the systematic slaughter of millions, Hitler tried to ensure that the genes of the 'unfit', mainly Jews but many others as well, would not make it to the next generation.

Curious to think in these post-holocaust days that eugenics was once considered to be a respectable enterprise. Members of eugenics societies included the eminent economist John Maynard Keynes; John Harvey Kellogg of Kellogg's corn flakes fame; Lord William Henry Beveridge, producer of the Beveridge report on social insurance in the United Kingdom; psychologists Cyril Burt, Hans Eysenck and Charles Spearman; the sexologist H. Havelock-Ellis; and geneticist Ronald Fisher.

Undoubtedly, many eugenicists probably felt that they had humanity's best interests at heart. However, today most would probably feel that even positive eugenics with its attempt to coerce or interfere with an individual's freedom of choice of sexual partner is an infringement of civil liberties and therefore abhorrent. Eugenics societies are still with us today, but technology has presented us with different if related issues. Currently there is controversy about the role of genetic engineering in determining human traits. It is already possible to screen foetuses for genetic disorders, and soon it will be possible to replace 'defective' genes to produce a healthy infant. Such gene therapy, as it has been called, has been heralded as being of potential benefit for humanity, but some worry that genes might be replaced that are not medically deficient, merely undesirable. If it were possible to detect genes that influence criminality, or antisocial personality, would it be ethical to change such genes for the common good? Would it be morally right to genetically manipulate genes for intelligence, or good looks?

The eugenics controversy has cast a shadow over the use of Darwinian theory in explaining human behaviour (see box 1.3); it has been all too easy for all evolutionary theories to be dismissed as inherently racist, supremacist or otherwise politically incorrect. This is unfortunate. Darwinian thinking could well prove to be the framework that unites the social sciences (Wilson, 1998) in the same way that it unified the disparate areas of biology in the early part of the last century (see chapter 2). We must not reject it simply on the grounds that some people have used it for nefarious means, any more than we should reject sub-atomic physics for its role in the production of nuclear weaponry. The fact that we do not like the implications of a particular theory does not affect its truth. On the other hand, it would be a mistake to think that science exists in a vacuum, and it is incumbent on all of us – including scientists, perhaps *especially* scientists – to guard against those who might wish to use the results of science for their own political ends.

Nothing is commoner than the remark that man differs from the lower creatures by the almost total lack of instincts and the assumption of their work by reason. (James, 1890, p. 389)

He went on to add that human behaviour might be characterised by more instincts than other animals rather than fewer, an idea that has been embraced by modern evolutionary psychologists such as John Tooby and Leda Cosmides. James's argument relating to instincts was so influential that in 1921 psychologist Ellsworth Faris, a critic of the instinct approach, was able to comment that:

So well did he [James] argue for the existence of instincts in man that we may now say: Nothing is commoner than the belief that we are endowed with instincts inherited from the lower creatures. Whole systems of psychology have been founded on this assumption. (1921, p. 184)

Many students of psychology know of William James's work on memory, attention, consciousness and learning, but his views on instincts are less widely known. In fact, the concept of instinct was dropped from social scientists' terminology in the twentieth century partly because it was considered too imprecise a term to be scientifically meaningful (see Bateson, 2000). Furthermore, many so-called instinctive behaviours are capable of being modified by experience, in which case it is difficult to see where an instinct finishes and learning begins. A final reason why the concept of instinct fell out of favour is that a new approach to the social sciences denied their existence and saw culture rather than biology as being the principal determiner of human behaviour. This is what we turn to next.

The rise of culture as a causal force in human behaviour

Two of the instigators of the recent emergence of evolutionary thinking in psychology, John Tooby and Leda Cosmides, have called the traditional non-evolutionary social science approach the Standard Social Science Model (SSSM). The SSSM makes the following assumptions about human behaviour and culture.

- Humans are born as blank slates: knowledge, personality traits and cultural values are acquired from the cultural environment.
- Human behaviour is infinitely malleable: there are no biological constraints as to how people turn out.
- Culture is an autonomous force and exists independently of people.
- Human behaviour is determined by a process of learning, socialisation or indoctrination.
- Learning processes are general in that they can be applied to a variety of phenomena. The same processes underlie mate selection, for example, as underlie food selection.

Many of these ideas can be seen in the work of anthropologists such as Margaret Mead, sociologists such as Emile Durkheim and psychologists such as Albert Bandura. The establishment of the SSSM can be seen, at least in part, as a reaction to some of the more extreme claims of the biological determinists of the late nineteenth and early twentieth century (see box 1.1). Many took Darwin's theories and used them to demonstrate that certain races were less highly evolved than others. When experiments were performed to test these ideas they usually took the form of presenting individuals from such cultures with Western-style intelligence tests. On finding that the respondents tended to fail such tests spectacularly, it was adduced that this was evidence that they occupied a lower rung on the evolutionary ladder than did the people of the West. Of course, these studies were fundamentally flawed in that the tests were culturally specific, requiring individuals to spot missing components from gramophones and tennis courts (see Gould, 1981). Such ideas were common in *The History of Creation*, in which the great biologist and naturalist Ernst Haeckel stated that

The difference in rationality between a Goethe, a Kant, a Lamarck, a Darwin and that of the lower natural men – a Veda, a Kaffer, an Australian and a Papuan is much greater than the graduated difference between the rationality of these latter and that of the intelligent vertebrates, for instance, the higher apes. (1969)

Eugenicists and their kind used the results of such research to recommend all manner of atrocities such as forced sterilisation based on the premise that other races and cultures were not so 'highly evolved' and therefore wouldn't feel, for example, pain in the same way that the 'more evolved' Western people would.

This is a misunderstanding of Darwin's ideas. In fact, the notion that some organisms are 'more evolved' than others and therefore more important in some moral way dates back to Aristotle and the Great Chain of Being (see above). As we shall see in more detail in later chapters, Darwinian thinking explicitly denies such a notion. Humans are not descended from chimpanzees as is commonly thought; rather, chimpanzees and humans are both descended from a common ancestor. It is all too easy to believe that a chimpanzee is simply a more primitive version of a human, stripped of the bells and whistles that constitute humanity. On the contrary, chimpanzees by virtue of the nature of their evolutionary trajectory have their own particular adaptations (including, no doubt, psychological adaptations) that we do not. As an analogy, the railway train and the automobile share a common ancestor – the horse-drawn cart – but it makes no sense to assume that a car is a more sophisticated railway train (or vice versa) since each has its own specific adaptations to suit the purpose for which it was designed.

Cultural relativity

The founder of what was to become cultural relativism was the anthropologist Franz Boas (see chapter 14). Boas argued that many differences between people were due

Figure 1.4 Chimpanzees have specialised adaptations of their own

to differences in their culture and if one wished to understand people one must necessarily understand their culture. This represented a step change in the social sciences that is still of great importance today. No longer do we assume that, for instance, working-class people speak differently from middle- and upper-class people because they are biologically inferior; we know now that it is an effect of culture.

From these honourable beginnings cultural relativism dominated thinking to the extent that many social scientists developed an almost pathological fear of biological explanations of human behaviour, a disposition that sociologist Lee Ellis (1996) termed **biophobia**. There are various reasons for this. One is that once a scientific paradigm is established it is difficult for researchers to consider alternative explanations that lie outside the paradigm as they are seen as old ways of thinking. Another is that the eugenic atrocities of the Second World War made people fearful of censure; advancing explanations based on human nature was seen as advocating genetic determinism and eugenics, as the **sociobiology** movement soon discovered (see next section and box 1.3).

Despite the misgivings of the social scientists, outside psychology Darwinian thinking was alive and well in disciplines such as ethology (Tinbergen, 1951) and behavioural ecology (Krebs and Davies, 1978) (see box 1.2), but the orthodoxy within psychology was still cultural relativism. Even psychologists who studied animal behaviour – where Darwinism can be least controversially applied – tended to ignore species-specific behaviour. Learning theorists such as Pavlov, Watson and Skinner were concerned with studying the general mechanisms of learning, using the principles of classical and operant conditioning. This framework viewed human beings as just more complex versions of rats, pigeons and sea slugs and proposed that if we could understand these simpler organisms, then we could scale up the findings to understand humans. Interestingly, two researchers engaged in this enterprise, Keller and Marian Breland, found that animals' instinctive behaviour kept getting in the way of the supposedly species-general processes of association and reinforcement. Using Skinnerian methods they were engaged in training animals for the advertising industry teaching different animals to put dollars in piggy banks, for example. What they found was that despite their best efforts the animals kept reverting to instinctive behaviours instead of depositing them in the container as required: pigs attempted to root the dollars with their snouts (a natural pig behaviour) whereas raccoons would rub the coins together (an instinctive food-washing behaviour). Breland and Breland (1961) open their paper by stating that:

There seems to be a continuing realization by psychologists that perhaps the white rat cannot reveal everything there is to know about behavior. (p. 1)

It would be incorrect to attribute the failure of psychology to embrace Darwin as resulting solely as a result of the political correctness of the dominant cultural relativist school. Psychologists have tended to focus on proximate questions such as 'how do people form impressions of other people?', or 'how does memory work?' or 'what risk factors are important in the development of eating disorders?' rather than the ultimate questions for which a Darwinian framework is best suited. Given the types of questions that concerned psychologists cultural relativism – or what Tooby and Cosmides refer to as SSSM – provided a perfectly workable framework; there was

Box 1.2 The application of evolutionary thinking in four disciplines

Putting things in boxes can be as dangerous as it is useful. Below we have tried to describe each of the four main disciplines that apply evolutionary thinking to behaviour. The danger is that although there are differences in approach, subject matter and method there is a great deal of overlap too. The descriptions below should therefore be seen as a rough guide rather than the final word on the matter.

Ethology

Description

The term ethology is derived from the Greek ethos meaning character or habit. Although many people see ethology as the invention of Lorenz, Tinbergen and von Frisch, during the 1930s, the term has been around for at least 300 years. What Lorenz, Tinbergen and von Frisch did was to take a largely descriptive discipline and add academic rigour to it via systematic observation and recording of behaviour followed by analysis.

Approach

Observation of animal behaviour in its natural setting, i.e. observe the behaviour in the environment in which it evolved. Ethologists attempt to combine evolutionary/ functional explanations with causal explanations. Early 'classical' ethologists were more interested in instinct as opposed to learning and were highly influenced by Darwin. Late twentieth-century ethologists emphasised the interaction between genes and environment.

Key figures

Charles Whitman, Oskar Heinroth, Wallace Craig, Karl von Frisch, Konrad Lorenz, Niko Tinbergen, David Lack, Robert Hinde, Irenäus Eibl Eibsfeld.

Behavioural ecology

Description

Behavioural ecology grew out of classical ethology. It differs from ethology in that it frequently uses economic cost–benefit modelling to predict how animals should behave in a given environment. These models are then used to derive predictions and compared against actual animal behaviour.
While sociobiologists and evolutionary psychologists tend to emphasise genetic constraints, behavioural ecologists emphasise the flexibility that genes provide. In this way ecological pressures select behavioural responses.

Approach

It combines principles from ecology with an ethological approach to behaviour. Examines the abilities of animals to make 'economic decisions' concerning, for example, foraging, fighting or mate-seeking behaviour. Hence is concerned with optimising inclusive fitness. In the case of human behavioural ecology the discipline draws on anthropology to examine how cultures vary (e.g. marriage patterns) due to ecological pressures.

Key figures

George Williams, John Maynard Smith, John Krebs, Irven DeVore, Donald Symons, Richard Alexander, Nicholas Davies, Richard Dawkins, Robin Dunbar.

Sociobiology

Description

The term sociobiology had been around for at least twenty years before E. O. Wilson defined it more rigorously in his book *Sociobiology: The New Synthesis* as 'the systematic study of the biological basis of all social behaviour'. Grew out of developments in ethology during the 1960s and 1970s. Very much overlaps with behavioural ecology – in fact most of the names listed under sociobiology could also appear under behavioural ecology and vice versa.

Approach

Deals with the evolution of social behaviour and uses functional explanations of pro- and antisocial behaviour. The term functional is used here to mean how current behavioural responses occur because of the usefulness they had to an individual's ancestors. Considers human social organisation developed through natural selection. Most sociobiologists are interested in non-human species – but applying the concepts from this area to explain human behaviour led to heated debate during the latter years of the twentieth century.

Key figures

Edward O. Wilson, William Hamilton, Robert Trivers, Randy Thornhill, Margo Wilson, Martin Daly, David Buss.

Evolutionary psychology (Santa Barbara school)

Description

The birth of evolutionary psychology was marked by the publication of *The Adapted Mind*. It generally takes the principles of sociobiology and combines them with a cognitive mechanistic view of the mind, modularity. Most evolutionary psychologists research human behaviour. Those researching the behaviour of non-human animals are most likely to describe themselves using one of the terms above.

Approach

Usually uses experimental studies or the use of naturalistic data (e.g. survey data) to test predictions drawn from evolutionary theory. Some evolutionary psychologists will use techniques such as optimality modelling from behavioural ecology. Focus of explanation is frequently concerned with psychological mechanisms, unlike the three other disciplines mentioned.

Key figures

John Tooby, Leda Cosmides, David Buss, Robert Kurzban, Steven Pinker, Jerome Barkow.

no perceived need for a Darwinian psychology. Unlike biologists who study animal behaviour (next section), for whom Darwin is indispensable, psychologists could get on fine without him.

Sigmund Freud

Freud is an interesting case in the history of psychology. To many he is the embodiment of cultural relativism, with the great emphasis he placed on the role of the parents and family in the shaping of an individual's personality. However, Freud deserves mention for two reasons. First, unlike many subsequent psychologists Freud was interested in ultimate questions; he was preoccupied by finding out *why* people behaved as they did, not simply *how*. Second, although many of these accounts were distinctly non-Darwinian (e.g. the Oedipus complex in which a male child desires to kill his father), some of his ideas are much more in line with recent Darwinian psychology. For example, Freud's notion of the id as a set of inborn desires including the sexual imperative is one that has many parallels with evolutionary theory, and his view that our conscious selves might be completely unaware of our 'real' motives is one that is echoed in Robert Trivers's theory of self-deception. Freud wrote that:

The individual himself regards sexuality as one of his own ends; whereas from another point of view he is an appendage to his germ-plasm, at whose disposal he puts his energies in return for the bonus of pleasure. He is the mortal vehicle of a (possibly) immortal substance – like the inheritor of an entailed property, who is only the temporary holder of an estate that survives him. (Freud, 1914)

This idea that we as people are only temporary vehicles for our immortal germ-plasm (we might now call it our genes) which influences our conscious selves to fulfil its motives is at the heart of Dawkins's 'selfish gene' theory of behaviour. Dawkins even uses the same word 'vehicle' to describe the individual, as we saw above.

E. O. Wilson and sociobiology

Notwithstanding the aforementioned theorists, the first serious assault to apply evolutionary thinking to psychology was led by Harvard zoologist E. O. Wilson with the publication in 1975 of *Sociobiology: The New Synthesis*. This book laid the foundations for the modern evolutionary approach to the study of behaviour. Like ethology and behavioural ecology (see box 1.2), **sociobiology** developed as a branch of biology rather than of the social sciences and was defined by Wilson as 'the systematic study of the biological basis of all social behavior'. Note here that 'biological' should not necessarily be equated with 'genetic': there are many ways of applying biology to behaviour without recourse to genetic levels of explanation. To a materialist (see above) all social behaviour has its roots in biological functioning in the sense that social behaviour is ultimately due to brain activity (see chapter 9). But Wilson meant rather more than this. He argued that if behaviour affected reproductive success in a predictable way (and surely it does) and if particular behaviours are influenced by genes, then natural selection would, to some extent, have shaped human behaviour.

Sociobiology suffered a fair amount of controversy (see box 1.3) and for this reason, many, including Dawkins and Wilson himself, have suggested that evolutionary psychology is simply sociobiology rebranded to make it more politically palatable. But there are some differences between sociobiology and what is now known as evolutionary psychology, although whether these differences are so great as to warrant a name change is up for question (see box 1.2).

From sociobiology to evolutionary psychology

The term 'evolutionary psychology' was coined by a group at University of California at Santa Barbara led by John Tooby and Leda Cosmides. Indeed, if evolutionary psychology has a birthday it is in 1992 when together with Jerome Barkow they published *The Adapted Mind* (Barkow *et al.*, 1992). A collection of articles by multiple authors, this highly influential book acted as the foundation for much of what was to come later.

Tooby and Cosmides proposed that evolutionary psychology differs from sociobiology in that the former adopts a cognitive level of explanation (see chapter 9). Evolutionary psychologists, unlike sociobiologists, attempt to explain human behaviour in terms of the underlying computations that occur within the mind. This was an important addition as it meant that evolutionary psychologists as well as studying

Box 1.3 **Sociobiology, evolutionary psychology and political correctness**

Like all scientific endeavours, sociobiology and evolutionary psychology have both attracted a good deal of criticism. Unlike most scientific disciplines, a great deal of this has been from outside the scientific community. Even if you have only fleeting knowledge of sociobiology, the chances are that you will know of the controversy that surrounded it. Sociobiology was seen by many as promulgating dangerous forms of thinking such as eugenics or supporting racist and sexist ideologies. In 1984 a poster was produced requesting protesters to bring 'noisemakers' to a public lecture to be given by Wilson, 'the prophet of right-wing patriarchy'. At the

1978 meeting of the American Association for the Advancement of Science, Wilson was met with particularly vocal opposition. Demonstrators chanted 'racist Wilson you can't hide, we charge you with genocide'. Many accounts of this meeting state that a protestor poured a jug of iced water over Wilson's head (indeed the first edition of this book told the very same tale). Richard Dawkins – who was at the meeting – recalls that during a scuffle a glass (not a jug) of water was spilled (not poured) over Wilson's clothes (not his head). This provides a salutary lesson of how stories can mutate over retellings towards variants that are more emotionally engaging (see chapter 14 on memes).

Within the academic community, his own Harvard colleagues Stephen Jay Gould and Richard Lewontin were members of the Sociobiology Study Group, who criticised sociobiology on scientific and ethical grounds. Attempts to seek the biological basis of behaviour and culture, they claimed:

> [T]end to provide a genetic justification of the status quo and of existing privileges for certain groups according to class, race, or sex. Historically, powerful countries or ruling groups within them have drawn support for the maintenance or extension of their power from these products of the scientific community . . . Such theories provided an important basis for the enactment of sterilization laws and restrictive immigration laws by the United States between 1910 and 1930 and also for the eugenics policies which led to the establishment of gas chambers in Nazi Germany. (1975)

In 1986 a group of twenty social scientists, including the Cambridge ethologist Robert Hinde, the psychologist David Adams and paleoanthropologist Richard Leakey, drafted what was to become known as the Seville Statement on Violence (Adams *et al.*, 1986). This document attempts to refute the link posed by sociobiologists, and more recently evolutionary psychologists between biology and violent behaviour, particularly war. A précis of its main propositions is presented below.

- It is scientifically incorrect to say that we have inherited a tendency to make war from our animal ancestors.
- It is scientifically incorrect to say that war or any other violent behaviour is genetically programmed into our nature.
- It is scientifically incorrect to say that in the course of human evolution there has been a selection for aggressive behaviour more than for other kinds of behaviour.
- It is scientifically incorrect to say that humans have a violent brain. How we act is shaped by how we have been conditioned and socialised. There is nothing in our neurophysiology that compels us to react violently.
- It is scientifically incorrect to say that war is caused by instinct or any single motivation.

Although the Seville Statement on Violence was adopted by UNESCO and the American Psychological Association as a statement of contemporary research on the relationship between biology and violence it has also attracted much criticism. It has been suggested that few scientists would advocate the claims it attempts to rebut. Fox (1988) called the statement 'a shopworn denunciation of ideas that no one ever really had in the first place' (p. 4). So in many ways the Seville Statement on Violence is totally uncontroversial. More problematic, however, is not what it actually states but what it has been taken to mean. For example, a letter to Cambodia's *Phnom Penh Post* co-signed by a number of humanitarian organisations claimed that the Seville Statement on Violence refuted the link between genetics and violence based on 'scientific evidence'. But this cannot be the case because there is no good evidence that comes close to refuting such a connection (refute, remember, means 'prove to be incorrect' or 'falsify' not simply 'deny'). On the other hand, it might simply mean that a link between biology and violence has not yet been proved beyond any reasonable doubt. If this is the case, then it could also be argued that it is scientifically incorrect to propose a link between socialisation and violence as Adams *et al.* did. Beroldi (1994) proposes that the statement is a political rather than a scientific one. It has some value in damping down the enthusiasm of some of the more overenthusiastic adherents to biological determinism (most of whom are not scientists). However, it also does a disservice in making it appear that the science has disproved what it patently has not.

phenomena entertained by sociobiologists – such as mate choice, parental–offspring conflict and foraging behaviour – they could now study phenomena that were the preserve of cognitive psychologists such as memory, reasoning and perception, albeit with a thorough background of evolutionary logic. Whereas sociobiology was seen by traditional psychologists as somewhat peripheral, evolutionary psychology was now squarely in the centre ground of psychology, and was hard to ignore.

Probably more than anyone else it is Tooby and Cosmides (1997) who were responsible for the synthesis of adaptationism and modularity, they outline five principles that define evolutionary psychology.

Principle 1. The brain is a physical system. It functions as a computer. Its circuits are designed to generate behaviour that is appropriate to our environmental circumstances.

Principle 2. Our neural circuits were designed by natural selection to solve problems that our ancestors faced during our species' evolutionary history.

Principle 3. Consciousness is just the tip of the iceberg; most of what goes on in our minds is hidden from us. As a result, our conscious experience can mislead us into thinking that our circuitry is simpler than it really is. Most problems that we experience as easy to solve are in fact very difficult to solve – they require very complicated neural circuitry.

Principle 4. Different neural circuits are specialised for solving different adaptive problems.

Principle 5. Our modern skulls house a stone-age mind.

Of these five principles, numbers 1 and 3 are standard assumptions taken from cognitive psychology (and in the case of 3, Freud and his followers); and principle 2 is made by sociobiology, the principles that are unique to the Santa Barbara school are principle 4 which is modularity, and principle 5 which implies that behaviours that were adaptive in the past could be maladaptive nowadays. Both of these have proved to be controversial. In particular the philosopher of science David Buller (2005a, 2005b) has been critical of these two principles. Buller differentiates between evolutionary psychology as a field of enquiry which simply attempts to understand the relationship between evolution and behaviour, and the research paradigm Evolutionary Psychology (written with upper-case letters) which makes assumptions about the modularity and the EEA, this is what we refer to as the Santa Barbara school.

Modularity has a long and colourful history in psychology; the phrenology of Franz Joseph Gall (1757–1828) was, in essence, a modular psychological theory. Gall's theory proposed that the mind is made up of specific mental 'organs' or faculties, each being responsible for some aspect of behaviour. Gall proposed in the region of thirty-seven different faculties (plus a few sub-faculties), each of which is localised in a particular part of the brain. Some of these organs had romantic names and exotic functions such as philoprogenitiveness (parental love), approbativeness (the

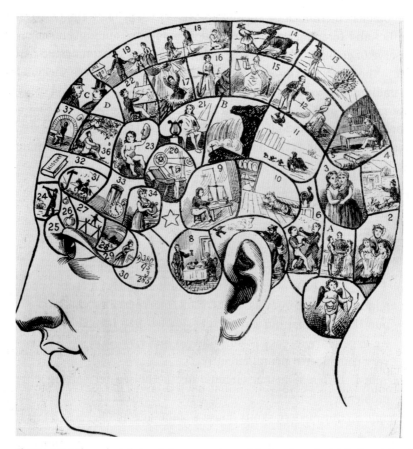

Figure 1.5 A Phrenologist's head. A precursor to modularity, phrenologists believed that different brain regions performed very specific functions and that they could 'read' a person's character by feeling for bumps on the head

desire for praise) and alimentiveness (concerned with appreciation of food and drink). Other organs were concerned with more prosaic tasks such as the perception of causality and time. The bumps that naturally occur on the cranium were thought to be indicative of these underlying organs and phrenologists believed that you could 'read' a person's characteristics by feeling the size of these bumps. While the specifics of phrenology have long been discredited, the idea that we might have mental faculties for specific behaviours lives on first due to the philosopher Jerry Fodor and then due to evolutionary psychologists such as Tooby and Cosmides.

The Modularity of Mind by philosopher Jerry Fodor was published in 1983. A slim volume of only 145 pages its small size belied the impact it would have on the cognitive sciences (a panel of cognitive scientists recently voted it the seventh most influential work of cognitive science in the twentieth century). Fodor's claim was that the mind was best thought of as being composed of mental modules, each of which was responsible for a certain aspect of human behaviour. For example, we might have a mental module that was responsible for the perception of human faces, a separate module for processing language and so on. Moreover, Fodor argued that these modules were innate and changed little over our lifetime. This notion was, and still is, controversial because many cognitive scientists saw the mind as being a large general-purpose computer with little innate knowledge and certainly no innate modules (see chapter 9).

Tooby and Cosmides saw the evolutionary logic in Fodor's proposition. When faced with a problem, natural selection, they argued, tends to produce specific solutions. Thus, our heart pumps blood, which is filtered by our kidneys and is sent to the lungs for gaseous exchange. Each bodily organ has one or only a few specific roles to play. Thus natural selection's usual modus operandi does not tally with the claim that the mind is a vast, general-purpose computing device (see chapter 9).

Some of Buller's criticisms of modularity can be arcane and beyond the scope of an introductory book, but one criticism – which echoes an earlier one by Panksepp and Panksepp (2000) – is that there is very little neurological evidence for mental modules in the neocortex: the part of the brain that is most closely associated with the behaviour of higher primates in general and humans in particular. We discuss the evidence for mental modules for theory of mind (chapter 6) and cheater detection (chapter 9).

Tooby and Cosmides's claim that modern humans possess a 'stone-age mind' has led to some confusion with many associating the Environment of Evolutionary Adaptiveness (EEA) with a particular period of time, the upper Pleistocene period from 1.8 million to 10,000 years ago. Tooby and Cosmides are adamant that this is incorrect.

[the EEA] is not a place or a habitat, or even a time period. It is a statistical composite of the adaptation-relevant properties of ancestral environments encountered by members of ancestral populations, weighted by their frequency and fitness-consequences. (1990b, pp. 386–7)

Many researchers more sympathetic to evolutionary psychology than Buller (e.g. Foley, 1995; Smith, 2007) have cause for concern about the notion of the EEA. Smith (2007) argues that even if it can be established that humans have a stone-age brain it might not be particularly helpful in understanding behaviour. His argument is that during our evolutionary past humans doubtless encountered many novel problems: such as how to deal with aggressive neighbours, when to leave a particular area as its resources become depleted and so on. What characterises human behaviour, Smith argues, is its ability to deal with novelty through mechanisms such as problem solving, language and cultural learning. Note that this is not an anti-evolutionary argument. Smith believes as many do that language, problem solving and the ability to imitate one another (culture) themselves evolved. Where he differs from the Santa Barbara school is in the extent to which a stone-age mind – should it exist – constrains our current and future behaviour.

Evolutionary psychology: present and future

In the first edition of this book we implied that the Santa Barbara version of evolutionary psychology was the only game in town; a decade later things have changed. While the assumptions of the Santa Barbara school are still popular – modularity, the relevance of the EEA to understanding modern behaviour – many other evolutionists are either agnostic about them or reject them entirely. For the purposes of this book we use the term 'evolutionary psychology' in the more inclusive sense which incorporates the modular approach (described above), those who adopt non-modular (but still cognitive) evolutionary approaches to the study of mind and behaviour, and old-style sociobiology. Where confusion is possible we refer to the modular approach as the Santa Barbara school, although many outside the confines of the University of Santa Barbara also use this approach (e.g. Steven Pinker, 1997).

Methods for evaluating evolutionary theories

In their classic paper, 'The spandrels of San Marco', Stephen Jay Gould and Richard Lewontin (Gould and Lewontin, 1979) levelled two criticisms at evolutionary theories of human behaviour. First they argued that many evolutionists are too keen to see behaviours (or physical structures, for that matter) as being adaptive. They lampooned this tendency with reference to Voltaire's Dr Pangloss from *Candide*, who saw everything as being for the best: 'observe, for instance, the nose is formed for spectacles, therefore we wear spectacles'. Second, they suggested that the adaptive explanations provided are frequently unsupported by any evidence and – because so little is known about our hunter-gatherer ancestors – it might be impossible to obtain any such evidence. This being the case, they suggest, adaptive arguments might be little better than Rudyard Kipling's whimsical 'just-so' stories which, for example, claim that the elephant got its trunk as the result of an ancestor getting its nose stretched in a tussle with a crocodile.

In the spirit of just-so stories, neuroscientist V. S. Ramachandran published a paper in the journal *Medical Hypotheses* claiming that males prefer blonde females because, among other things, their lighter skin makes it more obvious if they are infested with parasites. As we shall see in chapter 4, it is important to both sexes that they choose mates of high quality, and parasite infestation is likely to reduce the ability of a female to produce and rear offspring. Ramachandran later claimed that the article was a hoax designed to reveal the speculative nature of evolutionary thinking; his theory was intended to be a just-so story. Does Ramachandran's paper reveal evolutionary psychology to be no more than idle speculation and evolutionary psychologists to be gullible fools? It does not. First, the article was published in a medical journal rather than one dealing with evolutionary psychology or sociobiology. This is important because it means that the article would not have been subject to the scrutiny of evolutionists during the reviewing process. Furthermore, *Medical Hypotheses* is a journal designed for the publication of somewhat 'out there' papers as it says on its website 'the journal will consider radical, speculative and non-mainstream scientific ideas provided they are coherently expressed'. Second, Ramachandran's article's central argument, although speculative, is far from being total nonsense. Parasites are extremely debilitating and can severely lower an individual's fitness, as we discuss in chapter 3. Hence it makes sense for a male or female to attend to signals that might indicate the presence of parasites in a potential mate. It has been argued that adornments such as the peacock's tail might be present to indicate to a mate that its owner is relatively free from parasites (see chapter 4). Taken together these two points show that Ramachandran's hoax was nothing like that produced by physicist Alan Sokal. Sokal famously and deliberately set out to show the muddled thinking of cultural studies theorists by having a paper accepted by the journal *Social Text*. His paper 'Transgressing the boundaries: Towards a transformative hermeneutics of quantum gravity' was, as the title suggests, nonsense and this time *was* reviewed by experts in the field of cultural studies.

So how can evolutionary psychologists ensure that their research is not mere fantasy? There are a number of methods in addition to the usual ones used by psychologists to evaluate their theories (questionnaire studies, interviews, experiments and so on). One is to use research methods from behavioural genetics (see chapter 6) which attempt to separate out the effects of genes and the environment by conducting twin and adoption studies. One of the assumptions of this type of research is that because identical twins are genetically identical, any differences between them must be due to the environment. By comparing identical twins to non-identical twins and non-twin siblings behavioural geneticists have been able to estimate the extent to which genes are implicated in a wide range of traits and behaviours such as intelligence, personality, obesity, addictive behaviours and so on. Although behavioural genetics research can inform researchers that a particular trait is genetically influenced, it does not tell us whether that trait is an adaptation.

A second method, the comparative method, attempts to address more directly the problem of adaptation. Humans are under similar economic pressures to many other animals. Each needs to find and consume food, find a mate, rear offspring and so on. It is therefore likely that similarities exist between human and non-human species in terms of the way that they solve these particular problems (or more correctly the way that natural selection solved the problems for them). This is especially the case for our closest relatives the apes. One way, therefore, of testing an evolutionary theory is to look for analogues in primates and other species. Testing whether particular behaviours are adaptive is more easily done for non-human animals than it is for humans as it can be assumed that the animals are living under similar conditions to their ancestors. Thus evolutionists are able to observe certain traits and test whether, on average, they lead the individual to produce more surviving offspring.

Another method seeks cross-cultural evidence. If a particular trait is supposed to be adaptive, then we might expect to find it in all people irrespective of the particulars of their culture. With respect to Ramachandran's question, is the preference for blonde hair/light skin found in all cultures? Or are the gentlemen who prefer blondes found only in Western society? Finding that a trait is universal might again suggest that it is innate and therefore, possibly, a biological adaptation. However, this simple state of affairs is complicated because some evolved and adaptive behaviours are environmentally contingent; that is, they only arise under certain circumstances. A special type of cross-cultural research therefore looks at evidence from the dwindling numbers of hunter-gatherer communities that still exist across the world. The reasoning behind this is that these societies are living under conditions that are more similar to those that our ancestors experienced than those in the industrialised world (see chapter 8). Here we might determine whether a particular behaviour actually does seem to have fitness consequences in terms of them producing more surviving offspring. For example, one theory of why men tend to be more aggressive than women is that aggression was adaptive in the ancestral environment because it enabled men to compete with other men for the attentions of a mate. By studying existing hunter-gatherer societies we can determine whether, all else being equal, more aggressive men tend to father more children and that these children survive to reproduce themselves. This type of study is not without controversy, not least because contemporary hunter-gatherer people are not merely historical relics but have developed sophisticated cultures over the hundreds of thousands of years since the putative EEA.

The fourth method is that of mathematical and computational modelling. In this researchers create an abstract world in which 'individuals' with particular 'traits' compete with each other for dominance. This gives researchers some idea as to which particular traits or combinations of traits are optimal, and how different traits might interact with each other. One result from this work is that the success of a particular trait might be relative rather than absolute. Put differently it means that having a particular trait or behaving in a particular way might depend on what other traits are around in the environment and what other people do. For example freeriding (taking the benefits of social exchange without reciprocating) can be a very successful strategy for an individual to adopt, but only if the number of freeriders is small. As the number of freeriding increases, cooperators refuse to engage in social exchange, or become more wary, making freeriding an inefficient strategy.

Critics also point out that we know very little about the lives of our ancestors; however we do know *some* things about our ancestors based on surviving fossils and artefacts, such as that they lived in groups rather than alone; that they hunted and gathered and, later, engaged in primitive agriculture; that they practised sexual reproduction and prolonged childrearing; that they fashioned tools and weaponry; had rituals such as burial of the dead; wore clothing and ornamentation and so on. Furthermore, evolutionary thinking can be useful even if we know little about the evolutionary history of a trait. Take two facts about bipolar depression (see chapter 12). First, it is a debilitating disease that appears to reduce fitness (resulting in, in some cases, suicide); second, it is heritable. Only with knowledge of natural selection can we see that these two statements lead to a contradiction: if something is heritable and harmful it should be selected out of the gene pool. The fact that it is still with us suggests either that it is a relatively recent illness (but historical evidence suggests that it isn't) or that it has some hidden benefits to inclusive fitness that outweigh its obvious costs. Evolutionary thinking can therefore point out new and interesting questions for future research.

Agreement and disagreement in evolutionary psychology

Like sociobiology before it, evolutionary psychology has attracted a fair degree of criticism over the years, some of which is valid, some of which appears to be the result of common misunderstandings. In this section we present some of the most common criticisms with the aim of correcting some of the misconceptions.

Everything is an adaptation

First it is worth spending a few words discussing the nature of adaptation. Many evolutionary biologists follow Theodosius Dobzhansky (1970) by insisting that adaptation is a process rather than a thing and recommend the phrase *adaptive trait* to discuss a physical or behavioural trait. So adaptation is a process whereby a trait changes through the process of natural selection so that it functions more effectively in the current environment. A fish's tail fins are therefore adapted for swimming, a bird's wings adapted for flying and so on. Some of these cases are relatively clear-cut such as those just given, but in many cases it is not at all clear whether a given trait is an adaptation or not, and equally important, if it is an adaptation then what is its purpose? There is no designer that we can ask, so the ultimate arbiter as to what something is for is whether it causes the organism to leave behind more copies of its genes. From this view, childcare could be seen as an adaptation (or adapted trait) for ensuring that copies of genes in another person (the child) are protected from harm (see chapter 7) and survive. But many other traits are not adapted but are side effects of the way that the body was put together (sometimes referred to, following Gould and Lewontin – see above – as *spandrels*). A classic example is the recurrent laryngeal nerve that carries signals from the brain to the muscles of the neck, a distance of a few centimetres in most mammals. Instead, however, it descends from the brain down to the heart where it loops around the aorta and then returns back up, a distance of maybe half a metre in a human and five metres in a giraffe. It is clear that taking the scenic route serves no useful purpose, it is not an adaptation, rather it is a side effect (a spandrel) of the way that bodies evolved over history.

It is often said that evolutionary psychologists see all behaviours as adaptations (the notion of Panglossianism – see above) and it is true that thinking of the adaptive consequences of heritable traits and behaviours is a central part of evolutionary psychology. On the other hand there are many behaviours and traits that evolutionary psychologists believe are not adaptations. A fact that is often overlooked by critics is that not all evolutionary psychologists speak with the same voice. In any academic discipline there is disagreement, and evolutionary psychologists differ as to whether a given behaviour is adaptive, non-adaptive or the side effect of some other adaptation. For example in their book on rape co-authors Randy Thornhill and Craig Palmer disagree as to whether rape is a direct adaptation (Thornhill) or whether it is a side effect of the male drive for sex (Palmer). Jordania (2009) argues that music is an adaptation concerned with predator control whereas Steven Pinker argues that although music (and other arts) are cultural universals (see chapter 14) they aren't adaptations, rather they are by-products of adaptations. He suggests that music is the side effects of language processing (see chapter 10) and many visual aesthetic preferences a by-product of habitat selection (Dutton, 2009).

It is relatively easy to find a researcher who believes that X is an adaptation and produce a list which gives the impression that everything is an adaptation. However this would not indicate that there was any consensus (see Rose and Rose, 2001). Equally, critics could compile an even longer list of all of the things that evolutionary psychologists *do not think* are adaptive, but this would not make such interesting reading.

Evolutionary psychology espouses genetic determinism

Many critics have accused evolutionary psychology (and sociobiology) of genetic determinism; of suggesting that everything about us – our intelligence, personalities and sexual proclivities – is specified in our genes (see Lewontin *et al.*, 1984). This is simply not the case. As has been pointed out elsewhere in this chapter, evolutionists are at pains to emphasise the importance of the environment and culture in making us who we are. When evolutionary psychologists discuss the effect of genes on psychology they think in terms of predispositions rather than causes. Genes do not *cause* men to commit violent acts; if they do anything they *predispose* men to such acts; whether men actually carry them out will depend on their life-histories, cultural contexts and other genetic predispositions (such as conscience). This last point is an important one. Critics inevitably focus on the nasty side of evolutionary psychology – rape, violence, infanticide (see chapter 6) and so on – and rarely discuss the fact that evolutionists also propose predispositions for cooperation (see chapters 7 and 8), conflict resolution, morality (see chapter 6) and altruism (chapters 7 and 8).

Evolutionary psychology is reductionist

Reductionism is a dirty word in many circles but in fact it is one of the most important inventions in the history of science. Reductionism is simply the explanation of some property or behaviour in terms of simpler, more basic mechanisms and its application is what led human beings to discover that matter is made of atoms or that complex life was produced by natural selection. In his book *Darwin's Dangerous Idea*, philosopher Daniel Dennett distinguishes between 'good' (sometimes known as 'hierarchical') reductionism and 'greedy' reductionism. In good reductionism, phenomena are explained at lower levels but do not replace the higher levels, rather researchers from different disciplines work together to understand phenomena at all levels. Greedy reductionism eschews higher levels and attempts to explain everything in terms of the lowest possible level.

For example, we know that depression is manifested in terms of abnormal functioning in the brain and indeed studying the brains of people with depression has led to many useful insights about the nature of this illness. But it doesn't tell the whole story. We also know that life-events such as bereavement or unemployment can trigger episodes of depression and this cannot be determined by looking only at brains. Good reductionism seeks lower levels of explanation, but does not ignore the contributions of higher levels. So researchers should work together, psychologists investigating the environmental components of depression and neuroscientists investigating brain functioning, with results of all researchers being combined to form the 'big picture' of depression. While there are barriers to this utopian view – what E. O. Wilson calls **consilience** – not least the formation of a common scientific language that allows researchers from diverse fields to communicate, interdisciplinary research groups are certainly becoming more prevalent in the world's universities.

Evolutionary psychology is politically incorrect

Many have criticised evolutionary psychology for promulgating conservative, ethocentric or sexist accounts of human behaviour. As we shall see in chapter 4 a prominent theory in mate choice is that because of differences in the cost of sex to males and females (females can become pregnant, males cannot; males can sire many more children than can females, and so on) females are choosier as to whom they have sex with. Natalie Angier – an evolutionary biologist – argues that:

evolutionary psychology as it has been disseminated across mainstream consciousness is a cranky and despotic Cyclops, its single eye glaring through an overwhelmingly masculinist lens. I say 'masculinist' rather than 'male' because the view of male behavior promulgated by hard-core evolutionary psychologists is as narrow and inflexible as their view of womanhood is. (1999, p. 48)

First of all it is worth pointing out that most of the criticisms of evolutionary psychology focus on the mate choice literature. In fact, to many people the work on sex differences in mate choice *is* evolutionary psychology (notice that it is only a single chapter of this book). This is largely because this is the kind of stuff that gets in the newspapers. Second, even within the mate choice literature this is only one theory, although admittedly the most prominent theory. The success of evolutionary psychology should not be evaluated by the success of one particular theory in one particular topic area.

To return to Natalie Angier, her view is that evolutionary psychology not only reinforces sexual stereotypes but renders them immutable by shackling them to genes. But there is a deeper concern, if it is conclusively demonstrated that males and females are fundamentally, genetically different, then could this have effects on public policy? Should we forgive men's philandering because 'it is in their genes'? If, as Thornhill and Palmer assert, rape could be an effective reproductive strategy, should we be more lenient on rapists because 'they can't help it'? There are three responses to this question. The first is to appeal to a philosophical principle known as the **naturalistic fallacy**. To commit the naturalistic fallacy is to assume that because something is found in nature it is necessarily good or desirable in some kind of moral sense. Equating natural with good and unnatural with bad is fallacious. Many natural things are, from our perspective, bad such as tornadoes, cobra venom and faeces. On the other hand many unnatural things can be good (at least to some) such as mobile phones, electric guitars and red wine. Just because something is natural (whatever that means) does not necessarily mean it is desirable. Second, evolutionary psychology is still in its infancy, what researchers present are hypotheses supported by some evidence, not the *final word* on the matter. There is plenty of evidence supporting genetically specified sex differences but it by no means accounts for all of the data and, as we shall see in chapter 4, culture has a large effect too.

Third, even if we knew everything about our evolutionary predispositions, which we do not, it would be next to impossible (or at least undesirable) to specify a society based upon them. Just to take the example of rape, it may be in the evolutionary interests of some men to rape, but, it goes without saying, it is hardly in the evolutionary interests of the woman. Nor is it in the interests of her partner, her parents or her children. This is the problem with any kind of social Darwinism: legislating for the interests of one set of individuals will automatically legislate against the interests of another group of individuals. But it is worse than this. The gene-centred view of life (see chapter 2) shows that the interests of the genes and the interests of the individual are not always the same (consider, again, the unfortunate male red-backed widow spider) in terms of political decision making it seems more reasonable to prioritise the interests of the individual over those of their genes since it is individuals who are capable of suffering, not genes. If you want to engineer society, probably the best way is to decide on what kind of society we would like and throw it to the popular vote, as many of us already do.

So is evolutionary psychology politically incorrect? In many respects the question makes no sense. Science is not (or shouldn't be) political. There are two kinds of science, good science in which hypotheses are rigorously and dispassionately evaluated against the best evidence available and conclusions tentatively drawn, and bad science which fails on any or all of the above. If the science is good, disliking the results will not make them any less true.

Evolutionary psychology: the mind's new science

Notwithstanding all the argument and heated debate we, as psychologists, are convinced that evolutionary psychology has a great deal to offer in the attempt to understand how the mind works. E. O. Wilson may have put it rather too strongly when he suggested that 'biology will cannibalise psychology'. As we argued above, reductionism is a useful process but we need to be aware that we cannot explain everything by appealing to Darwinism (or biological phenomena such as the behaviour of neurons – see chapter 9). The majority of research psychologists in the world are focused on proximate questions such as how children learn to read, or how the mind changes as we get older, to name but two. Perhaps Darwinism will never help answer such questions (though it might). That said, we believe that some form of evolutionary psychology will prevail in the future, and the logic that it brings will not only help answer some outstanding questions, but present to us an entirely new set of questions that psychologists need to answer.

Summary

- Evolutionary psychology attempts to provide ultimate as well as proximate explanations of human behaviour. Proximate mechanisms are those that directly cause a particular behaviour (for instance we have sex because we enjoy it) whereas ultimate explanations are cast at the level of design by natural selection (we have sex because it leads to offspring).
- Although Darwin formulated the idea of evolution by natural selection, the concept of evolution is an old one. What was missing from these earlier accounts was a workable model of how change occurs. Darwin provided this mechanism with his theory of natural selection.

- Many early attempts to apply Darwinian thinking to human behaviour explained cultural differences in terms of biological differences between the groups. Some such theories led to social engineering programmes such as the eugenics movement which attempted to control reproduction for the good of the species.
- It has been claimed that much of twentieth-century psychology has been influenced by the cultural relativist position (what Tooby and Cosmides refer as the Standard Social Science Model, SSSM), the biological bases of human behaviour tending to be ignored or downplayed.
- Following the publication of E. O. Wilson's book the sociobiology movement attempted to formulate evolutionary explanations of human behaviour. Such attempts led to a great deal of scientific and political controversy.
- Opinions differ as to whether evolutionary psychology really is something new, or merely a rebranded sociobiology. One difference between sociobiology and evolutionary psychology is that the latter incorporates cognitive-level explanations such as modularity.

Questions

1. Recently there has been controversy about ability to screen foetuses for certain genetic abnormalities. If an abnormality is found the parents could then make the decision to terminate the pregnancy (this has happened with disorders such as Down's syndrome). Is this ethical? Is it ethical for parents to choose the sex of their children in this way? Is this ethically no more justifiable than eugenics?

2. The naturalistic fallacy suggests that you should not assume that just because something is true it must therefore be morally correct. The moralistic fallacy is the opposite: just because something is morally correct it doesn't mean that it is true. If one were to find evidence for something that seemed morally unpleasant (e.g. relationships between race and IQ) should this research be published? Should the research even be carried out? If you answered 'yes' to these questions, consider whether scientists should take special care when publishing such data, especially when discussing their ideas with the media.

3. Although eugenics is almost universally reviled nowadays, many of the advocates thought eugenics was for the greater good of society. To what extent might this be the result of our ethical principles changing over time, from those focused on the good of society to those focused on the rights of the individual?

4. The Great Chain of Being specifies, among other things, that there is a natural hierarchy where some individuals are more important than others. In modern terms we sometimes hear of people discussing some organisms being 'more evolved' than others. Discuss this principle. Does it make sense to describe humans as more

evolved than, say, bacteria, or snakes? Or, as some argue, given that all these organisms are well adapted to their environments, aren't they all equally evolved?

FURTHER READING

Cosmides, L., and Tooby, J. (1997). Evolutionary psychology: A primer. www.psych. ucsb.edu/research/cep/primer.html

The original Santa Barbara manifesto

Buller, D. J. (2005). *Adapting Minds: Evolutionary Psychology and the Persistent Quest for Human Nature.* Cambridge, MA: MIT Press. A staunch critic of evolutionary psychology, especially that of the Santa Barbara school.

Pinker, S. (2002). *The Blank Slate: The Modern Denial of Human Nature.* London: Allen Lane. The best account of the political and social implications of evolutionary psychology.

Wright, R. (1994). *The Moral Animal.* New York: Pantheon Books. An account of Darwin's theory and life which discusses some controversial applications of Darwinian theory, such as social Darwinism and sociobiology.

2 Mechanisms of evolutionary change

KEY CONCEPTS

natural selection • heritable variation • reproductive success • fitness • genes • chromosomes • Mendelian genetics • genotype • phenotype • mutation • DNA • heritability of characteristics • group selection • individual selection • gene selection • altruism • the selfish gene

Darwin's ideas have had a major impact on our understanding of the relationship between evolution and behaviour. In this and the next chapter we consider in more detail the foundations that he laid for evolutionary psychology and the contributions made by subsequent evolutionists. Since much of the work on the relationship between evolution and behaviour has been conducted on non-human species we consider a number of examples from the literature on animal behaviour. No understanding of evolution would be complete without considering genetics. What exactly a gene is and what it does are introduced.

Darwin's theory of evolution

Artificial selection

The Nobel laureate Herbert Simon once argued that a cow is a man-made object. What he meant was that domestic animals such as cows, chickens and dogs have been selectively bred for features that humans can make use of. In a similar way that humans have fashioned tools and other artefacts from natural materials, so they have fashioned living organisms to fulfil their needs.

Animal breeders have known for centuries that if you mate individuals that have desirable characteristics, then their offspring are also likely to have the favoured characteristics. If, for example, you breed large-breasted turkeys together and constantly select and breed from the progeny with the largest breast muscle, then over a number of generations you can substantially increase the amount of breast muscle in

Figure 2.1 Artificial selection has created a great range of domestic dog breeds from a primitive wolf-like ancestor in only a few centuries

your flock. Therefore, by choosing individuals with a particular feature you can, over a number of generations, create a change in the direction that you have selected.

Selective breeding has also been responsible for more radical changes in an organism's physical form. The wide variety of domestic dogs that we see today – from chihuahuas to St Bernards – have been created, in only a few hundred years, from a primitive wolf-like ancestor. The same applies to plants, with many quite different vegetables sharing a common ancestral root. As Mark Twain quipped, 'Broccoli is merely a cabbage with a college education.' Therefore, many organisms are the way they are today because their traits have been selected not by nature but by human beings, a process known as artificial selection.

Natural selection

In *The Origin of Species*, published in 1859, Darwin used the evidence of artificial selection to propose a theory of evolution that he called **natural selection**. This analogy, however, can be misleading. In artificial selection, there is a guiding hand; someone is deciding which traits are desirable and which ones are not. There is also an ultimate goal (e.g. to have plumper turkeys) and each generation selected is a step on the way to achieving this goal. In evolution, there is no omnipotent being choosing which organism should survive and which should be consigned to oblivion, and there is no ultimate goal that the selection process is trying to achieve (see Dawkins, 1986).

Most biologists consider that natural selection plays the most crucial role in evolution; but that is not to say they believe it is the only thing that has led to life being the way it is today. Processes as diverse as disease, climate change and extra-terrestrial collisions have played key roles in pruning the tree of life into its present shape, but natural selection (and, as we will see in chapter 3, sexual selection) leads not simply to change, but to adaptive change.

Natural selection and survival of the fittest

As we saw in chapter 1, natural selection is based on differential reproductive success of heritable characteristics that vary in a population. So individuals that happen to have genetically influenced advantageous characteristics in a given environment will be 'favoured' in terms of the number of surviving offspring they produce. Since individuals that survive to reproductive age are generally viewed as being physically fitter than those that don't (for example, they may have superior running ability or more acute hearing), this led to the term 'survival of the fittest' being used as shorthand for natural selection. Interestingly Darwin did not use this phrase in the original version of *The Origin of Species* but incorporated it into later editions at the suggestion of his friend and contemporary Alfred Russel Wallace from a suggestion by another contemporary Herbert Spencer (Wallace, 1864; Spencer, 1864).

In many ways 'survival of the fittest' is an unfortunate term since **fitness** means different things to different people (Dawkins, 1982; Dickins, 2011). In the years since *The Origin of Species* first appeared, fitness has been used in a number of different ways ranging from its original 'robust and hearty' type of meaning to a technical measurement of fecundity, often leading to debates where the protagonists have argued at cross-purposes (Dawkins, 1982). During the twentieth century, evolutionists began to use the term fitness as a measure of how successful an individual is at reproducing, that is its **lifetime reproductive success**. Hence if you have three surviving children in your life your fitness will be three. Later on, in chapter 7, we'll see that in recent years the notion of fitness has been expanded beyond consideration of an individual's own offspring.

Mendel and post-Mendelian genetics

Although Darwin solved the mystery of the mechanism by which evolution takes place, his solution was only partial. The problem was that Darwin had only a sketchy idea of the mechanism of inheritance, the way in which traits are passed from parent to offspring. Again, as we saw in chapter 1, it was Gregor Mendel's work on pea plants that led to the mechanism of inheritance – genes – being discovered. Here we expand on Mendel's findings and discuss developments in genetics that have occurred since his time.

Mendel's findings

The results of Mendel's experiments gave rise to three important findings that ultimately led to the development of the science of genetics. First, they showed that traits are caused not by a single gene, rather that genes operate in pairs; in sexually reproducing species, a single copy of each gene is passed to the offspring in each of the parental **gametes** (the male and female sex cells).

Second, his work revealed that the relationship between the genes that an individual possesses (now called the **genotype**) and that individual's physical structure (the **phenotype**) is rather more complex than it might appear. Two pea plants, for instance, might both have yellow peas, but the genes that specify that colour might be different; their phenotype is the same, but their genotype is different. This arises because one member of the gene-pair is **dominant** to the other, which is technically called **recessive**. Dominant simply means that the existence of a single copy is enough for that trait to be expressed, irrespective of the nature of the other copy. Mendel found that for pea plants, the yellow pea gene is dominant to green. This means that if a plant inherits a single copy of the yellow gene from either of its parents, then it will have yellow peas, even though it might also have a gene for green peas. The only way to obtain green peas is for the plant to inherit a copy of the green gene from *both* of its parents. In the notation used by geneticists the dominant gene is represented by the initial letter of the trait it specifies, thus the gene for yellow peas is denoted as Y. Rather confusingly, a lower-case version of the same letter is used to denote the recessive gene; thus in this case y is used for green. We can now see why two plants with different genes can have the same phenotype when it comes to a particular trait. A pea plant that has the genotype YY will have yellow seeds, as will a pea plant that is Yy; each has a different genotype, but the same phenotype. When an organism has two similar copies of a gene (such as YY or yy), it is said to be **homozygous** (homo = 'alike') for that trait; when it has two different copies (such as Yy), it is said to be **heterozygous** (hetero = 'different').

Finally, his experiments showed that inheritance is **particulate**, rather than the result of a process of blending (see chapter 1). For traits controlled by single pairs of genes such as seed colour in pea plants, the results are always one thing (e.g. yellow) or the other (e.g. green), with no half-measures permitted. Previously the problem with particulate theories was that they could not account for the contemporary observations (such as traits skipping generations – see box 2.1). Mendel's discovery that traits are determined by paired genes went a long way towards solving this problem. One of the curious things about this discovery is that nowhere in Mendel's

Box 2.1 Mendel's demonstration of colour dominance in pea plants

One of the mysteries of inheritance was why characteristics found in one parent were often not found in any of the offspring. If plants which breed pure for yellow peas are crossed with plants which breed pure for green peas, all of the resultant offspring will have yellow peas. If you then cross each member of this second generation with its siblings then some of the resultant offspring will once again have green peas. Again this observation is impossible for a blend model to explain, since yellow should never produce green when crossed with yellow.

It was observations such as this that led Mendel to formulate his theory. In the table we can see that pea plants that are pure breeding for yellow and green seeds are both homozygous. When these are all crossed with each other all possible offspring are heterozygous, but, because yellow is dominant, all are phenotypically yellow. When these are all crossed to produce a third generation, green re-emerges (the homozygous form yy) in the ratio 1:3 with yellow. Notice that the green colour, lost to the previous generation, is expressed since it does not have a copy of the 'masking' dominant gene (Y).

Generation 1

phenotype	yellow peas	green peas
genotype	YY	yy
gamete	Y	y

Leads to . . .

Y	Y	
y	Yy	Yy
y	Yy	Yy

Generation 2

phenotype	yellow peas (all offspring)	
genotype	Yy (all offspring)	
gamete	Y and y	

Leads to . . .

Y	y	
Y	YY	Yy
y	Yy	yy

Generation 3

phenotype	yellow peas	green peas
genotype	YY; Yy; Yy	yy
ratio of phenotypes	3	1

Note: It was the ratio of 3:1 (actual figures 6022:2001) in favour of yellow over green in the third generation that led Mendel to realise that the underlying genotypes YY, Yy, yY and yy were produced in the third generation.

Box 2.2 Mendel's original laws of genetics (using modern terminology)

1. Inheritance is particulate (i.e. parental genetic material is discrete and does not blend together), with each parent making an equal contribution to the progeny.
2. Characteristics are influenced by genes occurring in pairs (one contributed from each parent). The complete set of genes of an individual is known as its genotype.
3. Genes exist in at least two or more alternate forms that are called alleles. Where there are only two potential alleles at each locus then three types of gene combinations become possible. In the case of Mendel's pea plants, combinations of genes for pea colour exist as YY, Yy and yy. Where an individual has identical genes at a specific locus (e.g. YY and yy) it is said to be homozygous for that characteristic. In contrast, where an individual has different genes at a specific locus (e.g. Yy and yY) it is said to be heterozygous. The complete description of an individual's characteristics is known as its phenotype.
4. Dominant alleles override recessive alleles in their expression in the phenotype. Recessive genes can be expressed in the phenotype only when they occur in a double dose (the homozygous recessive condition, e.g. yy).
5. Only one of a pair of parental alleles is passed on to each of the offspring. Genes for different characteristics are passed on individually rather than being attached to each other (in the language of genetics they are **segregated**). This is sometimes known as Mendel's first law.
6. Phenotypic features that occur together in the adult will not necessarily appear together in the offspring. This is called **independent assortment** and is a result of segregation. This is sometimes known as Mendel's second law.

---

work did he state it explicitly (Hartle and Orel, 1992), although it is true that it is a natural conclusion to draw from his experiments.

Following a large number of breeding experiments with pea plants Mendel proposed a number of conclusions which have become known as 'Mendel's laws of genetics'. Mendel's laws are summarised in box 2.2.

It is important to realise that Mendel never saw a gene (nor did he use the term which came into existence in 1905); rather, he postulated that they must exist, based on their phenotypic effects in experiments such as that sketched in box 2.1.

Modifications of Mendel's laws

Although Mendel's 'laws' provided a framework for understanding the mechanism of inheritance, the picture was by no means complete. First of all, Mendel had no idea of how these units of inheritance were physically realised, or where they were located. Second, it soon became clear that there are exceptions to most of his original suggestions. To Mendel, sources of variation came from inheriting a mixture of parental genes. However, other processes of which Mendel was unaware have been uncovered since his time and these lead to a more complex modern-day understanding of genetics which includes other sources of variation.

Genes and chromosomes

During the 1930s it was discovered that genes are located in the nucleus of an organism's cells at specific locations on larger bodies called **chromosomes**. Each individual has a number of chromosomes which is typical of its species. In the case of humans the number is 46 (23 **homologous** pairs, one from each parent). One pair of chromosomes is the sex chromosomes – in humans, XX for females XY for males. The remaining 22 pairs are known as autosomal chromosomes and they have nothing to do with sex at all. The discovery of chromosome pairs provided a physical home for Mendel's paired genes. This means that a Yy pea will have its Y gene on one homologous chromosome, and the y on the other.

The number of chromosomes varies widely between species. Fruit flies of the genus *Drosophila* (a group of minute flies that have been used extensively to understand inheritance) have 8, dogs have 78 and some species of plants over 250.

A gene for a particular characteristic occurs at a specific point on the chromosome called its **locus** (plural **loci**). The purpose of the Human Genome Project was to identify the loci of all of the genes in our species; we may not know all the effects that a gene might have on the phenotype, but we now know where it is. Generally a locus is home to more than one alternative form of a gene; when this occurs the alternate forms are called **alleles**. In the above example we saw that the colour-determining gene can have two alternate forms, Y and y; these are alleles and as such will reside at the same locus on a chromosome.

Chromosome pairs become separated during sexual reproduction so that each sperm or ovum produced has half of the normal complement of genes (it is known as a **haploid** cell). The process of producing cells with half the number of genes/chromosomes is called **meiosis**. Meiosis ensures that when sperm and ovum fuse to form a fertilised egg or **zygote** the number of genes an offspring has is restored (that is, it is **diploid**). Note that when body cells divide they double the number of chromosomes they contain just prior to forming two new cells so that each new cell has the normal number of genes – a process known as **mitosis**.

Factors affecting the transmission of genes

During the early years of the twentieth century, evidence was uncovered that demonstrated that genes are not always passed on independently. Different genes may be

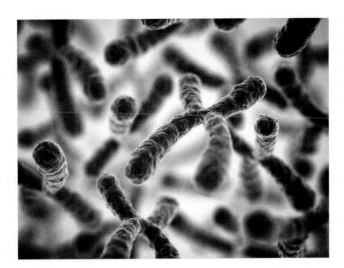

Figure 2.2 Human chromosomes. Each one comprises two identical chromatids joined at the centromere, which divides each chromatid into a long and short arm

linked together when they are passed on to offspring. If two genes are found on the same chromosome they are far more likely to be passed on together to offspring than if they appear on separate chromosomes. This means that genes may be linked together and a chromosome may be considered as a 'linkage group' of genes. The fact that genes occur in linkage groups does not, however, mean that all of the genes on parental chromosomes will be passed on together to the offspring. Prior to gamete (eggs and sperm) formation, homologous chromosomes pair up together and exchange genes at specific points.

This exchange of genes is known as **crossing over**. In this way genes become recombined and the genes that are passed on to offspring are said to have undergone **recombination**. Due to recombination each individual is not only genetically unique, but also has unique chromosomes (with the sole exception of identical twins). The closer together two genes are found on a chromosome, the more likely they are to be passed on together during recombination. This means the degree of linkage (the likelihood of genes being passed on together) is an indication of how close their loci are on a chromosome.

If we imagine a chromosome as a chain necklace with each gene represented by a link, then homologous chromosomes would be like having two chain necklaces with an identical number of links laid side by side. Although each link on one necklace is identical in length to its counterpart on the other, they may be made of different materials (representing the different genes on each). Now imagine breaking each necklace in a number of places and exchanging groups of links between them. Each necklace retains its original length but now differs at certain points. Note that the closer two links were on the original necklace, the more likely they will be to find themselves together on the new one. Today we know that the chain necklace view of genes is really quite a simplification since many characteristics are made up of parts of DNA taken from all over a chromosome.

Other exceptions to Mendel's laws

Linkage and recombination are the main reasons that the simple ratios Mendel predicted in breeding experiments frequently do not occur. And there are other reasons why Mendel's foundations of genetics have had to be modified over the years. Crossing over is a form of chromosome mutation that is common because it occurs every time a gamete is formed (there are other, somewhat less common, forms of chromosome mutation as well). Individual genes may also be subject to mutations but these are rare compared with chromosome mutations. A gene mutation involves the chemical structure of the gene being altered (by radiation, for example) but because genetic material is chemically quite stable the chances of a given gene mutating are one in thousands. However, given that each multicellular species has a very large number of genes (around 20,300 in the case of humans) this means that individual organisms will have quite a large number of mutations (perhaps as many as 100 in you and me). You need not worry about your 100 mutated genes, however, since the vast majority of these are **neutral**, that is, they have no phenotypic effect. When a gene mutation does have a phenotypic effect it is more likely to be detrimental than beneficial, but just occasionally a gene mutation can have a beneficial effect and this may be an important event for evolution (see below). In a sense then, each of us is a mutant; however, being a mutant is one of the reasons everybody is unique. At the level of the gene pool, mutations can be viewed as a source of variation in the population. Thus in modern-day genetics there are considered to be three sources of variation in a population that natural selection can work on:

- Mendelian variation due to the mixing together of parental genes.
- Recombination (also called chromosome mutation where genes are exchanged between chromosomes).
- Gene mutations.

As stated earlier, Mendel was fortunate in studying pea plants since they have a number of characteristics that could occur in either of two contrasting forms. He was also fortunate in that the characteristics he chose demonstrate a simple dominant/recessive relationship. Like a tossed coin which can only land heads or tails, peas are either green or yellow, they are round or wrinkled and their flowers are either red or white. Today we realise that many characteristics do not show complete dominance or complete recessiveness. In addition, many genes have more than one phenotypic effect; this is known as **pleiotropy** and many characteristics depend on more than one gene, that is, they are **polygenic**. Finally, the way that a gene is **expressed** in the phenotype may be altered by a **modifier gene**. So although Mendel laid its foundation stones, the builders of modern-day genetics have modified his original blueprints on many occasions.

Box 2.3 **The evolution of our species – from ape to early archaic**
Homo sapiens

Advances in **paleoanthropology** (the study of the fossils of our ancestors) during the last twenty years have radically altered our understanding of human evolution. Most experts today suggest that chimpanzees and humans diverged from a common ancestor around six million years ago. The ape-like fossils found by paleoanthropologist Tim White and co-workers between 1992 and 1994 led to a new species being named – *Ardipithecus ramidus*. Several subsequent fossil finds suggest that there may have been at least two different species of *Ardipithecus* (Lovejoy, 2009; White *et al.*, 2010). This is the earliest **hominin** (human-like ancestor) that has been uncovered and has features intermediate between humans and chimpanzees. *Ardipithecus* existed around 4.4 million years ago in Ethiopia. It had ape-like, long and strongly built arm bones but human-like, smallish canine teeth. The position of the **foramen magnum** (the hole in the skull through which the spinal cord passes) suggests that it walked upright on two feet. This suggests that one of the earliest major features of our ancestors following divergence from the ancestors of chimpanzees was **bipedalism**. Plant fossils found with *Ardipithecus* suggest that it was very much a woodland creature. In contrast, the 'next stage' of human evolution *Australopithecus* (various species found in a number of areas of Africa, McHenry, 2009), which begins to appear in the fossil record around 4.2 million years ago, is associated with drier savannah areas, as is generally the case for hominins thereafter. The *Australopithecines* eventually developed into two broad categories – a large 'robust' form which had a massive jaw, and a smaller, lightly built, 'gracile' form. Although the *Australopithecines* were clearly able to walk upright they had relatively shorter legs and greater wrist and ankle mobility than ourselves, allowing them to retain good tree-climbing abilities. It is believed that the *Homo* line descended from a species of gracile *Australopithecine* around 2.5 million years ago – again within Africa. The first of these was *Homo habilis* and it had a larger cranial capacity (and hence a larger brain) than *Australopithecus*. *H. habilis* used stone choppers and scrapers to remove meat from the bones of its prey (*H. habilis* was clearly a meat eater but there are debates over whether or not it was a hunter or scavenger). Although *H. habilis* probably spread to many areas of Africa it did not leave that continent. In contrast, the next species on the path to ourselves – *Homo erectus*, which began to appear in the fossil record around 1.8 million years ago – migrated north and eventually spread throughout much of the Eurasian continent. *H. erectus* had a brain size some 50 per cent larger than *H. habilis* and smaller molar teeth suggesting less reliance on uncooked plant food. It was distinctly more human-like than any previous hominin, having a less protruding face and making use of more complex stone tools. Artefacts and fossils from the Malay Archipelago suggest that

H. erectus built rafts or boats and constructed shelters with stone bases. *H. erectus* existed for at least 1.5 million years but at some stage less than 400,000 years ago 'archaic' forms of our own species *Homo sapiens* began to emerge. Although archaic *H. sapiens* had brains some 20 per cent larger than *H. erectus*, they were still 20 per cent smaller than modern *H. sapiens*. Anatomically modern *H. sapiens* probably have existed for around 150,000 years but precisely where they first evolved is a hotbed of debate.

From this brief description of the journey from ape to human we should not assume that a series of simple step-like changes occurred when one species evolved into another so that the former species no longer existed. Speciation (formation of a new species) is thought to occur when one population becomes geographically isolated from another for a lengthy period of time and is subjected to different selection pressures. After many generations the separated population becomes so different from their ancestors that they would no longer be able to breed together to produce viable offspring should they meet up once more. This is the point at which they are generally considered to be separate species. This is likely to have been the case during human evolution and indeed the fossil record shows that a number of hominin species are likely to have coexisted (Tattersall and Matternes, 2000; McHenry, 2009). A number of *Australopithecines* probably coexisted with each other and with *H. habilis*. Also there is clear evidence that *H. sapiens* coexisted with *H. erectus*, the latter only disappearing from the fossil record around 40,000 years ago.

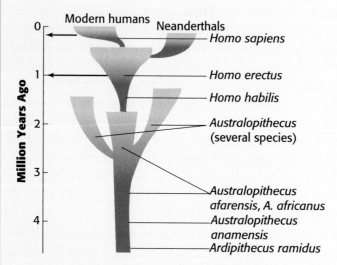

Human evolution from the first hominins to modern humans. The arrows indicate the two times when *Homo erectus* and *Homo sapiens* migrated out of Africa (after Goldsmith and Zimmerman, 2001, p. 278)

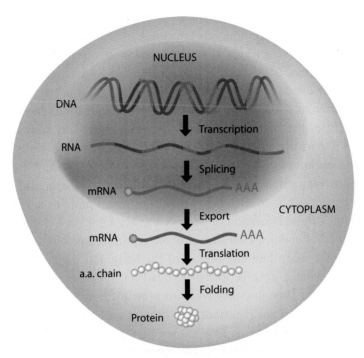

Figure 2.3 Production of protein from DNA double helix in nucleus of cell

Modern genetics

Genes and the structure of DNA

In order to comprehend the role that genes play in nature it is important to understand what a gene is and to appreciate the role that it plays in helping to create an organism. So what is a gene and what is its relationship to a chromosome?

A chromosome consists of a lengthy string of genes. Physically it is a double strand of the chemical **deoxyribonucleic acid** or **DNA**, the structure of which was discovered by Watson and Crick in 1953. DNA is a truly giant molecule, sometimes as long as two inches, and resides within the nucleus of the cell. In structure, DNA is the shape of a twisted ladder (the famed 'double helix') with each of the 'rails' – known as the backbone – being made up of alternating units of phosphoric acid and deoxyribose sugar. Each link of acid and sugar is connected to a base that may come in one of four forms: **adenine, thymine, cytosine** and **guanine** (A, T, C and G); each link of sugar, acid and base is called a **nucleotide** (see figure 2.3). The 'rungs' of the ladder are made up of paired bases. The properties of these bases are such that adenine can pair up with thymine, and cytosine can pair up with guanine. The bases code for the production of **amino acids** that are the building blocks of proteins. Each amino acid is coded for by a triplet or **codon** of bases (the amino acid lysine, for example, is coded for by the codon of AAG). We can think of each codon as a different word and a gene as a sentence made up of these words. It is the precise sequence of the one billion 'words' that makes up human DNA that the Human Genome Project was set up to uncover (see box 2.4). The use of three-letter words from an alphabet of four letters leads to 64 (4 × 4 × 4) different possibilities. This is more than ample for amino acid production since only a little over twenty amino acids exist in nature. This means that a number of slightly different three-letter words have the same meaning (like synonyms). For example, in addition to AAG coding for lysine so too does AAA. Although there are only around twenty different amino acids in existence, by stringing these together in various sequences hundreds of thousands of different proteins may be created. So, to return to the original question of what is a gene; a gene is a portion of DNA that, via its sequence of codons, codes for protein synthesis (see box 2.4). And proteins, of course, are the main building blocks of the body and brain. This at least is the classic view of what a gene is. Recently, however, it has been discovered that the vast majority of our DNA does not code for protein formation but that much of this non-coding DNA plays an important role in controlling the activity of the protein production portions. In fact it is now known that genes that code for proteins make up a mere 2 per cent of our DNA. These recent findings have led to debates about how we define what a gene is (Plomin *et al.*, 2008).

Despite such recent discoveries and debates it is still considered that the main function of DNA in all species is the production of proteins. But how does DNA do this? When a specific protein is required by a cell a portion of the double helix 'unzips' revealing a sequence of bases. Other, free-floating, bases within the cell attach to the exposed bases, forming a second type of molecule – **messenger ribonucleic acid**, or **mRNA** for short. This mRNA, once formed, detaches and travels to cell 'organs' called **ribosomes** where, via another form of RNA (transfer or **tRNA**), it forms the template for amino acid, and hence protein production. The formation of proteins from DNA is called **transcription**. DNA has one other main function – to make copies of itself, otherwise known as **replication**. Replication occurs when a strand of DNA fully unzips to form two separate strands. As before, free-floating bases attach to the exposed bases on the strand to form two new identical strands.

Each species may, in theory, be defined by the specific proteins that its DNA produces. Our own species has perhaps as many as 100,000 different proteins that make up the body and all of the chemical reactions within (although the base-pair sequence has been determined the exact number and sequence of proteins that our DNA codes for is yet to be resolved, see box 2.4). Given that a third of all protein-coding genes are **expressed** only in the brain (i.e. they only produce proteins here) many behavioural biologists believe that differences in personality and intellectual ability may, in part, be traced back to differences in the genetic code that we inherit from our parents (Plomin *et al.*, 2008).

Box 2.4 **The Human Genome Project – unravelling the code to build a person?**

Although a draft sequence of the human genome was originally published in February 2001, it was in April 2003 that the world woke up to hear the news that the entire human genome had been sequenced. Humans were not the first species to be sequenced – the DNA for thirty-nine species of bacteria had already been determined as well as a species of yeast, a nematode worm, the *Drosophila* fruit fly and a mustard weed. But unravelling our own DNA was arguably a quantum leap forward compared with sequencing these 'simpler' species. So now we know the precise base-pair sequence for human DNA and, as a consequence, we also know how many genes it takes to build a person. This is a major triumph of molecular biology. Indeed some evolutionists have claimed that this is the biggest scientific development the world has ever seen (Ridley, 1999; 2003). Others, however, have suggested that this breakthrough begs as many questions as it answers. One important question that we might ask is what does knowing the human genome sequence really tell us about how we are built? Another is, given that our genes vary from person to person at hundreds of different loci, whose DNA has been sequenced? Turning to the second question first, the Human Genome Project (HGP) has really produced the average or consensus human sequence for 200 people. The first question, unfortunately, is not so easily answered. Genes specify the sequence of amino acids that link up to form large molecules called polypeptides – biochemically one gene codes for one polypeptide. Proteins are then created by linking a number of these polypeptides together. Humans are built from proteins (based on 3 billion nucleotide base-pairs). You might think that knowing the base-pair sequence allows us to determine the polypeptide sequence and that this, in turn, allows us to determine the precise number of proteins that make up a human. Wrong. Polypeptides literally fold themselves up into various shapes in order to form proteins. But many polypeptides can fold themselves up in different ways resulting in different proteins. How precisely they fold themselves depends on the presence of a number of smaller molecules in a given cell, such as sugars, and on the presence of other proteins. This is why, although the base-pair sequence is now known, this information alone does not tell us the protein sequence. It also helps to explain why, although humans have perhaps 90,000–100,000 proteins, these are created from fewer than 22,000 genes (which incidentally is not enormously more than the fruit fly with 13,000 and the nematode worm with 18,000). In September 2011 the next step was announced – to identify at least one protein for each of the exons (protein-producing genes). This project, called the **Human Proteome Project** (HPP), was launched at the Geneva World Congress and it is anticipated that such knowledge will not only bring us a step closer to understanding the role that proteins play in body and brain development and function but will also help us to treat human diseases more successfully (Banku and Abalaka, 2012). Perhaps the results of the Human Genome Project should be seen as the beginning of the understanding of what it takes to build a human rather than the end point as many have suggested.

Since genes code for the synthesis of the building blocks of the body they are frequently considered to be the blueprints that dictate how an organism is built. As Oxford zoologist Richard Dawkins (1982) has pointed out, however, this analogy is an oversimplification; a better one is that genes make up a recipe for development. In a recipe for baking a cake, for example, the ingredients are specified by instructions prior to baking. The quality and availability of ingredients and the temperature and humidity of the oven, however, will all have an effect on the final product. In this analogy the recipe consists of the genetic code that is inherited and the other variables are equivalent to environmental input during development which, in ourselves, range from peer pressure and parental attitude to upbringing, through diet and illnesses to education. As Dawkins rightly points out, once it is taken out of the oven there is 'no one-to-one reversible mapping from words of recipe to crumbs of cake' (Dawkins, 1982). To Dawkins it is practically impossible to partition out the specific effects of individual genes. Nor is it easy to determine the precise effects of specific environmental variables on the outcome of a characteristic in an individual. Despite this it is possible to make an overall estimation of the relative contribution that genes make to individual differences.

Heritability of characteristics

As mentioned previously, animal breeders have long taken advantage of the emergence of individual differences in their livestock to breed for exaggerated features. The estimation of the extent to which we are able to breed for a characteristic is called its **heritability**. Canadian evolutionists Martin Daly and Margo Wilson define heritability as 'the proportion of the observed phenotypic variance that can be attributed to correlated variance in genotypes' (Daly and Wilson, 1983). Put simply, this is an estimation of the extent to which a characteristic in a population is due to genetic rather than environmental components. Daly and Wilson use egg production to illustrate the notion of heritability. In recent years egg producers have been able to increase the size of domestic hen eggs far more successfully than they have been able to increase the number of eggs produced by each hen. This is because there is more genetic variability available for egg size than egg number. Egg size therefore has a larger heritability than egg number.

Note that estimations of heritability must always be qualified by specifying the population or, in effect, the gene pool. As Daly and Wilson correctly assert, in a different population of hens heritability for these two characteristics might be equal or even reversed. This might be the case, for example, in the wild-living equivalent of modern-day domestic hens, the Red Burmese junglefowl. In domestic hens it may be that egg producers have pushed their flocks to a point where it is very difficult to increase further the number of eggs that a hen can produce in a year (which is around 365, incidentally) but that there still remains a greater degree of genetic variation for egg size. This means that under current rearing conditions there is little variation that can affect egg number. If a number of gene mutations were to arise and rearing conditions were greatly altered, then egg number might become more heritable. In contrast to domestic hens, for junglefowl the number of eggs laid is much smaller and varies with the seasons. Since junglefowl have not been selectively bred to produce so many eggs throughout the year, in populations of this sub-species it may be possible to push this number up greatly. So for Red Burmese junglefowl the number of eggs laid may be highly heritable when compared to their domestic cousins.

Studying the heritability of egg production certainly has practical implications – an egg producer's livelihood may depend on it – but when we turn our attention to human cognitive and behavioural characteristics the notion of a genetic basis for such features takes on social and political connotations. The idea of human abilities being largely inherited has been misused on a number of occasions during the twentieth century. It is important then that we are clear about the limitations of heritability studies. To say that a characteristic is estimated to have a high degree of heritability does not mean that little can be done to modify it by changing the environment. Adult height may be a highly heritable characteristic in humans, but it may be substantially reduced when a child is reared with a highly restricted diet. So how might we estimate the degree of heritability of human abilities? One method is to examine the phenotypic variation in people who are genetically related to different degrees. In such studies comparing the correlation between monozygotic (identical) twins with the correlation between dizygotic (non-identical) twins on various traits has been of particular use (McFarland, 1999). The idea here is that, since identical twins share 100 per cent of their genes, whereas non-identical twins share 50 per cent of theirs, we would expect the correlation for any trait between the former to be much higher than between the latter if genes play a prominent role in the trait. Studies of the correlation between IQ scores in twins, for example, suggest a correlation of around 0.75 for identical twins and around 0.38 for non-identical twins (based on five studies, see Alcock, 2001; see also chapter 13). This finding has been taken by behavioural geneticists as evidence that intelligence shows quite a high degree of heritability (Alcock, 2001). We should bear in mind, however, that 0.75 is not a perfect correlation (i.e. 1.0), thus leaving room for environmental influence. In contrast to intelligence, most studies of personality traits suggest that about 40 per cent of the variation is due to genes, thus leaving around 60 per cent due to environmental differences between individuals (Plomin *et al.*, 2008; Alcock, 2001; see also chapters 6 and 13).

Gene flow and genetic drift

Up until now we have considered natural selection to be the cause of change in organisms over evolutionary time scales. Today natural selection is certainly seen as the prime mover in evolution. However, other causes of change can occur in a population. When animals move from one population to another they may, by chance, have a genetic makeup different from the new population. If the new makeup confers an advantage in the new local environment then the population can alter quite rapidly. This process is called **gene flow** since new genes 'flow' into a new environment. Another force for change called **genetic drift** consists of changes in a population that may build up by chance because they are selected neither for nor against. Genetic drift may operate in all populations but is believed to be a significant factor only in very small ones since each chance mating will have a bigger impact. Occasionally, however, genetic drift might have a major impact on a population due to a process called the **founder effect**. This means that when a new population is started by a small number of individuals, as might happen when a group of rodents colonises an island for the first time, then they are likely to have only a small proportion of the genes from the population they left behind. In these circumstances the founder effect may mean that genetic drift is initially of great importance. This means that under some conditions, processes other than natural selection can lead to evolutionary change, but under most circumstances natural selection is the prime mover in evolution.

Levels of selection – the fittest what?

As we saw earlier, natural selection is frequently referred to as the survival of the fittest. But the fittest what? Species? Group of individuals? Individuals themselves? Since Darwin first introduced the notion of survival of the fittest, people have frequently taken this to mean survival of the species. As we will see when considering the relationship between evolution and behaviour, nothing could be further from the truth.

Group selection

In 1962 Scottish biologist Vero Wynne-Edwards published a book entitled *Animal Dispersion in Relation to Social Behaviour*. It was destined to be one of the most cited texts on evolution published in the twentieth century. But unlike Darwin's opus a century before, Wynne-Edwards' book became famous for being wrong. In *Animal Dispersion* Wynne-Edwards proposed that an animal's behaviour is shaped

Box 2.5 **The evolution of our species – the emergence of modern *Homo sapiens***

Currently two competing views exist as to where and when modern *Homo sapiens* emerged. The **multi-regional hypothesis** is the view that gradual changes in numerous Eurasian populations of *Homo erectus* led, via archaic *Homo sapiens*, to anatomically modern humans. In contrast, the **out-of-Africa** hypothesis suggests that a later African population of *H. erectus* led (again via archaic *H. sapiens*) to modern *H. sapiens* and that these then gradually spread out of Africa displacing earlier hominins.

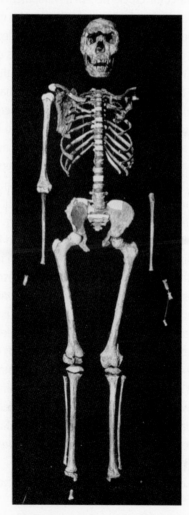

This skeleton of a *Homo erectus* boy (less than 12 years old) is the most complete specimen of an archaic human ever discovered. It was found in Kenya in 1984 and dated to around 1.6 million years ago.

If the former argument is correct, then our direct ancestors lived outside of Africa for well over a million years, but if the latter is correct, then we all share a recent common ancestor that lived in Africa between 100,000 and 200,000 years ago. It also suggests that our ancestors have only recently colonised the rest of the world (recently on a geographical timescale, that is).

Which hypothesis is correct? The advocates of the multi-regional hypothesis rely largely on their interpretation of the fossil record. The proponents of the out-of-Africa theory also rely on an interpretation of the fossil record but additionally they make use of another, more powerful tool – the **molecular clock**. Recent developments in molecular biology have led to the new sub-field of **molecular genetics**. Molecular geneticists have turned their attention to the genes that exist outside of a cell's nucleus in order to create their molecular clock. You may be surprised to discover that genes exist outside of a cell's nucleus. In the **cytoplasm** (the jelly-like material surrounding the central nucleus) of each human cell there are thousands of minuscule lozenge-shaped bodies called **mitochondria**. The mitochondria are responsible for providing energy for the cell via the controlled breakdown of sugars from food and are believed to have evolved from bacteria that invaded living cells around two billion years ago. Each mitochondrion has its own small single ring of genes that is passed on through the maternal line directly in the ova. This means that mitochondrial genes remain uncontaminated by sexual reproduction or selection pressures and the only changes that occur to their DNA sequence arise through random mutations (Dawkins, 2004; Oppenheimer, 2004). Since the mutation rate is well known for mitochondria (somewhat higher than for nuclear DNA), then, by comparing the variability in base-pair sequences between people from different geographical regions, molecular geneticists have been able to estimate when our most recent common ancestor existed. It is these changes in mitochondrial DNA that constitute the molecular clock and the figure that molecular geneticists have determined through this technique is around 150,000 years ago. The molecular clock is considered such a powerful tool because, whereas a fossil might have left descendants, all of our mitochondrial DNA certainly had ancestors (Goldsmith and Zimmerman, 2001). Since the mitochondrial DNA is only passed down via the female line the earliest common human ancestor of present living humans has been called 'Mitochondrial Eve' or sometimes 'African Eve'. Hence today many evolutionists support the later out-of-Africa argument and claim that African Eve was indeed the common ancestor of us all (Aiello, 1993; Lahr and Foley, 1994; Meredith, 2011).

by evolution to aid the survival and reproduction of its group. If many twentieth-century evolutionary theorists had been decidedly vague about the level at which natural selection operates, Wynne-Edwards was very clear. For him it operated at the level of the group. Wynne-Edwards used this **group selection** theory to explain many aspects of animal social behaviour. And it appeared to make a great deal of sense. Why else should songbirds give alarm calls to warn other members of their group that predators were present? Why else should the runt of a litter give up its life for its littermates? And why else should animals come together so frequently from communal roosts to communal migrations unless they were assessing the size of the population and using this information to control breeding so as not to overexploit resources? Animals, unlike humans, Wynne-Edwards argued, help the survival of the group (and hence the species) by only breeding when times are right. When times are hard, the group as a whole holds back and therefore survives into future generations. In Wynne-Edwards's eyes animals had evolved to be truly self-sacrificing or **altruistic**.

Such arguments make great intuitive sense and they appeal to our sense of fair play. Unfortunately natural selection has nothing to say about fair play. It is merely the name given to describe the process by which some individuals are better able to pass on copies of their genes to future generations than are others. Imagine a group where everybody breeds only when it is good for the group, producing fewer offspring at times when food availability is low, for example. Now imagine an individual in that population which has a mutant gene that makes it attempt to produce as many offspring as possible, selfishly ignoring the greater good of the group. It is this selfish individual which is most likely to pass on its genes under such conditions, not the altruistic ones (Dawkins, 1976).

Wynne-Edwards's thesis may well have done a service to the understanding of the relationship between behaviour and evolution in that it led other evolutionists to scratch their heads and decide whether it stood up to scrutiny. One evolutionist who scratched his more than able head and found the thesis to be wanting was George Williams. In 1966 Williams published a book on evolution called *Adaptation and Natural Selection*. In it he showed that when animals do cooperate it is almost always between close relatives. If animals were acting altruistically to their kin then they were really acting to promote copies of their own genes in relatives. If this is the case then it is not real altruism but ultimately selfish behaviour from the point of view of the gene. Williams's argument drew upon the most clear-thinking evolutionary theorists of his day and in bringing together their arguments (and adding a few of his own) *Adaptation and Natural Selection* severely dented Wynne-Edwards's notion of group selection.

Inclusive fitness

One of the foundation stones of Williams's argument was laid by another evolutionary theorist of the mid 1960s, Bill Hamilton, who proposed a theory which revolutionised the very way that we look at the relationship between evolution and behaviour. Hamilton (1964a, b), like Williams, held the view that selection worked on individuals. Clearly individuals may help to increase the survival of their offspring by looking

> ### Box 2.6 **Multilevel selection theory**
>
> Although today most evolutionary psychologists subscribe to individual- or gene-level selection theory, the notion of group selection is by no means dead and buried. A number of evolutionists have attempted to revive a form of group selectionism under the banner of **multilevel selection theory**. Multilevel selection is particularly associated with American evolutionists Elliot Sober and David Sloan Wilson (see for example Wilson and Sober, 1994; Sober and Wilson, 1999). Multilevel selection is a complex theory that proposes that groups, in addition to individuals, might be considered to be 'vehicles' in the language of Richard Dawkins. Although Sober and Wilson have sought to revive the group as a unit of selection, they do not propose that this replaces either gene- or individual-level selection – but rather that natural selection can act at all three levels (hence 'multilevel'). Drawing on both logical and empirical studies, Sober and Wilson argue that, when individual group members cooperate, the group can then outcompete other groups in terms of reproductive success. What sets this apart from Wynne-Edwards's group selectionism is the recognition that gene- and individual-level selection also occur. In this sense it appears to be a half-way house argument.
>
> This view is not without support from evolutionary psychologists and sociobiologists. E. O. Wilson, for example, has been favourable to multilevel selection theory (Wilson, 2005; 2012; Wilson and Holldobler, 2005). The gene-centred evolutionists such as Richard Dawkins (1994) and Daniel Dennett (1994) are yet to be convinced about multilevel selection, however. Dawkins in particular has argued that ultimately genes are the currency of natural selection – even though in the short term the group may appear to be the unit of selection. In his view what Sober and Wilson are advocating is not really a form of group selection. To Dawkins true group selection should see groups spawning other groups, which then compete with other groups still for survival. The winning group then passes on its 'genes' to the next generation. This is not really what Sober and Wilson have in mind with their model of multilevel selection.
>
> Multilevel selection may have kept the argument about the level of selection on the table, but it has a long way to go if it is to convince mainstream evolutionary psychologists. Due to its current standing in evolutionary psychology, in this book we adhere largely to the individual/gene-centred view of the relationship between behaviour and evolution.

after them. You don't need to be an evolutionary theorist to notice that parental care is common throughout the animal kingdom. Animals, in effect, invest time and effort in raising their offspring because having surviving offspring is what natural selection is all about (note that this suggests for many species individuals investing less time and effort in their offspring were less likely to pass their genes on). What Hamilton did was simply to expand this argument to consider the way that animals might treat other relatives. Since we share, on average, 50 per cent of our genes with each of our offspring, an act of heroism saving two children would save 100 per cent of our genes. However, we also share 25 per cent of our genes with each of our nephews, nieces and grandchildren and 12.5 per cent with each of our cousins and so on. Thus an act of heroism which saved, say, four grandchildren or eight cousins would also save on average 100 per cent of our genes. These great acts of heroism are extreme examples used for the sake of illustration. The main point is that an individual can also pass on copies of its genes indirectly by giving aid to relatives other than direct offspring.

Hamilton called the proportion of genes shared between two family members the **coefficient of relatedness** or 'r'. This value may vary from 1 to 0. Identical twins share all of their genes and have an r of 1, siblings and offspring have an r of 0.5, while for grandchildren, nephews and nieces it is 0.25 and for cousins 0.125. Using this information it becomes clear that there are now two ways in which an animal can aid the transfer of copies of its genes into the next generation: directly via offspring or indirectly through giving aid to other relatives. If fitness had come to mean the number of surviving offspring an individual produced, Hamilton now added the number of other relatives that an individual helped to survive, each of which is weighted by its 'r', to the equation to come up with a value that he called **inclusive fitness**. This means that inclusive fitness is equal to the sum of direct and indirect fitness. Since the 1960s experts interested in the social behaviour of animals have used Hamilton's notion of inclusive fitness to help explain some of the remarkable acts of apparent altruism within groups of closely related individuals. Apparent altruism directed at relatives has been called kin-selected altruism by Maynard Smith (1964).

So for Hamilton, parental care is just an extreme and highly common form of kin-selected altruism. This highly influential argument will be explored further in chapter 7.

Reciprocal altruism

By focusing on the individual's relationship with family members Hamilton and Williams may have helped to explain away many examples of apparent altruism in the animal kingdom. But not all examples of animals giving aid to others involve relatives. Among the primates there are well documented cases of individuals aiding non-kin. An example of this is that unrelated vervet monkeys which form regular grooming pairs will come to each other's aid in combat (Seyfarth and Cheney, 1984). Until this and other examples of altruism could be explained, group selection still had a foothold in evolutionary theory. In the early 1970s a student of Hamilton by the name of Robert Trivers came up with an argument as to how non-relatives could engage in apparently altruistic acts without resorting to a group selection explanation. He called his idea **reciprocal altruism**. Reciprocal altruism might be likened to 'you scratch my back and I'll scratch yours' but it is just a little more complicated than this. In Trivers's model there are a few prerequisites. It is necessary for animals to live in quite stable groups, to be relatively long lived and to be capable of spotting cheats. It is also important that the cost of the altruistic act is low compared to the benefit. To quote Trivers:

Whenever the benefit of an altruistic act to the recipient is greater than the cost to the actor, then as long as the help is reciprocated at some later date, both participants will gain. (Trivers, 1971)

Trivers's reciprocal altruism appears to work quite well for humans. Imagine, for example, that we are living on the plains of the Serengeti in Africa and that I have just killed a wildebeest. There is more meat than I could possibly eat before it either goes off in the heat of the African sun or is stolen by a clan of hungry hyenas. You may be starving but I can save your life at very little cost by giving you meat that is left over when I've had my fill. A week later our roles might easily be reversed and you may then save my life with your meat. In this way, if individuals regularly meet each other and enter into such a reciprocal arrangement then we may all gain.

Reciprocated acts of kindness are arguably one of the main features of human society, but isn't this asking rather a lot of animals? Just how common reciprocal altruism is in the animal kingdom has become an area of great debate in recent years (Clutton-Brock, 2009). Furthermore if aid is given when reciprocated aid is anticipated is this really a form of altruism at all? We will further explore both kin altruism and reciprocal altruism when we turn our attention to social behaviour in chapters 7 and 8.

The selfish gene

The reasoning that Williams, Hamilton and Trivers put forward to explain cooperation and altruism led some evolutionists to reassess the level at which selection operated. If evolution has endowed and even promoted behavioural responses which might benefit others because they share copies of our genes, then perhaps we shouldn't be focusing on the individual as the entity that selection acts on at all. Perhaps we should be focusing on the gene itself. This is the conclusion that Richard Dawkins came to in the mid-1970s. His book *The Selfish Gene* (1976) drew on the ideas of Williams, Hamilton and Trivers but it also made an original contribution to evolutionary theory. Whereas previous works had suggested that we should be focusing on genes if we want to explain behaviour and physical traits, Dawkins explicitly proposed that the unit of selection is the gene itself. In order to explain his thesis he introduced a number of new terms into the debate, in particular the **replicator** and the **vehicle**. Replicators are any entities which are able to make copies of themselves and vehicles are the entities which, on a geological timescale, briefly carry the replicators. In the context of life on earth we can think of replicators as genes and vehicles as organisms, including ourselves.

But why the 'selfish gene'? When we talk about people behaving selfishly we are using purposive and emotive language. In the context of his theory Dawkins uses the term selfish in a very specific way. Genes are considered selfish since alleles in the past which affected bodies to promote copies of themselves at the expense of others are the ones that are with us today. Genes that promoted copies of other alleles in the past were quickly removed from the population. A gene which is a particularly good replicator will leave many copies of itself and may continue for an indeterminately large number of generations. In this way, while the vehicle may be considered a transient survival machine, the gene which is most 'selfish' may in theory be immortal via copies of itself that it leaves. So selfish in this context merely means affecting the organism to make one's own replication likely with no purposive state intended.

But why did Dawkins reach such a radical conclusion? By the early 1970s both theoretical and observational work was making this conclusion highly likely to Dawkins. As far as theory was concerned, as Ridley has put it:

Given that genes are the replicating currency of natural selection, it is an inevitable, algorithmic certainty that genes which cause behaviour that enhances the survival of such genes must thrive at the expense of genes that do not. (Ridley, 1996)

As far as observational work was concerned, since Hamilton's classic work of the 1960s it had become clear that many behaviour patterns make a great deal of sense from a gene-centred perspective. Why, for example, should social insects lay down their lives for each other? Why should naked mole rats give up the right to breed to their 'queen' but brutally tear members of other colonies to pieces should they be unfortunate enough to wander into the wrong tunnel? And why should vampire bats regurgitate blood into the mouths of their starving colony mates? All of these and many other examples of extreme social behaviour could be explained only by recourse to the gene-focused theories of Williams, Hamilton and Trivers whereby copies of the genes for such responses ultimately benefit from the behaviour. From the gene-centred perspective the individual organism only makes sense as a transient survival machine (which is sometimes expendable).

You may feel unhappy to be called a transient survival machine. If you do, then you are not alone. Dawkins's notion of the selfish gene has not been universally accepted. In fact it has received criticism from a number of quarters. Much of the criticism has come from individuals who may not have a very clear understanding of how Dawkins uses the term 'selfish gene' (e.g. Midgley, 1979 and Hayes, 1995);

others have moral or political misgivings about this way of looking at life (e.g. Rose *et al.*, 1984); still others have purely theoretical reservations (e.g. Daly and Wilson, 1983). Dawkins dealt with many of his critics in a series of stylish rebuttals (Dawkins 1979a; 1979b; 1989) and over the last thirty five years the gene-centred view has had a major impact not only on how we explain behaviour but also on the sort of questions that we now ask (Ridley, 1996). Indeed, selfish gene theory is considered by some to be one of the foundation stones which led to the development of evolutionary psychology (Pinker, 1997; Laland and Brown, 2011).

It would be a mistake, however, to assume that all evolutionists interested in behaviour today are dyed-in-the-wool selfish-geners. The individual versus gene-level selection argument continues. As Daly and Wilson (1983) have put it, 'what we observe are individual organisms behaving, and it is their behavior that we wish to understand'. For most examples of behaviour, then, individual selection may be equated with gene selection since both benefit from the act. When it comes to considering altruistic behaviour, however, as we will see in chapter 7, genes may sometimes benefit even when there is a net cost to the individual.

This chapter has been largely about the relationship between natural selection, genes and behaviour. In the next chapter we introduce a new and powerful driving force which may help to explore the relationship between these three areas further: sexual selection.

Summary

- By the mid-nineteenth century the notion that organisms change was in the air. Many scientists considered the notion of evolution seriously but the mechanism for this was lacking. In 1859 Charles Darwin introduced just such a mechanism – natural selection – to the scientific community and the public at large. Natural selection is based on heritable variation and differential reproductive success. Hence individuals with characteristics which allow them to survive and outbreed others pass on such characteristics to future generations.
- Mendel's work on breeding in pea plants, once rediscovered in the twentieth century, led to a modern understanding of the particulate nature of genetic inheritance. Mendel demonstrated that genes act in pairs to determine an individual's characteristics via a dominance–recessiveness relationship. In Mendelian genetics, genes for different characteristics are passed on individually rather than being attached to each other. Mendel called this segregation. Features that occur together in the adult do not necessarily appear together in the offspring. This independent assortment is a result of segregation.
- Genes are found at specific locations on larger bodies called chromosomes that occur in pairs (one from each parent). The position of a gene is called its locus and

alternate genes that may occur at a given locus are called alleles. Individuals with identical genes at the same locus on each of a pair of chromosomes are said to be homozygous for that characteristic; conversely, where individuals have different genes at the same locus they are said to be heterozygous. The complete set of an individual's genes is known as its genotype and the description of all of its characteristics (both physical and behavioural) is called its phenotype.

- During sexual reproduction sex cells or gametes are produced which have half the number of chromosomes of normal cells due to a process called meiosis. Fusion of two gametes (a sperm and an ovum) leads to a fertilised egg which thereby has the normal number of chromosomes once more. New body cells are formed which have the normal number of genes by a process called mitosis.

- Mendelian genetics has been modified by discoveries of the twentieth century. Genes that occur on the same chromosomes are often passed on together – this is called linkage. Due to linkage, assortment is not entirely independent. Mutations and recombination are important sources of variation of which Mendel was unaware. Additionally, many characteristics are polygenic, that is a number of genes are involved in determining the trait. Alternatively, individual genes may be pleiotropic, which means that they have more than one phenotypic effect. The expression of a gene may be altered by another gene, called a modifier gene.

- The heritability of a characteristic is an estimation of the extent to which it may be bred for.

- Although natural selection is the main mechanism responsible for *adaptive* change, other processes may also lead to change. Examples of this are gene flow – the movement of individuals with different genes into new areas – and genetic drift – random changes that build up over time.

- Physically, chromosomes consist of deoxyribonucleic acid (DNA) which contains four alternating nucleotides (adenine, thymine, cytosine and guanine – A, T, C and G). These nucleotides code in three-letter codons for amino acids – the building blocks of proteins. In this way we can think of genes as functioning to code for protein production.

- During the latter half of the twentieth century evolutionists debated the level at which natural selection operates. Wynne-Edwards considered that individuals acted for the good of the group (i.e. group selection). Other experts such as George Williams and Bill Hamilton disagreed, arguing that individuals who act for the good of themselves and their relatives are more likely to pass their genes on to future generations (i.e. individual selection). Hamilton also suggested that individuals may pass on copies of their genes indirectly by giving aid to their relatives. The likelihood of them doing so may be related to the number of genes they share by common descent – their coefficient of relatedness (r). Maynard Smith called this kin selection. Kin selection has been used to explain the existence of self-sacrificing behaviour or altruism in ourselves and other species. Robert Trivers further suggested that examples of altruistic behaviour might be explained by a process of reciprocation – reciprocal altruism.

- The work of Williams, Hamilton and Trivers has led evolutionists to reconsider the level at which selection operates. In his book *The Selfish Gene* Richard Dawkins made explicit the notion of the gene as the unit of selection and introduced the concepts of the replicator and the vehicle. In the case of organic life, the replicator is the gene and the vehicle the organism. Debates concerning individual versus gene selection continue. For most purposes selection pressures which act on individuals will also act on genes directly. In the case of altruistic and selfish behaviour, however, this may not always be the case.

Questions

1. Old psychology and biology textbooks frequently suggested that animals' behaviour has evolved to aid the 'survival of the species'. Why is this notion problematic?
2. The notion of the selfish gene has been quite heavily criticised. Why do you think that people are unhappy with this term? You should be able to conceive of at least three different forms of criticism.
3. The 'out of Africa' hypothesis of human evolution suggests all modern human ethnic groups arose from a quite recent common ancestor. In contrast, the 'multi-regional' hypothesis suggests *Homo erectus* evolved into *Homo sapiens* separately in different geographical locations in our more distant past. If the multi-regional hypothesis were found to be correct what would this say about notions of a common human nature? Might it be argued that the multi-regional hypothesis is politically incorrect?
4. Robert Trivers's notion of reciprocal altruism has had a profound effect on our understanding of why humans help each other. But is reciprocal altruism really altruism? Present an argument for why it should be considered as altruism and an argument taking issue with this.

FURTHER READING

Dawkins, R. (1976; 1989; 2006). *The Selfish Gene.* Oxford: Oxford University Press. A clearly argued account of the relationship between evolution and animal behaviour which also made an original contribution to evolutionary thinking by arguing that natural selection operates at the level of the gene.

(1986). *The Blind Watchmaker.* Harlow: Longman. Argues persuasively that alternative explanations of complexity to natural selection do not stand up to scientific scrutiny.

Dennett, D. C. (1995). *Darwin's Dangerous Idea: Evolution and the Meanings of Life.* New York: Simon and Schuster. A wide-ranging and ambitious attempt to present a number of debates in relation to the importance of Darwinism as an explanatory tool.

Laland, K. N. and Brown, G. R. (2011). *Sense and Nonsense: Evolutionary Perspectives on Human Behaviour.* Oxford: Oxford University Press. A critical review of the various approaches that have been developed in order to explore to the relationship between human behaviour and evolution. Includes sociobiology, behavioural ecology and evolutionary psychology.

Plotkin, H. C. (2004). *Evolutionary Thought in Psychology: A Brief History.* Oxford: Blackwell Publishing. Lucid and accessible account of the history and current standing of the relationship between psychology and evolutionary theory.

3 Sexual selection

KEY CONCEPTS

sexual selection • female choice • parental investment • handicap hypothesis • parasite theory • Muller's ratchet • tangled bank • the Red Queen • arms race

Natural selection has become well accepted as the main mechanism of evolutionary change. Despite this acceptance, it is clear that it fails to explain why males and females of many species differ so much. In this chapter we consider the way that the behaviour of each sex might affect the behaviour of the other. This is the concept of sexual selection. We also consider why sex itself exists as a means of reproduction when so many species are able to do without it. Finally, we look at some examples from the animal kingdom of how the behaviour of each sex may be affected by sexual selection.

Darwin and sexual selection

During the writing of *The Origin of Species* Darwin realised that many animals had both physical and behavioural features which are very difficult to explain in terms of natural selection. Because they face the same ecological pressures, natural selection should drive the characteristics of males and females of a species in the same direction; and yet in many vertebrate species males are larger and more gaudy than their female counterparts. Furthermore, males generally engage in a greater degree of risk-taking behaviour. The elaborate feathers that make up a peacock's tail, for example, make him conspicuous to predators such as foxes and tigers and the piercing calls that he makes to attract females also inform predators of his whereabouts. Since natural selection was thought to promote anti-predator adaptations, it seems strange that such features should have arisen in his ancestors.

In addition to drawing attention from predators, the time and energy that many males spend in making courtship calls might otherwise have been spent on foraging and on other beneficial activities such as preening. This means that being attractive to females and spending time attempting to attract them must have real and potential costs. Despite these costs Darwin realised that traits which helped males to attract females would increase their chances of mating and thereby of passing on such features. So Darwin argued that features which helped you to breed might paradoxically sometimes be selected for, even up to the point of shortening your life. In 1871 with the publication of *The Descent of Man, and Selection in Relation to Sex* he developed a new selective force, **sexual selection**. Sexual selection applies to those characteristics that provide individuals with advantages in gaining access to mates. Hence if natural selection is survival of the fittest then we can think of sexual selection as 'survival of the sexiest'. Evolutionary psychologists have suggested that this is as true of our species as it is of others. A number of surveys of human mate preference, for example, demonstrate how men from a wide range of cultures find the classic hour-glass shape of young women particularly attractive (Buss, 2011). This makes sense when applying sexual selection theory since this shape is an indicator of fertility in women (human mate preferences will be discussed further in chapter 4).

Intrasexual and intersexual selection

Having introduced sexual selection in *The Descent of Man*, Darwin went on to outline how this competition for mates might take two different forms. **Intrasexual** selection consists of individuals competing with members of their own sex for access to the opposite sex. In most cases this means males fighting with each other for access to females. In contrast, **intersexual** selection consists of members of one sex attempting to impress members of the other; in this case the emphasis is on females since they are generally the ones that need to be impressed before they will assent to mating. Intrasexual selection is generally regarded as being responsible for males developing weapons to compete with each other such as large teeth and horns, greater musculature and a lower threshold for aggression when compared to their female counterparts (Clutton-Brock *et al.*, 1982). Intersexual selection, however, is believed to lead to the evolution of sexual ornamentation such as brighter plumage and courtship display in males in order to impress females (Andersson, 1982; Brennan, 2010). For their part, Darwin predicted that females should be choosy about which males they accept as mating partners; perhaps discriminating on the basis of male ornamentation and display. This means that for most species we can equate intrasexual selection with male–male competition and intersexual selection with **female choice**.

Do females have a choice?

In contrast to natural selection, the notion of sexual selection did not receive strong support during Darwin's day, even from those within the biological fraternity. While

Box 3.1 **Two forms of selection or one?**

From the moment Darwin introduced the notion of sexual selection into biology there has been a long-standing debate as to whether it really is a distinct and separate process from natural selection. Since each leads ultimately to increasing inclusive fitness (see chapter 2), then might they not both be labelled 'natural selection'? And, even for those who accept the argument of two separate processes, there remains one specific sticking point. Male weapons, such as enlarged teeth and horns, are frequently used to fight with each other *and* to ward off predators. This means that it is not always easy to determine the extent to which sexual and natural selection have contributed to the development of these features (Halliday, 1994). However, given that many examples of gaudy male ornamentation are likely to be driven in different directions by natural and sexual selection, we feel it is instructive to consider the two processes separately.

there was some acceptance that males might develop weapons such as tusks to compete with each other over females, many experts were distinctly sceptical about the idea of female choice. Given that females are smaller and less aggressive than males in most species, surely they were unlikely to have much choice when it came to sexual matters? In addition to this practical argument there were more serious theoretical concerns. In particular, Darwin was unable to explain why female preference should arise. Many examples of male adornment and courtship rituals were known to nineteenth-century naturalists, from the gaudy face of the mandrill to the exotic feathers of the birds of paradise. Although it might be argued that males which were successful in using such features to attract females would pass on such characteristics to their offspring, this still raised the question – what was in it for the females? Why should they choose gaudy males who would surely attract greater attention from predators? During the twentieth century a number of theories were advanced which attempted to answer these questions. It is useful to explore these theories in order to understand how sexual selection has gradually become of great importance to the understanding of the relationship between evolution and behaviour.

Theories of sexual selection

Sexy males and parental investment

In 1930 the English geneticist Ronald Fisher turned his attention to the relationship between female choice and male adornment and in doing so he rekindled interest in sexual selection. Fisher (1930) argued that ancestral females would have been attracted to males which had, for example, well-maintained tail feathers, since these might signal that they are likely to be good flyers. Furthermore, since such males had time to maintain such feathers, this was evidence of superior foraging and other abilities that would aid survival. For Fisher the feature chosen by females had to have some original survival advantage. Once the tail feathers (or whichever feature) had been selected, however, they could become exaggerated and evolve beyond their original function. Females who preferentially mate with males which show these inherited attractive features will, of course, produce more attractive sons since their offspring are likely to have the genes for such characteristics. Such sons would also be more likely to be chosen by females in the future. To Fisher, then, the most important trait that a male can offer a potential mate is his genes for being attractive. This suggests that once a feature has been chosen by females it may become progressively exaggerated with each generation since females will constantly be looking for individuals with the largest, brightest example of that feature. Fisher called this '**runaway selection**' since the feature runs away from its original function and becomes selected purely on the basis of its attractive qualities. In this way Fisher was able to put forward an explanation for the extreme tail feathers that we see today in peacocks. Eventually, according to Fisher, such superplumage would stop being exaggerated further because of its costs to survival; natural selection would therefore keep runaway selection in check. That is, there will be a trade off between attracting females and costs such as attracting predators.

Parental investment

Despite Fisher's efforts in this area, there was still an important piece missing from the theory. Darwin assumed that males would compete with each other for female attention and that females would be the choosy ones. But why should this be the case rather than the reverse? In 1972 Robert Trivers suggested that sexual selection is directly related to asymmetries between the sexes in the amount of effort that each parent puts into raising the offspring. He called this effort **parental investment**. Trivers (1972; 1985) chronicled the various ways that, for the vast majority of animal species, females invest a great deal more effort into producing offspring than do males. This asymmetry begins with gamete formation where males produce a large amount of low-cost sperm compared to the relatively small number of larger and more expensive eggs produced by females. Since an egg contains the material that provides for the initial development of the zygote it is approximately one million times larger than the spermatozoan that fertilises it. In contrast, a sperm provides nothing more than its genes. For most species this disparity of numbers means that, while females are limited in having a comparatively small number of eggs that may

Figure 3.1 A male elephant seal dwarfs the surrounding females and pups

be fertilised during their lives, males are limited only by the number of matings they are able to accomplish.

Asymmetrical gamete cost, however, is only the beginning of the inequality of investment between the sexes, since females generally put more time and effort into the rearing process. For mammals, this sexual disparity in effort can be enormous owing to the role that a female plays in terms of gestation, lactation and general nurturing. Since females invest so much in their offspring, Trivers argued that they should be very choosy about which males they allow to fertilise their eggs. For males, however, where the costs of reproducing are nearly always lower, Trivers predicted there should be far less discrimination and choosiness. A male that makes a poor mating choice loses very little (frequently no more than a little effort and a small amount of sperm). A female who makes a bad choice, however, will generally have to pay a much heavier cost for her mistake because she is generally the one left 'holding the baby'.

An extreme example of this sexual asymmetry is illustrated by the differing reproductive efforts made by male and female elephant seals (Trivers, 1985; Sanvito *et al.*, 2007). Male elephant seals (bulls) weigh in at almost 3,000 kg; females (cows), in contrast, are about a quarter of this size – typically around 650 kg. A bull elephant

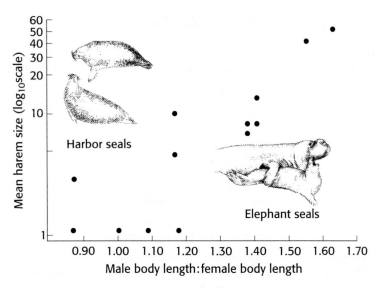

Figure 3.2 Harem size in relation to size of male

seal provides a few grams of sperm while the cow typically produces a pup weighing around 50 kg. During its first five weeks of life the pup will gain 100 kg and the cow will lose 200 kg. In contrast, the male puts his time and effort into inseminating as many other females as possible and defending his right to do so by threatening and fighting other males.

So, 100 years after Darwin first proposed the mechanism of sexual selection, Trivers suggested that choosiness in females is a direct result of their greater investment in offspring. Following Trivers's watershed paper of 1972, students of animal behaviour have paid more attention to the notion of female choosiness and its relationship to male traits. The repercussions of female choice are interesting when looking at characteristics in males. Is it possible that many present-day male characteristics may be the direct result of choices that their female ancestors made?

Female choice and male adornment

Most of the work on sexual selection since Trivers's paper on parental investment has been concerned with how females are able to assess a male's quality (Manning and Stamp-Dawkins, 1998; Brennan, 2010). One of the most controversial ideas came from the Israeli evolutionist Amotz Zahavi, who turned Fisher's idea on its head. Zahavi (1975) suggested that males might develop ornaments not to look attractive but, perversely, as an impediment in order to demonstrate their abilities to survive despite having such a handicap. According to this argument, males develop elaborate

Table 3.1 **Theories of evolutionary origin of male characteristics**

Theory and associated researcher	Theory proposes	Theory predicts
Runaway selection theory (Fisher, 1930)	Male adornments driven beyond original function by female preference for attractive features Male features not direct indicators of genetic superiority i.e. 'sexy sons'	Females will choose males purely on grounds of attractiveness
Parasite theory (Hamilton and Zuk, 1982)	Male adornments arose to display lack of parasites to females Male features signify genetic superiority i.e. 'healthy-offspring'	Females choose male features that demonstrate a lack of parasites and hence genetic quality
Handicap theory (Zahavi, 1975)	Male adornments are chosen by females for their conspicuous and costly nature Male features signify genetic superiority i.e. 'healthy-offspring'	Females choose males which show conspicuous and costly adornments as a sign of genetic quality

ornaments in order to signal 'I must be a good quality male if I can survive carrying this burden!' Hence to Zahavi male adornments allow females to assess their ability to survive and hence they are real signals of genetic quality. As with Darwin's original notion of sexual selection, despite initial criticism (e.g. Maynard Smith, 1978), what has become known as the **handicap hypothesis** has subsequently gained support from a number of experts (e.g. Andersson, 1986; Grafen, 1990; see also Zahavi, 2003).

The parasite theory and honest signalling

In a similar vein to Zahavi, but somewhat in contrast to Fisher's argument, in 1982 Bill Hamilton and his colleague Marlene Zuk proposed that male adornments evolved to demonstrate to females that they are free from parasites. They call this the **parasite theory** of female choice. Parasites, of course, may be anything from tapeworms and fleas to microbial life forms such as bacteria and viruses.

Given that parasites account for a larger proportion of fatalities than either predators or competitive conspecifics, so the argument goes, males which develop an elaborate healthy feature should be chosen by females since they are likely to pass on healthy genes to their offspring. To put it another way, if males with the fewest parasites are able to produce the most elaborate ornaments and if females choose males on this basis then they should be passing disease resistance on to their offspring.

The parasite theory differs from that of Zahavi in that, while both rely on males offering real signals of quality, the ornament is seen as a development to display health directly rather than as a handicap. The implication is clear, the more parasites have played an important role in your ancestry then the greater the pressure on you to signal your lack of them. The Hamilton–Zuk parasite theory raises a fundamental question about the signals that animals give to each other. In order for this theory to stand up it is necessary for males to be **honest signallers**. This means that, for females to benefit from the signals that male ornaments provide, it is necessary that these features really do correlate with parasite resistance rather than simply appearing to do so.

Evaluating theories on female choice and male adornment

Although the Hamilton–Zuk theory has been received favourably in recent years it is by no means universally accepted and there is still much debate surrounding sexual selection theory. Currently, the main sticking point is whether males' ornamentation has evolved simply to make them attractive to females or whether it serves as a signal of real quality. The former argument can be traced back to Fisher, while the latter is currently supported by the Hamilton–Zuk parasite theory. Matt Ridley (1993) refers to this debate as the 'Fisherians v. good-geners', although it has also been called 'sexy sons' v. 'healthy offspring' (see Cronin, 1991). For the 'good-geners' it is necessary to demonstrate that male adornments are widespread real signals of health and disease resistance in the animal kingdom. For the 'Fisherians' it is necessary to demonstrate that females favour males purely for their attractive features – their 'sexiness' – which a female can then pass on to her sons. Currently both sides can claim some support from the experimental literature (see box 3.2).

The studies outlined in box 3.2 are certainly consistent with the notion of parasites having played a role in male adornment, but they are not direct evidence of female choice. Might not male–male competition have provided the driving force for such plumage rather than female choice? Today there is quite clear evidence that female choice *is* involved in the development of male adornments. In swallows, for example, it is well established that females prefer males with longer tail feathers (Moller, 1988; 1990). This finding, in isolation, might be taken as evidence for either a Fisherian or a good-genes argument (Moller himself favours Zahavi's handicap hypothesis, which is a form of good-geners argument). In 1994, however, Norberg decided to determine whether or not male swallow tail feathers are a direct signal of a healthy feature or just a signal of sexiness. He placed a number of male swallows in a wind tunnel and discovered that those with longer tail feathers had improved flight performance due to an increase in lift. This suggests that the long tail feathers not only increase the attractiveness of a male but that they may do so because they are a real and direct

Box 3.2 Fisher versus Hamilton–Zuk – attractiveness versus good genes

One area of study, which appears to support Fisher's runaway selection hypothesis concerns **sensory bias** in females. Female sensory bias means that they pay particular attention to specific male features and that such an attention bias is inherited as a part of sexual selection. Basolo (1990) demonstrated, unsurprisingly, that female swordtail fish prefer males with the longest sword (an extension of the tail fin which only males of the species have). This would be predicted by both Fisherians and good-geners. What is surprising, however, was the finding that females of a closely related species called platyfish, a species in which neither sex has a sword, also prefer males with a long sword. In other words, these females prefer males of another species because they have the same sensory bias as their close relatives. The explanation for this curious favouritism appears to be that male platyfish used to have a sword, which they lost quite recently in evolutionary terms; but females still have the sensory bias for this feature (Basolo, 1995). Basolo suggests that the sword of swordtail fish does not signal a real health benefit but that it is simply a sexy male feature.

But surely if female platyfish currently have a sensory bias for a sword-like tail how can we explain its loss in the males of their own species? Haines and Gould (1994) may have provided the answer by studying a relative of both swordtails and platyfish – guppies. They found that guppies with shorter tails were better able to escape from an artificial predator than those with longer ones, despite the fact that females *preferred* the longer-tailed males! Perhaps the ancestors of each of these three related species had to solve different problems of predator pressure? Following an initial female preference for long tails in the common ancestor of all three species of fish, perhaps platyfish and guppies moved to areas where, due to specific predator pressure, the benefit of a shorter tail outweighed the advantages of having a sexy long tail. This scenario may be a good illustration of how natural and sexual selection may pull in different directions and how males might have to make compromises.

If Basolo's studies appear to lend support to the Fisherians, the good-geners can also draw on a number of studies to back their own stance. Zuk (1992), for example, has demonstrated that in tropical birds, the number of parasites a species has is directly proportional to the greater the degree of ornamentation seen in its males. Furthermore, it also appears that it is only those males who really have resistance to parasites that are able to produce the most striking ornaments (Zuk, 1992). Indeed it is now known that in a wide range of species including fishes, frogs, insects and birds it is the flamboyant species that are particularly troubled by parasites and within these species females show a clear preference for males which have the fewest parasites (see Cronin, 1991; Ridley, 1993; Willis and Poulin, 2000; Martin and Johnsen, 2007).

Figure 3.3 A male barn swallow's long tail is a sign of good health and attractive to females

indication of good genes. That is, they aid the development of an aerodynamically superior tail despite ecological pressures such as the presence of parasites.

We can see that a number of issues remain to be resolved with regard to the precise relationship between female choice and male adornment. In contrast to this debate, there is, however, general consensus that males and females differ both physically and behaviourally due to the process of sexual selection. Recently sexual selection theory has become an important yet controversial tool for the study of human behaviour. We will return to this debate in chapter 4.

What's so good about sex?

In order for sexual selection to operate, clearly members of a species must engage in sex. Sexual reproduction is so common that we tend to take it for granted that this is the normal way of producing offspring. But not all species use sex as a means of reproduction. Asexual reproduction is more common in the animal kingdom than people might think. Many unicellular organisms, for example, make clones of themselves by splitting into two; a process known as **fission**, and even among multicellular organisms, asexual reproduction is quite common (in which case it is called **parthenogenesis** or 'virgin birth'). In some multicellular species there may be both sexual and asexual periods during the life cycle, as is the case for aphids and water fleas, whereas for others parthenogenesis may be their only method of reproducing (in which case they are called **obligate parthenogens**). Examples of animals which are obligate parthenogens include certain species of fishes such as the Amazon molly and several species of whiptail lizard. To complicate matters further, in bees, wasps and ants (the hymenopteran social insects), female offspring develop from unfertilised eggs but males develop from fertilised ones. This means that the queen reproduces by both asexual and sexual means in the same season. Asexual reproduction is not, however, limited to insects and microscopic organisms; even among warm-blooded vertebrates such as domestic chickens, Chinese quail and turkeys, there are now well-documented cases of parthenogenesis on occasions (Crews, 1994; Parker and McDaniel, 2009).

Why bother with sex?

You might at this point be asking why so many species engage in asexual reproduction. But this is the wrong question to pose. As two of the world's leading evolutionary experts, John Maynard Smith (1971) and George Williams (1975), have pointed out, there are at least three heavy costs associated with sexual compared with asexual reproduction. First, there is 'the cost of meiosis' (Williams, 1975), which means that you throw half of your genes away with each offspring produced (see chapter 2). Second, there is the cost of producing males, which means that, in contrast to females, most males do not reproduce at all (which means that many of your offspring will fail to provide you with grandchildren). And third, there is the cost of courtship and mating during which a great deal of time and energy is used up which might have been spent feeding or avoiding predators. When these costs of sex are fully appreciated asexual reproduction suddenly appears to have a lot going for it. The real question is, if birds do it, bees do it, even parthenogenic fleas do it, why don't we all reproduce asexually?

The fact that asexual and sexual reproduction are both possibilities in such a wide range of species, and yet so many multicellular species rely on sex, suggests sex must have some clear advantage. Given the cost of meiosis alone (the loss of half of our genes with each offspring produced) as Maynard Smith (1971) has pointed out, when in competition with asexual reproduction, sex should win out only if it doubles the number of offspring produced. Imagine two females in a population, one of which reproduces sexually and the other asexually. Each time the asexual individual produces an offspring it will be a clone and therefore will have 100 per cent of its mother's genes. In contrast, each time the sexual female produces an offspring it will take, on average, 50 per cent of its genes from its mother and 50 per cent from its father. This means the sexually reproducing individual will have to produce twice as many offspring as the asexual one in order to pass on as many of its genes. Since this problem became apparent in the early 1970s evolutionary theorists have been struggling with the question 'what's so good about sex?' The answer, like so many things in evolution, is not straightforward. As Maynard Smith has conceded 'we have all the answers, we just can't agree on them' (personal communication).

Ratchets, raffles and tangles

Having explored the costs of sex we are now ready to ask the fundamental question – what is so good about sexual reproduction? Currently there are a number of theories that vie for our attention. Fisher himself advocated the influential idea that sexually reproducing populations would have an advantage in being able to evolve faster in a rapidly changing environment (Fisher, 1958). He argued that, by combining together genetic contributions from both parents, sexually reproducing individuals should show more variability in their offspring than asexual ones that would have to rely on fortuitous mutations to arrive. A sudden dramatic change in the climate, for example, would wipe out many more of the asexual individuals compared with the more varied sexual ones. A modification of Fisher's **faster evolution** argument is **Muller's ratchet.** This is the argument of Hermann Muller (1964) and states that each time a harmful mutation arises in an individual in an asexual population it will be passed on to all of its offspring. Like a ratchet that can only turn in one direction, each time a new harmful mutation occurs it is added to the population. With each new generation the number of these deleterious mutations accumulates. In sexual populations, however, on average only half of the offspring will inherit each parental mutation. If the mutation depresses an individual's reproductive success then it will eventually lose out to those individuals in the population that do not have it. This means that sex wins out because it helps to eliminate harmful mutations that would otherwise build up in the population.

Both Fisher's and Muller's arguments look at the evolution of sex from the viewpoint of the group or population. As we saw in chapter 2, however, evolutionists today consider natural selection as acting primarily at the level of the individual or even the gene. In 1975 George Williams, the champion of individual selection, proposed the **raffle analogy** to explain the advantages of sex. In this analogy having offspring is rather like having a number of raffle tickets which may or may not lead to the prize of surviving and reproducing in a given environment. Since sex leads to variation then each offspring is like having a new ticket with a different number. By comparison asexual reproduction is like providing all of your offspring with the same number on each ticket; the chances of winning will be greatly reduced if the environment should change. Williams's raffle analogy leads to the prediction that sex will be more common in highly unpredictable environments such as in streams and at high altitudes and latitudes while asexual reproduction will be more common in more stable environments. A number of observations appear to support Williams. Sexually produced aphids have wings which allow them to disperse, whereas asexually produced aphids which stay put do not. Clearly, if your offspring are going to travel then they are going to meet a variety of conditions and it may therefore pay you to provide them with greater variability.

The raffle analogy makes intuitive sense. Unfortunately, intuition is not hard evidence. When Graham Bell of Montreal University tested the prediction that sex would be more common where the environment is unpredictable he found quite the opposite. Sex, he found, is more common when the environment is *less* changeable such as in the seas and at lower altitudes and latitudes (Bell, 1982).

The effects of the living and the physical environments

The problem with Williams's theory may be that it relies too much on the predictability of the physical or **abiotic** environment. Others have subsequently built their arguments around the living or **biotic** environment. When you begin to consider the effects of predators, of parasites and of other members of your species then Bell's finding begins to make sense. Where abiotic conditions are predictable and less severe then they will be favourable to you. The problem is that they will also be favourable to other organisms. Under predictable conditions you will encounter the greatest competition from those closest to you, that is, other members of your own species. This means it may pay you to be a bit different. Hence sex is more common where physical conditions are favourable. Based on his findings Bell has developed his own theory to explain the existence of sex. He calls it the **tangled bank** theory after Darwin's description in *The Origin of Species* of the competition that takes place between the myriad of organisms living in an overgrown embankment. If Bell's theory is correct then, due to the competition that individuals within a species have with each other, we would expect to see continual change over a geological time scale. Unfortunately for Bell's tangled bank theory, the fossil record does not support this prediction. Species tend to remain the same for hundreds of thousands of generations and then quite suddenly alter very rapidly (Eldridge and Gould 1972; Maynard Smith, 1993).

The Red Queen

So where does this leave us? As we've seen with theories about sexual selection and even about why sex occurs at all, it seems that every time a new theory is put forward it is very quickly shot down. However, one of the exciting developments of recent years is that we may now be on the threshold of a general consensus, not only with regard to sex but also with regard to a number of other aspects of evolution. As with the theories about what choosy females are looking for in males, once again it's all to do with parasites. This is the theory of the **Red Queen** and, although it was introduced by Leigh Van Valen back in 1973, it has only recently made a major impact on evolutionary theory with regard to behaviour. The Red Queen is based on the notion that parasites and hosts are in a continual evolutionary battle or **arms race**.

Box 3.3 **Alice and the Red Queen**

Leigh Van Valen named his Red Queen theory of why sexual reproduction initially arose and why it is maintained in so many species after a passage in Lewis Carroll's *Alice through the Looking Glass*. At one point Alice meets the short-tempered Red Queen who constantly rushes around but never seems to get anywhere. When Alice is running around with the Red Queen but they don't seem to be making any progress she remarks, 'In *our* country . . . You'd generally get somewhere else – If you ran very fast for a long time as we've been doing', the Red Queen replies, 'A slow sort of country! . . . Now *here*, you see, it takes all the running *you* can do, just to keep in the same place. If you want to get somewhere else, you must run at least twice as fast as that!' The Red Queen theory suggests that evolutionary change on one side of the equation leads to counteracting change on the other side which in relative terms appears as a standstill.

Due to their short life span and their enormous numbers, bacteria, viruses and other microbial parasites evolve much more rapidly than their hosts. According to the Red Queen theory, the host produces variable offspring in retaliation to parasites so that, by chance, some of them will have resistance. It is this variability that, by lending resistance to at least some of the offspring, gives sex the edge in the population. Since each side in the arms race reacts to changes in the opposition's camp, then each ends up pretty much where it started off. Changes in the immune system of higher animals may even lead to circular warfare between host and parasite whereby a form of resistance, which may have been overcome in one generation, might re-emerge when the parasite has altered many generations later (see chapter 12). This may help to explain why many species remain largely unchanged over very lengthy geological periods.

As an armchair argument the Red Queen appears to stand up well, but does the empirical evidence substantiate it? Bell's finding that sex is more common when the environment is more stable fits in well with the Red Queen but this also fits in well with his own preference that it is competition between macro-organisms that maintains sex in a population. The acid test of the Red Queen is that sex should be more common where parasite pressure is greatest. Since many species can reproduce either sexually or asexually a good test would be to determine which method is favoured by a species that can do either under varying degrees of parasite pressure. One study that fulfils these criteria perfectly was conducted in New Zealand by Curtis Lively. It involves water snails of the species *Potamopyrgus antipodarum*. These snails live in both stable lakes and highly variable streams and they are able to make use of both asexual and sexual reproduction. Both the tangled bank and the Red Queen hypotheses would predict that sex should be more common in stable lakes whereas asex should be more common in the unpredictable streams. This of course makes it difficult to determine which hypothesis would be supported by finding sex more common in one environment over the other. Lively argued, however, that not only should sex be more common in the stable lake environment but so too would be the number of parasites. In strong support of the Red Queen, Lively (1987) discovered that in the lakes where rates of parasitism are high then sex is decidedly common, whereas in streams where parasitism is lower, asexual reproduction is more common. Lively and his co-workers have subsequently uncovered a similar finding with a small Mexican fish called a topminnow (Lively et al., 1990) and, more recently for a species of nematode (Morran et al., 2011). These findings lend clear support to the Red Queen and suggest that, although Bell may have been right to concentrate on biotic pressures as a driving force for sex, he may have been wrong about which biotic pressures. It's not the big organisms that are most likely to kill you, it's the ones you can't even see. In relation to our own species as Matt Ridley (1993) puts it

What killed your ancestors two centuries or more ago? Smallpox, tuberculosis, influenza, pneumonia, plague, scarlet fever, diarrhoea. Starvation or accidents may have weakened people, but infection killed them. (p. 63)

Currently the Red Queen is riding high. It may be that one of the most important consequences of the Red Queen lies beyond its effects on immunity from parasites – it lies in its effects on mate choice. Some evolutionists have argued that the Red Queen helps to explain why individuals of many species look for certain features in the opposite members of their population since these features are there to demonstrate a lack of parasites which might otherwise reduce reproductive potential.

Sex, evolution and behaviour

Armed with an understanding of the theories of natural and sexual selection we can now apply them to understanding behaviour. Understanding evolution as the differential survival of genotypes is quite easy when considering changes in **morphological** (physical) characteristics such as the number of eggs a hen lays or variability in, say, the length of a bird's tail feathers. Understanding the relationship between evolution and behaviour is more difficult. Unlike a leg bone, behaviour does not fossilise and cannot be studied directly (Slater and Halliday, 1994; Alcock, 2009). But if we consider an animal's behavioural repertoire as a part of its phenotype then we can begin to see how it may also be shaped by evolution. Laying more eggs may help you to pass on more copies of your genes. Having longer tail feathers may help you to escape a bird of prey and, for males, may also attract females of your species to you. But having long tail feathers to enable you to escape a raptor or to attract a female would be useless if you were unable to recognise other animals as being dangerous or potential mates respectively. Or to react appropriately to such stimuli. So, since

Figure 3.4 An African wild dog pack attack a wildebeast

behaviour has clear consequences for survival and for reproduction, genes which successfully modify an animal's behavioural repertoire are passed on to its offspring.

Of course, the consequences of an animal's behaviour are always contingent on the environment in which it lives. As we saw earlier we can break this environment down into abiotic and biotic components. Of the biotic components some will be potential food, some will be potential predators, some will be potential parasites but many will be members of your own species or **conspecifics**. Clearly, an animal's behaviour helps it to solve the problems of its abiotic environment; if it's too hot, cold, wet or dry it might be able to improve its immediate surroundings by digging a burrow and staying put until things improve. But today, most experts agree that the biotic environment is of greater importance in shaping an animal's behaviour (Drickamer *et al.*, 2002). Of this living environment, it is becoming very clear that an animal's conspecifics (or, strictly speaking, their ancestors) have been of the utmost importance in shaping the behavioural repertoire of a species (Alcock, 2009). After all, it is other members of your species that you will need to cooperate or compete with.

Cooperation is common among animal species; black-headed gulls band together to 'mob' larger carrion crows and drive them away from their nesting sites; African wild dogs form packs to bring down larger prey such as wildebeest and an individual ant could not survive without the combined and well-delineated efforts of its nestmates. But whereas cooperation is well documented in many species, competition is rife in all. Animals, in a sense, compete to become ancestors. Those individuals that successfully compete to pass on their genes to future generations become ancestors at the expense of others in the population. One of the most important elements of

> ## Box 3.4 **Female choice and male behaviour**
>
> We saw earlier how male elephant seals attempt to mate with as many of the females that come ashore into their territories as they can. Some males are far more successful than others in this activity. In fact, one study showed that as few as 4 per cent of males are responsible for 85 per cent of the matings in a breeding season (Cox and Le Boeuf, 1977). Since males compete with each other for access to females, being bigger and more aggressive is clearly a successful adaptive strategy for male elephant seals. Smaller and less aggressive males of previous generations were simply less successful; in this case it was the big bullies that left descendants.
>
> But what about the much smaller and less aggressive females? Is this one example where being much smaller than the males means that they really have no choice in the matter of reproduction? It turns out that even in elephant seals, females are able to influence which male mates with them. When a bull mounts a cow seal she gives out a loud call that can be heard by nearby males. If the suitor is a subordinate male then he will invariably be chased off by a larger one who then takes his place. In this way females are able to ensure that the largest, most dominant males inseminate them. It might be argued that females in the past which did not give out such calls left fewer aggressive male descendants than those that did so. In this way we can see how female behaviour can have an effect on both the male and female offspring that are produced. And we can see that, even in cases where males are much larger than females, female choice plays a role in reproduction.

competition is competition for mates. In this way we can think of genes as biasing behaviour in ways that produce more copies of themselves. Clearly, genes that alter behavioural responses in ways that increase mating opportunities are likely to spread at the expense of genes that fail to do so. We can see that female choice and competition between males may both be very powerful forces in the evolution of behaviour.

Female choice and male reproductive success

Females, arguably, exert an influence on the evolution of large size in male elephant seals and, as we saw earlier, female choice can lead to exaggeration of male features such as teeth and feathers. But is there any direct evidence of female choice affecting male reproductive success? Since the 1980s evidence has accumulated for the direct influence of female choice both on male physical features and on their reproductive success. Interestingly, the first clear-cut evidence of the importance of female choice involved precisely the feature that Fisher had suggested – elaboration of tail feathers (albeit not in peacocks). The African widowbird is a **polygynous** species (i.e. one male to several females – see chapter 4) that is found on the grassy plains of Kenya. In contrast to the mottled brown, short-tailed females, the jet-black male widowbirds have red epaulettes and, importantly, a very lengthy tail (on average 50 cm compared to the 7 cm average for females). Males maintain territories into which they attempt to attract females by sporadically leaping up above the long grass and showing off the magnificence of their fanned-out tail feathers. Females that land in a territory frequently mate with the resident male and afterwards build nests there into which they lay their eggs. It had long been suspected that females decide which territory to land in on the basis of the territory holder's tail length, when Scandinavian ethologist Malte Andersson (1982; 1986) decided to check this with an elegant field manipulation. It involved the use of scissors and super-glue. Having determined the number of nests in a range of territories, by cutting and gluing their tail feathers he created four different groups of males. One group had their tails extended to 75 cm; another had their tails reduced to 14 cm and two control groups were allowed to retain their original tail length (see figure 3.5). Following these manipulations, Andersson observed no change in the size of male territories, but in contrast found that females now preferred to nest in the territories of the long- to the short-tailed males by a ratio of 4:1.

Andersson's field experiment has frequently been cited as the first real demonstration of the power of female choice as a driving force for male adornment and reproductive success but it has not been without its critics. For one thing female choice was inferred from the number of nests produced in a male's territory rather than via the number of young fledged or from the number of matings observed. If Andersson's study is open to interpretation, then a series of follow-up lab-based studies appear to demonstrate the effects of female choice unequivocally. Haines and Gould (1994), for example, demonstrated that female guppies preferred males with longer tails even though a longer tail slows them down (see box 3.2). They discovered that when offered a choice between males of various sized tails, females chose both to spend more time with long-tailed males and to mate with them. Furthermore, the offspring produced also had longer tails just like their fathers. This finding is important because, as is the case for natural selection, for sexual selection to be accepted it is necessary that the features chosen are heritable.

Incidentally, in what may be thought of as the icing on the cake for supporters of female choice, just as Fisher originally suggested, one study has now demonstrated that peahens really do prefer to mate with peacocks with the most elaborate tail feathers (Petrie *et al.*, 1991). Whether they do so because it demonstrates 'good genes' or simply because it is 'sexy' is still open to debate, however.

Widowbirds, guppies and peacocks are just three examples from a literature that now abounds with such cases. In contrast to the ridicule that female choice was greeted with in the nineteenth century, today it is seen as an increasingly important

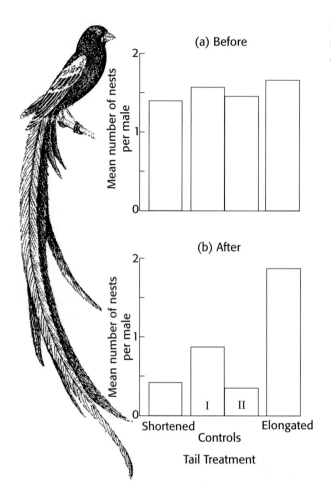

Figure 3.5 Average number of nests in each widowbird territory compared to male tail-length

element in explaining the evolution of both male and female behaviour (Graves *et al.*, 1985; Gould and Gould, 1997; Milan, 2010).

Competitive males – and female behaviour

If our ideas about the importance of female choice appear to have been strengthened in recent years we might also ask how well the other side of the argument stands up to scrutiny today. Do we still see males as the highly competitive sex? Throughout the animal kingdom it appears to be males that bluff and duel with each other. They appear to do so for resources such as territories or food, but ultimately all of the power struggles would be pointless without the presence of females. In the long run males compete for fertile females and they do so in many different ways. Lions, baboons and chimpanzees all form alliances in order to physically usurp other males and steal their mates (see chapter 4). American red-winged blackbirds and European robins

Box 3.5 Are you a bit Neanderthal?

A common put-down to someone we want to imply is both brutish and unattractive is to refer to them as 'a Neanderthal'. Interestingly, despite this commonly held view of how primitive and unappealing the Neanderthals were, it now appears that there might be some science behind such a remark. The Neanderthals were a sub-species of early *Homo sapiens* – *Homo sapiens neanderthalensis* (although some experts consider them to constitute a separate species – *Homo neanderthalensis*). In addition to a heavy, compact body they also had robust faces with large, wide noses and prominent brow ridges. Neanderthals (named after the Neander Valley in Germany where the first specimen was found) appeared around 130,000 years before present (YBP) in various parts of Europe and central Asia where they evolved from a different branch of *Homo erectus* (see boxes 2.4 and 2.5). They disappeared from the fossil record around 25,000 YBP suggesting perhaps that anatomically modern *Homo sapiens* drove them to extinction. Some of their genes, however, appear to have lived on and are with us today. In 2010 the **Neanderthal Genome Project** reported that modern humans living outside of sub-Saharan Africa typically have between 1 and 4 per cent of Neanderthal genes (Green *et al.*, 2010). This begs the question: what role did sexual selection play here? Is it conceivable for early anatomically modern humans to have found some features of Neanderthals attractive? We can only speculate that at least some of our ancestors found at least some of them attractive enough to form a romantic attachment.

Reconstruction of Neanderthal male

Figure 3.6 Red deer stags wrestling

defend territories and sing to lure females into them. And many species of frogs and toads wrestle with each other for the opportunity to fertilise a female's eggs even as she lays them.

One species which has been studied over many years in relation to male–male competition is the Scottish red deer. By making field observations over a number of years, field ethologist Tim Clutton-Brock and his co-workers have demonstrated that the relationship between sexual selection and reproductive behaviour is more complex than had previously been thought (Clutton-Brock *et al.*, 1982; Stopher *et al.*, 2011). As is frequently the case for members of the deer family, stags live in all-male herds outside the breeding season. At the beginning of the breeding season, however, they begin to threaten each other and engage in physical combat in order to compete for **harem territories.** Harem territories are similar to resource defence harems except that the territory is the stable home of a core group of females while a series of males are displaced over the breeding season. Also, males frequently attempt to round up and steal females from nearby territories. As with the elephant seals, males are much larger than their female counterparts, the does – about twice their size in fact. Additionally, males have much larger antlers. Stags that are successful in defending a harem must constantly be vigilant, however, since threats to their supremacy are common. Typically a stag will warn off challengers by producing some 3,000 loud roars each day. When an intruding stag makes a challenge the two males undergo a highly ritualised sequence of responses. This begins with a long series of roars – if the intruder cannot keep up he will normally withdraw at this point. If he does not back down then the next stage is parallel walking during which each stag appears to eye up the size and strength of his competitor. If at this point neither backs down then the competitors lock their antlers and a vigorous wrestling match ensues until one of the combatants is exhausted and retreats.

Due to their variability in size, in comparison to the does, red deer stags vary greatly in their reproductive success. Extensive field studies, however, have revealed that size can also pay dividends for females in the game of reproduction. Larger does are able to exclude smaller ones from the lushest parts of the territory and by improving their own grazing opportunities are able to increase the quantity of milk they provide for their suckling calves (Clutton-Brock *et al.*, 1982). This means that the calves of a dominant doe are most likely to build up the fat reserves necessary to survive the first winter. Furthermore, the most important predictor of an adult stag's reproductive success is his weight at the time of weaning. This means that the size and competitive behaviour of a doe plays a very important role in determining the success of her male offspring. This demonstrates how intrasexual selection can also be important to both sexes and that the female–female competition of one generation can have a knock-on effect on male–male competition in the next.

Perhaps it is too simplistic to consider each sex in isolation when assessing the effects of sexual selection on a species. Perhaps in order to understand the strategy of one sex we must always consider the strategies of the other and the ecological pressures that exist. Furthermore, field studies that have considered sexual selection demonstrate how it not only affects body size and weaponry but also levels of aggression and the social structure of a group of animals. The more we look at sexual selection, the more intertwined and all pervading we realise it is. In chapter 4 we come a little closer to home and consider the effects of sexual selection on mate choice in ourselves and our close relatives.

Summary

- In 1871 in *The Descent of Man, and Selection in Relation to Sex*, Darwin introduced the notion of a new selective force – sexual selection. Sexual selection leads to features that help individuals gain access to mates and takes two forms – intrasexual and intersexual selection. Intrasexual selection involves competition between members of one sex for access to the opposite sex, while intersexual selection involves members of one sex (usually males) attempting to attract members of the opposite sex. In nature these forces are believed to lead to elevated levels of aggression, greater body strength and the development of attractive features in males. For females sexual selection leads to choosiness over mates.
- In 1930 Ronald Fisher suggested that ancestral females selected males with good features that aided survival such as long tail feathers. Once females had selected

such features, over evolutionary time these features might become greatly exaggerated in males, since females are constantly choosing the most outstanding examples. These features might then become further exaggerated beyond their original function. Fisher called this 'runaway selection'.

- Robert Trivers suggested that females should be choosy about whom they reproduce with. Because they invest more in offspring than males, females have more to lose from making a bad choice. Males, on the other hand, lose very little if they make a bad decision and should therefore be less discriminating about sex. Trivers called the effort that each sex puts into producing offspring 'parental investment'. Due to gestation periods and nurturing activities such as suckling, the asymmetry in parental investment is greater in mammals than in other animals.

- Amotz Zahavi proposed that males develop elaborate features as impediments to demonstrate to females that they are able to survive despite having such a handicap – the 'handicap hypothesis'. In contrast to Fisher and to Zahavi, Hamilton and Zuk suggested that male adornments have evolved to demonstrate to females their lack of parasites.

- Many animal species reproduce asexually. Single-celled organisms frequently reproduce through fission (splitting into two new individuals) and many multicellular organisms reproduce parthenogenically (development from an unfertilised egg). As Maynard Smith and Williams have both pointed out, sexual reproduction has a number of costs that asexual reproduction lacks. These include the cost of meiosis (i.e. losing half of your genes each time you reproduce), the cost of producing males (many of which will not reproduce) and the cost of courtship. The realisation that such costs exist has made sexual reproduction an area of debate among evolutionists.

- A number of theories have been proposed to explain the existence of sexual reproduction. Fisher suggested that, since there is greater variability in sexually produced offspring, sex speeds up evolution. Muller suggested that sex gets rid of harmful mutations which would otherwise build up in a population. Williams suggested the raffle analogy whereby variation in offspring is like having a number of different raffle tickets. Because future environmental pressures are difficult to predict, it pays individuals to provide their offspring with different raffle tickets (i.e. variation). Bell proposed the tangled bank theory in which individuals have to vie with living (biotic) competitors rather than solving the problems of the non-living (abiotic) environment. Recently, however, attention has turned towards the Red Queen theory of sex as proposed by Van Valen. The Red Queen theory suggests that parasites and hosts are in a continual evolutionary arms race – the host produces variable offspring through sex so that, by chance, some of them will have resistance to pathogens.

- Behavioural patterns have both survival and reproductive value. Sexual selection theory and the notion of female choice have recently become important concepts for the understanding of behaviour. There is now clear evidence from a number of species, such as birds, fishes and marine mammals, that female choice has been a driving force in the evolution of male adornment and aggressive behaviour.

Questions

1. Some critics of evolutionary theory have suggested that the widespread existence of homosexual behaviour in both men and women means that human sexual behaviour is no longer related to inclusive fitness theory. How might an evolutionary psychologist deal with this criticism? You should be able to think of at least three explanations that might be suggested without dismissing inclusive fitness theory.
2. Female American jacanas (a species of wading bird) are larger and more aggressive than their male counterparts. This is known as an example of 'sex role reversal' in the animal kingdom. Based on this very brief information, what predictions would you make about the reproductive behaviour of both males and females of this species?
3. Arguably many traits might have arisen from either natural or sexual selection. An example of this might be birdsong. How might we distinguish whether a bird's song evolved via natural or sexual selection?
4. What's so good about sex?

FURTHER READING

Cronin, H. (1991). *The Ant and the Peacock: Altruism and Sexual Selection from Darwin to Today.* Cambridge: Cambridge University Press. Insightful and detailed history of the sexual selection debate.

Gould, J. L. and Gould, G. C. (1997). *Sexual Selection: Mate Choice and Courtship in Nature.* New York: W.H. Freeman and Co. A sociobiological/comparative account of how sexual selection may have helped to shape human evolution.

Milan, E. L. (2010). *Looking for a Few Good Males: Female Choice in Evolutionary Biology.* Baltimore: Johns Hopkins University Press. Presents a history of sexual selection in relation both to animal and to human behaviour.

Ridley, M. (1993). *The Red Queen: Sex and the Evolution of Human Nature.* London: Penguin. A very accessible account of the proposed relationship between parasites, evolutionary arms races and sexual selection.

Symons, D. (1979). *The Evolution of Human Sexuality.* New York: Oxford University Press. Applies Darwin's theory of sexual selection to human sexual behaviour and sex differences in behaviour in general; a theme which a number of subsequent books have followed up on.

4 The evolution of human mate choice

KEY CONCEPTS

mate guarding • provisioning hypothesis • male parental investment • cryptic oestrus • sexual dimorphism • polygyny • polyandry • reproductive value • sperm competition • sexy sons • Coolidge effect

What does a man look for in a woman? What does a woman look for in a man? To put it more crudely, what criteria do people use when looking for a sexual partner? In chapter 3 we considered sexual selection theory, that is, how morphological and behavioural differences may have come about by enhancing reproductive success. In order to have reproductive success humans need to make decisions about mates. Received wisdom suggests that men and women differ in their predilections for partners. Women want generous, emotionally stable and dependable men, and men – well, men want sexy women. The question is, does the evidence fit with this common-sense view and, if so, where did these differences come from? In this chapter we use sexual selection theory and evidence from other primates to explore the notion of mate choice, its roots and its consequences.

Testing the claims of evolutionary psychologists

Two of the main claims made by evolutionary psychologists are that there *is* a human nature and that ecological and social pressures of the past were responsible for the evolution of that nature (Pinker, 2002). If this is the case then it might be argued that mate preferences today reflect the decisions of our ancestors. People who made poor mate choices in the ancient past were less likely to pass on their genes than those who made good choices. Sexual selection should, therefore, promote 'good' mating choice strategies.

But, given that it is impossible to study the evolution of behavioural patterns directly, how might we explore the relationship between sexual selection, mate choice and human behaviour? One way is to compare ourselves with our primate relatives that shared a common ancestor with us. Comparing different species in order to add to our knowledge of anatomy, physiology or behaviour is called the **comparative method**. When behaviour patterns differ between closely related species then it might be argued that these differences can be traced back to differing ecological pressures (Clutton-Brock and Harvey, 1977; Krebs and Davies, 1981). Where behavioural patterns are similar it may suggest that the responses are ancient and might be traced back to a **common ancestor** (Wrangham, 1987). We will make use of the comparative method to examine human mating behaviour.

A second way in which we can study the evolution of human mate choice is by examining the degree to which such responses are common to separate human cultures. If they are the product of evolution then we might expect to see more similarities than differences. Over the last twenty years evolutionary psychologists have compared mate choice preferences in a variety of cultures with particular regard to the extent to which sex differences in mate choice are universal. We can think of these studies as examinations of the consequences of sexual selection on humans. We will consider these consequences after first considering the possible evolutionary roots of these responses by contemplating the behaviour of our relatives.

Origins of human mate choice: the social behaviour of our relatives

Given that we share a recent evolutionary past and hence a large proportion of our genes with other primates, perhaps an understanding of their social and sexual behaviour will provide us with a clue as to how our ancestors lived. It might also give us some insight into the evolution of human reproductive strategies. A number of species of primates have been used as models for human behaviour including common chimpanzees (and their relatives the bonobos), gorillas and baboons. There are two species of chimpanzee and these vary in behaviour both between species and between troops within a species: the common chimpanzee *Pan troglodytes*, of which there are several sub-species and their cousins the bonobos or pygmy chimps (*Pan paniscus*). The two species of gorilla – eastern and western – each have two sub-species giving us *Gorilla beringer graueri* and *Gorilla beringer beringer* (both eastern sub-species) and *Gorilla gorilla diehli* and *Gorilla gorilla gorilla* respectively (both western sub-species). Baboons comprise five species, all under the genus *Papio*. The social and reproductive behaviour of each of these primate genera is considered briefly below.

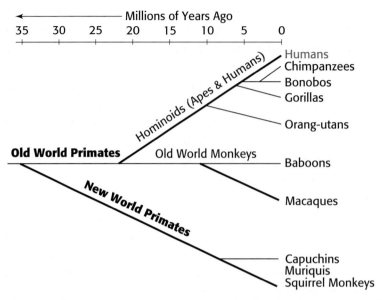

Millions of Years Ago

35   30   25   20   15   10   5   0

Humans
Chimpanzees
Bonobos
Gorillas

Hominoids (Apes & Humans)

Orang-utans

Old World Primates   Old World Monkeys

Baboons

New World Primates

Macaques

Capuchins
Muriquis
Squirrel Monkeys

Figure 4.1 Diagram of primate evolutionary tree – showing all of the primates mentioned in this chapter

Chimpanzees *Pan troglodytes*

Chimpanzees share over 98 per cent of their genes with humans and current thinking suggests we shared a common ancestor with them some time between six and seven million years ago (Dunbar, 2004; Strier, 2011). Chimps, like us, are highly social, primates that form groups of between 20 to 100 individuals. They have a **fission–fusion society**, which means that they frequently divide up into smaller groups of perhaps ten or fewer individuals while foraging and then recombine when a large food source is discovered (such as a tree that has just come into fruit). When this happens individual chimps often make 'pant-hoot' calls that bring others from afar. Males make up the permanent core of their society, forming a linear dominance hierarchy while females frequently leave to join another troop upon reaching sexual maturity (Goodall, 1986; Strier, 2011). The top-ranking male maintains his rank both through aggressive displays and through forming coalitions with other high-ranking males (often, but not exclusively, brothers). As the males have a strict dominance hierarchy most disputes are resolved by threats rather than physical attacks but these do occur at times. In the 1970s Jane Goodall documented a four-year 'territorial war' between two troops that only ended when one troop killed all of the mature males in the other troop. Male chimps have also been known to kill infants – an act that is believed by some to occur in order to bring a female back into oestrus more rapidly and ensure that any new offspring are likely to be those of the infanticidal individual (behaviour that is not uncommon among primates – Strier, 2011).

Mating patterns vary between troops but it is generally the case that dominant males do not have exclusive rights to receptive females, unlike their cousins the gorillas (although this can happen in some troops). When in oestrus, a female becomes distinctly attractive to the mature males, a number of whom will then mate with her. Oestrus is the time in a female's sexual cycle when mating is most likely to lead to fertilisation and is signalled via a swelling and reddening of the large areas around the vagina and anus (the **perineum**). Although oestrous females will generally mate with a variety of males, it is the more dominant members, and in particular the alpha male, who usually mate with her most frequently especially around ovulation (thereby increasing the chances of fathering offspring).

Despite being largely **frugivorous** (fruit eating), chimps do sometimes engage in group hunting of small mammals – an activity which is largely the preserve of males. On occasions when a male has made a kill he may offer some meat to other males that helped in the hunt but he may also offer some to a fertile female (Kuroda, 1984; Goodall, 1986; Stanford, 1998; 1999). Although it is a contentious area, it has been suggested that the giving of meat to fertile females increases the dominant male's chances of mating with her and while some anthropologists dispute this **meat for sex hypothesis** (Gilby *et al.*, 2010), recent studies do provide support for it (Gomes and Boesch, 2009). Hence, since the more dominant males are most likely to be the successful hunters, rank might indirectly provide reproductive benefits (Stanford, 1995; Gomes and Boesch, 2009; see also Mitani and Watts, 2001).

If rank order and hunting prowess are useful indicators of good genes for females and if females are able to choose which males they mate with, then we might ask: why do they mate with a number of males? Why not simply mate with a single dominant male? Perhaps this 'sharing of sexual favours' is a female strategy to reduce the possibility of infanticide and allow for sperm competition (Birkhead, 2000).

Pygmy Chimpanzees (Bonobo) *Pan paniscus*

Bonobos differ in their genetic material from humans by approximately 1.3 per cent, but they differ from common chimps by only 0.4 per cent (their genome was finally sequenced in June of 2012 – Prüfer *et al.*, 2012). It has been suggested that, since they live on either side of the Congo river (bonobos on the south side and common chimps to the north), the separate species evolved from a common ancestor prior to the formation of the Congo river around 1.5 million years ago. Despite its name, the pygmy chimpanzee, or bonobo, is not actually smaller than the common chimp but is a little slimmer and more **gracile** (fine-featured). Like common chimps, bonobos live in fission–fusion societies with the main group size generally varying from around 50 to 120 individuals (group size is slightly larger than common chimps possibly due to the greater availability of food sources in the great bend of the Congo river where they live in relatively high densities). Although they are more arboreal than

Figure 4.2 Male chimpanzees often collaborate in hunting

common chimps, they also spend a fair amount of time foraging on the ground where they are largely frugivorous. While being more arboreal, surprisingly bonobos also appear to be better able to walk bipedally than common chimpanzees, given their longer thigh bones and more centrally placed *foramen magnum* (Myers Thompson, 2002; see chapter 2). Again like common chimps they will, on occasions, kill and eat small vertebrates including small primates (Surbeck and Hohmann, 2008). In this case, however, although more common for males, both sexes are known to engage in hunting activity.

In direct contrast to common chimps, bonobo society is based around the adult females who form coalitions. Although an individual male is larger than a female, it is this female coalition that allows females to maintain control of the social group (Strier, 2011). Moreover, males remain with their mothers for many years and even in adulthood they frequently look to them for reassurance and support. While bonobos appear to be less aggressive than common chimps, they do form dominance hierarchies where having a high-ranking mother can boost her son's chances of reproductive success (Surbeck *et al.*, 2010).

Grooming and food sharing occur frequently between males and females, which is not generally the case for common chimps (outside of possible 'meat for sex' arrangements). Again there are records of female bonobos preferentially mating with males that have shared food with them (Kuroda, 1984). Given how frequently bonobos have sex, however, this is difficult to confirm. Also, unlike common chimps, bonobos have ranges that overlap with other groups. When two groups meet they may even combine for a while before separating and going their separate ways. This contrasts markedly with recorded antagonistic encounters between different common chimp groups.

Bonobos have a promiscuous mating system which, in addition to heterosexual pairings, also involves male–male and female–female sexual activity. Additionally, immature bonobos also take part in such sexual activity. Sexual activity in general is very common in this ape and appears to be used as a means to communicate reassurance, both helping to maintain group cohesion and dispel tension. It has been suggested that the fact that bonobos are less aggressive than their chimp cousins may be due both to the use of sex as a form of conciliation and the fact that groups are led by female coalitions (Nishida and Hiraiwa-Hasegawa, 1987; Strier, 2011). Despite this arrangement, when it comes to oestrus females, once again, like the common chimpanzee, the higher up the dominance hierarchy he is, the more likely a male is to be successful in the production of offspring (Surbeck *et al.*, 2010).

Gorillas *Gorilla beringer* and *Gorilla gorilla*

Gorillas shared a common ancestor with humans and chimpanzees around ten million years ago and currently share close to 98 per cent of their genetic code with us (Scally *et al.*, 2012). Gorillas are the largest of the primate order with mature males weighing up to 500 pounds. As with most primates, gorillas are highly social animals but unlike the two species of chimps they form **unimale** groups based around a mature silverback male and perhaps three mature females. Additionally there are likely to be one or two black-backed sub-adult males (8–12 years old) and a number of youngsters (less than 8 years old). The silverback protects the group from predators and threatens any other mature males that he encounters with the archetypal chest-beating display. Since he mates with each mature female, he will almost certainly be the father of any offspring produced in the group. The mature females form a linear dominance hierarchy with the first one to join the male having precedence. A high-ranking female spends more time close to the silverback as do her offspring – a situation that decreases the chances of predation since females are approximately half the size of males (Stewart and Harcourt, 1987). Grooming occurs throughout the group as is the case for many primate species. Eastern gorillas tend to form larger groups than western ones and may reach up to 30–40 individuals. The slightly smaller western gorillas live in groups varying from two to twenty individuals (see figure 4.3). Home ranges can be as large as 30 square kilometres, but unlike common chimps they do not defend these as territories. Sexually mature males and females leave the group – a situation that may well have evolved to avoid in-breeding.

Figure 4.3 Silverback western lowland gorilla eating vegetation

Both eastern and western gorillas preferentially consume fruit but both will also eat a wide range of vegetable material such as leaves, stems and bark. Additionally they consume invertebrates such as ants, termites and various grubs and larvae, but unlike chimps and bonobos they do not kill and eat mammals. Interestingly, gorillas of the rare western sub-species *Gorilla gorilla diehli* (only around 300 remaining) have recently been observed throwing sticks and grass at humans that were tracking them (Wittiger and Sunderland-Groves, 2007). While such behaviour is well documented for chimpanzees this was the first time this was observed for gorillas.

Baboons *Papio*

Although baboons share fewer genes with us than chimps and gorillas (around 94 per cent), a number of experts have claimed that they provide a better model for human social behaviour because they may well have shared similar ecological pressures. When the great African forests shrank between five and ten million years ago it is likely that the only primates to have left the trees for the newly expanding open grasslands were our ancestors and those of the baboon family. In this way baboons may be the only other savannah-adapted primates. In fact today various species of baboons are found in the open woodland and savannah of sub-Saharan Africa where early hominin fossils were also found. The classification of baboons has changed in recent years and might change yet again in the future but currently five separate species of Papio are recognised. These are: *P. hamadryas* (hamadryas baboon), *P. ursinus* (chacma baboon), *P. papio* (red baboon), *P. anubis* (olive baboon) and *P. cynocephalus* (yellow baboon). Given that *Papio hamadryas* appears to differ physically (with males having a large white mane) and to some degree behaviourally, from the other species, some authorities refer to the hamadryas baboon and all of the rest as 'savannah baboons' (see below).

Baboon troops vary in size from around 15 to over 150 individuals but in the case of the hamadryas baboon they can reach up to 750 (in which case there are various levels of sub-group). They typically inhabit a home range of several square kilometres. Their diet is largely vegetarian, but, as with chimpanzees, baboons will also kill and eat smaller mammals such as vervet monkeys. In fact, after humans, baboons are the most carnivorous of all primates. Once again hunting is largely (but not exclusively) a male preserve and, although baboons are not renowned for sharing their kills, in the case of the anubis baboon at least there are documented accounts of individuals donating meat to other troop members (Strum, 1987; Strum and Mitchell, 1987). When this does occur, as with chimps, it is claimed that the oestrous females are most commonly the favoured recipients (Strum, 1987; Strum and Mitchell, 1987).

Baboon society is **matrilineal**, that is, social relationships are based around female members of the group with relationships being sustained over three generations. For all non-hamadryas species males generally leave the troop on reaching maturity. There are two types of mating systems in Papio. For the hamadryas baboon each troop is made up of a number of unimale units where one male has the attention of between two and eleven females (that is, it is like the gorilla, a 'harem' system). In the case of all other baboon species, males compete for access to females and there is an overall dominance hierarchy for males in the troop. In these non-hamadryas species males and females form parallel dominance hierarchies with dominant males having first access to oestrous females. Recent research suggests that individual 'rank' depends as much on the status of an individual's family within the troop as it does on individual merit. Hence having high-status kin pushes an individual up the rank order (Bergman *et al.*, 2003). As with chimps (and indeed with non-human primates in general), females in oestrus can easily be spotted by the red swollen perineum area and once again this signal appears to be attractive to mature males. Dominant male baboons of a number of species attempt to limit the access of other males by forming consort relationships with females in oestrus. This involves following a female around and mating with her intermittently during her fertile period, while simultaneously chasing off other potential subordinate suitors. For obvious reasons such male behaviour is known as **mate guarding**.

While males can show a great deal of aggression towards other males they do show some care for infants including protection from other individuals, carrying and grooming behaviour (Anderson, 1992). In some cases these males may be the infant's father but in others it is thought that such caring behaviour towards an infant might make them more attractive partners for the female who might then mate with them. This demonstrates that, despite being much smaller than the male, female baboons, as in so many other species, exhibit a degree of choice in whom they mate with.

Reconstructing human behavioural evolution

Are humans different?

Having looked briefly at the social organisation and reproductive behaviour of chimps, bonobos, gorillas and baboons, can we now use their behaviour to help understand how sexual selection might have acted on our early ancestors? There are three related areas that we can consider – diet, social behaviour and reproductive strategies. According to some researchers, diet (or rather a change in diet) may help us to understanding much about these other features in our species. The arguments that might be developed from such field observations are rather convoluted and require that we consider all three together.

Meat-eating ancestors

Most experts today consider that, for more than three million years, our ancestors lived in small troops of hunter-gatherers on the open savannah (McHenry, 2009; Leakey and Lewin, 1992). As with chimps, bonobos, gorillas and baboons, they were likely to have exploited a range of plant foods. Additionally, however, there is clear evidence that meat has been of long-standing importance in our ancestral diet (Wrangham, 2009). Both our teeth and our gut show tell-tale signs of this. Although chimps, bonobos and baboons do eat some meat, their typically primate gut is clearly the product of an almost exclusively vegetarian ancestry. They have, for example, a relatively lengthy large intestine, which breaks down vegetable material, and a short small intestine, which breaks down protein-rich foods such as meat. In contrast, our relatively long small intestine and the cutting edges of our incisors, canines and premolars all suggest that meat played a prominent role during our savannah-dwelling ancestry. In fact, unlike chimps, there are a number of nutrients, in particular vitamins A and B12, which we are no longer able to synthesise from a plant-based diet. Today these vital nutrients are only available to us through animal products. Also, quite conclusively, fossilised animal bones from over two million years ago show clear signs of having been butchered by the tools of our early ancestors (Leakey and Lewin, 1992; Wrangham, 2009). Moreover, primatologist Richard Wrangham has suggested that our ancestors (*Homo erectus*) began to cook meat as long ago as 1.6 million years – releasing energy-rich and more easily digested nutri-ents (Wrangham, 2009; Wrangham and Carmody, 2010). According to Wrangham, this led to a reduction in the size of our teeth compared to the great apes (and may have facilitated an increase in brain size – Martin, 1983 – see below). Whether cooked or raw, throughout humanity today the amount of meat in the diet is considerably higher than in any of the 200-odd other species of primate (Tooby and DeVore, 1987; Wrangham, 2009).

The provisioning hypothesis

While we differ somewhat from our primate relatives in our dietary needs it is obvi-ous to anyone who has ever looked at monkeys and apes that there are other, more dramatic, ways in which we differ. One area where humans differ from chimps and baboons lies in the lack of an oestrous swelling in females. As we will see, some experts consider that this difference is one of a number of human features which may be directly related to the point when meat became an important constituent in our diet. Some evolutionists have suggested that meat eating might have led to an early division of labour along gender lines when it came to food production. Evolu-tionary psychologists John Tooby and Irv DeVore (1987), both of whom came from a background in anthropology, have attempted to reconstruct human behavioural evolution. The conclusions that they reached are most conducive to what has been called the **provisioning hypothesis** (see box 4.1 and Buss, 1999).

   Given our largely vegetarian primate past, we might ask why did our ancestors leave the trees and begin to incorporate meat into their diets? There are debates as to whether our ancestors and those of baboons left the rainforests in order to exploit the open grasslands or whether we were elbowed out of the diminishing rainforests by other primates that had superior arboreal adaptations (see, for example, Dunbar, 2004; Strier, 2011; Leakey and Lewin, 1992). Whether we jumped or were pushed it really makes no difference, in either event, both groups clearly became adapted to the challenges and the opportunities provided by the open savannah. One suggestion is that when our early human-like ancestors, or hominins, left the shelter of the rainforests and began to live on the open savannah they, unlike baboons, made use of their primate features to take serious advantage of the animal life that lived there (Tooby and DeVore, 1987; Wrangham, 2009). Given that our common ancestor with the chimpanzees was likely to have been an occasional meat eater, as are common chimps and bonobos today, then perhaps early hominins put such arboreal primate features to use in hunting. These features include good stereoscopic visual acuity, highly manipulative hands and a large brain. All of these characteristics might have been put to good use both to track prey and to aim missiles at it.

   This change to open savannah hunting may have had important consequences for both sexes. As we noted earlier, male chimps are known to exchange meat

Box 4.1 Bipedalism and pair-bonding part 1 – the provisioning hypothesis

Over the years anthropologists have wondered why, when the great apes habitually knuckle walk, did our ancestors develop upright bipedal locomotion? Why they did so is an unresolved debate. Some have argued that it freed the hands for tool use; others have suggested that it allows one to see further than when crouched or knuckle walking (Diamond, 1992). In 1981 anthropologist C. Owen Lovejoy proposed that this development was linked to monogamy and the aid that our male ancestors gave to our female ancestors (1981a; 1981b; 1988). In what became known as the **provisioning hypothesis** Lovejoy proposed that hominins formed pair bonds to increase the food supply to infants (which by primate standards were born relatively immature – see box 4.2). In order to bring provisions back to the female and their offspring males went off to find food such as small reptiles, amphibians, nuts, fruit and eggs and this necessitated freeing up the hands. Hence selection processes allowed us to develop full bipedalism (which the great apes can achieve for brief periods). Lovejoy suggests that, since *Australopithecus afarensis* was known to walk upright, bipedalism, pair-bonding and the provisioning are all inextricably linked in our early evolutionary history. While this model helps to explain a number of human features it has been criticised on the grounds that monogamous pair-bonded species tend to have little or no **sexual dimorphism** (a term introduced by Darwin – see later). That is, there is no size difference between males and females (since males are not competing for 'harems' as in gorillas and savannah baboons), yet it has been claimed that fossil evidence suggests *Australopithecus afarensis* demonstrated a high degree of sexual dimorphism (some authorities consider males to have been approximately twice the size of females, e.g. McHenry, 1991). This level of sexual dimorphism is normally associated with polygynous mating systems in other primates (such as the gorilla). Lovejoy and his co-workers have subsequently reanalysed such fossils and suggest that levels of sexual dimorphism in *A. afarensis* were similar to modern-day humans (Reno *et al.*, 2003), supporting the notion of monogamy.

The provisioning hypothesis was later further developed to integrate two previous ideas with regard to the relationship between food supply and explanations of why humans diverged from the other anthropoid apes: the 'Man the Hunter' and the 'Woman the Gatherer' hypotheses (Buss, 1999). The hunting hypothesis proposed that ecological pressures presented by hunting led men to develop complex tools, weapons and communication in addition to bipedalism (Washburn, 1968; Ardrey, 1961). In contrast, the gathering hypothesis suggests that the evolutionary pressure that led to these human developments came from the problems presented to women who went out to gather food and who benefited from the mutual exchange of vegetable items (being bipedal also allowed them to carry infants and babies, Tanner and Zihlman, 1976; Tanner, 1981). Of course such hypotheses are not mutually exclusive and there might be some truth in both. It is certainly the case that in today's foraging societies, hunting is largely a male preserve and the gathering of plant foods is largely a female concern but whether or not this is directly related to bipedalism remains an area of debate (Marlowe, 2007; Miller, 2009; Videan and McGrew, 2002).

for sex on occasions (and possibly baboons and bonobos). Interestingly, males of modern-day hunter-gatherer societies who are prolific hunters are the ones who are seen as the most attractive by the women of such bands. In fact in those societies, which are polygynous (i.e. where males have more than one mate – see below), the best hunters have the most wives and are more likely to have extra-marital affairs (Hill and Kaplan, 1988; Smith, 2004). If women preferred males that were most able to provide them with meat, then we could see immediately that, over evolutionary time, sexual selection would increase hunting prowess in males since females would be choosing their mates on such a basis.

Why only men?

Sexual selection may have acted to improve hunting prowess in men, perhaps by increasing upper-body strength. It may also have improved the manufacture and use of weapons and tools in males and might even have favoured the formation of male coalitions in order to exploit large prey through cooperative hunting (Washburn, 1968; Washburn and Lancaster, 1968; Hill, 2002). If meat had become an important part of the human diet, however, might we not also expect women to have become good hunters? Up to a point they may have been. Women also have large brains, hands that can grip with precision and good stereoscopic vision. Moreover, it is not unheard of for women in modern forager societies to engage in hunting occasionally (Estioko-Griffin and Griffin, 1981; Waguespack, 2005). Also, as we have seen, female bonobos are known to engage in hunting on occasions, so this is by no means male-limited behaviour for primates. But the problem for women as hunters is that control over the reproductive cycle is a recent human invention. For our female ancestors, certainly as judged by their role in the majority of present-day forager societies, hunting was a less likely option since for most of their (usually short) adult lives they would either be lactating or pregnant. Of course being pregnant or nursing a baby would not be a great encumbrance when gathering plant food. For this reason it has been argued that this hunting–gathering sexual division of labour is likely to be ancient (Tooby and DeVore, 1987; Waguespack, 2005). This is not to say that women never engaged in hunting or that men never gathered plant food. The argument is about how each sex is likely to have foraged habitually.

How, then, is this related to the oestrous swelling (or lack of it) in women? A number of researchers have argued that a shift towards hunting by men may have had a knock-on effect on the oestrus cycle of women (see for example, Badcock, 1991). From this point on the argument becomes somewhat convoluted and decidedly speculative. Unlike plant foods, meat is a highly economic food source. In addition to its high calorific content, it contains all of the amino acids necessary for the human diet and the essential fatty acids required for brain development (Martin, 1983). Clearly women would benefit just as much from meat as men. However, as we have seen, women bear a child-rearing burden that would not be entirely compatible with big-game hunting. We saw earlier that some male primates exchange meat for increased access to females. Perhaps while male hominins took advantage of the game available on the savannah, female hominins took advantage of the males. Perhaps by forming a long-term sexual relationship with a good hunter, a woman and her offspring would benefit from the food provided in return. Remember that in forager societies it is the best hunters that are the most successful in attracting women and are arguably those most likely to pass on copies of their genes (Hill and Kaplan, 1988; Smith, 2004). In this way, meat may be linked to the formation of strong pair bonds between men and women, with a male helping to provide for his partner and for their offspring.

Note that according to this argument the long-term pair bonds formed would have benefited both male and female partners. Such an argument would have to be weighed against the benefit of desertion and possible missed mating opportunities elsewhere for both sexes. Also infanticide is not uncommon in forager societies when a woman takes a new husband (Dunbar, 2004). In other words there are both costs and benefits to forming long-term pair bonds (see later).

Cryptic oestrus

As we have seen, along with primates in general, chimpanzee and baboon males are particularly attentive to females who show an oestrous swelling on the rump – a feature that is lacking in human females. Richard Alexander and Katherine Noonan (1979) have suggested that by concealing their period of oestrus (which they call 'cryptic oestrus') women may have made men attentive to them continually, since only in this way would males be able to ensure that they father a partner's offspring. You may, however, have spotted a problem with this argument. If human females conceal oestrus why would males be attracted to them? British sociologist Christopher Badcock (1991) may have an answer to this dilemma. He suggests that rather than never appearing to be in oestrus, women appear to be permanently in that state.

Box 4.2 **Bipedalism and pair-bonding part 2 – why do men help out?**

Arguments concerning pair bond formation in humans raise one big question. If female apes can rear offspring without help, why should female hominins (and arguably present-day women) rely on male aid in rearing their children? Or to put it another way, why do human males bother to help out when their primate relatives generally get away with doing little or nothing? One idea, which was originally proposed by Stephen Jay Gould (1977), is also based around the evolution of bipedalism. Gould has suggested that this change to habitual bipedalism led to a narrowing of the pelvic girdle and that this, in turn, meant that a large-brained baby could only be passed through the pelvis at a highly immature stage (given our lifespan, human babies should be born at 21 months rather than 9). So human infants are delivered in a relatively immature and helpless state. This means that they require almost constant attention for a considerable period compared with any other animal. Females dealt with this problem, so the argument goes, by forming long-lasting pair bonds with male partners who were prepared to help provide for the offspring. Technically this is called high **male parental investment** (or MPI – see chapter 7).

However, if women don't even show a regular oestrous swelling then how is Badcock able to make such a claim? Interestingly, in the gelada monkey, females provide another ovulation signal – they have swollen breasts at this stage in their cycle. By all accounts this swelling is attractive to males. Human females, in contrast to all other primates, have permanently swollen breasts during their fertile years. In this way human females may be providing a false oestrus signal and are therefore permanently sexually attractive to men. A woman who was presumably able to keep a man around who would help to provide for her and her offspring by forming a long-term sexual relationship would be at a selective advantage over one who was unable to do so.

Thus the development of oestrus signals (which we might call dishonest oestrus) outside of genuine oestrus may have come about via sexual selection. If this is the case then we can think of a woman's shape as being the equivalent of a peacock's tail, evolving to suit the preferences of the opposite sex. Note that in this case we are dealing with male choice. Males in general are not normally particularly choosy about sex, but once they begin to invest in offspring, that is provide parental care, then they may become choosy about long-term commitments (Buss, 2011). This constant female sexual attraction may well be a unique human feature and it may have led, in turn, to a unique long-lasting pair bond.

Clearly, given as we have seen our primate relatives do not generally engage in monogamy (with the possible exception of serial monogamy in the hamadryas baboon), the changes that led to the formation of a long-lasting pair bond would have required a degree of psychological re-plumbing in both sexes. Like a chick that becomes imprinted on its hen, it would be necessary that these partnerships involved a desire for the couple to spend much of their time together. This pair bond that evolved might therefore be called sexual imprinting or, in colloquial language, 'love' (see chapter 11). Thus, in addition to explaining the sexual division of labour, greater upper-body strength in men and dishonest oestrus in women, the provisioning hypothesis may even explain the very reason we fall in love.

We can see that some evolutionists have used the behavioural and anatomical features of our primate relatives to make suggestions about how sexual selection might have had an effect on our own criteria for choosing a mate and other aspects of our evolution.

Science or speculation?

Some readers might have found the arguments based around the provisioning/'meat for sex' hypothesis somewhat speculative. Indeed, the arguments presented here are by no means cut and dried. At present the provisioning hypothesis does appear to explain a number of features that set us apart from other primates. In the future, however, new evidence or other arguments could arise which might weaken it. We should also bear in mind that in most forager societies, plant-based foods provide the majority of calories consumed – which means that females also provide provisions to males (as well as to offspring). The provisioning hypothesis today can be taken to mean that pair bonds are based on mutual provisioning that aids the production of offspring. Furthermore, we must be careful when using behavioural evidence in comparative studies since, as we have stressed, direct observation is not an option in evolution (Wrangham, 1987; Potts, 1996). When dealing with purely anatomical features, however, we can be a little more confident in making use of the comparative method since physical features are ultimately there to provide support for behaviour and may be quantified more accurately than behaviour. Modern men *are* larger than women and do have greater upper-body strength. Women certainly *did not* develop an oestrous swelling following divergence from the great apes unlike many of our primate relatives. There *is* a modern sexual division of labour along hunting and gathering lines in extant forager societies and long-term male–female pair bonds, where males invest highly in offspring, *are* a cross-cultural phenomenon. How precisely these human features are causally related through sexual selection, however, is an area of debate and speculation. These areas of greater certainty are largely physical and quantifiable features. And, as we will see later, studies of comparative anatomy have led some evolutionists to some surprising conclusions.

Table 4.1 **Mating system categories**

Category	Description	Examples	Distribution
Monogamy	Individuals mate with one partner	Dwarf antelopes Humans	90 per cent of bird species; but rare in mammals
Polygamy	Individuals mate with more than one partner. There are two forms of polygamy	Polygamy can be sub-divided into polygyny and polyandry – see below	See below
Polygyny	A form of polygamy where individual males mate with more than one female	Bighorn rams Gorillas Elephant seals Wood frogs Humans	The most common mating system found in mammals
Polyandry	A form of polygamy where individual females mate with more than one male	American jacanas Red-necked phalaropes Galapagos hawk Humans	Very rare. Found in some bird species

Sexual dimorphism and mating systems

We have seen that sexual selection can lead to differences both in behaviour and in physical form between the sexes and some would argue that this is also true for our own species. We have also seen how diet may have an impact on sex differences. As was noted above, frequently this means that males of a species are bigger than females. Clearly, the difference in size between males and females is not an all-or-nothing phenomenon. Human males are about 20 per cent bigger than their female counterparts; in gorillas males are almost twice the size of females, but in gibbons the sexes are virtually the same size. Current theory suggests that the greater the increase in male size relative to females the greater the competition between males for access to groups of females. Species in which the largest and strongest males monopolise groups of females are said to be polygynous. Hence polygyny is a form of polygamy where one male has access to a number of females but each female is normally limited to one male (the reverse situation where one female monopolises a number of males is called **polyandry** and is very rare – see table 4.1). In monogamous species where a lasting pair bond is formed (such as in gibbons) sexual dimorphism is likely to be low since, once paired up, males are no longer in competition for further mates. Examples of mating systems are provided in table 4.1.

Mating systems vary greatly between human cultures (you will notice that humans are represented in all of the categories in table 4.1). Because humans vary so much between cultures in their mating strategies some social scientists have claimed that our reproductive behaviour is culturally determined and hence unrelated to our evolutionary past (e.g. Mead, 1949; 1961). This is a question that evolutionary psychology is beginning to address and to which we now turn.

Human mating strategies

We began this chapter by asking what men and women look for in a potential partner. Under the provisioning hypothesis we suggested that, following a shift towards meat in the diet and a sexual division of labour, our species began to form long-term pair bonds, with males investing heavily in their offspring compared with their primate relatives. As we stated earlier, evolutionary explanations for current human practices are highly speculative and are currently characterised by a great deal more theory than data. One person, however, who has sought to redress the balance is David Buss of the University of Texas who has spent the last twenty five years researching in this area and has drawn some controversial conclusions.

Buss's work on mate choice criteria is startlingly different from previous studies. It is not startlingly different because he asks essentially new questions or because he applies radically new theories to explain his findings. Duplicating studies going back at least to the 1930s, Buss and his collaborators present men and women with a list of eighteen characteristics that they might find desirable in a serious long-term partner. These include financial prospects, social status, attractiveness, ambition and sense of humour. The task of respondents is to rate each of these attributes on a scale that ranges from 0 (irrelevant) to 3 (indispensable). Where Buss's work differs radically from previous studies is in the sheer size and range of the operation. Whereas previous studies had used samples of dozens or a few hundred, in their largest study Buss and his co-workers sampled around ten thousand people and they included subjects from every habitable continent. The range of different cultures chosen (37 in this case) is at least as important as the actual numbers sampled. Uncovering differences between the relative ratings of various attributes both within and between the sexes in a single culture is clearly of interest. It tells you about that culture. However, by using only one culture we are unable to determine to what extent such a pattern is culture specific. In large-scale cross-cultural studies universal similarities might be taken as evidence of a species-specific response. And species-specific responses are important to evolutionary psychologists since they may be taken as evidence that they are related to evolutionary process (Brown, 1991; see also chapters 1 and 14 of this book). So what have Buss and his co-workers discovered? The findings can

Table 4.2 **Human mean mate preference scores in 9,474 people from 37 different cultures. Rating scores potentially vary from 0.00 (irrelevant or unimportant) to 3.00 (indispensable)**

Characteristic	Male rating for females	Female rating for males	Degree of sex difference	Degree of cross-cultural variation
Love	2.81	2.87	Low	Low
Dependability	2.50	2.69	Low	High
Emotional stability/maturity	2.47	2.68	Moderate	Moderate
Pleasing disposition	2.44	2.52	Low	High
Good health	2.31	2.28	Low	High
Education/intelligence	2.27	2.45	Moderate	Low
Sociability	2.15	2.30	Low	Moderate
Desire for home and children	2.09	2.21	Low	High
Refinement/neatness	2.03	1.98	Low	High
Good looks	1.91	1.46	High	Moderate
Ambition and industriousness	1.85	2.15	High	High
Good cook and housekeeper	1.80	1.28	High	High
Good financial prospect	1.51	1.76	High	Low
Similar education	1.50	1.84	Moderate	High
Favourable social status	1.16	1.46	Moderate	Moderate
Chastity	1.06	0.75	Low	High
Similar religious background	0.98	1.21	Low	High
Similar political background	0.92	1.03	Low	Low

Source: adapted from Buss *et al.*, 1990.

broadly be divided into long- and short-term mating preferences and are summarised in table 4.2.

Long-term mate choice preferences

How might we interpret these findings? In exploring this table we can see that there are a number of areas in which the sexes differ in their responses. In other areas males and females appear to want the same things. At this point it may be useful to tease out and explore some of the figures under a number of topic headings in relation to the proposals that evolutionary psychologists have put forward.

Preferences for financial resources, industriousness and social status

The mean scores suggest that women rate social status, industriousness and financial prospects highly in potential male partners and that men regard such features as of lesser importance in women. Moreover, it is well established that men of particularly high occupational status are able to attract and marry particularly attractive women (Dunn and Searle, 2010; Elder, 1969; Taylor and Glenn, 1976; Daly and Wilson, 1983). Evolutionary psychologists such as Buss (1999; 2011) claim that this supports the notion that, since ancestral females invested so highly in their offspring, they would have benefited greatly from choosing mates that were able to provide for them and their offspring. Clearly, resources may be assessed directly (in today's society this generally means indications of financial well-being) or they may be inferred from social status and level of industriousness.

Although women in all cultures favour these characteristics more highly than men do, the degree of difference between the sexes varies between cultures. Women in India, Iran and Nigeria, for example, value financial prospects more highly than do those in South Africa and Holland. This cultural difference is more difficult to explain than the sex difference. Perhaps differences between cultures with regard to access that women have to education and other means of independence from men might help to explain this observed variability. This very point has been suggested as a criticism of Buss's findings by social constructionist Alice Eagly and her co-workers. Eagly has uncovered evidence that the preference for males with resources is negatively correlated with the degree to which the women of a particular culture have access to financial resources (Eagly and Wood, 1999). In other words, in some cultures women have to have preference for males with resources since they are unable to gain them themselves. At the time Eagly saw this correlational finding as suggesting that social roles are more important than evolved dispositions for mate characteristics. As evolutionists Robert Kurzban and Martie Haselton have pointed out, however, evolutionary psychologists (including Buss himself) generally see human mate behavioural adaptations as structured to 'respond contingently to local social and ecological factors' (Kurzban and Haselton, 2006). This is a point that Eagly now accepts, and in fact she now regards herself as a social-evolutionary interactionist (Eagly, personal communication; see also Eagly and Wood, 2011).

Preference for good looks

While both sexes demonstrate a clear preference for physically attractive partners, cross-culturally males rate this more highly in a partner than females. Furthermore, and surprisingly to many people, what males find attractive in females is pretty universal. They like large eyes, good teeth, lustrous hair, full lips, a small jaw and a low waist-to-hip ratio (i.e. the hour-glass shape) (Ford and Beach, 1951; Johnston and Franklin, 1993; Singh and Luis, 1995; Singh and Singh, 2011; Cunningham *et al.*, 1995). Some cultural anthropologists find it hard to believe that men from different cultures find similar features attractive in women. In fact, although there *is* cultural variability in a number of features such as overall weight, colour of hair and height (Swami and Salem, 2011; Cunningham *et al.*, 1995; Ford and Beach, 1951), the characteristics that are claimed to be universal have one important feature in common – they correspond to youthfulness.

We might ask why should men favour these features and why should physical attractiveness be universally rated more highly by men than by women? In the words of David Buss, 'To be reproductively successful, ancestral men had to marry women with the capacity to bear children' (Buss, 1999, p. 133). According to Robert Trivers, men in the past who found fertile women attractive would be likely to pass this preference on when in competition with men who found infertile women attractive. Trivers's theory of parental investment predicts just this difference. But men face a problem that women do not have when it comes to choosing a fertile partner – women have a limited period of fertility. Whereas a man may be fertile from early teens right into old age, a woman is fertile from perhaps her mid teens only until her late forties. A number of studies have now uncovered a clear relationship between signals of general fertility in women and what men find sexually attractive (Malinowski, 1929; Cross and Cross, 1971; Singh, 1993; Buss, 1995; Sugiyama, 2005). Such signals are related to high levels of circulating sex hormones necessary for fertility: oestrogen and progesterone. And these, in turn, are correlated with clear skin, full lips, lustrous hair and a low waist-to-hip ratio. They are also correlated with youthfulness. So, the argument goes, men who made mate choices on the basis of these youthfully attractive features left more surviving offspring than men who didn't.

The relationship does not, however, work in reverse since, given a man's lengthy period of fertility, there would not have been the same pressure on ancestral women to seek out signals of youthfulness. In fact, as we saw above, since women have a clear preference for good financial resources and a high social status in men, then it may pay them to seek older partners who are more likely to have climbed the slippery pole of success. This notion is supported by a number of studies of age preference in lonely-hearts columns in a variety of newspapers (see, for example, Kenrick and Keefe, 1992; Waynforth and Dunbar, 1995; Pawlowski and Dunbar, 1999). Such studies demonstrate not only that men generally look for women who are younger than themselves and that women generally prefer older men, but, interestingly, as men grow older they prefer women who are increasingly younger than themselves. As they age, women, in contrast, still expect to date older men. Again such a proclivity is certainly consistent with an evolutionary explanation for mate choice.

The fact that men look for increasingly younger women (relative to themselves) as they grow older may well be a mating strategy that is unique to humans. Other primates such as chimpanzees and orang-utans appear to favour older more experienced females (Stumpf *et al.*, 2008). Human male mating preferences may have resulted from an almost unique feature of women – that is, they can expect a lengthy period of life beyond their fertile years. Why women become infertile in their mid years is a matter for speculation. One possibility is that, given how arduous childbirth became following the evolution of bipedalism, it may have paid women to shift their investment to their grandchildren beyond a certain age.

This means that, unlike other primates, men have a twofold problem in making mate choices. First, they have to determine whether the potential partner is in oestrus and second, they have to decide whether she is within the correct age range to potentially bear offspring.

Arguably, ancestral males who chose females of childbearing age who had the longest period of fertility ahead of them would have an advantage over males who were unable to do so. Evolutionists call the number of children that a person of a given age and sex is likely to have in the future **reproductive value**. It is important to distinguish between female reproductive value and fertility. Fertility refers to the likelihood of a female producing an offspring from a given mating whereas reproductive value is the potential for future offspring production. This may appear a pedantic distinction to stress, but for males making a long-term commitment, it may be of great importance. A woman of thirty might be as fertile as a girl of 16, but the 16-year-old is likely to produce more offspring in the future than the 30-year-old. This difference may also be relevant when considering short-term mating opportunities (see below).

Before leaving 'good looks' behind we should note that, although women do not rate physical attractiveness as highly as men, they do, as table 4.2 shows, consider it to be of some importance. However, there is a fair degree of cultural variability in the importance that women place on physical attractiveness in men. How might evolutionary psychologists explain this? In contrast to some areas where cultural variability for features is not yet well understood, a simple explanation has been proposed for this case. It appears that women place greater emphasis on physical attractiveness in parts of the world where parasites are most common (Gangestad and Buss, 1993; Park and Schaller, 2009). Since physically attractive cues such as symmetrical faces and bodies are believed to be good indicators of parasite resistance (Hamilton and Zuk, 1982; Park and Schaller, 2009, see also chapter 3 above), then it may make sense for women in these parasite-ridden cultures to be more choosy about partners on the basis of physical attractiveness.

Preference for love and dependability

Romantic love was long thought by social scientists to be a recent invention of Western culture (Symons, 1979; Jankowiak and Fischer, 1992). If evolutionary psychology has achieved anything, it is the destruction of this myth. Love may not make the world go round, it may not be easy to define scientifically, but it is certainly something that everybody can experience (see, for example, Jankowiak and Fischer, 1992). We would be very surprised if any reader of this book has never been in love. In Buss's study, both sexes report love as an essential requirement for long-term partnership (figures for both sexes are very close to the maximum '3'). Wanting to engage in a long-term relationship with someone that we feel we are in love with is such an obvious state of affairs that you might feel it needs no explanation. However, forming an enduring pair bond is a very rare state of affairs for a mammalian species. What purpose might love serve?

As we discussed above, it is clear that women generally favour resources and men favour youthful, attractive looks. Gaining a partner who demonstrates such characteristics is only the first step towards successful reproduction, however. If a man has a surplus of resources but deserts a woman immediately after sex or a woman is very beautiful but has multiple sexual partners, then in neither case will their partner be satisfied with the outcome. In other words, for long-term relationships to work, both partners require signals of commitment. Signals of love may provide this commitment. Signals such as promises of undying fidelity and dependability are also rated very highly by both sexes. Signals such as buying gifts for a partner, or listening to their woes. In other words, channelling time and effort into a relationship is what people in love expect from their partners. If the ultimate function of falling in love is to produce offspring in which both parents will invest, then the sexual imprinting that we call love may be a feature which sexual selection has led to in our species (see provisioning hypothesis earlier).

Preference for chastity

Chastity, in Buss's study, is defined as 'no previous experience in sexual intercourse' (Buss, 1989, p. 19). Chastity appears quite low down the list for both sexes. Crucially, however, it is substantially more important for men seeking a long-term partner than for women. Why should this be the case? In all **placental** mammals the embryo develops inside the female uterus. This means that, whereas an offspring that a female gives birth to must be hers, it may not necessarily be that of her long-term partner. In humans there is an extra problem for males. As we saw earlier, in the case of chimps, bonobos and baboons (and indeed of mammals in general) females give off visual and olfactory signals when they are ovulating. Ancestral human females, in contrast, began, at some point, to disguise their ovulatory signals. This means that, whereas in other primates a male may be able to pay close attention to a female during oestrus and possibly engage in mate guarding, for ancestral men who had to deal with other matters, such as hunting, there was an increased potential for cuckoldry. Some evolutionists have even suggested that this increased possibility of cuckoldry may have been the very reason that marriage was invented since it acted to increase a male's certainty of paternity (Alexander and Noonan, 1979). This male-centred view contrasts with the widely held view that marriage developed primarily to ensure joint investment in offspring.

By rating no prior sexual experience as a relatively important criterion for long-term mate selection, males may be attempting to reduce the possibility of cuckoldry. In contrast, since females know that any offspring they deliver must be their own we can expect chastity in a partner to be of lesser importance to them. This fits in well with what we would expect from a knowledge of sexual selection theory. However, if males have such a great fear of investing in another male's offspring then there is a problem with the figures that are revealed by Buss *et al.*'s study and you may have spotted it. Although males rate this characteristic more highly than females, why is it so low down the list of priorities? Moreover, we might also ask, why, if this is an inherited feature, does its importance vary so much between different cultures – so much so that it is the most variable characteristic between cultures in the entire study? In China, India and Iran, for example, chastity is considered to be of great importance in a potential wife; yet in Finland, Norway and Sweden it is considered largely unimportant.

Some anthropologists explain differences in chastity and in sexual permissiveness in general in terms of random differences between cultures, which may suggest that it is free from evolutionary influences (Mead, 1949). This is part of the Standard Social Science Model (SSSM; Tooby and Cosmides, 1997; see also chapter 1) and is often referred to as the **arbitrary culture theory** (Alcock, 2009). It is true that cultures do vary in how sexually permissive they are, but such features of human life also vary within cultures over time. Since the 'sexual revolution' of the 1960s and the invention of freely available and reliable contraception, being a virgin bride has become less common in the West. And it might be argued that since women have been able to engage in sex with comparative freedom from its reproductive consequences, their attitudes and behaviour have become more similar to those of men (Ruse, 1987; Crooks and Baur, 2013).

Interestingly, in the Scandinavian countries where premarital sex is least frowned upon, the provision of welfare systems with regard to supporting unmarried mothers is the most generous. This is particularly true of Sweden where women enjoy greater economic independence from men than virtually anywhere else in the world. Perhaps economic independence is a precursor of sexual independence (Posner, 1992; Elman, 1996). Extending this line of reasoning, we might suggest that it will be in those cultures where women are financially dependent on men that we can expect to see chastity rated as very important for them. This would certainly be the case for China, Iran and India where women earn substantially less than in the West. It does not, however, explain why chastity is so important for men in some cultures (such as China).

The findings with regard to chastity suggest that one cultural shift, such as a change in economic status for women, might have a knock-on effect on other cultural variables such as what is morally acceptable. Such cross-cultural findings might also suggest that some areas are difficult to explain purely in terms of evolutionary principles. We return to this important point at the end of the chapter.

Emotional stability and pleasing disposition

Although evolutionary psychologists are apt to concentrate on the differences between the sexes, you will note from table 4.2 how similar men and women are in many of the things that they want. Apart from a partner who is in love with them, both sexes want someone who is emotionally stable and of a pleasing nature. Moreover, after 'love' and 'dependability', these personal qualities are the most highly rated by both sexes. In a word, we all want a partner who is going to show kindness towards us. Forming a long-term relationship with a shifty, unreliable person of appalling disposition would not have boded well for our ancestors. Cues that suggest kindness, however, would certainly be regarded as conducive to mutual investment in offspring (although our ancestors may not have conceived of it in quite this way).

In summary, most of what people want from a long-term partner is surprisingly similar between the sexes. The areas where the greatest divergence appears, however, are exactly those Trivers's theory of parental investment predicted (Trivers, 1972). That is, men do appear to place greater emphasis on physical attractiveness and women place a premium on signals of wealth and status. Both sexes require indicators of commitment and therefore, in a subject that treats relationships in such a cold and calculated light, it seems reassuring to discover that both men and women value love as of primary importance. At least that is the picture when considering long-term relationships. When we consider less permanent affairs things begin to look less romantically rosy.

Short-term mate choice preferences

So far we have considered the preference that each sex has when looking for a partner with whom a lengthy commitment is intended. However, all societies have their fair share of short-term sexual relationships (whether sanctioned or not), so it is necessary to consider these also. Evolutionists interested in human behaviour have long considered whether humans are psychologically adapted to commit to long-term relationships (whether monogamous or polygamous) or whether it is in our nature to attempt to have multiple short-term partners (Badcock, 1991; Wright, 1994; Campbell, 2008). Of course, such claims assume that there is a genetic component to our mating strategies – that is, that mating patterns are adaptations. When considering behaviour, just how big an impact evolution has had on our psychological wiring is an area of great debate. In contrast, when considering physiological and anatomical peculiarities, few would disagree that such features are largely genetically determined. And it is recent studies of the reproductive physiology and anatomy of males that have provided some surprising insights into the sexual strategies of both sexes.

Size of testes and mating strategy

As we saw earlier, differences in the level of sexual dimorphism between various species may provide clues both to the mating strategy and to levels of inter-male competitiveness of a species. Another area where males vary between species and which may provide further clues as to differences in sexual behaviour is in the size of their testes. Once again we can make use of the comparative method to see how sexual selection may have acted on primate species differentially. Gorillas, in contrast to their enormous body size, have relatively small testes, whereas chimpanzees have extremely large ones. The reason for this difference becomes clear when we realise that the amount of sperm produced increases with the size of the testes. In chimpanzee society, where sexual dimorphism is quite low, high ranking males do not monopolise a group of females but instead attempt to pair off with individual females during their period of oestrus. As we have seen, female chimpanzees show a large oestrous swelling during this fertile period of their cycle and may mate with a number of males at such a time. Such multiple mating behaviour in female chimps means that their reproductive tract will often contain sperm from more than one male. This female mating strategy has led the males to engage in **sperm competition** so that those able to produce the largest quantities of sperm are most likely to inseminate a female and thereby pass on their genes (Short, 1979). Hence sexual selection has driven chimpanzees' testes to their current enormous size. In contrast to chimpanzees, as we saw earlier, silverback gorillas that are able to defend a harem from the attentions of other males produce relatively small quantities of sperm since their sperm will not have to compete with that of other males. This explains why their testes are so small (see figure 4.4).

Thus in males a large body size relative to females indicates polygyny (multiple mating partners for males) whereas large testes compared to closely related species indicates polygamy (multiple partners for both sexes). The finding of a relationship between testes and body size in relation to mating strategy raises the question – what sort of mating strategy do these measurements suggest in our own species? It turns

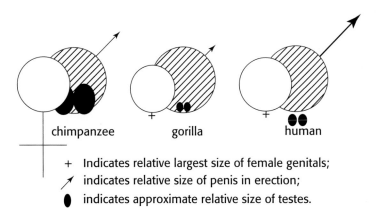

+ Indicates relative largest size of female genitals;
↗ indicates relative size of penis in erection;
● indicates approximate relative size of testes.
Large circles indicate approximate relative body size of sexes.

Figure 4.4 The relative body and testis size of apes and humans

out that we are intermediate on both measures. In terms of body size, humans are a little more dimorphic than chimps and decidedly less so than gorillas. In terms of testis size humans are four times larger in volume than gorillas, relative to body size, but only a third the size of chimpanzees. By these measures then, in our ancient past, human males may well have competed for females partly via strength and size and partly via sperm competition. In order for sperm competition to occur, some human females must have routinely mated with more than one male within a matter of days. This means that we may be able to infer something about the mating strategy of both sexes by studying the anatomical detail of one sex. The relative size of male testes suggests that human females were less promiscuous than chimps but more promiscuous than gorillas.

Pre- and extra-marital activities

The current workings of human testes suggest that, although all modern human societies recognise and encourage the formation of long-term pair bonds of various sorts, our ancestors of both sexes engaged in extra-marital activities (Baker, 2006; Shackelford *et al.*, 2005). Such a finding poses two big questions. Why might short-term relationships have been of benefit to each sex? And what do men and women look for in a short-term partner – is it the same as in a long-term partner, or something quite different? In other words, we need to consider the costs and the benefits of engaging in casual sexual relationships.

Costs and benefits of short-term relationships to men and women

One of the most revealing studies of the difference between men and women in their reactions to casual sex (at least in the West) was also one of the simplest. Clark

> ## Box 4.3 **Altering sperm production**
>
> The finding of a relationship between testis size and human promiscuity is also supported by the finding that a man's sperm count rises quite dramatically when he has been away from his partner for some time (Baker and Bellis, 1989; 1995; Shackelford *et al.*, 2005). The rationale being that when ancestral males spent some time away from their mates, upon their return they increased their sperm production in order to compete with other males that might have had sex with their partners. So in addition to producing relatively large amounts of sperm, human males are also able to alter the amount they produce depending on how long they have been away from their partners. Again such a male adaptation is difficult to explain without resorting to sperm competition being driven by ancestral females having more than one partner over quite short periods of time.
>
> Before we begin to feel let down by the lack of fidelity that this suggests for our female ancestors we should also bear in mind that it takes two to recombine their genes: both sexes are equally tainted by such findings! As Buss puts it:
>
> > Ancestral women must have sought casual sex for its benefits in some contexts at some times at least, because if there had been no willing women, men could not have evolved the psychological mechanisms attuned to short-term opportunities. (1995)

and Hatfield (1989) simply had attractive male and female students walk around a university campus and ask students of the opposite sex whether they would sleep with them. The responses of men and women could hardly have been more different. While 75 per cent of males agreed to sleep with a woman they had met only minutes before, every one of the females approached declined the offer! This study provides striking confirmation of what most of us would have guessed. Men see an invitation for casual sex with an attractive unknown woman both as a compliment and an opportunity. Women see it as a threat and an insult. David Buss and Donald Symons both consider that this difference in behaviour reflects differing psychological adaptations in men and women with respect to sex. They argue that men have evolved to be licentious and to find casual sex particularly appealing in order to increase their chances of producing extra offspring at little cost (Symons, 1979; 1989; Buss, 2003). Women, in contrast, they suggest, have evolved to be more coy about casual sex because, as Trivers realised, they have more to lose if they make a poor choice.

How many partners?

Although historically most studies of sexual relationships have focused on married couples, there is now supportive evidence for the views of Symons and Buss.

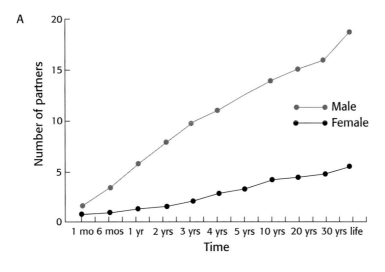

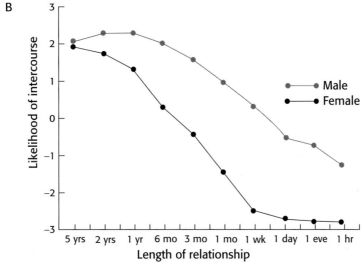

Figure 4.5 Number of sexual partners desired by males and females over various periods of time

Cross-culturally, women desire fewer lifetime sexual partners than men. One particular study conducted by Buss and his colleague David Schmitt (1993) revealed that, during a period of one year, women would ideally like to have one sexual partner whereas men would prefer to have around six. During a period of three years women would like to have two whereas men would ideally like to have around ten (see figure 4.5). One reason for this difference might be the greater costs and lower benefits that such behaviour holds for women when compared with their male counterparts. Unlike a man, a woman is unlikely to increase the number of offspring she has by increasing the number of partners she has. Moreover, a single woman who engages in short-term sexual relationships runs the risk of desertion (leaving them 'holding the baby') and a married woman who engages in extramarital sex runs the risk both of her husband's wrath and of his desertion. Furthermore, cross-culturally, promiscuous women are regarded as less 'marriageable' than monogamous or chaste ones (Buss, 2003). By being openly promiscuous a woman might reduce her chances of gaining a high-quality long-term partner.

In a very real sense, then, the benefits that men gain from short-term relationships might also be seen as the costs that women incur from such liaisons. That is, a reduction in the level of investment in the offspring by males at the expense of females. However, given that human testes reveal an evolutionary history of multiple partners for both sexes we must ask – what is in it for women?

What is in casual sex for women?

Until recently it was widely considered that, while extra-pair copulations might benefit males, the best strategy for a female must surely be to find a partner who would stick by her, and to stand by him. In recent years this view has changed. It has changed partly because of the findings with regard to human sperm production, but also due to two further developments. First, it has been suggested that, under certain conditions, women might also benefit from multiple pre-marital or extra-pair post-marital matings (Buss, 2003) and, second, there is growing evidence that cross-culturally women are by no means as monogamous as was once considered (Wrangham, 1993; Buss, 2011). Indeed in the USA, for example, confidential surveys suggest that somewhere between 20 and 50 per cent of married women have engaged in an extra-marital affair (Kinsey *et al.*, 1953; Glass and Wright, 1992). Also in England, via genetic testing, Baker and Bellis (1995) have found that about one in five children could not be the offspring of their supposed fathers. Given the findings that women appear to be less monogamous than was once thought, we might ask what possible benefits might they gain from brief sexual encounters.

Evolutionary psychologists have suggested that women may gain both material and genetic benefits for their offspring from casual sexual relationships. By having more than one sexual partner a woman may derive benefits such as food and other gifts. Recall that it has been argued that female chimps and baboons may sometimes exchange sex for food – a process which biologists call **resource extraction**. Indeed, anthropologists have found that in forager societies such as the Trobriand Islanders where casual sex is permitted or, at least, not heavily frowned upon, women generally act as mistresses only as long as their lovers bring them gifts (Malinowski, 1929). Furthermore, Buss has found that women rate having an extravagant lifestyle and generosity more highly in a temporary lover than in a permanent partner (Buss and Schmitt, 1993). These findings suggest that there may be material benefits to women in casual sexual relationships. Buss even suggests that,

These psychological preferences reveal that the immediate extraction of resources is a key adaptive benefit that women secure through affairs. (1995)

In terms of genetic benefits, there are a number of ways in which a woman may benefit from casual sex, whether she is married or not. A woman can increase the variability of her offspring by mating with more than one man (Smith, 1984). Furthermore, by taking a secret lover who is physically superior to, or of higher status than, her husband, a woman can potentially improve the status of the male offspring she produces. In support of this, Baker and Bellis (1989) have found that, when a married woman has an affair, her lover is almost invariably of higher status than her husband. Some evolutionists have even suggested that when women cuckold their partners they do so with more attractive men than their husbands (Meston and Buss, 2009; Simpson *et al.*, 1993; Wright, 1994). This may be of benefit if such women pass on these attractive features to their sons who would then have improved chances of attracting women. For obvious reasons this notion has become known as the **sexy sons** hypothesis (Fisher, 1958; Gangestad and Simpson, 1990).

Do women have a self-knowledge of their market value?

A final factor, which, it has been suggested, might affect a woman's likelihood of becoming promiscuous, is her perceived level of attractiveness to males. Some evolutionists have proposed that, as a girl grows up, the feedback she receives from males provides her with a self-knowledge of her level of attractiveness – her 'market value' (Trivers, 1972). This self-knowledge, Robert Trivers speculates, may then affect her reproductive strategy. Females who perceive themselves as less attractive might be more likely to engage in casual sexual relationships since they are less likely to gain a long-term high-quality partner (Harris, 1998). For those who receive feedback suggesting that they are particularly attractive, however, it may make more sense to hold out for a high-status male from which they are likely to gain a high level of investment (Trivers, 1972; Wright, 1994). This is a controversial notion but one for which there is some empirical support. Walsh (1993) has found that the less attractive a woman feels she is, the more partners she is likely to have. Moreover there is clear evidence that the most beautiful women in a given society do tend to marry the most powerful men (Kanazawa and Kovar, 2004; Symons, 1979).

Clearly, the sexual strategy that a woman adopts reflects a number of complex interacting factors – and we haven't even considered the importance of inherent personality variables (see chapter 13). Men, in contrast, it has been suggested, are less context dependent in their proclivities for casual partners (Buss, 2003). The potential reproductive benefits that men gain from casual sexual relationships should not blind us to the fact that they also might incur costs and need to weigh up their options. A man who has a relationship with another man's wife risks injury or even murder at the

Box 4.4 **Context and reproductive strategy in women**

If women are able to gain both material and genetic benefits for their offspring from casual sexual relationships, we might turn our earlier question on its head and ask why is it that most women enter into long-term relationships? Cross-cultural studies of human relationships have shown that reproductive behaviour is strongly dependent upon context. Whether a woman chooses a path of casual sex, long-term marriage or some sort of mixed strategy depends on a number of social and economic factors. Such factors include the availability of men with resources, the age and attractiveness of a woman and, of course, a woman's ability to gain resources herself (see end of chapter). In societies where women outnumber men, such as where warfare accounts for the death of many men (e.g. the Aché or the Yanomamö), women may adopt short-term mating strategies in order to gain a little from each partner (Symons, 1979). This may also be the case in inner-city ghettos where, due to high levels of male unemployment, men have little to invest (Buss, 2003, 2011). Also, following divorce, an older woman with children may become less attractive to males which might lead her to shift her strategy to multiple casual partners.

But a woman's mating strategy does not only depend on the circumstances of her adult life. There is now clear evidence that the likelihood of a woman engaging in casual sex is related to whether or not her father was present during her childhood. The daughters of divorcees are distinctly more likely to be promiscuous than those of parents who stay together. Startlingly, it has also been found that girls whose father is absent during development begin to menstruate at an earlier age than those who have a father present (Draper and Belsky, 1990). Might this be an adaptation to extract resources from male sexual partners at as early an age as possible? Might the presence or absence of a father during childhood be the prime factor in determining whether or not a woman becomes promiscuous in adult life? An evolutionary explanation might suggest that, during development, a girl uses such cues to determine her best strategy within the society in which she finds herself. According to this type of argument, in societies (and strata of societies) where men routinely form relatively short relationships with women it may pay female offspring to anticipate such a male strategy and act accordingly in later life.

This line of reasoning may appear to make sense. However, we should also bear in mind that a girl whose father is absent during childhood is likely to be less wealthy than one whose father is present. This may then have the knock-on effect of reducing the probability of meeting and attracting 'high-quality' men who might be prepared to form long-term relationships with her. This does not disprove an evolutionary-based argument, but it does demonstrate that we do not have to evoke one to explain this finding.

hands of her husband. Daly and Wilson (1988), for example, have found that a large proportion of male/male homicides are the result of sexual jealousy. Furthermore, in a number of societies it is permissible for a man to kill another man who has slept with his wife (and to kill the wife). Even when a man engages in a short-term sexual relationship with an unmarried woman he might not be safe from violence. In a number of societies he might be attacked and beaten by her brothers and father (Daly and Wilson, 1988). Finally, by engaging in short-term relationships a man may reduce the chances of his offspring surviving since he is unlikely to provide investment for them (or protect them from infanticide at the hands of other men, Dunbar, 2004). Despite such possible costs, universally, men do appear to engage in short-term sexual liaisons more frequently than women (Hunt, 1974; Hite, 1987; Baker and Bellis, 1995; Baker, 2006). Such a finding appears to provide support for the views of Symons and Buss.

Monogamous or polygamous?

Are we now in a position to answer the question – are humans monogamous or polygamous by nature? Given no constraints, would people naturally gravitate towards long-term committed relationships or towards multiple short-term sexual encounters? And would the sexes differ in respect of this? Cross-cultural studies suggest that in reproductive matters we are a highly flexible species and that, unlike other species, our sexual strategy cannot easily be pigeonholed. Evolutionary psychologists are only just beginning to scratch at the surface of the determinants of this flexibility both within and between cultures. The degree of sexual dimorphism suggests at least a partly polygynous past. Moreover, human testes bear witness to the possibility of promiscuity as one strategy that might be adopted by either sex given the right context. There is, however, a further, more clearly psychological finding, which suggests that, like the males of other species, men may be the real sexual opportunists; it's called the Coolidge effect (see box 4.5).

Cultural variability and developmental flexibility

The large-scale studies of Buss and his contemporaries have told us a great deal about what men and women want from a sexual partner. However, they have also revealed substantial cultural differences. As Buss (2011) has commented with regard to his own data, sex differences are generally smaller than cultural differences. Women may value men who can help to support them – at least in societies where they have a lower access to financial and other resources than men (i.e. in most societies). In societies where women now have greater financial independence, such as in the

> ### Box 4.5 Male preference for novelty – the Coolidge effect
>
> As with women, how beneficial long- and short-term sexual relationships are likely to be to men will depend on a number of factors such as how financially independent women in their society are and a male's own position with regard to status, attractiveness and resources. One area where male and female psychological wiring appears to differ universally, however, lies in a male's response to novel partners. If women may have had a less monogamous ancient history than we used to think, then men actually have a specific adaptation that is difficult to explain without an evolutionary history of 'straying'. While male birds and mammals generally require a period of rest following intercourse before being able to mate once again with the same female, it has been known for some time that if a novel female is introduced they will regain their sexual potency very rapidly (Jordan and Brooks, 2010). Moreover, by constantly changing the female that a male is with, he can continue to copulate for much longer than had he remained with the same one. This male interest in novel females is known as the **Coolidge effect** and is now also known to be a cross-cultural feature of human males (Symons, 1979; James, 1981; Hamer and Copeland, 1998). No parallel effect has been uncovered for females, which might suggest that it is a specific male adaptation. But then again it hasn't really been studied in human females.

Scandinavian countries, however, male status and resources are valued less. Such a finding reminds us of the degree of developmental flexibility that allows humans to adjust to social and economic circumstances. Yes, for long-term relationships women do want emotionally stable and dependable men who are well-off and of high status. But the relative importance of these features varies between cultures – and we will need to look more closely at specific cultural variables if we wish to understand why they differ so much (Benton, 2000).

As far as men are concerned, when considering a long-term partner they are surprisingly similar to women. They seek emotionally stable and dependable mates. Where they differ from women lies in their substantially higher rating of physical attractiveness. Men certainly do favour attractive young women. We should also note, however, as table 4.2 demonstrates, that good looks are given a lower rating than dispositional factors such as a pleasant personality and sociability. Furthermore, it should be noted that women also want attractive partners – although good looks are of lower priority to them. It is when we consider short-term casual relationships, however, that the sex differences really appear. Men substantially lower their standards for casual sex partners, while women retain, or even increase, theirs (Buss, 2003). This might be explained by differences in the potential costs and benefits of casual sex to men and women. But even here there is likely to be a fair degree of cross-cultural variation, if the variability on emphasis placed on chastity is anything to go by.

Humans have a fair degree of cross-cultural variability in the features that they favour in a partner. However, what of the universality of the Coolidge effect in human males? Does this mean that it is in a man's genes to philander? Findings concerning the anatomy and physiology of human testes and even those concerning what leads to increased sexual arousal in men merely inform us of what our genes may *allow* us to do. They do not *force* us to behave in a particular way. Clearly, unlike other species, humans bring a sense of sexual morality into relationships and the practices that are acceptable *do* vary between societies. Many couples engage in successful long-term monogamous relationships, but others choose not to. One of the difficulties for evolutionary psychologists will be to determine which factors are pre-eminent in the development of a person's reproductive behaviour. Such factors include social, cultural, economic, personality, childrearing and peer-group practices. Of course, all of these may, in turn, be influenced by our evolutionary past. It may be in our genetic ancestry to philander under some circumstances. But perhaps, our moral development and sense of free will make us the one species that can choose not to obey such genes.

Summary

- One way of illuminating our understanding of humans is by studying our living relatives – the comparative method. Comparisons with chimps, bonobos, gorillas and baboons reveal a number of substantial differences. Humans eat far more meat than monkeys and apes and, due to a lack of an oestrous swelling, a woman's oestrus cycle is a complete mystery to men. Some evolutionists have suggested there may be a relationship between these two human features. Under the provisioning hypothesis, it is suggested that when humans left the forests and began to live on the open savannah there was a shift towards bipedal locomotion and an increase in hunting for males. Females, who were now involved in nurturing for much of their fertile years, specialised in gathering plant foods but also gained meat from males and entered into long-lasting pair-bonded relationships with them which involved a substantial increase in male parental investment. Neonate survival benefited from the lengthy pair bond that may have been a result of this change.
- Darwin called the degree to which the sexes differ in physical characteristics sexual dimorphism. Usually this means larger size for males. Polygynous mating systems (one male to a number of females) generally lead to a large degree of sexual dimorphism since males compete for 'the prize' of a number of female mates. In monogamous species the sexes may be very similar in size since, once paired up, it does not pay a male to compete for further females.

- Another area which may provide clues as to differences in sexual and aggressive behaviour is variability in the size of a male's testes between primate species. Relatively large testes, which produce large quantities of sperm, suggest a degree of polyandry since the sperm from two or more males will have to compete in the uterus. Chimps have relatively large testes and a low level of sexual dimorphism; gorillas have small testes and a high degree of sexual dimorphism. This suggests that chimps engage in sperm competition and that females mate with a variety of males, but gorillas do not engage in sperm competition and are highly polygynous with large dominant males defending a harem of females. Humans are intermediate between gorillas and chimps with respect to body and testis size. This suggests that ancestral human males engaged in both physical and sperm competition to some degree.
- For long-term relationships both men and women look for loving and dependable partners who have a kindly disposition and are in good health. Where the sexes differ lies in men's greater emphasis on good looks and women's preference for status and wealth. Men also place a greater emphasis on chastity in a partner than women, a finding which varies between cultures.
- While both sexes may gain from the mutual investment in offspring that is normally associated with a long-term relationship, both may also gain from short-term sexual liaisons. Men may increase reproductive output through extra-pair or multiple matings. Women may be able to extract some degree of resources from each of a number of partners and might improve the quality and variability of their offspring via extra-pair copulations. Costs may also be incurred from multiple and extra-pair copulations, however, such as damage to a person's reputation, desertion or violent retribution from a partner or their relatives.
- The reproductive strategy of an individual (i.e. long- or short-term relationships) will depend on a number of factors such as the availability of suitable partners and the perceived attractiveness and age of a person. Evolutionary psychologists have recently suggested that a woman's mating strategy may be influenced by the nature of her parents' relationship during her childhood. In societies where the father is not present during a girl's childhood she is likely to adopt a more promiscuous adult strategy as men are less likely to enter into long-term commitments in such societies.

Questions

1. For 99 per cent of mammalian species males make little or no investment in the offspring beyond the 'gift' of a small amount of sperm. In songbirds, however, the vast majority of males help to feed the offspring following hatching. Based on the

concepts introduced in this chapter, why do we find this difference in levels of male parental investment?

2. In terms of behaviour, what effects might high male parental investment have on both the males and the females of a species?

3. According to Buss, cross-culturally men prefer younger female partners and women prefer older male partners. Why should it be this way around? Is it possible to defend an argument that this is an arbitrary cultural phenomenon?

4. Some evolutionists have argued that the Coolidge effect (see box 4.5) suggests males may benefit (in terms of inclusive fitness) from having multiple sexual partners. Could an evolutionary argument be made that females should also demonstrate a Coolidge effect?

FURTHER READING

Brown, D. E. (1991). *Human Universals*. New York: McGraw-Hill. Social anthropologist describes how he slowly became convinced that the standard social science model is fundamentally flawed. Records and describes a range of cross-cultural universals from facial expressions to sex differences in aggressive response.

Buss, D. M. (2004). *The Evolution of Desire* (2nd edn). New York: Basic Books. Considers sexual and mate choice behaviours from an evolutionary standpoint. Fast becoming a seminal work in evolutionary psychology.

Crooks, R. L. and Baur, K. (2013). *Our Sexuality* (12th edn). Belmont, CA: Wadsworth. The seminal academic work on human sexuality integrating psychological, social and biological components.

Strier, K. B. (2011). *Primate Behavioral Ecology* (4th edn). Upper Saddle River, NJ: Prentice-Hall. Sophisticated and comprehensive account of primate ecology for those wanting to study all aspects of primatology.

Swami, V. and Salem, N. (2011). The evolutionary psychology of human beauty. In V. Swami (ed.). *Evolutionary psychology: A Critical Introduction* (pp. 131–82). Oxford, UK: Wiley-Blackwell. Critically reviews the evidence for universal human preferences for attractiveness – mainly focusing on female beauty.

5 Cognitive development and the innateness issue

KEY CONCEPTS

nativism • empiricism • constructivism • epigenetic landscape • imprinting • critical period • sensitive period • Machiavellian intelligence • theory of mind • autism • Williams syndrome • neuroconstructivism • biological preparedness • cortical plasticity

Evolutionary psychology often makes strong claims about innateness, that the child is born with innate (inborn) mental modules that enable it to develop competencies in areas that have strong fitness implications. For this reason, early cognitive development has become one of the battlegrounds for evolutionary psychologists and their critics. In this chapter we evaluate the modularity hypothesis, introduced in chapter 1, and look at developmental evidence for and against this particular claim of evolutionary psychology. As a result of some evidence that apparently contradicts the notion of innate modules some have concluded that evolutionary psychology itself is untenable. Others, however, propose that modularity is not an essential component of evolutionary psychology and that evolutionary psychology can progress without a commitment to modularity.

Nature, nurture and evolutionary psychology

One of the central debates of developmental psychology is the so-called 'nature versus nurture' debate. This asks to what extent human behaviour is the result of environmental factors (nurture) and to what extent it is the result of innate biological factors (nature). This question has a long history, starting at least as early as the Ancient Greek philosophers, and has been revisited by a variety of thinkers ever since. Throughout history the pendulum of opinion has swung in favour of one or other of these forces as new theories are developed and evidence accumulated. Recently the evolutionary approach has led to a renaissance in nativism as a means of explaining human behaviour and, in particular, that human development is constrained by the existence of innate mental modules.

Innate similarities and innate differences

The nurture position has been perhaps most famously summarised by the behaviourist psychologist J. B. Watson in the early part of the twentieth century who claimed:

Give me a dozen healthy infants, well-formed, and my own specified world to bring them up in and I'll guarantee to take any one at random and train him to become any type of specialist I might select: doctor, lawyer, artist, merchant-chief, and, yes, even beggar man and thief, regardless of his talents, penchants, tendencies, abilities, vocations, and race of his ancestors. (1925)

The above quotation seems to be a fairly unequivocal statement of a belief that innate mental faculties do not exist and, were it true, might be seen as sounding the death knell for nativism in general and evolutionary psychology in particular. In fact, taken in isolation, all it states is that innate mental faculties play no role in the formation of individual differences (see chapter 13). This is important because current thinking in evolutionary psychology draws a distinction between the claim that differences between individuals are innate and the claim that similarities between individuals are innate. These two claims, it is argued, are logically independent. To see why consider the following example (adapted from Block, 1995). It is well established that the fact that most of us are born with five digits on one hand (rather than four or six) is entirely due to the genetic programme that dictates the development of the individual's hand. Conversely, that some of us might have fewer than five digits is almost totally the result of the environment, for example a finger might have been lost in an accident, or some toxin might have interfered with the individual's growth during prenatal development (as was the case with Thalidomide). This means that environmental factors account for almost all of the differences between individuals in digit number, even though genetic factors account for the majority of us having five digits. Incidentally this means that if we were to calculate the heritability of having five fingers it would be zero (see chapters 2 and 6 for more on heritability). This is because heritability is a measure of the variation in some trait due to genes, not the extent to which something is 'inherited'. Since the variation of finger number is almost entirely environmental, there is no variation due to genes and so the heritability would be zero. A point worth bearing in mind and one that we will return to in the next chapter.

Look at Watson's argument again. Even if he were correct his claim does not necessarily undermine either nativism or the claims made by evolutionary psychology. For example, some theorists have suggested that natural selection has endowed us with an innate faculty for learning language (see Pinker and Bloom, 1990; Pinker, 1994; see also chapter 10). Using the same argument as we did for the number of digits it is entirely possible that the ability to speak a language is due to the presence of an innate 'language organ' as it is sometimes called, whereas individual differences in language skills could be entirely due to environmental factors such as educational opportunities, brain damage and so on. So even if Watson could train his infants into a career of his choosing it does not rule out the notion of evolved learning mechanisms. As we shall see in chapters 6 and 12 the evidence from behavioural genetics research shows that there are strong genetic influences on individual differences too, so Watson was also wrong in this regard.

What does 'innate' really mean?

Evolutionary psychology has a strong association with nativism (see chapter 1), but the problem is that words such as 'nativism' and 'innate' are taken to mean very different things by different people. To claim, for example, that language is innate is obviously false. Newborn babies cannot speak or understand language, and the particular language that is learned by a child will depend on the linguistic environment in which he or she grows up. So when Noam Chomsky or Steven Pinker argues that language is innate they are not arguing that babies are born with full knowledge of language; they mean that children are born with predispositions that enable them to acquire language efficiently (see chapter 10).

The evolutionary psychology tradition that gained prominence in the 1990s – the Santa Barbara school – proposes that the mind is made up of innate mental modules. These are specialised processing units that are domain specific, that is, they are responsible for particular types of data such as language, physics, faces, cheater-detection and understanding mental states. Moreover, these modules are present because they were engineered by natural selection. It is important to note, however, that such modules are not necessarily supposed to map onto specific brain regions in the manner of Gall's phrenological theory of human psychology (see chapter 1). It is entirely possible that processes such as language involve the use of brain systems that comprise a range of widely distributed regions.

One argument for the existence of mental modules derives from an analogy between the mind and the body. The human body is composed of organs that perform quite specific tasks: the heart pumps blood; the lungs are responsible for gaseous exchange; the kidneys selectively filter out waste from the blood and so on. One reason for this is proposed by Cosmides and Tooby:

As a rule, when two adaptive problems have solutions that are incompatible or simply different, a single general solution will be inferior to two specialized solutions. (1994, p. 90)

According to Cosmides and Tooby we should expect the mind to contain evolved mechanisms that are specific to particular problems that our predecessors faced in the ancestral environment, in addition to any general-purpose learning algorithms. For example, humans, like many other social animals, need to be able to identify members of their species (known as conspecifics). Identifying a person as our mother, sibling, or sworn enemy would drastically alter how we would respond to them. According to Cosmides and Tooby, there is a good chance that natural selection would have provided us with mechanisms specifically designed to enable us to memorise and recognise human faces (see later).

What is the evidence for innate modules?

A number of lines of evidence have been used to evaluate the claim that humans are born with innate mental modules. Two of these are developmental in flavour and therefore appropriate for this chapter. The first comes from examining the competencies of newborns and young infants. If we find that some abilities are present at birth or emerge shortly after then this might suggest that they are innate. (The opposite, however, is not true: just because something emerges later in life does not mean that it is *not* innate, e.g. pubic hair.) The second line of evidence comes from developmental disorders. Some disorders that manifest themselves in infancy or early childhood are characterised by the impairment of specific abilities with the comparative sparing of others. It has been claimed that this is because the disorder damages some mental modules (such as those responsible for acquiring language) but spares the others. The rest of this chapter is dedicated to evaluating both of these types of evidence.

The early emergence of specific competencies

One of the obvious tests for the innateness of an ability is whether it occurs at birth or soon after. Human newborns seem so helpless that it is easy to believe that, apart from a few simple behaviours and reflex actions, they have no real cognitive abilities whatsoever, and that all of the competencies that they have as older children are slowly acquired by interacting with the environment.

This perspective was advanced by the most famous developmentalist of all, the Swiss psychologist Jean Piaget (1896–1980). He saw his view as an alternative to the extreme environmentalism of the philosopher John Locke (and later Watson and Skinner, see chapter 1) and the extreme nativism of Descartes (and later Chomsky and Fodor, see chapters 1 and 10). Rather, Piaget saw development as a process whereby the child actively constructs its understanding of the world.

Piaget's developmental theory

One of Piaget's most important contributions was his suggestion that there was much in common between psychological development and biological development. Modern

> ## Box 5.1 Stage theories of development
>
> A number of theories, but in particular Piaget's theory, postulate that development progresses in a stage-like manner. It is important to know what this means since it can be somewhat different from what people mean colloquially when they say that a child 'is going through a stage'. Stage theories usually specify that the child's knowledge changes drastically at one or more points in development. Piaget's theory suggests large qualitative changes in knowledge, rather than changes which are merely quantitative, such as learning a new fact about the world or a set of new facts. Such changes often have a marked effect on behaviour, for example, in Piaget's theory the ability to adopt the perspectives of others (but see later in this chapter). Stage theories are often domain general, so a change affects many domains (e.g. person perception, language, physical reasoning) rather than being specific to a particular domain. Domain specific theories that postulate qualitative change are often referred to as phase theories. Stage theories require changes to be rather sudden; the child's understanding of the world changing noticeably over a few weeks or months, followed by a more gradual increase in knowledge.

geneticists do not see genes as determining physical and behavioural development (see chapter 2); rather they are seen as guiding the process of development in a probabilistic manner. So behavioural geneticists discuss a 'developmental timetable', which involves a series of likely milestones (such as when the first clumsy steps will be taken or the utterance of the first spoken words). Such a developmental sequence does not proceed along a fixed pathway but depends on a large amount of environmental feedback. Likewise, Piaget believed that psychological development was neither the result of impressions made via the senses (as Locke suggested), nor the execution of some innate plan. Experiences matter, but that which is learned from experience is constrained by what was already present in the infant's pre-existing mental structures.

The epigenetic landscape

One question that Piaget sought to address was the observation that although children have very different experiences, they nevertheless tend to develop in a very similar way, for instance, reaching the major developmental milestones at approximately similar ages. In order to explain this phenomenon Piaget drew upon the work of geneticist C. H. Waddington (Waddington, 1975) who proposed that development could be thought of in terms of an **epigenetic landscape**. Figure 5.1 shows such a landscape. The ball is at the top end of a valley that subdivides a number of times, and the path of the ball represents the particular developmental trajectory taken by

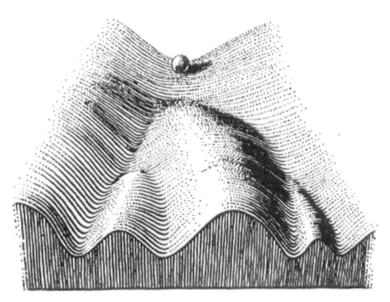

Figure 5.1 The epigenetic landscape

an individual child. As the ball rolls through the landscape, different environmental conditions might lead to perturbations in the ball's trajectory, but it will tend to return to its original path. Only extreme environmental activity would cause the ball to switch pathways and go down a different valley. Therefore, although environmental conditions can affect the path that the ball takes, these effects are always constrained by the structure of the landscape.

To relate this back to human development it suggests that although experiences can affect psychological development, the nature and size of the effect is constrained by the structure of that which is already present (the topography of the epigenetic landscape). These constraints serve as a buffer and children will tend to turn out similar to each other despite often having quite different learning experiences (we return to similar accounts in chapter 6 and chapter 14).

Learning about the physical world

Like all other animals, humans exist in a world that obeys the laws of physics in which unsupported objects fall to the ground, solid objects cannot pass through one another, and getting from A to B requires one to pass through all of the points in between. Understanding these and many other physical principles is essential if the individual is to negotiate the world in an effective manner. If evolution has shaped the way that the mind works we might expect such understandings to emerge early in life.

The Piagetian infant has no understanding of physics. A cynic might counter this by saying that nor do most high-school students. This is, however, incorrect as all clinically normal children have an intimate understanding of the physical world. Not the school physics of inclined planes, frictionless surfaces and masses which take up no space, but the common-sense physics that enables us to move around the world, throw things, use containers for liquid and reason about the behaviour of objects. It has been suggested (McCloskey, 1983; Slotta *et al.*, 1995) that it is our deep understanding of common-sense physics that makes learning school physics so difficult. The real world does not have frictionless surfaces; air resistance is a factor in most interactions and concepts such as heat and energy have formal interpretations very different from their meanings in common language. Learning school physics is hard because we first need to unlearn our intuitive physics.

One of the most basic assumptions of adult physical knowledge is that objects endure independent of our ability to perceive them, something that was investigated by Piaget and is known as object permanence.

Object permanence

Although not an empiricist, Piaget believed that the infant has to learn practically everything about the physical world, even the basic assumption that objects continue to exist when they are out of sight. Piaget was led to this position partly because his theoretical starting point was to assume as little innate knowledge as possible, and partly because he believed that he had evidence for it. In one of his studies an infant (younger than ten months) is seated opposite a desirable object such as a soft toy. Under normal circumstances the child shows interest in the toy and attempts to reach towards it. If, however, an opaque screen is placed between the infant and the toy, blocking its view, the infant quickly loses interest in the obscured object, treating it as if it had ceased to exist. (Older children behave differently, they simply reach round the screen to retrieve the toy.)

Piaget's interpretation of these results is that, to the infant, the object no longer exists which is clearly very different from adults' understanding of the physical world. We know, or at least believe, that objects continue to exist independently of our ability to perceive them. Of course over a longer time scale we adults often place objects so that they are out of sight and subsequently forget that they exist. The banknote that we placed in the back pocket of our trousers and is ruined by a journey through the washing machine; the key that we left on top of the table that we thought was in our purse; and the piece of wedding cake that we find in the pocket of our suit-jacket the next time we use it. When this sort of thing happens the discovery of the found-object will often bring to mind the occasion of its placement, or, if we cannot remember, we assume that something must have led to its appearance. We put forward such explanations exactly because of the way we assume the world to work:

Box 5.2 **Habituation procedures**

Habituation procedures allow us to have insight into the minds of infants by capitalising on the fact that infants, just like adults, eventually find repetition boring. If the same thing happens repeatedly then, no matter how interesting it was initially, the infant slowly loses interest, and indicates this lack of interest for all to see by averting its gaze from the repetitive stimulus. We can therefore think of habituation as learning not to attend to a stimulus.

If we present a stimulus – say for example a short animation – repeatedly to two groups of infants they will eventually show signs of boredom. We then present each group with a different animation – call them animation A and animation B – and measure the amount of interest (how much they are looking at the animation, how long it takes them to become bored). Suppose that the infants who had animation A showed significantly more interest than those receiving animation B we might therefore assume that animation A was seen by the infants as being more different from the original animation than animation B. We can therefore obtain some measure of how infants categorise the world. Of course in the study described perhaps animation A was just more interesting to all concerned than animation B, so the study will have to have various control conditions to rule out such possibilities.

things do not spontaneously pop into existence. We also assume that when we search for something that is no longer where we put it, that the object must be *somewhere*: things do not just pop out of existence either. These assumptions are fundamental to the adult's intuitive theory of physics, but not, according to Piaget, the intuitive physics of the infant.

The problem with Piaget's interpretation of the results is that they do not demonstrate conclusively that the infant has no understanding of the permanence of objects. For example, the hidden object might simply have become less salient, the infant simply forgets that it is there. Alternatively, maybe the infant knows that the toy is still there, but does not know how to go about retrieving it.

Piaget's original study is therefore inconclusive since there are a number of alternative accounts other than the radical one that the infant believes the object has disappeared from existence. One of the big problems in research on infancy is that we cannot simply ask infants what they think as we might with adults, this is why Piaget used infants' searching behaviour as an index of what was going on in their minds. Recently techniques have been developed which enable us to probe infants' thought processes in a more systematic way using techniques such as **habituation procedures** (see box 5.2).

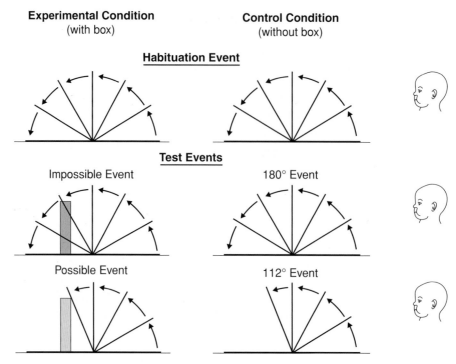

Figure 5.2 The apparatus used by Baillargeon

Studying object permanence using habituation studies

A number of studies has used this habituation procedure on the object permanence problem (see Bower, 1974), but the most widely cited and elegant study was conducted by Renée Baillargeon (Baillargeon, 1987; 1991) using infants of around four months of age. Figure 5.2 shows an outline of the equipment used. The infant is seated opposite a device in which a screen rotates through 180° away from the infant. Video cameras are focused on the infant's head to enable the time the infant spends looking at the screen to be measured.

The screen moves through its cycle over and over again until the infant shows signs of boredom by looking away from the screen. This initial habituation phase is then followed by one of four alternatives depending on the experimental condition being run; for the moment we will just focus on the two critical ones. Following habituation, a block is placed behind the screen of a height such that it is clearly visible to the infant as the screen starts to move up, but becomes obscured when the screen is at about 60° through its rotation. Once the block is in position the screen is again rotated, in one condition the screen stops at the point at which it would make

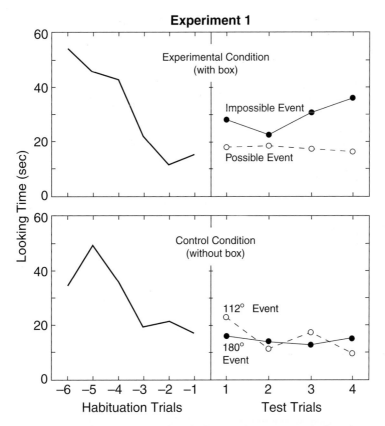

Figure 5.3 Data from Baillargeon (1987). Showing the responses of infants (mean age 4 months 14 days) to the apparatus shown in figure 5.2. The left-hand panels show habituation (looking times decrease as the babies become bored), the right-hand panels show looking times in the test phase. The upper-right panel shows that babies look longer at impossible events (where the box apparently disappears) than possible ones (where the screen is stopped by the box)

contact with the (obscured) block at 112°, in the other condition the screen continues to rotate as if the block were no longer there. In both conditions, interest is measured by amount of looking. Think of what Piaget's theory would predict. The Piagetian infant, remember, believes that once something is out of sight it no longer exists. If this were the case then the infant should not be at all surprised by the screen rotating through 180° in the test phase because as soon as it is obscured by the screen it ceases to exist and cannot therefore stop the screen. Indeed, the Piagetian infant should find the condition where the screen stops more interesting since this is more different from the habituation phase because the screen moves through a smaller angle and is therefore perceptually more distinct. In fact, Baillargeon found that infants attended longer to the 180° condition than to the condition where the

> ## Box 5.3 Other physical principles held by infants
>
> Using habituation techniques Elizabeth Spelke and colleagues (Spelke *et al.*, 1992) have suggested that by 4 months of age infants have a number of expectations of the physical world which she refers to as principles. These principles state that
>
> - Objects move as wholes on continuous paths. In other words objects maintain their shape and if going from A to B have to pass through all the points between. (This could be called the 'No Teleportation' principle.)
> - Objects cannot pass through one another or occupy the same point in space or time. (This could be called the 'No Ghosts' principle.)
> - Objects cannot act on each other unless they come into contact. (This could be called the 'No Telekinesis' principle.)
>
> Infants are not born with all the principles that they will eventually possess; some learning must take place. For example Spelke *et al.* (1992) found that 6-month-olds, having been habituated to an object falling onto a platform, were surprised when on a test trial the object subsequently came to rest inches above the table. Four-month-olds, however, showed no such surprise, indicating that their knowledge of gravity was not fully formed.

screen was stopped by the obscured block, indicating that this was surprising to them. Baillargeon interprets these results as suggesting that, just like adults, infants expect objects to endure even though they are out of sight – something that is in sharp contrast to Piaget's prediction.

It is worth mentioning the two other conditions. In these conditions the screen behaved in exactly the same way as it did in the other two conditions, but no block is used. These conditions were to ensure that it wasn't simply something about the movement of the screen, but was rather due to the interaction between the block and the screen. In these two conditions infants showed more attention to the condition where the screen stops at 112°, than when it carries on through its full rotation, presumably because the screen stops for no apparent reason.

This early knowledge of how the physical world operates is by no means a talent unique to human infants. Psychologists Marc Hauser and Susan Carey (Hauser and Carey, 1998) have shown that adult cotton-top tamarinds (new world primates) have similar assumptions about the physical world to those of a 5-month-old human infant. They also share with human infants basic number skills such as the knowledge that one plus one is two, two minus one is one, and one plus two is more than two (Wynn, 1993). The similarities between non-human primates and human infants should not be too surprising since the survival of both animals depends upon an understanding about the way that physical objects behave and is therefore likely to have been influenced by natural selection.

Human infants therefore may well be born with certain expectations about the way that the physical world operates. This makes evolutionary sense. Imagine a population of infants who have no fear of heights. Now imagine a genetic mutation arises in one individual in this population which provides that individual with a seed of a fear of heights. If having this fear of heights increased the infant's chances of surviving to maturity compared to its peers then it can be seen that such a mutation would, over a number of generations, spread rapidly throughout the population.

Should we be surprised by the talents of young infants? In one sense we should not be. The physical world is very stable, and objects have obeyed the same rules for billions of years. In evolutionary terms it would make sense for people to be given a head start in acquiring these rules by endowing them with psychological constraints that make learning easier. What is learned as a result of these constraints is a common-sense theory of physics.

Is this evidence for innate knowledge?

The early emergence of knowledge of the physical world might be taken as supporting the existence of an innate physics module. But as we have seen, many of the physical principles (e.g. gravity) seem to emerge in the first six months, rather than them being present from birth (recall, however, the point made above regarding puberty: the fact that some ability is not present from birth doesn't mean it is not innate). Carey and Spelke (1994) suggest that babies are born with a set of innate physical principles that serve to guide their developing knowledge of the physical world based on their experience. In the next section we present a more detailed theory of how nature and nurture interact in this way when we discuss how babies learn about people around them. As for whether it is evidence for innate *modules*, as some evolutionists have claimed, we discuss that later in this chapter.

Recognising conspecifics: a comparative perspective

People are important to the human infant. They are the objects that provide nurturance and protection; they also represent the things that they will ultimately have to get along with when they are older. Ethologists have noted that this is also the case for many species of social animal. Nobel prize-winning Austrian ethologist Konrad Lorenz (figure 5.4) is famed for uncovering an early attachment process which he called **imprinting**. In Lorenz's notion of imprinting, following birth, precocial animals (those that are born in a mature state such as geese and lambs) enter a **critical period** during which they rapidly learn the visual (and other) characteristics of their mother. At around twenty-five hours following hatching domestic chickens and geese, for example, will have learned the specific characteristics of their mother and from this point on will avoid other adults of their species. Lorenz saw this special learning process as the outcome of natural selection since those individuals that rapidly became attached to their mother would be more likely to benefit from the protection that she provides and thereby pass on their genes for this specific early learning process. He also suggested that the young emerge without a preference as to what the imprinting object might be since in the natural world the object will almost certainly be their mother (Konrad Lorenz imprinted young geese on himself; one of the most endearing pictures of Lorenz shows him swimming in a lake surrounded by his own clutch of goslings).

Subsequent ethologists have demonstrated that this early learning period is less circumscribed than Lorenz imagined. Cambridge ethologists Pat Bateson and Robert Hinde (Bateson and Hinde, 1987), for example, discuss imprinting as occurring during a more plastic **sensitive period** when chicks are more likely to learn the characteristics of their mother. In their view this period depends very much on what sort of external input the chicks receive. Being kept in the dark and viewing an imprinting object later may extend this period for up to several days after hatching. Other researchers have also modified our notion of specificity of the imprinting object; Johnson and Bolhuis (1991) have, for example, demonstrated that chicks, given the choice, will develop a preference for a hen-like object. Despite modifications to Lorenz's original idea of imprinting, present-day ethologists would agree that he was broadly correct in his assertion that its primary function is to enable recognition of, and attachment to, the mother by the young individual and that such a process is a product of natural selection (Workman *et al.*, 2000).

Evolution has therefore endowed some non-human animals with a 'quick and dirty' approach to recognising their parents which basically says 'attach yourself to whatever you perceive during a very early sensitive period within certain broad constraints'. In the natural environment this works very well since the first thing that a newly hatched chick will see is likely to be its brooding mother, it only tends to go wrong in unnatural environments where chicks are raised in incubators.

To return to human development, clearly the ability to recognise conspecifics is crucial for a baby's survival and future development; perhaps even more so than it is for chicks, given the importance of social interaction in human life. How, then, do babies discriminate people from other objects, and how do they discriminate between different people? Evidence suggests that, just like adults, babies use faces to inform them whether or not something is a person, and which particular person it is.

Figure 5.4 Konrad Lorenz and friends

Infants' preferences for faces in general

There has long been evidence that face-like stimuli are interesting to infants. Fantz (1961) compared newborn infants' looking times at a variety of different visual stimuli; each presented to the infant in pairs. The stimuli consisted of patches of colour, patterns such as bull's-eyes and checkerboards, and stimuli which looked like simple faces. Fantz found that infants spent significantly more time looking at the stimuli that resembled faces than any of the others.

Fantz's results might be taken as suggesting that infants are born with some knowledge of what a human face looks like, but how detailed is this knowledge? Do infants need to learn anything about faces apart from being able to discriminate among them (e.g. who is 'mother', who is 'father'?). As an analogy, you might prefer red wine to blackcurrant juice, but this does not make you a wine connoisseur,

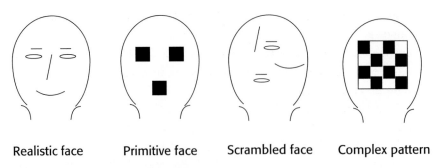

Realistic face   Primitive face   Scrambled face   Complex pattern

Figure 5.5 Stimuli used by Johnson and Morton

because the stimuli are radically different. Similarly, preferring faces to chessboards does not tell us how detailed this knowledge is. To investigate this, Johnson and Morton (1991) conducted a similar study, but they were interested in whether Fantz's study indicated that infants were born with a fully functioning face identification system, or whether they were born with only sketchy knowledge of faces, the details being filled in by experience of faces in the world. Johnson and Morton, like Fantz, used a preferential looking paradigm in which the infant was presented with stimuli shown in figure 5.5.

As can be seen, one of the stimuli is a simple checkerboard pattern, to control for stimulus complexity. Another stimulus was a 'realistic' face containing all of the components of a real face (eyes, nose, mouth) depicted in a relatively realistic way. Another was a primitive face, just dark patches in the same configuration as a normal face. The final stimulus contained the same components as the realistic face, but scrambled up into a non-face-like configuration. This condition was to ensure that any preference for the realistic face was due to the configuration of the components, not simply the appearance of the components themselves (a similar control was used by Fantz). The subjects for this experiment were neonates and 4-month-old infants.

Johnson and Morton's results show that for neonates both the primitive face and the realistic face elicit approximately equal looking times, indicating that they are equally interesting, and both of these are preferred to the other stimuli. The results are rather different for the 4-month-olds, although the primitive face is still more interesting than the checkerboard pattern and the scrambled face, the realistic face elicits much longer looking times.

Johnson and Morton interpret these results as suggesting that infants are born with some preference for face-like stimuli, but it is by no means fully specified; experience is still needed to flesh out the details. They propose that learning about faces involves two processes which they call **CONSPEC** and **CONLERN**. CONSPEC, it is suggested, is an innately specified set of principles that are responsible for directing attention towards stimuli that resemble human faces, but this knowledge is crude and cannot distinguish between primitive and more detailed face-like stimuli. Perhaps the most important thing in learning is that you attend to the appropriate information; conspec ensures that this happens. Guided by CONSPEC, CONLERN fleshes out the primitive representation based on experience of looking at faces and forms a more realistic representation of what a face is like.

This fleshing out process can be illustrated by research showing that at 6 months human infants can discriminate monkey faces as well as human faces but by 9 months this ability to discriminate monkey faces disappears (Pascalis *et al.*, 2002) unless exposure to monkey faces continues (Pascalis *et al.*, 2005). Similar results were found for Japanese macaques (*Macaca fuscata*) who learn to prefer monkey to human faces when given experience of monkey faces or prefer human to monkey faces when given experience with human faces. This further suggests that the mechanisms that underpin conspecific recognition in humans are considerably older than our species, being found as it is in species who share a common ancestry with humans 25 million years ago. Whether these mechanisms exist in more distantly related primates or outside the primate order remains an open question.

Recognising specific people

The research above shows that even newborn babies are social animals in that they are motivated to look at face-like stimuli. Moreover, within this general preference for faces, it appears that some faces are preferred over others. Research suggests that newborns show a preference for their mother's face (Bushnell *et al.*, 1989; Walton *et al.*, 1992) rather than the face of a stranger. It should be pointed out here that there is almost certainly nothing special about the mother, the preferential allocation of attention seems to be towards the person with whom the neonate has had the closest contact in the hours following birth, this is usually (but not always) the biological mother.

Babies' knowledge of faces seems to be quite sketchy however, as the preference disappeared if the mother and the non-mother were wearing identical wigs, suggesting that the infant was using cues such as the outline of the face more than the internal features (see figure 5.6).

These results showing a preference for significant people are consistent with the predictions of modern evolutionary theory that organisms able to recognise close relatives and distinguish them from non-relatives will derive a selective advantage (as we saw with imprinting above).

Care must be taken when interpreting the results of these studies. They do not suggest that neonates in any way recognise their mother in the way that adults

ONE-MONTH-OLD   TWO-MONTH-OLD   **Figure 5.6** How infants scan the human face

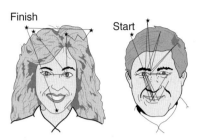

do. Face recognition is a complicated process that involves, among other things, a knowledge that the face denotes a unique individual, some knowledge about that person and often some emotional response to them. What we are seeing here is just a preference for one stimulus over another, and a relatively small preference at that. There is no reason to assume that the neonates' preference for their mother's face indicates that they assume that this mother is a unique individual. The mother's face could merely be a collection of stimuli that is attractive to the infant as a result of repeated exposure. Moreover, and alluded to above, the preference is a small one, as research by Bushnell *et al.* (1989) shows that it is fragile and can be disrupted by superficial changes. It takes children many months before they really respond to familiar faces in a predictable way. Neville *et al.* (1993) conducted brain-imaging studies on 6- and 12-month-old-infants' face-processing abilities. It was found that 6-month-olds used a variety of brain regions across both hemispheres for faces, whereas at twelve months processing had become more localised in the right hemisphere, more like that of adults. This suggests that although infants are competent face processors, this ability undergoes much refinement over the months as a result of experience. (It also shows that face recognition is lateralised – see chapter 11.)

Whatever is happening here, it is clear that the mechanism is more complex and extended than one of simply imprinting on an object in the way that chicks do. Despite these differences, the processes share more similarities with imprinting in domestic chicks than most people would have expected. In both humans and domestic fowl there is evidence of an inherent preference which may serve to orient the individual towards conspecifics in general and parents in particular (Dudai, 2002). Furthermore, in both there is now evidence of quite specific early gazing preferences towards the head or facial region of the parent.

Acquiring knowledge of what conspecifics look like is only one step on the way to complex social interaction, in the next section we review evidence of how infants begin to learn about people as psychological entities who have emotions, thoughts, goals and desires.

Mind-reading: the development of a theory of mind

Humans live, and have always lived, in complex social groups (see chapters 7 and 8). One advantage of this is that groups provide safety from predators, but they also enable collective action that can achieve so much more than we can when acting alone. Hunting, for example, is one instance of such coordinated action; acting in groups, humans can successfully kill and carry home a large animal. But such coordinated action brings additional problems. Once prey has been killed, how should it be distributed? Some equitable way of sharing is of benefit if group members are to continue to participate in the hunt. But if every member always gets an equal portion, what is to stop a certain member putting a little less effort into the hunt? Hunting is often dangerous and expends a lot of energy and it makes sense for an individual to hold back a little if they are guaranteed the same return as their more enthusiastic companions. Living in social groups, therefore, has a particular set of selection pressures that act on the group members. Not only do individuals need to understand the physical environment, but it would benefit them enormously were they to evolve a way of understanding the actions, intentions and beliefs of their conspecifics. If an individual could read the minds of others and discover what they were thinking it would give it and its offspring a tremendous competitive advantage. Among other things, it would be able to detect when it was being deceived, and also be able to deceive and manipulate others with less chance of detection. This ability to manipulate and deceive others has been labelled **Machiavellian intelligence** by primatologists Andrew Whiten and Richard Byrne of the University of St Andrews (Whiten and Byrne, 1988). They first used this term to describe the way that chimpanzees were observed to manipulate others to achieve their own ends.

Deception and manipulation are, cognitively speaking, complex and demanding processes to engage in successfully. Being honest is rather simple; all you need to do is to report what you know to be the case about any particular state of affairs. Successful deception, on the other hand, requires you to take into account the mental states of the person or people you are attempting to deceive. The child with a chocolate-smeared face who steadfastly maintains that she has not been raiding the biscuit tin fails to deceive because she fails to take into account what her accusing father can see to be the case. Of course true mind-reading does not and probably could never exist, but approximations of people's mental states can be made. The child above might make the assumption that because her face is covered in chocolate and because her father is looking at her face, he therefore has the knowledge that she has been eating chocolate. Facial expressions also leak otherwise hidden emotions and intentions into the outside world. Social animals, particularly humans, have learned to pick up on these cues to enable them to represent mentally what is going on in the minds of others, an ability that psychologists refer to as **theory of mind** or **mind-reading.**

Theory of mind and false beliefs

The acid test for the presence of a theory of mind is the false belief test. This is simply the knowledge that someone can hold a belief which is either different from current reality or different from what you yourself believe to be true. If, and only if, someone passes this test can we be sure that they have an understanding of the mental states of others. The other person's belief has to be different from our own because otherwise we could pass the test simply by reporting what we knew to be true, something which requires no understanding of other people's mental states.

A number of tests has been developed to demonstrate that people can deal with false beliefs, one of these is the deceptive box test developed by Perner *et al.* (1987). A child is shown a Smartie container (a tube that usually contains chocolates) and is asked what she thinks is in there, to which the child invariably answers 'Smarties'. The tube is then opened to reveal that it unexpectedly contains pencils. The child is then asked what someone else who had not seen the contents of the box would think was inside. The average 4- or 5-year-old would say, like us, that another person would think that there were Smarties in the tube; however, a younger child (usually under four years of age) would say that the other person would believe that there were pencils in the box. Even though it is made clear that the other person had no prior knowledge of what was in the box. Further, if after the unexpected contents have been revealed, the younger child is asked what she *initially* thought was in the box she will often say that she thought that there were pencils in the box, even though only a few seconds earlier she had clearly ventured that she thought that it would contain Smarties! Younger children therefore not only have difficulty reporting other people's thoughts they also have difficulty reporting what they initially thought when it is different from their current knowledge-state. Research has also ruled out alternative interpretations of this phenomenon: it does not seem to be a simple failure of memory, since children failing the Smarties test have no problems with state-change tasks where no false beliefs are involved (Gopnik and Astington, 1988). Also ruled out is the explanation that children might be trying to 'save face' in some way. Wimmer and Hartl (1991) conducted an experiment that recruited Kasperl, a puppet from German television who was notorious for making mistakes. In this experiment, the puppet rather than the child is asked what he thinks is in the box, to which he answers 'Smarties', after Kasperl is shown that the box contains pencils, the child is asked what Kasperl thought was in the box when he first saw it. As in the standard task, younger children claim that Kasperl initially thought that the box contained pencils. Note that here there is no loss of face on the part of the child as it was the puppet that made the mistake. Moreover, it is unlikely that the children are trying to save the puppet's embarrassment as getting things wrong was Kasperl's *raison d'être* on his TV show.

How does theory of mind develop?

Other similar tests for theory of mind such as the unexpected transfer test (Wimmer and Perner, 1983) and the Sally-Anne test (Baron-Cohen *et al.*, 1985) are all passed at roughly the same age, which some have taken as suggesting that theory of mind develops in a stage-like manner (see box 5.1 above). However, others have criticised this interpretation (see Mitchell, 1996), suggesting that since the test is all-or-none (you either pass it or you don't), it has the effect of making what might be a gradual developmental profile look like a sudden stage-like shift. An analogy for this might be a driving test in which all you found out was whether you passed or failed, you were given no feedback on how many errors you had made. Imagine that you failed three times before passing on the fourth attempt. Does this necessarily mean that your driving suddenly and drastically improved in a stage-like fashion between the third and fourth attempts? No. More than likely your driving gradually improved over all four attempts, but because you either pass or fail the test, this gradual improvement was hidden until you reached the pass threshold on the fourth attempt.

Similarly, because children of four years tend to pass standard theory of mind tests it does not imply that children younger than four, who fail the test, have no theory of mind. As with the driving test example, it is possible that younger children have some knowledge of false beliefs, but find performing the task too demanding cognitively to reveal their nascent understanding. Evidence in support of this interpretation comes from Baron-Cohen (1995) who used the Sally-Anne task. In this task a doll (named Sally) hides a marble in a box and then leaves. Unknown to Sally, a second doll, Anne, comes in and moves the marble from the box to a basket alongside it. The child is then asked where Sally, on her return, will look for the marble – in the box or in the basket. Consistent with the finding from the deceptive-box test, children of about four years will correctly report that Sally will look in the box because, after all, this is where she last saw it. Younger children, however, report that Sally will look in the basket where they know the marble currently resides. However, careful observation of the child's eyes reveals that they consistently look at the box before reporting the incorrect location. This has been taken as suggesting that younger children have some understanding of false belief, but the current location, perhaps because of its greater salience, wins out and they answer the question incorrectly.

It is probably a mistake to think that passing the false belief task represents the child crossing the rubicon where they go from not having to having a theory of mind. Even before children are able to pass the false belief test they make many attributions that relate to mental states. For example a 3-year-old, on being told that a character is looking for a cat and looks under the table, will explain the action by saying that the character *wants* the cat and *thinks* that it might be under the table (Wellman, 1988). Furthermore, there is still much to learn about people and their states of mind once one passes the false belief test. The 'second order' false belief task developed by Baron-Cohen (1989) introduces another actor into the frame and asks the child what he or she thinks that person X would think person Y would do is passed at an older age than the standard task. Other tests suggest individual differences in theory of mind ability. The 'reading the mind in the eyes test' (or just 'the eyes test') (Baron-Cohen *et al.*, 1997) requires participants to judge people's mental states from pictures of their eye regions (e.g. whether the person is 'aghast', 'fantasising', 'impatient' or 'alarmed'). This test reveals a number of individual differences, perhaps the most interesting being that females are slightly better at it than males (see chapter 6).

The role of experience in developing a theory of mind

Experience of interacting with people seems to be an important factor in the development of theory of mind. Ruffman *et al.* (1998) present evidence that children with older siblings tend to pass false belief tests at a younger age than either children without siblings or children with younger siblings. A possible explanation for this finding is that children with older siblings might be forced into situations where there is more need to think about the mental states of others. Younger siblings are often in competition for resources such as food, toys and parental attention, and the ability to get what you want by deception or other forms of manipulation is likely to be advantageous.

Experience may be necessary, but it is not sufficient for a working theory of mind. Many researchers (see Leslie, 1994) believe that there is an innate component to theory of mind. This is not to suggest that experience is unnecessary, rather it suggests that children will always grow up to understand the minds of others in terms of the direct causal influence of mental states. Evidence that experience is not enough for theory of mind to develop comes from sufferers of the disorder known as autism.

Is theory of mind modular – the case of autism

Further evidence that theory of mind is a domain specific mental module comes from research on individuals with autism who appear to have impairments in this ability. Autism is a disorder which, among other things, affects the sufferer's ability to engage in social behaviours – indeed the crude stereotype is of someone who treats others as if they were automata, rather than human beings with thoughts and feelings.

A wealth of research has consistently demonstrated that sufferers from autism have difficulty passing standard theory of mind tests when compared both to clinically normal children and children who suffer from other disorders such as Down's syndrome and Williams syndrome (Baron-Cohen *et al.*, 1985). Children suffering from Down's syndrome, for example, seem to have no more difficulty passing a standard test such as Sally-Anne (see above) than normal children when matched for a variety of measures including mental age (usually verbal ability is used). Autistic children, on the other hand, matched using the same criteria will often fail such a task. So a Down's syndrome child with a mental age of 5 or 6 will pass standard false belief tests whereas an autistic child is likely to fail them.

Autistic children who systematically fail tests of theory of mind can show reasonable performance on other tasks such as perspective taking and other tests of visuo-spatial ability. They also seem to have reasonably good physical reasoning ability. This is shown by their good performance on embedded figures tasks (see figure 5.6) where the goal is to find the target shape embedded in a more complex shape (Jolliffe and Baron-Cohen, 1997).

Not all autistic individuals fail simple false belief tests, many – particularly those with reasonable general intelligence – and sufferers of a related condition known as Asperger's syndrome will pass such tests. However, as pointed out earlier, tests such as Sally-Anne are all-or-none tests, you either pass them or you don't, and they are thus not very sensitive to more subtle variations in theory of mind. All they tell you is that the participant has a theory of mind equivalent to that of a clinically normal 4-year-old. More sensitive tests (such as the eyes test) or more difficult tests (such as the second order theory of mind test) reveal that even high-functioning autistics and Asperger's sufferers show impaired theory of mind.

There is therefore good evidence that people with autism and Asperger's syndrome have impairments to their ability to understand the mental states of other people, with some other cognitive abilities apparently spared (this is true especially for people with Asperger's syndrome and people with high-functioning autism). Further support for the modularity hypothesis could be found if there are people who appear to suffer from the mirror image of autism, that is they have preserved theory of mind with impairments in spatial ability, a so-called double dissociation. It has been claimed that sufferers of another developmental disorder – Williams syndrome – might represent such a case.

Autism, sex differences and cognitive development

A theory advanced by Baron-Cohen (e.g. 2002) has proposed that some of the cognitive and behavioural features of autism can be considered as a 'cognitive style'

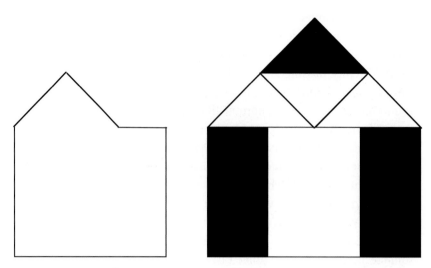

Figure 5.7 Embedded figures tests. Can you find the shape on the right in the figure on the left?

rather than a deficit and that this cognitive style can be characterised as an extreme version of the cognitive style demonstrated by clinically normal males. We know, for example, that males are worse than females on some of the tests where people with autism show impairment (such as theory of mind tests), and males are better than females on tests where people with autism show better than expected performance (such as the embedded figures test). This observation led Baron-Cohen to propose two dimensions that enable us to better understand the difference between people with autism and clinically normal individuals, and the differences between males and females, he refers to these dimensions as 'empathizing' and 'systemizing' (each spelled with a 'z' rather than an 's' in the Oxford and American style). Empathizing is similar to theory of mind (described above), it is a predilection to explain entities in terms of mental states (such as thoughts, beliefs and emotions), systemizing, on the other hand, is a tendency to explain entities as rule-governed systems and a preoccupation with classification. Examples of such entities includes mechanical artefacts, weather systems, mathematical and musical notations, political and social systems.

Typically when we think of people, we think of them in empathizing terms, that is as entities that can be explained by considering their thoughts, beliefs and emotional states. Inanimate objects and events such as a clock, are usually explained in systemizing terms (we don't usually think of clocks as 'wanting' to tell the time or 'believing' that it is half past four). That said, we can try to understand animate beings via systemizing and inanimate objects via empathizing. An example of the first, is the approach of cognitive psychology, which tries to understand people as rule governed information processors (see chapter 9). However, if you consider the complexity of

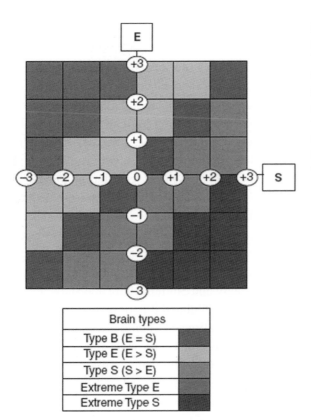

Figure 5.8 Simon Baron-Cohen's conceptualisation of different brain types. The vertical axis shows increasing empathizing ability, the horizontal axis shows systemizing ability. The diagram shows how people might vary along these axes; people who are high on systemizing (S) and low on empathizing (E) have extreme male brains, and vice versa for extreme female brains

Brain types	
Type B (E = S)	
Type E (E > S)	
Type S (S > E)	
Extreme Type E	
Extreme Type S	

this task, it is not surprising that when trying to understand people we usually defer to empathizing. Conversely, inanimate objects can also be understood by empathizing. People often describe computers or recalcitrant cars as if they were animate beings ('I can't get my computer to talk to the server', 'my car doesn't like starting on cold days'): both are complex devices, and in lieu of a good understanding of their internal workings (necessary for systemizing) an account based on empathizing will do the job.

In Baron-Cohen's account systemizing and empathizing are independent cognitive styles so one could be high on one and low on the other, high on both, or low on both (see figure 5.8).

Figure 5.8 is a hypothetical diagram of how empathizing and systemizing vary. A person with high E and S would be towards the upper right hand corner, a person low on E but high on S (such as a person with autism) would be towards the lower right hand corner. According to Baron-Cohen's theory women would, on average, be towards the top left-hand quadrant, with men typically towards the lower right.

We have already seen some evidence that men tend towards systemizing and women empathizing, further supporting evidence is presented below.

Females and empathizing

- Above we saw how infants of only a few days old orient towards face-like stimuli (Johnson and Morton, 1991); it appears that even at this early age there are reliable, if small, sex differences (Haviland and Malatesta, 1981). More recent research on day-old babies confirms that boys look longer than girls at a mobile while girls look longer than boys at faces (Connellan *et al.*, 2001). At 12 months, girls engage in more eye contact with their mother than boys, with the amount of eye contact being inversely related to the level of prenatal testosterone to which children were exposed (Lutchmaya *et al.*, 2002). This last research suggests that although male and female are distinct categories, there are degrees of maleness and femaleness that might be the result of the action of hormones. Women are also better at decoding non-verbal cues such as facial expressions and tone of voice (Hall, 1978).
- Cross-culturally, males engage in more approach behaviours in infancy (Rothbart, 1989), are more aggressive (Eagly and Steffan, 1986) and show more dominance in their social interactions by early childhood (Charlesworth and Dzur, 1987).
- Across the span females are more attracted to intimate relationships than are males (Berndt, 1986) and are more concerned with love and intimacy in sexual relationships (Buss and Schmitt, 1993). Additionally, cross-cultural research suggests that females of all ages are more person-centred and males more object-centred (Eibl-Eibesfeldt, 1984).
- There is evidence that sex differences in nurturance and empathy have their origins in infancy. Hoffman (1977), for instance, found that infant girls respond with greater empathy than do boys to distress in other people while Simner (1971) demonstrated that infant girls are more likely than boys to cry when exposed to the cry of another infant, but no more likely to cry, for instance, after a loud noise. More recent research (Zahn-Waxler *et al.*, 1992) shows that girls generally respond with more empathy to the distress of another person than do boys.

Males and systemizing

- Boys are more likely than girls to choose toys that are susceptible to systemizing such as construction kits, and mechanical objects such as cars and trucks. Interestingly, rhesus monkeys with no prior experience show a similar sex bias when allowed to play with human toys (Hassett *et al.*, 2008).
- Males are better at tasks involving 3D construction (Kimura, 1999), and are better at mental rotation tasks (Collins and Kimura, 1997).
- Men are more interested in classifying animate and inanimate objects. Scott Atran (Atran, 1990) conducted research among the Aguaruna of Northern Peru on intuitive classification systems of local plants. It was found that men showed a

greater number of subcategories and their classification schemes were more consistent with one another than the schemes of women.

- Many of the occupations that rely on systemizing show a higher proportion of
males than females (some are almost exclusively male) including metalworking,
construction work and engineering (Geary, 1998).

As some of the research above indicates, there is good evidence that a considerable
amount of the difference between males and females is biologically based rather than
a result of social learning, although social learning doubtless plays a role in shaping
these sex differences.

Turning again to autism, what is the evidence that autistic people have an extreme
version of the male brain? We have already discussed impaired theory of mind
(empathizing) and superior performance on embedded figures test (systemizing). Further evidence is that people with autism frequently have preferences for a rule-based,
predictable regime (as do males); that people with high-functioning autism and people with Asperger's syndrome score highly on tests on intuitive physics (Baron-Cohen
et al., 2001); males and autistic people prefer 'closed systems' with controlled variables
such as computers, bird watching and train spotting (Baron-Cohen and Wheelwright,
1999); and that males are more interested in collecting and classifying than females,
people with autism showing even greater interest (Baron-Cohen, 2002).

The sex difference could be explained in terms of natural selection: men maybe
experiencing a selection pressure to develop systemizing in order to make better
tools or develop better hunting strategies, females experiencing a selection pressure
in order to help rear children. Alternatively the difference could be the result of
sexual selection. In a commentary on the website 'The Edge' David Geary suggests
that superior empathizing ability in females might be the result of female–female
competition:

Girls and women compete by gathering as much information on other people as they can get
and then using this information to attempt to organize their web of social relationships so
as to have better control of these relationships and through this access to what they want.
(Geary, n.d.)

What about autism? What does it mean to say that the brains of people with autism are
extreme versions of male brains? Could autism (especially high-functioning autism
and Asperger's syndrome) be an adaptive phenotype? Or is it a genuine deficit, albeit
one that has some assets (higher systemizing)? Temple Grandin (herself a person with
autism) speculates in her book *Animals in Translation* (Grandin, 2005) that people
with autism have a cognitive style that is closer to non-human animals. Like people
with autism animals tend to notice small details in the environment, details that clinically normal people would miss completely. Startling evidence from Allan Snyder's
laboratory at the University of Sydney suggests that normal people can exhibit
savant-like skills (these are systemizing skills such as correctly multiplying together

two large numbers) if certain regions of the brain (e.g. the frontotemporal region) are temporarily 'knocked out'. This is achieved through a non-invasive technique called Transcranial Magnetic Stimulation (TMS) which uses a rapidly fluctuating magnetic field to induce weak electric currents in particular brain regions. This can either stimulate or block the action of neurons in these areas. These results have still to be replicated, but they might suggest that we are all capable of savant-like skills (and of high degrees of systemizing) but other brain regions block this ability. If this is true, it might support Grandin's assertion that becoming less autistic-like was one of the changes that happened to humans as they evolved.

Williams syndrome: the extreme female brain?

Williams syndrome is a comparatively rare developmental disorder affecting around 1 in 25,000 live births. The symptoms include hypersensitivity to noise, premature ageing of the skin and cardiovascular problems caused by a narrowing of the major arteries, specifically the aorta, which, unless treated, can lead to premature death. Perhaps the most obvious physical characteristic, however, is their facial appearance. People with Williams syndrome tend to have a broad nose, full lips, large ears and sometimes a star-shaped patterning on the iris which have given rise to their colloquial name of 'pixie people'.

Psychologically, they are even more interesting with a profile of impairments characterised by peaks and troughs – some abilities being impaired and others being relatively spared. IQ is low, typically in the 50s or 60s with a range between 40 and 90. In particular, spatial ability is severely compromised with many sufferers finding it difficult to perform everyday tasks such as finding their way around their own house, retrieving a number of items from a cupboard, or tying their shoes. On the other hand, language tends to be well developed compared with their non-verbal IQ, although there is often a preference for ornate and florid words. One individual, when asked to list some animals, included ibex, pteranadon and yak as well as species new to science such as brontosaurus rex (Bellugi et al., 1990). Perhaps most strikingly, particularly in the light of what we have learned about autism, people with Williams syndrome seem to have highly developed social skills compared with their general intelligence. For this reason, many have described Williams syndrome as the mirror image of autism.

The cause of Williams syndrome

Williams syndrome is a chromosomal disorder caused by missing genes on one particular chromosome. Chromosomes, recall (see chapter 2) are just long strands of DNA located in the cell nuclei. During meiosis, they take on the shape of two sausages connected by a narrow region called the centromere. The arms are of different lengths, the long one being known as the q arm, the short one known as the p arm. In Williams syndrome some of the genetic material on the long arm of one of the chromosome 7 pairs has been deleted in the 11.23 region (see figure 5.7). These microdeletions, as they are known, mean that some important protein-assembling genes are absent. Currently, it is estimated that at least 20 genes are deleted. These include ELN which codes for the structural protein elastin which, as the name suggests, gives elasticity to many of the bodies organs (including the skin and major blood vessels). The deletion of ELN – on one of the chromosome 7 pairs, there is a working version of ELN on the other copy of chromosome 7 – leads to a deficiency in elastin which explains the premature aging of the skin and some of the cardiovascular problems suffered in Williams syndrome. Other deleted genes include GTF2I which may affect IQ, CYLN2 which is expressed in the cerebellum and LIMK1 which codes for protein, LIM-Kinase 1 which is associated with visuo-spatial ability (Frangiskakis *et al.*, 1996).

Williams syndrome: a modular account

A simple modular account might propose that sufferers of Williams syndrome have selective damage to the mental module(s) responsible for spatial cognition, with little or no impairment to those involved in social cognition (such as Theory of Mind). There is some evidence to support this. For instance, Karmiloff-Smith (1997) found no difference between Williams syndrome and clinically normal individuals on tasks measuring face processing ability. Tager-Flusberg *et al.* (1998) found that Williams syndrome sufferers perform better on 'the eyes test' than people with Prader–Willi syndrome matched for mental age. (Prader–Willi syndrome is a developmental disorder characterised by low IQ but no specific cognitive deficits.) This last study is important because it suggests that people with Williams syndrome are better at mental state judgements than would be expected given their mental age.

Sadly for those who like things nice and simple the true picture seems to be rather more complicated. For instance, research by Tager-Flusberg and Sullivan (2000) suggests that although people with Williams syndrome seem to have preserved social *perception* abilities they appear to have impairments of social *cognition*. So although they are good at recognising faces, and identifying expressions of emotional and other mental states (such as in the eyes test), they are no better than would be expected given their mental age at reasoning about mental events and causes. For example, one task asked children to explain why a character was crawling around wearing a leopard suit and growling, children with Williams syndrome were no more likely to

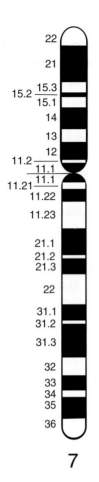

Figure 5.9 Chromosome 7. The microdeletions involved in Williams syndrome are on the long arm (q) in region 11.23, just below the narrow region or centromere

get the correct answer, that he was pretending to be a leopard, than mental age-matched controls.

Such evidence has been used to suggest that the social module might consist of a number of sub-modules, one of which deals with social perception and is preserved in Williams syndrome, another of which deals with social cognition that is impaired. This view is entirely consistent with the view of evolutionary psychologists (see Barkow *et al.*, 1992, p. 599).

Evidence against a modular account of Williams syndrome

There is other evidence, however, which appears to contradict the theory of innate modules. Research suggests that although children with Williams syndrome are good at recognising faces, they seem to do this in a different way to clinically normal individuals. It is well known that clinically normal individuals are particularly bad at recognising upside down faces, unless the face has something very distinctive about it such as a beard or an unusual hairstyle. This seems to be something peculiar to faces, since we have much less trouble identifying other inverted objects such as types of car or breeds of dog. Karmiloff-Smith (1997) found that people with Williams syndrome were better at identifying inverted faces than were clinically normal controls. Further research suggests that this is because sufferers from Williams syndrome use a different strategy for identifying faces than non-sufferers do. When normals recognise a face they seem to process it holistically – somehow the identity of the face emerges as a gestalt – whereas people with Williams syndrome appear to process faces on a feature-by-feature basis. Using imaging techniques Karmiloff-Smith *et al.* (1998) found that individuals with Williams syndrome used different brain regions when processing faces than normals.

A similar story can be told for the spared language processing ability of people with Williams syndrome. Karmiloff-Smith *et al.* (1998) found that, as well as the preference for baroque words, they have other linguistic abnormalities. For example, they find it difficult even to repeat sentences with embedded relative clauses such as 'the boy the dog chases is big' (where 'the dog chases' is the relative clause). Again this is taken as suggesting that it might be simplistic to suggest that Williams syndrome is characterised by a preserved language module. Karmiloff-Smith argues that this research shows that development is a more complex process than is given in the modular account and advances an alternative account known as neuroconstructivism.

Alternatives to modularity: Neuroconstructivism and domain relevant learning

Karmiloff-Smith suggests that the notion that children are born with innate modules has been overstated. Too much of the evidence is based on the abilities of either adults or older children; we find that an individual can't perform a particular task and assume that an innate module must have been damaged. Further, she suggests that modular theorists assume that, because a sufferer has some abilities preserved, then the brain (or mind) must be achieving these in the same way as it does for clinically normal individuals. It is known that the brain, especially the infant brain is capable of some degree of regeneration following injury, a property known as **cortical plasticity**. According to Karmiloff-Smith, cortical plasticity is rather more than a curiosity that occurs following trauma; it is an essential part of development and, in her view, contradicts the existence of innate modules. She argues that genes play a role in shaping components of the mind, but they by no means determine them. She refers to the study by Johnson and Morton (1991) described above. This, she argues, indicates that we do not have innate domain specific mental modules, rather we have innate domain relevant biases. These biases direct attention and aid learning which gradually makes the processes faster and more able to discriminate between different types of face-like stimuli. Module-like structures exist in the adult mind, but they are formed through experience rather than being innate. Her theory owes much to Piaget's constructivist notion of the interaction between incoming information and the knowledge structures that we possess, and has therefore been labelled neuroconstructivism. The mind/brain constructs itself as a result of some genetically influenced developmental 'programme' and the information bombarding the brain via the senses.

Evolutionary theory, modularity and neuroconstructivism

Many evolutionary psychologists have used innate modularity as part of their descriptions of human behaviour (Cosmides and Tooby, 1992; Pinker, 1994; 1997). Some research into developmental disorders provides an important line of evidence for the claim that there are innate modules. Recent research by Karmiloff-Smith and colleagues calls into question some of this evidence. The view that the cognition of Williams syndrome sufferers is the result of impairments to innate modules is overly simplistic, and Karmiloff-Smith argues that the process of ontogenesis (the development of the individual) needs to be taken more seriously.

To what extent do the developmental data pointing to the importance of cortical plasticity undermine the evolutionary position? In *The Blank Slate*, Steven Pinker (2002) takes on those who use cortical plasticity to downplay the role of the genes at the expense of learning. For the genes to exert a powerful effect on the developing brain does not require them to specify every last detail of the brain's structure (nor can they, the brain is made up of billions of neurons and trillions of synaptic connections; a complexity too great for 30-odd thousand genes, see chapter 13). Nor does it require genes to specify which particular region is responsible for which particular job. Pinker uses the analogy of a computer's hard disk. The computer's operating system does not reserve specific areas of the disk for specific types of data, nor are individual files or applications stored on the same portion of the disk; rather a single file might be scattered all over a disk and reassembled by the operating system when the file is launched. (It is for this reason that computer users are supposed to defragment their disk from time to time, a process which reassembles files onto contiguous portions of the disk enhancing the performance of the operating system.) He suggests that the brain might be similar, using whichever region is most convenient. Under normal circumstances these might be similar across people (e.g.

language located in the left hemisphere) but when regions of the brain are damaged, other areas can be used as a substitute. However it appears that the brain's ability to do this is severely restricted even in the case of babies. Farah *et al.* (2000) report on a 16-year-old boy who suffered bilateral damage (damage on both hemispheres) to the temporal lobes and visual cortex following a bout of meningitis at one day of age. His verbal IQ was in the normal range, as were many of his other cognitive abilities, but he was completely unable to recognise faces, even those with whom he had had a great deal of experience (including the cast of his favourite TV show, *Baywatch*). It seems that following brain damage, the brain can switch processing to other areas that are somewhat similar (for example, it can localise language in the right hemisphere if the left is damaged), but it is by no means infinitely plastic.

Is modularity false, and would it matter if it was?

One of the big problems with the modularity debate is that neither side is unambiguously clear as to what they are advocating. From their point of view the modularity theorists sometimes seem to be suggesting that modules are innate and hard-wired, meaning that they are not changed as a result of development or experience (fixed neural architecture was one of the characteristics initially proposed by Fodor in 1983). Clearly *something* changes during development and if this isn't the modules themselves (assuming they exist) then it is incumbent on the modular theorists to explain what it is that changes and how this fits in with modularity. A recent paper by Confer *et al.* (2010) defends massive modularity but only as alternative to domain-general learning, the idea that knowledge is largely built up from experience with little innate knowledge to guide it. This is a very different position from that of the neurocontructivists which proposes the existence of innate knowledge.

To return to a point made in chapter 1, evolutionary psychology in its broadest sense does not live or die on the question of innate modules. While it is likely that some parts of our minds and some behaviours are innate, it is also likely that some parts are not. As Smith (2007) has pointed out, one of the things that has led to the human success story is their ability to repeatedly solve novel problems and it seems reasonable that this was achieved by a neuronal architecture that was modifiable rather than fixed.

In finishing this first chapter on development it is also pertinent to ask: if it is all about hard-wired modules why does development take such a long time in humans. Is it just about physical development or does cognition itself take time to reach maturity. This is the topic that we address in the next chapter, in which we ask the vexed question 'what is development *for*?'.

Summary

- Infants seem to have certain expectations of the way that the physical world operates. For example infants of at least three months of age have the knowledge that objects exist independently of their ability to perceive them. A number of other physical principles seems to develop in the first few months as if supported by innate learning mechanisms.
- Infants have preference for face-like stimuli from birth, and learn the details of human faces rapidly. Again, it seems that this is the result of innate learning mechanisms rather than innate knowledge per se.
- Young children have an understanding of the role of mental states as a cause of behaviour, despite the fact that these states cannot be seen. This skill becomes more sophisticated as children develop. This ability, known as theory of mind or mindreading, is measured by a number of tasks such as false belief tasks and more recently, the eyes test, in which participants are required to judge how people feel from looking at their eyes.
- It has been suggested that many of the symptoms of autism can be characterised as being the product of the 'extreme male brain'. This theory suggests that autistic people (and normal males) are superior at systemizing – understanding rule-based systems – but inferior when it comes to empathizing – intuitive psychology.
- Some argue that disorders such as autism and Williams syndrome, which have cognitive profiles characterised by peaks and troughs, provide evidence for selective impairment of mental modules. Further research shows that such selective impairments are not as simple as they first appear. For example, people with Williams syndrome although appearing to have intact face-processing abilities seem to process faces in a different way from clinically normal people.
- Karmiloff-Smith proposes a theory of neuroconstructivism that emphasises the importance of learning and a gradual process of modularisation rather than the existence of innate mental modules. Although denying the existence of innate modules, this approach is certainly not incompatible with an evolutionary approach to cognitive development.

Questions

1. How might our 'intuitive physics' make learning school physics difficult? How might we overcome these difficulties?
2. Baron-Cohen (2002) suggests that differences between males and females can be captured by the systemizing–empathizing axes. To what extent might this explain the lack of female engineers and lack of male kindergarten teachers? Accepting

Baron-Cohen's research, should we give up encouraging women to become engineers and just 'let nature take its course'?

3. To what extent does research showing that non-human primates are as good at recognising human faces as faces of their own species and vice versa suggest that the mechanisms for face recognition evolved in a common ancestor, rather than being uniquely human?

4. To what extent are the claims that *differences* between people are innate independent from the claim that *similarities* between people are innate?

FURTHER READING

Baron-Cohen, S. (1995). *Mindblindness: Essays in Autism and Theory of Mind.* Cambridge, MA: MIT Press. An excellent introduction to the study of autism as a deficit of theory of mind.

Baron-Cohen, S. (2004). *The essential difference.* London: Penguin.

Boden, M.A. (1994). *Piaget.* London: Fontana. An in-depth discussion of the work of Piaget and its relationship to other disciplines such as philosophy, cybernetics and cognitive science.

Gopnik, A., Meltzoff, A. N. and Kuhl, P. K. (1999). *How Babies Think.* London: Weidenfeld and Nicolson. A good, popular introduction to recent research on infants.

Karmiloff-Smith, A. (2000). Why babies' brains are not Swiss-army knives. In S. Rose and H. Rose (eds.). *Alas Poor Darwin: Arguments Against Evolutionary Psychology.* London: Jonathan Cape. A chapter containing a critique of the modularity hypothesis, with evidence from research on developmental disorders.

6 Social development

KEY CONCEPTS

life history theory • attachment styles • r–K continuum • C–F continuum
• principle of allocation • shared environment • non-shared environment
• behavioural genetics • group socialisation theory • moral development

Some early developmentalists were influenced by Darwinian thinking. John Bowlby, for instance, proposed that the child is born with certain biological needs and that normal development is dependent upon these needs being met. Failure to do so could result in a wide range of problems in later life including criminality, intellectual under-achievement, promiscuity and psychological disturbances. More recently an evolutionary approach known as life history theory has been used to understand human development. This perspective suggests that some individual differences might be the result of children deploying different evolutionary strategies based on their childhood environment. Behavioural genetics research has also been crucial in unravelling the effects of nature and nurture on the developing child. This has led to a controversial theory which states that socialisation is carried out in peer groups. Finally we also discuss evolutionary approaches to moral development presenting research that suggests that the function of the moral sense is to enable us to exist in groups with non-kin.

What is development for?

Childhood presents us with something of a paradox. Evolutionary theory teaches us that the only valid strategy in the game of life is to pass on more copies of your genes than your competitors, in which case it might seem strange that humans (and many other organisms) spend such a large amount of time being unable to reproduce. Furthermore, rearing offspring produces a considerable drain on parents' resources, reducing the survival chances of both parties (young orphans are unlikely to survive in many species). Given these basic facts it would seemingly make evolutionary sense for childhood (defined as that part of the life cycle where the individual is sexually immature) to be as short as possible in order to maximise reproductive opportunities and minimise the burden of parenting. So why is it that human beings (and other primates) have such a long childhood? Assuming that evolutionary theory is correct, how can we explain such a long period of sexual immaturity? Put another way, what is childhood *for*?

Life history theory and development

Mammals are by no means unique in having a protracted period of sexual immaturity. Consider the life history of the butterfly. This organism has two distinct life histories, that of the immature caterpillar and the adult butterfly, each of which has a distinct physiology and function. A caterpillar is an eating machine; it is designed to consume as many calories as possible to enable it to become a successful butterfly. A butterfly on the other hand is a sex machine; its function is to mate with other butterflies in order to propagate its genes. The physiology of these two stages of life is consistent with their separate functions. The caterpillar has jaws and a digestive system to enable the efficient conversion of food into stored energy which is stored in its expandable body. The butterfly, on the other hand, has mouthparts designed to sip nectar – nature's own high-energy drink. This food is necessary for the strenuous activity of flight which, in turn, enables the animal to disperse, mate with non-kin and lay eggs in new regions. A caterpillar is therefore *for* reproduction, but only indirectly, because it cannot itself reproduce, instead it stores up energy that increases its reproductive chances when reproduction becomes an option.

Of course, human beings do not have physiologically distinct stages in their lives; children are much more similar to adults than caterpillars are to butterflies. But the same evolutionary logic can be applied: childhood is ultimately *for* reproduction. Adopting this simple perspective enables us to see that many of the behaviours and traits present in childhood might not be of direct benefit to the child, but might be beneficial to the adult that the child will ultimately become. Other behaviours and traits are concerned directly with the child's survival to make sure that he or she actually reaches adulthood.

Life history theory

A number of researchers including James Chisholm and Jay Belsky (Chisholm, 1999; Belsky, 1997) have developed the idea that childhood is for reproduction by adopting a theoretical framework known as life history theory. Life history theory describes

Table 6.1 **The different components of fitness**		
Somatic effort	(1)	Survival, maintenance
	(2)	Preparations for reproduction (e.g. growth, development, learning, maturation, etc.)
Reproductive effort	(3)	Reproduction
	(3a)	Production of offspring (increases offspring quantity)
	(3b)	Rearing of offspring (increases offspring quality)

Source: Chisholm (1999)

development in terms of the decisions made by organisms in order to maximise their inclusive fitness.

A naive view of development is that it is essentially a passive process. The child's developmental trajectory (assuming the organism is human) is seen as being under the control of a multiplicity of environmental experiences, particularly those within the family. The word 'socialisation' – used to describe the process whereby the child gradually becomes a member of society – indicates that this is something that is done to the child rather than something that the child does itself. In contrast, life history theory argues that sexually immature individuals play a much more active – although not necessarily conscious – role in determining their optimal developmental path.

Life history theory argues that at any point in time an individual should invest effort in order to maximise fitness. Fitness, however, consists of a number of components that are often grouped into two categories, **somatic effort** and **reproductive effort** (see table 6.1). Somatic effort includes feeding, avoiding predation, learning and – for juveniles – growth and maturation. Reproductive effort, on the other hand, includes producing offspring and rearing them (for those organisms whose reproductive strategy includes a protracted period rearing offspring).

What makes the organism's task difficult is that investing time and effort in any one of these activities necessarily prevents time being invested in one of the others. For instance, when an organism is foraging for food it is not devoting time to mating. Moreover, activities directed towards enhancing one component might actually reduce fitness on another. For example, as we saw above, rearing offspring places demands on the parent's time and resources that decrease the parent's chances of survival. An organism has therefore to choose how much of its time and resources it spends engaging in each of the fitness-enhancing activities. This is known as the **principle of allocation**. Dennett (1995, p. 128) summed the challenge of life by saying 'if you wanna live you gotta eat'. Following Dennett, Chisholm characterises the principle of allocation by proposing that:

[I]f you wanna live and you wanna grow and develop and wanna have babies (and your babies to have babies) you gotta eat more. What if there is no more? Then you gotta decide what to do: continue living, continue growing or have babies. Can you do all three? If you cannot, what gives? (1999, p. 38)

It can be seen that a rational animal needs to choose carefully how to allocate its time if it is not to become an evolutionary cul-de-sac. What makes the animal's task harder is that there is no single globally optimal method for allocation. As we shall see, how much time an organism should invest in, say, childrearing is dependent upon the prevailing environmental conditions. It has been claimed that the environmentally contingent nature of allocation gives rise to a number of individual differences in behaviour (as well as differences between species). We discuss environmentally contingent differences further in chapter 13.

Parents' choices: offspring quality versus offspring quantity

One particularly pertinent decision that many organisms have to make relates to the trade off expressed in table 6.1 between maximising the quality of offspring over quantity. Why is this a trade off? Simply because resource and time limitations mean that the more offspring you have, the less you are going to be able to devote to each individual: one of the fundamental laws of nature is that time and resources are always limited.

In chapter 7 we will consider how an organism's reproductive strategies can be classified using the r–K continuum. Organisms adopting the r selected strategy focus on producing as many viable offspring as quickly as possible and investing minimal resources in their upbringing. This strategy is employed by many species of fish that produce many millions of fry – the technical name for baby fish – and leave them to their own devices. Only a small percentage will survive to sexual maturity but because the initial number is so large, enough will reproduce for it to be a worthwhile strategy. At the other end of the scale is the K selected strategy. Here only a small number of offspring is produced, but the parents invest heavily in the care and upbringing of each individual such that a high percentage of individuals will make it to adulthood. Whether a species employs an r or K selected strategy depends primarily on the chances that the offspring will die as a result of harsh conditions (e.g. being eaten); when this is high, r selection is optimal (see chapter 7).

The r–K continuum is mainly used for classifying reproductive strategies between different species; when describing different strategies that occur *within* a species life-history theorists use a related scheme (known as the C–F continuum) that specifies whether the organism should maximise current reproductive fitness or future

Box 6.1 Infanticide as an adaptive strategy

Not every baby is nurtured and protected by his or her parents; infanticide – the deliberate killing of young offspring – has existed throughout history and is not unknown today, even in industrial society. Stories of parents killing babies or allowing them to die are greeted with bewilderment: how could someone behave in such a callous manner, surely there must be something psychologically wrong with such people? Research suggests that the answer to this last question is that it depends on how old the child is when it is killed.

Technically (although not legally) infanticide can be divided into neonaticide (the killing of a newborn) and filicide the killing of babies and children older than one day. Why make such a distinction? Isn't each act equally immoral and repugnant? Certainly that is the view of most people, but the distinction was made because research indicates that whereas mothers who kill older infants and children have frequently suffered psychological problems prior to the killing (e.g. depression), mothers of newborns have not (Resnick, 1970). Daly and Wilson (1984) argue that infanticide – as cruel as it might seem – might be the result of an implicit cost–benefit analysis made by a parent who believes her baby is unlikely to reach maturity either because it possesses abnormalities, or the particular conditions are unfavourable (e.g. famine, many other children, death of a spouse). Rearing children is an expensive business and under such circumstance the best strategy in terms of inclusive fitness might be to focus attention on other children, or wait until times are better and try for another child. Daly and Wilson's data indicate that the women who commit neonaticide tend to be those who are least likely to be able to rear their offspring to maturity because they are themselves either young or unmarried or lack other social support (see chapter 7).

reproductive fitness. Having a large number of offspring maximises current reproductive fitness (because there are immediately many copies of your genes), whereas investing heavily in few offspring maximises future reproductive success. (The best-of-all-possible-worlds strategy to invest in many offspring is not possible for the majority of individuals due to resource and time constraints.)

Again, the best strategy for an individual to adopt is dependent upon the nature of the environment. The claim is that when the environment is uncertain and the chances of offspring reaching maturity are low, it is often optimal to maximise current fitness; conversely, in predictable environments where there is a high chance of offspring surviving to maturity it might be best to maximise future reproductive fitness. Under extreme circumstances there is evidence that parents might adopt the cruellest strategy of all, infanticide (see box 6.1).

Box 6.2 **A life history account of play**

If life history theory is correct and animals are under pressure to allocate their time and resources adaptively, then how do we account for the prevalence in all higher mammals of apparently functionless behaviours such as play? After all, play seems to provide no direct benefit to the individual in terms of inclusive fitness. Is play purely functionless (in which case its existence is a serious challenge to life history theory), or does it have some hidden benefit? Evolutionists have addressed this question by suggesting that play is a strategy designed to enhance future reproductive success by fostering the development of skills that will be important in adulthood. Play fighting, therefore, provides a safe way to practise skills that will be useful in adulthood (although, as we shall see later, the most useful type of play might depend upon factors such as the sex of the individual).

According to life history theory, an animal investing in the future is doing so at the expense of maximising current fitness (e.g. survival) so play should only occur in situations when the environment is comparatively stable and unthreatening. Consistent with this prediction is the observation that when times are hard, juvenile mammals play much less than when times are good (presumably because they are allocating their time and energy to maximise their immediate survival (Fagen, 1981)). Research on kittens apparently contradicts this finding. Bateson *et al.* (1990) found that female cats who had been placed on restricted diets weaned their offspring earlier than those on normal diets. This is sensible because the best thing for cats to do in food-reduced situations is to discharge any additional demands on their metabolism – such as hungry kittens – as quickly as possible. However, the early weaned kittens actually played *more* than those of mothers whose diets were normal and were therefore weaned for longer. This is apparently in contradiction to the predictions of life history theory: the kittens should be maximising their current survival chances not their future reproductive chances by engaging in play.

This result, however, is only superficially counter to the predictions of life history theory. Bateson *et al.* found that early weaned kittens engaged in more object play, which is important for the development of hunting skills, at the expense of social play which has a longer-term reproductive benefit. The kittens were therefore maximising their immediate survival chances by allocating their time and effort to activities that enabled them to survive in a situation where they could not rely on their mother to provide them with food. Such studies undermine the misconception that genes must necessarily lead to behaviour that is fixed and inflexible; as we can see, flexibility is often built into the system, with behaviour being contingent upon the environmental.

Maximising fitness from the point of view of offspring

What effect do the reproductive strategies adopted by parents have on their offspring? Recall that, although children cannot invest directly in reproduction, they can still 'choose' to allocate their time and resources to maximise current survival or to maximise future gain by investing in activities such as play and exploration. Again, how much they should invest in one or the other is environmentally contingent. When conditions are harsh (e.g. food is scarce, the chances of predation are high), the best thing might be to maximise current survival; when times are good it might be better to maximise future success by exploiting learning opportunities.

In their 1982 paper Patricia Draper and Henry Harpending applied life history theory to development by investigating the effects of being reared in a home where the father was absent. Previously it had been noted (Whiting, 1965) that being reared in a home where the father is absent following divorce leads to precocious sexual development. In particular, boys in father-absent homes show more aggression than those who grow up in homes where fathers are present, are more rebellious and, in adulthood, view women in a sexually exploitative way. Girls in absent-father homes show a precocious interest in sex, have negative sexual attitudes towards men and have difficulty maintaining long-term monogamous relationships.

Draper and Harpending suggested that the economic disadvantages and uncertainty caused by living in a single-parent compared to a two-parent family meant that maximising current reproductive fitness would be more effective than maximising future reproductive fitness. Children in fatherless homes, by maturing earlier and showing an early interest in sexual activity with multiple partners, are simply adopting a reproductive strategy designed to maximise their inclusive fitness by producing offspring early and at a high rate. Such tendencies, they argued, are formed in response to the presence or absence of an investing father during a critical period between the ages of five and seven years.

Life history theory has also been applied to an area of psychology known as **attachment**. Attachment has been one of the most widely researched areas of social development over the last fifty years. Before discussing life history approaches to attachment, we shall spend some time describing the background to the theory and its key predictions.

Attachment theory

British developmentalist John Bowlby (1951; 1969), was concerned with the factors that affect emotional and social development. Human infants are particularly helpless (technically known as altricial) and the attachment system evolved as a means of increasing the infant's chances of survival and thus ultimately enhancing reproduction (see chapter 7).

Central to Bowlby's theory of attachment was the idea that children form a **working model** of the self and others as a result of their early experiences with the mother. The working model is a mental representation that includes both cognitive and affective components and is used to guide the child's subsequent behaviour. Bowlby proposed that children who grew up in secure environments with responsive and sympathetic mothers would establish a working model that included the belief that relationships were worthwhile and that people were generally to be trusted. Children who grew up with unresponsive or abusive mothers, or if the mothers were absent, would have working models that led them to view relationships and other people with suspicion. The formation of a working model was thought by Bowlby to have a critical period between the ages of about six months and three years. This means that experiences within the critical period are all important when it comes to the formation of the working model, with later experiences being much less important.

Despite recent criticism, Bowlby's ideas have stimulated a great deal of research and many developmentalists today draw on his model of attachment; one such researcher

Figure 6.1 Developmentalist and father of attachment theory, John Bowlby (1907–90)

was psychologist Mary Ainsworth. Ainsworth (1967) developed a procedure known as the **strange situation** in which the immediate effects of maternal separation are studied under laboratory conditions. Children are taken into a room which contains a number of toys. When the child is comfortably playing a stranger enters the room and shortly afterwards the mother leaves. The mother returns a little later and engages the child in play while the stranger slips out. The mother then leaves once more and the stranger returns. Finally, the mother returns once more. The infants frequently cry when the mother disappears; this is quite normal – what is of interest is how they respond when she reappears. Based on their response to the mother's disappearance and reappearance, Ainsworth originally classified infants into three categories **secure attachment, insecure avoidant** and **insecure resistant** (see table 6.2). Subsequently other categories were added based upon observation such as disorganised attachment but for the purposes of this discussion these additions are not relevant so we do not discuss them further.

As you can see from the table the majority of infants are categorised as securely attached, although the actual proportion varies from culture to culture, indicating perhaps that cultural differences in childrearing practices has an effect on infants' behaviour.

Table 6.2 **The three principal attachment styles. The different forms of attachment are sometimes thought of as a continuum with anxious avoidant individuals at one extreme, anxious resistant at the other and securely attached individuals somewhere in the middle; hence they are also known as Types A, B and C**

Type of attachment	Typical behaviour in 'strange situation'	Typical behaviour in later childhood and adulthood	Approximate proportion in each category
Secure attachment (Type B)	Cries when the mother disappears seeks attention when she returns and resumes playing following being comforted	Generally form long-lasting and stable relationships	2/3
Insecure avoidant (Type A)	Shows little attention to mother; does not show much distress when she disappears and as easily comforted by stranger as by mother	Generally form more ephemeral relationships than securely attached individuals	1/4
Insecure resistant (Type C)	Infants remain very close to mother; show anxiety when she disappears and is not easily comforted when she returns	Generally tend to overcommit to few relationships	1/10

Applying life history theory to attachment

The attachment theories of Ainsworth and Bowlby, and the resulting evidence is clear: insecurely attached children – whether as the result of maternal deprivation or poor parenting – are more likely to suffer from mental illness, engage in deviant activities and are generally less successful in life. Although securely attached children are in the majority – accounting for around two-thirds of children studied – this still means that one-third of people are insecurely attached in one way or another.

From an evolutionary perspective, this number is very high given that insecurely attached children are generally less successful than securely attached children. Why has natural selection permitted such an apparently perverse state of affairs to continue? One possibility is that rather than the behaviours that accompany insecure attachment being thought of as deviant and maladaptive, they might be optimal given the environment in which the child is reared. This is the essence of the life history approach to development.

According to some theorists (Belsky, 1997; Belsky et al., 1991; Chisholm, 1996; 1999) Ainsworth's attachment styles can be seen as adaptive reproductive strategies given a particular environment. Attachment experiences provide children with information relating to the amount of risk in their environment, which is used as an index of their reproductive value. Put bluntly, attachment enables the child to predict the future. Or at the very least it provides information that enables the child to guess at future circumstances and adjust his or her behaviour appropriately in order to select the optimal reproductive strategy. The stress felt in early childhood as a result of a disruptive family life might indicate that the parental environment is risky, and hence serves to trigger a different strategy from that of a low-stress family life.

Jay Belsky's life history theory of attachment

Psychologist Jay Belsky (Belsky, 1997) proposes the following adaptationist account of the three principal attachment styles. As this was originally proposed with Steinberg and Draper (Belsky *et al.*, 1991) it is often referred to as the BSD theory.

Secure attachment

Belsky argues that the parenting style that leads to secure attachment represents the emphasis of parenting over reproduction or, put differently, of maximising quality rather than quantity of offspring. Parents will therefore bring up few children but spend a great deal of time, effort and resources providing for them. For their part, children respond to this high investment environment by forming the beliefs that the world is a benevolent place, that other people can be trusted and that relationships are emotionally rewarding and enduring. These beliefs would orient children towards forming close relationships with others, including romantic relationships. When they reproduce, such children are likely themselves to be sensitive parents who invest heavily in their children, so long as the economic situation allows it.

Research into adults classified as securely attached by the Adult Attachment Interview indicates that they tend to report higher levels of relationship security than do insecurely attached individuals. Secure men engage in more supportive relationships with their partners (Ewing and Pratt, 1995); the romantic relationships of secure men and women are longer lasting than those of insecure people (Hazan and Shaver, 1987); and secure partners are more likely to marry in the first place (Kirkpatrick and Hazan, 1994).

Insecure-avoidant attachment

Recall that children who are categorised as insecure-avoidant tend to treat the mother with some indifference: they show little distress when she leaves the room in the strange situation experiment, and little joy when she returns. What use might such a strategy be with respect to that child's inclusive fitness? Belsky (1997) proposes that in situations when the predicted availability of resources is low and others cannot be trusted, maximising future reproductive fitness might be inefficient. What is the point, for instance, of getting married and bringing up a few children if your spouse leaves you and either takes away the children that you have invested in so heavily, or fails to contribute his (or her) resources to your offspring? With this in mind, it might be profitable to adopt a lifestyle ultimately directed towards maximising current reproductive fitness. Such individuals might therefore engage in opportunistic relationships not fully committing to their partners and perhaps even exploiting them. Furthermore, such individuals might have a series of sexual partners and might begin mating at a comparatively young age.

Evidence suggests that insecure-avoidant individuals are more willing than others to engage in sex in the absence of an enduring relationship (Brennan *et al.*, 1991), are more likely to have had dated more than one person (Kirkpatrick and Hazan, 1994) and are more likely to have experienced the break-up of a relationship (Feeney and Noller, 1992). Furthermore, avoidant mothers are more likely to be ambivalent and unsupportive towards their children and show the least responsiveness and affectionate behaviour when reunited with their children during the strange situation (Crowell and Feldman, 1988; 1991). There is some evidence that insecure-avoidant children reach sexual maturity earlier than do those categorised as secure. Moffitt *et al.* (1992) presented evidence that family conflict at age seven was predictive of earlier onset of puberty in girls. It seems that environmental cues might influence biological aspects of maturation as well as psychological characteristics.

Insecure-resistant attachment

Insecure-resistant children are the least numerous of the three main attachment categories and tend to be very clingy and attention demanding. In particular, they seem to be very demanding of the mother, and it is difficult for anyone else to comfort the child. Belsky proposes that such children are being driven into a null reproductive strategy, where they are destined to have no children. Superficially, this might seem like a maladaptive strategy, as the individuals will pass on no copies of their genes directly. Recall, however, that you don't need to reproduce yourself in order for your genes to go forward to the next generation (see chapters 2 and 7). Having a child might ensure that 50 per cent of your genes go forward to the next generation, but a niece or nephew carries 25 per cent of your genes as a result of you sharing 50 per cent of your genes with your sibling. Thus helping the offspring of a close relative can help to increase your inclusive fitness if, for whatever reason, you are unable or unwilling to have children yourself.

Belsky's life-history explanation for this form of attachment is the most speculative of the three although there are precedents in the rest of the animal kingdom. For example, it is known that other animals born either physically or behaviourally

Table 6.3 How the three principal attachment styles arise out of an interaction between the parent's reproductive strategy and the child's resultant developmental strategy

Attachment style	Parental reproductive strategy	Child's developmental strategy
Secure	• Long-term • Able and willing to invest • High parenting effort • Unconditionally accepting, sensitive, responsive to the child	• Maximise long-term learning, quality of development • Maintain investment from 'rich' parent
Insecure avoidant	• Short-term • Unwilling to invest • High mating effort • Dismissing, rejecting of child	• Maximise short-term survival • Avoid rejecting, potentially infanticidal parent
Insecure resistant	• Short-term • Unable to invest • Parenting effort with inadequate resources • Inconsistent, preoccupied but not rejecting of the child	• Maximise short-term maturation 'quantity' of development • Maintain investment from 'poor' parent

Source: Chisholm (1996)

sterile will help their siblings or parents to rear offspring (Dawkins, 1976; 1989; 2006 – see also chapter 7). However, there is little direct evidence for this particular part of Belsky's theory, partly because comparatively few individuals fall into this category. Some evidence is found in questionnaire studies. Females classified as anxious-resistant tend to admit to 'mothering' their partner, rather than engaging in a typical romantic relationship (Kunce and Shaver, 1994). Furthermore, firstborns, particularly if they are female, are more likely to be resistant than children born later – consistent with the idea that some children may be behaviourally 'sterile' to help out with their younger siblings.

James Chisholm's life history theory of attachment

Like Belsky, Chisholm (1996; 1999) proposes that the child's attachment style is a response to the particular reproductive strategy adopted by his or her parents (see table 6.3). Again, like Belsky, Chisholm suggests that secure attachment is a response to heavy parental investment signalled to the child by the relative absence of stress within the family. Such children show this secure attachment by engaging in behaviours that maximise long-term aspects of their development (e.g. engaging in play and exploratory behaviours, forming close relationships with peers). Avoidant attachment styles are formed in response to parents who are *unwilling* to invest perhaps because they have adopted a parenting strategy of maximising the quantity of offspring, and/or they are investing in their other children. In the face of such a parental strategy, children will seek to maximise their short-term survival at the expense of exploring relationships. Children should avoid such parents due to the high risk of neglect, abuse or – in most extreme cases – death. Resistant attachment styles, on the other hand, are the result of parents who are *unable* rather than just unwilling to invest in their offspring. The child attempts to extract all of the meagre resources that it can get from its parents by being clingy and demanding.

Evaluation of life history explanations of attachment

The life history approach has strong similarities with that of Darwinian medicine (see chapter 12) which also makes the claim that many apparent forms of dysfunctional behaviour are perfectly functional when inclusive fitness is used as a currency rather than society's expectations. Further recall that the currency of inclusive fitness is the number of genes that are passed on to the next generation rather than the well-being of the particular individual whom the genes use as their transient vehicle. A strategy that maximises the number of genes that replicate themselves will win out even if this ultimately leads to an individual who is miserable and is frowned upon by society. It might help at this point to consider the suicidal tendencies of the male red-backed widow spider we discussed in chapter 1: he dies to give his genes the best possible chance.

Remember also that the claim is that such strategies would have been adaptive in the ancestral environment rather than the environment in which the overwhelming majority of individuals is studied (e.g. industrial or post-industrial society). This presents a particular difficulty in testing these theories. If we were studying non-human animals most of whom, we assume, are living under circumstances close to those in which they evolved than the average twenty-first-century human, we could do the appropriate cost–benefit analysis and work out whether each of the strategies was adaptive given the particular conditions under which the offspring was raised. Because cultural evolution has changed our environment so much, it is difficult to do the same thing with human beings. However, Waynforth *et al.* (1998) investigated the pre-industrial Mayans of western Belize and the Aché of eastern Paraguay to test the effects of – among other things – father absence. The Aché and Mayans were used because, it is assumed, living in a pre-industrial society their culture is thought to be closer to that of our ancestors than that of Europeans and North Americans who are usually the subject of such studies. The results were mixed. Most importantly they found that the patterns of father absence and age at first reproduction did not fit the simple life history model. Individuals reared in father-absent families did not tend to reproduce any earlier than those reared in families where the father was present. They suggest that more complex models need to be formulated that take into account mediating factors such as kin help, mating effort and parenting effort.

More recent evidence has shown a fair amount of support for the BSD theory and some of its variants (e.g. Chisholm's theory). For example, Belsky *et al.* (2010) found that 65 per cent of girls categorised as insecure at 15 months of age using the Strange Situation test experienced menarche (onset of puberty) at less than 10.5 years of age compared to 54 per cent of those categorised as secure at 15 months. The insecure group also completed puberty early as well. A similar study by Belsky *et al.* (2010) found that maternal harshness at 15 months predicted early menarche – as before – but also greater sexual risk taking in adolescent girls. Measurement of maternal harshness was achieved by the responses that their mothers gave to a questionnaire. 'Harsh' mothers tending to spank their children for doing something wrong, believed that children should respect authority, should be quiet when adults were around, believed that praise spoiled the child and did not give many hugs.

In a study of 4,553 British women Nettle *et al.* (2011) found that early pregnancy was accounted for by environmental risk factors such as low birth weight, short duration of breastfeeding, separation from mother in childhood, frequent family residential moves and lack of paternal involvement. Social economic status and the age of the participants' mother when they were born were controlled for in this study.

Not all evidence supports the BSD hypothesis, for example studies by Ellis *et al.* (1999) and Miller and Pasta (2000) failed to find results in the predicted direction. But the weight of the evidence currently supports the BSD hypothesis. There are however two important considerations. The first is that it is possible genes that lead to early menarche and/or sexual risk taking are somehow associated (either through pleiotropy or some form of linkage) with genes that lead to maternal harshness. If this were the case it would give a similar pattern of results. This is not as far-fetched as might be imagined. To take the pleiotropy version of the story (one gene with multiple phenotypic effects). Imagine that there was a gene that led females to display the characteristics described in the BSD hypothesis (early menarche, early sexual activity, risky sex, multiple partners, etc.). Further imagine that this gene also had the effect of making the mothers somewhat harsh towards their offspring (beating them, showing them less love than is typical and so on). Now a mother who has this gene is likely to pass it on to her offspring specifically, for this argument, her daughters. The researchers measure the mother's maternal harshness at time 1 and find that she is harsh, they measure her daughter's age of onset of puberty at time 2 and find that it is early and conclude that mother's behaviour at time 1 is causing her daughter's behaviour at time 2. Incorrectly! In fact the mother's behaviour has nothing to do with her daughter's behaviour, underlying both the mother's and the daughter's behaviour is the effect of our hypothesised gene. If you think that this sounds implausible you must remember that pleiotropy is the rule rather than the exception. But it needn't even be a single gene. Multiple genes can be linked together, for example by being close to one another on a chromosome, meaning that they also tend to get passed on *en masse* rather than individually – in fact this is Richard Dawkins's definition of a gene (see Dawkins 1976; 2006). If you think that the traits of maternal harshness and early age menarche are unlikely bedfellows you could consider the gene(s) to be gene(s) of *low parental investment* which maximise current rather than future reproductive success in which women have more children (as a result of earlier and greater sexual activity) and invest in them less (which manifests itself as maternal harshness). We can consider this as there being two phenotypes – although really it is more likely to be a continuum – when times are harsh the environment favours the low investment (C) when times are good it favours the high-investment (F) strategy. In an attempt to separate these two entirely different explanations, Mendle *et al.* (2006) conducted a Children-of-Twins study (CoT). They recruited a group of adult female identical twins all of whom had daughters. They were selected so that one twin had experienced family disruption, such as divorce, and the other had no disruption. They then compared the age of menarche of the disrupted twin's daughter to that of the child from the twin with the intact family. The logic here was that if early menarche was genuinely a response to environmental disruption the daughters from the disrupted family should show earlier menarche than those from the intact family. On the other hand, if early menarche were the direct effect of low-parental investment genes, as discussed above, there would be no difference. Children of twins were used to maximise the genetic similarity of the children. The study failed to find any support for the BSD hypothesis as there was no difference in pubertal timing between the two groups.

A different methodology found evidence for BSD, however. Tither and Ellis (2008) compared older and younger sisters from the same disrupted family, the families were selected such that the older sister had reached, or was close to reaching menarche at the point at which the disruption happened while the younger sister was still some way from puberty. The BSD prediction was that the younger sister would show earlier puberty as she had longer in the disrupted environment than the older sister. In support of the BSD hypothesis they found that for disrupted families the younger sister experienced menarche significantly earlier than the older sister, whereas for non-disrupted families it was the older sister who experienced (slightly) earlier puberty. The effect of disruption on menarche was enhanced when the family showed serious paternal dysfunction. Again in line with the predictions of BSD. It has to be said that although the principal results were significant, the effect sizes were small. Notwithstanding this, it is difficult to explain these results without assuming that family disruption plays some role in accelerating puberty, although it remains a possibility that some combined genetic and environmental model offers the best explanation of the data. Some children may be predisposed to develop more rapidly in the face of a disrupted childhood than others. So far this has not been tested.

Finally, there needs also to be more work developing the model with respect to differences between males and females as to what constitutes an optimal reproductive strategy. As we saw in chapter 4, there are substantial sex differences in mating strategy because men and women are subject to different constraints. It seems likely that the same environmental circumstances (e.g. father present or absent, parents maximising quality or quantity of offspring) might have differential effects on the best strategy for males and females (Maccoby, 1990). This argument is very important from the perspective of evolutionary psychology. In chapters 3 and 4 we discussed how males and females might be under different pressures with respect to reproduction. Females are much more restricted than are males in the number of offspring that they can produce, they typically release one egg every month and should they fall pregnant are then 'infertile' during the subsequent period of gestation and lactation. For their part, although men can potentially father thousands of offspring – and therefore have much more to gain – they are also less likely to obtain a sexual partner (because other men might be 'commandeering' more than one woman) and therefore have much more to lose. Furthermore, a woman is always certain that she is the mother of her child, a man is always less than 100 per cent certain that he is the father. Such differences indicate that the optimal reproductive strategy might be different for males and females under the same set of environmental conditions.

The effects of parenting

Parents, as we have discussed above, provide not only food and shelter for their offspring, but also emotional support and a safe base from which their children can explore the environment. The bond between parent and child is a powerful one; parents regularly claim that they would do anything to protect their children, even if that meant killing someone else (but see box 6.1). From the point of view of evolutionary psychology the power of this bond should come as little surprise. Genes that ensure that parents will protect their children are more likely to be passed on than those that do not (see chapter 7 on kin altruism). For their part, babies that love their parents are also going to be at an advantage over those that do not as this will tend to keep them physically closer to their parents and hence safer.

So far we have looked at parenting in terms of the investment in children (life history theory) but much of the psychological literature sees parenting as being much more than the provision of resources (physical and emotional). For instance, since Freud psychologists have focused on the effect of the child–parent relationship on psychological well being with researchers such as John Bowlby and, more recently,

Figure 6.2 Nurturing behaviour in males is common, though not a sex-typical characteristic

Mary Ainsworth (see above) carrying on this tradition. A recent book by the British psychologist Oliver James (2002) coyly echoed Philip Larkin's poem in its title *They F*** You Up: How to Survive Family Life* and argued that many psychological problems can be traced back to the effects of parenting and family life. Such a notion is compelling. After all, children spend a large amount of their time with their parents, especially in the early years, and surely this must have an effect.

Behavioural genetics: separating nature from nurture

One of the big problems in studying the effects of parental behaviour on offspring is that parents potentially influence their children in two entirely separate ways. First there is the effect of the genes: a biological parent shares with each child 50 per cent of his or her genes by common descent so parents obviously exert a genetic influence on the child. Second, in most families, there is the social influence on children of growing up in close proximity to their parents. The fact that these two influences frequently co-occur means that if children resemble their parents in their behaviour we don't know whether it is due to shared genes, social learning or some combination of both.

Behavioural genetics attempts to estimate the relative contributions of genes and the environment by conducting studies on twins and other siblings. Identical twins (or monozygotic twins) are the result of a single fertilised egg and therefore share 100 per cent of their genes whereas non-identical (or dizygotic) twins are the result of two separate fertilisations and share 50 per cent of their genes, just like normal siblings. By comparing the similarities and differences between these different types of twins, it is possible to estimate the effects of nature and nurture on individual differences in behaviour. For instance the amount of variation between individuals can be calculated by looking at the differences between identical twins reared apart on the trait because, since they are genetically identical, it follows that any difference between them must be due to the environment. The results of such studies estimate that the environment accounts for between 50 and 60 per cent of the variation among them on a variety of traits (see chapter 12). It therefore follows that genes account for 40–50 per cent of the variation. It is important to point out that such statistics do not differentiate between the direct effects of the genes and the indirect effects of the genes. For instance, people judged to be attractive are generally more assertive, a finding that is explained by the observation that attractive people are generally treated with more deference than less attractive people (Jackson and Huston, 1975 – see box 6.3). Even if there were no direct genetic influence on assertiveness we can see that there is an indirect one; genes influence attractiveness which leads to individuals being treated differently, which affects their personality. In the data of behavioural genetics research, both show up as effects of the genes.

Before we move on it is important to point out that estimates of heritability can sometimes be misleading (see chapter 2). Consider the example presented by Richard Lewontin (see chapter 2). He asks us to imagine buying a packet of seeds from the local garden centre. The seeds are genetically diverse, i.e. they are not clones. We divide the seeds in half and plant them in two identical trays. Both these trays are treated exactly the same (the same light, temperature, etc.) but one tray is given good nutrients, the other poor nutrients. The seeds grow into plants and after a period of time we observe two things. First, that the average height of the plants in the tray containing good nutrients is greater than the average height of the plants in the poor nutrient tray. Second, if you examine the plants within each tray some are bigger than others. If we are to account for these differences then the between-group difference is entirely due to the environment (one rich, one poor) since there is no net genetic difference between the two groups (we divided the packet randomly). However, if we wish to explain the *within*-group difference then this is entirely due to genetic differences among the seeds, some are genetically taller than others. We know this because all the seeds within a tray were treated identically. So here is the lesson. Research on a particular population – let's say middle-class children – might reveal that there is very little environmental contribution to differences in

> ## Box 6.3 Behavioural genetics and the effects of the genes on the environment
>
> Many think of the contribution that genes and the environment make to development as being independent; the genes have some initial effect and then the environment has its own separate effect uninfluenced by the genes. This is not the case; behavioural geneticists show how the genes can have a radical effect on the environment that the child experiences. There are three types of gene environment interactions.
>
> **Passive interactions** occur because, in cases where children are reared by their parents, they will tend to be similar in personality, intelligence and temperament to their parents. Hence, an intelligent child will, on average, be reared in a household with intelligent parents who might surround the child with books or engage the child in intelligent conversation. Thus children inherit not just 'intelligent genes' from their parents, but also an environment that is intellectually stimulating.
>
> In **reactive–evocative interactions**, children with a certain genetically influenced trait will tend to be treated differently by people. We know, for example, that children who are judged attractive are punished less harshly for misdemeanours than those who are more homely (Dion, 1972; Landy and Aronson, 1969) and that people judged attractive are generally more assertive (Jackson and Huston, 1975). Thus the way that people treat a child (which constitutes part of a child's environment) will be, in part, affected by genetically linked dispositions.
>
> Finally, **active interactions** occur because children tend to seek out people who are similar to them. Thus, active children who like sport will tend to band together, as will children who like intellectual pursuits and so on. If any of these traits are associated with some underlying genetic influence (like the two just mentioned), then we might say that the genes are influencing the environment in which children grow up.

intelligence, most of the variation is explained by genetic differences. This might lead you to conclude that any differences in intelligence *between* groups – say middle class children and working class children is also genetic. But this may not be the case, as Lewontin's thought experiment demonstrates, differences within groups may be genetic, but differences between groups could be entirely environmental. A study by Turkheimer *et al.* (2003) shows that this is not just hypothetical. He studied several hundred identical and non-identical twins and found that the environment accounted for most of the variation in intelligence for poor children with genes having little effect, but for well-off children the situation was reversed. One possible explanation for this is that for poorer children, even small differences in their environment might have large effects on intelligence (the availability of books, parental involvement, etc.) but the environment for well-off children is already so good that any differences in the environment have little effect. To return to Lewontin's example, giving a plant some fertiliser is going to improve its growth but there comes a point where improvements in the environment cease to have any additional effect, at this point any differences in plant size will be down to genetic differences. The overall message, however, is that the results of behavioural genetic studies are complex and can be misinterpreted. When thinking about such studies it is helpful to return to Lewontin's simple example (see also chapter 13).

Having sounded a note of caution against oversimplistic interpretations of behavioural genetics we can further explore the way that behavioural geneticists explore environmental influence. Behavioural geneticists divide the environment into two separate forces: the **shared environment**, which consists of the influences common to all siblings (the fact that they have the same parents, or might go to the same school), and the **unique** or **non-shared environment**, which consists of all the influences that are specific to an individual (experiences with teachers, peers, childhood illnesses and also differences in the uterine environment). These three effects – the genes, the shared environment and the non-shared environment – are considered to be the only effects on development, and therefore sum to 1 (or, if you prefer, 100 per cent). The effect of the shared environment can be estimated in a number of ways. One is by comparing the difference between identical twins reared together (who share genes and the same environment) with those reared apart (who share only their genes); any difference between these two groups would give the effect of the shared environment. Another is to measure the similarity between adopted 'siblings' – unrelated individuals adopted at an early age by the same family. The assumption here is that because they share no genes by common descent any similarities between them must be the result of their shared environment.

The results of these diverse pieces of research lead to the same conclusion: the shared environment accounts for little or none of the variation left over when you take out the genetic effects. One might think that identical twins reared in the same household would be more similar to each other than those reared apart; in fact there is very little difference between them (Plomin *et al.*, 1994). Other research indicates that unrelated children who are adopted and brought up as siblings in the same family environment are no more similar to each other than any two unrelated children chosen at random from a population (Plomin and Daniels, 1987). The measures in these studies were the heritability of personality, cognitive skills and mental illness. At most the data suggest that the shared environment accounts for 10 per cent of variation among people (Turkheimer, 2000).

If genes account for 50 per cent of the variation among people and the shared environment between 0 and 10 per cent, what accounts for the missing variation? Given that the three causal factors on variation among people – genes, shared environment, non-shared environment – sum to 1, it stands to reason that it must be the **non-shared environment** that is accounting for these differences.

Figure 6.3 Children may learn more from their peers than their parents – even at a young age

Group socialisation theory and environmental influence

In her book *The Nurture Assumption* and in a previous article in the journal *Psychological Review* (Harris, 1995; 1998) Judith Harris used the results described above to claim that the missing 40–50 per cent of variation is primarily caused by the influence of other children. The book in particular caused a storm and the Society for Research in Child Development voted it the fifth most controversial since 1950.

Harris admits that in the initial stages of infancy parents do have an important influence. In the earliest years infants learn a lot from their parents, they will usually acquire their first language from parental input, for example, but as soon as they start to mix with other children they learn things which override the earlier parental influences. Children of immigrants, for instance, might initially learn the language of their parents but later learn the language of their peers (assuming that these two are different). These children will be bilingual and will often switch back and forth between their parental language and the language of their community (the technical term is **code switching**), depending on who they are with at the time. In most cases the child's native language (the one that they are most comfortable with) will become the language of his or her peers, rather than the parental language, despite having learned the parental language first. A related situation occurs when families move to a different part of the country: parents soon notice to their dismay that their child starts to talk less like them and more like the child's peers.

Harris argues that parents are remarkably poor role models for how children should behave. In all cultures, parents do many things that children would be punished for doing. Parents swear, fight, consume alcohol, stay up late and take part in dangerous activities – usually things that children are prohibited from doing. If a child were to emulate an adult, she wouldn't get very far before she came unstuck. As Harris puts it:

A child's goal is not to become a successful adult, any more than a prisoner's goal is to become a successful guard. A child's goal is to become a successful child. (1998, p. 198)

Put differently, children want to be successful in the eyes of their peers and behaving like an adult probably won't help them to achieve this.

Group socialisation and evolutionary psychology

If Harris is correct (and she does have a number of critics) can we make sense of this in evolutionary terms? Why for instance shouldn't children want to imitate adults? Would this not enable them to learn more rapidly than learning from other children? If children learned from adults, they surely would not need to make the same mistakes that adults made, wouldn't culture also advance at a more rapid rate, benefiting us all? According to Harris, there are four reasons why children might have evolved to be socialised by their peers rather than by their parents.

(1) Younger members of human and non-human primate species tend to be the innovators (see Rowe, 1994). Cultural innovations – such as fire and weaponry – have the potential to increase our inclusive fitness. If we learned from our parents we would be shielded from potentially beneficial innovations, which would reduce our fitness compared with those who learned from their peers (see chapter 13).

(2) If children learned everything they knew from their parents their skills and ideas would all be very similar. Having children learn from their peers increases the variation of knowledge that is in the culture; variation is useful if the environment suddenly changes (see chapter 13).

(3) Children can't count on having parents to learn from. In the ancestral environment many parents were killed and the chances that a child would have both parents for very long were relatively small. Such children would be doomed if they counted on their parents for education. However, there will nearly always be a peer group to learn from.

(4) Parents and children have different, often competing, interests (see chapter 7). It is not in the child's interest to learn what the parent might want them to learn, because this is unlikely to be what's best for them.

So far most of these evolutionary justifications for group socialisation theory amount to little more than speculation. The first two points do make some form of sense, but it must be remembered that the benefits of culture must ultimately be to the individual (or rather his or her genes – see chapter 2) if natural selection is to act on them, not the species or society as a whole. Point 3 also contains much truth, but in the ancestral environment orphans would probably have suffered rather more than an absence of someone to learn from; they could well have starved. And if some kindly relative stepped in and provided food and shelter then the child could have learned from them. Finally, point four is also true, parents and children do indeed have competing interests much of the time. But children's interests compete with those of other children as well; it is not as if children constitute an organised coalition against parental exploitation.

Evaluation of group socialisation theory

Harris makes two separate claims: (1) that parents have little or no long-lasting socialising effect on their children, and (2) that the missing 50 per cent of variation not accounted for by genes is the result of peer interactions (group socialisation theory). Do either of these two claims stand up? The claim that parents have little or no long-lasting effect is only partially borne out by the data. The data seem to show that growing up in the same parental environment does not seem to make children any more similar to one another (e.g. Plomin and Daniels, 1987) but this does not show that parents have no effect. In fact, although parents seem to think that they tend to treat all of their children the same, this is neither the view of their children, nor is it the view of independent observers who have rated parental behaviour to different offspring (Reiss et al., 2000). Put simply, parents treat different children differently so parental behaviour would contribute to the non-shared rather than the shared environment (Plomin, 2011). So parents might have an effect, they just don't have the effect of making siblings more like each other.

Other researchers have proposed that because the results show no effect of the shared environment; there must be an interaction between parental behaviour and children's personalities (Vandell, 2000). Interaction is used here in the statistical sense which means that the effect of a particular variable (in this case parental behaviour) is dependent upon another variable (in this case the child's genetic make-up). A particular parental behaviour would therefore have an effect on each individual child but because each child responds in a different way the effect cancels out when summed across many children. For instance, permissive parenting might cause some children to become irresponsible because there are no constraints on their behaviour, and others to become ultra-responsible because they have to assume control over their own lives. Each form of behaviour is having an effect, but when you add the individual effects together they cancel each other out so it looks like there is no effect of the shared environment (see Pinker, 2002). Such an effect is unlikely but by no means impossible and might still rescue the notion that parents have a long-lasting effect on children. So far, however, there is little evidence to support the claim that parental effects are truly interactive.

The second claim regarding the importance of peers might well depend upon which area of behaviour is under question. There is evidence that attitudes, values and other culturally specific behaviours such as accent are strongly influenced by the peer group rather than parents, but the mechanisms by which peer groups can influence variation in personality is harder to explain (see chapter 13). One way that Harris suggests this could happen is that siblings might join different peer groups, with perhaps one child joining a group of children who are responsible and hard working and the other joining a group of anti-establishment slackers. In order for this to work, however, the motivation to join each group must not be on the basis of genetic propensities; if it were, the effects of the peer group would show up as effects on the genes (see box 6.3). To see why, remember that heritability estimates do not differentiate between the direct effect of the genes (e.g. genes that 'code' for assertiveness) and the indirect effects of the genes (genes that 'code' for attractiveness that leads to assertiveness because of the way people treat them). If group membership were just an indirect effect of the genes it would therefore show up as an effect of genes, rather than an effect of the unique environment, which is what we are trying to explain. So we are looking for an effect that would essentially drive identical twins apart on a variety of personality traits. Harris's other suggestion is that the roles within a particular peer group – whether you are a leader, joker, peacemaker or the butt of everyone's jokes – might have this effect. This might work because there may be competition for particular roles which might mean, in the case of identical twins, that one twin might be the leader, with the other forced into some other role (because there can be only one leader). Harris acknowledges that there is little evidence to support this particular mechanism but it seems that the environmental influence on children might be more capricious and dependent on chance than might at first be thought. Pinker (2002) proposes that chance events throughout life – being in the right place at the right time, or vice versa; catching an illness; minor differences in the uterine environment or subtle variations in brain chemistry when the brain is being wired up – might ultimately explain why identical twins are different, and thereby account for the effect of the unique environment on us all (see chapter 13).

Ultimately Harris's theory may be proved wrong or too extreme, perhaps the null effect of shared environment might be genuinely due to interactions between parental behaviour and children's personalities. Whatever is the case we must ensure that the effects of the genes are taken into account when studying socialisation and development and that the effects of nurture are no longer merely assumed, but tested directly.

Differential susceptibility to rearing influence

Above we have presented two seemingly contradictory theories. The modified attachment theory suggests that children use parental behaviour as a way of choosing (unconsciously) a reproductive strategy designed to maximise their fitness given the particular constraints of the environment, in short, parents matter. Group socialisation theory, on the other hand, suggests that children should not be influenced by parents, rather they should be influenced by the group: in short, parents do not matter. Can we reconcile this apparent disparity? Or is one theory simply incorrect? A recent theory has been put forward by Jay Belsky which might suggest that, to some extent, both could be correct. Belsky (e.g. 2005) argues that some children might be more susceptible to parental influence than others, and that this differential susceptibility might in itself be an adaptation. The logic is as follows. Imagine a stable world in which very little changed from generation to generation. In such a set of circumstances it would make sense for children to imitate and be otherwise influenced by their parents, after all, parents are the experts on the way the world works and they have negotiated it successfully enough to have children. This kind of world would be one in which children who learned from, and were influenced by their parents would outcompete those who chose to go it alone. In such a world, hard times in early childhood would suggest that times would be hard when they were adults so adopting a reproductive strategy such as those described above would be adaptive.

On the other hand, consider a very different world in which there is a large amount of change within a generation. In such a world it would make less sense to learn from your parents since the strategies you acquire from them could soon be useless. Furthermore, hard times might be rapidly followed by good times, so to adopt a reproductive strategy based upon parental behaviour might be suboptimal. Such a world would benefit children who were less influenced by parents and perhaps more influenced by their peers (see Harris's points above).

Finally consider a world which is a combination of the two. Sometimes there are long periods where comparatively little changes, sometimes there are times of rapid change, but it is impossible to predict when the world might be stable and when it might be unstable. What kind of child would that favour, one who was influenced by his or her parents or one who was not? Belsky's argument is that it does not favour one kind of child, rather it favours parents having different types of children:

some who are susceptible to parental influence (to prosper in the stable world) and some who are less susceptible (to prosper in the unstable world). To see why, consider that, evolutionarily speaking, a child is simply a parent's way of passing his or her genes on to the subsequent generation (grandchildren), and if the world is capricious then having different kinds of children might maximise the parent's chances of having grandchildren. This theory is therefore consistent with the claim that parents matter (because some children are genetically predisposed to be influenced by parents) and the claim that parents do not matter (because some are predisposed to be less susceptible to parental influence).

Due to its relative newness this theory has little direct evidence, but it might clear up the contradiction that some data (such as the attachment data) support parental influence whereas other data (such as the behavioural genetic data) suggest that they do not. Some more direct evidence is presented by Caspi *et al.* (2002). These researchers conducted a longitudinal study of a cohort of boys in New Zealand. Two of the things that they were interested in were the effects of maltreatment on children and the effect of a different version of a gene that codes for the enzyme monoamine oxidase A (MAOA). MAOA metabolises (breaks down) neurotransmitters such as noradrenaline (also known as norepinephrine), serotonin and dopamine and one version of the gene is associated with low MAOA activity. What is interesting about this research is that there is an interaction between parental influence on a particular child, and the version of the gene that that child has. Children who had the gene that led to low MAOA activity were much more sensitive to parental influence than those that had the alternative gene.

There needn't be a genetic difference between children in order to find that some are more susceptible to parental influence than others. It is possible that some environmental effects (e.g. during embryogenesis or beyond) might affect the expression of particular genes. In chapter 13 we discuss the effects of birth order on personality. Frank Sulloway presents some evidence that later-born children might be different in their personalities (more creative, less conventional) than firstborns. If Sulloway's birth order effect is real – and it is controversial – it might be the result of genes being switched on or off as a result of hormones in the uterus, the constitution of these hormones varying depending on whether or not the mother has had children before. Thus parents (unconsciously) see to it that their children vary in the extent to which they can be influenced, with laterborns being less malleable than firstborns.

This is extremely speculative, and the mechanism is unclear but Belsky's theory does make some evolutionary sense and it might help to clear up some of the contradictions in the parental influence data. Before finishing on this topic one crucial prediction of this theory is that the environment is sometimes stable, sometimes not. Is there any evidence that this is the case? One possibility is that the ice-ages provided such an environment. As we shall see in chapter 14 ice ages could be quite capricious, with long periods of stability punctuated by comparatively rapid fluctuations in temperature. Such changes would have affected the indigenous animals and plants, leading to the necessity to develop different hunting and gathering techniques and different ways of preparing food, not to mention ways of keeping warm during the cold snaps. So far there is no strong evidence for this proposition, although computational modelling might at least suggest whether having different susceptibilities to parental influence is indeed beneficial under capricious environmental conditions.

Moral development

In his book of the same name journalist Robert Wright described human beings as *the moral animal*, by which he meant that we are alone in the animal kingdom in having an explicit sense of right and wrong. Moreover, this sense is not merely cognitive it is accompanied by powerful emotions. When someone else commits an immoral act we often feel angry or disgusted at their actions whereas feelings of guilt or shame or embarrassment often accompany occasions when we behave immorally. On the other hand, those who show great morality, such as Nelson Mandela or Gandhi, are often revered. And who has not experienced the great swell of pride when we ourselves do someone a good turn? The fact that morality is a cultural universal (Brown, 1991 – see chapter 14) and that it triggers such powerful emotional responses has been taken as suggesting that it is part of human nature. In the next section we address the question of what evolutionary purpose morality might have.

What is the evolutionary function of morality?

Throughout this book we have emphasised the importance of a gene-centred view of evolution: human nature evolved to facilitate the propagation of the genes and that, in most cases, is best served by aiding the survival and reproduction of the individual that serves as a vehicle for these genes, or their close relatives (see chapter 2). This being the case it seems, on the face of it, to be somewhat paradoxical to suggest that natural selection might have endowed us with a moral sense. What possible advantage could it have for the individual and his or her genes to behave in a moral way towards non-kin? Surely such a behaviour could only be understood by invoking group selection: the behaviours are of benefit to the species as a whole. In fact there is no contradiction, it seems that a moral sense has some clear advantages to the individual, although as we shall see, not all of the benefits are entirely concerned with what is traditionally thought of as morality. In secular state societies the conventional view of morality owes much to philosophers such as John Stuart Mill who contributed to the foundation of liberal democracy. Crucial to this view is that something is only immoral to the extent that a human being suffers (or might potentially suffer) as the consequence of some deliberate action by another. But even in liberal societies, people's judgements of the morality transcend those prescribed by that society, as can be seen in the following example.

In the late 1990s and early 2000s an exhibition called Bodyworlds by Gunther von Hagens toured Europe and the UK. The exhibition contained human corpses preserved by a process called plastination which literally turns flesh into plastic. Among the exhibits was a skinned male body, his cranium split in half to reveal his brain, crouching over a chessboard as if pondering his next move, and – most notoriously – a pregnant woman sliced down the middle to reveal the unborn foetus inside. Bodyworlds produced a storm of protest and moral outrage throughout Europe and not just among conservatives and religious fundamentalists; many atheists and liberals also admitted to feeling pangs of moral concern at the exhibition; after all, these were once living, breathing human beings. The problem is to determine just where the immorality of Bodyworlds lies. The 'models' are dead so cannot suffer, and they freely agreed to the subsequent process of plastination and exhibition when they were alive (von Hagens still signs up potential subjects during his exhibitions). So according to the standard model there is no contravention of morality and the detractors recognise this. Although many felt there was something immoral about the exhibition, they had no argument to show exactly why it was immoral.

Bodyworlds represents an example of what psychologist Jonathan Haidt (Haidt et al., 1993) calls **moral illusions** by analogy to visual illusions such as those shown in figures 9.3a and 9.3b (p. 254). In visual illusions there is a difference between what seems to be the case and what is the case by objective criteria (such as measurement of size, colour, light intensity). By analogy, although to many people Bodyworlds appears to contravene moral principles, in fact by objective criteria from the standard model it contravenes none.

Moral illusions have been studied experimentally by Haidt (Haidt et al., 1993) by presenting participants with scenarios such as the one below.

A family's dog was killed by a car in front of their house. They had heard that dog meat was delicious, so they cut up the dog's body and cooked it and ate it for dinner.

As for Bodyworlds such stories were judged immoral (most participants judged that the protagonists should be stopped or punished) but participants faltered when asked to justify why. Haidt suggests that people's intuitive notion of morality overlaps with the standard view but also includes other judgements that are not part of the standard model. Drawing on work by anthropologist Richard Shweder (Shweder et al., 1997) he argues that people's intuitions span three distinct spheres of morality. Morals of *autonomy* are concerned with avoiding harm to the individual, including restricting their freedom and protecting their rights and property. This form of morality is closely related to reciprocal altruism (see chapter 8). A group in which everyone cheated, lied and stole from one other would soon collapse as everyone would opt out of social exchanges. Cross-culturally the moral sense places prohibitions on cheating, lying, stealing, murder and thus enables us to reap the benefits of group living. Morals of *community* relate to the issues of harm and disrespect to the in-group and the social hierarchy. This includes showing disrespect to elders and the cultural traditions of a particular group. Morals of *divinity* uphold that which is considered holy or sacrosanct in order to prevent it from defilement (Rozin *et al.*, 1999).

To return to moral illusions. According to Haidt and his colleague Paul Rozin transgressing each of these spheres of morality automatically triggers its own distinct emotional response without first passing through conscious reasoning processes. Although we frequently think of morality as being due to conscious deliberation, quite often this doesn't seem to be the case. This is the reason that people *feel* that a moral transgression has occurred but cannot consciously justify their response. Recent research using fMRI scans supports the role of emotions in moral decision making (Greene and Haidt, 2002; Greene *et al.*, 2001; Greene *et al.*, 2004). These emotional responses differ depending upon the particular realm of morality that has been violated. Transgressions of autonomy (such as cheating) invoke anger; transgressions of community invoke contempt and transgressions of divinity (which is concerned with purity) invoke disgust, which can be thought of as an emotion that guards against contamination. Positive emotions too are associated with morality. Consider the esteem in which one holds altruists, or the reverence inspired by martyrs who commit the ultimate sacrifice for the beliefs of the in-group.

Morality might therefore be a system that protects the individual's sense of fairness, hierarchy and purity and enables us to thrive within our groups and engage in reciprocal altruism (see chapter 8). This research is still very much in its early stages, but if it is correct it shows how morality is rather more than a rational cognitive process and is intimately related to emotional responses to particular transgressions.

The origins of morality

If morality is essential for group living it should emerge early in life as children are as much social animals as adults; certainly children of three years of age have some concept of right and wrong (Yuill, 1984). There is also some evidence that morality might reveal its origins in infancy. Research suggests that babies find happy facial expressions pleasurable and pained facial expressions stressful (the babies were attached to instruments that measure stress levels) (Hoffman, 1978; Zahn-Waxler and Radke-Yarrow, 1982; Radke-Yarrow and Zahn-Waxler, 1986). Hoffman (1982) argues that originally morals might be selfish, pained faces trigger an 'empathic distress' response in a baby who then acts to reduce their stress by acting to alleviate the person's pain. This simple mechanism means that infants are able to engage in apparently prosocial behaviour before they are able to distinguish between 'self' and 'other'.

Although this research might explain certain moral universals, it does not explain why morals vary from culture to culture. For instance, the cow which is widely consumed in the West is sacred in the Hindu religion. How can we explain such variability of moral values?

Why are morals so variable?

Although it has been suggested that a moral sense might be part of human nature (see above) the specific nature of moral values varies from person to person and from culture to culture (apart from a few universals such as murder and rape: see Brown, 1991 and chapter 14). Why might this be? If morals are so useful (and we must assume that they are) why didn't natural selection just wire in strong moral sentiments?

One answer has been provided by evolutionist Robert Wright (1994), who draws on William Hamilton's explanation of why reciprocal altruism seems to vary so much in the population. Wright suggests that perhaps the optimal moral strategy is contingent upon the particular historical, cultural and social context in which the individual finds him or herself. As we saw in our discussion on life history theory, when the optimal strategy is contingent, hard wiring makes little sense. If, for instance, you are born with a very strong moral sentiment, you might find yourself outcompeted by conspecifics who are prepared to cheat, steal and lie. On the other hand, if you were to be born with few moral sentiments, you might be ostracised by a community of high-moralists. In the same way that it might pay to adopt a 'wait and see' approach to reproductive strategy, the same might apply to morality (we return to this general principle in chapter 13).

This is an ultimate reason why morals vary from culture to culture. Haidt and Joseph (2004) present a proximate one. They are concerned to address the problem of why certain morals seem to be universal (anger at being cheated, loyalty to your group, compassion towards the suffering) yet the form of some of these varies from one culture to another. They propose that there are five moral domains that are innate, and that these can be modified by cultural learning. These domains are a kind of mental module (see chapter 1), although they see modules as being rather more flexible entities than some (e.g. Tooby and Cosmides, 1997). They subscribe to a version of modularity proposed by Dan Sperber called **teeming modularity** in which modules can be modified by environmental input, can spawn other modules and are, to some extent, under conscious control.

Table 6.4 shows a list of these domains with their characteristics. The first row lists the possible adaptive challenge that drove the evolution of the particular moral domain. The second and third rows relate to the nature of the triggers to that module. The **proper domain** (see box 9.3) are the triggers that the module was designed (by natural selection) to respond to, the **actual domain** are the things that trigger the module by virtue of it resembling the proper trigger in some significant way. A fly landing in a spider's web can trigger the spider out of its hiding place with the goal to

Box 6.4 Theory of mind and morality

Behaving in a moral way and making decisions about the morality of the behaviour of others is not simply a matter of slavishly following rules. Frequently we are required to make decisions that have moral implications, even if it is simply a matter of whether you should jump a queue at the supermarket or pocket a small sum of money that is lying on the floor in a cafeteria. Confronted with such situations we can not always draw upon explicit rules; we make decisions based upon whether someone would suffer and how much. For instance we might be more likely to keep money we found in an expensive restaurant than if it was in a soup kitchen because we might think that in the first instance the person who lost the money would be less likely to miss it. Judging how people might feel as a result of our actions requires a fully operational theory of mind (see chapter 5) as we need to imagine how someone might feel as a result of our actions. Consistent with this interpretation we find that children start to appreciate the nature of morality around four years of age, around the time that theory of mind starts to manifest itself in an adult-like form (Yuill, 1984).

One question that might be prompted by discussion of theory of mind is whether sufferers of autism show deficits in moral reasoning ability. So far there has not been a great deal of research on this issue, but it is likely that sufferers of autism find moral reasoning tasks such as that above demanding. The experiences of Temple Grandin might be instructive here. Temple Grandin is a high-functioning autistic individual who has published widely in her career as an academic in the department of animal sciences at Colorado State University. Despite her intellectual achievements she admits that she finds the social world something of a mystery. She relates how she developed a set of explicit rules to help her in her interactions with others, some of them were concerned with morality, others are concerned with other forms of social transgression (from www.autism.org).

- *Really bad things* Examples: murder, arson, stealing, lying in court under oath, injuring or hitting other people. All cultures have prohibitions against really bad things because an orderly civilised society cannot function if people are robbing and killing each other.
- *Courtesy rules* Examples: not cutting in on a line at the movie theatre or airport, table manners, saying 'thank you' and keeping oneself clean. These things are important because they make the other people around you more comfortable. I don't like it when somebody else has sloppy table manners so I try to have decent table manners. It annoys me if somebody cuts in front of me in a line so I do not do this to other people.
- *Illegal but not bad* Examples: slight speeding on the freeway and illegal parking. However, parking in a handicapped zone would be worse because it would violate the courtesy rules.

> - *Sins of the systems (SOS)* Examples: smoking pot and being thrown in jail for ten years and sexual misbehaviour. SOSs are things where the penalty is so severe that it defies all logic. Sometimes the penalty for sexual misbehaviour is worse than killing somebody. Rules governing sexual behaviour are so emotionally based that I do not dare discuss the subject for fear of committing an SOS. An SOS in one society may be acceptable behaviour in another; whereas rules 1, 2, 3 tend be more uniform between different cultures.

eat the fly (proper domain), but inedible seeds or prodding fingers can elicit the same response (actual domain). Triggers from the actual domain need not be adaptive. To take harm–care, Haidt and Joseph suggest that there is a real evolutionary benefit to responding with compassion to our own offspring (see chapter 7) but other stimuli (baby seals, other people's offspring) resemble our own offspring sufficiently to trigger the module. Note that there is no real adaptive value to feeling compassion for seals (it is arguable if there is adaptive value in feeling compassion for the offspring of others). These five basic modules can therefore be modified by cultural learning. Morals are similar from culture to culture because we all share the same basic modules, they vary because culture varies and pushes the module in different directions. Take purity. Some cultures proscribe the eating of certain foodstuffs, whereas other cultures might proscribe racism. Both of these proscriptions hook in to the purity/sanctity module giving rise to a feeling of disgust if the idea of eating meat or racism is entertained.

These are early days for this kind of research, and this represents work in progress. Some might argue for rather more than five innate morality modules, and some might wonder why emotions and behaviours designed to protect marital fidelity are not seen as adaptive (a function of it being listed in the actual, rather than the proper, domain). The partnership involved in rearing children and the potential implications for inclusive fitness if that partnership fails seem at least as important as someone cheating you out of some food.

Universal morality?

A similar approach to that taken by Haidt is that of primatologist and psychologist Marc Hauser and co-workers (Hauser *et al.*, 2007). They presented participants with scenarios describing particular moral dilemmas involving a runaway train. For example, is it permissible to guide a runaway train heading towards six people round a branch line on which one person is standing? Box 6.5 shows the stimuli, it might be worth trying out the experiment yourself before reading further. The data show that people will generally opt to kill one person if it saves five in the case of Denise (see box 6.5) but are much more reluctant in the case of Frank. What's the difference?

Table 6.4 A proposed list of five moral 'domains' taken from Haidt and Joseph (2004)

	Harm–care	Fairness–reciprocity	In-group–loyalty	Authority–respect	Purity–sanctity
Adaptive challenge	Protect and care for young, vulnerable, or injured kin	Reap benefits of dyadic cooperation with non-kin	Reap benefits of group cooperation	Negotiate hierarchy, defer selectively	Avoid microbes and parasites
Proper domain (adaptive triggers)	Suffering, distress, or threat to one's kin	Cheating, cooperation, deception	Threat or challenge to group	Signs of dominance and submission	Waste products, diseased people
Actual domain (the set of all triggers)	Baby seals, cartoon characters	Marital fidelity, broken vending machines	Sports teams one roots for	Bosses, respected professionals	Taboo ideas (communism, racism)
Characteristic emotions	Compassion	Anger, gratitude, guilt	Group pride, belongingness; rage at traitors	Respect, fear	Disgust
Relevant virtues [and vices]	Caring, kindness, [cruelty]	Fairness, justice, honesty, trustworthiness [dishonesty]	Loyalty, patriotism, self-sacrifice [treason, cowardice]	Obedience, deference [disobedience, uppitiness]	Temperance, chastity, piety, cleanliness [lust, intemperance]

Box 6.5 Moral reasoning

The stimuli below were presented to participants as part of the experiment conducted by Hauser *et al.* (2007). You might find it instructive to try the questions out yourself. The responses of participants are at the bottom of this box.

Picture	Description

Denise is a passenger on a train whose driver has fainted. On the main track ahead are 5 people. The main track has a side track leading off to the left, and Denise can turn the train onto it. There is 1 person on the left hand track. Denise can turn the train, killing the 1; or she can refrain from turning the train, letting the 5 die.

  Is it morally permissible for Frank to shove the man?

Frank is on a footbridge over the train tracks. He sees a train approaching the bridge out of control. There are 5 people on the track. Frank knows that the only way to stop the train is to drop a heavy weight into its path. But the only available, sufficiently heavy weight is 1 large man, also watching the train from the footbridge. Frank can shove the 1 man onto the track in the path of the train, killing him; or he can refrain from doing this, letting the 5 die.

  Is it morally permissible for Frank to shove the man?

Ned is walking near the train tracks when he notices a train approaching out of control. Up ahead on the track are 5 people. Ned is standing next to a switch, which he can throw to turn the train onto a side track. There is a heavy object on the side track. If the train hits the object, the object will slow the train down, giving the men time to escape. The heavy object is 1 man, standing on the side track. Ned can throw the switch, preventing the train from killing the 5 people, but killing the 1 man. Or he can refrain from doing this, letting the 5 die.

  Is it morally permissible for Frank to shove the man?

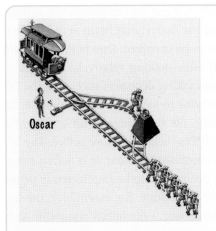

Oscar is walking near the train tracks when he notices a train approaching out of control. Up ahead on the track are 5 people. Oscar is standing next to a switch, which he can throw to turn the train onto a side track. There is a heavy object on the side track. If the train hits the object, the object will slow the train down, giving the 5 people time to escape. There is 1 man standing on the side track in front of the heavy object. Oscar can throw the switch, preventing the train from killing the 5 people, but killing the 1 man. Or he can refrain from doing this, letting the five die.

Is it morally permissible for Frank to shove the man?

Percentage of participants (N=5,000) judging that it was morally permissible to shove the man in each of the stories: Denise = 85%, Frank = 12%, Ned = 56%, Oscar = 72%

First consider the difference between Oscar and Ned; the two scenarios are very similar but people are generally more accepting of Oscar's scenario (where the man is behind a heavy weight but nonetheless dies) than Ned's (where there is no weight, just the man). Rather like the Haidt study mentioned above, people can see that there is *some* difference between the stories of Ned and Oscar but they can't articulate why. Hauser uses this as evidence for the fact that moral judgements are not necessarily (or even commonly) based on conscious reasoning. People act as if they are following a rule but they do not know what it is. The rule is known as *the principle of double effect* which states that it is permissible to do someone harm for the greater good (e.g. kill one to save five) but only if that harm is as a by product of the action not a means in itself. Two other rules seem to suggest why so few people thought that Frank's action of pushing the fat man off the bridge was acceptable. In addition to the principle of double effect it also seems that people judge situations where a new threat is introduced (pushing the man) more harshly than situations where an existing threat is being redirected (the runaway train). Additionally, people are less happy with creating a threat by direct personal means (e.g. physical contact with the individual) rather than at a distance. Consider the following scenario:

Five people are dying in hospital each as a result of a different organ failing (kidneys, liver, etc.). In the waiting room is a healthy man with fully functioning organs. Is it therefore permissible to use this healthy man's organs to save five?

Most people are not only adamant that this is most definitely *not* morally permissible, they tend to find the idea outrageous because all three principles (double effect, new threat and personal contact) apply.

The cognitive neuroscientist Josh Greene has explored the differences between these moral decisions by examining the underlying brain activity. He has found evidence that two brain systems seem to be involved. One is the dorsolateral prefrontal cortex (DLPC) which is associated with making relatively dispassionate utilitarian decisions. This is largely involved in making decisions such as in the Denise dilemma, where most people are happy to kill one to save five. In the more emotive dilemmas such as Frank's (pushing the fat man off the bridge) a different brain region – the ventromedial prefrontal cortex (VMPC) – becomes more active. The VMPC is associated with decisions that have high emotional content. It is active, for example, when a desirable reward is offered and it seems also to be implicated in people's reluctance to sanction pushing the fat man off the bridge. So, essentially, the hypothesis goes, that presentation of one of the above moral dilemmas results in a shouting match between the dispassionate, utilitarian DLPC and the emotionally charged VMPC and which shouts the loudest determines which course of action the person considers morally acceptable (Greene and Haidt, 2002).

Further evidence of the involvement of these two brain regions is presented in a study by Koenigs et al. (2007). They found that people with damage to the VMPC tend to make more utilitarian decisions (e.g. more likely to assent to the fat man being pushed off the bridge) presumably because damage to the VMPC enables the DLPC to win the shouting match. Furthermore, it appears that the VMPC may also be functioning abnormally in people with psychopathy (Finger et al., 2008) and that prisoners diagnosed with low-anxiety psychopathy are more likely to make utilitarian judgements (Koenigs et al., 2012).

Are moral sentiments such as the above universal? In the aforementioned study Hauser found no effect of sex, religion or ethnicity which suggests that it might be. Perhaps more convincingly, Hauser gave similar dilemmas to the ones above (with locally relevant changes involving crocodiles and canoes) to the Kuna, a tribe in Central America that has little contact with the Western world, and found that they appear to have the same intuitions.

Hauser's approach is rather different to that of Haidt, although like Haidt he stresses that much of moral reasoning is intuitive and emotional he also proposes that conscious deliberation plays a role too. In terms of moral development, Hauser makes a comparison between morality and Chomsky's principles and parameters theory of language development (see chapter 10) in which innate moral principles guide the acquisition of moral values (Hauser et al., 2007). Cultural variability in morals can be explained by the different demands placed on the individual by different culture, whereas cultural commonalities exist because we all share the same innate moral principles.

It can be seen that there are similarities with the approaches of Haidt and Hauser, both emphasise the role of innate moral intuitions (domains in Haidt's terminology, principles in Hauser's) that are modified by culture and learning. Hauser sees this process of learning as involving parameter setting as is the case of Chomsky's theory of language (again see chapter 10) whereas Haidt is less clear about the specific mechanisms involved. In terms of specifics, fitting Hauser's work dilemmas into Haidt's scheme shown in table 6.4 is difficult, although it is possible that Hauser's judgements reside in the moral domain of suffering. Further research needs to be conducted to determine to what extent suffering involves Hauser's three principles outlined above. Despite these differences, it is becoming increasingly clear that morality rather than being a uniquely human invention – something that separates us from other animals – is an essential requirement of living in groups and very probably part of our biological endowment. It seems that morality is part and parcel of human nature rather than being something that merely enables us to rise above it.

Summary

- A life history theory of development claims that, from an early age, children are monitoring their environment and making decisions about their future reproductive value. Based on their assessment of the environmental conditions they can choose to maximise current reproductive success or future reproductive success.
- Attachment theory (Bowlby, 1969) claims that early attachments (relationships with caregivers, usually the mother) can have a substantial effect on subsequent personality and behaviour. Central to this theory is that a child forms a 'working model' of the self and relationships that is used to guide subsequent behaviour. Secure working models generally lead to more satisfactory and stable relationships in later life than insecure ones. Ainsworth proposed there are three attachment styles, secure (Type B), insecure-avoidant (Type A), insecure-anxious/resistant (Type C). A large amount of evidence suggests that individuals exhibiting insecure attachment styles will generally suffer more psychological and relationship problems later in life.
- Life history theory applied to attachment theory suggests that rather than insecure attachments being dysfunctional (as was often thought) they might be considered adaptations. In the ancestral environment, insecure attachments might have led to children adopting strategies that were designed to maximise their fitness. Chisholm's theory proposes that one factor that children are monitoring is the amount of risk and uncertainty in the environment. If the level of risk is low, they will tend to adopt a strategy that maximises future reproductive value, if it is high they will attempt to maximise current reproductive value.
- There are reliable sex differences in personality and behaviour, many of which seem to emerge at an early age. In particular, females are more nurturing than males and males more likely to take risks than females. Evolutionary theory explains such differences by proposing that they are the result of the two sexes being under different constraints with respect to reproduction. Males need to compete with each

other for a sexual partner and are therefore under pressure to take risks, whereas females are more likely to be the ones left rearing children and are therefore under more pressure to nurture. Although there is evidence that these personality differences have innate bases, learning seems to play a role as well.

- In contrast to many developmentalists (including those applying life history theory to development) Harris (1995; 1998) argues that the parental environment is of little consequence in its effects on children's development. Her theory, group socialisation theory, suggests that the principal source of environmental influence is from the peer group. Group socialisation theory is controversial; many agree that peer groups are important, but remain unconvinced of the unimportance of parental influence.

- Morality is often thought of as something separate from human nature, but recent theories suggest that it is an essential requirement for a species that lives in groups of non-kin. Morality is not merely a cognitive judgement or rule following, but is tied to strong emotions such as anger, disgust, shame, pride and reverence.

- Some recent theories of morality argue that there is an innate component to the basic judgements of good and bad. Although there may be some morals that are universal (e.g. those that prohibit murder) the majority appear to be learned. Wright has explained this by proposing that when the environment is uncertain it makes sense to build flexibility into the system rather than hard-wiring particular moral values.

Questions

1. To what extent do you think parents and peers influence children's development? Think of examples of influences that your parents might have had on you, and also influences that might have come from your peers.

2. Try and think of decisions that you (or others) might have made that have had a moral dimension. Do these fit into Haidt's five domains of morality outlined in table 6.4? If not how might you characterise these? Does Haidt's framework need to be extended, if so how?

3. To what extent are environmental risk factors of early sexual behaviour merely triggers to adaptive developmental trajectories rather than direct causes? How does this differ from the way that it has traditionally been thought of? Assuming that this is true, how might this affect public policy and the way that such individuals are viewed?

4. Between and within species reproductive strategies can be explained by the extent to which an individual is maximising current or future fitness (the C–F continuum). How does this relate to research and theory of sexual reproduction explained in chapter 3 such as the red queen hypothesis?

FURTHER READING

Harris, J. R. (2009). *The Nurture Assumption: Why Children Turn Out the Way They Do.* (Revised edition) New York: Simon and Schuster. A still controversial book that unleashed group socialisation theory to a general (as opposed to technical) readership. This version is revised with additional material.

Hauser, M. (2006). *Moral Minds.* New York: Springer. Introduction into recent research on evolution and morality.

Pinker, S. (2002). *The Blank Slate: The Modern Denial of Human Nature.* London: Allen Lane. The chapter on children is a lucid discussion of many of the themes discussed here.

Wright, R. (1994). *The Moral Animal.* London: Abacus. A readable introduction to evolutionary psychology, with a focus on the evolution of moral sentiments.

7

The evolutionary psychology of social behaviour – kin relationships and conflict

KEY CONCEPTS

inclusive fitness • direct and indirect fitness • coefficient of relatedness • kin altruism • parental investment • parent–offspring conflict • K- and r-selection • parental manipulation

To many people human behaviour is social behaviour. Linguistic communication is meaningless unless used between at least two people; sex by definition involves more than one person (usually, although not invariably, two); child rearing and sibling relationships are clearly social and most working practices occur in groups. Humans do engage in some solitary activities – reading a book or taking a bath, for example, are not normally social events. But even by primate standards, we are an extremely socially integrated species. So it's not surprising that some evolutionary theorists have suggested that evolutionary psychology may have the greatest impact on social psychology (Neuberg *et al.*, 2010; Wilson, 2012). Social behaviour can broadly be divided into pro- and antisocial patterns of response. Both can be found frequently in interactions that involve kin. Social scientists have long sought to explain why such love–hate relationships exist in families. Evolutionary psychologists think they have the answer – to them it's all about evolved psychological mechanisms that would have aided inclusive fitness during the EEA.

Social psychology and evolutionary theory

Social psychology is a well-developed area of psychological enquiry. During the twentieth century, social psychologists developed theories to account for, among other things, group conformity, in- and out-group stereotyping, intergroup aggression, social concept and attitude formation (Hewstone *et al.*, 2012). Moreover, it has been very successful in testing these theories in both the lab and field. So what can the evolutionary approach bring to improve our understanding of human social behaviour?

At the least, the evolutionary approach can provide an interesting new perspective, which might help to derive new models and suggest new ways of testing them; at best, it might radically alter the very way that we consider human behaviour. Despite its successes at explaining various aspects of human social behaviour, by taking a largely SSSM stance (see chapter 1), conventional social psychology has yet to develop a well-accepted general theory which connects its disparate findings. In the words of two American evolutionary psychologists, Jeffry Simpson and Douglas Kenrick, social psychology has developed a series of **minitheories** but lacks an overarching theory that can bring these together (Kenrick and Simpson, 1997). By adding the ultimate level of explanation to the fabric of social psychology, the evolutionary approach may provide the framework on which the various findings of the field might be woven together. That is, it might provide a **metatheory**. Evolutionary psychologists consider that this will be achievable through an integration of evolutionary theories which pertain to social behaviour (Archer, 1996; Wilson, 2012). We can identify five such theories (Buss, 1999). The first of these is the theory of sexual selection, which we dealt with in chapters 3 and 4 and may be traced back to Darwin himself (1871). Of the remaining four theories, three are attributable to Robert Trivers and one to William Hamilton:

- Kin altruism/inclusive fitness (Hamilton, 1964a, b)
- Parental investment (Trivers, 1972)
- Parent–offspring conflict (Trivers, 1974)
- Reciprocal altruism (Trivers, 1971)

In this chapter we consider the first three theories in relation to social behaviour (Trivers's reciprocal altruism is considered in the next chapter).

Charity begins at home – inclusive fitness theory and kin altruism

Social psychologists generally define altruism as selfless behaviour conducted on behalf of others without regard for one's own self-interest (Bierhoff, 1996; Hewstone *et al.*, 2012 – see box 7.1). Note that such definitions include intentionality on the part of the altruist. In contrast, evolutionists define altruism purely in terms of the act performed, not the intention behind it. In this way ethologists have no problem in discussing examples of apparent altruism in animals.

Table 7.1 lists a number of well-documented acts of apparent altruism in the animal kingdom. In all of these cases, it is now known that the individual who provides a benefit to others does so to its relatives. Note that in table 7.1, r, which may vary from 0 to 1, equals the proportion of genes shared between two relatives by common

Table 7.1 Documented acts of apparent altruism in the animal kingdom

Species	Beneficial act	Relationship to altruist and proposed reason for altruistic act	Source (example)
Ants (many species)	Soldier caste ants do not breed themselves but defend the colony with their lives. Likewise worker caste ants do not breed but care for their younger siblings.	Soldier (and worker) castes are sterile and are more closely related to their sisters ($r = 0.75$) than they would be to offspring ($r = 0.50$) they produced themselves	Wilson (1975)
Wild dogs of Africa	Adult male and female dogs bring back meat from kills and regurgitate to other members of the pack	All dogs in pack are closely related and thereby feed young relatives and older infirm ones	Schaller (1972)
Florida scrub jays	Individual males help feed and defend nestlings which are not their own	Scrub jays feed their younger siblings ($r = 0.50$). It is difficult to eke out a living on the harsh scrub land – so helpers at the nest at least ensure that some of their younger relatives survive	Woolfenden and Fitzpatrick (1984)
Dwarf mongooses	Female dwarf mongooses suckle the young of other females	Dwarf mongooses live in closely related group and nurse each other's offspring	Rood (1986)
Naked mole rats	Mature females help to raise the young of the nest's 'queen' rather than breed themselves	Colony members are highly inbred (mean $r = 0.81$). Younger females are rendered temporarily sterile by pheromones released by the 'queen'; may be playing a 'waiting game' whereby they will have a chance to breed when she dies	Sherman *et al.* (1991)

descent (full siblings, for example, share 0.5 of their genes and identical twins share 1.0).

As we saw in chapter 2, why acts of self-sacrifice or 'altruism' such as those outlined in table 7.1 occur at all has long been an area of debate among evolutionists. Since the 1960s, however, there has been a growing consensus as to why individuals of social species frequently appear to act altruistically. Most recorded examples of self-sacrificing behaviour involve giving aid to relatives with which the altruist shares a varying proportion of their genes (note that this is true of all of the examples in table 7.1).

In Hamilton's terminology we can expect 'actors' to show self-sacrificing behaviour for 'recipients' (relatives) when the cost to the actor is less than the benefit to the

Figure 7.1 A Florida scrub jay

recipient. This has become known as 'Hamilton's rule' and can be reduced to this simple formula:

$$c < rb$$

Here c is the cost to the actor, r is the coefficient of relatedness between the actor and the recipient and b is the benefit to the recipient. Ultimately, these costs and benefits are measured in terms of inclusive fitness.

Hamilton introduced the notion of kin altruism as an explanation of self-sacrificing behaviour, and today we look at animals as inclusive fitness maximisers rather than simply as individual fitness maximisers (see chapter 2). Modern-day evolutionists consider the genes which are passed on to the next generation via an individual's own offspring as their **direct fitness** and those which are passed on via aid to other kin as their **indirect fitness**.

This means that if a human being rears two children and helps other (non-descendant) kin then they are boosting both their direct and indirect fitness. For worker ants and most naked mole rats, however, the only way they may be able to raise their fitness will be indirectly through providing care for younger kin which are not their offspring. Taken together direct and indirect fitness equal inclusive fitness. In this way Hamilton argued that we can predict that animals are likely to provide care for others who share genes with them by common descent and that the amount

Box 7.1 **Kindness to relatives – is it altruism?**

Altruism stinks of fallacy (Catatonia, 1998)

If most cases of altruism involve acts between relatives so that those involved are helping copies of their own genes to be passed on indirectly, then this raises a rather large question – is such behaviour really altruistic? To most social psychologists altruism is concerned with a willingness to help others at a cost to oneself (Bierhoff, 1996; Hewstone *et al.*, 2012). If we consider self-sacrificing behaviour from a traditional human individual perspective then we can certainly term beneficial acts to others (be they relatives or not) as 'altruism'. You may recall that this level of explanation is known as proximate causation and that this is the normal level of causation as used by social scientists. Social scientists interested in evolutionary explanations, however, also use ultimate causation, which may be defined as 'causation on a generational time scale' (Daly and Wilson, 1983; see also chapter 1). Thus ultimate causation is concerned with the likelihood of copies of genes being passed on. Clearly, acts that aid copies of shared genes in relatives are ultimately selfish. Thus, whether we consider an act as altruistic or not depends on whether we are discussing it at a proximate or an ultimate level of causation. A beneficial act towards a relative is altruistic when considered at an individual (i.e. proximate) level, but when using a gene-focused level of explanation (i.e. ultimate) then the very same act may be considered as selfish!

of care given will increase as does the proportion of these genes shared. But why did Hamilton add 'by common descent' to his explanation of kin altruism? Members of a population may share the majority of their genes without being closely related. Siblings may share 99 per cent of their genes with each other and with other members of their species. They will, however, share only 50 per cent on average from their common parentage (Dickins, 2011). In this way 'r' (the coefficient of relatedness – see chapter 2) can be thought of as the probability that an allele (gene) shared by two individuals is 'descended from the same ancestral gene in a recent common relative' (McFarland, 1999). If an individual shows altruism to those that share the same gene by common descent, rather than those that share the gene simply by being members of the same population, it is the former strategy that evolutionists consider will be favoured by natural selection. John Maynard Smith coined the term **kin selection** for this part of natural selection that promotes the favouring of relatives. Although Hamilton is rightly credited with developing inclusive fitness theory, it is historically interesting to note that the eminent evolutionary biologist J. B. S. Haldane had come close to developing this theory during the 1930s when he scrawled the idea on the back of a beer mat in a London pub that he would risk his life for at least an identical twin or eight cousins. Although Haldane later went on to briefly outline this idea in the mid 1950s (Haldane, 1955) he did not develop it, and evolutionists had to wait another decade before Hamilton's work changed the course of evolutionary thinking.

Today, evolutionists interested in behaviour tend to look at animals as nepotistic strategists rather than individual strategists. In the words of ethologist John Alcock, 'Hamilton's explanation for altruism rests on the premise that the unconscious goal of reproduction, from an evolutionary perspective, is to propagate one's distinctive alleles' (Alcock, 2005, p. 564). Note that Alcock is making it explicit that ethologists do not consider it necessary for animals to be in any way conscious of their actions towards relatives. It is sufficient merely that they act appropriately. Under natural conditions it is nearly always immature animals which are in greater need of aid than their mature relatives. For this reason we can expect the giving of aid to younger, more vulnerable individuals by their older or less vulnerable relatives to be widespread in the animal kingdom. All of the examples given in table 7.1 would certainly fit this prediction.

Can kin altruism explain human acts of self-sacrifice?

For most social scientists the idea that animals help their kin in the interests of shared genes by common descent is not problematic. However, applying the same reasoning to our own species has led to a number of quite vociferous debates. On one side of the debate a number of social scientists have continually argued that, due to our intelligence and complex culture, our self-sacrificing behaviour is free from genetic influence (Sahlins, 1976; Harris, 1979; Bierhoff and Rohmann, 2004). On the other side, sociobiologists and, more recently, evolutionary psychologists have proposed that any genetically influenced responses which habitually lowered inclusive fitness, such as laying down one's life for complete strangers, would be likely to be removed from the population long ago (Wilson, 1975; Brown, 1991; Sigmund and Hauert, 2002). This does not mean that humans continually act to increase their inclusive fitness but that we have developed the type of mind which tends to do things that aided inclusive fitness in our past and may frequently do so today (see later). A major question facing evolutionary psychologists is: how well does Hamilton's reasoning fit in with current human behaviour?

Many of the early studies of kin altruism involved social animals such as those described in table 7.1. In recent years, however, despite the misgivings of some social scientists, a number of evolutionary psychologists have applied this model to examples of human social behaviour where individual actions may have a bearing on the survival of others. During the first Gulf War of 1990, for example, Shavit *et al.* (1994) studied altruistic behaviour with regard to air raids in Israel. They found that individuals were more likely to share air raid shelters with relatives and to call up kin to see whether help was needed. In contrast, when it came to lesser forms of aid such as giving advice about preparing for air raids, individuals were more likely to aid friends than relatives. Such a finding suggests that people may rely more on friends for companionship but, when it comes to life-threatening circumstances, charity really does begin at home (Shavit *et al.*, 1994; Badcock, 2000).

As well as making use of naturalistic observations psychologists have also begun to use social–psychological rating scales to test Hamilton's kin selection theory in humans. Burnstein *et al.* (1994), for example, asked participants to make hypothetical decisions with regard to giving aid either to relatives or to non-relatives under either life and death conditions or where a small favour was involved. In a series of such studies, Burnstein *et al.* manipulated a number of characteristics of the hypothetical recipients such as sex, health, wealth and level of kinship. Over all of these studies participants' decisions followed precisely the predictions made by Hamilton's inclusive fitness theory. Not only did they favour relatives over non-relatives but also their favouritism towards relatives was stronger under life and death conditions and younger, healthier relatives were particularly favoured. Interestingly in other studies of hypothetical decisions to give aid to friends or relatives Stewart-Williams (2007) found that for low-cost aid, friends were given as much aid as kin but that when this shifted to high-cost aid, kin were favoured and the closer the kin relationship, the greater the aid provided (see also Roberts and Dunbar, 2011).

Adoption and fractions – Sahlins's criticisms of kin altruism

Despite these positive findings some acts of human kindness appear to run counter to Hamilton's notion of a species of nepotistic strategists. Take adoption. If humans are designed to aid relatives then why is it that we sometimes choose to look after individuals other than our own children and even treat them as we would our own? Adoption practices have been used by critics of the evolutionary approach to human behaviour as an example of behaviour patterns that appear to run counter to inclusive fitness theory. One such critic, anthropologist Marshal Sahlins, suggested in his influential book *The Use and Abuse of Biology* (1976) that Hamilton's notion of kin altruism is fundamentally flawed. Sahlins made two main criticisms. First, he suggested that, because most hunter-gatherer cultures have not invented the fraction, then they are incapable of calculating 'r' and hence would be unable to act appropriately towards relatives. And second, he suggested that adoption practices of hunter-gatherer societies do not reflect patterns that kin altruism theory would predict. In particular, Sahlins claimed that the adoption practices of the islanders of the central Pacific (Oceania) are quite arbitrary rather than occurring to aid relatives. How might evolutionists deal with such claims? The first of these criticisms demonstrates a misunderstanding of how evolutionists use the notion of kin altruism.

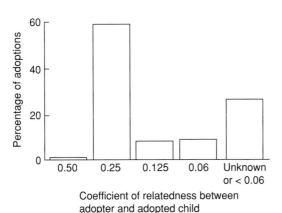

Figure 7.2 Coefficient of relatedness between adopted children and their adopters, based on eleven Oceanic societies studied by Silk (1980; 1990)

Sahlins is a distinguished social anthropologist. Unfortunately, however, his argument showed a poor understanding of the proposed relationship between natural selection and behaviour. It is not necessary for an organism to have insight into either how or why it does anything. It is merely sufficient that it generally behaves in ways that are likely to increase its inclusive fitness – and nothing more. Humans do not require an understanding of fractions in order to give aid to their relatives. As is the case for behaviour in general, the argument that people frequently favour relatives is one that is considered to work via heuristics (rules of thumb – see chapter 9) rather than via a detailed analysis of how and why certain acts should be performed. A logical extension of Sahlins's argument would have dam-building beavers understanding the principles of civil engineering and spiders understanding trigonometry in order to construct their webs! Richard Dawkins makes much the same point in his withering attack on *The Use and Abuse of Biology* in the second edition of his book *The Selfish Gene* (Dawkins, 1989). Today this argument is known as 'Sahlins's fallacy' (Workman, 2014).

While Sahlins's first criticism may be dismissed quite easily as a fallacy, his second must be taken more seriously. In Oceania around 30 per cent of children are adopted. If such adoptions really do occur arbitrarily then this would throw serious doubt on the use of kin altruism as an explanation for adoption in these societies. One anthropologist who has been more sympathetic to the evolutionary approach, Joan Silk, decided to undertake a formal analysis of the relationship between adopters and adoptees. Using samples from eleven different Oceanic cultures, Silk uncovered support for the kin altruism argument, demonstrating that the majority of adoptees were cared for by the genetic equivalents of aunts, uncles and cousins (Silk, 1980; 1990 – see figure 7.2).

In contrast to Sahlins's claim, in Oceania the coefficient of relatedness typically reported between adopters and adoptees actually provides support for a kin altruism hypothesis.

Adoption in the West today – all you need is love

In Western society today, where the state controls adoption, most examples of this practice occur between unrelated individuals. Does this suggest that kin altruism has been jettisoned from this process in the industrialised countries? In a sense it does. In terms of giving aid to non-relatives and expecting no reward from such adoptees then we must accept that this constitutes altruism and that such behaviour is currently unrelated to inclusive fitness. Such a finding, however, should not be taken as evidence that our adoption practices are completely unrelated to the evolutionary pressures that our ancestors faced. You may recall that one of the central tenets of evolutionary psychology is that, rather than expecting all current behavioural practices to increase inclusive fitness, selective processes have led to the development of a mind which in the ancient past would generally have done so. During our own ancient past (the environment of evolutionary adaptedness or EEA) it may have made adaptive sense to adopt young orphaned individuals since, as members of your small tribe, they would most probably have been relatives of some degree (Silk, 1980; Alcock, 2009). This means that today we may be left with the legacy of such urges even though they may no longer be appropriate (in an evolutionary sense). Some evolutionary psychologists have argued that the sort of mind which tends to feel sympathetic towards helpless youngsters, and develop a desire to give aid to them, is one which has arisen from a history of kin-selected altruism (Alcock, 2009). We saw in chapter 3 how an evolutionary approach to childrearing might help to explain the existence of romantic love between men and women. Steven Pinker has suggested that kin altruism may also help to explain love of family members.

The essence of love is feeling pleasure in another's well-being and pain in its harm. These feelings motivate acts that benefit the loved one, like nurturing, feeding and protecting. (1997, p. 400)

Strong feelings of pleasure derived from nurturing younger, more helpless, individuals might be with us today because they generally aided our inclusive fitness in the ancient past in much the same way that a romantic attachment would have. Perhaps Lennon and McCartney (1967) were right when they said, 'All you need is love' – but perhaps not for quite the reason they intended.

Today a number of evolutionary psychologists consider that kin altruism may have played a major role in moulding the social behaviour of many animal species including our own. It is important to realise, however, that animals do not run around searching out more and more distant relatives in order to give them smaller and smaller slices of their investment pie. In most cases parents put effort into raising offspring because these are not only the ones with which they share a large proportion of their genes but also the most likely to be at the most appropriate stage in their life cycle.

Box 7.2 **How do animals recognise kin?**

If we and other species do channel resources towards our relatives then this surely suggests that many species must be able to recognise just who their relatives are?* How are they able to do this? As far as our own species is concerned it is clear that all cultures are fascinated to know who they are related to and to what degree (Brown, 1991). Language certainly allows humans to pass on such information. But how might other species recognise kin? Since the advent of the modern-day evolutionary/functional approach during the 1970s ethologists have developed and tested a number of proposed mechanisms for kin recognition. Scottish ethologist Peter Slater (1994) suggests there are four possible mechanisms that might allow for kin recognition:

(1) **Context-based discrimination**. Here recognition is based on location. Many rodents and birds, for example, feed offspring that live in a particular nest or burrow.
(2) **Discrimination based on familiarity**. Here 'signatures' (sensory cues) are used for identification which are thought to be learned during development. American toad tadpoles, for example, will associate with other tadpoles that developed in the same clump of spawn and are therefore likely to be siblings.
(3) **Phenotype matching**. In this case, unlike the above category, it is not necessary for individuals to have shared experiences but rather that an individual learns about its own or its close relatives' characteristics and then uses such information to determine whether a novel individual also has a similar signature. Experimental evidence suggests that mice are certainly able to discriminate between unfamiliar kin and unfamiliar non-kin.
(4) **Genetic systems**. This category covers two related proposed mechanisms of recognition. First, genes may be used as kinship markers which produce signals that aid animals in their decisions concerning potential mates. In particular, these may include genes that are involved in the production of the molecules on the surface of body cells (the **major histocompatibility complex** or **MHC**). Experimental evidence suggests that mice prefer to mate with individuals that differ in their MHC from themselves. In so doing they may be more likely to produce offspring with particularly healthy immune systems. Second, there may be specific **recognition genes** – an idea originally proposed by Richard Dawkins. The idea here is that if an animal had a gene for altruism and if that same gene could also signal its presence via, in Dawkins's hypothetical example, producing say a 'green beard', then two related individuals might recognise such a gene from a common ancestor and act altruistically towards each other. It should be realised that the notion of recognition of genes is currently highly speculative and that such genes would really have to do three things:

- code for a phenotypic signal
- code for recognition of such a signal
- code for the correct social response (altruism)

Although most genes are probably pleiotropic this is asking a lot from a gene.
* Note that, in addition to allowing animals to 'know' who to channel aid towards, a second advantage to kin recognition is that it might aid in decisions over who to mate with. Breeding with close relatives is likely to lead to a number of genetic defects (although breeding with more distant relatives might actually lead to certain advantages such as increasing the value of 'r' in an animal's offspring). In this way current theories concerning animal behaviour strongly suggest that kin recognition would confer at least two clear advantages to an individual.

In the fifty years since Hamilton proposed kin selection theory a large number of lab and field studies have demonstrated that social animals really do aid kin. In addition to the examples presented at the beginning of this chapter there are now a large number of well-documented cases of animals providing aid for relatives who are not their offspring. It is now known, for example, that, in addition to Florida scrub jays, there are around 200 other species of birds that have helpers at the nest. Despite myriad well-documented observations of aid to non-descendent kin, such examples pale into insignificance when compared with the extent of parental care found throughout the animal kingdom.

Although, as mammals, we tend to think of parental investment as providing milk and protection for offspring, the exact form of aid given varies quite extensively between species. How this varies depends on a number of factors such as the evolutionary history of the species and current ecological pressures.

Parental investment and family life

Robert Trivers was well aware of the selective pressure on parental care. He also realised that, although there are many well-documented cases of organisms giving aid to relatives other than their own offspring, direct parental care is far more widespread throughout the animal kingdom. As we saw in chapter 4, Trivers called the time and effort that individual parents put into rearing each offspring 'Parental investment'. Put formally, Trivers defined parental investment as

any investment by the parent in an individual offspring that increases the offspring's chance of surviving at the cost of the parent's ability to invest in other offspring. (1972)

Whereas parental investment should increase the survival chances of a given off-spring, in Trivers's model this fitness benefit needs to be weighed against the cost of investing in other offspring.

How much should parents invest?

How much investment should we expect parents to provide for each of their offspring? There are a number of factors that need to be considered here. First, we need to consider the number of offspring typically produced by an organism's species. Clearly the larger the number of offspring produced the smaller the investment that can be given to each individual. Tapeworms produce millions of microscopic offspring but provide each with almost nothing. Female chimpanzees, in contrast, produce only one offspring around every four to five years, but nurture that individual for several years. These are two quite different strategies. The first involves producing enormous numbers, the vast majority of which will certainly perish, in the hope that one or two will, by chance, make it to reproductive age. The second involves an enormous effort being put into a very small number of offspring in anticipation that each will have a good chance of reaching sexual maturity. Ecologists call the production of vast numbers of offspring at little cost per individual **r-selection** and the production of very few at great cost per individual **K-selection** (Drickamer *et al.*, 2002).

In reality most organisms fall somewhere between tapeworms and chimpanzees so that K to r-selection is really a continuum. Whether an organism favours the r end (produce them as frequently and cheaply as possible) or the K end (lavish great effort on each one) of the continuum depends on the ecological pressures and body plan of its species. K-selected species are adapted to stable environments and tend to live longer and have a larger body size. Since stable environments are believed to lead to strong intraspecific competition (see chapter 2), such selection pressures favour quality over quantity in such species. K, incidentally, refers to the carrying capacity of the environment (the number of organisms that the environment can sustain). In contrast, r-selected species are generally found where, due to unpredictable conditions, it may pay a parent to produce large numbers of offspring which develop very rapidly whenever conditions are conducive. In this case r is derived from the reproductive rate of the population.

The strategy of birds and mammals is generally one of a great deal of parental care, that is, very much towards the K end of the spectrum. But even here we find a fair degree of variation. Although rodent pups are suckled by their mother they are produced in large numbers and weaned at quite a young age. The long-lived, large-brained primate species of monkeys and apes, however, have the longest period of dependency in the animal kingdom. Our closest relatives the chimpanzees may be cared for by their mothers for a third of their lives, during which they will learn much about the social behaviour of the troop from them and from their peers (Strier, 2011).

Box 7.3 Parental investment in spiders – the ultimate sacrifice

Amaurobius fenestralis

There is a family of funnel weaver spiders known collectively as the Amaurobiidae. There are five species of such spiders living in northern Europe. The Amaurobiidae are unremarkable to look at, each being around one centimetre in length. They live in holes in trees and in crevices in artificial structures. There is, however, something about their reproductive behaviour that you may find both fascinating and gruesome. Having mated in their second year of life, females of the Amaurobiidae lay their eggs in a tightly spun feeding chamber and shortly thereafter enter into a state of torpor. The spiderlings initially gain sustenance from the egg yolk that their mother has kindly provided for them. But this soon runs out and the voracious spiderlings leave the feeding chamber in search of more food. All they find is her torpid body. So they eat their mother. An Amaurobiidae spider really does give her all for her offspring. But how can such an excessive degree of sacrifice ever have evolved? Prior to Hamilton's development of inclusive fitness theory, such extreme self-sacrifice would have been explained by many as an act which 'promotes the good of the species'. Today most ethologists ask what is in it for the genes rather than for the species. The Amaurobiidae spiders may be an extreme example of kin-selected altruism. Most parents don't let their offspring eat them. But this bizarre example serves to demonstrate just how far nepotistic behaviour can go given the right circumstances. In the environment of the Amaurobiidae females the chances of meeting a male are quite slim and it may make adaptive sense to breed just once and make the ultimate sacrifice for your offspring.

Humans, of course, have a primate heritage. This means that, even before the evolution of *Homo sapiens*, our ancestors had internal fertilisation, a lengthy period of immaturity and extensive parental investment (Smith, 1987). In all human societies studied women invest more in their offspring than do their partners. As we saw in chapter 3, evolutionists explain this difference partly in terms of greater certainty of maternity than paternity – a sex difference that is true for all species with female internal fertilisation – and partly in terms of simply which sex is left holding the baby. Therefore two further factors which help to determine just how much an individual is likely to invest in each offspring are the evolutionary history of its species and its own sex. This means that if you are the female of a long-lived, internally fertilised species in which there is a lengthy period of development during which a great deal of learning takes place, then you are likely to invest greatly in each of your offspring. It is hardly surprising that humans, and in particular women, put so much effort into raising offspring. But what can this knowledge tell us about the social behaviour of humans? Social behaviour begins in the family.

The family – the result of parental investment?

Most social scientists explain the existence of families in terms of historical and economic factors, but evolutionary psychologists explain it as the result of two main dispositions: dispositions to mate and dispositions to favour kin (Smith, 1987). Canadian evolutionary psychologist Martin Smith suggests that human families exist in order to enhance the inclusive fitness of their members. Following a theme initiated by Richard Alexander (1974; 1980), Smith goes so far as to suggest that humans are 'genetically disposed to form families that display several common features' (Smith, 1987, p. 231). The problem with this claim is that although human families exist as a universal phenomenon they do vary in structure quite considerably. Some families are built around a polygynous marriage with one father and several mothers, others are built around a monogamous couple, and, in a few cultures, there may even be two fathers and one mother – a polyandrous marriage system. Smith's response to this claim of variability is to argue that, cross-culturally, similarities are greater than differences. Such similarities include greater parental investment by women than men, differential investment in offspring depending on their projected reproductive potential and a tendency for women to marry men with the greatest resources. Where differences do occur they are seen as the outcome of an interaction between innate dispositions and differing social pressures. But in all human societies mothers invest heavily in their offspring and most fathers do also. For humans such investment is not simply a matter of feeding. It also involves a great deal of protection and, importantly, teaching. One way that Alexander (1974) suggests parents might be able to increase their inclusive fitness is by teaching appropriate moral codes to their offspring. In

> ## Box 7.4 The Cinderella Effect – the downside to parental investment?
>
> Controversially, Canadian evolutionary psychologists Martin Daly and Margo Wilson have suggested that there may be a downside to parental investment theory when considering the treatment of stepchildren. Making use of epidemiological data from Canada, the United States and the UK, Daly and Wilson have spent more than thirty years investigating the 'Cinderella effect', that is, the notion that step-parents lavish less care and attention on stepchildren than on their own biological offspring. While they are clear in their findings that most stepchildren are not mistreated by their step-parents they have uncovered evidence that the risk of maltreatment is distinctly higher from such 'non-biological' parents. Drawing on Trivers's parental investment theory, Daly and Wilson suggest that parental care is regulated by discriminative parental solicitude built around psychological adaptations to allocate resources to their genetic offspring. This means parents are less likely to guide resources to their stepchildren than their genetic ones and more likely to neglect or abuse the former than the latter. Examples of their findings include the fact that infanticide by stepfathers is 120 higher for step than for genetic offspring (Daly and Wilson, 1998). Moreover, a child under the age of 3 living in a family with one step-parent is seven times more likely to be abused than one living in a family with two biological parents. To Daly and Wilson the greater likelihood of such maltreatment of non-genetic offspring may be a remnant of the male primate adaptive strategy of killing the offspring of other males in order to increase the possibility of fertilising a female. The Cinderella effect has been questioned by critic of evolutionary psychology David Buller (2005a) who argues that abuse by genetic parents is likely to be underreported to the point where Daly and Wilson's findings can be overturned. Unfortunately for Buller this and a number of other disputable assumptions weaken his criticism (Daly and Wilson, 2007) and a number of independent studies appear to support the findings of the Canadian evolutionists (Anderson, 1999; Tooley et al., 2006). Of course this difference in levels of investment in genetic and non-genetic offspring does not prove that this is an adaptation (or even a remnant of a primate adaptation). But it does appear to be a cross-cultural phenomenon making a purely cultural explanation less likely (Daly and Wilson, 1998; 2005; 2007).

particular, he has suggested that, as a consequence of Trivers's theory of parent–offspring conflict, parents will tend to teach their children to behave benevolently towards each other. Alexander calls this **parental manipulation**, since it is the parents' genes that will benefit from such cooperative behaviour.

Parents help to mould the social and moral behaviour of their offspring

In the West we typically reward our children when they are polite, hardworking and law abiding. Smith and Alexander would argue that this is the best way for children to gain lucrative employment and a high-quality partner. From an evolutionary perspective Smith views 'these end points of socialization as intermediate steps in achieving the real goal of parenting: the maximization of inclusive fitness through the maximal production of grand-children' (Smith, 1987, p. 235). In other societies children might be socialised to take on quite different moral codes. In the Yanomamö of South America, for example, tribal warfare is common and 44 per cent of men have killed another person (see chapter 8). Killing is seen as a sign of manhood and those who have killed have on average two and a half times as many wives and three times as many children as non-killers. Pacifists are not common in Yanomamö society – pacifists don't get wives (Chagnon, 1988; 1992; 1997; 2012). It is not surprising to find that in this culture boys are socialised to meet conflict with an aggressive response.

This is not to say that the Yanomamö have a totally different, heartless code of morality or that males in the West are not capable of acting violently (see later). In all societies studied males demonstrate higher levels of aggressive behaviour than females (Daly and Wilson, 1994). Biologists attribute this, at an ultimate level, to competition for females and at a proximate level to physiological factors such as raised levels of testosterone relative to females (Daly and Wilson, 1994; Gorelik and Shackelford, 2012; Liddle *et al.*, 2012). The point is that, under the social and economic conditions of the Yanomamö, it may be a good strategy to bring up your sons to be competent in the use of violence (a good strategy, that is, if you want grandchildren). In this way aspects of what is socially acceptable in an individual may be the outcome of an interaction between genetic dispositions and parental manipulation to fit in with societal norms.

Parent–offspring conflict

'Blood is thicker than water' is a phrase commonly used when family members want to pressurise an individual into favouring relatives over friends. Certainly, the extent to which family members will pull together under conditions of adversity can be astonishing and impressive. Evolutionists consider that they have explained, at an ultimate level, why this state of affairs arose using inclusive fitness theory. However, anyone who has ever lived in a family will recognise that this picture of domestic bliss is rarely a constant one. Personal experience tells us that how harmonious a family is varies greatly from one family to the next. But rare indeed is the family that never quarrels. If Trivers, Alexander and Smith are right that the very existence of the family arises out of increased opportunities for kin altruism to occur, then why is family conflict so common?

Social psychologists traditionally explain conflict between parent and offspring as the maladaptive effects of poor role models and as the outcome of a lack of conflict resolution strategies (Straus, 1971; Straus *et al.*, 1980; Deaux and Wrightsman, 1983). In short, conflict is seen as a dysfunctional state of affairs. Evolutionary psychologists, however, see some conflict as a natural outcome of inclusive fitness theory. This is because at the very heart of Trivers's theory of parental investment there exists a contradiction. The same theory that predicts benevolence based on the coefficient of relatedness, paradoxically, also predicts periods of serious conflict between family members.

Shortly after he suggested that parental care should be viewed as an investment in copies of an organism's genes, Trivers realised that natural selection operates differently on the two generations involved. When the parent of a K-selected species, say an ape, gives birth to a single offspring then clearly it pays both her and her offspring for her to invest heavily in it. Since they share 50 per cent of their genes by common descent ($r = 0.5$) we can expect the mother to suckle her newborn offspring and generally provide a great deal of care for her. The problem arises when we reach the point of weaning: the point at which a female is ready to breed again. As the infant grows she becomes better able to feed and fend for herself. Eventually there will come a time when it would pay the mother ape to produce another offspring and transfer her investment to him. For the mother this occurs at the point when the cost in terms of fitness exceeds the benefit. Because the first offspring shares 50 per cent of her genes with her newborn brother (assuming they have the same father) she should not be indifferent to his welfare. However, in inclusive fitness terminology, we can think of her as sharing 100 per cent of her genes with herself. This means that it will benefit her to have her mother continue to invest in herself right up until the point when the benefit to the new sibling is at least twice the cost to herself.

We can see that the point when it would pay the mother to shift investment to the new offspring comes at a much earlier time for the mother than it does for the older offspring. Hence we can predict parent–offspring conflict to happen regularly at certain times in development (Trivers, 1972; 1974). Moreover, in addition to conflict with the mother we can also predict that there will be rivalry between siblings during this period and, to a lesser extent, beyond (except in the case of identical twins, siblings always 'share more genes with themselves' than with each other). Using Trivers's way of thinking about development of social behaviour it might be argued that, although it may pay siblings to provide aid for each other when compared to nonrelatives, investment by the parents in one offspring can always be seen as investment taken away from another. Rivalry may be most acute when a newborn child appears and draws investment away from the older offspring – but throughout life it may pay offspring to gain a little more investment than their siblings. Not

Figure 7.3 Trivers's model of parent–offspring conflict (Based on Trivers, 1972). The graph demonstrates the ratio of the benefit to the offspring and the cost to the mother in relation to offspring age

perhaps to the extent that they would generally see their siblings expire – they do after all share 50 per cent of their genes – but certainly they are unlikely to favour them over themselves.

Figure 7.3 demonstrates Trivers's model of when parent–offspring conflict should take place. In the first section of the graph (bottom left) you will see that when an offspring is young, the ratio of the cost to mother to the benefit to offspring is low (less than 1). Remember that the cost to the mother is a measurement of her not investing in another offspring. However, as the offspring ages the cost to the mother increases faster than the benefit to the current offspring. Between 1 and 2 it makes sense for the mother to invest in another offspring, while it still pays the current offspring to reap the benefit. This is the period of predicted parent–offspring conflict. Beyond 2, when the cost to the mother is more than twice the benefit to the offspring then it pays both to allow her to invest in another offspring.

Conflict at times other than weaning

This model of conflict over weaning may appear to be rather esoteric. The question is, does the predicted discord occur in the natural world? And does it do so at the predicted time? As with Hamilton's theory of kin selection, when Trivers proposed his parent–offspring model it made sense on paper but the acid test is: does it work like this in the real world? In recent years, evidence has accumulated that this *is* what happens in the real animal world. Conflicts over weaning have been well known to livestock farmers for centuries, but until Trivers proposed his model it had not occurred to anyone why in ultimate terms this conflict should be so intense at this stage. Recent observations suggest that Trivers's model works quite well. Evolutionary psychologists Robin Dunbar and Louise Barrett of the University of Liverpool have studied this conflict and see it occurring in a wide range of species. Tantrums are used by a wide variety of infant animals including pelicans, starlings, baboons, rhesus macaques, zebra and chimpanzees as an attempt to increase maternal investment (Barrett and Dunbar, 1994; Barrett *et al.*, 2002; Maestripieri, 2004; Goodman *et al.*, 2012). And the conflict appears to reach a peak at the time of weaning as the mother increasingly rejects attempts from offspring to be fed from her and begins to redistribute her efforts towards breeding once more (Hinde, 1977; Barrett *et al.*, 2002; Goodman *et al.*, 2012). The time course for this rejection fits in well with Trivers's prediction. To date, however, this area has not been addressed in any detail for human mother–infant relationships. In contrast to the lack of studies around the time of weaning, there is now good evidence that the intense conflict that was predicted by Trivers may also occur both much earlier and much later on than this for our species (see below).

Conflict at puberty – who should reproduce?

Evolutionary theory predicts that parents should want to see their children grow up to make them grandparents. However, a mother might not be keen on seeing her daughter make her a grandmother too soon. This may often be the case because an immature girl may not make an ideal parent. It might even be the case due to vanity on the part of the older woman. But there is another, more gene-centred, argument as to why a mother might not want to become a grandmother too soon. Evolutionary anthropologist Mark Flinn has suggested an extension of Trivers's theory of parent–offspring conflict which may occur at the time when a daughter first reaches puberty (Flinn, 1989; 2011; Quinlan *et al.*, 2003). The problem arises essentially for the same reason that it occurs at the point of weaning – in terms of boosting inclusive fitness, there may be a cost/benefit asymmetry between mother and daughter. The scenario goes like this. Imagine that you are a thirty-something mother with a teenage daughter living at home. She may now be of reproductive age. But so are you. Given limited resources, who would you rather has a baby – yourself or your daughter? Using inclusive fitness theory you should choose yourself because every offspring you produce will have 50 per cent of your genes by common descent whereas every offspring that your daughter produces will have only 25 per cent of your genes by common descent. At this stage in life it does not make sense to shift strategy to the role of grandmother. Of course, once a woman is beyond reproductive age herself then the conflict should vanish since it is in the interests of both generations for the daughter to reproduce.

Once again, as in the theory over weaning conflict discussed above, this model may sound rather theoretical and not necessarily a 'real-world' scenario. There is, however, at least circumstantial evidence that supports this hypothesis. Flinn has reported that in Trinidad agonistic encounters are significantly more frequent between a mother and her teenage daughter if the older woman is still of reproductive age (see figure 7.4). Moreover, Flinn has also found that no girl of reproductive age in this society became

---

Box 7.5 **Conflict in the womb – an arms race of raging hormones**

Since Robert Trivers originally suggested that parents and offspring should not always live in perfect harmony the conflict that he predicted has cropped up in some surprising places. In 1993 evolutionary geneticist David Haig even suggested that this disharmony might occur prior to the birth of the infant. Extending Trivers's argument back to this prenatal stage of development, Haig has argued that, up to a point, we should view the foetus as a parasite and the mother as host where resources are concerned. Up to a point, that is, because clearly it is in the interest of both parties for the foetus to be born. However, the mother would like the foetus to appear without taking too much in the way of nutrients out of her so that she will be able to reproduce again as soon as possible. Haig has documented two main ways in which the foetus and mother compete for resources. First, foetal cells invade the artery that supplies blood from the mother to the placenta, destroying the muscle cells there, which would otherwise allow the mother to control constriction of this artery. This then allows the foetus, via release of its own hormones, to divert more of the mother's blood to itself. A knock-on effect of this is a rise in blood pressure as the foetus grows and demands more blood – in some cases leading to the potentially life-threatening condition of pre-eclampsia. Second, there is a battle over blood sugar between mother and foetus during the latter stages of pregnancy. In the three months prior to parturition the foetus directs the placenta to secrete increasing quantities of the hormone **human placental lactogen** (hPL) into the mother's blood. This counteracts the effects of insulin that the mother is producing in larger and larger quantities in order to direct blood sugar into her own cells. In a sense, there is an arms race over the sugar supply with both sides secreting hormones in order to counteract the sugar-grabbing hormones of the other side (Haig, 1993; 2002). Interestingly (and just to complicate matters), there is now evidence that growth of the embryo and placenta are under control of paternal rather than maternal genes so, like a general who oversees the battlefield without taking part directly in the action, the father may also be involved in this arms race.

Although the foetus appears to be winning the arms race for resources in a number of ways, it does not have it all its own way. Recently Haig has suggested that a large proportion of embryos (30–75 per cent) may be spontaneously aborted in the first two weeks of development and that this process occurs when the mother's body, picking up on chemical cues, decides that it is of low quality (Haig, 1998; 2002). The proposed mechanism for elimination of the embryo is via changes in levels of the female sex hormone **progesterone**. If a pregnancy is to progress, then high levels of progesterone are required. Progesterone is produced by the egg follicle or **corpus luteum** in the ovary after the release of an egg. Normally, progesterone production in the corpus luteum declines after two weeks as the follicle begins to break down. If there is a growing embryo in the uterus it is necessary for it to release a hormone at this point – **human chorionic gonadotrophin** (hCG), which has the effect of maintaining the corpus luteum and hence progesterone production. Haig has suggested that it is those embryos not able to produce sufficient quantities of hCG that are eliminated from the mother's body since they do not stand up to her quality control procedure. Perhaps the mother, via her hormones, may have ultimate control during the early stages, but as the foetus grows, like most parasites, it slowly begins to gain a controlling influence.

Figure 7.4 Conflict between mother and daughter is likely to be higher in families where both are of reproductive age

pregnant while living with her mother until the mother's last-born child was at least 4 years old. Such a finding suggests that there may be a reproductive suppression mechanism, which is in some way controlled by the mother – perhaps via pheromones. If this is the case, then we might question why the daughter has not fought back and evolved a way of ignoring such a means of suppression. The answer may be that it might not pay her to do so. The reason is that there is an asymmetry built into the equation. Although the mother has a coefficient of relatedness, or 'r' (see above) of only 0.25 with her grandchildren, the daughter has an r of 0.5 with her siblings (assuming the same father). This means that while her mother is still of reproductive age it may not matter to her whether it is she or her mother who reproduces. In fact, given the inexperience and lack of personal resources during the teenage years, it might often be a better strategy for the daughter to delay her personal reproduction and play more of a 'helpers at the nest' role until both she and her mother are older.

This means that reproductive suppression by the mother might partially suit both parties. Note that from this argument we can make at least two predictions. First, we can suggest that household agonistic encounters are more likely to be initiated by the mother than by the teenage daughter, and second we can predict that there should be fewer of these encounters involving teenage sons than daughters. As an overall prediction we might also suggest that mothers will generally be more involved in family conflicts than fathers. This last prediction might be complicated, however, by questions of uncertainty of paternity in some cases. Such hypotheses remain largely to be tested.

Do families exist to maximise inclusive fitness?

In the eyes of evolutionists such as Trivers, Alexander, Smith, Dunbar, Barrett, Daly, Wilson and Flinn, families exist ultimately to boost the inclusive fitness of their members. Family units may increase opportunities for the creation and care of children. Moreover, they increase nepotistic opportunities and allow parents to manipulate their offspring into conforming to the type of moral behaviour which, given the societal norms, is likely to lead to the production of grandchildren – at the appropriate time.

But does this knowledge inform us about human social behaviour? A knowledge of theories of kin selection, parental investment and parent–offspring conflict suggests that from details of family size, sex and age of offspring we will be able to predict when parents are likely to have acute periods of conflict with their offspring and when sibling rivalry is most likely to be a particular problem. When asking questions concerning the relationship between pro- and antisocial behaviour within families with regard to boosting inclusive fitness, however, we should ensure that we are clear whose inclusive fitness we are discussing. Perhaps, in human families, some conflict is almost inevitable.

Evolutionary psychologists are currently arguing that humans have evolved psychological mechanisms that help us to understand and predict family interactions. Much of our social life, however, involves interactions with non-relatives and many of the decisions that we have to make involve them. Can inclusive fitness theory also be of benefit here? We turn to this and other questions with regard to social behaviour between non-relatives in the next chapter.

Summary

- Evolutionary psychologists have used the concepts of inclusive fitness theory, evolved psychological mechanisms and kin altruism to help explain social behaviour in ourselves and other species. Inclusive fitness is an estimate of the number of genes that individuals pass on both directly via their own offspring and indirectly via their effects on the survival of other kin.
- Kin altruism (also known as nepotism) is the term used for self-sacrificing acts towards kin. The tendency to provide aid to relatives appears to be related to the proportion of genes shared by common descent (i.e. the coefficient of relatedness – 'r'). Although aid to other relatives is well documented in the animal kingdom, most examples of aid consist of parents providing care for their own offspring. Today evolutionists explain many acts of social behaviour in animals in terms of nepotistic strategies.
- Parental investment consists of the amount of time and effort that an individual puts into rearing each of its offspring. In some species a large number of offspring are produced but very few resources are provided for each. Such a strategy is known as 'r'-selection. In others a great deal of effort is spent on each of a small number of offspring, a strategy called 'K'-selection. Today evolutionists see r to K as a continuum that ranges from little investment to a very great deal. Humans and other primates are at the extreme end of K-selection.
- As a direct consequence of parental investment theory, siblings are predicted to be in conflict with their parents at certain times in their lives. Such parent–offspring conflict is predicted because parents may want to divide resources more equally among their offspring than each offspring would ideally like. This conflict may be most acute at three particular points in the development of the family unit. First, there may be conflict between the foetus and the mother during gestation as both compete for limited resources. Second, the mother may want to wean the offspring at a time earlier than the offspring would prefer in order to shift investment towards future offspring. Finally, there may be conflict between a mother and her teenage daughter over who should reproduce if the mother is still of reproductive age.

Questions

1. Mark Flinn has predicted that there will quite often be conflict between a woman who is still fertile and her teenage daughter. Based on the material in this chapter can you think of other reasons for conflict between offspring and parents during this time in life?

2. According to Alcock (2009) 'bridewealth' (where a man is expected to donate resources such as cattle or money to the family of his fiancée) occurs in 66 per cent of societies studied by anthropologists and yet in only 3 per cent of societies is a 'dowry' (where the bride's family must pay the groom's family) the norm. Why might this be the case? What features of a society might help to determine whether bridewealth or dowry payment becomes the norm?

3. The female funnel weaver spider *Amaurobis fenestralis* lays its life down for its offspring. How might this behaviour be controlled and how might it have evolved?

4. Under the 'Cinderella effect' it was suggested that the greater likelihood of maltreatment of non-genetic offspring may be a remnant of the male primate adaptive strategy of killing the offspring of other males in order to increase the possibility of fertilising a female (see box 7.4). How might we gather evidence to support or refute this proposal? Can you think of any problems with this proposal?

FURTHER READING

Hewstone, M., Stroebe, W. and Jonas, K. (eds.) (2012). *Introduction to Social Psychology*. Oxford: Blackwell. General multi-author text which covers all of the core topics of social psychology.

Schaller, M., Simpson, J. A. and Kenrick, D. T. (2006). *Evolution and Social Psychology (Frontiers of Social Psychology)*. New York: Psychology Press. Multi-author text that demonstrates what an evolutionary approach can bring to social psychology. The most detailed evolutionary social psychology textbook currently available.

Trivers, R. L. (1985). *Social Evolution*. Menlo Park, CA: Benjamin/Cummings. A classic work on the relationship between social behaviour and evolution by one of the major figures in the development of sociobiology and subsequently evolutionary psychology.

8

The evolutionary psychology of social behaviour – reciprocity and group behaviour

KEY CONCEPTS

reciprocal altruism–direct reciprocation • xenophobia • gift economy • game theory • prisoner's dilemma • evolutionarily stable strategy • tit-for-tat • stereotyping • ethnocentrism • self-concept

Most animals live relatively solitary lives, occasionally meeting up only to copulate, threaten or fight with each other. But some species live in groups where they constantly interact. Students of animal behaviour have long asked what benefits do individual organisms accrue from living in such social groups? According to evolutionist Richard Alexander, 'Complex sociality should be expected to arise only when confluences of interest produce benefits that override the costs of conflicting interests' (Alexander, 1987, p. 65). He sees the seeds of animal social behaviour as arising out of the need for cooperative defence and the production of mutual offspring. In recent years theories concerning altruism, which have been developed to explain animal social behaviour, have also been used by evolutionary psychologists to study human social behaviour. So do we thrive in the company of others for the same reasons as other social animals?

Why are we kind to other people?

In chapter 7 we outlined the ways in which self-sacrificing behaviour towards relatives may, in the long run, aid an individual's inclusive fitness via direct and indirect selection. Yet it is a common feature of our species that we frequently show kindness to those with whom we share no genes by common descent. We have all heard stories of soldiers laying down their lives to save their comrades in battle and there are many well-documented examples of individuals diving into dangerous waters to save the lives of non-relatives. On a more mundane level, in many countries throughout the world, blood is given freely to be dispensed to complete strangers

Table 8.1 **Documented acts of apparent reciprocity between non-relatives in the animal kingdom**

Species	Beneficial act	Relationship to altruist and proposed reason for altruistic act	Source (example)
Olive baboons	A subordinate male baboon distracts a dominant male who is in a consort relationship with a female in oestrus. While this is occurring another male copulates with the female	Generally non-relatives. The act is reciprocated later, i.e. the male who mates with the female will distract a dominant male on a future occasion while his friend mates with the consort female of a dominant male	Packer (1977)
Vampire bats	A well-fed bat regurgitates blood into the mouth of another hungry individual that has begged to be fed	Such acts are frequently recorded between non-relatives. On another occasion the roles may be reversed	Wilkinson (1984)
Green wood hoopoe	Individuals help to rear nestlings which are not their own offspring	Some of the helpers at the nest are relatives of the breeding pair but others are not. Helpers ensure that there will be sufficient numbers in future generations to aid the helpers when they breed themselves	Ligon and Ligon (1978)
Dolphins (various species)	Injured dolphins are assisted, supported or carried to safety	Likely not to be close relatives in many observed cases. Again may be reciprocated at a later date	Trivers (1985)
Vervet monkey	Individuals come to the aid of other specific individuals giving alarm calls	Group members form special reciprocal relationships with other non-relatives	Seyfarth and Cheney (1984)

and the giving of money to charity is considered abnormal in no known society. If natural selection promotes genetic 'selfishness' then why do humans engage in self-sacrificing behaviour towards non-relatives? Has free will developed in our species as an emergent property of the brain which takes us beyond our 'genetic imperative' and into acts of true altruism or can evolutionary theories fully explain such behaviour?

Reciprocal altruism

As we saw in chapter 7, Hamilton, Trivers and Alexander all claim that the evolutionary approach to families can help to explain the universal existence of both cooperative and conflict-related behaviours. There are, however, examples of apparent self-sacrificing behaviour which occur outside the family context. Take a look at table 8.1.

Table 8.1 strongly resembles table 7.1. In all of the cases presented here, however, there is suggestive evidence of aid being given to non-relatives.

You may recall from chapter 2 that Robert Trivers called beneficial acts that are later repaid by the beneficiary 'reciprocal altruism'. As with Trivers's notions of parental investment and parent–offspring conflict, development of the theory pre-dated documented examples of behaviour that might constitute reciprocal altruism. Note that all of the examples given in table 8.1 were published after Trivers's 1971 classic theoretical paper. According to Trivers, the evolution of reciprocal altruism in an animal society relies on a number of prerequisites:

- The cost of the altruistic act to the recipient should be lower than the benefit to the actor.
- Animals should be capable of recognising each other in order both to reciprocate and to detect cheats (non-reciprocators).
- Animals should have a reasonably long life span in order that they may repeatedly encounter specific individuals and thereby allow for incidents of reciprocation to occur.

Reciprocal altruism or direct reciprocity?

In recent years, given that the aid is returned, many researchers have begun to replace the term reciprocal altruism with **direct reciprocation** or simply **reciprocation** or **reciprocity** (Clutton-Brock, 2009). This terminology neatly sidesteps arguments as to whether the behaviour is really altruistic (how can it be if ultimately the benefit to the actor outweighs the cost?). The dolphins, primates, bats and social birds that are detailed in table 8.1 would certainly fit Trivers's prerequisites for direct reciprocation. This alone, however, does not prove that this is what is occurring in all of these cases. As Cambridge University zoologist Tim Clutton-Brock has pointed out there are at least two other ways of explaining the giving of aid to non-relatives – **mutualism** and **manipulation**. According to Clutton-Brock (2009) for reciprocation to occur the assistance has to have 'net costs at the time that it is provided, which are offset by subsequent benefits'. In contrast, in the case of mutualism and manipulation 'the benefits of assistance exceed the costs involved at the time that it is provided'. In the case of mutualism both individuals benefit from cooperation at the time of the act (such as cooperative hunting in wolves) and hence there is no immediate cost–benefit asymmetry that is later repaid. Note, given there is no delay, there is no opportunity to cheat (freeride). For manipulation, one individual, such as a dominant conspecific may coerce another into providing aid and once again there is no reciprocity. Alternatively, a non-dominant conspecific might simply be so persistent in its calls for aid that the actor succumbs to providing this in order to escape the constant begging behaviour. Indeed this explanation has been suggested for the case of blood sharing in vampire bats as outlined in table 8.1. Moreover, it has also been suggested that bats that do provide blood to conspecifics are generally related, which means that we cannot discount kin selection (Clutton-Brock, 2009).

We can ask two questions about reciprocity in the animal kingdom. First, does it exist, and, second, how common is it? Direct reciprocation would necessitate evidence that the same individuals repeatedly assist each other, that the frequency of assistance given reflects the frequency of assistance received and finally that there are immediate costs to the actor that are later recouped from the initial beneficiary. This is a tall order for non-human animals and, while most animal behaviourists today would agree that direct reciprocation does exist in the animal kingdom (especially among primates), outside **Homo sapiens** it is likely to be a rare phenomenon (Clutton-Brock, 2009; Hammerstein, 2003).

Reciprocity and human evolution

Trivers (1985) considers that reciprocity is likely to have played an important role in hominin evolution. He bases this conclusion on a number of arguments. First, all existent societies fulfil the three prerequisites he laid out (see above); second, humans throughout the world have been observed to give aid to friends in a reciprocated manner; and third, the emotional system that we have developed underlies such acts (emotions may play an important role in cooperation, Hammerstein, 2003, see chapter 11). In Trivers's own words:

We routinely share food, we help the sick, the wounded and the very young. We routinely share our tools, and we share our knowledge in a very complex way. Often these forms of behavior meet the criterion of small cost to the giver and great benefit to the recipient. Although kinship often mediates many of these acts, it never appears to be a prerequisite. Such aid is often extended in full knowledge that the recipient is only distantly related. (Trivers, 1985, p. 386)

Altruism in stone-age cultures

During the twentieth century many anthropologists, sociologists and social psychologists spent a great deal of time in the company of present-living stone-age cultures. Given that such people live in pre-industrial conditions, it was hoped that an understanding of their cultural practices might throw some light on the sort of lives that our ancestors led. One question that intrigued many of these social scientists was to what extent do such people exhibit altruistic behaviour? Are the people of stone-age cultures more or less self-sacrificing than ourselves?

Figure 8.1 The bottlenose dolphin is a species which has been observed displaying complex cooperative behaviour in the wild. One eyewitness account describes how an individual struck by an electroharpoon is helped to the surface for air by other members of its group (see Pilleri and Knuckey, 1969)

Three societies which have been studied quite extensively are the !Kung San bush people of Botswana in southern Africa (see for example Lee, 1972; 1979), the Northern Aché of eastern Paraguay (see, for example, Hill, 2002; Hill and Hurtado, 1996; McMillan, 2000) and the Yanomamö of Brazil and Venezuela (see, for example, Chagnon, 1997; 2012). Evolutionary psychologists consider that the concept of direct reciprocation may be used to help understand the social behaviour of these societies. We examine each, in turn, briefly.

The harmless people – the !Kung San

The !Kung San, who are a monogamous people, live on the open savannah/desert of the Kalahari in small nomadic bands of perhaps between twenty and fifty individuals. In all there are believed to be 87,000 individuals spread over Botswana and Namibia (the Kalahari covers parts of both countries). Although in 2005 the government briefly moved the Botswana population off their land, this decision was overturned in a famous court ruling in December 2006 which led to their return to the Kalahari. It is now believed that, other than this one brief interlude, the San have been living

---

Box 8.1 **Blood donation – a criticism of reciprocity in humans**

As with kin altruism, the notion that people engage in self-sacrificing acts towards friends ultimately because they are likely to benefit themselves has been criticised by a number of social scientists. One area of criticism lies in blood donation. One critic of the evolutionary approach, Peter Singer, has argued that blood donation is a form of pure altruism because the donor does not normally meet the recipient and cannot therefore anticipate repayment (Singer, 1981). Such acts are certainly not easily explained by Trivers's (1971) original definition of reciprocal altruism (nor indeed by Hamilton's (1964a, b) definition of kin altruism). Certainly humans, unlike vampire bats, do not expect to receive blood from the recipient of their earlier donation. So do we have to accept that blood donation is a form of true altruism that transcends evolutionary considerations? Perhaps it is – but Richard Alexander (1987) has proposed an explanation that may be thought of as an extension of Trivers's reciprocal altruism. He suggests that, rather than the donor being repaid directly by the recipient, by impressing others with his apparent self-sacrificing behaviour they may be more likely to cooperate with him in the future. In this way humans may have extended reciprocal altruism into more complex multi-party relationships than other species.

Although Alexander has addressed Singer's blood donation argument directly, he is making a more general point: that is, we may have evolved psychological mechanisms that make minor good deeds feel rewarding – especially when they are observed by others. Such a state of mind may have had fitness benefits for our ancestors. Alexander's explanation does not disprove the 'pure altruism' argument, but it does, as John Alcock (2009) has pointed out, lead to testable predictions – the acid test being that people who engage in acts such as blood donation will generally ensure that others find out about their actions. In support of this prediction, Bobbi Low and Joel Heinen of the University of Michigan report that people are significantly more likely to contribute to fundraising drives if they receive a badge to demonstrate their involvement (Low and Heinen, 1993). Perhaps when we wear blood donation badges or AIDS sympathy ribbons today we are reflecting behaviours that helped our ancestors to attract cooperation from others.

---

in this region of Botswana for at least 22,000 years (Wells, 2003). Along with the Inuit (Eskimo) and the Aboriginals of Australia, the !Kung San are one of few hunter-gatherer societies that has retained a lifestyle that was common to all peoples prior to the invention of agriculture some 10,000 years ago (Lee, 1979). Each San band forages within a home range of around 5,000 square kilometres where there is a clear division of labour: men hunt, women gather. On average meat provides 40 per cent of the calories consumed, but during a successful hunting season this may rise to

Figure 8.2 !Kung San bushpeople by huts, Kalahari, Botswana, southern Africa

90 per cent, enabling individual tribe members to eat around two kilograms of meat each day. Alternatively, during a lean period this may drop to below 20 per cent. The women gather over one hundred different types of plant food, but the monogo fruit tree forms a staple part of their diet.

!Kung men vary quite considerably in their hunting prowess, but all meat killed is shared. The band will frequently produce four or five two-man teams which hunt simultaneously, but only one of these needs to be successful in a big game hunt to provide meat for the entire band. When a pair of hunters kills, say, a wildebeest, each hunter will divide his share among his relatives who, in turn, share with their next of kin. Given that band members are all either blood relatives or related through marriage, in this way everybody receives some meat. This habit of sharing is considered to be of great social significance. A lapse of such generosity is considered a grave social sin and individuals who fail to comply lose status and prestige. Even acting in a boastful way about kills is considered a social taboo. Anthropologists have labelled the food-related behaviour of the !Kung San a **gift economy**, where, rather than take part in overt trading, individuals regularly give each other gifts of food (Lee, 1979).

The benevolent behaviour of the successful hunters of the !Kung San towards the unsuccessful might appear as pure altruism to the outside observer. It is clear, however, that such benevolence is expected to be reciprocated should the roles be reversed. Social anthropologist Marvin Harris (1985) considers that such reciprocal hunting arrangements make a great deal of sense in the unpredictable environments of the savannah and desert. Following a large kill, any meat that cannot be consumed by the hunters will go off very quickly. Handing it out to relatives might aid your inclusive fitness. Handing it out to friends may ensure future reciprocation.

Clearly we need to be careful not to assume that the well-developed blend of kin altruism and reciprocation that surrounds meat distribution in the !Kung San is the pattern found in all 'primitive cultures'. However, such a system appears to be widespread, at least among forager peoples (Harris, 1985; Hill, 2002).

The sharing people – the Aché

The Northern Aché are a forager people that live in the rainforests of eastern Paraguay. They are a polygynous society – so much so that when asked who their father is, children often identify two or three men. Until the 1970s they had no real contact with the outside world. At this point there were only around 560 left spread over ten to fifteen different bands (Hill and Hurtado, 1996; McMillan, 2000). Bands typically have between fifteen to sixty individuals but frequently engage in fission–fusion behaviour (not unlike some of our primate relatives – see chapter 4). They are nomadic, moving camp on an almost daily basis. Although their world is changing rapidly now, certainly prior to very recent times, they spent approximately 25 per cent of their time hunting and gathering (Hill, 2002). As in forager societies in general gender roles are quite strict – men hunt and women gather (Marlowe, 2007). In recent years some of the Aché have become forager-horticulturists, whereas others have continued a predominantly forager's lifestyle (those considered here).

When on a foraging expedition both sexes set out early in the morning together but after a while they separate with the men fanning out while the women continue on their way. The men specialise in hunting game or honey. If they find honey – they call the women to it – if they find game, they call men to help them. In the afternoon they meet up at some prearranged rendezvous where the women have prepared a temporary camp. The women bring plant food and grubs whereas the men bring monkeys and larger prey such as armadillos, pacas and deer. When hunting, men will spend around seven hours a day after game, whereas the women spend about two hours foraging. The women will have sex with a number of men and although they do become married, marriages are often short-lived especially among the young adults. All men that a woman has had sex with leading up to the child's birth are expected to help provide for the offspring – but if she has sex with too many, then extreme uncertainty of paternity can lead to none of them giving aid. So clearly both sexes play a cost–benefit game. They are not without sexual jealousy – and if a married man considers his wife is having an affair he may beat her. If he leaves marks on her, she may boast how much her husband must really love her.

The Aché are renowned for their egalitarian sharing with meat, plant food and honey being shared throughout the band. According to Kim Hill, who has studied the Northern Aché for many years, cooperative hunting and sharing of food reduces the amount of variability in daily intake and increases the variability in individual diet (Hill, 2002; Gurven *et al.*, 2002). Such generosity, especially in the case of meat, is of course remembered (and likewise meanness). Sharing might also be related to the fact that most game requires cooperation to capture. There are well-documented examples of members of the Aché sharing beyond what appears to be reasonable tit-for-tat like behaviour and anthropologists have argued about why this might be the case. Whatever the case anthropologists have been very impressed with the sharing behaviour of the Aché. While manipulation and mutualism may be involved in foraging and sharing practices, it is clear that reciprocity is well developed in this tribe (Hill and Hurtado, 1996; Hill, 2002).

From the description of the share-and-share-alike behaviour of the !Kung bushmen and the Northern Aché some anthropologists have suggested that our Pleistocene ancestors were benevolent and modest noble savages (see Pinker, 2002). One book from the 1950s went so far as to describe the !Kung as 'the harmless people' (Thomas, 1959). Unfortunately, those who subsequently observed the !Kung and the Aché in great detail over lengthy periods have found that murder rates are higher than in American inner cities (Pinker, 2002; 2011). In particular in the case of the Aché, despite their reputation for egalitarian food sharing, more than 40 per cent of all adult deaths and over 60 per cent of child fatalities are due to violence by other Aché. It is known that if a child loses its primary father, then its chances of survival are greatly reduced. It is not unheard of for an orphan to be buried alive with his deceased parent. Also mothers will sometimes kill their own infants if they are fatherless. Such harsh treatment is not uncommon for forager people as we will see when considering the Amazon Yanomamö.

The fierce people – the Yanomamö

The Yanomamö are polygynous tribespeople who live in the rainforests of the Amazon basin. In addition to foraging, they have developed slash and burn agriculture and this may help to explain why, unlike the nomadic !Kung and the Aché, permanent villages are set up where crops are grown. The formation of settlements and the growth of crops in individually owned 'gardens' has led to the development of a more complex economy than that of the !Kung San and the Aché. Trading practices occur both within and between villages. To the untrained observer, it appears that the Yanomamö regularly give gifts to each other. However, all such gifts are remembered and it is incumbent on the recipient to reciprocate at a later date. An important

Figure 8.3 Yanomamö warriors from allied villages lining up to raid a common enemy group

facet of this trading is that a 'gift' must always be reciprocated by a *different* gift of (approximately) equal value.

Because the Yanomamö live in relatively permanent settlements, each village has become specialised in the production of different goods. One village may, for example, become expert at producing clay pots while another may be good at producing cotton yarn. This specialisation and the trading of such artefacts means that, in effect, each side gains something that would be more costly to make for themselves (given the time it takes to learn to make something new). Such an arrangement fits in extremely well with the principles of reciprocity. That is, reciprocation is delayed and the benefit to each party outweighs the costs. Indeed, this division of labour is considered by some to be an important step in human cultural evolution, making each society 'more than the sum of its parts' (Ridley, 1996, p. 42).

As is generally the case for polygynous societies, a small number of Yanomamö men have several wives while the remainder are either married to one wife or remain as bachelors. When a man takes a wife she is expected to be subordinate to him. If he is unhappy with her behaviour then he is at liberty to beat her or even to shoot an arrow into her (provided the arrow is aimed at some non-vital part!). But if the Yanomamö men sometimes act violently towards their wives, this is positively charitable when compared with the way that they treat the men of other villages. These Amazonians are renowned for their frequent violent raids on each other's villages (when not involved in trading), which are most usually conducted on the premise of avenging some past killing or abduction. Such raids are not without fatalities; when they occur, as many men are killed as possible and as many women are abducted as possible (the Yanomamö call themselves 'the fierce people'). Almost half of Yanomamö men have killed another man and it is these killers who are most successful at attracting wives and lovers (Chagnon, 1988; 2012).

The Yanomamö are not alone in engaging in violent raids. But then again nor are the !Kung San or the Aché, who, despite their high murder rate, adhere quite strictly to practices of food sharing throughout the band (Keeley, 1996; Hill and Hurtado, 1996). Why, we might ask, do we find such variability between cultures? As you may recall, many social scientists of the twentieth century suggested that differences between societies reflect random cultural factors (a hypothesis known as the 'arbitrary culture theory', which is part of the SSSM, see Sahlins, 1976; Alcock, 2009). Today, however, evolutionary psychologists suggest that the extent to which food sharing extends beyond the family is dependent on their method of gaining food and their mating system. And just to complicate matters, as we saw in chapter 4, food and sex may well be interrelated. In societies that rely solely on foraging, a man cannot store up anything with which to barter. However, you can store up the notion of the gift of meat. As evolutionist Jared Diamond has suggested, in the savannah you can't store meat in a fridge but you can store it in the bellies of your friends (Diamond, 1997). Thus acts of reciprocity over food may make a great deal of sense for nomadic people like the !Kung San and the Aché.

In cases like the Yanomamö, in addition to demonstrating prowess in hunting and in intertribal conflicts, a man who is successful in agriculture and trade is also likely to be successful in competition for wives. It is well established that among primates, females can best increase their reproductive output by gaining access to resources such as food and males can best increase theirs by gaining access to females (Trivers, 1972). This means that the polygynous nature of Yanomamö society may be a direct result of successful males being able to hold resources, an option perhaps not available to the nomadic !Kung San men. Hence, giving food away freely does not make economic sense to the primitive slash-and-burn Yanomamö farmers.

Although the introduction of primitive agriculture may have reduced the level of simple food sharing, like all cultures studied, in times of need the Yanomamö are known to aid friends in addition to relatives. In particular, when intratribal disputes occur both friends and relatives of each protagonist quickly become involved as people take sides. When such disputes escalate into violence, serious injury and even mortality, frequently it is the secondaries that are struck down rather than the principal protagonists (Trivers, 1985).

Taking into account trade and violent disputes, we can see that reciprocity can be both a very serious and a complex business in stone-age societies. And, if you think that modern, post-industrial, societies are less reliant upon it, then just consider one

Player A

Cooperate   Defect

Figure 8.4 The prisoner's dilemma – 'pay-off matrix' showing four possible outcomes

Player B

	Player A Cooperate	Player A Defect
Cooperate	R = 3 Reward for mutual cooperation	S = 0 Sucker's payoff
Defect	T = 5 Temptation to defect	P = 1 Punishment for mutual defection

concept that all modern countries have developed: money. Without the development of aid being reciprocated later, then money would not work.

Evolved predispositions to reciprocate?

Such field studies of widely dispersed stone-age societies suggest that Trivers's concept of reciprocity is an important evolutionary human development. Drawing on such anthropological studies (and building on earlier theoretical work of Trivers, 1985 and of Cosmides and Tooby, 1992) Kim Hill (2002) has suggested that human cooperation based around reciprocity is based on three evolved predispositions. First there is a predisposition to seek cooperative solutions that will benefit all parties relative to non-cooperators; second, a predisposition to share cooperatively acquired resources with all of those deemed to belong to the same group; and third, a predisposition to punish non-reciprocators even if the punishment is costly.

Today most social scientists would agree that humans do engage in acts of reciprocal aid. The only debate is whether this is due to evolved predispositions or a cultural invention in each society (Ridley, 1996). Reciprocal back-scratching appears to be rife across widely separated human cultures – although the precise form that it takes may be related to economic factors specific to a given society. Clearly, since everybody in the group will benefit, cooperating makes sense. Or does it? During the middle years of the twentieth century a number of mathematicians suggested that cooperation might not make sense. They based this argument on a game.

Prisoner's dilemma and reciprocation

There is a branch of mathematics that deals with the decisions that people are predicted to make depending on the strategies of others. It's called **game theory**. The

---

Box 8.2 **Prisoner's dilemma in the absence of a brain**

You might think that engaging in prisoner's dilemma requires some degree of intelligence and is therefore unlikely to be seen outside humans and other large-brained animals. But one recent study demonstrates how it can occur in life forms that are so simple they don't have a brain at all (Turner and Chao, 1999). We often think of bacteria as bugs that infect our bodies (see chapter 12). Many bacteria, however, are themselves infected by viruses. A virus which invades a bacterium is called a **bacteriophage**. One particular bacteriophage exists in two forms. One form, which we might label 'cooperator', produces by-products that help the reproductive success of other viral particles. The other form, which we can call 'defector', produces very few of these useful by-products but makes use of the by-products of the first form. A single bacterium may be invaded by either form of the virus or by a mixture of both forms. Interestingly, when we look at the reproductive success of each virus form it is found to depend on which other individual virus forms are present. If we set the reproductive value of a cooperator form that finds itself in a bacterium with other cooperator viruses as 1.00 (equal to mutual reciprocity or R), then its reproductive success falls to 0.65 when in the presence of defector viruses (this is the sucker's payoff or S). Moreover, the reproductive success of defectors that find themselves in bacteria infected by cooperator viruses works out at 1.90 (which may be seen as the defector's payoff or T), while for defectors that find themselves in cells already infected with defectors the value is 0.83 (mutual defection or P).

Here we find that $T > R > P > S$, the usual pattern in a prisoner's dilemma. A real prisoner's dilemma in a microcosm.

---

whole idea about game theory is that it examines problems the world presents in both simplified and universal ways. One of the main aims of game theory is to find a solution to a problem which, given what everybody else is doing, cannot be bettered. This accepted solution is known as the Nash equilibrium after the Nobel-prize-winning Princeton mathematician John Nash, about whom the film *A Beautiful Mind* was made. Having been developed by economists to predict what people are likely to do with investment decisions, John Maynard Smith introduced game theory into animal behaviour to explain the relationship between behaviour and evolution. Subsequently it has been developed to help understand the evolutionary basis of human decision making.

But what, you might ask, has this got to do with reciprocation? One particular hypothetical scenario that game theory has been applied to solving is called **prisoner's dilemma**. As you'll see, it may be likened to the problems surrounding reciprocity.

In prisoner's dilemma two criminal suspects are arrested by the police and placed in separate questioning cells. Each is told that if they implicate the other they will be rewarded and set free while the other will receive a harsh sentence. If, however, neither talks then both will receive a light sentence. In game theory terminology implicating the other is called 'defection' and refusing to talk is called 'cooperation'. The outcome or **payoff** for each player is generally symbolised by one of four symbols: T is the temptation to defect; R is the reward each receives if they cooperate; P is the punishment they receive if both defect; and S is the sucker's payoff – that is, if you cooperate when your partner has defected. In this set-up it is important that the payoff decreases from T through R and P to S. This makes sense when we consider that T has to involve a 'temptation' (i.e. it is the biggest payoff – but only if the other party does not defect which leads to the P payoff, the second smallest payoff). It is also necessary that the payoff for mutual cooperation R is greater than the average payoff for cooperation and defection – otherwise there is no real incentive to cooperate. Mathematically we can express the payoff in prisoner's dilemma as $T > R > P > S$. In practice the game is played for points – providing values for each of these will help. Typically the following values are given:

$$T = 5; R = 3; P = 1; S = 0$$

We can represent the four possible outcomes in a 'payoff matrix' (see figure 8.4). Note that the points gained are given for Player B in the above example, not Player A (although in the case of mutual defection or cooperation both players will have equal scores).

Now here's the dilemma. Both players should realise that rationally they should defect – but this makes each worse off than if they both cooperated. But why can we expect that each would defect? Think about it. If you are playing this game you must consider what your partner might do. If your partner cooperates, then by defecting you will gain 5 points; if your partner defects then you will have to defect in order to gain the 1 point for punishment rather than the 0 that is a sucker's payoff. The dilemma boils down to the fact that you do not know what your partner is going to do. Prisoner's dilemma suggests that people should not cooperate.

At this point you might be thinking that prisoner's dilemma sounds like a little game which has nothing to do with real social behaviour. However, as Matt Ridley puts it, prisoner's dilemmas are all around us:

Broadly speaking any situation in which you are tempted to do something but know it would be a great mistake if everybody did the same thing, is likely to be a prisoner's dilemma. (1996, pp. 55–6)

Thus, deciding whether or not to buy a round of drinks, deciding whether or not to repay the favour of babysitting, considering the tipping of a waiter and, perhaps most importantly of all, deciding whether or not to remain faithful in a relationship – these may all be thought of as the equivalent of prisoner's dilemmas. Put crudely, the dilemma that players face lies in deciding whether to reciprocate (cooperate – in a sense the equivalent of reciprocation) or to cheat (defect). If as Ridley claims, prisoner's dilemmas are all around us and if the only logical act is to defect/cheat then how can we explain the regular reciprocation that we encounter in human societies (and in at least some social animals)?

This same problem occurred to students of economics before Trivers had even proposed reciprocal altruism. Many claimed that we should not expect to see cooperation under such circumstances. And yet, all around us people do cooperate. The mathematicians who initially explored prisoner's dilemma in the 1960s also found that people often cooperated on the game even though this seemed illogical. They concluded that people just don't act rationally – that they weren't sophisticated enough to realise that double defection is the only logical response (Rapoport and Chummah, 1965). But if prisoner's dilemma is a model of the sort of decisions we face all of the time then surely we should have evolved to play the game rationally? The answer came when animal behaviourists pointed out that real-life social relations are rarely like a one-off game of prisoner's dilemma but that social animals encounter each other repeatedly and *remember* what happened on the last encounter. So social life is more akin to a series of such games where the same players meet each other frequently.

Whereas in 'one-shot' prisoner's dilemma, defection is the only logical option, when the game is played repeatedly by the same two players ('**iterated prisoner's dilemma**') they will frequently fall into a pattern of mutual cooperation. In this way both continually gain three points. When this is compared with the average score that is achieved via a mixture of the other three outcomes then both players will gain. That this pattern is rational stands up to the test of mighty computers. When different computer programs are played against each other typically the winner is one called 'tit-for-tat'. In tit-for-tat (or TFT) the strategy is to cooperate on the first move and thereafter do whatever your opponent did on their last move. Other, more complex, programs have been written involving a number of contingent rules depending on what your opponent does and that may involve switching strategies suddenly. But TFT apparently beats all others (Axelrod and Hamilton, 1981). This may help to explain why people often try to cooperate even in one-shot games of prisoner's dilemma – they (and their ancestors) were unlikely to find themselves in positions where their social behaviour has no possible future repercussions.

But why exactly is tit-for-tat so successful against all other strategies? Political scientist Robert Axelrod, who has been at the forefront of examining prisoner's dilemma, considers TFT to be an **evolutionarily stable strategy** (or ESS). An ESS is a strategy that cannot be bettered provided sufficient members of a group adopt it (Maynard Smith, 1974). Axelrod believes that tit-for-tat is an ESS because it has three strengths:

- it is nice – i.e. it never defects first, which means it encourages cooperation;
- it is retaliatory – i.e. defection occurs immediately after the opponent has defected;
- it is forgiving – i.e. if a previously defecting opponent then cooperates it will immediately also cooperate (1984).

Today many social scientists consider that tit-for-tat describes well a common strategy that people employ when deciding how to respond to others. In addition to helping to describe and explain general incidents of social responses, it has even been used to help explain behaviour during warfare – both for the escalation of violence (Chagnon, 1983) and in some cases its dissipation (Axelrod, 1984).

Mutual constraint in warfare

You might be surprised to hear that a TFT strategy can lead to reductions in violence during human warfare. Most soldiers do not have the repeated contact with individual members of the opposing army to allow for a positive tit-for-tat to develop. However, during the trench warfare of the First World War, company units faced each other over 'no-man's-land' for lengthy periods of stalemate. Frequently, during these encounters, it became obvious that troops were beginning to fire over the heads of their opponents. Once such a gesture was made, reciprocal shoot-to-miss strategies were very quickly set up (Axelrod, 1984; Trivers, 1985). Clearly, both sides realised that they were encountering the same individuals repeatedly, which meant that they were in a position to remember the previous actions of their combatants. Moreover, individuals of both sides would be better off by cooperating. Interestingly, on occasions when the unwritten shoot-to-miss agreement was broken, retribution was always swift – typically the number killed would also be killed by the opposition. Likewise, a return to restraint was met with reciprocity. The behaviour of troops under such conditions is eerily similar to the behaviour of the iterated prisoner's dilemma computer program designed to play with a tit-for-tat strategy. Sadly, for innumerable young men, when the senior officers eventually realised what was happening, they began to move units around and started up raiding parties, both of which strategies put an end to what might have developed into a relatively painless war.

Violence and xenophobia

The degree of sacrifice that individuals are prepared to undergo for friends and family may be quite astonishing. As we have seen, via reciprocation, this tendency may be extended to an entire group where few genes are shared by common descent. It might be argued that this arose because, for the vast majority of our evolutionary history, we lived in forager societies of small bands where everybody was likely to have been a relative or close friend of some degree or to have had an interest in supporting mutual offspring. There is, however, a flip side to this coin.

Most human societies have demonstrated hostility towards some separate group at some point in their past (Archer, 1996). Social psychologists have long known that the roots of **xenophobia**, or hatred of strangers, may be traced back to identifying strongly with one's own group and negatively **stereotyping** those of other groups. Over a century ago American sociologist William Graham Sumner introduced the notion of a 'we–they' partition that he called **ethnocentrism**. In his book *Folkways*, published in 1906, Sumner described how membership of a group might lead, on the one hand, to pride and self-sacrifice and, on the other, to contempt and aggression towards other groups. Most modern-day social psychologists studying in-group/out-group attitudes trace the concept back to Sumner – but Darwin got there first:

The tribes inhabiting adjacent districts are almost always at war with each other [and yet] a savage will risk his own life to save that of a member of the same community. (Darwin, 1871, pp. 480–1)

Since Sumner's day, much theoretical and empirical work has been devoted to describing and explaining in-group/out-group bias – a phenomenon which appears to be universal (Brown, 1991; Rabbie, 1992). Today the prevailing approach appears to be a social–cognitive one. Social-cognitivists view stereotypes (both positive and negative) as cognitive schemas and social categories that influence perception of our own group and that of others. Such schemas help to simplify the world and make it easier to understand (see chapter 9). But they are more than just cognitive short-cuts. They also have emotional implications. What is unfamiliar may be seen as dangerous and negative. What is familiar may be seen as friendly and positive. Indeed, according to social psychologists, our own view of ourselves – our **self concept** – may be constructed partly out of our membership of social groups, so it's not surprising that we tend to view our own groups as positive (Bierhoff, 1996).

In-group loyalty and out-group hostility

Today social psychology has constructed well-developed theories as to why we form positive and negative attitudes in relation to the 'us' and 'them' labels during our lifetimes. However, studies from social psychology do not tell us why we seem to have this universal propensity to develop such a psychological dichotomy. Perhaps the evolutionary perspective will finally explain why this occurs.

Most evolutionists today agree that during much of human evolution we lived in relatively small groups. Estimates of size vary but average sized groups were probably somewhere between twenty and two hundred individuals (Caporael and Baron, 1997). This view is supported by both fossil and artefact evidence (Lewin, 1998) and by observations taken of current living pre-industrial people (Lee, 1979; Chagnon, 2012; Hill and Hurtado, 1996, see earlier). Within such groups, judging by the behaviour of these extant societies, it is likely that smaller coalitions would have formed which would have been in competition with other members of the larger group for resources relevant to reproduction. At times of hardship, however, the entire group may have banded together to compete or even fight with other tribes. Again this is supported by evidence from at least some pre-industrial societies (as discussed above). Human ancestors may well have had a long history of decision making over when to cooperate and when to compete and to do so at the appropriate level. Despite this competition, as prisoner's dilemma demonstrates, cooperation is frequently preferable to defection.

Among others, Ed Wilson (1975) has argued that, although small, highly related, groups of intelligent and long-lived individuals can make for a well-developed system of mutual aid, there is a downside to such a system. If ancestral human societies were largely based around acts of kin altruism and reciprocation, then selective pressures would also have led to the evolution of psychological mechanisms to spot cheats and to be suspicious of strangers until we are reassured that they are not freeriders. Indeed there is clear experimental evidence that our reasoning under social circumstances does initiate a search for cheats (Cosmides, 1989 – see chapter 9).

If, however, we spent much of our evolutionary past in quite close-knit groups which were in competition over resources with other small groups, then on balance it might have benefited our ancestors to be wary of members of other bands. According to Wilson, real or imagined threats to the group may help to forge a sense of group identity and mobilise tribal members. In his own words, under such circumstances:

Xenophobia becomes a political virtue. The treatment of nonconformists within the group grows harsher. History is replete with the escalation of this process to the point that the society breaks down or goes to war. No nation has been completely immune. (Wilson, 1975, p. 290)

Some evolutionists have suggested that the tendency to perceive sharp distinctions between in-group and out-group members is crucial to the formation of enduring coalitions and might therefore be an adaptation in itself (Krebs and Denton, 1997). It is certainly well established, both through field observation and by experimental manipulation, that the formation of a group identity can lead to positive in-group and negative out-group stereotyping. Many studies have demonstrated that out-group members are treated less charitably, with their misfortunes being attributed to the personal failings of the group members whereas failings of in-group members

Box 8.3 **Freeriding and the evolution of cooperation**

The evolution of cooperation among non-kin is greatly compromised by the existence of freeriders. Freeriders reap the benefits of cooperation without paying the costs and thus place themselves at a competitive advantage by exploiting cooperators. Many (e.g. Tooby *et al.*, 2006) have argued that, given the inherent disadvantages of cooperating with freeriders, cooperation could not have evolved unless mechanisms for detecting and dealing with freeriders also evolved. We discuss the detection of freeriders in chapter 9, but on the topic of dealing with freeriders (once detected) research suggests that there are at least two ways of dealing with them. The first is punishment. Cooperators feel a desire to punish those whom they perceive are failing to pull their weight (Price *et al.*, 2002). But punishment is not always an option as it is not always possible to identify the specific individual who is freeriding. In such cases cooperators respond by withdrawing cooperation completely.

Withdrawal of cooperation in the face of freeriding is supported by a wealth of research in experimental economics. For example in 'public good' games a group of individuals is given a sum of money that they can 'invest' in a common pool. After everyone has invested, a third party contributes additional money based upon the amount already in the pool (e.g. by multiplying the total by 1.5). This money is then shared out equally among all participants irrespective of the size of each individual's initial contribution. The process then repeats itself for a number of iterations. In such a situation group profit is maximised if everyone puts in the maximum amount each time and so long as everyone contributes individual profits are maximised too.

In the early stages of public good games participants generally invest a large proportion of their stake in the common pool (as predicted above), however over repeated iterations contributions decrease until little or no money is being invested towards the end of the game. Fehr and Schmidt (1999) conducted a meta-analytic study of twelve public good games and found that the average contribution in the early stages was around 40 per cent of initial stake, but in the final round 73 per cent of participants made no contribution at all. In post-experimental interviews participants indicated that the decline in contribution was due to them withdrawing their cooperation as a response to the low or non-existent contributions of others. Thus as Tooby *et al.* (2006) point out:

> The greatest cost that freeriders inflict is the loss of all the potential gains from n-party exchanges that otherwise would have been achieved if freeriding had not triggered antiexploitation motivational defenses among cooperators. (p. 120)

The importance of punitive sentiment in maintaining cooperation is shown by further research using public good games; when individuals are allowed to levy punishments (in the form of fines) on freeriders, cooperation drastically increases (Fehr and Gächter,

2002). In such a situation only 20 per cent of participants failed to cooperate in the final round of a public good game (contrasted with 73 per cent in non-punishment conditions, see above). The importance of punishment in ensuring cooperation is highlighted in research by Ostrom (1990), which found that sophisticated monitoring and punishment systems were found in all successful real-life common-pool institutions. Punishment, or at least the threat of it, therefore seems to be important for the maintenance of cooperation (see also Fehr and Gächter, 2000).

Box 8.4 Criticisms of Edward Wilson's views on xenophobia

You may recall from chapter 1 that some of the ideas expounded by E. O. Wilson in his book *Sociobiology: The New Synthesis* (1975) were heavily criticised at the time of its publication. One specific area of criticism concerned Wilson's ideas on xenophobia and his suggestion that it may, in some sense, be 'in our genes'. Allen *et al.* (1975), in quite a savage attack, charged Wilson with propagating the view that xenophobia and warfare are natural and thereby predestined suggesting that he was attempting 'to provide a genetic justification of the *status quo* and of existing privileges for certain groups according to class, race or sex'. Clearly, we need to be sensitive about such arguments. To state that xenophobia may have served a purpose in our ancestral past does not commit us to developing such feelings today or imply that, were we to do so, they should be considered morally acceptable. To have the potential to develop a trait should not be equated with inevitability. Genes exert their phenotypic effects via an interaction with the environment. Change the environment and the phenotypic effects may be greatly altered, even reversed (see chapter 2).

Moreover, it should also be realised that Wilson was being largely descriptive rather than prescriptive. Evolutionists are not suggesting that the development of racist attitudes is predetermined, only that strong identification with a specific group may have been one strategy that helped our ancestors to survive in competition with other groups. This, in turn, might also help to explain why many people are so easily indoctrinated into nationalistic causes today. Knowledge of such a potential might even help us to educate our children not to hold such views.

are frequently put down to bad luck (Buss, 1997; see also chapter 9). A classic example from social psychology, which demonstrates just how easily children can be indoctrinated to form in-group/out-group stereotypes, involved the random allocation of schoolboys into artificial groups.

Natural group formation – the Robbers' Cave experiment

In Oklahoma in the mid-1950s, social psychologist Muzafer Sherif and his co-workers conducted an experiment which demonstrated just how quickly groups can form and how strong the social glue may quickly become (Sherif, 1956). They randomly divided twenty-two boys into two groups at a 'summer camp' in Robbers' Cave State Park (in reality the camp was a social psychology experiment set up to study group behaviour). The boys, who had never met before the experiment, all came from different schools but had similar backgrounds – all were white protestants who had average or just above average intelligence. The boys were allowed to name their own groups and became the 'Rattlers' and the 'Eagles'. The two groups arrived separately and were kept in cabins in different locations in the park for the first week. In fact, during this period each group was led to believe they were the sole occupants of the camp – the idea being to bring the two groups together in competitive games after a week and see how they interacted. At least that was the plan.

In the event, the two groups heard each other playing in the distance and both immediately wanted to show the others 'who was boss'. When the two groups were brought together to play a series of games, competition soon spilled over into aggression and violence. Name-calling quickly progressed into physical fighting and, while between-group hostility was spiralling out of control, individual boys were seen to act in defence of other group members. The only thing that relieved the hostility was the introduction of an imaginary third group. Sherif and his collaborators told the boys that a group of unknown boys from outside the camp had been vandalising the camp water system and that both groups were needed to check the entire water pipeline. This, and a number of other tasks that required the collaboration of the two groups, gradually led to a truce between them.

Despite this armistice, the boys remained closer to their group members than to those of the other group. You might argue that this study only serves to illustrate at a slightly more extreme level what all of us probably already know. Anybody who has ever played a team sport or been a member of some sort of gang will recognise both the loyalty felt by the boys to their comrades and the hostility they vented on their competitors. But Sherif's study also teaches us the important lesson that if we want to resolve group conflict then one way to do so is by presenting a common enemy. When this occurs then suddenly the out-group can become incorporated into the in-group.

Group formation based on minimal information

If the Robbers' Cave experiment demonstrated how easily we can be sucked into arbitrary groupings, then Henri Tajfel's studies of in- and out-group discrimination

18	17	16	15	14	13	12	11	10	9	8	7	6	6
5	6	7	8	9	10	11	12	13	14	15	16	17	18

Figure 8.5 Example of an allocation matrix from Tajfel's experiment

at an English high school in Bristol have served to illustrate that this process can even occur between individuals who remain anonymous to each other (Tajfel, 1970). Tajfel's experiment involved the allocation of rewards to others and consisted of two phases. In the first phase, a researcher showed a group of boys from the same school forty slides consisting of clusters of dots and asked them individually to estimate how many dots they had seen on each slide. Their scores were then taken away by the researcher and assessed. At this point the boys were told that some individuals constantly overestimate the number of dots while others consistently underestimate. The boys were then taken into separate rooms where each was given a code number. Each boy was told either that he was an 'underestimator' or an 'overestimator' at the task (in reality they were randomly assigned to these group labels). The second phase of the study then began and consisted of a decision task whereby each boy had to assign points to pairs of other subjects. In order to do this every boy was given an eighteen-page booklet, on each page of which was printed a matrix consisting of series of number pairs (see figure 8.5). These number pairs represented possible paired allocations of points, the upper number going to the boy whose label (overestimator or underestimator) and code number were indicated on the top row and the bottom number going to another boy whose label and code were attached to the bottom row. Importantly these points could be exchanged for money. In this way each boy had to allocate points to two other (anonymous) boys each time they turned over a new page. The only information with which they were provided in order to make their decisions was whether each of the pair to be rewarded was an overestimator or an underestimator. Note from figure 8.5 that the range of paired numbers allowed for each participant to allocate the paired recipients either virtually equal amounts (such as 11 and 12 points) or a range of unequal amounts (such as 9 and 14 or, more extremely, 6 and 18).

Given that the boys did not know to whom they were allocating points, Tajfel and his co-workers were unsurprised to discover that they allocated the points roughly equally when the upper and lower labels belonged to the same 'group' (i.e. over- or underestimators). In marked contrast, however, when they were of differing groups they allocated unequal amounts – favouring those in the same group label as themselves (Tajfel, 1970; Tajfel *et al.*, 1971). This result was surprising, since it was clear evidence of favouring of the in-group over the out-group even though the identity of both group members was unknown to each decision maker. Tajfel called this behaviour **minimal intergroup discrimination**, that is, they were discriminating in favour of some individuals on the basis of arbitrary and anonymous group member-ship alone.

Although Tajfel's finding astonished social psychologists in the early 1970s due to the sheer lack of information that the boys used to discriminate between in- and out-group membership, it has subsequently been replicated many times and appears to be a robust effect (Brewer and Crano, 1994).

Like Sherif's Robbers' Cave experiment, Tajfel's results suggest that we don't have to seek out like-minded compatriots, we just have to have something (anything) that allows us to feel part of a group. In the words of John Archer:

It seems that people will latch on to almost any cue to distinguish in-group and out-group members. (1996, p. 33)

Although, in terms of competition, Sherif and Tajfel's experiments demonstrate how extreme in- and out-group prejudice can become, the incidents of violence were mild compared to the sort of acts that frequently occur during warfare. Seemingly, these social psychology experiments are a long way from serious 'real-world' conflicts. Or are they? If we stand back for a minute and consider, it becomes clear that the difference is one of degree, not kind. The boys at Robbers' Cave, for example, may not have wanted to see members of the other group dead – but they did seriously try to hurt each other and both groups expressed a view that they would rather they had the camp to themselves. If this level of hostility can develop after only one week in individuals randomly allocated to groups then it may help us to understand how different racial and religious groupings such as the Israelis and Palestinians, both claiming precedence to parts of Israel, can develop murderous hatred towards each other. It might also help to explain the extreme degree of 'altruistic' behaviour required for the suicide bombing raids that have occurred under such conditions. Altruistic, that is, to the members of your own group.

The reasoning above is an example of the kind of argument that has been developed by social psychologists to help explain intergroup hostility and cooperation. The component that evolutionary psychologists would like to add to the equation is the notion that, in our ancestral past, in-group/out-group discriminations would have had inclusive fitness consequences. Perhaps suicide bombings serve to illustrate just how far kin altruism and direct reciprocation might develop. Such actions might also serve to demonstrate the serious downside to the evolution of human social behaviour.

In conclusion

The argument above is an example of an ultimate level of explanation that evo-lutionists are attempting to bring to the analysis of all social behaviour. Currently, rather than examine each specific area of research that traditional SSSM social

> Box 8.5 **A real prisoner's dilemma – Philip Zimbardo's**
> **prison experiment**
>
> In the latter years of the twentieth century a whole series of social psychology studies
> were built on the findings of Sherif and Tajfel. Such studies confirmed not only how
> quickly 'us' and 'them' concepts can become established but also how badly otherwise
> normal individuals might then treat non-group members. A dramatic example of this
> was the 'prison simulation experiment' of Stanford psychologist Philip Zimbardo and
> his colleagues (Haney *et al.*, 1973). In this study college students were randomly
> allocated to role-play the parts of 'prisoners' and 'guards' in a mock-up of a prison
> wing. Zimbardo and his colleagues monitored the behaviour of both groups via video
> and audio equipment in order to study how group identities developed. The experiment
> was designed to last for two weeks, but due to the harsh treatment meted out by the
> 'guards' to their increasingly despondent captives it had to be terminated after only six
> days. During this period the guards frequently resorted to psychological bullying,
> commanding the prisoners to do pushups at random intervals and refusing their
> requests to go to the toilet. In contrast to the way the guards treated their charges,
> they very quickly formed a cohesive group which worked effectively together.
> Effectively, that is, with regard to keeping their 'prisoners' subservient. For their part,
> the prisoners became so demoralised that they demonstrated clear signs of depression
> and helplessness – so much so that Zimbardo and his colleagues held a number of
> debriefing sessions over the year following the experiment to help them overcome such
> feelings.

psychologists have tackled, evolutionary psychologists are attempting to introduce concepts largely derived from sociobiology to help understand human social responses. In particular, evolutionary psychologists suggest that the fundamental reasons for pro- and antisocial behaviour may be traced back to inclusive fitness theory (see chapter 7). More specifically, the theories of kin and direct reciprocation have been applied to help explain why people give aid (or not) to others. Such concepts may have been modified by humans, however, as with the development of language and complex culture people develop insight into the reasons why they help others – and why they sometimes feel hostility towards them. Reputation and a conscious awareness of the result of our actions may have taken altruistic behaviour to a new level of complexity. Conversely, such an understanding may also have led to tit-for-tat spirals of aggressive acts between and within human social groups.

For much of the twentieth century, most psychologists considered questions concerning human social behaviour as if Darwin had not existed. Even today there is a reluctance from many social scientists to apply evolutionary principles to human behaviour (see, for example, Wallace, 2010 – see also chapter 1). If, however, the ultimate level of analysis does gain acceptance in mainstream social psychology then a powerful tool may be made available for the development of novel testable hypotheses concerning pro- and antisocial behaviour in our species (Schaller *et al.*, 2006).

Summary

- Evolutionary psychologists have used the concept of reciprocal altruism/direct reciprocation to help explain cooperative behaviour in humans and other species. Direct reciprocation consists of self-sacrificing acts between two unrelated individuals that are based on delayed reciprocation. Well-documented cases of reciprocity are known in non-human species including the giving of regurgitated blood between vampire bats and mutual aid in vervet monkeys.

- It is likely, however, that reciprocation is rare in animals when compared to kin altruism (see chapter 7). In contrast to its rareness in other species, some evolutionary psychologists consider that reciprocation may be one of the foundation stones of human social behaviour.

- A branch of mathematics called game theory has been used by evolutionists to model the behaviour of humans and other species under simplified versions of social decision-making scenarios. One hypothetical scenario called prisoner's dilemma asks players to make decisions concerning cooperation or defection with regard to a fellow player. Computer simulations involving a series of prisoner's dilemma interactions suggest that one strategy – 'tit-for-tat' – is the most successful. In tit-for-tat a player begins by cooperating on the first encounter and thereafter responds in kind to whatever the other player has done.

- Tit-for-tat has been labelled an evolutionarily stable strategy, or ESS. An ESS is a strategy that cannot be bettered provided sufficient members of a group adopt it. Humans who play prisoner's dilemma repeatedly most frequently also develop the ESS tit-for-tat strategy. This might suggest that, as a general strategy, humans seek a willingness to cooperate but also bear a grudge when this cooperation is not reciprocated.

- Evolutionary psychologists trace the fear of strangers, or xenophobia, back to competition over limited resources between small close-knit groups of individuals living in our ancestral past. Intergroup hostility may also be related to the type of mind that has developed under the pressures that an evolutionary history of kin altruism and reciprocation creates. Controversially, some evolutionists have proposed that the tendency to perceive sharp distinctions between in- and out-group members aids the formation of coalitions and might under some conditions have been an adaptive strategy.

Questions

1. Some evolutionary psychologists have argued that intergroup hostility (and even warfare) may stem from in-group/out-group bias. What might be the limitations of this argument when considering warfare? Make a list of competing hypotheses that might be used to explain warfare. How might we test between these alternative hypotheses?

2. Which of the following might be considered to be acts of true altruism (you should be able to defend your answer):
   (a) A man saves his son from a burning building.
   (b) A man saves his friend from a burning building.
   (c) A woman gives all of her savings to charity.
   (d) A pop star adopts and raises a child from a poor undeveloped country.

3. Table 8.1 presents evidence of examples of apparent reciprocity in the animal kingdom. Tim Clutton-Brock has suggested, however, that many examples of apparent aid between non-kin can be accounted for by mutualism or by manipulation. Choose one of the examples provided and suggest what sort of observations might allow us to distinguish between these three ways of explaining this social behaviour.

4. E. O. Wilson was criticised by Allen *et al.* for suggesting that xenophobia may, in some sense, be 'in our genes'. Do you find this argument convincing? Even if he holds such a view on purely scientific grounds, considering their potential implications, should he have published such statements?

FURTHER READING

Alcock, J. (2009). *Animal Behavior: An Evolutionary Approach.* Sunderland, MA: Sinauer. An up-to-date evolutionary approach to understanding animal behaviour including material on social behaviour and a final chapter which explores human social behaviour from an evolutionary perspective.

Alexander, R. D. (1987). *The Biology of Moral Systems.* New York: Aldine de Gruyter. A detailed examination of the relationship between moral behaviour, emotions and evolution set in social contexts. Explores in some depth the notion of reciprocation as applied to human societies.

Chagnon, N. (2012). *Yanomamö: Case Studies in Cultural Anthropology* (6th edn). Wadsworth, CA: Belmont. A personal account of a technologically primitive people by an anthropologist who lived among them. Describes and seeks to explain social behaviour of a pre-industrial society via a case-study approach.

Ridley, M. (1996). *The Origins of Virtue.* London: Viking Press. A very readable account of the relationship between evolution and behaviour, focusing on cooperation and other aspects of social behaviour.

Evolution, thought and cognition

The ability to respond to and act upon the environment was a big step in evolution, requiring sophisticated mechanisms of perception, monitoring and decision making. In the twentieth century, a new form of psychology was developed – cognitive psychology – which described these control processes in terms of their underlying computations. Traditional theories of cognition have tended to emphasise proximate causes, explaining behaviour in terms of the cognitive processes that underlie it rather than ultimate ones. Evolutionary approaches to cognition attempt to explain behaviour at the ultimate level in terms of behaviours that might have been ancestrally adaptive. In doing this they seek the adaptive significance of certain behaviours and ask what specific problems the cognitive system was designed to solve. Cognition is therefore seen as adaptive and apparent maladaptive behaviour is either the result of differences between the current world and the EEA, or necessary trade-offs in the evolution of mind. In this chapter, we discuss the nature of cognitive theorising, which focuses on explaining behaviour as a result of mental computation. We then investigate the impact of evolutionary thinking on theories of cognition investigating the important areas of memory, reasoning and decision making.

What are minds? What are brains? And what are they for?

Psychologists, particularly cognitive psychologists, are familiar with discussing minds, whereas neuroscientists are familiar with discussing brains. What is the difference and if there is a difference, does it matter? To many, particularly dualists such as the philosopher Descartes, there was a difference and it certainly mattered. In fact, to Descartes it was all about matter and the lack of it. In his view brains were material objects meaning that they were made of the same kind of stuff as the rest of the body and indeed the physical world. They doubtless did a lot of important work, but what they didn't do, in his view, was to think. Thinking was done by a different kind of thing completely, a thing called the mind and unlike the brain it was not a material object, it was not made of matter but of some mysterious 'substance' that Descartes referred to as *res cogitans*: Latin for 'thinking stuff'. (The name he used for common or garden matter, including the brain, was *res extensa*, Latin for 'extended stuff'.)

Nowadays most psychologists and philosophers have rejected the view that there are two fundamentally different kinds of substance involved in cognition (the dualist position) and accept that mind and brain are fundamentally the same kind of thing. This view suggests that everything is ultimately the result of matter and material processes and is therefore known as **materialism**. It is the materialist view that is espoused in this chapter. We can express the relationship between mind and brain in different ways. Steven Pinker refers to the mind as 'the information processing activity of the brain'. In other words the mind is what the brain does. Another way of thinking about it is that the mind is how the brain appears to itself, which emphasises the way in which mind tends to be equated with conscious activity and self-awareness. However you think about it, it is important to recognise that the fundamental assumption of materialism is 'whatever is in the mind is also in the brain'. There is no special place or set of processes that we could consider to be 'of the mind' that are not ultimately manifested in brain activity.

But why do we have brains, and what are they for? When psychology students are asked this question they usually struggle for an answer. This is surprising as many of them have been studying psychology for two years. It is a bit like physiology students having an intimate understanding of the heart: its tendons, muscles, neural pathways, valves, blood vessels and distinctive sound without ever being told that its function is to pump blood. The very thing that brings order to what might otherwise be a random collection of different types of meat. So what is the brain for? One answer is that it is an organ of decision making. Yes it is also for perception, although perception is merely a way of making use of environmental information in order to make fitness-relevant decisions – avoiding predators, finding food, finding an attractive mate and so on. It is also involved in memory but memory is – as we shall see later – a way of using past events to predict future ones, again the better to make good decisions. And so on. In this chapter we discuss these issues, relating them to standard phenomena of cognitive psychology, such as perception, memory and reasoning, in an attempt to understand the reasons why the mind operates the way it does, and why it sometimes seems to fail us.

Cognition and the evolution of thought

The human mind is breathtaking in its power and complexity. It enables us to navigate three-dimensional space with an ease that would embarrass any robot, entertain thoughts about things that we have never before experienced, and share these thoughts with others by packaging them up using the medium of language. The benefits of having a powerful mind are obvious; culture, language, creativity and complex problem solving, but there are also less obvious costs.

First, a powerful mind is the result of a powerful brain, and human brains are metabolically costly, gobbling up some 20 per cent of the body's energy while accounting for only 3 per cent of its mass. Second, it increases the weight of the head, making death from a broken neck or other 'whiplash' injuries much more likely than in other primates. Third, the larger head required to accommodate the human brain means that birth is difficult for both mother and baby – an alarming number of infants and mothers die from birth complications, particularly in societies without advanced medical care. This problem is compounded by the fact that the human pelvis is narrower than in our primate relatives due to the biomechanical requirements of bipedalism (see chapter 4).

That the brain developed despite these costs is clear evidence that the brain didn't get bigger by accident, there must have been advantages in order to outweigh these costs. Exactly what were these advantages has been the topic of much debate within evolutionary psychology but in general evolutionists believe that the minds of our ancestors evolved particular **computational mechanisms** that enabled them to deal effectively with the demands of their environment.

The notion of computation is the cornerstone of the discipline known as cognitive science which sees the brain as a computer. It is important to stress that this is not merely a usefully metaphor or analogy; cognitive scientists do not see the mind as *like* a computer, they see it literally as *being* a computer. Many people are uneasy with this notion, often raising objections that computers need to be told what to do (by a program) whereas the mind learns for itself, or that computers work by slavishly applying algorithms to a problem whereas humans work by 'intuition'. This is presumably because they have in mind the type of computer that sits on their desk at home. But hard disks and microprocessors are just one way of building a computer; another way is to do what nature does and build a brain. To make this clearer it might help to know that the word *computer* was originally used to describe people whose job it was to crunch numbers, sometimes with the help of machines such as abacuses or other calculating devices. As technology improved the word was used to describe the machines themselves rather than their operators. Charles Babbage's analytical engine first described in 1837 was perhaps the first design for a general programmable computer: input and output were achieved using cards with holes punched in them, information was processed by metal drums with pegs in them

Figure 9.1 Trial model of the analytical engine conceived by pioneering computer scientist Charles Babbage in 1834. Only part of the actual machine was build (pictured)

and the whole thing was powered by steam (see figure 9.1). Although the analytical engine was never built due to its complexity, and although it was mechanical rather than electronic; it was nonetheless as much of a computer as a modern day PC or Mac. This is because it engages in *computation* a process defined by a set of mathematical principles devised by, among others, the British mathematician Alan Turing; so long as something engages in computation, it is a computer irrespective of what it is made from or how it is constructed (in his 1976 book *Computer Power and Human Reason* computer scientist, Joseph Weizembaum shows how to build a computer out of toilet roll and some pebbles). Thus when we describe the brain as a computer we are referring to the abstract process of computation just as when we describe the heart as a pump we are referring to its abstract property of moving fluid from one place to another by a particular sequence of actions. To argue that the brain is not a computer because it doesn't resemble current artificial computers is like arguing that the heart cannot be a pump because it doesn't resemble the thing you use to inflate your bicycle tyres. (There is a debate about what computation means, and whether the brain engages in it, see Fodor, 2000, and the reply by Pinker, 2005).

The **computational theory of mind** as this position is known provides cognitive scientists with a powerful way of understanding how the mind works. For example, vision can be understood in terms of the computational processes that render a coloured, three-dimensional representation of the world from light of different wavelengths falling on the retina. Researchers can then test theories as to how this might be achieved by turning their theories into computational models and running them on a desktop computer. A further assumption of cognitive science is **substrate neutrality**: the nature of the hardware – whether it is neurons or silicon (or toilet roll!) – makes no difference to the computation being carried out (in terms of input and output, factors such as time taken might vary).

Of course, if we want to properly understand human psychology, we will want to understand the substrate: how neurons process information. One of the roles of neuroscience is to take abstract computational theories of vision or memory and work out how they might be implemented in a neural architecture. Notice that this is what Dennett calls 'good' reductionism (see chapter 1): theories at the biological level enhance rather than supplant theories at the higher computational levels (see box 9.1).

Most cognitive scientists defer to the computational theory of mind but not all cognitive scientists defer to Darwinian theories of cognition. What might Darwin bring to the cognitive sciences? Most conspicuously, evolutionary cognitive science brings some commitment to innately specified mental machinery (which might mean proposing innate mental modules or innate learning mechanisms – see chapter 5). Perhaps more importantly an evolutionary explanation attempts to understand the mind/brain by asking what it is *for*, or more correctly what problems particular components of the mind might have been designed to solve. In the rest of this chapter, we discuss how evolutionary thinking might be applied productively to four of the key areas of cognitive science: visual perception, memory, categorisation and reasoning.

Vision

The branch of the cognitive sciences to which evolutionary thinking has been applied with the least controversy is visual perception. The vision scientist David Marr (see box 9.1) revolutionised the field when he asked what the visual system is designed to do (see the above discussion on what the brain is for). The answer might seem obvious: to enable us to see the world as it is, but this doesn't really help since there are many instances where we clearly do not see the world as it is.

Figure 9.2, for instance, shows two visual illusions. In the first all that is there are three circles with wedges cut out, yet we can't help seeing a triangle; it is as if the space in the middle is somehow denser than the surrounding space. In the second the parallelograms that make up the tables are the same size and shape even though the one on the left looks longer and slimmer than the one on the right.

Box 9.1 **David Marr and levels of explanation**

In chapter 1 we argued that evolutionary psychology was reductionist in the 'good' sense (Dennett, 1995), that it explains behaviour at different levels with lower levels contributing rather than replacing descriptions at higher levels. Consistent with this view, David Marr (1982) suggested that a complex organism or artefact could be described and explained at three levels.

(1) The level of *computational theory*. What is the thing for? What is its function? For example a computer program might be designed to add up a list of numbers.
(2) The level of *representation and algorithm*. How is the above achieved at the abstract computational level? For example, what steps does the computer program go through to add up the numbers?
(3) The level of *hardware implementation*. How is this computation described in step 2 implemented on the actual physical substrate of the machine? Is the computation done by neurons, microprocessors or mechanical wheels and punch cards? How does this substrate achieve the computation?

Given the difficulties of understanding the human mind in terms of the behaviour of neurons most cognitive theories of mind have, understandably, tended to focus on the second level or representation and algorithm. One of Marr's great contributions was to propose that if we are to properly understand some aspect of human thought and behaviour we need to have some idea as to the function or purpose of this behaviour. Throughout this book we have been suggesting that one of the benefits of adopting an evolutionary approach to psychology is that it focuses on the function of behaviour. Thus evolutionary psychology can provide us with our computational theory (to use Marr's term). As we shall see later on, Cosmides and Tooby argue that decades' worth of research on logical reasoning failed to take into account what the mechanisms engaged by these tasks was for. They make sense of the data by arguing that at the level of computational theory, the process that solve logical tasks were actually designed to detect freeriders or cheats.

In other words, the area of the retina that is covered by the two tabletops is the same but our brain somehow contrives to make them look different. If our visual system were truly designed to represent the way that the world is then we should see no triangle and the tables would look the same shape. And visual illusions do not just apply to shapes. Colour, we know, relates to the wavelength of light reflected from a particular surface; if the surface reflects short wavelength light it appears blue, if it reflects longer wavelengths it appears red. Yet the wavelength of light depends not just on the nature of the surface, it also depends on the wavelength of the ambient light. On a sunny day the wavelength of light reflected off a 'red' shirt, for example,

Figure 9.2 Some visual illusions. In the one on the left you see a triangle where there is no triangle, and in the one on the right, are the tabletops the same size and shape or different?

Figure 9.3a Shadow illusion by Edward Adelson. Believe it or not, the two squares, A and B, are exactly the same shade and colour even though A looks much darker

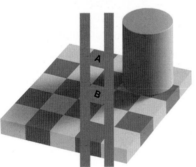

Figure 9.3b Proof that the two squares are the same. Each square blends perfectly with the horizontal bar

will be different at noon from at sunset and dusk. The fact that the shirt appears to be the same colour at all times of the day is a testament to the compensatory effects of the visual system. A good example of this is shown in figure 9.3a (from Adelson, 1993). Look at the squares A and B. The square marked A looks grey and the square marked B looks like a white square in shadow, a kind of grey but not as dark as A. You guessed it. They are exactly the same colour. Don't believe it? Well 9.3b shows the proof of this. The two vertical lines are, as you can see the same colour as both squares, they blend in perfectly when they touch the squares. The squares probably still look a little different, this is the illusion, they look different, but they are the same colour, in other words the wavelengths of the light leaving the squares is identical for A and B. This illusion shows that the visual system can distinguish real, permanent patterns such as physical objects (the grey and white squares) from transient patterns such as shadows.

Are these just exceptions? Maybe the visual system really is designed to represent the world as it truly is but fails on a handful of contrived illusions? Marr's position is that such illusions are not exceptional, nor are they design faults; on the contrary, they show how well designed the visual system is. Marr argues that the visual system is not merely designed to represent the way things are in the world, rather vision 'is a process that produces from images of the external world a description that is useful to the viewer and not cluttered with irrelevant information' (1982, p. 473). Take the notion of colour outlined above. We see the colour of objects as uniform across different conditions of luminance because it helps us in our day-to-day activities to maintain a perception of the world as being filled with stable enduring objects. If the colour of objects changed with moment-to-moment changes in luminance it would become difficult to track objects across time and space and identify objects as ones that we had (or hadn't) seen before. The tables in figure 9.2 look different because the visual system is compensating for the foreshortening that occurs when objects are viewed at an oblique angle. If the two objects were real tables (rather than simply drawings) then because of the viewing angle, the left-hand table really would be longer than the one on the right is wide. The visual system is giving us information about the size of the object that we are viewing by compensating for the foreshortening effect. We see an illusory triangle because our visual systems are designed to 'fill in' missing information to create a whole object. Think how disadvantageous it would be if a tiger walking behind long grass were identified as a set of narrow individual tiger-slices rather than a large, somewhat dangerous whole tiger. The way that we see the world is designed to enable us to make good decisions and act upon them effectively.

Once adaptationist thinking is applied to vision we realise that representing the world as it actually is is not the primary goal of perception; the primary goal of perception is action and visual illusions do not reveal bugs but features. Taking their lead from Marr, some cognitive scientists have argued that the same logic can be applied to other areas of cognition, including that other flawed psychological process – memory.

Evolution and memory

In the 1993 film *Groundhog Day*, weatherman Phil Connor (played by Bill Murray) is forced to relive the events of a single same day over and over again. Connor is, however, the only one who is aware that all this is happening; all of the other characters, including love-interest Rita (played by Andie MacDowell) are blissfully unaware that they are stuck in a time loop. Connor eventually turns this to his advantage – he has designs on Rita and uses the fact that history is repeating itself to modify his behaviour so that she eventually falls for him. The unique events of *Groundhog Day* illustrate the principal function of memory – to use the past to predict the future. Of course, we don't literally experience exactly the same events over and over again as did the characters in *Groundhog Day* but most events have enough similarities to previous ones for memory to put those who have it at a distinct advantage to those who do not.

One of the pioneers of memory research was Herman Ebbinghaus (1850–1909). Ebbinghaus studied memory by stripping his experimental stimuli of all meaning and emotional content by using visually presented nonsense syllables such as PUX, ZAT and RIQ. By doing this, Ebbinghaus believed that he would be able to test the basic processes of memory free from other systems such as those responsible for processing meaning and emotion. Although this seems a reasonable assumption, there is a real danger that one ends up merely testing the capability of a system rather than its function. Whatever human memory evolved to do (and it is likely that it was not one single thing – see later) it was certainly not to remember nonsense syllables, since written language is a comparatively recent invention. It is therefore, perhaps, unsurprising that the picture of memory that Ebbinghaus's research paints is that of a limited, fallible and somewhat fragile system.

Often contrasted with the work of Ebbinghaus is the more naturalistic work of the British psychologist Sir Frederick Bartlett (see Bartlett, 1932). Rather than using meaningless symbols, Bartlett presented his participants with meaningful materials such as pictures and passages of text and tested their recall sometime after. Again, memory comes out as appearing somewhat unreliable. In particular, he found that people's recall of textual information is prone not just to omissions but also to intrusions where culturally specific information would be falsely recalled. For example a passage in an Inuit folk tale that described a group of men going hunting for seals was misremembered by Bartlett's British participants as them going fishing, presumably because they were unaccustomed to the concept of seal hunting.

Although Bartlett's work attempted to present stimuli that were more ecologically valid it is no more likely for memory to have evolved to memorise long passages of text verbatim than it is to remember nonsense syllables. So what is memory for?

What is the function of memory?

Although researchers such as Ebbinghaus and Bartlett contributed much to the study of human memory, they also tended to isolate it from the rest of human behaviour. But

Box 9.2 **The problem of free will**

The cognitive approach to psychology frequently leaves some people feeling uncomfortable. If the mind is nothing more than a biological computing machine where does that leave our free will? Are all our choices predetermined? The idea that free will is contrasted with determinism is a common one and it is important to point out the problem of this form of thinking. A deterministic system is one in which (1) if you understand completely the starting state of the system and (2) you understand completely the rules by which the system operates then it is possible to predict with 100 per cent accuracy the state of that system at any point in the future.

Assuming that the universe were a deterministic system, then if we knew the state of the every particle in the universe at some point in time (say a few billions of years ago) and if our physics were perfect, then by applying the laws of physics we would be able to predict the formation of planet earth, the origins of life, the evolution of human beings and even the fact that you are reading this book at this precise moment.

It follows, therefore, that if the universe is deterministic and our brains are part of that universe, made up of complex aggregations of atoms and molecules, then our thoughts are as determined and therefore as predictable as everything else. This usually makes people feel uncomfortable, and many seek solace by assuming that the universe is not deterministic. After all, they argue, quantum physics suggests that there is genuine uncertainty: physics does not operate like a clockwork mechanism. In an indeterministic universe there would be genuine unpredictability. For example, particles subjected to identical forces might move off in one direction or another, with no possible way of telling which in advance. It would be as if someone flipped a coin or threw dice in order to determine what happened next. This would certainly lead to the universe becoming unpredictable – exactly how unpredictable depending on how much randomness there is – but does indeterminism rescue our concept of free will? Some argue that it does. But consider what indeterminism means for freedom. It would be as if a coin were being tossed in the brain. Given a set of circumstances with two courses of action X and Y, in some cases the coin would come down heads and we would choose X, in other circumstances they would choose Y. But randomness does not seem like free will either, free choices are motivated, not the result of a random coin flip. So neither determinism nor indeterminism rescues our concept of free will. Is free will therefore an illusion? On the face of it, some research seems to suggest that it might be.

One famous study was conducted by Libet (1985). Libet connected his participants up to an EEG machine that measured brain activity and asked them to consciously decide to move a finger whenever they felt like it. During this part of the study participants were staring at a fast moving clock so they could register exactly when they had the subjective experience of deciding to move their finger. When their hands moved it broke a beam of light so the actual timing of the hand movement could be accurately registered as well. Things became interesting when the results of the EEG were studied. For all participants a swell of brain activity reliably preceded the conscious decision to move the finger by 350–400 milliseconds. This suggests that some set of unconscious processes occurs *before* the conscious decision to move the finger.

In another study by Brasil-Neto *et al.* (1992) participants were asked to choose to move either their left or right index finger in response to a click. During this, transcranial magnetic stimulation (TMS) was applied to the motor cortex in either the left or right hemisphere. The effect of TMS here was to stimulate the motor cortex to initiate action in either the left or right finger (recall that due to the wiring of the brain, the left motor cortex controls the right-hand side of the body and vice versa). Even though participants were not in control of their actions (TMS was) they stated verbally that it was they who decided which finger they moved.

So is free will an illusion? Not necessarily, but it does mean that we should probably revise the way we think about free will and consciousness. Free will and consciousness are not entities that exist outside the material world; they are part (perhaps a special part) of the computational machinery of mind which, in turn, is produced by the brain. Although it might seem strange that conscious will might not be in full control of the minutiae of behaviour, this might derive from a misunderstanding of what consciousness is for. One way of viewing consciousness is as the manager of a company who has to control every aspect of the business. But it is also possible that our conscious selves only become involved in decisions that cannot be dealt with automatically. In the Libet study, our conscious selves might simply send an instruction to lower level processes which states 'at some point move the finger and let me know when this has been done' leading to a lag between the decision and the awareness of it. Likewise in the TMS study a similar instruction ('move one of the fingers when you hear a click and let me know when this is done') results in the reply that a finger has been moved as requested, even though this finger was moved – unbeknownst to consciousness – by magnetic stimulation. Like many managers, your conscious self knows only what it has been told happened, not what actually happened (Wegner, 2003).

memory did not evolve simply to store and retrieve information, it evolved to store and retrieve information for some purpose, that purpose being to support complex behaviour. As an analogy, consider another information storage and retrieval system: the library. Many libraries contain archives consisting of large repositories of books, journals and other materials kept away from public view. If you wish to obtain something from the archive, you need to speak to a librarian who will fetch you the relevant item from the store. An important criterion in the design of an archive is that librarians are able to retrieve relevant information quickly (you have many customers

Figure 9.4 Sir Frederick Bartlett

and you don't want to keep them waiting by spending a long time looking for each item). One way of increasing efficiency is to have the items that you think will be more likely to be requested in the future within easy reach, and use the less accessible places for infrequently borrowed items. How can you predict which items will be more likely to be requested in the future? One way is to use past information about borrowings. Research on libraries shows that books that were popular in the past are likely to be popular in the future, therefore one way of increasing future efficiency is to place high-frequency items in easily accessible locations, and low-frequency items in the more difficult locations.

Although memories are vastly different from libraries, it seems that similar principles hold. The psychologist and cognitive scientist John Anderson of Carnegie Mellon University proposes that human memory is optimally adapted to the structure of the information retrieval environment. For instance, we know that the speed at which an item such as a word is retrieved is predicted by the frequency at which the word was encountered in the past; high frequency words being faster than low frequency words. Anderson (see Anderson and Milson, 1989) argues that this is evidence of adaptive design. The mind is simply doing what an intelligent librarian would do and predicting which items will be useful in future by using information relating to its usefulness in the past, and organising the system so that useful items can be accessed more rapidly. Just like Phil Connor memory uses knowledge about the past in order to maximise future gain.

Anderson and Milson provide a similar account for **priming**. If a person encounters a particular word (e.g. 'dog') then he or she will be able to access that same word much faster next time they encounter it. This is called priming (more technically it is called 'repetition priming') because the presentation of the word 'primes' the system for future encounters. Perhaps more interestingly, not only is the word itself primed, but words that are semantically related are also primed. For example after we experience the word 'dog' the words 'cat', 'bark' and 'leash' will be retrieved more quickly than if we had received the word 'table'. Again, this is interpreted as memory trying to predict what words might come up in the near future based on previous co-occurrences of the concepts that underlie these words.

Klein *et al.* (2002) extended Anderson's work on memory, arguing that memory evolved to support the decision-making process. Throughout our lives humans make many millions of decisions and most, if not all, of these decisions will require more information than is available in the environment; this additional information is provided by information stored in memory. Of course, there are many different types of decisions – including habitat selection, mate choice and predator avoidance – each with its own particular solutions and constraints. Some decisions, for example, need to be made rapidly, whereas others can be made more leisurely but demand greater accuracy. For this reason, Klein *et al.* propose that there will be separate memory systems depending on the nature of the decision being made.

Different types of memory support different types of decision

Rather than talking about a single memory system, many psychologists prefer to think of memory as consisting of a number of separate sub-systems, all of which might have their own particular function. One long-standing division in memory research is that between **episodic** and **semantic** memory systems (Tulving, 1972). Episodic memory refers to the storage of specific experiences that one has had, whereas semantic memory stores generalised facts about the world. For instance specific memories of a vacation in Paris: the trip up the Eiffel Tower, or a meal at a café on the Champs Elysées would be retrieved from the episodic memory store. General knowledge about Paris such as that it is the capital of France or that it contains the Louvre art gallery would be stored in – and hence retrieved from – semantic memory.

To confuse matters slightly, recent research suggests that one can have semantic facts about oneself – kind of semantic episodic memories. For instance, Klein *et al.* (1996) report of a student W. J. who, following a blow to the head, had little recollection of any of her experiences in the months prior to her accident. However, her memory for general facts about this part of her life was preserved. For example, she could recall the names of her teachers and the classes she attended, but could not remember any particular experiences or people from those classes. To account for this, Klein *et al.* propose a further distinction between **inceptive** and **derived memories**.

Inceptive memories are true episodic memories in that they represent information stored at its inception with no further processing. They are therefore a hotchpotch of different types of information encoded as part of the episode and include accounts of events, perceptual information (colours, textures, shapes), proprioceptive information (how things physically felt) and emotional content. These inceptive memories may undergo further processing and inference, to produce derived memories, which can be thought of as summaries of concrete experiences. Consider the following example. During social interaction we frequently meet new people and we form inceptive memories of our experiences with them. As was noted above, these memories will be rather complex affairs containing specific details of the person, snatches of conversation, perceptual information about how the person looked and sounded and our emotional responses to them. Subsequently we might form derived memories of that person in which we form a summary of them in terms of a list of traits. For instance, we might classify them as warm, friendly and industrious, or as cold, calculating and antisocial. Why might we do this? Klein *et al.* argue that certain decisions might require information to be in such a distilled and abstracted form to enable rapid processing. In dealing with the physical and social worlds, it is important that we make decisions quickly – the world doesn't always wait for us to ponder how we should respond to it. The memory subsystems responsible for producing and storing derived memories might have evolved to maximise speed at the cost of accuracy.

Inceptive memories, on the other hand, are preserved because although they are slow and costly to process (because of all of their detail) they might be beneficial in situations where accuracy rather than speed is of the essence. For example, in courtship when one wishes to appear attractive towards a potential mate – as Phil Connor did in *Groundhog Day* – one might benefit from poring over one's detailed inceptive memories of prior encounters in order to effect an appropriate response.

Memory, stereotypes and categorisation

It has been proposed that stereotypes are another example of the cognitive system's attempt to maximise speed and ease of computation at the cost of accuracy. For example, we have a stereotypical idea of birds that captures the essence of most if not all of the members of this category. For instance in groundbreaking work by the psychologist Eleanor Rosch (see Rosch, 1973) such stereotypes (technically referred to as **prototypes**) reflect the properties of frequently encountered members of that category. When you are asked to think of a bird you will probably think of a small flying animal that has a beak, feathers and lives in trees such as a robin or sparrow (at least you will if you live in North America or Europe). You will be unlikely to think of a large, flightless bird that lives on the ground such as an ostrich. Such prototypes, it is argued, are formed because they permit rapid processing and work in the majority of cases. If, when asked to think of a bird, you brought to mind all of the birds that you know about, the processing will be much more time-consuming, computationally costly and might slow decision making down too much (Pinker, 1997).

Categories such as birds are uncontroversial; more controversial are categories for particular groups of human beings based upon, among other things, their sex, sexuality, ethnicity or social class. Society frowns upon these types of category for two reasons: first, because they do not properly capture the diversity of people within these groups and second, they are thought to cause prejudice (see chapter 8 on in-group/out-group judgements). Do these criticisms reveal such categories to be maladaptive? The second criticism does not really bear on the issue. Stereotypes might lead to prejudice, but prejudice is not in itself evidence of maladaptiveness. Recall that the hallmark of an adaptation is that it increases inclusive fitness; being prejudiced against other members of society need not affect inclusive fitness at all. Repugnant though it might seem to many people, making snap judgements about how a type of person might behave can be as useful as making snap judgements about types of animal (e.g. whether it is a predator or prey) or plants (e.g. whether it is food or poison). On the first criticism regarding diversity, the whole point of categories is that they necessarily reduce information to enable faster decisions; this means that they fail to capture subtle nuances. Are categories of people then somewhat accurate? There is some evidence to suggest that they are. With a few important exceptions, people's categories of other people (including those based on ethnicity, class, sex and sexuality) represent the average category member with some degree of accuracy (Lee *et al.*, 1995). One important exception is that the people must have some first-hand knowledge of the people under question, rather than it just being hearsay or propaganda (which is, of course, the source of a great deal of prejudicial stereotyping). So our categories of people do seem to have some grounding in reality in a similar way to our categories of animals, plants and inanimate objects. They might not be considered ethically nice, but they are efficient and this is a good enough reason for natural selection.

When our memories are fallible: an adaptive account

Human memory is amazing, and we should be in awe of its capabilities, so why is it that we often have cause to curse it? As users of memory we are painfully aware of its limitations: we forget important appointments; have distorted recollections of the past and are often seemingly unable to remember the name of a familiar person, frequently at a point that causes maximum embarrassment. John Anderson recounts that in discussions with computer scientists on how research on human memory

Table 9.1 **Schacter's seven 'sins' of memory**

Memory problem	Description	Example
Transience	The gradual weakening or loss of memory over time	Not being able to remember in detail what you did several years or even weeks ago
Absent-mindedness	A breakdown at the interface between attention and memory. It is not a failure of memory *per se* because we never actually adequately stored the appropriate information	Forgetting where you left your keys. Forgetting a lunch appointment
Blocking	Failing to retrieve information that we know we know. For example, the infuriating 'tip of the tongue' phenomenon	Not being able to remember the name of a familiar person or favourite song
Misattribution	Forgetting the source of information	Incorrectly remembering that someone told you a story when in fact you read it in a book
Suggestibility	Incorrect memories as a result of leading questions or comments when we're trying to recall a past event	After viewing a tape of a car crash and then being asked: 'How fast was the car going when it *smashed* into the tree'? Use of the word 'smashed' often leads to higher estimates of speed (Loftus and Palmer, 1974)
Bias	Unconsciously editing or re-writing past events	Recalling the break-up of a relationship in a way that makes us look more positive
Persistence	The repeated recall of disturbing or unpleasant events	Rerunning a car crash or the results of some embarrassing incident. Post-traumatic stress disorder

Source: Schacter (2001)

might help the design of better information retrieval systems he is often told that 'of course we wouldn't want anything as unreliable as human memory' (1990, p. 42).

Such prejudices present us with something of a paradox. If memory is the product of evolution why does it apparently fail so often? Is this evidence against the claim that memory is the product of natural selection, or can we think of such failures as being the flip side of sensible adaptations?

Psychologist Daniel Schacter (2001) proposes an adaptive explanation for why memories are fallible by listing what he calls the seven sins of memory (see table 9.1).

It should be mentioned here that Schacter's use of the word 'adaptive' (in common with that of John Anderson) is somewhat less specific than the way it is used by evolutionary biologists (and psychologists). By adaptive Schacter means that they are sensible given the environment in which we live rather than thinking of them as *adaptations*, i.e. shaped by natural selection. However, he does suggest that natural selection might have played a role in crafting human memory. We discuss potential adaptive explanations for each of these seven sins in turn.

Transience. According to Schacter, transience is adaptive because not all experiences and information will have future benefit. Memory is vast but its capacity is still limited, so storing every single event in vivid detail is probably impossible and certainly undesirable. Most of the time, the information that memory 'throws out' will be well judged and you will not be aware of its absence. As we saw above in the work of John Anderson, whether or not you remember a particular item depends (among other things) on how frequently it was presented in the past, and how recently it was last encountered. An item that has been encountered frequently or recently is assumed to be important and therefore given a high priority, rarer items are pushed to the back of the queue because it is assumed that they are unlikely to be required. Transience is just an extreme example of this; items deemed to be unimportant are either pushed so far to the back of the queue that they are inaccessible or are removed completely.

Absent-mindedness is adaptive, according to Schacter, because we cannot attend to everything at once and the most important prerequisite as to whether we store something is whether we attend to it. Hence, the cognitive system needs to decide what we should attend to and what we should not and consequently what is stored. Absent-mindedness occurs when we fail to give a potentially important item our full attention.

Blocking has a similar explanation to transience. Normally the names or words that are 'on the tip of our tongue' are ones that are low in frequency or ones that we haven't used for some time. Therefore many of the effects of blocking might be due to the gradual decay of memories making them less accessible. Furthermore, Schacter proposes that a further cause of blocking might be **inhibition**. Above we saw that words can be primed (made active) as a result of encountering a semantically related word. Consider what would happen if this process went unchecked. We encounter the word 'dog', which primes the word 'cat' this in turn, would prime other words, say 'mouse', which itself might prime 'cheese'. And 'dog' would not only prime 'cat'. Think of all of the knowledge you have of dogs, and all of the experiences that you have had that involve dogs! It is clear that left unchecked you would be swamped by thousands of memories and associates, which is not a very good design for a system that is supposed to enable rapid decision making. To counter this, memory has inhibitory processes that stop activation from spreading uncontrollably by reducing the activation of some memories in a principled way. Thus we are left with only a handful of memories which, in most cases, are likely to be the most useful. The downside of this, Schacter proposes, is that occasionally the wrong item is blocked and we end up being unable to retrieve the information that we need. As for transience, we are only aware of the negative aspects of inhibition (tip of the tongue) less so of the positive.

Misattribution and suggestibility. The adaptive perspective, outlined above, suggests that memory is not simply an archive of our experiences as if we were recording our lives using a video camera. Memory is designed to support future action based on past experience and as such, as we saw above, much information is thrown out of memory or ignored. This can lead to serious problems if we are trying to remember the face of a criminal, and research shows that eyewitness testimony is frequently flawed. Again, think of what it might be like if we remembered *everything* in detail. Witness the amazing memory feats of S. V. Sherashevski studied in the early part of the twentieth century by neurologist A. R. Luria (1968). Sherashevski had an incredible memory. For instance, he could faultlessly recall a list of seventy words or a matrix of fifty numbers in any order, after the briefest of exposures. Perhaps more strikingly, Sherashevski could remember such words or numbers many years after having seen them, again in any order and without error. Such a memory might seem like a blessing but it was a curse for Sherashevski. Although he had an amazing memory for detail, Sherashevski had problems forming abstractions. Above we argued that the process of forming derived memories such as mental categories enables rapid decision making by throwing out detail that is deemed irrelevant to future action. Sherashevski's memory didn't appear to do this efficiently, he could often remember the details of an experience but had difficulty forming the derived memories that are so important in our day-to-day life. The usefulness of memory is as dependent on what it throws out (or ignores) as on what it stores.

The downside of forming derived memories is, of course, that we often cannot recall when or where we originally learned something, or we 'remember' things that did not happen. For instance, if we are presented with words that are strongly associated with the word 'rough' such as 'coarse', 'jagged', 'sandpaper', 'smooth' but do not present the word 'rough' (known as the critical lure) then people will frequently report seeing the word 'rough' in the list, even though it never appeared (Roediger and McDermott, 1995). Such 'false memories', it has been suggested, occur because of the process of abstraction; we forget the details and are left with the impression that we actually saw the lure word.

Bias. Generally, our memories tend to portray us in a positive light. So when we remember events we might overestimate our contribution to successful events and underestimate our contribution to unsuccessful ones (something which social psychologists refer to as **cognitive dissonance**). According to Schacter, this might fulfil the function of promoting psychological well being as it is known that people with positive recollections of past events tend to do well in life, and those who have negative recollections are more likely to suffer mental illness. Furthermore, evolutionist Robert Trivers (see Trivers, 1976) explains biases such as cognitive dissonance as part of a more general phenomenon of self-deception. In many situations (such as in wooing a potential mate – see chapter 4) we wish others to believe that we are competent, sincere, honest and kind. For their part others are likely to have evolved sophisticated methods for detecting cheats and liars (see later) and are thus sensitive to the leakages that might occur when someone is telling barefaced lies. Given this set of circumstances, what better way of preventing someone from detecting your 'lies' than for you yourself to believe them to be true?

Persistence describes the way that we often suffer recollections of unpleasant, embarrassing or traumatic events. Who hasn't lain awake at night fretting over some mistake that was made during that day? More seriously, post-traumatic stress disorder (PTSD) is a very debilitating mental illness that can seriously affect the sufferer's ability to live a normal life. How can we consider such intrusions to be adaptive? Schacter argues that one of the many functions of memory is to learn from negative events as well as positive ones and the majority of negative memories, although unpleasant, would not be so severe as to result in PTSD. Memory, by making negative events prominent, is warning you not to make the same mistake again (see chapters 11 and 12).

Schacter's adaptative account of the 'sins' of memory attempts to show how many of the apparent weaknesses of our memory are in fact simply the downside of some beneficial feature. As we pointed out, Schacter's use of adaptation does not necessarily imply that he believes in natural selection but it certainly fits well with current evolutionary approaches to cognition.

The 'adaptive memory' approach

The adaptationist accounts of memory discussed above focus on the processes of storage, retrieval and abstraction, the only evolutionary criteria are to design a system that (1) enables the future to be predicted from the past and (2) rapid and (usually) reliable decision making based upon limited information. They make few appeals to the adaptations that might have evolved in the Environment of Evolutionary Adaptedness (EEA – see chapter 1). A recent approach to the study of memory does just this and has become known as the adaptive memory approach (Nairne *et al.*, 2007). Researchers using this approach claim that memory has evolved not only to be an efficient mechanism for supporting decisions but is more sensitive to certain kinds of content than others, particularly things that would have been important to the lives of our ancestors. They propose an additional variable to those that cognitive psychologists have previously shown made concepts memorable such as concreteness, imageability and frequency that they term s-value (for survival value – see Nairne and Pandeirada, 2008). Concepts that are high in s-value are those that are related to survival, reproduction, navigation, sex, social exchange and kinship. In a series of experiments Nairne and colleagues show that memory can be enhanced in situations that trigger perceptions of s-value. Perhaps the most striking result is from a related study by Weinstein *et al.* (2008, Experiment 2) presented participants with the following scenario.

In this task we would like you to imagine that you are stranded in the grasslands of a foreign land, without any basic survival materials. Over the next few months, you'll need to find steady supplies of food and water and protect yourself from predators.

They then presented participants with a list of twelve randomly selected words such as 'priest', 'slipper', 'tomb' and 'macaroni' which they were asked to rate as to how relevant they would be to achieving the above task. Following a delay participants were then asked to unexpectedly recall the words. The results demonstrated that participants recalled significantly more words in the above condition than if the words 'grasslands' was replaced by 'city' and the word 'predators' replaced by 'attackers'. This result is interpreted as the result of evolved mechanisms for dealing with life in the grasslands (including predator avoidance) which increases the memorability for any items presented together with this scenario, even when some of those items (such as slipper and macaroni) are irrelevant to the scenario. The results are even more striking when you consider that the participants were from St Louis and London and presumably have much more knowledge about dealing with cities than the savannah.

Is memory adaptive, did memory evolve?

Anderson and Schacter make a strong case for the adaptive character of memory without making strong claims that its adaptations were the product of natural selection. Klein *et al.*, however, go the extra step to place the study of memory squarely within the remit of evolutionary psychology. Memory, they argue, evolved to support behaviour by storing and searching for information in a way that enables us to make the choices we need to make in an ever-changing world. In the next section, we look more closely at how evolutionary psychology has informed the area of decision making.

The more recent 'adaptive memory' perspective provides compelling evidence for domain specific memory processes relevant to ancestral humans. These are early days for this approach but the effect has been replicated a number of times and could potentially revolutionise the way that cognitive psychology studies memory which has traditionally focused on content neutral processes such as imageability, depth of processing and familiarity.

Reasoning and decision making in an uncertain world

Human beings make a vast number of decisions throughout their lives. Some of these have rather trivial consequences (which television programme you should watch), others have more far-reaching repercussions (which university to go to, or decisions about health or finance). In the 1970s Amos Tversky and Nobel Laureate Daniel Kahneman published some startling work suggesting that people are rather poor at making decisions in situations that involve some degree of uncertainty. In particular, Tversky and Kahneman proposed that much of our reasoning under uncertainty involves the use of **heuristics**. Heuristics are short-cut solutions to a problem, which are usually fast and easy to apply but which do not guarantee a correct solution. They are usually contrasted with **algorithms**, which are often computationally expensive, but guarantee a correct answer. Two of the heuristics that Tversky and Kahneman studied are those of **representativeness bias** and **base-rate neglect**.

Fallacies concerning representativeness

Before we discuss the representativeness heuristic, try the following problem.

Linda is 31 years old, single, outspoken and very bright. She majored in philosophy. As a student, she was deeply concerned with issues of discrimination and social justice, and also participated in anti-nuclear demonstrations. Which of the following statements about Linda is more probable?

(1) She is a bank teller.
(2) She is a bank teller who is active in the feminist movement.

When Tversky and Kahneman (1982) presented this problem to an undergraduate population, the majority (around 85 per cent) of them chose (2) as being more likely than (1). But this can't be the case, because in order for Linda to be a feminist bank teller, she has first to be a bank teller, so (2) is always going to be a subset of (1). Tversky and Kahneman call this tendency to select statements such as (2) the **conjunction fallacy** because people apparently forget (or don't realise) that in order for A *and* B to apply to something (the conjunction of A and B) A has to apply first, and is therefore more likely. Tversky and Kahneman explain the existence of the conjunction fallacy by suggesting that people are misled by what seems to be representative of the real world. In the problem above, Linda seems rather unlike a stereotypical (or prototypical – see above) bank teller and rather like a stereotypical feminist and so participants tend to choose (2) in preference to (1).

The following is another example of a bias that can be explained by the representativeness heuristic. Suppose you toss a coin six times. Which of the following

Figure 9.5 Amos Tversky and Daniel Kahneman

is more likely (H = heads, T = tails): HHHTTT or HTTHHT? Most people estimate the second of these runs of tosses to be more likely than the first. In fact, they are both equally likely. You can prove this to yourself quite simply by applying basic probability theory. The likelihood that a tossed coin comes down heads is 1 in 2 or 0.5, the same as the likelihood of it coming down tails. This means the chance *any* single run of six tosses is going to be 0.5*0.5*0.5*0.5*0.5*0.5 = 0.015625, or 1 in 64 irrespective of the whether each result is a head or a tail.

Why is it that people think that some patterns are more likely than others? Tversky and Kahneman again use the representativeness heuristic to explain this phenomenon. Somehow, the sequence of tosses in the second example looks more representative of a random process than the first. Our idea of randomness seems to require the number of heads and tails to be approximately equal (which prohibits a run of all heads) and that these heads and tails should be distributed in a haphazard fashion. This prohibits the first which looks far too neat and tidy.

A closely related phenomenon can be demonstrated again using a sequence of coin flips. Suppose that you have some money to bet on the toss of a coin. A coin is tossed six times, and each toss has so far turned up heads and you have the opportunity to bet on the next toss. Do you put it on a tails or a heads? As you probably realise, it makes no difference, because each toss of the coin is independent of what came before, the chance of winning is 0.5 whether you place it on a heads or a tails. Many people forget, or don't realise, this and exhibit what is known as the **gambler's fallacy**. This is the belief that a run of losses *must* be followed by a run of wins in order for the sequence of events to have the even distribution of the stereotypical random process. We know better, as do the owners of the casino.

Base-rate neglect

When you toss a fair coin the outcome of the toss is independent of anything that happened previously; as we saw above the chance of a coin coming down heads is 0.5 irrespective of how many heads (or tails) have come before. Few events in the real world are like this. In most cases the probability of something happening depends upon something else happening first, which is itself less than certain. In such situations, when estimating the likelihood of the second event happening, it is important to adjust it with respect to likelihood of the first event happening.

Here is an example taken from Tversky and Kahneman (1973). A group of participants was presented with the following cover story.

A panel of psychologists have interviewed and administered personality tests to 30 engineers and 70 lawyers, all successful in their respective fields. On the basis of this information, thumbnail descriptions of the 30 engineers and 70 lawyers have been written. You will find on your forms five descriptions, chosen at random, from the 100 available descriptions. For each description, please indicate your probability that the person described is an engineer, on a scale of 0 to 100.

Another group received the same text with the initial proportion of engineers and lawyers reversed (i.e. there were 70 engineers and 30 lawyers). The descriptions presented to participants were purportedly the result of a series of 'personality tests' but were in fact generated so that they were either compatible with stereotypes of engineers and lawyers, or were neutral (they supported neither one stereotype nor the other). Two of these descriptions are presented below, the first intended to sound like a description of a stereotypical engineer, the second intended to sound neutral.

Jack is a 45-year-old man. He is married and has four children. He is generally conservative, careful and ambitious. He shows no interest in political and social issues and spends most of his free time on his many hobbies, which include carpentry, sailing, and mathematical puzzles.

Dick is a 30-year-old man. He is married with no children. A man of high ability and high motivation, he promises to be quite successful in his field. He is well liked by his colleagues.

Both groups of participants rated Jack as being very likely to be an engineer, with no significant difference between the groups. This is anomalous. Given that in one condition engineers are more abundant than in the other, you should expect there to be some effect of prior probability, in fact there was none. This is perhaps even more striking in the neutral condition. If the description of Dick really offers no clue as to his occupation, then participants should use the base rate information alone. In the above examples, they should rate the chance of Dick being an engineer as 30 out of 100; in fact, the median response for both groups was 50 out of 100.

Participants' failure to take prior probabilities (or base-rates) into account is in direct contradiction of a statistical principle known as Bayes theorem. Bayes theorem enables us to calculate the probability of something happening or being true taking into account a string of prior events, each with a probability of occurrence less than 1 (i.e. less than certain). This sounds complex but is in fact quite commonplace. For example the probability that a person will be in work today will depend upon the probability that the bus was not delayed, the probability that she awoke in time to catch the bus and so on.

The following is a more concrete example first used by Casscells *et al.* (1978) and originally presented to a group of staff and fourth-year students at Harvard Medical School.

If a test to detect a disease whose prevalence is 1/1000 has a false positive rate of 5% [that is, the test indicates that 5% of those tested have the disease, even though they do not], what is the chance that a person found to have a positive result actually has the disease, assuming that you know nothing about the person's symptoms or signs?___%

The correct Bayesian answer to this problem is 2 per cent but only 18 per cent of the Harvard-educated participants gave an answer close to this. Forty-five per cent of these distinguished participants said the answer was 95 per cent; completely ignoring the base-rate information. The correct answer can be calculated by using Bayes theorem, but you can see why it is 2 per cent intuitively. The disease affects only 1 in 1,000 individuals, so in a random sample of 1,000 people only one of them would have the disease. Imagine that we tested all of these 1,000 people using the above test. Now remember that the test gives a false positive 5 per cent of the time which means that of those 1,000 people 50 of them would show up as having the disease even though they were completely healthy. The person who actually had the disease would also test positive, so overall 51 people would show as having the disease but only one would really have it, 1 expressed as a percentage of 50 is 2 per cent.

In case you think that this is merely of academic interest, many tests for the presence of diseases such as HIV and cancer have a less than 100 per cent hit rate. Without any understanding of the importance of prior probabilities, it is easy to think that if you test positive after being given a test with a 99 per cent hit rate then it is 99 per cent certain that you have the disease. Bayesian statistics tells a different story. The evidence, however, indicates that people fail to take base rates into account, even highly educated participants from Harvard Medical School, whom you would think should know about the importance of prior probabilities in medical decision making. Of course, it would be hoping too much to expect someone with no understanding of probability theory – particularly Bayesian probability theory – to look at the problem, mull it over and, after careful consideration shout '2 per cent!' but we should expect them to at least make some adjustment and arrive at an answer that approximates the correct Bayesian solution.

Evolutionary explanations of reasoning under uncertainty

The traditional approach to explaining reasoning under uncertainty has often been called the 'heuristics and biases' approach. From this perspective people can be seen to fail to reason appropriately, usually because they use some 'quick and dirty' approximation to the solution which leads to 'cognitive illusions' (Piattelli-Palmarini, 1994b). A cognitive illusion, like a visual illusion, is where the mind 'sees' something different from what is objectively the case. People have been quick to seize upon the results of the heuristics and biases tradition as suggesting that humans are irrational beings, packed full of suboptimal heuristics which guarantee that they make poor decisions. Certainly, the results suggest that we should be wary of our intuitions when it comes to making estimations of likelihood when the problems are presented as they were in Tversky and Kahneman's studies, but should we be surprised by these results? In one sense, we should not. Statistics are a very useful tool for understanding the relationships between variables, but are a recent invention. The concept of variance, for instance, was first introduced in 1918 by the statistician Ronald Fisher (who is, incidentally, the same Ronald Fisher who was largely responsible for the modern synthesis of Darwinism and Mendelian genetics – see chapter 2).

It would be a mistake to see the enterprise undertaken by researchers of the heuristics and biases tradition as demonstrating that we are irrational decision makers. Their goal is to understand how people reason under uncertainty and the errors that people make inform us as to how they think. Unfortunately, it is all too easy to interpret these results as suggesting that we always make errors. Kahneman and Tversky acknowledge that 'although errors of judgement are but a method by which some cognitive processes are studied, the method has become a significant part of the message' (Kahneman and Tversky 1982, p. 124).

Recently evolutionary psychologists have become interested in the errors such as those described above. If biases can be thought of as illusions (see above) then maybe, like visual illusions they are not really bugs in the system but adaptations. Alternatively, maybe we are presenting to people problems that their minds are not adapted to cope with, like trying to remember a 20-digit number, nonsense syllables or long passages of text.

Frequencies versus single-case probabilities

Cosmides and Tooby (1996) and Gigerenzer (1991) suggest that problems such as the bank teller problem and the Harvard Medical School problem are unfair because they ask for predictions about a single individual or event. In their view, people can consider base rates so long as the information is presented in an appropriate way. Some of our reasoning mechanisms, they argue, 'do embody the aspects of a calculus of probability, but they are designed to take frequency information as input and produce frequencies as output' (Cosmides and Tooby, 1996, p. 3). In support of this position, Gigerenzer (1991) presented the bank teller problem, after giving the description of Linda as for the original problem the problem was changed so that it was based on frequencies rather than estimating the likelihood of a single individual.

There are 100 persons who fit the description above (that is, Linda's). How many of them are:

(1) Bank tellers? __ of 100
(2) Bank tellers and active in the feminist movement? __ of 100

In contrast to the original version of the problem where 85 per cent rated (2) as being more likely than (1), all of the participants chose the correct answer, rating (1) more highly suggesting that recasting the problem as frequencies makes the problem easier.

Cosmides and Tooby (1996) likewise rewrote the Harvard Medical School problem so that it was based on frequencies rather than a single case.

1 out of every 1000 Americans has disease X. A test has been developed to detect when a person has disease X. Every time the test is given to a person who has the disease, the test comes out positive. But sometimes the test also comes out positive when it is given to a person who is completely healthy. Specifically, out of every 1000 people who are perfectly healthy, 50 of them test positive for the disease.

Imagine that you have assembled a random sample of 1000 Americans. They were selected by lottery. Those who conducted the lottery had no information about the health status of any of these people. Given the information above, on average, how many people who test positive for the disease will actually have the disease? ____ out of ____

When people are presented with the question in terms of frequencies rather than probabilities or percentages, 76 per cent get the correct answer (compare this to the 18 per cent who got it correct in the original study). Similar results can be obtained in other puzzles involving base rates. For example, if the 'feminist bank teller' problem is expressed in frequencies, then people are much more likely to accord with the laws of probability. Cosmides and Tooby argue that in such cases people use Bayes's rule when reasoning, but they do not mean that people necessarily compute it, as shown in box 9.2. Rather they suggest that people behave *as if* they are computing Bayes's rule, and leave open the specifics of exactly how this is implemented in people's minds.

So what is the problem with single-case probabilities? Why should it be that people behave like good statisticians when base rate problems are presented in terms of frequencies, but like imbeciles when they are presented as probabilities of single events? In Douglas Adams's *The Hitch-Hiker's Guide to the Galaxy* the most powerful computer ever made, Deep Thought, gave the answer to the Ultimate Question of the meaning of Life, The Universe and Everything as 42. It then responded to the puzzlement of its operators by pointing out that the quality of the answer depends on the nature of the question that has been asked; if you don't ask the right question, you can't expect to get the right answer. Deep Thought then helped to design an even more powerful computer whose sole purpose was to come up with the question to the Ultimate Answer. This story illustrates the principle known by computer scientists as 'garbage in, garbage out' (or GIGO). In other words, if you input the wrong sort of data (or the wrong question) into a computer, you cannot expect the computer to magically come up with the correct answer. Cosmides and Tooby's explanation for the paradoxical state of affairs presented above is that the human mind is good at dealing with frequency data, and hopeless at dealing with probabilities of single events.

But this is only half the answer, a proximate answer, why should it be that that we didn't evolve a mechanism for dealing with single case probabilities? First, it is most definitely the case that humans and other animals are capable of making judgements about the relative likelihood of success when making the decision as to where to go hunting or gathering based on past success rates. To make a decision like this it is necessary that the animal can store information relevant to relative frequencies. Evidence suggests that many non-human animals seem capable of storing and using such frequency-based information (see, for example Real, 1991).

According to Cosmides and Tooby (1996) a method for evaluating single-case probabilities did not evolve because they are essentially meaningless. In order to meaningfully estimate a probability of likelihood we always require a particular **reference class**. The problem with single events or cases is that the reference class is potentially infinite. In the United Kingdom, people are told that the chances of winning the national lottery are lower than the chances of being struck by lightning. But what are any one individual's chances of being struck by lightning? It depends on the reference class. If you live in an area renowned for thunderstorms and spend a lot of time outside then your chances are increased over someone who spends little time out of doors. Many have argued, therefore (see Gigerenzer, 1991) that it is impossible to judge the probability of a single event; they are, in effect, meaningless. Further, what does it mean to discuss the probability of a single event occurring? To take the example of Linda described above. Linda is either a bank teller or she is not a bank teller. To say that there is a 70 per cent chance that she is a bank teller is meaningless. The claim made by Cosmides and Tooby our ancestors might have derived some benefit from evolving frequency sensitive mechanisms, mechanisms based on single events are likely to have been of less use, and – supposing that they evolved – would have conferred little advantage on their owners (Cosmides and Tooby, 1996).

There is some debate about this point. Some have argued that although it does indeed make little sense to discuss the probability of a single individual person being a bank teller it can make sense to say this if the probability is basically a shorthand for a frequency (Vranas, 2000) which is the way that it was used in the original Harvard Medical School problem, or is simply a way of expressing confidence. On this last point, suppose you tell your tutor that you are 90 per cent sure that you are going to attend a seminar tomorrow. Do you mean that in situations similar to the one you are in now you have, in the past, attended a seminar nine times out of a ten? Or do you simply mean that you are very confident that you are going to attend? The point is that although statisticians may claim that we are reasoning irrationally by using single-case probabilities they are often a shorthand for frequencies or merely a way of using the language of probability to express confidence in an event occurring.

Taking this a little further, the assumption behind the Linda problem is that people are reasoning irrationally because they fail to recognise that the set of bank tellers who are active in the feminist movement has to be a subset of the set of bank tellers. Technically we would say that the set of feminist bank tellers is *nested within* the set of bank tellers. But this is a very unfamiliar style of question to most people. In most problems that have two alternative answers the answers are mutually exclusive: 'would you like pasta or pizza for dinner?' It would seem rather odd if someone were to ask you whether you would like pasta or spaghetti for dinner because, of course, spaghetti is a type of pasta (or, more formally, spaghetti is nested within the category of pasta).

Supposing someone did ask whether you preferred pasta or spaghetti what would you think? Very probably that they used the word 'pasta' to refer to some other pasta that was not spaghetti (penne or farfalle, for example). To give people a choice of two options one of which is nested within the other violates the conversational rules – technically known in linguistics as **pragmatics** (see chapter 10) – that are essential if we are to understand one another. There is a good chance that in the Linda example people assume that the two options are not mutually exclusive and instead read the problem as 'what are the chances that Linda is (1) a bank teller who is active in the feminist movement, (2) a bank teller *who is not active in the feminist movement*'. The italics showing where the participants are using inference to prevent the options violating conversational rules. There is simply no way of knowing a priori which of these two alternatives is more likely but given the description of Linda it makes sense to infer that she is more likely to be active in the feminist movement than not.

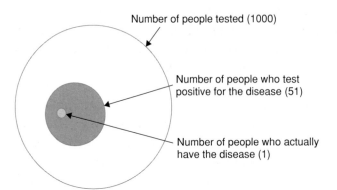

Number of people tested (1000)

Number of people who test positive for the disease (51)

Number of people who actually have the disease (1)

Figure 9.6 The nested nature of the Harvard Medical School problem

Ignoring the nested nature problems that contain a degree of uncertainty can help explain people's responses to some of the other problems. For example an alternative account for why the so-called frequentist version of the Harvard Medical School problem devised by Cosmides and Tooby is successful is because it draws attention to the fact that it deals with nested sets when it states 'out of every 1,000 people who are perfectly healthy, 50 of them test positive for the disease'. it is explicitly demonstrating that the 50 is a subset of the 1,000, and further that 1 person is a subset of the 50 (1 in 50 = 2 per cent), see figure 9.6.

More recent research has found that people can solve the Harvard Medical School problem if participants' attention is drawn to what is known as the 'nested sets' nature of the problem. The structure of the problem is shown in figure 9.6: it can be seen that the people testing positive is a subset of the sample, and the people who actually have the disease is a subset of this. A number of researchers (see Sloman *et al.*, 2003) have pointed out that expressing the problem using frequencies draws attention to the nested structure of the problem whereas expressing it in terms of single-case probabilities focuses attention of the individual rather than the structure of the problem as a whole. When the problem is expressed in terms of single cases (1 in 1,000 and so on) but is so designed as to draw attention to the nested structure of the problem a similar success rate is found as for those that use frequencies (Sloman *et al.*, 2003).

Evaluation of evolutionary theories of reasoning under uncertainty

The evolutionary view and the heuristics and biases tradition are usually portrayed as in direct contradiction to one another. A review by Samuels *et al.* (2002), however, argues that this is not necessarily the case. That people exhibit biases in their reasoning is not disputed by either side, nor is the fact that people can often reason correctly when the conditions are favourable. Most of the apparent disagreements, according to Samuels *et al.*, are differences in emphasis: the heuristics and biases tradition tending to emphasise the irrationality of human reasoning, whereas the evolutionary group tend to stress its adaptive rationality. Another difference is that the evolutionary approach emphasises ultimate explanation whereas the heuristics and biases tradition seeks explanations in terms of proximate mechanisms.

Above we also presented one particular evolutionary account as to why people can be good on some kinds of problems and poor on others. This particular account stated that we are good when reasoning about frequencies and poor when reasoning about single-case probabilities because single-case probabilities are largely meaningless due to their lack of a reference class. However, others have demonstrated (Evans *et al.*, 2000; Sloman *et al.*, 2003) that in problems similar to the Harvard Medical School problem (1) a similar success can be found using single-case probabilities as using frequencies *if* attention is drawn to the structure of the problem, and (2) frequencies can be as difficult to solve as single-case problems in some situations.

Conditional and logical reasoning

Conditional reasoning refers to problems that use an IF/THEN format. These are used in social interaction in the making of social contracts or promises. Imagine someone were to say to you IF you give me the money THEN I will get you the concert tickets. You give them the money and receive no tickets. Clearly the person has broken their promise to you and has contravened the conditional rule. But conditionals are not only used in the making of promises, they are also used in specifying causal relations among events. A rule such as IF you drink beer THEN you get a headache is an example of one such causal rule. Suppose you don't drink beer but still get a headache, has the rule been broken or not? Logically speaking the answer is no because the rule doesn't exclude that you might get a headache by other means (such as reading books on logic for example). However if you find someone who *has* drunk beer and does not suffer from a headache, then the rule has been broken. Suppose that you drink beer and get a headache, does that prove the rule? No, according to philosopher Karl Popper (1959) because truly to test a hypothesis you need to try to falsify it; you can never prove a scientific theory to be true, only show it to be false. If you put forward the hypothesis *all swans are white* then no matter how many confirmatory instances you find you never prove that it is true because the next swan you find might be black (as indeed some swans are) and the rule will be broken.

Wason's selection task

In 1966 the psychologist Peter Wason presented participants with a task to see if they reasoned in accordance with the laws of logic. The task used rather abstract

Table 9.2 **Percentage of choices in the abstract version of the Wason selection task**

Cards chosen	E & 3	E & 4	E	E, 4 & 3
Expressed logically	*p* and *not-q* (correct)	*p* and *q*	*p* only	p, q and not-q
Percentage of participants choosing this response	4	46	33	7

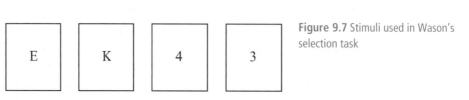

Figure 9.7 Stimuli used in Wason's selection task

conditionals; participants were presented with the conditional rule *if a card has a vowel on one side, then it has an even number on the other*. They were presented with four cards (see figure 9.7) and asked which of the cards would they need to turn over to check to see that the rule was not being broken. Table 9.2 summarises typical results of this experiment (data from Johnson-Laird and Wason, 1970).

The task can be interpreted as a problem of logical implication, *p* implies *q* (written as $p \rightarrow q$), which can also be read as IF *p* is the case THEN *q* is also the case. If our goal is to find out whether the rule is being obeyed, then the only cards that bear upon this are the *E* card and the *3* card. To see why, it is worth spending a few moments stepping through the problem. Turning over the *E* card (*p*) is necessary because if you find that it is not an even number (*not-q*) the rule is falsified. Turning over the *K* (*not-p*) card is pointless; it does not matter what is on the other side because the rule says nothing about consonants. The *4* (*q*) card might be of initial interest; after all if you find that there is a vowel on the other side it would add support to the rule. However, according to Popper it should be avoided because it can never falsify the rule, only confirm it. Finally, the *3* card (*not-q*) should be turned, because there is a chance that there might be a vowel on the other side, in which case the rule is falsified. As we can see from table 9.2 only 4 per cent made the correct choice with the majority seeking confirmation rather than refutation by turning over the *E* and *4* cards (*p* and *q*).

Griggs and Cox (1982) used a task very similar to the one above but obtained rather different results. They used a rule that was familiar to the participants in their study, namely the laws about the minimum legal age that people are allowed to consume alcohol. The rule was *If a person is drinking alcohol, then they must be over nineteen years of age*. They were presented with four cards as above containing *beer* (*p*), *coke* (*not-p*), *16 years of age* (*not-q*) and *twenty-two years of age* (*q*), and were asked to imagine that they were police checking for under-age drinkers. When presented with this version of the task most subjects correctly chose the *p* and *not-q* cards.

Participants' success at this task is not simply attributable to it being less abstract than in Wason's version. Manktelow and Evans (1979) presented participants with the statement, *Every time I eat haddock then I drink gin* and then gave them cards *haddock, cod, gin* and *whisky*, and found no improvement over the standard task that used letters and numbers. Even the under-age drinking example only works when presented with a suitable context. Pollard and Evans (1987) found that if the police cover story was omitted, performance decreased towards that of the abstract tasks. So why do people sometimes reason logically and at other times not? Many explanations have been provided (see, for example, Evans and Over, 1996) but here we focus on just two. The first, supplied by Cosmides and Tooby argues that the concrete version of the task triggers **Darwinian algorithms** used for detecting cheats, whereas the abstract version of the task does not. The second account, provided by Mike Oaksford and Nick Chater argues that the responses to the abstract task can be seen as rational if we assume that people are dealing with probabilities rather than logic.

Domain specific Darwinian algorithms

Cosmides (1989) suggests that one of the main differences between the under-age drinking task and the other tasks mentioned above is that the under-age drinking task makes sense to people because it appeals to their knowledge of, and concern to catch freeriders. Recall that earlier in this chapter we presented Trivers's argument that in order for reciprocal altruism to exist, people need to be effective cheat detectors. Cosmides suggests that people perform well on the under-age drinking task because it triggers mental circuitry (or mental modules – see box 9.3) responsible for detecting people who renege on social contracts. Other tasks such as the abstract version using even and odd numbers do not trigger this circuitry and give rise to a different pattern of results (see also Gigerenzer and Hug, 1992). There is some evidence that this is not simply a foible of Western culture. Cosmides and Tooby (1992) have replicated the results of this study with a foraging people from Ecuador.

Further evidence suggests that the facilitation effect is specific to situations where the goal is to detect cheaters, rather than being concerned with social contracts in general. Cosmides (1989) found that participants showed much less facilitation when the goal was to detect altruists (those who pay the cost but do not reap the benefit) and Gigerenzer and Hug (1992) showed participants were not so good at reasoning about social contracts which did not specifically involve cheating. This is what might be expected, given Trivers's claims about group life. Engaging in reciprocal altruism means that you need to check that no one is cheating you, but there is no reason to

> ## Box 9.3 What is the domain of a module?
>
> One of the key claims of the synthesis of evolutionary psychology and modularity is that modules can respond to things for which they were not originally adapted. A bizarre example of this is that Nico Tinbergen reported that sticklebacks he kept in his living room responded aggressively to a red post-office van that visited his house and was clearly visible to the sticklebacks through the window. This represents a misfiring of a mental 'module' that sticklebacks use as part of their mating behaviour (male stickleback have a red colouration and males usually respond aggressively to other males).
>
> Sperber (1994) deals with this issue by proposing a distinction between what he calls the **actual** and **proper** domains of a mental module. The actual domain of a module is anything that satisfies its entry requirement; the proper domain, on the other hand, is the stimulus (or stimuli) which by virtue of it triggering the module gives adaptive value. So for the stickleback example, the proper domain of the releasing behaviour is the red colouration of male sticklebacks leading to competitive behaviour, whereas the actual domain consists of lots of things, including red post-office vans. Many of the stimuli in the actual domain will have no fitness consequences (such as post office vans). Some, however, may have negative fitness consequences. For example some orchids mimic female bees leading to male bees copulating with them hence wasting valuable sperm (and time) and putting themselves at risk of predation. Orchids do this in order to use the bees to fertilise the flower by transmitting pollen.

Table 9.3 **Summary of results from abstract, cheat detection and altruist detection tasks. Note that the data for the altruist detection task vary depending on whether the word used is altruist (28%) or selfless (40%)**

Task	Correct choice	Percentage of participants choosing correct answer
Abstract	p & not-q	4
Cheat detection	p & not-q	74
Altruist detection	not-p & q	28–40

Source: Cosmides and Tooby (1992)

check that you aren't getting more than your fair share. That is for others to worry about.

Manktelow and Over (1990) present evidence of facilitation in the selection task in cases where no cheating is involved, such as 'If you clean up spilled blood then you must wear rubber gloves.' People solve this unsavoury example, concerned with the avoidance of contamination about as well as they solve the under-age drinking example. Cosmides and Tooby (1992) acknowledge that the mind may well contain a large number of innate, domain-specific mental modules for detecting contamination as well as cheating.

Optimal data selection

A rather different account of the results of the Wason task from the one above is that of Optimal Data Selection proposed by Oaksford and Chater (1994). Neither is an evolutionary psychologist, in fact both take issue with many of its fundamental assumptions (see Chater and Oaksford, 1999), but the basics of their theory is not incompatible with the Darwinian framework. Oaksford and Chater argue that one of the reasons for the disparity in performance between the under-age drinking task and the abstract Wason task is that they are concerned with different domains. In the abstract task you are asked to determine the truth or falsehood of a rule (known as an **indicative** task). Problems such as the under-age drinking task are concerned not with the truth but with obligations, and are known as **deontic** tasks. In an indicative task, you are given some statement like *all swans are white* to which a natural response might be to gather data to test the rule which might be rejected on the basis of finding contradictory evidence. Deontic tasks are different. If you are told that people under nineteen are not allowed to drink beer, then finding someone breaking the rule does not make the rule false. To use another example, you cannot prove that the speed limit does not exist by driving faster than it mandates; anyone believing that they have done so will probably be advised to discuss the results of their experiment with the judge.

Oaksford and Chater suggest that the under-age drinking task and the abstract task yield different results because the tasks have two entirely different solutions, by virtue of one being indicative, the other being deontic. Importantly, however, they argue that people's intuitions with respect to the indicative task (such as that originally presented by Wason using letters and numbers) reveal that they are adaptive as opposed to maladaptive (again the word 'adaptive' is not intended, by them, to imply that it is an adaptation).

In their theory, participants presented with indicative tasks act to reduce their level of uncertainty about the world. In the abstract Wason task, people are much more likely to choose the *q* card rather than the *not-q* card that is, as we have pointed out, not the correct choice from the perspective of falsification, but Oaksford and Chater argue that falsification is an incorrect normative model of what participants should be doing. They suggest that in the indicative task, *q* might be more informative than *not-q* because of a principle known as the rarity assumption. The rarity assumption is based on the notion that, in most cases, finding out something which is true about an entity is more informative than finding out something which is not true. The rarity assumption dictates that in the overwhelming majority of cases the chances of something happening or being the case are much lower than the chances of the same thing *not* happening or not being the case. This means that positive information is more useful to you in arriving at a solution than negative information.

Imagine that you are playing the game of twenty questions where you have to guess the name of an animal. If you find out that the animal is a bird, this is more useful to you than to find out that it is not a bird, because there are vastly more non-birds in the world than birds. If people are rational beings, they should therefore seek positive rather than negative evidence because the former is more informative and more likely to enable them to arrive at a conclusion. Oaksford and Chater propose that behaviour in indicative problems (where they are seeking the truth) can be explained by assuming that participants are acting to increase their Expected Information Gain (EIG). In the Wason task participants are therefore not reasoning irrationally or maladaptively when they choose the q card over the *not-q* card because the rarity assumption suggests that the q card is the more informative and will thus increase their EIG. The rational choice in indicative tasks is therefore not p and *not-q*, but p and q.

What about deontic tasks? Recall that deontic tasks are not about proving the rule true or false, they require you to take some perspective towards the rule, such as trying to enforce it. Here the rarity assumption does not apply, instead – when you are trying to detect violators – there is a high value placed on catching the violator and, using decision theory, the rational choice would be to choose p and *not-q*, which is what we find in tasks such as the under-age drinking task.

Information gain can explain a wide range of logical reasoning tasks, much wider than can a cheater detection theory, and it does this with a few assumptions about the statistical structure of the world, and the relative values of different types of information. Currently, however, it cannot explain why cheater detection tasks show facilitation, but altruism detector tasks do not. Additionally, given the strong evolutionary pressures on us to detect freeriders (Trivers, 1976) it would be somewhat surprising if natural selection had not played some role in the development of cheat detectors.

Notwithstanding this, Oaksford and Chater's argument that behaviour on the Wason task reflects people's desire to maximise information gain has some evolutionary precedents (although Oaksford and Chater would shy away from such claims). Psychologist George Miller even goes so far as to refer to humans as **informavores** suggesting that they consume information in an analogous way to the way they (and other animals) consume food. A recent approach to the study of human cognition has investigated these claims further. For instance some have suggested that human information-seeking behaviour in information-rich environments can be understood if we assume that humans are adapted to maximise their rate of gain of information

(Pirolli and Card, 1999; Sandstrom, 1994; Reader and Payne, 2007). Foraging theory has also been applied to decision making, and it is this research that we address next.

Understanding differences within deontic tasks – the return of cheater detection

Optimal data selection can explain the difference within indicative tasks and between indicative and deontic tasks, but it cannot explain differences found *within* different types of deontic tasks. Similarly a recent criticism of cheater-detection theory (and evolutionary psychology more generally) by David Buller (2005b) takes the cheater-detection hypothesis to task for – he claims – ignoring the difference between indicative and deontic tasks (but see Cosmides *et al.*, 2005). His alternative explanation, based on a domain-general mental logic, can explain only the differences between deontic and indicative tasks not differences within deontic tasks. To understand why there might be differences in deontic tasks one must understand why we have them in the first place. Deontic rules, recall, relate to obligations or societal rules. These rules are presumably there to maintain stability within a community, for example the maxim: do not take more than your fair share (with punishments meted out for those who violate the rule) is there to maintain harmony. If resources are limited and if everyone is to get a share of the resources then it makes sense to place limits on how much each person can reasonably take. If the rule did not exist then some people would take more than what they were due and the resource would soon be depleted leaving others without. If violations went unpunished (a toothless law) then even fair minded people would probably start to take more than they deserved ('if they do it, then why shouldn't I?') with a similar depletion of the resource. The almost inevitable depletion of a shared resource because of people taking more than they are due is called 'the tragedy of the commons'.

According to Cosmides *et al.* (2010) violations of such deontic rules regulating social exchange should only be detected when (1) a cheater has benefited from cheating, (2) the person did it intentionally rather than accidentally, and (3) cheating by violating the rule is possible. If all of these conditions are met, the cheater-detection algorithm will fire and people will solve the deontic rule correctly; if any one of these criteria is not met, then the cheater-detection system will not fire and people will show reasoning errors such as those for the original Wason selection task. In a series of experiments Cosmides *et al.* (2010) showed this to be the case. In one example (Experiment 4) participants were told that they were given a task of checking for cheating in allocating children to one of two schools. The rule was:

If a student is to be assigned to Grover High School, then that student must live in Grover City.

They were given additional information that the people allocating children to schools were volunteers and they were concerned that some of these people might have vested interests, e.g. they might be the parents of children going to one of the schools. In some cases they were told that people in Grover paid higher taxes to support their school which was thus better than the rival school, Hanover High (benefit to cheating) in others that the schools were the same (no benefit). In some conditions they were told that the students were identified by name (possibility of cheating), in others that they were identified by anonymity code (no possibility of cheating). Finally intention was manipulated, some participants were told that volunteers had been overheard planning to break the rule whereas other participants were merely told to check for mistakes. Cosmides *et al.* found that people reasoned correctly more frequently in conditions where there was motivation, benefit and possibility of cheating than in conditions where these were absent.

Summary of logical reasoning

The literature on logical reasoning is large and complex and many attempts have been made to understand why people reason logically in some situations but not others. The cheater-detector theory described above is one of the most successful, not only because – unlike its competitors – it explains the differences between conditional and deontic tasks (Cosmides, 1989) and differences between different kinds of deontic tasks (Cosmides *et al.*, 2010) but because it gives a good evolutionary rationale for why these differences exist: they engage mental processes designed for detecting freeriders. It should be made clear that a cheater detector is not just a convenient fiction, a just-so story constructed post-hoc to explain a pattern of results – a cheater detector is an evolutionary necessity. Game theoretic research (see chapter 8) and mathematical modelling are clear that cooperation between non-kin could not have evolved without some ability to detect and deal with freeriders. We know that cooperation evolved so cheater detection must have also evolved. This is a point that is often missed by critics of the theory (e.g. Fodor, 2000) but an important one.

Foraging theory and adaptive decision making

Foraging theory (or optimal foraging theory – see Stephens and Krebs, 1986) is an approach to the study of animal behaviour developed by behavioural ecologists. The question that they ask is quite simple: given that animals (including humans) need to satisfy many needs (for example, feeding, mating, rearing offspring) and have only a limited amount of time to do them, how do they manage their time in a sensible way?

As the name implies, foraging theory has been most widely applied to food-foraging behaviour where it asks how animals manage to allocate their time exploiting richer, rather than poorer food patches taking into account costs such as the energy expended while foraging. Foraging theory has demonstrated that animals are very efficient at finding and exploiting high quality food patches, as might be expected given the importance of energy and nutrition to an animal's survival. It has also shown that animals are flexible foragers, able to modulate their behaviour based on internal factors such as need and external factors such as risk of predation. For instance, under normal circumstances, animals might avoid food patches where there is a high risk of predation. This is one reason why squirrels avoid venturing out into areas where there is no cover such as fields. However, when needs are high, such as when the animal is extremely hungry, they may risk foraging in open spaces. Foraging theory shows that the animals are in fact making some quite complex calculations, assessing the risk of predation and weighing it against the risk of starvation; the risks, it seems, are always calculated risks.

Foraging theory and decision making

In the realm of human cognition, there is some evidence that people behave in ways that are not unlike these animals. One long-standing finding in the reasoning/decision-making literature is that, all else being equal, people prefer alternatives where the outcome probability is known to those where it is unknown. For example, imagine that you have two boxes – box A contains 50 white balls and 50 black balls, box B contains 100 black and white balls of unknown proportion. If you draw a black ball from one of the boxes you win $100, if you draw a white ball you win nothing. Which box would you choose? Consistent with the above, most prefer box A where the distribution of the black and white balls is known. One possible explanation for this behaviour is that people view the box B as probably containing fewer black balls than white so therefore go for box A where they know they have a 50 per cent chance of winning. But this doesn't seem to be the case. Following the withdrawal of a ball from box A, participants are then instructed to replace the ball in box A (so that the distribution of balls is back to 50–50) and are then told that they can choose again but this time a *white* ball wins. If people did genuinely believe that in the original task white balls outnumbered black balls in box B, they should now choose from box B, but they don't, as before, the majority choose from box A again.

Generally the results of such tasks indicate that people prefer choices where their chances of success are known in advance. Rode *et al.* (1999) conducted an experiment to test the generality of this principle. They presented participants with one of two boxes, as above, where the distribution of balls was either known or unknown. No money was at stake in this part of the lottery; instead, if participants drew a specified number of black balls they would progress to a next stage where they had the chance of winning $20. Rode *et al.* manipulated two variables, need and expected value. Need corresponded to the number of black balls that needed to be drawn consecutively to go on to the next stage, a large number of black balls was high need, a small number represented low need. Expected value was the proportion of black balls to white balls, the more black balls there were the higher the expected value (the more chance of success). Rode *et al.* found that when the expected value of the known box was above the need then participants tended to choose the known box; however, when the expected value was below what was needed they would tend to choose the unknown box. Therefore, like squirrels and other animals, it seems that people are not always risk-averse; when needs are high human beings might also make risky choices.

Evolution and cognition

One of the unifying principles of the diverse theories described above is that human cognition evolved to support action. The visual system did not evolve to show us how the world actually is; it evolved to provide us with a useful representation that supports action. Likewise, memory is not designed to represent a veridical representation of the past but rather stores information that supports us in our day-to-day lives. And the processes of reasoning and decision making were not designed to enable us to answer textbook questions, they were designed to make rapid decisions that allowed us to flee from predators, attract a mate or detect cheaters.

The cognitive powers possessed by humans are unparalleled in the animal kingdom, but we are rather more than brains in a vat, the mind was designed for a purpose and it is that purpose that evolutionary psychology is attempting to find. So far, we have not considered language, one of the most ubiquitous of human activities and another miracle of evolution; this is what we consider in the next chapter.

Summary

- The cognitive approach to the study of psychology sees behaviour as resulting from the operation of internal mental processes. A number of authors have suggested understanding how the mind works can be helped by understanding what it was designed to do (Marr, 1982).
- Evolutionary psychologists see the mind as being adapted to solve problems that were encountered by our Pleistocene ancestors, rather than the problems that we

meet today. This means that our mind is not adapted to perform many tasks that have arisen in recent times, such as reading, memorising telephone numbers and mathematics. Many phenomena that initially appeared to suggest that human cognition was maladaptive have recently been re-evaluated within an evolutionary context.

- Our visual and memory systems did not evolve to present us with a true description of the world; rather they evolved to give us a useful description of the world that supports our actions upon it.

- The modern approach to evolutionary psychology proposes the existence of innately specified, domain specific mental modules that have been shaped by natural selection. Modules have been proposed for a variety of human activities such as detecting freeriders and forming categories that enable rapid processing and decision making.

Questions

1. Make a list of instances where your memory has failed. Do they fit in with Schacter's Seven Sins of memory outlined above.

2. There is a phenomenon known as flashbulb memories where people report very detailed memories of events that accompany high emotions (especially traumatic events). For example, people often have very detailed episodic memories of what happened on September 11th 2001 during the Twin Towers atrocity. Can you think of any evolutionary benefit for why people have detailed memories of traumatic events?

3. Look at some visual illusions (there is an excellent collection at www.michaelbach.de/ot); which of these might be the result of visual adaptations, which side effects of adaptations and which failures of the visual system?

4. When people fail to solve problems (e.g. in logic or statistics) it is usually thought that it is a failure in mental processes. Discuss the evidence that people are solving such problems correctly, they are just solving a different kind of problem.

FURTHER READING

Barkow, J. H., Cosmides, L. and Tooby, J. (eds.) (1992). *The Adapted Mind: Evolutionary Psychology and the Generation of Culture*. New York: Oxford University Press. Multi-authored volume containing a number of classic articles on evolutionary psychology.

Dennett, D. C. (1996). *Kinds of Minds: Towards an Understanding of Consciousness*. London: Weidenfeld and Nicolson. Well-written book exploring the evolution of thought and consciousness.

Nairne, J. S. and Pandeirada, J. N. S. (2008). Adaptive memory: Remembering with a stone-age brain. *Current Directions in Psychology*, 17(4), 239–43. A short paper that provides an overview of the recent adaptive memory approach to cognition.

Pinker, S. (1997). *How the Mind Works*. London: Allen Lane. A readable exposition of the modern evolutionary approach to the study of the human mind.

10 | The evolution of language

KEY CONCEPTS

learnability argument • ostensive communication • Universal Grammar (UG)
• parameter setting • inflectional morphology • derivational morphology
• FOXP2 gene • specific language impairment social grooming hypothesis
• social contract hypothesis

Without language, social interaction would be impoverished beyond recognition. It enables us to reveal our innermost thoughts to others, or, if the mood takes us, to disguise them with misinformation and lies. With language, action can be coordinated so that a group of people can act as one – even if chimpanzees could conceive of a pyramid they still couldn't build one because they lack the ability to coordinate action through language. Language also, as we shall see in chapter 14, enables hard-won knowledge to be passed on to others – including our children – enabling culture to proliferate in ways that would not have been possible in our languageless ancestors. When language evolved it was evolutionary dynamite. Not only did it vastly extend the range of things that ancestral humans were capable of, enabling them, perhaps, to outcompete other hominins around at the time, but it is also likely to have had an impact on the evolution of the brain itself. It is unlikely that our languageless ancestors had brains identical to ours but lacking the appropriate language circuitry; it is more likely that the gradual increase in communicative sophistication led to huge leaps in the way that the mind worked. So great are the advantages of language to our species that surely it must have been the product of natural (or sexual) selection. This chapter begins by outlining the modular account of language, currently popular within evolutionary psychology. We then go on to discuss when in our evolutionary history language might have emerged and finally we present some accounts as to why language evolved.

Is language specific to human beings?

There is no doubt that non-human animals communicate with each other in the sense that they have evolved particular ways to convey information such as their particular psychological state to others (think of a growling dog), but animals communicate other information as well. The work of Austrian ethologist Karl von Frisch on the dances of honey bees is a celebrated example. Von Frisch discovered that after finding a profitable food patch bees would return to the hive and engage in an elaborate dance to communicate the physical location of the food source and the estimated quantity of nectar to be had. After witnessing the dance, the bee's hivemates would 'decide' whether to exploit the patch, taking into account its distance and potential yield. Another classic example of complex communication in non-human animals is that of vervet monkeys who have been shown to use different vocalisations to indicate the presence of different types of predator such as snakes, cheetahs and eagles (Cheney and Seyfarth, 1982). It is not only primates who appear to be able to do this. Prairie dogs (a ground-living member of the squirrel family) appear to have a range of distinct warning calls made in response to specific stimuli. They will, for example produce different calls to coyote, red-tailed hawk, deer and humans. Perhaps even more surprisingly, when prairie dogs were presented with unfamiliar objects such as a European ferret or a black oval they all gave the same call independently of one another (Slobodchikoff, 2002) and were even able to incorporate the colour of the predators into their vocalisations (Slobodchikoff *et al.*, 2009). In this case the 'predators' were three similar-looking women wearing different coloured clothing. Giving the same call is important because it suggests that their calls are genuinely referring to particular attributes of the stimuli (colour, for example, or shape) rather than just making random vocalisations. It suggests that the prairie dog communication system has rules for generating new 'words' and that these rules are shared by the community – something that is essential if you need to be understood.

The researcher who carried out these studies (Con Slobodchikoff of Northern Arizona University) speculates that prairie dogs have some (possibly innate) rules that enable them to produce calls to novel stimuli, although the details of this are obscure. Why might prairie dogs have evolved such a sophisticated system of alarm calls? One possibility is that prairie dogs are preyed on by many different kinds of other animals including coyotes, badgers, domestic cats and dogs, ferrets, owls, eagles, bobcats, snakes and, of course, humans. With such a variety of predators a flexible system of warning calls would help them to flee from predators. Presumably, as with vervet monkeys, the appropriate response to a particular predator varies as a result of the specific nature of the predator.

Whether any of these (and other) instances of communication constitute language is a long-standing debate, although currently the majority opinion is that they do not. (Things do seem to be changing – slowly – here as researchers study more animals in more detail.) With respect to the criteria presented in box 10.1 no animal communication system yet meets all seven (Aitchison, 1989); the principal difference being that human language is much more creative and flexible than animal communication systems. Honey bees, for example, are geniuses at giving directions to sources of nectar, but appear unable to use their sophisticated dances to communicate

Box 10.1 What is language?

Producing a definition for language is not easy but here are some fairly widely accepted criteria that help to identify whether a form of communication is or is not a language (Aitchison, 1989).

Use of vocal auditory channel. Fairly self-explanatory, a language should use verbal communication. In fact this is probably one of the weakest and most controversial of the criteria, because it rules out the sign language used by the hearing impaired, which is certainly a language by all other criteria (and enables communication as complex as spoken language). It also rules out written communication. As Aitchison points out, this criterion captures the essence of human language rather than being a necessary feature, and is of little use for deciding whether animals have language.

Arbitrariness. Languages use symbols that need bear no relationship to what is being discussed. The word 'dog', for example, does not physically sound like a dog. The word 'minuscule', meaning very small, is a much larger word than is 'huge', meaning very big. Similarly, one can shout the word 'quiet' with no disruption of its meaning. Some animals do appear to have the property of arbitrariness in their communications.

Semanticity. Language means something. When we hear the word 'chair', we know that someone is referring to a particular type of object (and we also assume that the person has some intention behind referring to the chair).

Cultural transmission. Languages are handed down from generation to generation; they are not usually generated spontaneously (although there is evidence that this has happened with some sign languages). Languages are, among other things, cultural artefacts and as such are jealously guarded by their speakers.

Spontaneous usage. Language is spoken freely, not only under duress. Even human babies seem to have an overriding desire to babble; it is not something that their parents need to encourage in them.

Turn taking. Apart from very specific contexts such as a lecture or a soliloquy in a Shakespearean play we don't tend to speak for very long periods at a time, neither do we tend to talk while someone else is speaking; we take it in turns. Again, turn taking is something that happens very early in life, seemingly without tuition (most of the time!).

Duality or double-articulation. Languages are double-layered. The component sounds of a word such as d-o-g are meaningless by themselves; they only acquire meaning when they are placed in a very specific order.

Displacement. Language can refer to things that are not there. Either because they are no longer present (temporal displacement), they are some distance away (spatial displacement) or they are totally hypothetical. When we say 'If it rains tomorrow I will stay at home' we are referring to a hypothetical state of affairs.

Structure dependence. All human languages are fussy about how words go together. The meaning of 'have a nice day' is dependent on the words occurring in a particular sequence and its meaning is not some average of the meaning of the words. In contrast, many vocalisations made by animals (and humans) require no structure. The howls of pain produced by a person having hit their thumb with a hammer certainly communicate their suffering, but no structure is required for this communication to occur.

Creativity. Language is infinitely expressive, we do not have a set number of responses like some dumb Artificial Intelligence program. When something novel happens we are able to describe it, or at least attempt to.

other potentially useful information such as the existence and location of a rival hive. Vervet monkeys can signal the presence of predators but do not appear to use their calls to convey information about the quality of potential mates, habitats or sources of food. Human language, however, is used to communicate information relating to every realm of human experience.

Human language and the combinatorial power of grammar

The process of forming a one-to-one mapping between sound and object such as that displayed by vervet monkeys was an important step in the evolution of language. One might even imagine a situation whereby this ability is extended and refined to lead, ultimately, to a human-like vocabulary which contains many thousands of words. The average literate person knows between 50,000 and 100,000 words; however if you remove words that share a common morphological root – such as walk, walking, walked, and compounds made of known words (wrist-watch, pencil-case) – the average American high-school graduate knows around 45,000 words (Nagy and Anderson, 1984). Having a different word for each concept is fine as far as it goes, but given the large number of things that we might wish to talk about we would soon find ourselves running out of space to store all the words we know and time in which to learn them all. Furthermore, if for each idea there had to be a distinct 'word' how would you ever say anything new? You could always invent a new word, of course, but since no one else would know what the word means they wouldn't be able to understand you. Language's second trick is even more impressive than an extensive vocabulary; it gives us a means of obtaining limitless powers of expression from a comparatively small set of words: grammar.

The communication structures of other animals, as far as we know, do not have grammar, which is why vervet monkeys and honey bees are stuck within their limited 'linguistic' universe, unable to 'say' anything that hasn't already been 'said' by others

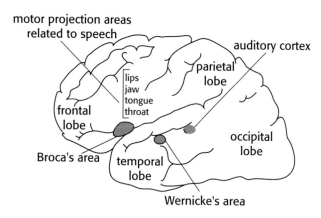

Figure 10.1 Regions of the brain involved in language processing showing Broca's area, Wernicke's area and the related areas involved in hearing and articulation

a thousand times before (although prairie dogs might be an exception). Interestingly von Frisch recounts an experiment where he placed sugar water some distance up an antenna only a short distance from the hive. When bees were shown the source they flew back to the hive and duly gave directions by the usual choreographic means. This led to a host of bees buzzing around the base of the antenna, apparently unable to find the source. Von Frisch concluded that: 'The bees have no word for "up" in their language. There are no flowers in the clouds' (von Frisch, 1954, p. 139).

Pinker and Bloom – an evolutionary theory of language acquisition

In their landmark paper 'Natural language and natural selection' (1990) the psycholinguists Steven Pinker and Paul Bloom argued that language has many of the characteristics of complex organs such as the human eye or hand. Like the eye, language has positive fitness implications in that it enables information to be transmitted more efficiently than by non-linguistic means, but it also allows different forms of information to be transmitted. The properties of displacement and creativity (see box 10.1) mean that we are free from making fixed responses about the here and now. With language we can refer easily to past events, speculate on the future and discuss any issue that might come to mind, again things that are difficult using non-linguistic communication.

Pinker and Bloom argue that natural selection is the *only* known mechanism that can produce the adaptive complexity that we see in language. A particularly difficult problem for non-selectionist theories is how to explain all the costs associated with the specialist hardware that language requires. The comprehension and production of language uses a large amount of costly neural material in dedicated brain regions such as Broca's area and Wernicke's area (see figure 10.1).

Furthermore, the design of the vocal tract required to make complex articulation possible also has the unfortunate side effect of making dying from choking a distinct possibility. (Non-human mammals and, indeed, pre-linguistic babies are able to swallow and breathe at the same time.) If language did not arise by natural selection, it is hard to explain how our ancestors could have borne these costs without them being offset by some very special advantages.

In the next few sections we examine some of the evidence for Pinker and Bloom's argument. First, we discuss the fundamental building blocks of language, the sounds, or phonemes that are used to transmit meaning. Second, we discuss how words are learned and what assumptions children need to make when learning a word. Finally, we present Chomsky's work on grammar which suggests that language learning is supported by an innate language 'organ'.

Learning the sounds of language

With few exceptions – such as the sign languages of the deaf – languages transmit meaning through the medium of sound. Why should this be the case when – as generations of people with hearing impairments have demonstrated – a combination of gestural and facial expressions can serve just as well; what is so special about sound? First, using sound enables multitasking; your hands can get on with other work while you talk. Second, you don't have to be looking at the person with whom you're communicating, which means that you can attend visually to other things while communicating and others can easily attract your attention with warning cries for example. Third, you can communicate in the dark – an important attribute in our ancestral environment of equatorial Africa, where it is dark for approximately twelve hours a day every day.

Although sound is the medium of choice for all languages not all languages use the same sounds. Each language contains a particular set of minimal acoustic building blocks known as phonemes (such as 'b', 'a' and 'm') and languages differ as to how many phonemes they use. English, for instance, uses around forty different phonemes (depending on dialect), Polynesian, however, uses only eleven phonemes and Khoisan (a language of southern Africa) as many as 140. Some phonemes such as the 'click' of Bantu languages as used by the !Kung San (the exclamation mark representing one of those clicks) sound alien to English speakers' ears, but to speakers of other languages English itself uses sounds that are difficult to pronounce. For example the 'th' sound in English words such as 'thick' or 'the' is difficult for many non-native speakers who often approximate by using 's' or 'z'. Some phonemes are not only difficult to pronounce for a non-native speaker, they are indiscriminable from other phonemes in the language, even after 500 trials of training (Pinker, 1994,

p. 264). Two-month-old infants, however, are able to discriminate between all of the phonemes in all of the world's languages (Kuhl *et al.*, 1992). This is not so surprising because the very presence of different phonemes in a particular language depends upon the ability of babies to distinguish them in the first place. However, infants learn rapidly and this ability starts to decline around 6 months of age as they home in on their native phonemes, where 'native' simply means the sounds that they are exposed to. For instance, older babies in a Spanish-speaking environment will start to treat the phonemes 'v' and 'b' as the same, just as their parents do, whereas younger babies show a discrimination. So, before a baby utters its first word it has already learned a great deal about the language spoken around it. Babies, it seems, are predisposed to attend to language-like sounds from birth, as we would expect if language were an evolved instinct. But phonemes are just the building blocks of language, they don't in themselves contain any meaning; for this they need to be combined to produce words and how children learn words is what we turn to next.

Learning words

Learning words seems easy. A person points at an object, says its name aloud and the child gradually learns to associate the sound pattern with the object (this is one of the claims made by Skinner's behaviourism). However, as we shall see, this simple case of word learning (known as **ostensive communication** or **ostension**) only appears easy because it is supported by a variety of cognitive mechanisms. Learning by ostension is more complex than it seems and to illustrate this point philosopher W. V. O. Quine devised the 'gavagai problem' (Quine, 1960). Quine invites us to imagine that we are travellers in a foreign land accompanied by a guide; we cannot speak a word of his language, and he cannot speak a word of ours. Suddenly as we rise to the crest of a hill a rabbit dashes out in front of us. The native points at the rabbit and shouts 'gavagai'. What does he mean? Most people assume that gavagai must be the local word for rabbit, but why do we assume this? Gavagai might be an exclamation of surprise such as 'blimey'; maybe he is referring to its colour or the way that it is moving, or maybe he is merely shouting 'there goes my dinner'. There is no way of telling what he means, but we make the assumption that he is naming the whole object. Young children learning words face a similar problem. When, for instance, a parent points at a brown furry animal and calls it a dog there is nothing in this act that tells the child that the parent is referring to the type of animal rather than giving that particular dog's name ('Fido') or passing some comment on its shaggy coat. In the absence of this additional information the child has to provide his own by making assumptions about the naming process.

Constraints on word learning

Ellen Markman (1989) suggests that the child makes (at least) three assumptions when learning words. First, the child makes the **whole object assumption**: the child assumes in the absence of any other evidence that when an object is named the person refers to the whole object, not its parts, colour or some other attribute. Second, the child makes the **taxonomic assumption**, when an object is named the child assumes that the person is referring not to that specific object ('Fido') nor to its very general category (mammal, animal or living thing) but at a medium level of generality known as the basic level (Rosch *et al.*, 1976). Basic level categories usually contain items that resemble each other in crucial ways. For example, 'table' is a basic level category whereas 'furniture' is at a higher level of abstraction. Although tables differ somewhat in size and shape, they are quite similar and much more similar to each other than the members of the 'furniture' category which contains tables, beds and wardrobes. Finally, children make the **mutual exclusivity assumption**. If a child already knows the name for an object and it is referred to by another word, then the child assumes that the second word is referring to some other aspect of the object such as its colour, manner of movement, material and so on, rather than assuming that it is a synonym.

To demonstrate this, Markman presented 3-year-olds with an array of objects which included familiar objects (cups) and unfamiliar objects (tongs). When children were shown a set of tongs and told that it was *biff* and asked to collect more *biffs* the children assumed that *biff* must be the name for tongs (whole object assumption) and collected more, even though the tongs were different in subtle ways (taxonomic assumption). However, when shown a pewter cup and told that that was *biff* the children, knowing that the object already has the name 'cup' assume that it must be something else about the object that is *biff* rather than its name (mutual exclusivity). Generally they assume that it must be the unusual material that it is made out of and choose other pewter objects as examples of *biff*. Here we can see mutual exclusivity operating which enables children to infer word meaning from context.

Children's sensitivity to the attention of others in word learning

The behaviourist model that word learning is solely the formation of an association between two stimuli (object and sound) has been shown to be false; further, word learning by ostension requires special mechanisms if the child is not to drown in a sea of hypotheses about what people mean when they name an object. It also appears that sounds are only associated with objects under particular circumstances. For instance if an infant is playing with a novel toy and hears a novel word she only assumes that the word is the name for the toy if someone uses the word while they themselves are attending to the toy (Baldwin *et al.*, 1996). Similarly, if a child is looking at a novel object and an adult produces a novel name, the child will shift attention to the adult's eyes to see what it is that the adult is attending to. This research shows that learning the meaning of words is rather more than the formation of associations between sound and object and involves assumptions and the sharing of attention that are probably inborn. The importance of innate knowledge is even more prominent when we consider the way that children acquire the grammatical structures of language, which is what we address next.

Acquiring grammar: Chomsky, innateness and the Universal Grammar

In the 1950s, Noam Chomsky of MIT (Chomsky, 1957) made the outrageous claim that language learning is impossible. What he meant was that given the amount of information that children have to go on, learning was not possible without extra information coming from elsewhere, an argument known as the **argument from the poverty of the stimulus** or the **learnability argument**. He reasoned that children learn language so quickly and with so few errors that they cannot be merely learning language by trial and error as behaviourists such as Skinner suggested or by another general learning mechanism such as analogy (see Chomsky, 1959). The only way that language could be learned was if children are given support by innate knowledge which fills in the blanks left by messy human speech.

To illustrate this, we will use one of Chomsky's most celebrated examples, that of turning statements into questions. Suppose you are given the following statement:

(1) The man is playing football.

We can turn this into a question that asks what the man is doing by simply taking the 'is' and moving it to the beginning of the sentence as in example 2.

(2) Is the man playing football?

Now Chomsky asks us to imagine that the child is attempting to discover (or induce) the linguistic rule that turns statements into questions simply by observing instances of statements and questions as above. Imagine that the child encounters a different sentence to turn into a question.

(3) The man who is wearing shorts is playing football.

The problem is that the word 'is' appears twice; which one should the child take? A child familiar with simple sentences such as those like Sentence 1 might be tempted to take the first 'is' to produce

*(4) Is the man who wearing shorts is playing football?

Figure 10.2 Linguist Noam Chomsky

Which is ungrammatical (denoted by the asterisk). If children simply worked out grammatical rules by trial and error – as many early theories claimed – then we should expect to see such errors at least some of the time, but we don't. Why not?

According to Chomsky this is because children do not just perceive utterances as linear streams of words, they perceive them as hierarchically structured. Implicitly children parse utterances into higher level units such as noun phrases and verb phrases. In the first sentence 'The man' is a noun phrase, containing information about the subject of the sentence, 'is playing football', on the other hand, is a verb phrase which contains information about what the man is doing. In the second sentence, the noun phrase is rather longer 'the man who is wearing shorts' because 'who is wearing shorts' is saying something about the man (noun) rather than about the action he is performing (verb). Because the question requires the child to ask what the man is doing (the verb phrase), the 'is' that is moved has to be the one that relates to the verb phrase rather than that of the noun phrase. (Note that if we wanted to ask a question about the man – whether he is wearing shorts – we would move the 'is' from the noun phrase to end up with 'is the man who is playing football wearing shorts'.) The overwhelming majority of people who can speak a language have probably never even heard of noun and verb phrases, and they are things that do not come naturally to students of grammar and linguistics in the first instance, but everyone is implicitly aware of their existence, otherwise they would not be able to speak in grammatical sentences.

This is a classic example of the learnability argument; the information needed to turn statements into questions is not something that is given to children in the linguistic environment, nor do parents explicitly teach children about verb and noun phrases. But this information must come from somewhere and Chomsky argues that it is innate.

There is one crucial question: do children produce grammatical rather than ungrammatical utterances when turning statements into questions? Crain and Nakayama (1986) conducted an experiment in which 3-year-olds were required to ask a Jabba the Hut puppet whether, for instance, the dog who is wearing the blue collar likes playing fetch. In the majority of cases, children were able to turn such statements into grammatical questions, and never made errors such as those in sentence 4 where the incorrect 'is' belonging to the noun phrase is moved to the front of the sentence.

Other evidence shows that babies are capable of understanding complex syntactic structure. Katherine Hirsh-Pasek and Roberta Golinkoff (1991) showed that babies between 13 and 15 months of age who were in the one-word stage of language production could nevertheless discriminate between similar sounding but syntactically distinct phrases. The infants were seated in front of two televisions, each of which showed a film in which a pair of adults dressed up as Cookie Monster and Big Bird from television's Sesame Street performed simple activities. A voice-over said, 'Oh look! Big Bird is washing Cookie Monster! Find Big Bird washing Cookie Monster!' (or vice versa). Careful measurement showed that the babies spent reliably longer looking at the screen that matched the action rather than the other (foil) screen that showed a different but closely related action (for instance Cookie Monster is washing Big Bird). This shows that even before infants are able to string words together, they are able to understand the different roles of subject, verb and object.

The Universal Grammar

Chomsky argues that language learning is supported by a language organ which contains knowledge of the Universal Grammar (UG) which is the abstract specification that underlies all human languages. Languages differ syntactically in many ways, some put the verb between the subject of the sentence and its object (like English, which is therefore known as a Subject Verb Object or SVO language); others put the verb first and then the subject and then the object (such as Gaelic); whereas still others put the subject then the object followed by the verb (German is such an example). Table 10.1 shows the proportion of each of the logically possible six orderings of subject, verb and object in a sample of 402 of the world's languages. As can be seen, the majority of languages are SOV or SVO, with OVS and OSV being extremely rare. Notice also that in 96 per cent of this sample the subject is placed before the object.

Table 10.1 Proportion of languages adopting each of the six logically possible word orderings from a sample of 402 of the world's languages

Word order	Number of languages	% Languages
SOV	180	45
SVO	168	42
VSO	37	9
VOS	12	3
OVS	5	1
OSV	0	0
Total	402	

Source: Tomlin (1986)

Languages vary in other ways. English, for instance, is fussy about the order in which words appear in sentences; change the word order and you change the meaning of the sentence. Other languages such as Latin and some Australian aboriginal languages such as Warlpiri are more relaxed about word order, instead who's doing what to whom is conveyed by the use of special affixes (sounds that are added on to the end, beginning or in the middle of words).

Although languages vary significantly in their syntax there are certain abstract properties that all languages share. Languages differ in the orders of subject, object and verb, but all languages use these syntactic components; all languages have structures which perform the function of nouns, verbs, adjectives and prepositions; all languages have other features such as a topic and a head. These similarities exist, according to Chomsky, because they are part of the newborn's innate knowledge of language contained in the Universal Grammar.

How do children learn the particulars of the language spoken around them? Chomsky proposes that the child has a group of mental switches – called parameters – that are 'flicked' as a result of linguistic experience and it is this parameter setting that makes language learning so fast. As a simple example, a child's UG tells the child that there are subjects and objects, but there is a free parameter which allows SVO, VSO or SOV (for example). If the child's linguistic environment were English then, as a result of exposure to language, the parameter would be set to SVO; on the other hand, if the child were growing up in a German-speaking environment it would be set to SOV.

Chomsky and his followers argue that even when children make grammatical errors many of these are not simply random. It is proposed that many errors made by English children would be perfectly grammatical in some other language. Some errors made by young children in English have been shown to be perfectly grammatical in German. What is happening here? Remember that the Universal Grammar contains the abstract specification for all human languages that exist, have existed and (presumably) some that have never existed as well. The Universal Grammar enables the child, based on impoverished input, to induce the correct rules of the particular language that he or she is hearing and thereby become a member of the linguistic community.

The above is a much simplified account of a complicated theory and there is much debate, even among Chomskyians, as to how the process of parameter setting actually works, and to what extent parameters can be unset (say if the child moves to another linguistic environment). In fact it appears that children are quite flexible in this regard and are able to acquire new languages with great ease up until around age seven, after which this ability gradually declines (Pinker, 1994).

Chomsky and evolution

Although Chomsky argues that language learning is supported by innate psychological mechanisms, he was reticent to accept that these mechanisms were shaped by natural selection. Rather, he suggested that the language organ evolved for some other purpose and was co-opted, or exapted, for its current purpose. More recent proposals by Chomsky and co-workers (Hauser *et al.*, 2002) expand upon this idea by delineating the 'faculty of language in the broad sense' (FLB) from 'the faculty of language in the narrow sense' (FLN). FLB refers to what we would commonly call language (verbal communication) and includes all of the cognitive operations that support this, such as fine motor control, auditory perception, planning, parsing and so on. FLN delineates only those features of language that are specific to language itself. This would therefore exclude many of the aforementioned features of FLB as they are used for non-linguistic purposes and can be found in non-linguistic animals. One possible candidate for a cognitive operation that is specific to language is recursion. Recursion is what we use when we produce (or comprehend) embedded clauses. For example we could say:

'Throw the spear at the mammoth'

Or, to be more specific

'Throw the spear at the mammoth with the large tusks'

Or, even more specifically

'Throw the spear at the mammoth with the large tusks that is running towards you.'

Each additional clause ('with the large tusks', etc.) adds information as to which mammoth one should throw the spear at. This is one of the important combinatorial features of grammar, as we saw above. Hauser *et al.* leave it as an open question whether recursion is the *only* feature that is in FLN (there could be others), and also whether recursion is specific to language. They raise as a possibility that recursion could have been developed for spatial navigation and was co-opted for language use. So far there is no evidence that this is the case, although if homologous (same feature by common descent) examples of recursion can be found in non-human animals it would provide evidence for the notion that recursion was co-opted. If this were the case would it suggest that language did not evolve but was merely co-opted? In a review of Hauser *et al.*'s paper Jackendoff and Pinker (2005) argue that even if it were true that *all* the underlying cognitive operations of language were co-opted, it would still not deny that language evolved. Natural selection usually works by modifying what is already present rather than creating new structures. Perhaps the most famous example is that the ossicles of the mammalian ear (the hammer, anvil and stirrup) evolved from bones that originally functioned as part of the reptilian jawbone. But the current adaptive function of the ossicles is clearly to transmit sound vibrations in order to enable auditory perception, the fact that they might have, at one point, served a different function is largely irrelevant to the debate.

Whether co-opted or not, many now accept that language involves a complex design of interacting parts that surely could not have evolved by accident. But if language is 'in the genes', where are these genes? What progress has been made in identifying how the language organ is specified in the genome? We will return to this point after first evaluating Chomskyian theory.

Evaluation of Chomskyian theory

In evaluating Chomsky's contribution to the evolution of language, we must carefully delineate several claims. The first claim is that language acquisition is impossible if it were to simply rely on species-general learning mechanisms (Skinnerian mechanisms) such as the forming of associations, reinforcement and punishment, this is the learnability argument outlined above. The second claim is that extra information is provided to assist the process of language learning in the form of species-specific structures and processes: a universal grammar of some sort. The third is that language acquisition is facilitated by the specific principles and parameters proposed in Chomskyian theory such as the exotically named 'trace erasure principle', the 'ergative case parameter' and the 'nominal mapping parameter'. Whereas practically all psychologists and linguists agree with the first claim – the evidence both empirical and logical is overwhelming – there is, however, more debate with regard to the specific nature of this extra information. Whether, for example, our minds contain an abstract representation of grammar that is gradually fleshed out by a process of parameter switching, or, as some have argued, language is acquired by statistical extraction of linguistic regularities (see next).

As in many areas of human inquiry, the language acquisition camp tend to cleave into those who consider themselves to be Chomskyian and those who are anti-Chomskyians. This is unfortunate. Scientific theory should not be treated as dogma, one should not be forced to either accept it or reject it wholesale the way one might do with a religion or a political ideology. On the contrary, we should explicitly reject such a temptation as unscientific; we should accept those parts of the theory that explain the relevant phenomena and are supported by the evidence and reject those parts of it that do not and are not.

Non-modular evolutionary accounts of language acquisition

There are a number of theories that propose that language evolved through a process of natural selection but eschew the argument that language is acquired through the action of innate, domain-specific, mental modules espoused by Chomsky, Pinker and others. Evolutionist Michael Tomasello (see Tomasello, 1999) proposes that language is like any other cultural artefact handed down by our ancestors and needs no domain-specific language organ in order to explain its acquisition. Instead, he proposes that species-specific cognitive, social cognitive and cultural learning processes can account for language learning (see chapter 14). Unlike other domain-general theories of language learning, such as that proposed by behaviourists, in which children passively acquire language through experience, Tomasello proposes that language learning is the result of children actively attempting to understand adult communication in a context of attention sharing. Although grounded in evolutionary theory, Tomasello argues that the principal difference between humans and non-humans is humans' ability to identify with their conspecifics (i.e. theory of mind – see chapter 5), and it is this that enables language learning.

Tomasello argues that Chomsky and Pinker have underplayed the role of imitation in language learning, and overplayed children's ability to form general rules aided by innate knowledge such as the Universal Grammar (Tomasello, 2005). Central to this view is the creativity enabled by inductive processes and rule formation. As we shall see when we discuss the Wug test, 3-year-olds are able to inflect novel nouns to make them plural. Some evidence by Akhtar and Tomasello (1997) suggests there are severe boundaries to this creativity. Given a sentence like 'The ball is getting *dacked* by Ernie' (where 'dacked' is a novel verb) and asked 'What is Ernie doing?' children find it difficult to give the correct answer (*dacking*); instead they tend to stay close to the form of the verb that they heard. Tomasello argues that this is because children's language is a lot less to do with abstract rules than Chomsky and others believe. He suggests that children acquire schemas such as those called **verb islands** which consist of a verb familiar to the child and one or more slots that can take nouns. So a child might have a representation _____ kicked _____ with the slots on either side able to take a number of nouns with which the child is familiar. This endows flexibility, but – at least for young children – the verb at the centre of the construction cannot be changed.

Tomasello presents some interesting evidence for his theory, but so far it has not yet been used to explain many of the linguistic anomalies that led Chomsky to propose a language-specific learning mechanism (such as the ease with which children turn statements into questions mentioned above). The idea is intriguing but it needs a thorough examination before becoming mainstream. Consistent with Tomasello's theory is that people with autism – who have impaired theory of mind, see chapter 5 – show language delay and frequently never develop language to the level of clinically normal individuals. However, sufferers from the related condition Asperger's syndrome may also show substantial impairments in theory of mind but have few difficulties in their ability to learn language.

The search for language genes

Recent research on a language disorder known as **specific language impairment** (SLI) has been widely touted as evidence for the genetic basis of the language organ. Specific language impairment, as the name implies, is a disorder that targets certain aspects of language production – particularly certain aspects of grammar – with no obvious profound sensory or neurological impairment (Bishop *et al.*, 1995). Speech is effortful and often unintelligible with many word-order and other grammatical errors evident. The KE family from Birmingham in the British Midlands were studied in the late 1980s by psycholinguist Myrna Gopnik and colleagues (e.g. Gopnik, 1994; Gopnik and Crago, 1991; Crago and Gopnik, 1994). Sixteen out of thirty members of the extended family were affected by a particularly severe form of SLI leading them to produce sentences such as:

'It's a flying finches they are'.
'Carol is cry in the church'.
'A Patrick is naughty'.

As the quotations above emphasise, SLI sufferers seem to have particular problems with **inflectional morphology**. Inflectional morphology is the process whereby words are modified to indicate grammatical features such as number, tense, agreement and aspect.

Gopnik (1994) tested sufferers on a test known as the 'Wug' test. We know from extensive research that children of 3 and 4 years of age are able to inflect novel

Box 10.2 **Can non-human animals be taught language?**

Some researchers have tried to teach animals something akin to human language: an area of research that has excited much debate and controversy. The research has normally focused on the attempt to teach non-human primates, usually common chimps but also bonobos (pygmy chimps – see chapter 4) and gorillas, non-verbal languages such as sign language or specially developed languages using pictographic tokens. Spoken languages were abandoned after it was realised that the vocal systems of non-human primates are incapable of making the range of sounds necessary for a properly verbal language. What is at stake here is a number of theoretical issues but most importantly for this chapter, whether Chomsky is correct in his arguments that language is the result of an innate language organ (animal language researcher Herbert Terrace even provocatively named one of his chimps Nim Chimpsky). If other animals can be taught language, then the most likely conclusion would be that innate knowledge is not essential for language learning. Given that non-human primates don't normally use language, it would be somewhat wasteful for them to have a language organ kicking around doing nothing (or waiting for human scientists to attempt to teach them language), and natural selection punishes profligacy mercilessly. Early attempts to teach primates language include Sarah (Premack and Premack, 1972), who communicated using plastic chips containing symbols, and Washoe (Fouts *et al.*, 1984), who was taught a version of American Sign Language (ASL). Sarah and Washoe were quite successful in comprehending and producing 'utterances'. For example, Washoe produced utterances such as 'baby in shoe' and 'open hurry' (when standing outside a door). However, these examples of creative language use are often outnumbered by meaningless utterances and word-salad. Human infants make mistakes too, but far fewer than would be expected if they were merely combining words at random (Brown, 1973). More recent attempts have met with more success. In particular a team led by Sue Savage-Rumbaugh claim to have successfully taught non-human primates the rudiments of language. Of particular interest is Kanzi, a bonobo whose adoptive mother Matata was undergoing language training using a keyboard consisting of symbols known as lexigrams. Kanzi showed little interest in the keyboard during Matata's training but later, after Matata had been sent off for a period of time, Kanzi showed that he could use most of the ten lexigrams that had been on Matata's keyboard. This was surprising, since usually it takes many hours of special training for apes to learn the lexigrams. Kanzi proved himself a prolific learner and can now produce over 200 words and is able to 'comprehend' over 500. He is also able to carry out instructions correctly such as 'give the pine needles to Kelly' (Savage-Rumbaugh *et al.*, 1993). The animal language controversy polarises researchers like few other debates in psychology. Its supporters claim that although the 'languages' learned by non-human primates are nothing like as complex as those spoken even by young children, the difference is one of degree not type. Many other linguists and cognitive scientists argue that impressive though the animal feats are, they are really little more than clever parlour tricks and bear little resemblance to real languages (Pinker, 1994).

Sue Savage-Rumbaugh and the bonobo Kanzi. Kanzi was taught to communicate using lexigrams (also pictured) and was known by the lexigram 太

Suppose, for a moment, that this research was successful and animals were trained to use language; would this undermine Chomsky's position? Successfully training an animal to use language might be taken as evidence that a language organ was unnecessary for language learning. Presumably natural selection has not equipped languageless animals with such a faculty in the chance that it will be needed at some point in the future. However, it is worth bearing in mind that apes are typically subjected to an exhaustive regime of language training, each being presented with trail after trail of carefully constructed paired associates with teams of researchers taking it in turns to give them instruction. This is very different from the messy and incomplete language curriculum human children experience. Under such circumstances the learnability argument does not apply since language is not being learned in the same way that children learn language.

How should evolutionists treat this research? With some ambivalence. At one level evolutionary psychologists are interested in the kinds of things that organisms do in the wild. This is one of the great differences between an evolutionarily inspired discipline such as ethology and behaviourism which pays little lip service to Darwinism. It is surely interesting that chimps and gorillas can show aspects of linguistic competence (assuming that they can – which many believe is a big assumption) but the training regime required to instil this provides good evidence that such animals were not 'designed' for language (or at least not a language like human language). As psycholinguist and philosopher Jerry Fodor points out: 'That a dog can be trained to walk on its hind legs does not prejudice the claim that bipedal gait is genetically coded in humans. The fact that we can learn to whistle like a lark does not prejudice the species-specificity of birdsong' (Fodor *et al.*, 1974).

The Wug Test

Figure 10.3 A sample question from the Wug test

This is a Wug.

Now there is another one.
There are two of them.
There are two___.

nouns for (among other things) plurality (Berko, 1958). In the Wug test the child is given a picture of an unfamiliar object that is given a novel name such as Wug, and then shown a further picture representing two such objects and told 'Now there are two of them, there are two___' and the child is encouraged to inflect the name to produce the plural, Wugs (see figure 10.3).

Gopnik's research demonstrated that even adult sufferers of SLI find the Wug test demanding. Not only do they frequently fail to use the correct suffix, when they do, it is frequently mispronounced to produce words such as 'Wugs' (where the final phoneme is an unvoiced 's' as in 'buss' rather than a voiced 'z').

Certain forms of SLI appear to be genetic in that they run in families (as is the case for the KE family). The pattern of inheritance suggests that it is the result of a single dominant gene on an autosomal (i.e. non-sex) chromosome (see chapter 2). More recent research suggests that the gene responsible for SLI lies on chromosome 7 (the same chromosome where the Williams syndrome deletions occur, see chapter 5). Specifically it appears that the damage is in region 7q31 in an area comprising 70 different genes that was called SPCH1 (Fisher *et al.*, 1998). Further research (Lai *et al.*, 2001) suggests that the crucial gene seems to be one known as FOXP2. FOXP2 is not unique to humans but the specific version present in humans is subtly different from those present in other animals. Comparative genetic research by Enard *et al.* (2002) suggests that the gene reached its current state 100,000–200,000 years ago.

More recent research has capitalised on the ability to use DNA samples from extinct species, specifically *Homo neanderthalensis* or Neanderthals for short (see chapter 3). This research is particularly exciting as it enables us to better understand our closest relative and ourselves. The research suggests that Neanderthals possessed exactly the same variant of FOXP2 as modern humans, further reinforcing the notion that Neanderthals possessed language of some form. Other research suggests that rather than FOXP2 reaching its current state before the anatomically modern human and Neanderthal lineage split from one another, the genetic evidence can be better explained by assuming gene flow between humans and Neanderthals: in other words the two groups interbred (Coop *et al.*, 2008 – and see chapter 3). If this is the case, and it is by no means certain that it is, then it suggests that Neanderthals 'got' the FOXP2 gene from humans rather than the other way around as Neanderthal DNA is not present in indigenous Africans but FOXP2, and of course language, is.

All of this raises the question – is FOXP2 the grammar gene? Almost certainly it is not. As we have seen before, the disruption of a single gene can have wide-ranging effects on behaviour (pleiotropy), but this does not mean that that gene is *for* a particular behaviour. As psychologist Richard Gregory has pointed out many times, removing a component from a radio can result in the radio howling uncontrollably, this does not mean that the component is a 'howl suppressant'. More recent research has indeed shown that FOXP2 has a variety of phenotypic effects. This is partly because FOXP2 (and other FOX genes, of which there are many) codes for a transcription factor, this is a protein that binds to other genes potentially affecting their expression (how the gene exerts its phenotypic effect). So a mutation in FOXP2 such as that suffered by the KE family would have a variety of effects, particularly on the brain where it seems to have its most profound effects. Indeed as well as the aforementioned language problems the KE family also had difficulty moving the lower face, especially the mouth and lower lip. Moreover, they also had significantly reduced verbal and spatial IQ. Curiously other research shows that if mice are engineered with non-functioning version of FOXP2 then they show either a reduction in or absence of ultra-sonic vocalisations that are usually produced when pups are removed from their mothers (the extent of this deficit depending on whether one or both copies of the gene are damaged). However, as with the KE family, other effects are also noted including motor problems and, in those where both copies were damaged, premature death (the KE family had a functioning copy of FOXP2 on the other chromosome). Research on FOXP2 is still ongoing; it certainly does seem to play a role in language, and other forms of communication.

Specific language impairment as a problem with inflectional morphology

Notwithstanding this, some researchers have tentatively argued that the damaged gene found in SLI sufferers may be one of many genes that are responsible for, among other things, building the language organ (Pinker, 1994). Gopnik argues that sufferers might have an impairment in their ability to learn the rules that enable words to be inflected properly. In English, nouns and verbs are either regular or irregular. Regular verbs, for example, are inflected by adding '-ed' to indicate that the action occurred in the past, or with '-ing' to indicate that it is ongoing with respect to some frame of reference (e.g. I am walking to the park). For their part, regular nouns are inflected with '-s' to indicate that there is more than one of them. Irregular nouns and verbs, on the other hand, are as the name might imply, unpredictable. The excerpt from a poem by Phoebe Cary below illustrates the dangers of trying to make predictions of the past tense forms of irregular verbs.

Sally Salter, she was a young teacher who taught,
And her friend, Charley Church, was a preacher who praught;
Though his enemies called him a screecher who scraught.

Some research suggests that irregular and regular words are learned in different ways. Because irregular verbs and nouns are unpredictable, they have to be learned by rote. This means that there is a separate entry for each form in the mental lexicon, despite them having the same meaning (e.g. there would be an entry for 'teach' and 'taught' with a marker to show that one was present tense, the other past tense). Regular nouns and verbs, on the other hand, have a single entry and a rule is invoked to change the entry in order to inflect it appropriately (e.g. we would have a single entry for 'walk' and general rules would add the '-ed' or '-ing' where appropriate). Gopnik's argument is that the process responsible for learning the appropriate rule is faulty in SLI sufferers, and they therefore have to approach all words as if they were irregular. This is a monumental task. Although irregular verbs and nouns are among the most frequent in the English language they are also relatively few in number, just over a hundred. Imagine what a feat it would be to have to learn the correct suffixes for each one of the tens of thousands of regular words.

Some experimental evidence for this claim can be found by using another task normally conducted on children. We have mentioned inflectional morphology, which changes words to fulfil new grammatical roles. **Derivational morphology**, on the other hand, enables new words to be made from old. The word 'microwavable' is a recent example. The noun microwave became a verb to microwave and the **morpheme** '-able' added to the end to create a new word meaning 'capable of undergoing the action of being microwaved'. One form of derivational morphology is a process called compounding in which two or more distinct words (as opposed to words plus morphemes such as microwavable, downloadable and googleability – the likelihood that something can be found using a search engine) are combined to describe or name a new concept. Common examples of colloquial compounds are head-hunter, man-eater and toothbrush. Like aspects of inflectional morphology, the compounding process develops early in life and even 3-year-olds are masters at generating new compounds. What happens when we form a compound? It is believed that we take the mental representation of the relevant words from our lexicon and join them, making sure that we obey the compounding rules of our particular language. For instance in English, the most important word or 'head' as it is known occurs in the second position in two-word compounds, for example a football is a type of ball (ball being the head) not a type of foot. In Celtic languages such as Welsh the head comes first, as in the popular Welsh sport *pêl droed* in Welsh, which literally translates as 'ball foot'. Now, according to the theory of regular and irregular nouns and verbs mentioned above, regular nouns and verbs have only one entry (which is close to the present tense or singular form), whereas for irregular nouns and verbs all of the different forms are stored. This means for regular verbs and nouns only the uninflected form can occur in the compound (because this is the only form stored), whereas any version of an irregular verb or noun should be able to appear.

Psychologist and linguist Peter Gordon (Gordon, 1985) showed that when encouraged to form compounds, 3-year-old children behaved as predicted. For instance when asked what one might call a monster that eats mice, children would either say a 'mouse-eater' or a 'mice-eater'. Both singular and plural forms are stored as separate words in the mental lexicon, therefore either is available to enter the compounding process. Regular words, however, are stored in only one form, the singular form, therefore only this word can be made into compounds. Sure enough, when children were asked what one would call a creature that eats rats they said 'rat-eater' but never said 'rats-eater'. Returning to specific language impairment if, as Gopnik argues, sufferers of SLI have slavishly to learn all forms of regular nouns and verbs then they should have separate lexical entries for 'rat' and 'rats' (unlike non-sufferers who would only have 'rat'). This would predict that, unlike Peter Gordon's 3-year-olds,

SLI sufferers would be as likely to say 'rats-eater' as 'mice-eater' and this is indeed what they were found to do (Van der Lely and Ullman, 2001).

Is specific language impairment really an impairment specific to language?

Even researchers sympathetic to evolutionary approaches to the basis of language deny that the gene associated with SLI is a gene *for* grammar, although some have suggested that it might be one of many genes that specify some components of the language organ. Others, however, raise another possibility. Paula Tallal and colleagues have found that sufferers from SLI have particular difficulty perceiving rapid bursts of sound (Tallal *et al.*, 1985). Perhaps, she reasoned, this deficit led to SLI sufferers having problems discriminating phonological features that occur for only a brief amount of time. Such a deficit could well lead to impoverished input and therefore poor language learning. Consider the Wug test again. The inflections on the ends of words in English tend to consist of comparatively short bursts of sound: the /s, /z and /is found in plurals such as 'dogs', 'cats' and 'horses' and the /ed that signifies that a regular verb is past tense, and what's more they tend to be unstressed.

If a sufferer's ability to perceive rapid sounds were impaired in such a way, they might miss these crucial components of the English inflectional system. Laurence Leonard (1992) presents evidence that this may be the case. In Italian, for instance, many inflectional affixes are comparatively long, tend to be stressed and the stem form often can't stand alone. For instance, in Italian 'scrivo' means 'I write', 'scrivi' means 'you write' but the stem 'scriv' never appears alone. An English-speaking sufferer could reasonably mishear 'rats' as 'rat', but an Italian-speaking sufferer could not confuse 'scrivo' with 'scriv' because 'scriv' is not a word.

Leonard found that Italian sufferers of SLI tend to perform well on tests such as the Wug test where the affixes are long and stressed, and poorly on those that are unstressed (see table 10.2).

To confuse the issue somewhat, research by Myrna Gopnik (1997) investigated Japanese sufferers of SLI. As for Italian, Japanese has an inflectional system where the affixes constitute many syllables. For example, the affix 'mashita' is a polite past-tense inflection which would hardly slip by unnoticed in the way a swallowed '-ed' affix might in English. Table 10.3 clearly shows that even when affixes are conspicuous such as in Japanese, SLI sufferers show a reduced performance when compared with unimpaired controls.

A more recent account of SLI developed by Michael Ullman (2001a; 2001b; 2004; Ullman and Pierpont, 2005) may go some way towards clearing up these inconsistencies. He bases his account on the distinction between procedural and

Table 10.2 **The performance of English and Italian sufferers from SLI and controls on a variety of inflection tasks. Note in many cases the Italian SLI sufferers are equivalent to the controls. Age is in years and months. The participants were matched on language ability by using Mean Length of Utterance (MLU)**

	% correct	
	SLI	MLU controls
English speakers		
Articles	52	62
Plurals	69	96
Third singular	34	59
Regular past	32	65
Irregular past	65	77
Age range	3 yrs 8 mths–5 yrs 7 mths	2 yrs 11 mths–3 yrs 4 mths
Italian speakers		
Articles	41	83
Plurals	87	89
Third singular	93	93
Noun–adjective	97	99
Age range	4 yrs–6 yrs	2 yrs 6 mths–3 yrs 6 mths

Source: Leonard (1992)

Table 10.3 **Participants' ability to produce correct tense marking. Participants were given items such as 'Every day I walk to school.' 'Yesterday I _____.'**

% correct	English (England)	English (Canada)	French (Canada)	Japanese	Greek
Impaired	38.3	52.3	46.7	48.1	20.0
Controls	91.7	93.5	96.4	97.9	87.1

declarative knowledge (Ryle, 1949; Anderson, 1983). Declarative knowledge relates to facts about the world ('Paris is the capital of France') whereas procedural knowledge relates to the ability to apply rules and procedures such the ability to drive a car; these types of knowledge being served by anatomically distinct brain structures. In terms of language, acquiring words requires the use of declarative memory, whereas acquiring grammar – as it is a rule-based system – principally requires the use of procedural memory. Ullman's claim is that people with SLI have impairment in the brain structures responsible for acquiring procedural knowledge (such as the basal ganglia, Eichenbaum and Cohen, 1991) with the structures serving declarative memory preserved. Thus people with SLI find word learning comparatively easy, but have difficulties acquiring the grammatical rules required for learning syntax and inflectional morphology. So from this point of view, specific language impairment is not specific to language, sufferers also show deficits in procedural memory that are non-linguistic (such as learning a sequence of finger taps, Bishop, 2002).

Where does this discussion leave us with respect to the evolution of language? Does the finding – if it is correct – that SLI is not a language-specific deficit cast doubt on the notion that language evolved? Does it suggest that language learning is served by general learning algorithms rather than specific ones (contra to Chomsky)? The answer to both of these questions is no. When SLI was first discovered in the KE family it led to much excitement, maybe here was an example of a deficit that was purely concerned with acquiring language. If it had been found to be so it would have been strong direct evidence for the domain specificity of language learning. However, evidence that SLI is not specific to language doesn't count as evidence that language learning is not domain specific. We know that there are many domain-general aspects to language learning such as the ability to discriminate sounds, memory, the ability to control motor actions and so on, if it is finally concluded that SLI is not language specific, it simply puts it in a large category of deficits that affect language and other things as well.

Finally, a few words of caution. First, one of the problems with studying SLI is that it seems to be a fairly heterogeneous category of disorders. Not all SLI sufferers (in fact a very small minority) suffer from the dysfunctional FOXP2 gene possessed by the KE family. The apparent inconsistencies found in the research might be the result of researchers testing a family of disorders with different aetiology. Second, and echoing a point made previously, genes tend to be pleiotropic (see chapter 2) and finding a gene that has only a single effect is very rare indeed. We need to determine which effects of a gene have fitness consequences and which do not in order to decide which ability the gene was actually selected for.

When did language evolve?

Language doesn't fossilise so it is hard to say with complete certainty whether a particular ancestral hominin did or did not possess language, and to what degree of sophistication. However, evidence from the anatomy of early hominins and the types

Box 10.3 **Language development and life history approach**

The development of language is traditionally seen as being one of a progression towards linguistic competence: children's vocalisations start off as prelinguistic coos and wails, progress through language-like babbles to one-word then two-word utterances, and then as vocabulary expands and grammatical complexity increases their speech becomes ever more adult-like.

Viewing children as universal novices, and childhood as merely an apprenticeship to adulthood, has had a long history in developmental psychology, but has recently been challenged by some evolutionists. In chapter 6 we saw how some researchers have adopted a life history approach to development. These researchers argued that children's behaviour should be understood in two ways: (1) as an attempt to maximise their own survival and (2) as an attempt to increase their reproductive fitness when adults. We gave the example of a caterpillar which has its own unique morphology compared to that of the adult (meaning we cannot merely study caterpillars are miniature butterflies), but are nonetheless trying to maximise their reproductive fitness when adults (by piling on the calories and so becoming a fit and healthy butterfly).

A recent paper by Locke and Bogin (2006) suggests that we might likewise view language development in the same way. Rather than seeing child language as merely a lesser form of adult language they ask what a child's language does for the child and how this might influence their reproductive chances as adults. Locke and Bogin argue that *Homo sapiens* has a more complex life history involving more stages than our primate relatives. Whereas chimpanzees have infancy, a juvenile and an adult period we have infancy, childhood, a juvenile, an adolescent period and an adult period. They explain these two extra periods (childhood and adolescence) as specific adaptations, which are part and parcel of the evolution of language. In a sense they are claiming that these two extra periods are there to support language – in another sense they are claiming that language is the very reason we have all of these stages.

The graph below shows a graph comparing the length of each developmental stage for humans and their ancestors, for example the average age at which the eruption of the first permanent molar is shown (this is taken as marking the end of childhood and the beginning of juvenility in humans). It can be seen that humans have a relatively long period of childhood and a period of adolescence.

Locke and Bogin claim that one reason for these two extra stages is to allow for linguistic competence to develop. In terms of language, childhood is a time of engaging in new extrafamilial friendships. By age six the child is physically able to produce the adult range of vowel sounds. This is a period when complex games are learned and

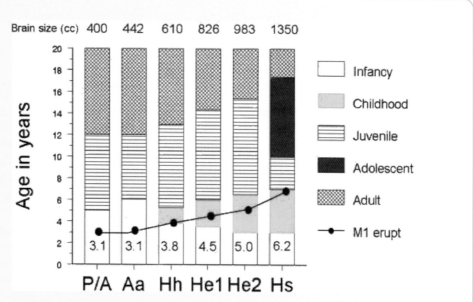

The different stages of development for a number of hominins. P/A = Pan and *Australopithecus aferensis* (e.g. Lucy), Aa = *Australopithecus africanus*, Hh = *Homo Habilis*, He1 early *Homo erectus*, He2 late *Homo erectus*, Hs = *Homo sapiens* (modern humans). M1 erupt is the average age at which the second set of teeth erupt.

there is verbal competition. There is also a growth in verbal creativity and sex differences emerge in how language is used. Boys tend to speak more assertively and get more attention; girls tend to speak more softly and become more involved in interpersonal relationships. Perhaps the most important development is that of displacement – i.e. the ability to talk about things that are not present. So Locke and Bogin see childhood as an important development in a number of ways that allows greater linguistic ability to become apparent and ultimately increases both direct and indirect fitness. Later on adolescence, a period where individuals are sexually mature but still not fully adult-like in physical stature and socioemotional competence, is seen by the authors as a stage where language is used for intra-sex competition (male–male, female–female) and courtship in preparation for adulthood. In a nutshell, by slowing down development and adding two stages to development, *Homo sapiens* achieved greater verbal competence and hence a selective advantage. The table shows the key characteristics of language at each of these stages and the proposed function.

Stage	Approximate duration (there are considerable sex differences)	Starts at	Language characteristics	Function
Infancy	0–36 months	Birth	Coos and babbles, first words	To increase parental investment by engaging parent
Childhood	36 months–6 years	Eruption of deciduous teeth	Fluency increases, self-referential	Creating and maintaining independent from parents
Juvenility	6–10 years	Eruption of first permanent molar	Pragmatic advances: gossip, storytelling. Verbal 'duels' particularly in males	Competition between group members, fostering of alliances and friendships
Adolescence	10–17 years	Adrenarche (maturation of adrenal glands, associated with onset of puberty)	Increase in complexity. Use language to compete with others, impress the opposite sex (esp. for males)	Develop social networks and explore romantic relationships
Adulthood	17 years +	Adult stature and social skills develops	Much of the above still present	Develop and maintain networks, foster romantic relationships, instruct children

The different stages in human development according to Locke and Bogin (2006).

of cultural artefacts that they produced goes some way towards helping us to answer this question. It used to be thought, for instance, that Neanderthals (discussed earlier) present in Europe around 200,000 years ago did not have language, despite them having larger brains than modern humans. The reasoning for this was that a crucial bone, the hyoid bone, was located too high up the vocal tract to enable certain vowel sounds to be produced. (The hyoid bone acts as a brace for the tongue and larynx giving a greater range of vocal expression than would be possible were it not present.) However, a recent discovery found a Neanderthal with the hyoid bone in a suitably low position to enable such vowels to be produced. This and the recent finding that Neanderthals possessed the same variant of the FOXP2 gene (see above) as modern humans suggests that Neanderthals did possess language.

Human brain size began to expand relative to body size some two million years ago (Boyd and Silk, 2000; Deacon, 1997 – see also chapter 2) and it is possible that this expansion coincided with the evolution of language. Some have argued that *Homo erectus* – the ancestors of the Neanderthals and *Homo sapiens* – which appeared in Africa nearly two million years ago – might have had the capacity for some language. Wynn (1998) observes that endocasts (casts taken of the inside of the cranium) of *Homo erectus* suggest that two brain regions thought to be crucial for language – Wernicke's area and Broca's area (see figure 10.1) – are similar to those in modern humans. Other evidence, however, suggests that *Homo erectus* might not have had sufficiently fine control over breathing to enable a full spoken language (Wynn, 1998; MacLarnon and Hewitt, 1999).

Exactly when language evolved is still uncertain, but even if *Homo erectus* were not capable of a language as sophisticated as that of modern humans, it remains a possibility that they had primitive language skills. The wings of an archaeopteryx might not have enabled the delicately controlled flight of a modern bird, but they permitted a form of gliding flight good enough to increase their fitness. Maybe the language of *Homo erectus* was primitive but good enough to confer an advantage over conspecifics with poorer or non-existent language.

The evolution of languages

In a similar way that paleoanthropologists have made attempts to construct the family tree of *Homo sapiens* (see chapter 2), so comparative linguists have attempted to recreate the evolution of the languages spoken today. Figure 10.4 shows a schematic representation of the current thinking in this area. This is only part of a tree representing the Indo-European language family which includes most of the languages traditionally spoken in Europe and the Asian sub-continent. This reconstruction was made possible by a discovery in 1786 by Sir William Jones, a British judge stationed in India. Jones was studying Sanskrit, the ancient language of India, and noticed that there were marked similarities between this language and ancient Greek and Latin (and also other modern languages). See table 10.4.

Jones's conclusion was that Sanskrit, Latin and Greek must have all had an even older common ancestor, a language that became known as Proto-Indo-European (PIE). It seems that the speakers of PIE spread throughout most of Europe and Asia, leaving perhaps only a few islands of non-Indo-Europeans (Basque and Finnish,

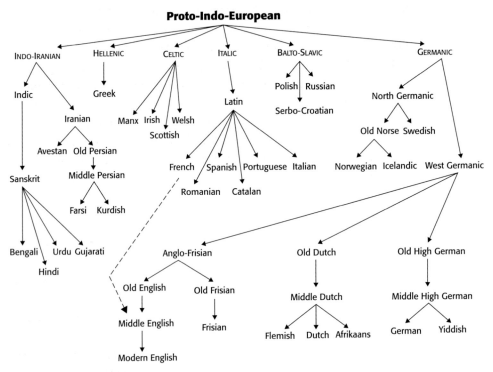

Figure 10.4 The descent of language, the Indo-European family tree

Table 10.4 Sanskrit compared to other Indo-European languages ancient and modern

English	mother	three	me	brother
Sanskrit	matar	tri	me	bhrator
Latin	mater	tres	me	frater
Italian	madre	tre	me	fra
Spanish	madre	tres	me	hermano
French	mère	trois	moi	frère
Greek	meter	treis	me	phrater
Dutch	moeder	drie	mij	broeder
German	mutter	drei	mich	bruder
Norwegian	mor	tre	meg	bror
Lithuanian	mater	tri	manen	brothar
Celtic	mathair	tri	me	brathair

for example, are not Indo-European languages). British archaeologist Colin Renfrew (1987) proposed that the Indo-Europeans originated in Anatolia (Modern Turkey) in the Fertile Crescent around 7000 BC. They were farmers (the Fertile Crescent is thought to be the birthplace of agriculture) and therefore were able to reproduce more rapidly than the hunter-gatherers who presumably inhabited Asia and Europe at the time (see chapter 14). It is also more than likely that the Indo-Europeans mated with these hunter-gatherers, absorbing them into their advanced culture.

What about all the other language families? Opinion differs as to the identity of the other language families, but some claim that there are seven families in addition to Indo-European.

These are listed below.

(1) *Afro-Asiatic* including Hebrew, Maltese, Libyan and Ethiopian;
(2) *Sino-Tibetan* languages spoken which include Chinese, Tibetan, Burmese and Eskimo;
(3) *African* languages which include the Bantu group of languages, and Kohsian group;
(4) *Asiatic* languages which counts Turkish, Lapp, Pushtu (spoken in Afghanistan) and Hungarian;
(5) *Caucasian* languages (the name refers to Caucasia, a region in central Asia) which includes the languages spoken in Chechnya and Georgia;
(6) *Oceanic* (sometimes called Australian languages) including the languages of New Zealand, Polynesia, Micronesia, Melanesia, Hawaii and Fiji;
(7) *Native American*. The languages spoken by Native Americans including Cherokee and Kamanchi.

Historical linguists such as the late Joseph Greenberg (1987) attempt to reconstruct the ancestors of all this diversity. By carefully analysing the words used in different languages he grouped together all languages apart from Sino-Tibetan and Oceanic into an ancestor language he called 'Nostratic' (the word is from the Russian meaning 'our language'). The remaining languages were grouped under the banner 'Dene Caucasian' which is the ancestor of Chinese, Tibetan, Burmese and several other languages of South and East Asia. The ultimate goal is to construct the common ancestor to these two language super-phyla. This work is very controversial and many linguists argue that such reconstructions go way beyond the available data. However, there is some supporting evidence from research examining biological similarities between people. For example, one claim is that all the native languages of North and South America derive from only three ancestors (as a result of three separate waves of immigrants entering via the Bering land bridge). This has found support from investigations of genetic and other biological similarities among modern natives (Cavalli-Sforza, 1991).

Why did language evolve?

If language evolved as a result of natural selection, one obvious question is why did it evolve? What were the particular pressures that led to our linguistic ancestors being favoured over their languageless conspecifics? First of all, it is important to re-emphasise that language, like the human eye, almost certainly did not evolve as a result of one huge mutation (a macromutation) that led us from having no language to having a full-blown language as we know it today. More likely, language evolved from non-linguistic vocalisations similar to those we see in non-human primates, gradually becoming more complex over the generations.

In a way, the question is difficult because there are so many candidates, as biological anthropologist Terrence Deacon notes:

From the perspective of hindsight, almost everything looks as though it might be relevant for explaining the language adaptation. Looking for the adaptive benefits of language is like picking only one dessert in your favorite bakery: there are too many compelling options to choose from. What aspect of human social organization and adaptation wouldn't benefit from the evolution of language? (1997)

The aspect of language that language researchers have tended to focus on is information transfer, specifically in its use in coordinating hunting or for teaching other people new skills. Recently, however, this view of what language might have been for originally has been challenged by a number of evolutionists, each of whom argues that language evolved for primarily social reasons. We discuss three such theories of the social origins of language next.

Gossip and language evolution

Evolutionist Robin Dunbar of Oxford University (1993; 1996) proposes that information transfer – although important – might not have been evolution's original motivation for producing language. He argues that language evolved as a means of maintaining social bonds through gossip.

Social gossip, he suggests, fulfils in humans a similar role to that provided by grooming in other primates: as a means of forming bonds between members of a community. This is part of a more general claim that intelligence evolved in order to maintain large group sizes; the more individuals you live with the more demands are placed on you to keep track of each individual and of the relationships among them. To meet these cognitive demands, he suggests, there needs to be an increase in brain size. In support of this general claim, Dunbar (1993) plotted the ratio of neocortex (the part of the brain believed to be used for higher cognitive abilities, including language) to total brain volume against the mean size of their group for a range of

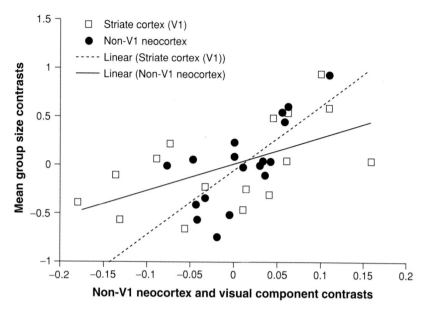

Figure 10.5 Ratio of neocortex to group size in a number of non-human primate communities

non-human primates. Humans were not included at this point, since estimating the group size for humans is difficult – for instance it could range from a few tens of people in an extended family group to several million in a large city. The graph is shown in figure 10.5 and it can be seen that there is a strong positive correlation between group size and neocortex ratio, suggesting that the social brain hypothesis might have some credibility. If the value for human neocortex size is plotted on the same graph we find that the predicted mean group size for humans is around 150 individuals.

Dunbar provides some evidence that 150 is a good estimate of human group size. Many hunter-gatherers, for example, live in bands of between 100 and 200 (with a mean of around 150). (The size of hunter-gatherer groups seems, in fact, to be trimodally distributed with overnight camps of a few tens of individuals, and tribes being a few hundred to a couple of thousand individuals; bands are an intermediate grouping of people.) He also suggests that people in the Western world are able to call on an average of 150 individuals for help (if, for example, they needed to borrow money).

So Dunbar's argument is that one of the pressures that led to the development of the brain is the need to remember all of the people that we know and interact with them in an efficient manner. But what has this got to do with language? Well, it has been suggested by Dunbar and others (see Dunbar, 1993) that in non-human primates the social glue that holds a group together is provided by grooming. Many primates such as baboons and chimpanzees will groom each other putatively to remove ticks and other parasites from their bodies, but also as a means of forming and maintaining relationships. The amount of grooming that a primate needs increases in direct relationship to the size of the group of which the individual is a member, so much so that some primates can spend as much as 20 per cent of their daytime engaged in grooming activities.

It has been estimated that if humans were to maintain group sizes of 150 individuals by using one-on-one grooming then they would need to spend around of 50 per cent of their time grooming. This figure is too high for us to attend to all of the other daytime chores, so Dunbar argues that our ancestors developed a new form of social grooming – language. Language enables us to engage more than one person in conversation and we can also 'groom' while performing other activities such as hunting and gathering. Given that the average group size for non-human primates is 50 and that for humans is 150, it follows that if humans are to spend no more than 20 per cent of their time engaged in social grooming, language must be three times more efficient than one-to-one grooming. Research by Dunbar *et al.* (1995) indicates that the maximum number of conversational partners that is typically possible is around three.

Dunbar presents some interesting evidence for his language-as-social-grooming hypothesis. Studies of language use suggest that it is most often used for gossiping and other social chitchat rather than for other means (such as giving instructions or information transfer for example). Dunbar *et al.* eavesdropped on people's conversations and calculated that between 60 and 70 per cent of the time conversations were of a social rather than pedagogical nature. Interestingly women were no more likely to engage in social conversation than were men.

Evaluation of the social grooming hypothesis

Dunbar proposes that language evolved for two reasons (1) to exchange social information and (2) to enable individuals to interact with more people at any one time. Many linguists and psychologists would accept the first proposition that language evolved for primarily social reasons rather than, say discussing hunting techniques or transmitting information about the physical world. The second proposition is, however, more contentious. It may be the case that larger groups lead to more surviving offspring but it remains an open question as to whether it was the ability to form larger groups that originally gave our linguistic ancestors an advantage over non-linguistic hominins, or whether group size was merely a side effect of the evolution of language. In support of this last point, Derek Bickerton (2007) asks why it was necessary for something as complex and costly as language to replace grooming – which is, at root, a fairly simple activity. What is the purpose of syntax, semantics and the like, and couldn't one have simply got away with making soothing, cooing vocalisations to facilitate social bonding? In other words, the selective pressure (the need for social bonding) does not specify the particular design features of language.

The social contract hypothesis

In contrast to Chomsky and Pinker, who have tended to focus on syntax as the hallmark of human language, Deacon (1997) focuses on another aspect of language – that of reference. He argues that the key difference between human language and animal communication is that human languages use symbols (words) to refer to objects. He argues, therefore, that the main phenomenon that needs explaining is the shift from non-symbolic to symbolic communication. He suggests that the mechanism for such a shift is likely to be sexual selection rather than natural selection, observing that in other species it is sexual selection that leads to the more radical shifts in communication patterns.

He suggests that our mating arrangements placed our ancestors under a unique set of pressures. Human relationships are, in the main, monogamous and stable with the males playing a role in the provisioning and care of offspring. Such a state of affairs is a recipe for disaster – especially when males are away from females for periods of time, as happens in hunter-gatherer communities – because it leaves the way open for freeriders: males who copulate with females and leave other males to pick up the tab in terms of providing for the young (see chapter 4).

This situation would not last for long because the cuckolded males, uncertain of the parentage of their partner's offspring would quickly stop providing for them and the whole system would collapse. What prevented the collapse was marriage. In order to prevent (or at least reduce) mistrust, couples made public and binding promises to each other as a way of reassuring each of the partners that they would not copulate with anyone else. According to Deacon, the only way in which such a promise could be made was through symbolic language because not only did it refer to the here and now, but also to future events ('as long as you both shall live...'). Symbolic language thus permitted the formation of social contracts, which enabled groups to stay together, which enabled the specialisation of male and female roles in terms of the provisioning of food (men hunt, women gather – see chapter 4) and permitted the moderately high male parental investment.

Evaluation of the social contract hypothesis

Again, this is an interesting if highly speculative hypothesis. Certainly Deacon presents a credible set of evolutionary pressures that might have favoured symbolic communication, but it is not at all clear whether language pre- or post-dates the type of social structures that he describes. It could well be that language evolved prior to the sort of society described by Deacon for entirely different reasons. Language then enabled social contracts and therefore monogamy, male parental investment.

The big problem with this hypothesis is that one of the most impressive features of human language, that which Hockett (Hockett and Altmann, 1968) calls prevarication (lying), but is better described as *stimulus freedom* (Trask, 1999). As far as we know most if not all forms of non-human animal communication are closely tied to a particular stimulus: a dog growls because it is angry, a vervet monkey calls because it sees an eagle, a bee dances because there is a nectar source and so on. One of the great strengths of human language is that the utterance doesn't need to be tied to a particular stimulus. We can cry wolf, tell tall tales and say 'I love you' when we don't mean it. We can also make promises that we can't or don't keep (as today's divorce statistics indicate). Although language might provide a disincentive to infidelity because other people who witness the indiscretion might well be able to inform the injured party, perhaps this, as much as promises and rituals, is evidence of language's ability to act as a glue to keep monogamous social structure together.

'The mating mind' and language evolution

Like Deacon, Geoffrey Miller (2000) argues that language was under the control of sexual selection rather than natural selection and evolved as a means of showing off how good our genes are to our prospective partners. At the heart of Miller's argument is Zahavi's notion of honest signalling that certain phenotypes evolved to indicate our underlying genetic fitness to potential mates and competitors (see chapter 3). Miller uses this line of reasoning to explain apparently functionless (in terms of natural selection) aspects of human behaviour such as art, creativity and also language. Of course, language is not functionless, far from it, but Miller's argument is that language may have originated as a means of enabling the process of competing for a mate; it was only later that it was used for all its other purposes. Miller points to the process of verbal courtship as an example of the importance of language in the dating game. Men, he suggests, are like verbal peacocks, using language to impress women during courtship. For their part, women use language less as a tool during mate selection (although they do use it for this purpose of course), rather as a method for holding an already existing relationship together. Through language, Miller argues, women endeavour to prove to men that they are still the best option and thus try to prevent them mating with other women. As we saw in chapter 3, when we discussed the Red Queen hypothesis (Ridley, 1993), male ornamentation such as horns or the peacock's tail seem to have evolved to their large size by virtue of their role in influencing female choice. Likewise the role of language in courtship might have increased its complexity beyond that necessary for mere survival.

Research by Miller suggests that males are more than ten times more prolific than women at producing works of art, and are at their most productive when at their peak age of sexual activity. Men also tend to have larger vocabularies than do women and use more complex words. Women, however, on average score more highly on tests of verbal fluency than do men. This might be seen as evidence against the theory; surely if men are the ones who attempt to court women through language it is they who should have the higher verbal fluency. Miller addresses this anomaly by suggesting that women need good verbal skills in order to choose a good mate by making an accurate judgement of a potential partner's ability.

Evaluation of Miller's theory

Miller's hypothesis is controversial, not least since there are many pressures that might lead to women being artistically less productive than men (time spent childrearing, being economically disadvantaged, having different societal expectations). But it does attempt to account for the existence of apparently functionless forms of behaviour such as poetry, storytelling, verbal wit as well as music and art. However, as with the other two hypotheses, it is not clear whether the use of language as a way of attracting a potential mate was an original causal factor in the development of language, or whether it was something that appeared after language evolved. The peacock's tail, for example, would originally have evolved for functional reasons (functional that is in terms of natural selection) before sexual selection distorted it beyond recognition. Likewise, language might have originally appeared for reasons other than to impress potential mates, with sexual selection only acting upon it later.

Evaluation: language and social interaction

Each of the hypotheses outlined above suggests that language evolved for reasons that were inherently social. This is a comparatively new area, and it is therefore not surprising that the hypotheses are somewhat speculative and, as yet, have little hard evidence to support them. Perhaps tellingly, none of the advocates of these hypotheses is a trained linguist, and it is probably the case that a thorough evaluation will be possible only when a number of researchers from different backgrounds (including psychology, ethology, biology, neuroscience, linguistics, archaeology and palaeontology) sift over the claims and evidence.

Until then, we can start to sketch out what a theory of language evolution might look like, what kinds of things it would have to explain. First it would have to explain some of the complexities of language. Language is an effective medium for expressing thoughts and for giving precise instructions; a theory would have to explain why such complexity was necessary. As we saw above there are questions as to why these attributes are required in order to groom, make promises or impress females. On the last point, one might raise the objection that the peacock's tail is not necessary for impressing females but that is why it seems to exist (Zahavi, 1975 – see chapter 3 in this book). But a peacock's tail is relatively trivial compared to language, requiring only that an existing functional organ be made bigger and brighter, compared to the wholesale restructuring of brain and vocal tract required for language.

Second, and related to the first point, it would need to explain the costs of language – the metabolic costs of language processing; the extra brain matter required which makes for a heavy head and increases the risk of broken necks; the descended larynx which makes choking more likely and so on.

Third, it would have to pin down *who* actually benefits from language. Quite often when thinking about information transfer we think of the listener as benefiting rather than the speaker: the speaker gives instructions and the listener learns. But that can't be right because it falls foul of the freerider problem discussed in chapters 6 and 7. If other people benefit from an action that we perform, then that action will not be evolutionarily stable, unless we (ultimately) benefit more. More correctly, genes for language would be outcompeted by genes for no language if they place themselves at a fitness disadvantage. Unless, that is, we speak exclusively to biological relatives who are likely to share those genes (Hamilton, 1964a, b), which we don't. One possible solution is a form of reciprocation (see chapter 8, Trivers, 1971): every speaker is, at some point, a listener so the costs and benefits even out. Another, raised by Thom Scott-Phillips (Scott-Phillips, 2006) is that language is a selfish activity. Drawing on a classic paper by John Krebs and Richard Dawkins (Krebs and Dawkins, 1984) Scott-Phillips suggests that many of the features of language use are indicative of it benefiting the speaker more than the listener. The first line of evidence is concerned with the concept of cheating. In chapter 9 we examined evidence that humans evolved mechanisms for detecting and punishing freeriders (Cosmides, 1989), if listening were freeriding we might expect people who listened too much to be considered selfish and punished accordingly. However, the opposite is true, with people who talk too much being considered the selfish ones. His second line of evidence is anatomical: there are many adaptations for speaking (such as the descended larynx) but far fewer for listening (Lieberman, 1984). As an example of this Rico, a border collie, is able to respond to over 200 words, but is unable to utter a single one (Kaminski *et al.*, 2004). The benefits to the speaker have been proposed as being status (Dessalles, 1998) and the aforementioned mating opportunities (Miller, 2000). Perhaps more interestingly Phillips uses Krebs and Dawkins's work to suggest that language is a form of manipulation. By using requests, demands, seduction and a variety of other means language gives us the possibility of taking control of the nervous systems of others to achieve our own ends. Not all instances of linguistic communication need be like this, as Krebs and Dawkins themselves point out.

Contrast the Bible-thumping oratory of a revivalist preacher with the subtle signals, undetected by the rest of the company, between a couple at a dinner party indicating to one another that it is time to go home. The former bears the hallmark of signalling designed for persuasion, the latter of a conspiratorial, cooperative whisper. (1984, p. 391)

Summary

- There is much evidence that language has some innate basis. Chomsky argues that we have an innate language organ that comes complete with abstract information as to the way that language works in general. Babies are therefore born with certain expectations as to how language works and language learning, according to Chomsky, is simply a matter of parameter setting – deciding, for example, whether their language is head first or head last.
- Although a nativist, Chomsky denies that language is the result of natural selection. Pinker and Bloom (1990) take an evolutionary perspective on language and argue that Chomsky's theory should be placed squarely within an evolutionary framework.
- There is some evidence that specific language impairment might provide evidence for the underlying genetic basis for language, although it is still not clear at what level the damaged gene might have an effect (e.g. at the level of grammar learning, or at more perceptually based levels).
- Research suggests that language may well have been around for almost two million years, as there is some evidence that *Homo erectus* could well have had language, although this language is likely to have been more primitive than that of modern humans.
- There are a number of hypotheses suggesting that language evolved to fulfil a social function such as social grooming (to bind large groups together), the making of social contracts (to enable monogamy and male provisioning) and the use of language to impress potential mates. While each of these hypotheses has its merits, each is still highly speculative and requires more evidence from different areas of research (such as linguistics and anthropology).

Questions

1. Some have suggested (e.g. Pinker, 1994) that because the criteria for language (see box 10.1) are based on human language it tends to belittle animal communication systems reducing them to failed languages. What are the pros and cons of producing

criteria such as these? Would it make more sense to produce a set of criteria for all communication systems (human and non-human)?

2. Given that we can say anything we want regardless of its truth, why should we believe anything that anyone says? In other words, what are the mechanisms that keep what we say (generally) honest?

3. When someone speaks who benefits, the speaker or the listener? Try to answer this question by thinking of different contexts in which people speak and listen (e.g. lectures, phone conversations, gossip). Also if it is the listener who benefits why do we chastise people from talking too much but not for listening too much (or do we)?

4. FOXP2 has been widely touted as a gene for language (or specifically, grammar). What is the evidence for and against this claim?

FURTHER READING

Aitchison, J. (1998). *The Articulate Mammal* (4th edn). London: Routledge. Not concerned with the evolution of language, but a good resource for information on language in general and a thorough and critical examination of Chomsky's theory of language acquisition.

Dunbar, R. (1996). *Grooming, Gossip, and the Evolution of Language.* Cambridge, MA: Harvard University Press. A good discussion of Dunbar's social grooming hypothesis of language evolution.

Fitch, W. T. (2010). *The Evolution of Language.* Cambridge: Cambridge University Press. Comprehensive coverage of recent thinking on the evolution of language.

Pinker, S. (1994). *The Language Instinct. How the Mind Creates Language.* London: Penguin. Certainly the most readable introduction to an evolutionary perspective on language. Particularly useful are chapter 4, on Chomsky's theory of language, and chapter 11 on language evolution. But it is worth reading in its entirety.

11 | The evolution of emotion

KEY CONCEPTS

universal emotions • emotional expression • emotional experience • emotion and motivation • James–Lange theory • limbic system • amygdala • orbitofrontal cortex • lateralisation of emotions • autonomic nervous system • display rules preparedness theory • positive and negative emotions

Evolutionary psychologists maintain that the mind was designed to solve specific problems that our ancestors faced on a regular basis. If this is the case then, in addition to cognitive mechanisms, surely emotions also serve an adaptive purpose. Such a notion can be traced back to Darwin, who in 1872 argued that emotional expressions are common to all cultures. Following a century when this claim was either disputed or, more commonly, ignored, most psychologists today accept that at least some basic expressions are shared by all cultures. But such a conclusion raises a number of further questions. If certain emotional expressions are universal then this suggests that they are adaptive – but how can a facial expression aid survival and reproduction? Moreover, if we all express basic emotions in the same way does this mean that we all experience emotions in the same way? If we do, how might these specific internal states also be adaptive? In this chapter we consider the evidence that emotions are innate and universal from three areas of research – comparisons between different cultures, comparisons between ourselves and our primate relatives, and the neurological bases of emotions. Finally, we examine the proposed functional explanations for specific emotional states.

What are emotions?

If you ask a number of psychologists today what is meant by the term 'emotions' you will probably receive as many definitions as the number of psychologists you ask. Most, however, would not dispute a definition that incorporates positive and negative feelings which involve physiological, cognitive and behavioural reactions to internal and external events. Evolutionists might agree with such a definition but would point out that this is a proximate definition of emotions, while they are more interested in ultimate explanations – why such mechanisms came about. One evolutionary psychologist who has a special interest in emotions is Randolph Nesse of the University of Michigan. Nesse, a psychiatrist by training, has explicitly defined emotions in relation to their evolutionary functions:

The emotions are specialized modes of operation shaped by natural selection to adjust the physiological, psychological, and behavioral parameters of the organism in ways that increase its capacity and tendency to respond adaptively to the threats and opportunities characteristic of specific kinds of situations. (1990, p. 268)

This is a particularly appropriate definition for our purposes since not only does it incorporate the ultimate level of analysis, it also suggests that each emotional state will be related to quite specific circumstances that our ancestors faced. You might like to refer back to Nesse's definition when considering the rest of this chapter as we explore what evolutionary psychology has to say about the 'ins and outs' of emotions – that is, both their internal experience and external expression.

Why do we have emotions?

In chapter 9 we saw how certain cognitive processes may be thought of as adaptations which help us to solve the sort of problems that our ancestors regularly encountered. But humans and other animals are more than just problem-solving automata. Cognition is motivated to some specific end, whether that is to obtain food, avoid injury or predation, to find a suitable sexual partner, to protect offspring, or to avoid exploitation by others. Evolutionists argue that emotions fulfil this crucial motivational role. Works of science fiction frequently present emotions as a weakness, if we could act out of pure, cold logic like Mr Spock from the original series of *Star Trek*, then, being unencumbered by the baggage of emotions, we would be better able to perform the various acts that help us to live long and prosper. But herein lies the problem, without emotions to motivate cognition why would we do anything at all? Think about it for a second. You work hard on your course because of your *desire* to obtain a good qualification (and also, perhaps, because you *fear* poor performance), you help someone in distress because you feel *compassion* towards them, you cooperate with others in order to avoid the *shame* and *guilt* of being labelled a freerider and so on. Actually the fictional figure of Mr Spock is really a con. He does have emotions – albeit a little different from our own. Although he rarely shows warmth or anger he frequently describes events as 'fascinating' and 'intriguing'. In other words, there are many things which he finds rewarding because they are interesting (this incidentally is also true of the *New Generation* equivalent of Mr Spock – Data – and of *Star Trek*

Voyager's 'emotionless' Tuvok and *Enterprise*'s T'Pol). Finding something rewarding (or indeed the opposite – punishing) means that we must, at some level, have an emotional response to it. In fact American psychologist Carroll Izard (1977) considers 'interest' to be *the* most frequently experienced emotion. Emotions motivate us to do things. A human without emotions would be akin to having the most complex computer ever invented sitting around doing nothing, not because it wants to do nothing, but because it is unable to want or not want to do anything! This is as true of emotions such as anger, fear and sadness as it is of interest. Emotions are the driving forces that propel us to make use of the cognitive abilities we have.

Such a statement is nothing new. What evolutionary psychology might add to this understanding is the notion that emotions exist to make us want to do the sorts of things that made our ancestors successful, in an inclusive fitness sense, and to avoid doing the things that would have made them less successful. If this is the case then we might be able to develop a more precise understanding of the function of each specific emotion (Nesse, 1990; 2009). But where did this idea come from and what might the evolutionary approach tell us about the relationship between emotions, evolution and behaviour? In this chapter we will explore both the current thinking among evolutionists on specific emotions and the historical roots of treating emotions as the products of natural selection. So, when it comes to emotions, whose shoulders do modern evolutionary psychologists stand on?

Darwin, James and Freud and the early study of emotions

Many psychologists today consider the pioneering American psychologist William James as pre-eminent in considering emotions as 'instinctive'. But, as is so often the case, it was Darwin who first considered the notion. Twelve years prior to James's famous essay on emotions, 'What is an emotion?' (1884), Darwin published *The Expression of the Emotions in Man and Animals*, in which he explicitly stated not only that emotions served the purpose of aiding survival and reproduction in our ancestors, but that they are currently used in the same way cross-culturally (1872). Darwin was not alone, however, in considering emotions to be universal. During the last thirty years of the nineteenth century, Darwin, Freud and James all spilt much ink on the topic of human emotions and their universality.

The purpose of emotions in humans as seen by Darwin, James and Freud

Darwin (1809–82), having observed the same emotions on the faces of individuals from a range of different isolated cultures, argued that such expressions must be inherited rather than learned. Darwin saw emotions as internal psychological

Box 11.1 Emotion and motivation

Emotion, motivation and cognition are often considered to be the big three areas that psychologists study. We considered cognition in chapter 9, but the remaining two are often seen to overlap. Emotion and motivation are both associated with arousal and goal-directed behaviour (Buck, 1988). How might we distinguish between these two concepts? Ross Buck of the University of Connecticut has made a special study of motivation and emotion. He sees motivation as 'a potential for the activation and direction of behavior inherent in a system of behavior' (Buck, 1988, p. 9). In contrast, he suggests emotional states have three components not normally associated with motivation:

- Emotions involve *feelings* such as anger, fear and happiness
- Emotions are associated with *expressive behaviours* such as smiling or crying
- Emotions are associated with *peripheral physiological responses* such as changes in heart rate or sweating

(Buck, 1988; see also Kleinginna and Kleinginna, 1981a; 1981b)

Although Buck's definition might help to distinguish between the two, we should also bear in mind that, in some respects, the two may be considered as part and parcel of each other in that we only react emotionally when something affects our progress towards our motives and goals (Lazarus, 1991). If this is the case then perhaps we cannot have one without the other. But which came first – are we motivated because we feel emotional about something or do we develop an emotional state because we feel motivated towards a goal? This chicken-and-egg scenario is difficult to resolve – but, given that we have little difficulty in attributing motivations to animals but often feel uncomfortable using emotionally laden terms, then it might be argued that emotions evolved later to help serve motivations. In this chapter when we use the term emotion we take it for granted that there will also be motivation involved.

states, the expressions of which are rudimentary vestiges of behaviour handed down from our ancestors (Workman, 2014). More specifically he argued that human facial expressions had a common evolutionary origin with our primate relatives. In *The Expression of the Emotions in Man and Animals*, Darwin introduced three principles around which he considered emotions to be based:

(1) Serviceable associated habits. This means that, when in a specific emotional state, a person is likely to demonstrate the same type of expression and the same type of body posture. Interestingly, although Darwin saw expressions as having value for our primitive ancestors, he believed that they were no longer functional in modern humans.

(2) Antithesis. Here the idea is that the expression of positive and negative emotions occur in pairs – so a relaxed and open body posture is seen in someone who is happy and friendly whereas the opposite – a tense posture – is seen in an angry person in an aggressive state. Moreover, when trying to disguise our feelings we may unconsciously attempt to present a body posture which is the opposite of the way we are really feeling.

(3) Direct action of the excited nervous system on the body independently of the will. When in a strongly aroused state, our facial expression, intonation and body posture all let others know about our internal state. Hence, we tremble with fear, we withdraw physically from a disgusting scene and our whole body may shake when we laugh at something overwhelmingly funny. All of these things occur without conscious effort.

James (1842–1910) specifically developed Darwin's ideas arguing that, rather than the physical signs of an emotion following an internal state, the reverse is the case. So we feel fear because we tremble, rather than the other way round (James, 1884). In this way humans were seen to have evolved to react to our inward and outward bodily signs of emotions. In particular, James argued that the brain monitors the state of the viscera (that is 'gut feelings') and then we react to these signs with the appropriate internal state. This idea was also put forward independently by Danish psychologist and philosopher Carl Lange (1885/1912) at around the same time and hence came to be known as the James–Lange theory of emotion. This theory was well accepted by psychologists for forty years until it was criticised by physiologist Walter Cannon who, in 1927, observed that individuals who had had their viscera accidentally severed from the central nervous system still felt emotions. Although the James–Lange theory is no longer central to the psychology of emotions, experimental evidence from Ekman and colleagues suggests that there is an element of truth in it. Subjects told to pull certain faces then reported that they began to feel the emotion depicted by such expressions (Ekman, 1992).

Freud (1856–1939), like James before him, was very much influenced by Darwin and applied his principles to understanding and treating people who had serious emotional problems such as **hysteria**. He specifically used the idea of antithesis to help describe the behaviour of some of his patients. Freud also developed the concept of human behaviour being very much driven by the pursuit of pleasure and the avoidance of pain – the pleasure–pain principle, which he traced back to Darwin.

Although, in contrast to much of twentieth-century psychology, Freud considered emotions as central to understanding human behaviour, his work has been heavily criticised by mainstream psychology and, with the exception of Christopher Badcock of the London School of Economics, Freud's ideas have not had a major impact on the writings of evolutionary psychologists (Badcock, 2000).

Twentieth-century rejection of universal emotions

Despite the ideas of Darwin, James and Freud, during most of the twentieth century emotions were largely ignored by social scientists. Many of those who did consider them took either a behaviourist stance, seeing all of behaviour as the outcome of conditioned learning (Skinner, 1957, see chapter 10), or in a similar vein, treated human behaviour as almost infinitely malleable. This latter SSSM view of emotional expression was particularly associated with husband-and-wife team Gregory Bateson and Margaret Mead (see, for example, Mead, 1928). These social anthropologists took issue with Darwin's innate view of emotions and Mead, in particular, argued vigorously that each culture develops its own unique set of emotions. She even claimed that in at least one society – Samoan – there was no such emotion as sexual jealousy. Today it is difficult to imagine how great an impact this blank-slate view of human nature had on the development of the social sciences. The SSSM that prevailed throughout much of the twentieth century may well have been one of the reasons that many psychologists shied away from investigating the universality of human emotions. If each culture has its own set of emotions then this would have been a fruitless task. Today, however, much of Mead's work on cultural differences in emotions has been discredited due to problems of objectivity and preconceptions. According to the anthropologist Derek Freeman, Mead was duped by two Samoan girls who engaged in a game of misleading her about the emotions and general practices of their culture (Freeman, 1983, 1999; Ekman, 1998; see also chapter 14). Freeman's own study of Samoan society revealed that sexual jealousy was as common there as anywhere else. Indeed, during the last thirty years there has been growing evidence that Darwin was correct in his view of the universality of human emotions – at least as far as expressions are concerned (see box 11.2).

The nature and function of emotions

Following the work of researchers such as Freeman and Ekman there has, since the 1990s, been a growing interest in reconsidering emotions not as culturally specific phenomena, but as adaptations. As we'll see later, today a number of researchers have been strongly influenced by Darwin's ideas on emotion.

Emotional expression and emotional experience

Psychologists are generally on much firmer ground when discussing emotional expression than the internal subjective states that we all experience. Facial expressions and body language can at least be observed and, to a degree,

Box 11.2 Six universal facial expressions?

Almost 100 years after Darwin first proposed that emotional expressions are universal, Paul Ekman and his colleague Wallace Friesen provided evidence that helped to validate this view. In the late 1960s, Ekman and Friesen reported that the members of an isolated society living in a remote part of New Guinea – the South Fore tribe – were able both to identify and to copy a number of facial expressions as used by Westerners. The tribespeople were also able to confirm that they used specific expressions under the same sort of circumstances as people in the West. Moreover, when Ekman and Friesen presented photographs of the tribespeople using various facial expressions to denote specific emotions to their students back in the United States, the latter were immediately able to identify such emotions (Ekman and Friesen, 1967; 1969; 1971). This is strong evidence to support Darwin's belief that many emotional expressions are innate and universal since the possibility of an isolated tribe developing and using by chance exactly the same facial expressions under the same circumstances as ourselves is extremely small.

On the basis of these observations and studies in over twenty other countries Ekman and Friesen suggest there are at least six basic universal facial expressions to denote human emotions – Surprise, Anger, Sadness, Disgust, Fear and Happiness.

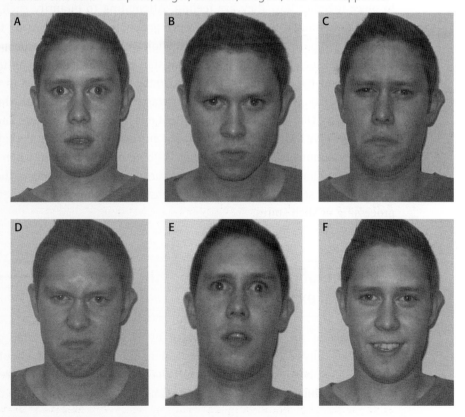

(A) Surprise, (B) Anger, (C) Sadness, (D) Disgust, (E) Fear, (F) Happiness

> Since the time of Ekman and Friesen, a number of other studies has confirmed the universality of basic human facial expressions, although there is some dispute among these 'basic emotion theorists' as to how many of these we have. Philip Johnson-Laird and Keith Oatley (Johnson-Laird and Oatley, 1992), for example, have suggested that there are five universal emotions – all of Ekman and Friesen's bar 'surprise' – while Carroll Izard suggests there are eight (Izard, 1977; 1992; 1994). Clearly, we all show more than between five and eight different emotional facial expressions – most emotion theorists suggest that the large number that we all demonstrate is due to blending or mixing of these basic emotions, rather like the way that a very large number of hues may be produced from a small number of primary paint colours (LeDoux, 1996).

quantified. Comparisons can also be made between ourselves and our primate relatives – if similar expressions are observed under broadly similar circumstances then this might help us to understand the roots of such emotions (see box 11.3). How a person really feels inside, however, is very difficult to determine – we can only use what they say and the expression and intonation they use as indirect indications of their internal state. Then, using our own experience of emotions, we can attempt to piece together how they are feeling. Attempting to quantify such internal states in the lab is fraught with problems since people notoriously portray themselves in a dignified and positive light. In fact, although we are often told to be more open about our feelings, social life would grind to a standstill if everybody continually reported their moment-by-moment internal state to the world. Also, at least in Western industrialised society, we are frequently embarrassed (another emotion) when asked about our emotions. Due to this we keep many of our feelings to ourselves and modify much of what we give away to others about our current internal state. Perhaps a better way to study emotions is to examine what is going on in the brain when we experience them. If emotions really are innate universal features of humans then perhaps we can expect to see a designated neural substrate for the generation, recognition and processing of such states.

Seeing emotions in the brain – the biology of emotional experience

As we saw in the definition provided by Nesse, there are three components to emotions – physiological, psychological and behavioural. Much of the work on emotions involves the psychological/behavioural dimensions but recent advances in **neuroimaging** techniques (i.e. brain scans) have allowed scientists to gain insights

Box 11.3 **Similarities between ourselves and other primates in facial expressions provide clues about the origins of human facial expressions**

Darwin was very taken by the highly expressive faces of primates and saw parallels with humans in the 'grinning' and 'laughing' faces that they frequently pull.

> Young orangs, when tickled, likewise grin and make a chuckling sound. (1998 [1872], p. 132)

Having observed similar facial gestures in humans and primates under broadly similar circumstances, Darwin suggested that a number of these gestures may have arisen from a common simian ancestor. Observational work by British and German ethologists Richard Andrew (1963a; 1963b) and J. van Hooff (1967; 1972), respectively, have helped to flesh out this original suggestion.

A. Chimpanzee smiling

Andrew sees primate facial expressions as a secondary consequence of the vocalisations they produce when in an emotional state. The shrill shriek that a number of monkeys make when in fearful circumstances, for example, necessitates pulling back the lips into a 'fear-grin'. Such a grin is common to monkeys and humans. Andrew argues that, having evolved in order to allow the relevant sound to be made, such a facial gesture may often be used silently by ourselves and other primates today.

Van Hooff, likewise, has observed and documented **homologous** (shared derived) expressions in humans and other primates. He sees two dimensions in pro-social gestures – 'friendliness', which involves a non-threatening baring of the teeth, and 'playfulness', which involves an open mouth and a staccato vocalisation. To put it in human terms, friendliness involves smiling and playfulness involves laughing. In this way smiling and laughter form a continuum with two dimensions. According to van Hooff, the silent bared-teeth display originated as an appeasing signal and later evolved into a friendly gesture in a number of primate species including our own. The open-mouthed vocal gesture, however, may be used as an invitation to play (all primates studied engage in playful activity). Van Hooff's scheme for the evolutionary development of laughter and smiling is shown below.

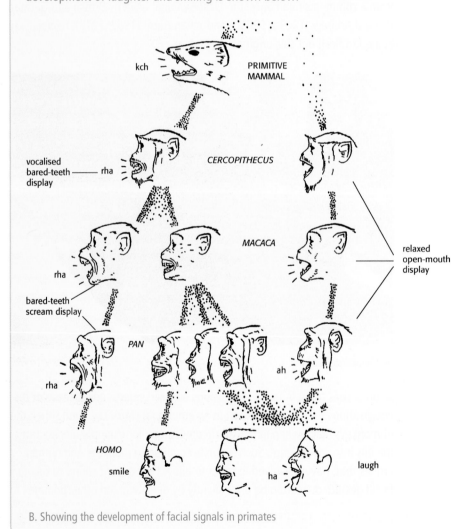

B. Showing the development of facial signals in primates

The evolutionary development of laughter and smiling from primitive primates to humans was suggested by van Hooff. On the right we see the development of laughter, in the centre smiling and on the left anger (from van Hooff, 1972).

Although the precise origin and specific function of given facial gestures is still an area of debate, there is clear evidence that we do share a number of such signals with other primates and that we do use them under broadly similar social circumstances (see for example, Parker, as cited in the 1998 edition of *The Expression of the Emotions*).

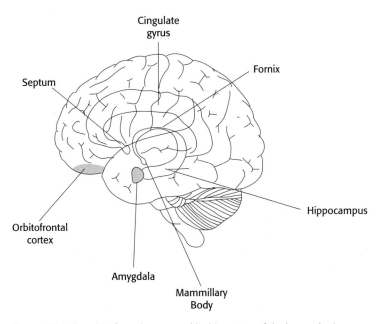

Figure 11.1 The orbitofrontal cortex and limbic system of the human brain

into their physiological bases. Using PET (positron emission tomography) and fMRI (functional magnetic resonance imaging) scans, neuropsychologists have begun to uncover what is going on in the human brain when experiencing or viewing emotions. This is a new and revolutionary way of objectively studying emotions. So far, two quite specific areas of the brain have been implicated in emotions – the **amygdala** and the **orbitofrontal cortex**. We will consider each in turn.

The amygdala

The amygdala is an almond-shaped bundle of neurones found in each cerebral hemisphere about an inch in from each of your ears (see figure 11.1). It is an important part of the **limbic system** – a group of components which lies deep within the brain (part of the subcortex) and is concerned with emotions. It has been known for a number of years that the limbic system and, in particular, the amygdala, is involved in emotions, since humans with damage to this area and animals that have been lesioned here show inappropriate emotional responses. Humans with damage to the amygdala, in particular, appear to be unable to recognise fear in the faces of others (Calder *et al.*, 1996; Atkinson, 2007). Moreover, they have profound problems with memory (LeDoux, 1996; McGaugh, 2004; Toates, 2011). Brain scans of undamaged individuals have now confirmed that the amygdala is active during the perception of emotional faces and particularly so when viewing fear (Morris *et al.*, 1998). Interestingly, Blair *et al.* (1999) have demonstrated that, in addition to increased activation when viewing fear, PET scans also show an increased activation of the amygdala when perceiving sad but not angry faces. What these findings tell us about the nature of emotions is open to debate. Does the emotional state cause increased activity in the amygdala or does increased activity in the amygdala cause the emotional state that we feel? In either event, it is fascinating to note that the two are clearly related.

The orbitofrontal cortex

The cortex of the brain consists of a six-millimetre-thick convoluted sheet of neurones which forms the outer surface of the brain covering the structures below (the subcortex referred to above). The cortex is responsible for many of our higher functions such as language processing, reasoning and consciousness. Each part of the cortex is described neuranatomically by its position relative to the centre of the brain. The orbitofrontal cortex consists of the outer covering of the brain just above the orbits of the eyes – hence the name. Just above the orbitofrontal cortex are the frontal lobes which consist of a large amount of cortex in each cerebral hemisphere that is involved in controlling behaviour (see figure 11.1). The orbitofrontal cortex receives information from the cortex of the frontal lobes and from the sensory systems. It also has extensive communication with the limbic system below. In a sense, the orbitofrontal cortex may be said to be kept very much informed about what is going on in the outside world and what is going on internally with regard to planned behaviour. Furthermore, it is able to affect the activity of the limbic system and, in particular, the amygdala. It is not surprising then that it has been known for some time that the orbitofrontal cortex is, in some way, very much involved in emotion. Damage to this area leads to profound changes in emotional response and to personality in general (Kringelbach and Rolls, 2004). In the case of this area of the brain, however, a neuroimaging technique (or a technique related to neuroimaging) has been used in a novel way to illustrate how the orbitofrontal cortex may be involved in emotional responses in a patient who died over a century ago.

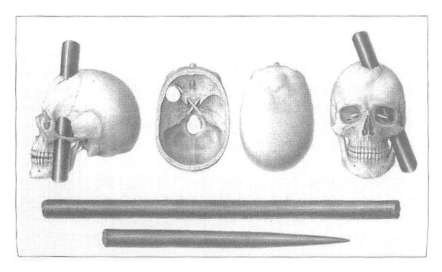

Figure 11.2 View of the crowbar's path through Phineas Gage's skull engraved for inclusion in a mid-1800s medical journal account of the case

Phineas Gage – an early study of serious brain injury

One of the earliest documented cases of damage to the orbitofrontal cortex occurred in the middle of the nineteenth century and involved railway foreman Phineas Gage. Back in 1848 Phineas was working on one of the new railroads that was being constructed throughout North America at the time. One day he came across a large boulder which was lying in the area where the new track was to be laid. In order to remove this rock he drilled a hole and filled this with dynamite. He then took a large tamping iron to ram the dynamite into place. Unfortunately, a spark caused by friction of the iron against the rock ignited the dynamite, causing it to explode. The explosion sent the bar through Phineas' left cheek and through the front of his brain, leaving via the top of his head and landing some 300 feet away. Neuropsychologist Antonio Damasio and his co-workers used a high-power computer to reconstruct the damage that must have occurred to the front of Phineas' brain and were able to confirm that his orbitofrontal cortex would have been largely obliterated (Damasio *et al.*, 1994).

There are two fascinating things that can be said about Phineas Gage following his accident. The first is that he survived it. In fact, after briefly losing consciousness, he was able to walk to a wagon that was to take him to the doctor; the second is that, after recovering, he was a changed man. Whereas prior to the accident he was considered to be a serious and industrious man who was thoughtful and well respected, following it he became irritable, childish and thoughtless (Harlow, 1848). Figure 11.2 shows the position of the tamping iron as it passed through his skull.

This was perhaps the first clinical evidence that quite a specific portion of the cortex is heavily involved in emotion and personality.

A small number of cases similar to Phineas Gage's (see box 11.4) have subsequently been reported in which the orbitofrontal cortex has likewise been seriously damaged (the number is small because most people receiving such a serious injury would be unlikely to survive). In each of these, distinct changes in emotional response have also been observed (Carlson *et al.*, 2000; Carlson, 2012). The list of emotions affected is lengthy and includes problems of anxiety, apathy, irritability, impulsivity and a general lack of thought for others. Such a large list makes it unlikely that the orbitofrontal cortex is specifically involved in one or two emotional states. It appears more likely that this area of the brain is involved in integrating and appreciating subtle social and emotional cues such that the ability to distinguish between trivial and important decisions becomes seriously impaired (Damasio, 2003; Carlson *et al.*, 2000).

The findings with regard to the amygdala and the orbitofrontal cortex may be taken as evidence for the existence of an innate biological organisation of emotional processing. Since brain organisation is largely the outcome of selection pressures then evolutionary psychologists would argue that these findings support the notion of emotions being the product of evolution (LeDoux, 1996; Izard, 2009).

The chemistry of emotions – adrenalin, the sport commentator's hormone

Although the brain (and nervous system in general) is very much the seat of human emotions, its activity is modified by the release of hormones from **endocrine glands** into the bloodstream. While the release of these hormones is very much controlled by the central nervous system, we should also bear in mind that these chemicals are taken by the blood stream to the brain where they affect its activity. An example of this is the activity of the hormone that all self-respecting sports fans know about – **adrenalin** (also known as **epinephrine**). When challenging emotional events occur, the amygdala sends messages to the **autonomic nervous system** or ANS (the part of the nervous system which regulates the activity of the internal organs). The ANS, in turn, causes the release of adrenalin into the bloodstream from the **adrenal glands** just above the kidneys. This adrenalin is the 'fight or flight' chemical which prepares target organs such as skeletal muscles for action. So, when frightened or excited, a part of the brain causes the hormone adrenalin to be released – and this, in turn, prepares the body for the challenge. The question is, does the amygdala provide us with the feeling of anxiety, excitement and general readiness for action, or does the adrenalin that is 'pumping away' somehow cause these feelings? Once in the

Box 11.4 **Lateralisation – the asymmetrically emotional brain**

Although the left and right cerebral hemispheres of the forebrain appear as structural mirror images of each other, functionally they are quite different. This functional difference is known as **lateralisation**. The study of lateralisation began in the middle of the nineteenth century when it was observed that, whereas damage to the right hemisphere has little effect on language abilities, damage to the left leads to quite profound linguistic deficits (Springer and Deutsch, 1998; Corballis, 2009 see also chapter 10). Since this time, many claims have been made with regard to the differing functions of the two hemispheres. Following over 150 years of research, the most robust findings are that the left hemisphere is especially associated with the recognition and processing of language and the right plays a major role in emotions (Springer and Deutsch, 1998; Corballis, 2009). Although initial work on the involvement of the hemispheres in emotions suggested that this was the sole domain of the right side, more recent research has demonstrated that the left hemisphere also plays an important role.

Before discussing these findings it is necessary to understand something of the methodology employed by researchers interested in lateralisation. One way of testing how well the two hemispheres are able to recognise emotional expressions is by presenting visual representations of expressions to each hemisphere. This may sound quite complex but is, in fact, quite an easy experiment to perform. Primary visual input from each lateral field (i.e. the area of vision clearly to the left or right of centre when you look straight ahead) is projected only to the visual processing centres of the opposite cerebral hemisphere. This means that visual input from the left visual field is initially sent only to the right hemisphere, the reverse being true for the right visual field. So by presenting pictures to either lateral visual field and recording a person's response, we can gain some insight into the workings of each hemisphere separately. Quite a speedy response is required since, given a little time, the two hemispheres will pass information back and forth between them (**inter-hemispheric transfer**) via a large bundle of neural fibres known as the **corpus callosum**.

One way of using this 'half visual' field method is to present participants with a chimeric face consisting of a neutral half-face on the one side and an emotional one on the other side (see below). When presented with a pair of such chimeras, one above the other (one with the emotion on the left and one with the emotion on the right) and asked which face shows the greatest emotional intensity, a number of researchers have demonstrated that the one with the emotion on the left side is the most expressive (Levy *et al.*, 1983; Springer and Deutsch, 1998; Watling *et al.*, 2012). This suggests the right hemisphere is, indeed, superior at recognising expressed emotions. We might call this the right-hemisphere hypothesis for emotional processing. Some researchers, however, have suggested that, while the right hemisphere is better able to recognise negative emotions, the left hemisphere is superior when it comes to positive emotions (see for example, Reuter-Lorenz and Davidson, 1981). This notion of a left-hemisphere superiority for positive expressions and a right-hemisphere superiority for negative ones is called the **valence hypothesis** and appears to contradict the right-hemisphere hypothesis. Workman *et al.* (2000; see also Workman *et al.*, 2006 and Taylor *et al.*, 2012) have produced experimental evidence using a series of chimeric faces which suggests there may be some truth in both hypotheses. When presented with six different expressive chimeras – happiness, sadness, surprise, disgust, fear and anger – they found that, superimposed onto an overall right-hemisphere advantage, there is a shift back to the left when viewing pro- as opposed to antisocial expressions. The pro- and antisocial way of grouping emotions is somewhat different from the positive and negative dichotomy that has traditionally been used. Workman and his co-workers suggest that the fundamental difference between the two hemispheres when involved in emotional processing lies in a pro-social/approach/left hemisphere and an antisocial/withdraw/right hemisphere dichotomy.

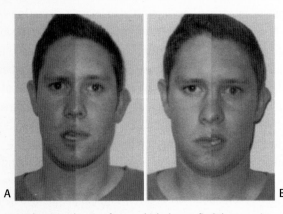

A   B

Two chimeras showing fear – which do you find the more intense expression: A or B?

Just to complicate matters further, Richard Davidson and his co-workers at the University of Wisconsin have suggested that, although the right hemisphere is superior at recognising emotional stimuli, the left may be more involved in experiencing it (Davidson and Sutton, 1995). Clearly, the question of the lateralisation of emotions requires further research.

bloodstream adrenalin, in addition to affecting the gut and the muscles, also travels to the brain where there are a number of widely dispersed receptor sites that are affected by it. In the brain adrenalin has a number of effects – including, via its action in the temporal lobe, helping to strengthen memory formation and an effect on the amygdala (Carlson, 2012; Toates, 2011). The amygdala sends neural fibres to higher centres in the cortex and receives feedback from these areas. This means that the exact cause of the fight or flight response and how we eventually perceive this activity is extremely difficult to disentangle.

In addition to adrenalin, other hormones are released during emotional states. Testosterone and cortisol, for example, are both related to stressful events in life and to memory formation (Carlson, 2012). Following a fight between two male mammals, for example, the loser will show reduced levels of circulating testosterone and elevated levels of cortisol – the reverse being the case for the victor (Toates, 2011). Cortisol and other related hormones (the **corticosteroids**) are believed to strengthen memory formation (McGaugh, 1992; Barsegyan *et al.*, 2010), so an animal which has been defeated is unlikely to forget who the victor is and make the same mistake again. Evolutionists explain this effect on memory formation as part and parcel of the function of emotions – that is, hormones that are secreted might not only prepare us physically for events but may also ensure that positive and negative encounters are remembered, since they are likely to have had survival and reproductive consequences for our ancestors (see later).

Learning and cultural display rules can modify emotional response

Despite the move towards resolving the differences between cultural relativists and evolutionists by Paul Ekman (see box 11.5), the notion of universal emotions is still a controversial one among many social scientists (LeDoux, 1996; Izard, 2009). It is certainly the case that there are cultural differences in the use of facial expressions and in emotional responses to various stimuli. We all frequently hide or modify our true internal state when in public. In fact, just which emotions we should display in public, and to what extent, varies quite considerably between societies. In Japanese culture, for example, there is a general discouragement of the public display of any emotions other than happiness. Consequently, since Japanese people smile a great deal on the streets and rarely show an unhappy face, they may appear to outsiders to feel negative emotions less frequently than, say, Europeans or North Americans. The emotional expressions (and frequency and intensity thereof) that a particular culture permits are known as its **display rules** (Ekman *et al.*, 1972). In this way how much emotional expression an individual demonstrates depends, in part, on the display rules of that individual's culture. This does not mean that different cultures *feel* different levels of emotional range and intensity, but that how much they display in public is largely determined by their cultural norms. In fact there is some experimental evidence that, when on their own, individuals from cultures where negative emotions are frowned

Box 11.5 Criticisms of the universality of emotions – human pigs and false smiles

While the notion that basic human emotional expressions are universal and therefore derived from a common evolutionary ancestor has gained a fair degree of support from psychologists over the last thirty years, it is not without its critics. Fridlund (1992), for example, argues that facial expressions are social tools that we use largely during communication rather than for showing our true feelings to others. If this is the case, then each society may have developed different expressions to mean different things during normal communication. Smiling, for example, is sometimes used to express sarcasm. Likewise, laughter, under the right circumstances, may be used as a threat. A more hard-line version of this argument is that emotions are products of society rather than of biology (see, for example, Averill, 1980; Harré, 1986). This is the social constructionist or SSSM view of 'human nature' (see chapters 1 and 14). James Averill, for example, has described an emotional state that is observed among the Gururumba who live in the highlands of New Guinea which is called 'being a wild pig'. In this state villagers spend some time running wild like an undomesticated pig. They may be violent and steal things – although they rarely really hurt anyone or take anything of real value. After a while the 'wild pig' returns to a normal village activity and life continues as before with no recriminations. Since this wild pig state is unknown in other cultures, Averill uses this example to support his view that most emotional reactions are socially constructed (Averill, 1980; LeDoux, 1996).

If evolutionary psychologists are to claim that human emotions are universal then they will need to address such arguments. One way of dealing with such examples is Ekman's proposal that we should distinguish between basic expressions common to all cultures and other bodily movements that are learned and may incorporate these fundamental expressions. In this way, the culture-specific expressions can be placed at a level above the basic universal emotions (Ekman, 1980; 1992). This means that, in Ekman's view, much of the disagreement may be more apparent than real since social constructionists are focusing at the level of learned cultural differences while the basic emotion theorists are focusing at a more basic level of innate responses. Ekman further concedes that basic expressions can be consciously modified to take on different meanings under different social circumstances (see also 'display rules' above).

upon show these expressions as often as individuals from cultures where such emotional displays are acceptable. At least this has been shown for Japanese individuals as far as expressions of anxiety and disgust are concerned (Ekman *et al.*, 1972).

We should also bear in mind that, as in virtually all human responses, emotional responses can be modified by personal experience. While certain animals that might have posed a danger to our ancestors tend to be those about which we are most likely to develop a phobia, such as snakes and spiders (both of which are poisonous in many parts of the world), whether or not we develop such a phobia depends very much on our early experience with them. Being frightened by a spider or a snake as a young child may lead to the full-blown anxious fear that we call a phobia; however, being reassured by an adult that they are unlikely to cause harm may mean that a child grows up without developing the phobia (Buck, 1988). An acquired response such as a fear of dogs following being bitten is called a conditioned emotional response. In many cases, since the conditioned response is learned, the learning may be reversed by classical conditioning whereby positive experiences are paired with the phobic animal. Having some plasticity in a fear system makes sense since how dangerous such animals are will vary greatly from one part of the world to another. The fact, however, that classical conditioning is frequently unsuccessful as a treatment for snake and spider phobias supports the hypothesis that these responses are partly inherited because of the threat to our ancestors. This notion of being born with a propensity to acquire a phobia about certain animals or objects rather than others has been called **preparedness theory** (Seligman, 1970; Buck, 1988; Ohman and Mineka, 2001).

Another area where humans demonstrate plasticity of emotional response lies in what we find physically attractive. Here there is a great deal of scope for modification during development. In some cultures, for example, scars or tattoos are considered very attractive bodily adornments while in others they may be seen as ugly disfigurements (Carlson *et al.*, 2000). Additionally, what a given culture finds attractive or ugly may change quite rapidly over time and may even differ between different sub-sections of a society. In Western culture today, for example, the emotional response to tattoos has recently changed, at least for younger members of society, who frequently regard them as 'cool' and sophisticated rather than as blemishes.

So while emotions may be universal in the sense that all cultures appear to have the same basic range of internal states and external signals, there is clearly a fair degree of malleability built into the level of response to external stimuli in our species. If we are to accept that emotions are adaptations then this raises the question of what precise functions they might serve.

Proposed functional explanations for specific emotional states

So far we have suggested that our current repertoire of emotions arose from the selection pressures that our ancestors faced. To summarise, three areas of research appear to support this contention:

- different cultures use the same basic emotional expressions under similar circumstances

- our primate relatives use similar facial expressions under similar circumstances
- humans have quite specific neural hardware devoted to recognising and processing emotions.

There is, however, another way in which such findings can be explained without evoking natural selection: that is, emotions may have come about as epiphenomena of evolutionary processes. Recall from chapter 2 that this means they might be the by-products of other adaptations without adaptive significance. Randolph Nesse (1990; 2011) sees this explanation as highly unlikely since emotions are not only shared by people of different cultures, they also have clear fitness repercussions as we have seen. Clearly, becoming emotionally attached to partners and to offspring are generally prerequisites to passing on our genes. Likewise, being able to react emotionally to signals of danger would have consequences for gene replication. Indeed, people with serious emotional problems are frequently unable to look after themselves, let alone form stable attachments and rear offspring (see chapter 12). Such findings suggest the epiphenomenon explanation is less likely than the adaptation one.

The function of specific emotions

Nesse, following on from previous evolutionists, attempted to specify quite specifically the 'situations and selective forces that have shaped each emotion' (Nesse, 1990, p. 269). In a similar vein, Barbara Fredrickson of the University of Michigan and (as we saw earlier) Paul Ekman of the University of California have also brought an evolutionary perspective to bear on human emotions (see for example, Fredrickson, 1998 and Ekman, 1994; 1998). Although there is much overlap, there are also differences in the approaches of the three evolutionists. The following discussion, which draws heavily on the work of Nesse, Fredrickson and Ekman, considers the possible adaptive function of the core 'positive' and 'negative' emotions: fear, anger and sadness on the one hand and love and happiness on the other. We begin with negative emotional states.

Negative core emotions – fear, anger and sadness

Negative emotions are believed to have evolved in order to allow us to respond appropriately to aversive stimuli. Negative emotions differ in fundamental ways from positive ones in that the former appear to be both more abundant and more specific (Fredrickson, 1998). Fear and anger, for example, are generally related to very specific events, whereas happiness and love are more ephemeral and may be considered to be more general. Nesse has suggested this greater specificity for negative emotions has come about because there is a larger number of different types of threats than there are types of opportunities. Another difference may be thought of as an asymmetry of the consequences of not responding to positive and negative circumstances. Not responding to a life-threatening situation might have had dire consequences for our ancestors. Not responding to opportunities would have had less serious consequences. Ignoring a mating opportunity might allow for other opportunities at a later date. Ignoring a charging rhino does not allow for any future opportunities. Today a number of evolutionists have argued that selection pressures for negative emotional responses would have been both stronger and more specific than those for positive ones (Pratto and John, 1991; Fredrickson, 1998; 2006).

If there is one core emotion that has clear survival implications it must be fear. People who have no fear do not make for good ancestors. Ekman (1994; 1998) sees fear as one of the fundamental emotions. Nesse, however, sees a number of sub-types of fear, each of which, he argues, would have quite specific ways of augmenting fitness. Panic and agoraphobia, for example, may be seen as adaptations which prepare the body, both physiologically and psychologically, for attack. Blood circulation is re-routed to the muscles, and the mind becomes highly focused on finding escape routes. A number of evolutionists have argued that 'negative' emotions such as fear and anger generally serve to narrow the focus of attention and increase vigilance (see Fredrickson, 1998). Anyone who has ever felt either intense fear or complete rage will be aware that, once we are attending to the object of such negative emotions, we are not easily distracted from them.

Other evolutionists have considered that negative emotions are related to urges to take quite specific action. Such urges have been labelled **specific action tendencies** (Frijda, 1986; Lazarus, 1991; Tooby and Cosmides, 1990b). Whereas fear is manifested by the urge to retreat, anger is clearly related to the urge to attack and injure. In either case the tendency to take action is quite specific. But how does sadness fit in with this idea? Unlike fear and anger, sadness is a negative emotion for which it is difficult to imagine a 'specific action tendency'. What is it that people do when they are feeling sad? It might be argued that sadness creates 'the urge to withdraw from action' (Fredrickson, 1998, p. 303). It has also been argued that sadness is a form of self-punishment that motivates us towards protecting children and other loved ones (Wright, 1994). In either event surely we can't label these as specific action tendencies? Perhaps, as both Ekman and Fredrickson have suggested, we should not anticipate all emotions fitting a single, general-purpose model but instead we should consider separate theories for separate emotions (Ekman, 1994; Fredrickson, 1998). Even some of the proponents of the specific action tendency model have noted its limitations for some emotional states (see for example, Lazarus, 1991).

It may be difficult to pin sadness down to a specific action tendency but our problems with this emotion do not end there. How people regard the state that we call sadness is also more difficult to pin down cross-culturally than fear and anger. American anthropologist Robert Levy has even reported one culture – the Tahitians – where, he argues, the people have neither the concept of sadness nor even a word to describe it. Interestingly, despite lacking the term of sadness, the Tahitians are clearly capable of feeling this emotion. When rejected by a lover, for example, they take on the appearance of being sad and frequently become lethargic in the way that we would recognise as sadness. They consider such a state to be a form of illness, however, which is unrelated to the rejection (Levy reported in Ekman, 1998). This suggests that not having a concept of an emotion does not necessarily mean that such a state is alien to a culture. At this point it is worth flagging up another problem with the concept of sadness, that is, at what point do we consider the state of sadness to have developed into the more long-term condition of depression? This issue (along with the negative emotion of anxiety) will be considered when we address mental illness in the next chapter.

Although negative emotions are often viewed as adaptive in that they help us to deal immediately with adverse events, one curious aspect of the state of anger that Nesse has highlighted is that it often involves spiteful threats or acts which may incur a cost to the actor. This is particularly the case when the target of the anger is a friend who has let us down. To put it in the language of Robert Trivers, we may feel incensed when anticipated acts of reciprocation fail to materialise (see chapter 8). Nesse sees this form of anger as a problem for evolutionary theories of behaviour since it may lead to costly and apparently irrational behaviour. Under such circumstances, as Nesse puts it, 'How can anger possibly be adaptive? Why not just ignore the person who will not cooperate and look instead for a different reciprocity partner?' (1990, p. 277). The answer Nesse suggests is that such anger, paradoxically, might, in the long run, be rational. Anger directed towards friends who have treated us badly might signal to them that a defection has been detected and that this 'will not be tolerated'. This behaviour might persuade the defector to make amends or, failing this, it will at least demonstrate that the casualty is not open to further acts of exploitation (see chapter 8). Such an explanation is a little speculative, but without having this form of outrage in our repertoire people would certainly be easy prey for exploitative 'friends'. Incidentally, Nesse also suggests the negative emotions of guilt and 'self-punishment' have evolved partly in order to restore a relationship following a defection. Thankfully, for the most part, friendly relationships promote positive emotional states.

Positive emotions – love and happiness

Most of the theoretical and empirical work on emotions has concentrated on the negative emotions. Barbara Fredrickson (1998) thinks there are three main reasons for this bias – that is, positive emotions:

- are fewer and less differentiated than negative ones,
- do not generally create problems for people,
- make for less precise prototypes than negative ones.

In contrast to some evolutionists, Fredrickson considers that positive emotions may be the product of quite strong selection pressures. Developing a theme first introduced by Derryberry and Tucker (1994), she turns the narrowing of focus argument for negative emotions on its head and suggests that positive emotions serve to expand an individual's attentional focus and knowledge – or to use Fredrickson's own terminology, to 'broaden our mindset'. Fredrickson considers four basic emotional states: joy, interest, contentment and love (see also Ekman, 1992). The first three of these may be seen as components of happiness but Fredrickson considers these to be sufficiently distinct to merit individual consideration.

Joy is generally associated with safe and familiar contexts and frequently with the achievement of goals (Izard, 1977). To Fredrickson, joy embodies the urge to be playful. Engaging in play, as ethologists have long argued, promotes the development of both physical and intellectual skills (Fagen, 1981; see also chapter 8). It also enables you to find out about the various strengths and weaknesses of other members of your social group relative to your own (Fagen, 1981). In this way the playful behaviour that is the outcome of feeling joyful may serve long-term social and intellectual functions.

Interest, the main emotion of our 'emotionless' Mr Spock, is a state that all mentally healthy people feel every day of their lives. Without it we would be unlikely to engage in exploration and thereby increase our knowledge of the world. In fact it is almost impossible to conceive of life without 'interest'. Some experts are unconvinced that interest *is* a basic emotion (Lazarus, 1991). But as Fredrickson points out, interest is more than just attending to something in a detached way – it involves an urge that is rewarding and pleasurable. Again, like joy, interest tends to have long-lasting intellectual consequences and is likely to broaden our 'mindset' (Fredrickson, 1998; see also Fredrickson, 2006 and Johnson *et al.*, 2010).

Contentment is generally seen as a low arousal positive state. So does this positive state also fulfil Fredrickson's model of expanding an individual's mindset? If contentment involves a desire to become inactive, then such an argument is less obviously applicable when compared to joy and interest. Fredrickson argues, however, that contentment is a state which creates the urge to 'savour and integrate recent events and experiences' (1998, p. 306) and that this, in turn, increases receptiveness. This is a slightly more convoluted argument than for joy and interest, but again it does fit in with her main thrust of broadening rather than narrowing perspectives.

Love is quite a vague term used to describe a number of emotionally positive states that involve being strongly attached to another person. Clearly, we don't love our mother or our children in the same way that we love our lover – but all of these relationships/states share the urge to be close to the target of our affections and a feeling of pleasure when in their company. How well do such feelings fit in with Fredrickson's model of broadening a person's mindset? Fredrickson sees love and the various positive emotions associated with it as helping to 'build and solidify an individual's social resources' (1998, p. 306). Such social resources might be drawn upon later. This implies that love may play a role in the development of reciprocal altruism – a not unreasonable assumption. Clearly, if love has arisen via selection processes, then it must have affected inclusive fitness. Reciprocal acts that seal a friendship may be a part of this, but surely a more direct route for affecting fitness would be via love's effects on mates and family. Trivers certainly sees the various states of love as means of helping to increase our inclusive fitness (Trivers, 1985). Passionate love is an obvious state which is likely to boost our direct fitness (provided that love is reciprocated, of course), whereas love of family members and of other relatives puts one in a psychological state that is likely to boost both direct and indirect fitness (see chapters 2 and 7).

In Fredrickson's model, positive emotions have been shaped by selection pressures, not because they allow for immediate life-preserving responses but because opening people up to new experiences puts them in a mental state to build for the future. In this way positive emotions may be seen as adaptations since they make us likely to 'build resources during safe and satiated moments by playing, exploring, or savoring and integrating' (1998, p. 313). This is an attractive idea, but is there any empirical evidence to support it? Fredrickson cites two indirect pieces of evidence to support her theory. First, there is some evidence that people with **bipolar depression** ('manic-depression', see chapter 12) are particularly creative during their manic (extremely happy) phase (Jamison, 1993; 2011); and second, lab-based studies have demonstrated that, when a positive emotional state is induced into normal participants, their attentional focus may be broadened (Derryberry and Tucker, 1994, cited in Fredrickson, 1998).

Like Barbara Fredrickson, Randolph Nesse also considers positive emotions as important adaptations. His view overlaps with Fredrickson's but draws more directly on the ideas of Hamilton (1964a, b) and Trivers (1971) with regard to the origins of 'altruistic' behaviour (see chapters 7 and 8). Nesse sees affectionate emotions as having evolved to provide aid to family members who share an individual's genes and a useful element of the reciprocity equation in the case of non-kin relationships. In Nesse's words:

Darwinian success for humans depends substantially on social success and social success depends substantially on successful negotiation of reciprocal relationships. (Nesse, 1990, p. 274)

Interestingly, Nesse also suggests that positive emotions might have become more important in our recent evolutionary history stating that 'Positive emotions may now be more often useful than negative ones because life is safer than it was' (Nesse, 2009, p. 160). Since the 1990s, at least some evolutionists have begun to consider the importance attached to positive emotions and they have done so by drawing on evolutionary theories that were developed to help explain pro-social behaviour during the latter years of the twentieth century.

Does the theory of universal human emotions stand up to scrutiny?

As we have seen, in recent years evolutionary psychologists have begun to propose functional explanations for common human emotional states. In the case of negative emotions such as fear and anger, some evolutionists have suggested that these states prepare us to deal with aversive conditions. For positive emotions, it has been proposed that the feelings of love, joy, interest and contentment allow for the build-up of knowledge, relationships and resources. It has also been suggested that such emotions (along with negative ones such as anger and guilt) may have arisen as a part of the evolution of altruistic behaviour which is ultimately related to boosting inclusive fitness.

Some might argue that such ideas are currently quite speculative. We should be aware, however, that it is the specifics of such arguments that are speculative rather than the general argument that emotions are adaptations. Very few would argue today that selection pressures played no role in the origins of human emotions. One of the problems with the idea of specific action tendencies being related to specific social circumstances, however, is that we frequently find ourselves in a state of mixed emotions. When insulted and challenged by an aggressive individual we are likely to feel anger, fear and anxiety in varying measures. Also, we should bear in mind the fact that different emotional states can have the same behavioural outcome. Crying, for example, can occur during extreme happiness as well as sadness (LeDoux, 1996). Moreover, as some cognitivists have asked, if these emotions really are universal then why is there disagreement over their precise number and nature (Ortony and Turner, 1990)? Indeed, a number of psychologists see emotions as involving higher cognitive appraisals rather than simply as hard-wired universal responses.

To be fair to them, Ekman, Nesse and other 'basic emotion theorists' are aware of all of these potential problems and have themselves accepted that cultural and cognitive factors can and do modify emotional responses (see box 11.5). Furthermore, as LeDoux has pointed out, much of the debate concerning differences between the basic emotion lists of different researchers may be more apparent than real. Different terms may be used by separate researchers to describe the same emotions – joy and happiness, for example. Also, claiming that there are certain emotions that are common to all people does not deny that an individual can have more than one at the same time. Finally, in their defence, the evolutionists can now point to the evidence that homologous areas of the brain in ourselves and other species deal with fundamentally the same

Box 11.6 Nesse's proposed 'phylogeny of emotions'

Strongly influenced by Darwin's ideas on the evolution of emotions, in 2004 Randolph Nesse proposed what we might call an evolutionary tree of emotions (i.e. its phylogeny). The suggestion here is that ancient organisms began with arousal that evolved to deal with threats and opportunities. Later on in evolutionary history these became more differentiated in order to deal with adaptive challenges for each species. This eventually led to complex socially evoked emotional states in our species – such as romantic love, pride and shame.

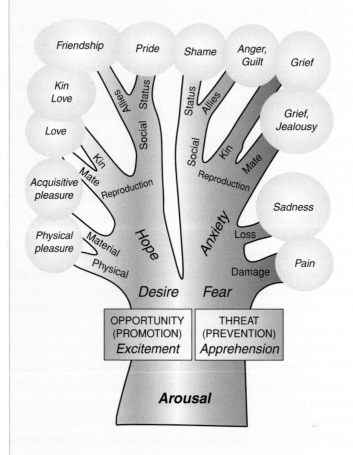

Note that as Nesse has pointed out this illustration is a simplification since 'the tree will be different for different species, the actual pathways would have many dead-ends, and selection can undifferentiate specific emotions to deal with more general situations. Also, of course, the diagram should be in about twenty dimensions.'

emotions. Such findings are difficult to explain without recourse to an evolutionary explanation, lending support to argument of an innate biological organisation of emotions. An example of this is the cross-species involvement of the amygdala in fear reactions (LeDoux, 1996).

Are all emotions adaptations?

If we accept that some emotions are universal and have arisen from selection pressures then does this mean that we have to accept that all emotions are adaptations? We saw earlier how Randolph Nesse has argued that the epiphenomenon explanation is unlikely for the core emotions but this does not mean that we can dismiss it for all forms of emotional experience. The great sadness that is felt when a loved one dies might, as some have suggested, be adaptive in that it makes us withdraw from action and conserve energy at appropriate times such as during a famine, but bereavement may also be an emergent property of having an emotional brain. It might be that bereavement serves no adaptive function but is simply the price we pay for having the positive emotions associated with love and attachment. If this is the case then it is also possible that some other negative emotions are not adaptive in themselves but are the result of the removal of the source of positive emotion (and vice versa). Determining which emotional states are adaptations and which are emergent properties will be a very difficult task for evolutionary psychologists to deal with. At least we can see that having focused on cognitive processes for so long, evolutionary psychologists are finally beginning to turn their attention to what drives these processes – emotions.

Summary

- In 1872 Darwin published *The Expression of the Emotions in Man and Animals*. In this ground-breaking book he argued that there are a number of emotional expressions which are innate and common to all cultures – universal emotions. Such expressions include sadness, anger, surprise and enjoyment. Although Darwin backed his theory of the universality of emotional expression with a great deal of personal observation, most twentieth-century social scientists disputed this claim, adhering instead to the notion that each society develops its own range of expressions. During the latter years of the twentieth century, however, evidence accumulated which supported Darwin's contention.
- The universality of human emotions is supported by three forms of evidence. Comparison with other primates suggests a common evolutionary ancestor; cross-cultural studies suggest that different cultures recognise and experience the same

basic emotions; and certain areas of the human forebrain appear to be particularly associated with emotional states. Specifically, the amygdala is highly active during the state of fear and an area of the cortex, the orbitofrontal, is believed to be involved in the appreciation of social and emotional cues in others. These findings suggest an evolved neural substrate for emotional processing.

- Alongside Darwin, Sigmund Freud and William James also considered emotional states to be the products of evolution. Darwin proposed three principles around which emotions are based. These are: (1) serviceable associated habits – a specific emotional state will predictably lead to a specific expression and posture; (2) antithesis – positive and negative emotions occur in paired opposites; (3) direct action of the excited nervous system on the body independently of will – facial expressions and body postures related to emotions occur without conscious effort and provide cues that allow others to have insight into our internal state. Freud suggested that much of human behaviour is driven by the pursuit of pleasure and the avoidance of pain. James proposed that emotions are the result of the brain monitoring the state of the body and then responding with an emotional state, rather than the reverse.

- A number of social scientists have been critical of the notion that human emotions are universal. Some cultural relativists have proposed that emotions are the products of culture rather than biologically evolved states. This social constructionist view of emotions is based on the fact that in some societies there are apparently complex emotional states that are not found in others. Evolutionists such as Paul Ekman counter these claims by proposing that we should distinguish between basic emotions common to all people and culture-specific ones which involve putting these emotions together in ways that each culture has learned. Ekman also claims that, although all peoples experience a similar range of emotions, the expressions that a person shows in public may be determined by the 'display rules' of that culture. In this way, in comparison to Westerners, individuals from the Far East may be dissuaded from exhibiting sadness or anger in public but they may show these expressions when alone.

- Evolutionists such as Randolph Nesse, Barbara Fredrickson and Paul Ekman have proposed particular functions for specific emotional states. Negative states such as fear and anger may have evolved in order to place people in the correct psychological and physiological state to deal with aversive circumstances. These internal states may make likely appropriate behavioural responses, which have been called specific action tendencies. Positive emotions such as love and the components of happiness have received less attention than negative ones. Fredrickson and Nesse, however, have both suggested that positive emotions might serve the function of placing us in the appropriate psychological state to help build up social relationships. Nesse has developed this argument in relating it to kin altruism and reciprocation, while

Fredrickson has proposed that, in contrast to negative emotions which narrow attention, positive emotions serve to 'broaden our mindset'.

Questions

1. Martin Seligman has argued that we are biologically prepared to develop phobias to some animals such as spiders and snakes due to their posing a danger to our ancestors – i.e. 'preparedness theory'. Make a list of the strengths and the limitations of this theory. How might we go about testing the 'preparedness theory' of phobias?
2. List the different ways in which the term 'love' is used to describe quite different feelings in our species. In what ways might each of these examples of strong feelings ultimately be related to inclusive fitness?
3. Does human romantic love differ fundamentally from animal sexual imprinting?
4. What does the case of Phineas Gage tell us about the foundations of human emotional states? This case is often presented to demonstrate the materialist nature of internal emotional states. What does this mean and how might it be criticised?

FURTHER READING

Damasio, A. B. (2003). *Looking for Spinoza: Joy, Sorrow and the Feeling Brain*. Fort Worth: Harcourt Brace College Publishers. Discusses the relationships between brain and emotional states and presents these in a way that a nonspecialist reader can digest.

Darwin, C. (1998). *The Expression of the Emotions in Man and Animals*, 3rd edn with Introduction and Afterword by Paul Ekman. London: HarperCollins (originally published in 1872). Darwin's original and lucid account of the relationship between evolution and emotions brought up to date by the incorporation of a number of commentary boxes by Paul Ekman.

Evans, D. and Cruse, P. (Eds) (2004). *Emotion, Evolution and Rationality*. Oxford: Oxford University Press. Specialist multi-authored text that explores the relationship between emotions and rationality within an evolutionary framework. Considers in particular which emotions are helpful and which potentially detrimental.

LeDoux, J. E. (1996). *The Emotional Brain: The Mysterious Underpinnings of Emotional Life*. New York: Simon and Schuster. Very accessible account of the relationship between the brain and emotion.

12 | Evolutionary psychopathology and Darwinian medicine

> ## KEY CONCEPTS
>
> evolutionary psychopathology • Darwinian medicine • pathogen • aetiology • pathogenesis • trait variation • immune system • verification module • smoke detector principle • affective disorders • social competition hypothesis • schizophrenia • personality disorders

Life on earth has existed in some form for well over three billion years. Given this lengthy period of evolutionary change, why is it that modern-day humans still suffer from colds, fever, morning sickness, personality disorders, anxiety and depression, and the most serious of psychiatric illnesses – schizophrenia? Surely natural selection has had time to rid us of such problems? One of the major contributions that evolutionary psychologists have made in the last twenty years lies in reconsidering the symptoms of mental and physical illnesses in one of three ways based on a knowledge of evolutionary theory. They suggest that symptoms may be adaptations, they may be due to constraints on evolutionary processes or they may be due to a mismatch between our evolutionary heritage and our current environment. Our susceptibility to infectious diseases, for example, is now seen as a pathogen–host arms race that, due to the vast asymmetry in life-cycle time and in sheer numbers, humans can never win. Darwinian medicine leads to the counterintuitive conclusion that perhaps sometimes unpleasant symptoms should be left to continue because they are good for you. It is in the field of psychiatry, however, that evolutionary psychology may have its greatest impact as, for the first time, psychologists are asking why the propensity for mental illness is so widespread in our species.

What are evolutionary psychopathology and Darwinian medicine?

Evolutionary psychopathology and Darwinian medicine are overlapping but slightly different concepts. Psychopathology is the study of mental illness – so we can think of evolutionary psychopathology as the Darwinian approach to the study of mental illness (Baron-Cohen, 1997). Darwinian medicine is also concerned with improving our understanding of mental illness by applying evolutionary principles but is somewhat broader since it also encompasses non-psychiatric health problems (Nesse and Williams, 1995). In recent years the term 'evolutionary medicine' has also come into common parlance (Gluckman *et al.*, 2009). In this chapter we will generally use the term 'Darwinian medicine' as shorthand for evolutionary psychopathology, evolutionary medicine and Darwinian medicine. In addition to being concerned with improving our understanding of health-related problems, as we'll see, proponents of Darwinian medicine have also considered how we might improve their treatment.

We might ask how Darwinian medicine differs from conventional medicine. In essence, it differs in the same way that evolutionary psychology differs from the traditional social sciences – that is, whereas conventional medicine deals with the proximate questions of 'how' and 'what', Darwinian medicine is concerned with ultimate 'why' questions (Nesse and Dawkins, 2010). This means that evolutionists are interested more in why each health-related problem continues to exist today rather than in the mechanism of causation. The best way to understand this difference in approach is by example. In this chapter we will consider the evolutionary approach to understanding and treating illnesses – both mental and physical. In order to illustrate how evolutionary principles may be brought to bear in this area we begin with infectious diseases and genetic disorders before considering serious mental health issues and personality disorders (Nesse, 2012).

Infectious diseases and the evolutionary arms race

When we complain that we are ill with an infectious disease we are really saying that our body has become host to a pathogen which is causing us a number of unpleasant symptoms. Such pathogens include viruses, bacteria and other microbial parasites such as protozoa and fungi. Conventional medicine seeks to understand the **aetiology** (cause) and the **pathogenesis** (mechanism) of each illness (McGuire *et al.*, 1992). Note that these are proximate levels of explanation – that is those that deal with *how* illnesses happen rather than *why* illnesses happen. From such a proximate level of understanding clinicians aim to develop treatments to help alleviate the symptoms and destroy the pathogen. Darwinian medicine, however, seeks ultimate explanations for the symptoms of disease in order to aid treatment. The evolutionary approach asks why such symptoms exist – what function, if any, might they serve? At this point it is important to realise that the proponents of Darwinian medicine are not attempting to replace conventional medicine but rather that an evolutionary approach might be used to provide an overarching framework for understanding health and illness (Gluckman *et al.*, 2009; Nesse, 2005; 2012).

Recall from chapter 2 that the evolutionary approach views the host–parasite relationship as an arms race conducted on an evolutionary time scale where each side struggles to gain the upper hand. Adaptations by one side lead to counter-adaptations on the other. One of the advantages of this approach is that symptoms may often be seen as adaptations. But therein lies a problem. Adaptations for which side of the equation – host or parasite? This question is not merely an academic one. Adaptations by the host are designed to destroy or expel the pathogen. Adaptations by the pathogen are designed to spread copies of itself to other bodies. Traditional medical practitioners tend to view all symptoms as pathological, that is, as problems which should be relieved (Nesse, 2012; Nesse and Dawkins, 2010). Evolutionists, however, have suggested that many of our symptoms may well be defence mechanisms which have evolved to protect us (Martin, 1997; Gluckman *et al.*, 2009). Perhaps we should concentrate on alleviating the symptoms which are designed to benefit the pathogen but allow the symptoms which are designed to kill it off to persist for a little longer. By allowing the latter symptoms to persist we might, in the long run, speed up recovery. Specific examples of viral and bacterial infections will help to illustrate this point.

Bacterial infections

Bacteria are single-celled microbial organisms. Many of them are free-living but others can only survive on or in the bodies of other organisms where they frequently cause debilitating symptoms. Bacterial infections lead the body to release a chemical called **leucocyte endogenous mediator** or LEM. This substance, in turn, leads to both a raising of the body temperature and to iron withdrawal from the bloodstream (and into the liver – leading to a reduction of up to 80 per cent of blood iron). These events may sound like bad news for us – and in a sense they are – we tend to feel both listless and feverish. However, since bacteria require iron to develop and multiply and since higher body temperatures help to kill them off, these uncomfortable changes are exactly what the doctor ordered to dispel the invader. Unfortunately for the sufferer, what the doctor frequently does order is **antipyretic** (fever suppressant) drugs and iron supplements. In fact, most doctors and pharmacists don't even realise that such treatments can help to maintain the illness (Nesse and Williams, 1995; Nesse, 2012).

Although many of the unpleasant symptoms that we exhibit may have evolved to dispel the pathogen, there are others that are clearly adaptations of the pathogen to aid its transmission. In the case of cholera (*Vibrio cholerae*), for example, the severe diarrhoea that develops within hours of contagion helps to pass the parasite on to others. The dehydration that stems from the diarrhoea can be fatal. The fact that cholera kills so many of its hosts might be viewed as a poor adaptation for the bacterium. It is passed on so quickly, however, that death of a host may not matter from the point of view of the pathogen.

> ## Box 12.1 **Is morning sickness an adaptation?**
>
> Until quite recently, most clinicians have considered the early proneness to nausea and vomiting in pregnancy (NVP) as a non-functional by-product of a woman's physical state at that point. In 1992, however, the medical researcher and evolutionist Margie Profit provided evidence that this 'morning sickness' may be an adaptation to protect the embryo from toxins and micro-organisms in food that might otherwise lead to deformities. Potential toxins are found in a wide range of plant foods such as cabbage, celery, oranges and bananas and micro-organisms can be common in meat. Such foods normally pose no problems to adults since the liver uses enzymes to convert the poisons in them into harmless substances which are excreted. Although the adult human is able to deal with these toxins, during its early stages of development the foetus is susceptible to them. Moreover, the mother's own immune system is 'down-regulated' in order to stop her body attacking the perceived foreign tissue of the foetus. Profit has suggested that the problem is resolved by the release of pregnancy hormones that lower the nausea threshold which is controlled by an area of the brain stem (the **chemoreceptor trigger zone**). This, in turn, makes women less likely to consume such foods and when they do so makes them more likely to vomit following their consumption.
>
> Profit's theory is supported by the finding that women who show little or no sign of morning sickness are far more likely to spontaneously abort their foetus than those who suffer from it (Profit, 1992). It is also supported by that fact that women are most likely to become aversive to meat during the early stages of pregnancy (Sherman and Flaxman, 2002; Flaxman and Sherman, 2008). Rather than being merely an unpleasant side effect of pregnancy, NVP might in reality be a well-developed adaptation to protect the developing foetus.

Bacteria may be uninvited microscopic guests but some pathogens are even smaller and decidedly simpler. As we'll see when we consider viruses it is not always the case that symptoms aid only one side of the equation.

Viral infections

If bacteria are microscopic then viruses are *sub-microscopic*, consisting only of a short strand of nucleic acid surrounded by a protein coat. Broadly speaking these pathogens may be subdivided into DNA and RNA viruses. The illness that we refer to as the 'common cold' is a rhinovirus which exists throughout the world in around 100 rapidly changing forms. This 20-sided (icosahedral) RNA virus enters the cells of the nasal passages where it rapidly reproduces asexually. New copies of the virus are then shed and released into nasal secretions from which they spread to others in their millions each time we sneeze. Clearly, the sneeze both expels the virus (which is good for us) and helps it to spread (which is good for the virus). We might ask who benefits from the behaviour of the host? The cold virus thus illustrates that in some cases symptoms might arise which benefit both host and parasite even though such symptoms may damage others in the population (Clamp, 2001; Goldsmith and Zimmerman, 2001; Gluckman *et al.*, 2009).

Fighting back – the immune system

If we have been locked in an evolutionary arms race with viruses and other pathogens for millions of years, we might ask what sort of long-term counter-measures have we developed? At some stage in our evolutionary history we came up with a master-stroke – we invented the immune system. To be more precise, our reptilian ancestors invented it and passed it on to all of their descendants. The part of the immune system that is found in the blood consists of an army of specially adapted white cells or **lymphocytes**. There are two main categories of these cells: B-lymphocytes, which are formed in the bone marrow, and T-lymphocytes, which develop in the thymus at the base of the neck.

The immune system is activated by the entry of large foreign molecules known as antigens into the body. Antigens may be any large molecule such as a protein or a sugar. Given that pathogens have such antigens on their surface, their appearance in the body causes B-lymphocytes to produce proteins called antibodies (antigen is short for antibody generator). These antibodies then circulate in the blood and bind (attach) to the antigens, marking them for destruction. When the surface of, say, a virus or bacterium has thus been 'marked out' by antibodies, it is then engulfed by other white blood cells called **macrophages** ('eaters of large things'). The T-lymphocytes also aid the process in a number of ways. When a pathogen is detected T-lymphocytes begin to proliferate and form various sub-classes that both help in the attack of the antigen and aid the B-lymphocytes in their production of antibodies.

This may sound like a successful, if somewhat complicated, system for dealing with foreign bodies. There is a problem, however. Antigens can occur in literally millions of different forms. Biochemists like to think of antibodies as locks and antigens as keys. This means that each invading pathogen may have one of a million different keys and our bodies have to produce the appropriate lock if we wish to destroy them. As Matt Ridley puts it, our body 'cannot keep armies of each antibody lock ready to immobilise all types of keys, because there is room for millions of cells of one type, one cell of each of millions of types, but not for millions of cells of millions of types' (1993, p. 72). The body solves this problem by keeping a relatively small number of each specific white blood cell. When a lymphocyte comes across an antigen that fits its locks, it then begins to multiply, producing vast numbers of identical ones to fight the foreign body. Over an evolutionary time scale we have developed an enormous number of slightly different white blood cells in the hopes that one of them will have the correct key for any antigen that appears in the body. Since sex increases the level of variability in the immune system, as we saw in chapter 3, such parasites have been used to explain the very existence of sexual reproduction (see the 'Red Queen' hypothesis in chapter 3).

The problem with developing a complex anti-parasite adaptation such as the immune system is that, of course, the parasites have hit back with their own adaptations. Some, like the bilharzia parasite, cloak themselves by attaching host cells to their surface so that they are ignored by the immune system. Others, such as influenza viruses, are so virulent that they are passed on by the time the immune system kicks in. Such counter-adaptations illustrate once more that evolution is more of a treadmill than a ladder.

HIV and AIDS – the virus that cheats the system?

Since the 1980s we have seen the evolution of one virus which has cheated the system. This pathogen does not attempt to avoid the attentions of the immune system, nor does it cloak itself, it simply attacks the immune system itself. The **human immunodeficiency virus**, or HIV, binds to the surface of the helper T-cells, gains entry and then destroys them. Since the helper T-cells coordinate the activity of the immune system, by taking out the T-cells HIV has played an ace card. Following contraction of HIV an individual may remain healthy for some time as new T-cells are produced to compensate for the death of others. Once T-cells are killed off at a greater rate than they are produced, however, the sufferer becomes progressively more susceptible to other pathogens such as bacteria, fungi and protozoa. Many of these pathogens are mild infections to healthy people but in the advanced HIV sufferer they are now able to multiply, causing serious symptoms. It is these secondary symptoms that medical experts call **acquired immune deficiency syndrome** or AIDS.

HIV and AIDS illustrate two important points with regard to host–parasite relationships. First, they show how our own behaviour can alter the evolution of pathogens – increased promiscuity and intravenous drug use have favoured the development of this highly virulent virus. And second, they illustrate that we cannot win the host–parasite arms race outright but only gain a temporary respite with each bug.

One final question that we might ask about infectious diseases is why is it that some pathogens are so virulent and debilitating and others far less so? Evolutionist Paul Ewald has proposed that the virulence of a pathogen is strongly influenced by

Box 12.2 **Genetic diseases**

It seems inconceivable that our own genes can cause us to be ill. Surely selection pressures will have removed mutant genes that cause illness from the human genome? Such a conclusion may make intuitive sense – there is, however, clear evidence that certain genes which cause illness are maintained in our species because, on balance, they are beneficial. The first of these was discovered at Oxford University in the late 1940s and has subsequently become the classic biology textbook example – sickle-cell anaemia (Ridley, 1999). Sickle-cell anaemia causes the sufferer to have an abnormality of the red blood cells (they become sickle-shaped rather than round), leading to problems in oxygen transportation and a whole series of unpleasant symptoms such as general weakness, impaired mental abilities and kidney damage. The disease only occurs in individuals who have two copies of the sickle-cell gene – one from each parent. Sickle-cell anaemia is found in people who live in areas where malaria is common and a single dose of the sickle-cell gene conveys a degree of resistance to this disease. Since most individuals have only a single dose of the sickle-cell gene, then it is maintained in the population due to this advantage of resistance to malaria. Sickle-cell anaemia reminds us that the effects of a gene are always contingent on not only the environment, but also the existence of other genes in the organism. This argument is known to geneticists as **heterozygous advantage**. That is, when the condition of having two different alleles which confer an advantage is found in a population, then the possibility of the homozygous condition will occur every so often (see chapter 2). This homozygous condition may be either neutral or harmful. We can think of heterozygous advantage as a special case of the pleiotropy argument presented below. Today, some evolutionists consider that many of the mutations which are maintained in the population and cause problems (either in a single or a double dose) may be the price we pay for the beneficial effects of such genes on ourselves or our relatives (Martin, 1997; Ridley, 1999; Gluckman *et al.*, 2009).

In addition to the heterozygous advantage argument there is a second, probably more common, way in which genes that cause damage to our health may be maintained in our species. If a harmful gene normally has its effects after the age of reproduction, then natural selection is unable to remove it from a population. In this way inherited diseases such as Huntington's chorea, which does not emerge until middle age, may be kept in the population. In Huntington's chorea there is a progressive loss of motor control and eventual death. Huntington's chorea is fortunately quite a rare condition, but it may be only the tip of the iceberg, as many other degenerative conditions such as Alzheimer's and osteoarthritis might also be maintained in our species owing to their late onset. It might even be the case that these late-acting diseases are so common because the genes which help to cause them may confer advantages early on in life. Perhaps people with the 'genes for' Alzheimer's are particularly quick-witted in early adulthood – or perhaps they are more athletic than their peers. We really have not, as yet, even begun to look for such advantages.

its method of transmission (1994; 2002). Those that are passed on directly by personal contact, he suggests, should be less debilitating than those that are passed on by a vector (an organism that acts as an unwitting go-between). The rhinovirus, for example, is more easily passed on if it allows the host to remain active, thereby making contact with others more likely. In contrast, the protozoan that causes malaria (*Plasmodium*) is transmitted by the anopheles mosquito and can lead to a chronically debilitating state which thereby decreases the sufferers' ability to ward off the attentions of these unpleasant insects. To put it crudely, killing the host may not matter as long as there are plenty of opportunities for the vector to take copies of the pathogen onto other hosts (Nesse and Dawkins, 2010). Each year up to three million people die of malaria, whereas the common cold is merely a mild inconvenience to most sufferers. Hence, an evolutionary approach may help to provide surprising insights into infectious diseases.

Psychiatric problems

Although parasites may have played a very important role in human evolution, it is psychological rather than physical problems which have been of greatest interest to evolutionary psychologists. During its short history, researchers into Darwinian medicine have already considered a wide range of mental health problems including depression and anxiety, schizophrenia and serious personality disorders (including psychopathy, Brüne, 2008). In short, all of the psychiatric problems that clinical psychologists and psychiatrists consider. We will consider each of these in turn. But first we need to consider, if natural and sexual selection promote positive changes, why haven't psychiatric disorders been removed from our species? An understanding of evolutionary theory helps us to understand that we still contract colds because we are in an unwinnable arms race with pathogens – but surely the existence of psychiatric disorders cannot be explained away so easily?

Why can't evolution rid us of psychiatric problems?

Two of the pioneers of the Darwinian approach to medicine, American evolutionists Randolph Nesse and George Williams, have suggested three ultimate reasons as to why many modern-day humans have psychiatric problems:

- Genes that predispose people to psychiatric disorders may also have inclusive fitness benefits.
- Environmental factors that cause psychiatric disorders may be novel when compared to our ancestral past.

- Some psychiatric disorders may be due to design compromises rather than genetic flaws.

We might label the first of these the *pleiotropy* argument – that is, many genes have more than one phenotypic effect, so the negative effects of a gene may be maintained in a gene pool because the positive ones outweigh them. A variation of this argument is that the harmful genes provide a benefit when combined with other genes, but that sometimes such genes are found in bodies that lack the necessary 'good' genes. The second argument we could call the *time lag* argument – that is, humans have developed a lifestyle that did not exist in our ancestral past too rapidly for selection pressures to have led to appropriate changes (also known as the **mismatch hypothesis**). Finally, we might call the third one the *compromise* argument – that is, selection pressures act on inclusive fitness, not on perfecting psychological (and physical) devices.

We might add to this list the *trait variation* argument. This is based on the notion of a **normal distribution curve**. This means that within a given population, individuals may be plotted along various dimensions for physical traits such as height, weight and hair colour and for psychological traits such as level of intelligence and personality factors (e.g. extraversion and neuroticism). A large number of factors determine an individual's position in the normal distribution of each characteristic measured. These include the combination of genes they inherit from their parents (sexual reproduction leads to unavoidable variation) and their life experiences. When such measurements are plotted for a population they generally produce a bell-shaped graph – the normal distribution – with most people in the middle of the range and progressively fewer individuals as we move to the extremes. There are, for example, very few Einsteins and very few seven-foot men. Thus if, say, an emotional trait like anger has evolved in a species such as our own, then there will be some individuals who are found at the extremes of the distribution who have too much or too little of it for their own good.

The pleiotropy, time lag, compromise and trait variation arguments are having a growing impact on the early development of Darwinian medicine and should be borne in mind when considering each of the topics discussed below.

We considered moment-by-moment internal states which we call emotions in chapter 11. In our discussion of psychiatric problems below, however, we are more concerned with pervasive and enduring emotional and mental states.

Anxiety – why worry?

We all recognise anxiety – it's a general feeling of apprehension about what might happen to ourselves or our loved ones. In colloquial terms we call it 'worrying'. In

Figure 12.1 Anxiety related to an exam may improve performance

some ways anxiety is one of the easiest psychological problems to explain within an evolutionary framework. Imagine the selective advantages that might accrue to the first individual to be born with a mutant allele which endowed him with the propensity to feel anxious in a population that previously lacked it. Right from birth he would want to attract his mother's attention if she left him alone. Throughout life he would be wary of eating unfamiliar foods or approaching strange animals. He would surely fare much better than his conspecifics who, even in the jaws of a predator, remained perfectly calm.

Clearly this is a simplification of how anxiety originally arose. It probably pre-dates hominin evolution (Nettle and Bateson, 2012) and there are likely be a whole series of genes involved in endowing us with the ability to experience this state. But the point remains the same. As Nesse and Williams put it:

In the face of threat, anxiety alters our thinking, behaviour, and physiology in advantageous ways. (1995)

When threatened, anxiety focuses our attention and prepares us for action in a way that would have been advantageous to our ancestors. The problem that needs to be explained, however, is why do so many of us have so much of it? One in seven American citizens will develop a clinical level of anxiety and even those of us who are not in this league on the anxiety scale have quite astonishing propensities to worry about all sorts of things. We worry about how good the weather will be on vacation; we worry about how well our soccer team is performing; we worry about what we should wear to a social engagement. Surely such trivial things cannot have fitness consequences?

The smoke detector principle

Nesse and Williams suggest that in order to understand just why we worry so much we need to consider how the mechanisms that regulate anxiety are likely to have been shaped by selection pressures. They point out that there is a cost–benefit asymmetry associated with being over- or under-anxious. If you compare the fitness consequences of not feeling anxious when we should with the consequences of feeling anxious when we shouldn't then it immediately becomes clear that we should err on the anxious side of the equation. Nesse and Williams call this the 'smoke detector' principle, where false alarms are cheap but ignoring a real warning might be deadly. In their words, '[T]he cost of getting killed even once is enormously higher than the cost of responding to a hundred false alarms' (Nesse and Williams, 1995; see also Nesse, 2012). Interestingly, the smoke detector principle is supported by recent research which demonstrates that for people with a low level of anxiety proneness long-term survival is reduced when compared with their more anxiety-prone peers (Mykletun et al., 2009; Bateson et al., 2011).

Turning the question on its head, we might ask: if anxiety is so useful to us then why haven't we evolved to be in a constant state of anxiety? The problem with this argument is that anxiety uses up time and energy, both of which might better be spent elsewhere. So, given a Pleistocene past teeming with predators, pathogens and competitive conspecifics, and where we had little control over climatic conditions, it may have made sense for our ancestors to have passed on a well-developed ability to worry – but only up to a point. The fact that many of these pressures currently exist at a lower level in the West does not mean that our propensity to feel anxious can simply 'unevolve'. Note that the smoke detector hypothesis is an example of a time lag explanation.

Even if we accept this line of reasoning, however, there are still those for whom anxiety is not just well developed – it is a debilitating illness or, as clinicians label it, a disorder. Can Darwinian medicine explain this widespread phenomenon? Perhaps the trait variation argument can help us here. This is certainly the view of some evolutionists. In the words of two proponents of Darwinian medicine 'Anxiety disorders, like disorders of other defence systems, are mainly disorders of regulation that entail excessive or deficient responses' (Marks and Nesse, 1994, pp. 69–70).

In addition to this trait variation explanation we might also resort to the time lag argument. One possibility is that some features of an anxiety disorder, for example, in agoraphobia (fear of leaving the home), the highly anxious feelings about leaving

Box 12.3 **Obsessive–compulsive disorder – an overactive verification module?**

Obsessive–compulsive disorder (OCD) is an example of a disorder, which according to Stevens and Price may be evidence of a verification module in our species, and one that can become overactive. Sufferers of OCD have two related problems (Berle and Phillips, 2006). First, they have obsessions – that is, recurrent thoughts and urges that cause anxiety. These may vary from being rather concerned that they haven't locked the front door to, in severe cases, feeling that they might have knocked someone over in the car. Second, they have compulsions to carry out repetitive acts – for example, in the first incidence going back to check the front door is locked two or three times or, in the second example, driving back five miles to check that there isn't an injured person lying by the roadside. Other examples of obsessions include recurrent thoughts about health and hygiene – sufferers may consider other people to be unclean or have a contagious disease (and interestingly OCD sufferers who have a health and hygiene problem often also have an overdeveloped sense of disgust, Berle and Phillips, 2006). In this case the compulsion may involve a great deal of hand washing. Hence the obsessive thoughts lead directly to the compulsive acts, which then reduce them (e.g. hand washing reduces fear of contamination). Unfortunately in the case of severe sufferers, the reduction in anxiety that is gained by performing the compulsive act is often short-lived and the obsessive thoughts frequently return.

Official figures suggest that around 2.5 per cent of the population suffer from OCD, which makes it a very common disorder (Kring *et al.*, 2010). One way to think about OCD is that it may be an exaggerated form of a normal internal state and behaviour of our species (i.e. we might explain it via the trait variation argument). This means that it may pay all of us to have some concern about hygiene, especially when it comes to preparing food, which might otherwise contain pathogens. A person who had no sense of food hygiene would be unlikely to leave descendants. It may also pay us to show some concern about how we treat others – for example feeling guilt at times may stop us behaving in ways that might exclude us from future reciprocation (see reciprocal altruism, chapter 8).

Stevens and Price (2000) suggest that OCD may be traced back to maintaining healthy resources and to the preparation of weapons that might be used in warfare or hunting. Clearly, if you get these wrong it might have inclusive fitness consequences, but for some anxious individuals such ritualised practices might become exaggerated.

But how might we test this idea? Stevens and Price suggest that we can use a comparative method both by making comparisons with other species and with present living forager societies (as described in chapter 4). With regard to other species, Stevens and Price suggest that repetitive, stereotyped behaviour patterns are common including continuous grooming and cleaning when placed under stress or given little stimulation. In such cases obsessive (or at least excessive) preening in birds, hair pulling in cats and compulsive paw licking in dogs are well-documented behaviours when these animals are put under stress. Perhaps the existence of these ritualised patterns in other species suggests that the roots of OCD are quite ancient. As our species evolved we developed more complex ways of being anxious (as we are able to conceive of future events and worry about them). On balance these more complex forms of anxiety may have given our ancestors a selective advantage by developing into a 'verification module' (i.e. one that looks for things to worry about in order to avoid problems before they occur). But they may also have opened the door to the disorder in individuals that have this module at 'the wrong setting' (see 'The smoke detector principle').

When considering present living forager societies, in support of Stevens and Price, anthropologists have recorded how hunter-gatherers take enormous care over their weapons and how they frequently have complex rituals before setting off on a hunt or to engage in warfare. This to Stevens and Price is evidence that we do have a verification module that prompts us to check and double check. If we add in the trait variation argument then some individuals who are prone to anxiety and have stressful life events may be led down the path to OCD and help to explain why 1 in 40 of our species currently suffers from this debilitating problem.

the home would have had a rational basis in our ancient past (Nesse and Williams, 1995). If, for example, an unpleasant close encounter with people from another tribe had caused you to retreat to a safe home base such as a cave, and if this was followed by a period of anxiety that kept you there for some time, then this might, arguably, have been an adaptive response. Eventually, it would have been necessary to leave such a base to forage for food, thereby breaking the cycle.

If we still have such responses within our repertoire today then, perhaps, highly socially anxious encounters might lead some people to retreat to their homes for an extended period. The difference of course is that this might become extremely extended as other people can bring to us the things we need to survive today. Perhaps the novel environment of today does not allow us to break such a rewarding cycle of withdrawal due to social anxiety. Such explanations for prolonged anxiety (i.e. anxiety disorders) are rather presumptive. Since, however, our environment has changed so rapidly over the short period of cultural history, it is not unreasonable to suggest that our anxiety responses may well manifest themselves in enduring ways which may not have occurred in our past. To put it another way there may be a mismatch between the environment in which our anxiety responses evolved and our current post-industrial environment (Nesse and Dawkins, 2010; Bateson et al., 2011).

Serious long-term anxiety is rarely an isolated psychiatric problem. In the words of clinicians it shows comorbidity with another possibly more serious and debilitating problem – depression.

Depression – an epidemic of modern times?

Depression is a very common mood problem which has been growing at an alarming rate since the middle of the twentieth century. Recent World Health Organization reports suggest that it affects 350 million people worldwide and that it is currently the world's third most common cause of morbidity (WHO, 2008; 2012). Psychiatrists and clinical psychologists distinguish between endogenous/clinical depression and reactive depression. Reactive depression can be very severe but is considered to be a normal response to life events that would make anybody unhappy, such as bereavement or disappointment. Clinical or endogenous depression, however, is either considered to be unrelated to life's events or is seen as an overreaction to them in its depth or longevity. Psychologists lump all clinical levels of depression together with serious mood disturbances as '**affective disorders**' (Kring *et al.*, 2010). The two main sub-categories are unipolar disorder and bipolar disorder. In unipolar (sometimes called major) depression there are generally alternating periods of depression and of relatively normal mood, whereas in bipolar disorder (sometimes called 'manic depression') there may be alternate bouts of mania and depression which may be separated by periods of normal mood.

Around one person in one hundred is diagnosed as having bipolar depression (Dawson and Tylee, 2001; Ustun and Chatterji, 2001) and onset is usually during their late twenties. During the manic phase there are periods of euphoria and high energy where grandiose plans may be conceived. A slightly less extreme form of mania known as hypomania may also occur. Money may be squandered, sex drive is often very high and sleep may become rare. At its extreme, mania may lead to delusions and hallucinations. Frequently, following a period of mania or hypomania the sufferer becomes exhausted. This exhaustion is frequently followed by a brief period of relatively normal mood before depression sets in. When depression does set in, however, it is usually severe. Rare indeed is the individual who has never experienced some form of depression as a reaction to disappointment or bereavement. But for the bipolar depressive the sense of bleak hopelessness is so severe that one in eight succeeds in suicide.

Unipolar depression is far more common with at least 5 per cent of the population suffering from it at some stage. Average age for onset is around forty and it is far more frequently diagnosed for women than for men. Unipolar depression is frequently associated with feelings of sadness, lethargy and social withdrawal. Sufferers may be preoccupied with thoughts of death and suicide, but are statistically much less likely to kill themselves than sufferers of bipolar depression.

Again, like anxiety, depression is such a frequent problem for our species that the possibility of its being an adaptive trait has been widely considered by evolutionists. In fact depression is *the* most researched area by proponents of Darwinian medicine. Given that a depressed person appears to be acting in such a maladaptive way, how might evolutionists explain this problem? Although evolutionists have argued for some time now that depression serves a function, it is only in quite recent years that a number of specific models have begun to emerge as to what that function might be. In their review of evolutionary explanations for this debilitating problem, Michael McGuire and Michael Raleigh of UCLA and Alfonso Troisi of the University of Vergata in Rome have identified three types of model which have been developed by evolutionists to explain depression. These are represented in table 12.1.

Given the sheer amount of theoretical work that has taken place into the relationship between evolution and depression, it is beyond the scope of this text to discuss all of the models presented in table 12.1 in detail. However, there are a number of points that can be explored in relation to these models. In particular a number of the arguments presented in table 12.1 draw on an influential evolutionary theory of depression that has been around since the 1960s (see below).

The first point to consider is that these explanations are by no means mutually exclusive – an individual, for example, might have developmental disruption *and* problems due to a loss *and* low social status. In this case then it would be surprising if they did not develop some form of depression. Also, since the form and intensity of depressive symptoms vary greatly between individuals, it is possible that different sub-types of depression (such as uni- and bipolar depression) are related to different explanations. It is also worth pointing out that a number of these separate models of the ultimate cause of depression overlap to a large extent. The 'depression as an adaptive trait', the 'failure to resolve interpersonal conflict' and the 'decline in social status' models are all related to a lack of social standing. In fact all three of these models draw on the long-term work of British psychiatrist John Price.

The social competition hypothesis

Long before the advent of Darwinian medicine, John Price argued that mood, in general, plays an important role in human status hierarchies and that this may be related to the social conditions of our early ancestors. More specifically, he suggested that depression is often observed in individuals who are unable to win a hierarchy struggle and yet refuse to yield (Price, 1967; Price *et al.*, 1994). Price calls this the **social competition hypothesis** of depression. This hypothesis is based on the notion that we share with our 'more primitive ancestors a mechanism for yielding in

Table 12.1 **Evolutionary models of depression**

Models emphasising ultimate causes	Model emphasising developmental disruption	Models emphasising ultimate–proximate cause interactions
(1) Depression is an adaptive trait. Views depression as an adaptive response to adverse conditions. It has, for example, been considered as a response to the intolerability of low social status which then prevents a person from challenging high-status individuals.	Infants have normal genetic information for development but some form of disruption leads to depression or an increased vulnerability for depression.	(1) Decline in social status model. Depression is due to a fall in status or inability to rise in social hierarchy. Note that this model overlaps with the depression as an adaptive trait model.
	Examples include effects of toxins on the developing foetus such as alcohol intake by the mother.	(2) Failure to resolve interpersonal conflict model. Depression results from a failure to resolve conflict with regard to dominance relationships. Depressive state enables individual to accept defeat.
(2) Pleiotropy explanation. Genes that increase inclusive fitness (for example, genes for attractiveness or creative thinking) may also lead to a state of depression as an epiphenomenon.	Adverse social effects may also be included in this model such as rejection by mother at an early age. This model is similar to more traditional psychological explanations for depression such as behavioural or psychoanalytic in that abnormal upbringing may be a key feature in increasing the likelihood of a disorder developing.	(3) Response to loss model. Depressive state is a reaction to interpersonal loss. Again fits in well with other psychological models but includes a consideration of the evolved neural hardware.
(3) Trait variation explanation. Depression may be due to the chance effects of genetic mixing that occurs at conception.		

Source: McGuire *et al.* (1997)

competitive situations' (Price *et al.*, 1994). According to Price, this is an involuntary subordinate strategy which serves to inhibit aggression, provides a signal that there is no threat and thereby expresses 'voluntary yielding'. Such an internal state and overt behaviour may serve to terminate conflict and allow for reconciliation. Price and his co-workers consider that when the voluntary yielding fails to occur then the state of depression, which would otherwise be transient, develops into prolonged depressive illness. Perhaps in today's society we are unable to express such voluntary yielding and the normally transient state of depression often develops into a long-term problem which may have been rare or non-existent in our ancient ancestors. This is another example of a time lag explanation. As we will see later there may be other reasons why long-term and more frequent states of depression are so common in today's society.

Price's model certainly fits in with the notion discussed in chapter 11 that feeling sad creates the urge to withdraw from action (Fredrickson, 1998; 2013). But is there evidence to back it up?

Depressed monkeys?

If the social competition hypothesis is correct and depression arose some time ago in our evolutionary past then we can predict that other extant primates will exhibit homologous responses. We might also predict that they are likely to share with us common proximate mechanisms for this state. McGuire, Raleigh and Troisi have uncovered evidence of a relationship between mood and status in vervet monkeys, which is mediated by the neurotransmitter serotonin. They discovered that alpha (highest-ranking) males in each group had levels of serotonin which were twice as high as in low-ranking subordinate males (Raleigh and McGuire, 1991). When such males lost their position, however, their serotonin levels fell dramatically (McGuire *et al.*, 1997). At the same time their behaviour altered. Whereas they had previously appeared 'confident' within their groups, they now huddled up and rocked back and forth refusing to eat. In fact their behaviour was remarkably similar to that of a seriously depressed human. Interestingly, these behaviours were removed when the monkeys were given the antidepressant Prozac (a selective serotonin reuptake inhibitor or SSRI) which boosts serotonin levels (McGuire *et al.*, 1997; McGuire and Troisi, 1998). And, incredibly, they also discovered that when the alpha male was removed from a group and another randomly chosen male was given Prozac, the latter became the new alpha male in every case!

The fact that in one of our primate relatives, the vervet monkey, there is a relationship between status, a neurotransmitter known to be involved in depression and an apparent depressive state adds weight to Price's social competition hypothesis in humans. Arguments about human internal states based on other species (even primates) are frequently criticised on the grounds that we are fundamentally different.

In this case, however, there is also supporting evidence from human studies of the relationship between status and serotonin and mood.

Machiavellians and moralists

Some studies of human social behaviour label males as either 'Machiavellians' who are relatively aggressive and competitive individuals or as 'moralists' who, in contrast, are more deferential. For Machiavellians social rank and serotonin levels are positively correlated, but for moralists there is a negative relationship between social rank and serotonin (Madsen, 1985; Madsen and McGuire, 1984). Put simply, in our own species, as in vervet monkeys, there is evidence that pushy high-status males have high levels of serotonin. Given that low levels of serotonin are known to be related to many cases of depression (Kring *et al.*, 2010) then this finding might be taken as further support for Price's social competition hypothesis. We need to bear in mind, however, that this evidence is indirect since the findings for Machiavellians and moralists were not concerned with levels of depression.

Currently the social competition hypothesis appears to have some experimental support and may help to explain many cases of depression in an evolutionary context. Perhaps one of the functions of serotonin is to mediate status hierarchies with low mood being an adaptive response to failure to gain status. The social competition hypothesis is unlikely to explain all cases of depression of course. It might even be criticised on the grounds that, with its emphasis on competition and status, it is a male-centred view of depression. Women do, however, also compete for status, albeit in a less overt way than men (Cashdan, 1996; Campbell, 2002; 2006). If the social competition hypothesis does help to provide insight into the ultimate cause of some forms of this debilitating illness then Darwinian medicine might help clinicians to identify potential cases of depression.

Is depression becoming more common?

It is a commonly held belief that depression is on the increase (see earlier). But does this notion stand up to scrutiny? The pooled data from nine different studies involving 39,000 people from five diverse areas of the world showed that in each area young people are more likely to suffer from major depression than previous generations (reported in Nesse and Williams, 1995). Furthermore, and perhaps counter-intuitively, rates of depression were found to be higher in the richer societies than in the poorer ones (WHO, 2008; Hidaka, 2012). So why is it that more of us, in the relatively comfortable and materially successful West, are becoming depressed? One way that evolutionary psychologists have explained this problem is by proposing that certain novel aspects of modern life, which would not have occurred in our ancestral past, currently increase the likelihood of depression. Two such novel aspects have been proposed by Nesse and Williams (1995) – mass communication and disintegration of communities.

One result of mass communication, according to Nesse and Williams, is that it effectively makes 'us all one competitive group'. This is particularly true of television and films, they argue, since, whereas in our ancestral past we would have compared ourselves with others in our relatively small forager group, today we constantly compare ourselves with images of the most successful on earth. If we are consistently bombarded with images of the rich, the beautiful and the talented then in comparison our own abilities pale into insignificance – so the argument goes. If our perceived status is based, as the social competition hypothesis would suggest, on how we view ourselves in comparison to others around us then this could lead to depression. Furthermore, we may also feel that our partners are less attractive when we compare them to such glamorous images, which may also make people feel dissatisfied and more prone to depression. This may be rather a speculative explanation for the rise in rates of depression over the last century but there is some empirical support for it. Evolutionary psychologist Douglas Kenrick found that if you expose individuals to photos of, or stories about, desirable potential mates they will thereafter decrease both their commitment to, and ratings of, their current partners (cited in Nesse and Williams, 1995). Perhaps mass communication helps to emphasise our lack of perfection and that of our partner when compared with the unrealistic images brought into our lives on a daily basis and this, in turn, leads to an increase in rates of depression.

With regard to disintegration of communities, Nesse and Williams suggest that in recent years '[e]xtended families disintegrate as individuals scatter to pursue their economic goals' (Nesse and Williams, 1995, p. 12). According to them the worst punishment that can be meted out to a human is to live in solitary confinement. And yet, because of the disintegration of the extended family (and even the nuclear family, often breaking down due to increased divorce rates), this is virtually what life is like for a growing number of people in the West. Again this idea is quite speculative – but it is certainly the case that marriage and close family ties can militate against depression (Kring *et al.*, 2010). However, the correlation between increased rates of depression and the increased break-up of the family unit does not prove that the latter has caused the former. One might argue the reverse or that other independent factors play a causal role in both.

Both of these ideas are attractive but both are a long way from being fully accepted as playing an important role in the recent rise in rates of depression. We should also bear in mind that at least part of the rise in reported rates of depression might be due to a rise in the awareness of the problem (Nolan-Hoeksema, 2007). It will be necessary for evolutionary psychologists to develop a means of testing such hypotheses more fully.

Box 12.4 Do women drive other women into a state of anorexia nervosa?

Given that both natural and sexual selection are considered to boost inclusive fitness, the fact that an estimated 10 per cent of young women in the developed world currently starve themselves into a state of emaciation (Steiger *et al.*, 2003) may appear to be quite a challenge for evolutionary psychology. The eating disorder known as **anorexia nervosa** is characterised by measures that control weight at a level at least 15 per cent below the healthy norm through dieting, use of laxatives and excessive exercise to burn off calories. It is also associated with a disturbed body image that leads to anxiety and depression over potential weight gain. This sounds an unlikely complaint for evolutionary psychology to address? Over the last thirty years, however, evolutionists have suggested a number of ways in which this behaviour might have arisen. Such explanations include the *reproduction suppression hypothesis* (Lozano, 2008) where females reduce their weight to avoid becoming pregnant (the menstrual cycle ceases when women lose substantial weight – a state known as **amenorrhea**) and the *parental manipulation hypothesis* where parents manipulate a female offspring in order that she shifts her reproductive investment from herself towards other siblings (i.e. it is maintained by kin selection; Voland and Voland, 1989). These explanations place the sufferer or her parents in a central causal role. Recently, however, evidence has accumulated that places a female's peers centre stage in the development of anorexia nervosa. First proposed by Abed in 1998, the *sexual competition hypothesis* is based on sexual selection and suggests that eating disorders are driven by high levels of female–female competition for the attention of potential partners. You may recall that sexual selection is concerned with gaining access to mates (see chapters 3 and 4). Given that fertility in females is associated with youthfulness and, given that youthfulness is associated with slimness, the sexual competition hypothesis suggests young women compete with each other for attention of potential mates by appearing to be youthfully slim. Although, at the time that it was proposed it was largely a theoretical explanation, a recent study by Abed and co-workers has demonstrated that in a sample of 206 young women those that displayed high levels of female–female competition were indeed also most likely to exhibit disordered eating behaviour (Abed *et al.*, 2012). Interestingly, this means that eating disorders might be driven by other competitive females (i.e. by intrasexual selection), a position that is in direct contrast to the commonly held feminist view that pressure from men leads to anorexia in women (Chernin, 1994).

Creativity – the function of mania?

The evolutionary models which suggest that low mood serves the general function of altering social behaviour in ways that may be adaptive (or would have been in the ancestral past) might help to explain unipolar depression but can they help to explain bipolar depression? Perhaps we need a different explanation for people who suffer from alternate periods of depression and mania.

One intriguing argument that has been proposed for manic depression suggests that there may be advantages associated with this illness. Psychiatrist Kay Redfield Jamison of Johns Hopkins University has proposed that manic depressive illness may have a genetic basis and that the genes predisposing a person to the illness also endow the sufferer with a compensatory advantage. This is a form of the pleiotropy argument that we outlined earlier. Jamison (1989; 1993; 1995; 2011) noticed that many famous artists, writers and musicians had a tendency to suffer from depression and mania, including William Blake, Lord Byron, Alfred Lord Tennyson, Sylvia Plath, Vincent van Gogh, Tennessee Williams and Robert Schumann. This led her to make a retrospective study of forty-seven distinguished British writers, painters and sculptors. In comparison to the 1 per cent of the general population that suffer from bipolar depression, Jamison found that an astonishing 38 per cent of her sample had been treated for bipolar depression. Jamison is not alone in this finding – other studies have confirmed this relationship between creativity and bipolar depression and have demonstrated that this problem runs in families (Ludwig, 1992; Jamison, 1995). Jamison uses an evolutionary argument to suggest that the energy, creativity and focus that accompany a manic state may have been of sufficient advantage that the individuals with the genes for such states were kept in a population because of the advantages they conferred on their ancestors. In support of her argument she was able to demonstrate that these famously talented people were most productive during manic or hypomanic states (Jamison, 1995). The depressive state that accompanies such creative periods may be seen as a pleiotropic effect of the gene (or genes) for this state. This argument may be thought of as the old 'mad genius' idea of exceptionally talented people also having psychiatric problems. This is rather a speculative argument and requires further testing. But if it does stand up to scrutiny then it could lead to a large practical dilemma for many talented people. That is, if bipolar artists are treated with drug therapy for their illness, might such treatment also tone down their creativity?

The downside of treatment

Darwinian medicine may help us to understand the ultimate causes of depression and anxiety but can it provide us with any guidelines so as to improve their treatment?

Figure 12.2 Lord Byron (1788–1824), one of many accomplished authors who have suffered from bipolar depression

There may be one unforeseen problem associated with a common practice in modern medicine. That is the widespread use of drugs such as Prozac to alleviate depression and anxiety. As health researcher Paul Martin, who is also a trained ethologist, has pointed out, if unpleasant states serve adaptive functions then suppressing these might be akin to suppressing coughs and fevers. In other words the immediate alleviation of the symptoms might lead to the problems ultimately lasting longer (Martin, 1997). Nesse and Williams have also considered this problem and further suggest that, if serotonin does play an important role in both status and depression, there might be problems in large hierarchical corporations if so many of their employees were taking antidepressants that boosted serotonin. It might be argued that, if lithium and antidepressants do help to even out the mood of bipolar people, such sufferers should also be made aware of the possible damping down of creative processes. Proponents of Darwinian medicine are not suggesting that, as with fever suppressants, antidepressants should never be prescribed but that we should be more aware of the potential drawbacks to their indiscriminate use (Andrews *et al.*, 2012). In the long run some sufferers might be better off if they allow these problems to run their natural course. However, in the case of suicidally depressed cases, then there is an argument for their short-term use.

Evolution-based therapy for depression: can knowledge of the EEA help us to solve the problem of depression?

Currently there is debate among evolutionary psychologists as to the degree to which depression is an adaptation (Watson and Andrews, 2002; Andrews and Thomson, 2009; Nettle, 2004; see also Toates, 2011). Whether it is adaptive or maladaptive we may still ask the question can evolutionary psychology help in treatment of this highly disabling problem? There is now evidence that it can. Evolutionist Stephen Ilardi and his co-workers have developed a fourteen-week six-step treatment regime for depression that is designed partially to mimic the conditions under which our Pleistocene ancestors lived. The regime includes increasing the amount of sunlight a sufferer receives each day while also boosting the amount of omega-3 fatty acid in the diet and adopting other measures such as spending more time with friends and family and in outdoor pursuits. Sleep patterns are also altered to be more in tune with ancestral habits. Remarkably Ilardi *et al.* (2007) were able to report a 75.3 per cent success rate for those undertaking the regime (compared with 22 per cent for a control sample). Such a success rate may be taken as evidence that one of the current causes of depression is the current mismatch between our lifestyle today and that under which our ancestors evolved (Ilardi, 2010).

Schizophrenia

Schizophrenia is arguably *the* most severe psychiatric illness and unfortunately is not uncommon. The World Health Organization (WHO) reported in 1992 that it affects between 1 and 1.5 per cent of the world's population – that's around 1 person in every 100 on earth today (Jablensky *et al.*, 1992). Most people will have met someone with schizophrenia; many will have a relative with the illness.

Schizophrenia literally means 'split-mind'. This split refers to a split in connections between cognitive, emotional and motivational processes and should not be confused with 'multiple personality disorder' – a rare problem where the sufferer behaves as if they have two or more separate personalities. People suffering from schizophrenia have a number of psychotic symptoms including hallucinations (usually auditory but also visual in some cases); delusions and disorders of affect (that is inappropriate emotional responses), and of thought (Kring *et al.*, 2010). The auditory hallucinations are usually voices which typically tell the sufferer to do things, or make comments about them. Frequently they hold bizarre beliefs, for example, that they are really another person such as a member of a royal family or even God, or that they are the centre of a sophisticated conspiracy. Many people with the illness are socially withdrawn and find it difficult to maintain relationships. In a sense the 'split' in schizophrenia is a split from reality. Schizophrenia is what many people colloquially

---

Table 12.2 **Changes to the classification of schizophrenia under DSM-5**

The Diagnostic and Statistical Manual of Mental Health, or DSM (produced by the American Psychiatric Association) is an international manual which is used by clinicians around the world to diagnose and classify mental disorders. In previous editions of the DSM schizophrenia was subdivided into five sub-types – 'disorganized' (incoherent speech), 'catatonic' (immobility and periods of excitement), 'paranoid' (suspicious and grandiose), 'undifferentiated' (a little of each of the others) and 'residual' (a lesser degree of symptoms). With the publication of the DSM-5 in May 2013 these sub-types were dropped due to the fact that there is a huge degree of overlap in symptoms between patients. Another problem is that sufferers of bipolar affective disorder can demonstrate many of these symptoms during manic periods. Today clinicians still look for these symptoms and many sufferers (but by no means all) may in theory be primarily associated with one of these categories. Technically, however, since 2013 to be diagnosed as having schizophrenia a sufferer must have one or more of the following symptoms for at least six months (including at least one month of active symptoms): delusions, hallucinations, disorganised speech and behaviour, and other symptoms that cause social or occupational dysfunction.

Source: Based on www.dsm5.org website

refer to as 'insanity' or 'madness' – but such terms have no place in the language of modern-day psychiatry and clinical psychology.

Like other health-related problems, clinicians distinguish between persons who have a chronic form of the illness (i.e. ongoing or recurrent) and acute (rapid onset but relatively short-lived and from which recovery is the usual outcome). Even in cases of chronic schizophrenia, however, there may be periods of relatively normal behaviour, or remission, when psychotic symptoms are either absent or much reduced. There are other schemes that have also been developed to distinguish between different forms of schizophrenia. One of the best known and most widely used of these is the American Psychiatric Association's Diagnostic and Statistical Manual, which is now in its fifth version – DSM-5 2013. Under previous editions of the DSM scheme there were five different sub-types of schizophrenia – disorganised, catatonic, paranoid, undifferentiated and residual. These have now been removed (see table 12.2).

Schizophrenia runs in families – so is it transmitted genetically?

It has long been recognised that schizophrenia tends to cluster in families. As table 12.3 demonstrates, genetic relatives of persons with schizophrenia are more likely to develop the illness than the general population. Furthermore, the closer the relationship (i.e. in terms of number of genes shared by common descent), the greater the likelihood of developing schizophrenia. The term **proband** refers to individuals

Table 12.3 **Summary of hereditary studies of schizophrenia**

Relation to proband	Percentage schizophrenic	Coefficient of relatedness (r)
Spouse	1.00	0.00
Grandchildren	2.84	0.25
Nieces/nephews	2.65	0.25
Children	9.35	0.50
Siblings	7.30	0.50
Dizygotic twins	12.08	0.50
Monozygotic twins	44.30	1.00

Source: Based on Gottesman *et al.* (1987)

in a genetics study who have the trait under investigation. Also remember that the coefficient of relatedness (r) refers to the proportion of genes shared between two individuals by common descent (see chapter 2).

When considering table 12.3 notice in particular that the spouse (not genetically related to the proband) is no more likely to develop schizophrenia than the rest of the general population. As the proportion of genes shared increases, however, so too does the probability of developing schizophrenia. Given the pattern uncovered here, it appears as if schizophrenia is largely genetically determined. There are, however, two problems with the 'all in the genes' argument. First, relatives who share the most genes are also likely to share much of their environment; and second, although the concordance rate is very high for monozygotic twins (who share 100 per cent of their genes), if it is purely hereditary then the rate should be 100 per cent. Despite these shortcomings it is clear that genes play a role in schizophrenia (the three- to fourfold increase in monozygotic when compared to dizygotic twins is the acid test here).

The diathesis–stress model

A diathesis means a predisposition towards developing an illness or abnormality (Kring *et al.*, 2010). The fact that schizophrenia runs in families but not in a perfect Mendelian manner has led many experts in the field to propose that some people may have a diathesis for the illness but that it will only be phenotypically expressed following stressful life events. This is known as the diathesis–stress model of schizophrenia (Kring *et al.*, 2010). It is certainly the case that the psychotic symptoms of schizophrenia tend to occur following stressful events in life. If we accept the diathesis–stress model then we can still use the term 'genes for schizophrenia'

Figure 12.3 All four of the identical girls known as the Genain quadruplets developed schizophrenia. The likelihood of this occurring due to chance alone is 1 in 2 billion. Such cases provide strong support for the argument that there is a genetic component in schizophrenia

provided we make it clear that such genes create a predisposition for the illness and do not make it inevitable. This might help to explain why many close relatives of sufferers (including identical twins) do not develop the illness themselves.

How do evolutionists explain schizophrenia?

Some clinicians who study the pathology of schizophrenia suggest that the illness is related to abnormalities of neurotransmitters such as dopamine or serotonin (Angrist *et al.*, 1974). Others propose that some form of brain atrophy is implicated (Chua and McKenna, 1995). Such explanations are important but do not tell us why the disorder is so common in our species. In recent years evolutionists have begun to propose ultimate explanations for the illness.

Schizophrenia is a difficult psychiatric problem for evolutionists to explain. Unlike anxiety and depression, the symptoms are not simply exaggerations of normal internal states, nor is there a straightforward relationship between the illness and positive traits such as creativity. In fact, due to their social problems, individuals with schizophrenia are at a procreative disadvantage which makes it all the more difficult to explain how there can be a genetic component to the illness (Kring *et al.*, 2010). A number of hypotheses have been suggested by evolutionists to explain why schizophrenia is maintained in the population. Three that have been proposed are the 'abnormal lateralisation of language', 'group-splitting' and the 'social brain' hypotheses. All three hypotheses suggest there may be compensatory advantages to having schizophrenia when viewed within an evolutionary framework.

Abnormal lateralisation of language hypothesis

Tim Crow, a psychiatrist from Oxford who has an interest both in neurology and in evolutionary theory, has suggested that schizophrenia is related to the evolution of lateralised language in our species. Lateralisation, you might recall, is the differential functioning of the left and right cerebral hemispheres (see chapter 11). Normal language lateralisation involves left hemisphere specialism during development (Hsiao and Man Lam, 2013). According to Crow (2005), while this lateralisation is maintained in our species because there are advantages to having an asymmetrically functioning brain, given just how complex this is in terms of **neurodevelopment**, for some people the pattern develops abnormally. For such people this leads to an inability to dissociate external voices from internal language. All of the symptoms of schizophrenia including paranoia and disordered thought then stem from this problem of language lateralisation. Hence for Crow schizophrenia is maintained in our species because the genes that lead to language development and functional brain asymmetry work well for the vast majority of us. Note this is not a group-level selection argument since Crow considers the genes that influence language lateralisation are passed on via close relatives that have managed to develop a normally functioning asymmetrical brain. Crow also suggests that the gene combinations implicated in schizophrenia when found in slightly different combinations (i.e. in the relatives of the sufferer) may then lead to high achievement in, for example, the arts. In this way the genes for schizophrenia may be maintained in our species.

Crow's hypothesis is supported indirectly by the finding that people with schizophrenia frequently have an atypical leftward shift in handedness distribution, that is, there are more left-handers than in the rest of the population (a sign of abnormal development of lateralisation). It should be borne in mind, however, that the vast majority of left-handed people do not develop schizophrenia.

A similar argument suggests that the phenotypic manifestation of the genes may have been different in the ancestral past when it conferred an advantage (or did not lead to a disadvantage). Some might argue that the novel stresses of modern life lead to the symptoms of schizophrenia today but would have led to some other phenotypic outcome in our past (an example of the mismatch hypothesis). The fact that the illness is also found in pre-industrial societies makes this argument less likely. Note that these latter suggestions are versions of the pleiotropy and the time lag arguments. Virtually all of the arguments proposed earlier to explain mental illnesses might be brought to bear on Crow's hypothesis. It will be necessary to find ways of devising tests that can distinguish between such hypotheses. Do relatives of people with schizophrenia have special abilities that we could measure for example? At present there is some evidence that the relatives of sufferers do have relatively high levels of accomplishment (Nesse and Williams, 1996). Such a finding is, however, a long way from verifying Crow's hypothesis.

Group-splitting hypothesis

Stevens and Price (2000) have suggested a novel evolutionary explanation for schizophrenia that they call the 'group-splitting' hypothesis. They propose that throughout recorded history many charismatic leaders from Adolf Hitler to David Koresh (leader of the Waco cult) may well have had schizophrenia. They claim that what we see today as a mental illness may be related to leadership which arises when members of a society become disaffected and look for a new leader who is going to suggest radical change. The group then splits off from society and follows the new radical leader. This means that in Stevens and Price's model the bizarre way of thinking and talking which reflects a very different world-view might be attractive to disaffected people looking to form a new society. In this way schizophrenia may be related to leadership which, with the associated raised status, might lead to increased mating opportunities and hence fitness benefits.

The group-splitting hypothesis is quite a radical notion but again, does it stand up to examination? It is certainly true that leaders such as Hitler, Stalin and, more recently, David Koresh did rise to positions of prominence among groups of disaffected people. Also Koresh, in particular, used his position to have sex with a large number of women – and thereby perhaps pass on genes related to his condition. If such circumstances happened regularly in our past then perhaps such a strategy might be adaptive. There are, however, three problems with this theory. The first is that only rarely in recorded history have disillusioned people followed a 'mad' charismatic leader like Hitler or Koresh making it unlikely that it is an adaptive strategy. Second, most people suffering from schizophrenia are not organised and coherent to the point of being able to form a cohesive group-splitting plan. Third and finally, we can't even be certain that any of these world leaders was suffering from schizophrenia – they may have been, but it would be very difficult to prove this. Stevens and Price might argue that in our ancient past group-splitting may have occurred on a more regular and local basis, which means that the state may have been adaptive during the EEA. It might also be argued that seriously disaffected people might not be in an ideal state of mind to make such decisions. Certainly, the writings and speeches of Hitler (or Koresh for that matter) are thoroughly unconvincing (and immoral) when examined today by anyone who is in a balanced state of mind. But their followers literally laid their lives down for such ramblings.

Social brain hypothesis

A third evolutionary argument of the existence of schizophrenia was proposed by Darwin-influenced South Africa psychologist Jonathan Burns in 2007. In *The Descent of Madness: Evolutionary Origins of Psychosis and the Social Brain* Burns proposed that, due to the intricacies of human social life where we constantly attribute internal meaning to the actions of others, we have evolved a brain of such complexity that in some cases neurodevelopment that underlies social cognition does not proceed properly. This has the knock-on effect of over-interpretation by some and, this in turn, leads to psychotic symptoms. In common with Crow, Burns sees schizophrenia as a secondary consequence of having a very complex brain but his argument differs in that it relates the illness not specifically to language lateralisation but to interpreting complex social behaviour.

Burns's proposal, like Crow's, is both speculative but, up to a point, compelling. Given that the human brain is the most complex entity that we are aware of in the universe, perhaps the neural circuitry underlying social cognition has pushed the mammalian brain to a point where for some people having the wrong combination of genes can lead them down the path of mental illness. As with Crow's proposal, however, the social brain hypothesis is not without problems. One problem is that, since sufferers often report hearing voices when alone, schizophrenia affects people outside of social settings. A potentially larger problem with this (and the other two evolutionary hypotheses outlined above) is that today many experts see schizophrenia as a cluster of different mental illnesses that have been grouped together due to some degree of overlap in symptomology rather than a single illness with a single cause (Kring *et al.*, 2010). In fact one extreme, yet quite commonly held view is that the 'illness' we label 'schizophrenia' does not exist at all, but that the symptoms are an extreme example of normal human internal experiences (Bentall, 2003).

Might paranoia be adaptive?

The 'abnormal lateralisation of language', 'group-splitting' and the 'social brain' hypotheses are not the only ones that have been proposed to explain schizophrenia within an evolutionary framework. One further theory proposes that the genes involved in the development of 'suspiciousness' may also have had positive effects in that they would have endowed the individual with a lowered susceptibility to freeriders (Nesse and Williams, 1995). Certainly people with paranoid schizophrenia are very suspicious and might well spot freeriders. The only problem with this explanation is that it is frequently difficult to convince people with schizophrenia that genuine friends really do care about their welfare. Another explanation suggests that schizophrenia is a form of autoimmune disorder whereby the body's own immune system attacks the brain, in which case the illness is a result of the pathogen–host arms race discussed earlier (Martin, 1997). Again, like the hypotheses discussed above, such explanations are quite speculative.

Genes underlying schizophrenia?

If schizophrenia has been maintained in *Homo sapiens* by Darwinian natural selection, then it has to be related to the genes we carry that code for brain development (see table 12.3). In 2007 an international team of Crespi, Summers and Dorus, after analysing the DNA from a series of human populations, identified twenty-eight genes that make individuals susceptible to the disorder. Crespi *et al.* (2007) suggest that having various combinations of these genes may well promote linguistic skill and creativity, but that having most or all of them leads to schizophrenia. Hence these genes might be maintained in the population because they provide people with advantages such as high levels of creativity but having too many of them might make a person susceptible to schizophrenia. Interestingly, this explanation fits in quite well with both the social brain and the abnormal lateralisation hypotheses (and perhaps even the group-splitting hypothesis). Perhaps these ideas for the evolution of schizophrenia are not mutually exclusive explanations but rather approaches that address the problem from different angles.

Evolutionary explanations that either view schizophrenia as an adaptation to a previous age or that suggest the genes associated with it may currently provide compensatory advantages either to the sufferer or to their relatives are not entirely convincing or well accepted at present (Brüne, 2004). As a problem that shows remarkable uniformity of both incidence rates and symptomology around the globe, however, explanations that ignore ultimate causation may well miss an opportunity to develop a unifying theory of the existence and maintenance of this most serious psychological illness.

Personality disorders

A personality disorder does not normally involve psychotic symptoms such as hearing voices or believing that you are a deity. Rather, personality disorders are 'longstanding, pervasive, and inflexible patterns of behaviour and inner experience that deviate from the expectations of a person's culture and that impair social and occupational functioning' (Kring *et al.*, 2010). To use a rather outdated term, people with personality disorders are neurotic rather than psychotic.

Table 12.4 Personality disorder clusters according to DSM-5

Cluster	Specific personality disorder
Odd/eccentric	Paranoid – intense suspicion of others, frequently hostile, often a high level of sexual jealousy.
	Schizoid – lack of warm feelings to others, indifferent, socially withdrawn, similar to residual schizophrenia.
	Schizotypal – serious interpersonal difficulties, odd beliefs including e.g. belief in magical events.
Dramatic/erratic	Borderline – impulsive, particularly in relationships, erratic emotions, argumentative and unpredictable.
	Histrionic – great show of emotions, but in reality emotionally shallow.
	Narcissistic – overblown view of own abilities, highly self-centred, lack of empathy, opinionated.
	Antisocial – highly dishonest, destructive, manipulative, irresponsible and in many cases aggressive.
Anxious/fearful	Avoidant – oversensitive to criticism, highly anxious in social circumstances.
	Dependent – lacks both a sense of self-confidence and of autonomy, highly dependent on partner.
	Obsessive–compulsive – preoccupied with rules and details, tend to be work orientated but poor at completing projects due to drive for perfection; often called a 'control-freak' due to inability to give up control.

In contrast to schizophrenia, personality disorders may be more easily explained when viewed from an evolutionary standpoint, in part because they may be thought of as forms of thought and behaviour which many of us frequently exhibit, but taken to an extreme. DSM-5 recognises ten personality disorders which form three clusters – odd/eccentric, dramatic/erratic and anxious/fearful (see table 12.4).

Can evolutionary psychology explain personality disorders?

Looking at table 12.4, it is clear that people with personality disorders have certain features in common. They are frequently self-absorbed, and highly anxious. They may be unreliable and difficult. In short they do not make for ideal partners. Psychiatry today considers personality disorders as enduring abnormalities that people have in their dealings with others and with life in general. Such a view would suggest that people who have personality disorders are behaving in a maladaptive way. But are they? Psychologists trained in evolutionary theory are beginning to question this assumption – perhaps some forms of 'personality disorder' would have been adaptive in our ancestral past. Perhaps others would not have been adaptive but are an outcome of the mismatch between genes adapted for earlier conditions and today's environment. It may also be the case that genes associated with such disorders code for other, fitness enhancing, features. Note that these are forms of the *time lag*, *compromise* and *pleiotropy* arguments introduced earlier on in this chapter. As in the case of the problems discussed earlier, some of these arguments have been proposed to explain certain types of personality disorder. In particular, evolutionists Michael McGuire and Alfonso Troisi have suggested that some disorders might be adaptive while others may be viewed as impaired attempts to act adaptively (McGuire and Troisi, 1998; Troisi and McGuire, 2000). Their arguments are best illustrated by examining specific personality disorders – in particular we consider in some detail two disorders which may involve an excessive degree of social defection – antisocial and histrionic personality disorders.

Antisocial personality disorder – are psychopaths using an adaptive strategy?

Although some experts have argued that the terms 'psychopath' and 'sociopath' form a subdivision of the category antisocial personality disorder (Rutherford *et al.*, 1999), the terms are generally used as synonyms today. Here we use the terms psychopathy and antisocial personality disorder (APD) as referring to the same serious personality problem. Psychopaths are characterised by a lack of empathy, a callous approach to the suffering of others and a general disregard for their rights. They frequently exploit others without feelings of guilt or shame. They tend to have low levels of anxiety and seek novelty and instant gratification. Imagine being offered £100 now or £200 if you are prepared to wait for a year. Which would you choose? Unaffected adults generally choose to wait a year and make 100 per cent profit. Psychopaths choose the £100 now. In a sense their moral behaviour may be likened to that of an average 2-year-old in being very self-centred and unable to wait for gratification. However, unlike a 2-year-old, as adults they may develop subtle ways of achieving their aims via charm or deflecting blame onto others.

Could such self-centred behaviour possibly be adaptive? You might recall from chapters 2 and 8 that evolutionary psychologists consider much of our social behaviour as based around acts of reciprocation (Trivers, 1972; 1985). Aiding others in the expectation (conscious or otherwise) that such aid will be reciprocated, however, might allow for the evolution of non-reciprocating freeriders. Perhaps psychopathic exploitation is an evolved alternative strategy to reciprocation. Such an argument for persons with APD has been considered by a number of evolutionists (Mealey, 1995; 2005; McGuire *et al.*, 1997; Glenn *et al.*, 2011) but is particularly associated with McGuire and Troisi (1998). It is certainly the case that non-reciprocation is a primary feature of psychopaths (Mealey, 1995). For such a model to work, however, it needs to meet two minimum requirements. First, it is necessary that there is a genetic component to the 'disorder', and second it is necessary that the majority of people in a population are reciprocators. This second point is important because, if there is a sizeable proportion of freeriders in a population then it may not pay to be a reciprocator and the whole system breaks down. Is there any evidence that the criteria are fulfilled?

It is certainly the case that monozygotic twins show a significantly higher concordance rate for APD than dizygotic twins (Lyons *et al.*, 1995). Additionally, adoption studies reveal higher instances of psychopathy than would be expected by chance in the adopted children of biological parents with the condition (Ge *et al.*, 1996). Finally, the risk of developing the disorder is increased fivefold for first degree male relatives of psychopaths (Plomin *et al.*, 2008). All of these findings suggest that there is at least a genetic component to psychopathy. In terms of prevalence, many experts today consider around 3 per cent of adult males and 1 per cent of adult females may have the disorder (Kring *et al.*, 2010). This means that about one person in fifty is considered to be suffering from the disorder. In the words of McGuire and Troisi:

In a society made up primarily of reciprocators, genes for cheaters can enter the population and remain, provided persons with such genes reproduce. (1998, p. 191)

Also, in support of the evolved cheater strategy hypothesis, they suggest that the greater prevalence of psychopathy among males may be a result of 'selection favoring stronger migratory tendencies among males than among females'. In other words, freeriding may be a better strategy for males than females because by moving from group to group more frequently they are less likely to be detected. Finally, it has been assessed that around 50 per cent of psychopaths currently remain undiagnosed (i.e. 'detected'), which might suggest that it is a successful strategy for many.

Balancing and shifting theories of psychopaths

Building on the ideas of McGuire and Troisi in recent years two main theories have developed out of the original evolved cheater strategy notion. The **balancing theory** suggests that selection pressures from the social environment lead to different levels of a trait being observed (Buss, 2009; Glenn *et al.*, 2011). This means that some individuals that have the potential to develop psychopathic traits might boost inclusive fitness by doing so in some environmental circumstances. Examples of such circumstances might be when individuals with this potential find themselves in, for example, large densely populated cities. Under such circumstances engaging in exploitive behaviour is more likely to succeed due to the reduced chances of face-to-face encounters with the exploitee. In smaller, more intimate social settings the balancing theory would predict that psychopaths will be less common. Note that, while this sounds like a social theory of psychopathology it does depend on individuals having a genetic predisposition to APD which is then released by environmental input and can therefore be labelled a bio-social interactionist view. The balancing theory suggests that there may be genes that some people inherit that produce a diathesis which is then phenotypically expressed under the right (or wrong) environmental conditions. If, for example, a boy with the predisposition to psychopathy finds himself in a society where people succeed by being selfish and unfeeling, then he may develop into a psychopath. A more caring and intimate society might have led to a different phenotypic outcome.

The **contingent shift theory** is similar to the balancing theory, in as much as it also suggests individuals may have a range of environmentally conditional strategies that can lead to APD under the right (or wrong) circumstances (Ward and Durrant, 2011). It differs however in that it suggests that all individuals may have the propensity to develop psychopathy given the (in)appropriate circumstances (the balancing theory suggests that, due to specific genes, only a minority within the population will be capable of developing psychopathic strategies). Under the contingent shift theory *everybody* has the potential to develop APD since we have all inherited modules that may be calibrated by an adverse social environment to release callous and manipulative behaviour. In support of this Gao *et al.* (2010) uncovered a strong relationship between childhood abuse and later psychopathic behaviour.

We can see that there is circumstantial evidence supporting the notion that psychopathy is an evolved strategy. Such evidence is currently far from conclusive, however. As we can see one potential problem arises from the fact that, although many evolutionary psychologists agree that there is a genetic component to the disorder, the same authorities disagree over how the environmental–genetic interaction operates and the proportion of the population that might be expected to develop the disorder. It is certainly the case that high levels of conflict and criticism combined with low levels of parental warmth have been related to the development of the disorder (Ge *et al.*, 1996; Gao *et al.*, 2010). Such findings, however, do not provide conclusive evidence that it is an evolved strategy (and may even be taken as evidence that it is socially endowed).

The debate is also complicated by the suggestion of evolutionist Linda Mealey that there may be two fundamental forms of psychopathy, one of which is largely inherited and may be independent of environmental circumstances and another form which appears only when a person perceives themselves as socially disadvantaged (Mealey, 1995; 2005; see also chapter 13). Unravelling how this notion fits in with the theories presented above is unlikely to be an easy task. Given however the relatively high rate of this disorder cross-culturally, explanations that exclude ultimate causation are likely to be incomplete.

Histrionic personality disorder

A person with histrionic personality disorder (HPD) tends to be an attention-seeking, self-centred individual who is obsessively concerned with their appearance. Such people tend also to be overly dramatic in their actions and may engage in fantasy. They are frequently seductive in nature and make a great show of their feelings. In reality, however, they are generally emotionally shallow. Although they differ somewhat from psychopaths, people with histrionic personality disorder are also prone to social defection (i.e. a lack of reciprocation). Also, like psychopaths, the diagnosis has a prevalence rating of around 3 per cent but with females more frequently represented than males. Like APD, HPD appears to run in families, again suggesting a genetic basis (Coryell, 1980). According to McGuire and Troisi, histrionics may well be successful by evolutionary criteria in that they frequently 'acquire mates, marry, have children, command resources, and invest in kin' (McGuire and Troisi, 1998, p. 193). How they manage to avoid reciprocation appears to be via bouts of feigned illness – they are frequently characterised as hypochondriacs. Despite their shallow nature, histrionic individuals tend not to show the levels of aggression that are often associated with psychopaths.

In addition to APD and HPD, McGuire and Troisi also consider persons with attention deficit/hyperactivity disorder (ADHD) and 'malingerers' as potential non-reciprocation strategists. Although neither category forms a discrete type under DSM-5, both feature in a number of personality disorders. Under their scheme, at least some personality disorders might be adaptive strategies which may be akin to parasitic microbes in their exploitation of the normal human condition.

One of the most interesting findings about people with these exploitative personality disorders is not their behaviour but the internal states they report. What stop most of us from exploiting our friends are the feelings of guilt and shame that would follow such a lack of reciprocation. Some evolutionists have even argued that such feelings are adaptive precisely because they drive us against committing antisocial acts which, in the long run, might exclude us from reciprocation circles (Wright, 1994). People with APD, HPD, ADHD and malingerers do not appear to have the same depth of feelings of shame, remorse and empathy – in fact in the case of psychopaths they may lack these feelings completely.

Other personality disorders – social navigation with a leg in plaster

Even if we were to accept uncritically that the aforementioned disorders are adaptive, there are others for which it would be difficult to defend such an argument. It is certainly difficult to see borderline, narcissistic and paranoid personality disorders as adaptive strategies. For these, however, McGuire and Troisi have another card up their sleeve. They suggest we should view such disorders as attempts to act adaptively.

> ## Box 12.5 Why aren't we all psychopaths?
>
> If these personality disorders are successful by evolutionary criteria then we might ask why we aren't all freeriders. There are probably two answers to this. First, selection pressures may well lead to the strategy being successful when it appears at a low rate – that is, it may be the result of frequency dependent selection with selection forces countering the strategy when too many in the population use it (discussed further in chapter 13). And second, although 50 per cent of psychopaths may remain undetected, this means that 50 per cent are detected. Note that this suggests psychopathy, in game theory terms, might be an evolutionarily stable strategy (ESS – see chapter 2). As Robert Trivers has suggested, the moment that reciprocal altruism began to evolve as a social strategy then the possibility of cheating the system also arose – this, in turn, would lead to selection pressures favouring the ability to spot cheats. If we have evolved to be vigilant with regard to freeriders then the strategy may be both a risky and a condition-dependent one.

This does not mean that the individuals concerned are consciously aware that they are attempting to behave adaptively, merely that, finding themselves with serious problems, they make the best of a bad situation – in terms of 'social navigation'. In the words of McGuire and Troisi:

[T]hese disorders can be likened to the circumstances of a person who has a cast on one leg and is trying to cross the street rapidly in the face of oncoming vehicles. This person hops, jumps, and even crawls if necessary, and it is this behaviour that is adaptive. (1998, p. 196)

The personality disorders that McGuire and Troisi consider as attempts to act adaptively include borderline, narcissistic, paranoid, avoidant and dependent (see table 12.4). According to McGuire and Troisi (1998) people with such disorders demonstrate a limited capacity 'to read others' behaviour rules, to develop novel behaviour strategies, and to efficiently utilise self-monitoring information'. Such people frequently form unstable relationships and have inappropriately intense mood swings. Despite such problems, in the view of McGuire and Troisi, individuals with these disorders do attempt to achieve relatively normal goals. They try to form relationships and attempt to gain resources, for example. How they go about these aims is where they differ from others, since they may require, for example, unnaturally high levels of reassurance or may be unduly suspicious or even hostile.

According to McGuire and Troisi, the behavioural responses that we observe in people suffering from these disorders of thought and emotion are their way of dealing with their deficits. It might be argued that such an explanation does not require an evolutionary level of analysis and once again it has to be said that such an explanation is currently rather tentative. We also need to know why such disorders arise and why they are maintained within human populations. McGuire and Troisi suggest that people with these disorders may be at the extremes of natural trait variation. Another possibility, however, is that the genes which make such conditions likely to develop may be adaptive when found in combination with other genes, or that there may be other benefits associated with them – that is the pleiotropy or indirect benefit hypothesis. The fact that these disorders also tend to cluster in families again lends some support to such arguments.

The arguments that some personality disorders are adaptations remains largely to be tested, however. As McGuire and Troisi have pointed out, there is no evidence that people with these conditions have fewer offspring than persons without. They also point out that this is true of many other problems involving abnormal states of mind such as bipolar affective disorder. This may be a rude reminder that selection forces do not operate to make our lives happier or more comfortable but simply to boost our inclusive fitness.

Evolution and illness – explanation or speculation?

Alongside evolutionists such as Randolph Nesse and the late George Williams, Michael McGuire and Alfonso Troisi are strong proponents of the view that evolutionary theory should be applied to explaining both normal *and* abnormal behaviour. They propose that many abnormal conditions may ultimately either be found to be adaptive in the context in which they occur or should be seen as attempts to make the best of suboptimal circumstances (McGuire and Troisi, 1998; Troisi and McGuire, 2000). This ultimate level of analysis might prove to be a powerful tool when attempting to explain some psychiatric states. That is, the pleiotropy, time lag, compromise and trait variation explanations developed by evolutionists might help to elucidate many physical and psychological problems found in our species. However, even if this should prove to be the case we must be careful not to fall into the trap of assuming, because we can explain some health-related problems in this way, that the ultimate level of analysis will explain all of them. All of behaviour must have proximate causes – but it does not have to have ultimate causes. Sometimes, for a myriad of reasons, human physiological systems become dysfunctional. Sometimes in humans, things just go wrong.

As we have emphasised throughout this chapter, many of the ideas in Darwinian medicine are currently speculative. However, it is a new approach and this is not unusual at this stage of early development. Moreover, evolutionists are beginning to test hypotheses concerning Darwinian medicine. Thus far, there are clear signs of successes with regard to some physical, health-related, problems. Margie Profit's work on morning sickness, for instance, is an example of a parsimonious use of evolutionary theory to explain as an adaptation what had previously been considered as a functionless by-product of the state of pregnancy. So far, it has been less successful in explaining mental health problems – but then so has conventional medicine. The challenge for Darwinian medicine now is to formulate and test predictions concerning psychiatric illness and personality disorders.

Summary

- Evolutionary psychopathology, evolutionary medicine and Darwinian medicine are concerned with understanding physical and mental health-related disorders through evolutionary principles.
- The symptoms caused by microbial parasites such as viruses, bacteria, fungi and protozoa can be viewed as adaptations either of the pathogen to aid its multiplication or of the host in order to kill off or expel it. An understanding of which symptoms are designed to destroy the pathogen and which are designed to spread it might inform treatment of infectious diseases. The relationship between host and parasite has been portrayed as an evolutionary arms race of adaptation and counter-adaptation.
- Evolutionary explanations for current-day physical and mental symptoms include the notion that our bodies and minds are adapted to the pressures of a stone-age existence but are living under modern-day conditions – the time lag or mismatch argument. Other explanations include the idea that genes which cause illness might also have positive facets associated with them – the pleiotropy argument; that selection pressures act on increasing inclusive fitness, not on perfecting systems – the compromise argument; and that disorders might be viewed as the extremes of normal variation – the trait variation argument.
- Some evolutionary psychologists have suggested that the propensity to feel high levels of anxiety may be an adaptation that helped our ancestors to survive dangerous situations. They argue that the costs of being a little too anxious may well have been small when compared to the costs of not being sufficiently anxious – the 'smoke detector principle'.
- Affective disorders involve serious pervasive problems associated with depression or mania. In unipolar disorder a sufferer has periods of serious depression while in bipolar disorder there are alternating bouts of depression and elevated mood (mania, or in a lesser form – hypomania). It has been proposed that unipolar depression may be a result of a fall in status and that the associated withdrawal from social life might have been an adaptive reaction in our ancestral past. Bipolar depression is associated with creativity in numerous individuals – it has been proposed that the

genes related to this condition are kept in the population because of the advantages associated with the manic state.

- Rising rates of depression may be related to increases in mass communication which constantly show us highly successful individuals and may lead to a lowering of the perception of our own abilities. Another way of explaining rising rates of depression is the break-up of traditional family and community units.
- Schizophrenia, the most serious of mental illnesses, affects at least 1 per cent of the world's population. Symptoms include auditory hallucinations, bizarre false beliefs, paranoia, inappropriate emotional response and social withdrawal. There is strong evidence that schizophrenia runs in families, suggesting a genetic component. Rates of schizophrenia, however, do not follow simple Mendelian ratios, suggesting an environmental component. Evolutionists have suggested a number of explanations for schizophrenia including the notion that, with the evolution of language, the ensuing pattern of cerebral lateralisation may be open to disruption. Another evolutionary-based explanation is that highly original charismatic figures suffering from schizophrenia might be reproductively successful when they come to lead newly formed groups of people. Finally, there may be a relationship between having a highly complex 'social brain' and the evolution of schizophrenia.
- Personality disorders involve abnormal and inflexible patterns of inner states and external responses. In particular, antisocial and histrionic personality disorders involve self-serving behaviour patterns and a general lack of reciprocation of aid – freeloading. Evolutionists have suggested that a state of mind that leads to non-reciprocation might constitute an adaptive strategy in a species where a high level of reciprocal altruism is the norm.

Questions

1. Randolph Nesse has argued that in order to understand why mental illness is so prevalent in our species we need to study the relatives of people with such problems. What exactly is Nesse suggesting here?
2. Richard Bentall (2003) has suggested that schizophrenia is not a mental illness but rather an extreme of normal functioning. If Bentall were proved to be correct how would this affect the theories that schizophrenia is maintained in the population due to evolutionary processes as discussed in the chapter?
3. In the chapter it was suggested that evolutionary theory can be used to help explain antisocial personality disorder and histrionic personality disorder. How might evolutionary psychology be used to help explain problems with 'perfectionism'?
4. Can you think of any illnesses where an evolutionary-based explanation is unlikely to aid our understanding?

FURTHER READING

Brüne, M. (2008). *Textbook of Evolutionary Psychiatry. The Origins of Psychopathology.* Oxford: Oxford University Press. Explores why some people are more vulnerable to psychiatric illness such as anorexia and depression than others by considering the relationship between evolutionary processes and brain development. Suggests ways in which psychiatry can be improved through integration of evolutionary theory.

Gluckman, P. and Hanson, M. (2008). *Mismatch: The Lifestyle Diseases Timebomb.* Oxford: Oxford University Press. Two leading medical scientists argue that the mismatch between the environment of our evolutionary past and our current lifestyle leads to many problems both physical and psychological in this highly engaging textbook.

Horwitz, A., and Wakefield, J. C. (2007). *The Loss of Sadness: How Psychiatry Transformed Normal Sorrow Into Depressive Disorder.* Oxford: Oxford University Press. Argues that diagnoses of mood disorders are actually a mixture of appropriate responses to life events and cases where neurobiological systems have become dysregulated. The challenge for evolutionary psychiatry will be to determine where we draw the line between these forms of explanation.

Nesse, R. M. and Williams, G. C. (1995). *Evolution and Healing: The New Science of Darwinian Medicine.* London: Weidenfeld and Nicolson. The clarion cry for the application of the evolutionary approach to illness both mental and physical from two of its main proponents.

13 Evolution and individual differences

KEY CONCEPTS

personality • niche fitting • heritability • frequency dependent selection • intelligence • general intelligence (g) • multiple intelligences

A great deal of research in psychology has focused on differences among individuals. Psychologists have been particularly interested in individual differences in personality and intelligence, investigating the underlying causes of these differences and how they might affect other aspects of life such as career development, success in relationships and susceptibility to mental illness. Evolutionary psychology with its focus on ultimate questions asks a different question. What is the function, if any, of individual differences? Why, for example, are some people sensation-seeking extraverts while others are timid stay-at-home introverts? Why are some people smart and others less so? One answer could be that these characteristics reflect differences in upbringing; that they are the result of environmental rather than genetic differences. Intelligent individuals were given more educational opportunities than less intelligent individuals; extraverts were encouraged to be bold and so on. But this cannot be the whole story. Research has shown that many of these traits are heritable, suggesting that at least some of the variation in the aforementioned characteristics is down to the effects of genes. But this poses another problem. We know that natural selection promotes certain genes over others by virtue of their superior phenotypic effects, thereby reducing genetic variability in a species, so why haven't all of these genetic differences been removed from the gene pool? Is there some hidden benefit in having variability in personality and intelligence within our species? This chapter focuses on these (and other) questions, and in doing so it draws on material covered in previous chapters and points the way to the future of evolutionary psychology; an evolutionary psychology that views genes as dynamic, shaping the phenotype using decision rules that act upon environmental information.

Individual differences and evolution

It is obvious to anyone that people differ from one another. For example, people growing up in France will usually speak French and people growing up in China will tend to speak one of the Chinese languages such as Cantonese or Mandarin, and they will do this regardless of their genetic makeup (see chapter 10). The same applies to cultural practices, which vary widely across the world (see chapter 14). But when psychologists speak of individual differences they usually mean something more specific than these differences, they are usually referring to differences in intelligence and personality. There is a great deal of evidence that people exhibit differences in personality and intelligence that are stable over time and across different contexts (Cooper, 2012; Larsen and Buss, 2009). One might ask whether an evolutionary theory of individual differences is really necessary – might differences in personality and intelligence be just due to environmental differences like the cultural and linguistic variability pointed out above?

One reason why evolution might be important is that, as we saw in chapter 6, there is a considerable body of research indicating that many personality factors are to some extent heritable (usually between about 0.3 and 0.5 on a scale from 0–1) and intelligence has heritability coefficients of 0.4–0.7 (Loehlin *et al.*, 1998; Plomin *et al.*, 2008). The existence of moderate heritability coefficients suggests individual differences are at least partly due to genetic differences. This being the case it suggests that there is some benefit – in terms of inclusive fitness – to having variability in our offspring because, as we saw in chapter 2, disadvantageous phenotypes tend to be selected out of the population.

There is a potential paradox here. Much of this book has made the claim that selection pressures in the environment of evolutionary adaptation (EEA) led to the evolution of a human nature that was designed to solve the problems encountered by our hunter-gatherer ancestors (see Cosmides and Tooby, 1992; Pinker, 1997; Causey and Bjorklund, 2011). If this is the case then should we not by now all have the same personality and the same intellectual ability (barring brain damage and other unforeseen circumstances)? Does not the very existence of individual differences (particularly those that are apparently genetic in origin) completely undermine the notion of an evolved human nature that evolutionists such as Cosmides and Tooby have worked so hard to promote? No. Such a contention represents a misunderstanding of the very idea of a human nature. There are two possibilities that reconcile the apparent contradiction between the claim of an evolved human nature and the data on individual differences, and these are detailed below.

Individual differences make little difference as far as inclusive fitness is concerned and are therefore invisible to natural selection. Here it is suggested that we as humans tend to overemphasise the magnitude of the differences among us: a Martian studying our species might see us all as pretty much identical (barring gross differences such as sex). Thus there are no inclusive fitness benefits of tending towards one personality rather than another, or being more or less intelligent (within reason). Naturally, having a profoundly different personality (for example, having a personality disorder, such as psychopathy – see later and chapter 12) or having an abnormally low IQ might make a difference, but for the majority there will be little effect on fitness. In a sense this variability may be thought of as 'noise' in the system.

There is no single, globally optimal 'human nature'. Doubtless many of the problems faced by our ancestors had just one best solution. For example, having colour vision is better than not having colour vision; being wary of strangers is – for a child – better than treating them with equanimity; being on the look-out for potential cheats is more useful than checking for altruists (see chapter 9). In such cases it is easy to see how certain aspects of our nature might have become 'fixed'. There are many other problems, however, where the best solution (in terms of inclusive fitness) is less clear. Is it better to be bold and venturesome or cautious and considered; to be unremittingly selfish or to be generous with non-kin; to be good at understanding people or good at making tools? Each of the above might be a thoroughly adaptive way of behaving depending on the nature of the environment and what other members of your group are doing. This last point is important, as we shall see later; it might be in your own interests to behave somewhat differently from other members of your group, to exploit opportunities missed by others. Two such approaches that we discuss later are **niche fitting** and **frequency dependent selection**. Before we begin to discuss in more detail potential ways of resolving the above paradox, we first need to describe in a little more detail the nature of individual differences. We begin with personality.

Individual differences in personality

What is personality?

To understand personality, we need to make a distinction between **psychological states** and **psychological traits**. Suppose that a person behaves in a particular way, for example on a single observation that she becomes angry rather quickly. If she behaves in a similar way at different times and over different situations we might conclude that being quick to anger is part of her psychological makeup, known technically as a psychological trait. On the other hand, if this behaviour shows no temporal and situational consistency, then we might conclude it is merely a transient mood, technically known as a psychological state. Evidence for state dependency might be increased if there were some precipitating circumstances, for example the person was under stress. Differences in psychological traits (personality) can be thought of as differences in what people are motivated to do or how

Box 13.1 **How is personality measured?**

Personality is measured by personality tests, which are self-report tests that usually require the participant to respond to a set of questions relating to the specific aspect of personality under question. For example, if we are interested in measuring extraversion we might ask participants, questions such as: 'Do you usually stay in the background at social occasions?' (YES/NO), or they might be asked, 'Are you a worrier?' in order for their level of neuroticism to be determined. After completing a number of such questions the participant is given a score that records, for example, how extravert or neurotic he or she is. These questions are the result of extensive testing to determine whether they predict behaviour – whether they are a *valid* measure of personality (for example, do people who are categorised as extraverts using these measures really behave in an extravert manner (Cooper, 2012; Schultz and Schultz, 2005) and whether they are *reliable* (for example, if people complete the tests more than once is their personality measure the same in each case?). Here are some examples from a self-report personality questionnaire (in reality there are usually over 100 questions) that are designed to uncover how anxious/relaxed, extravert/introvert or friendly/unfriendly a person you are:

1. Are you outgoing?   YES NO
2. Does meeting new people make you happy?   YES NO
3. Do you have regular concerns about your health?   YES NO
4. Would it make you happy to have others fear you?   YES NO
5. Do you lose sleep at times due to work-related worries?   YES NO
6. Do you feel good when you hurt someone you love?   YES NO

Clearly such tests rely on honest answers. Many of these tests have 'lie detector' questions – if more than one or two of such questions are answered the 'wrong way' then the tester discounts the scores as unreliable. Such lie detector questions are ones that only 'a saint' would give a particular answer to such as:

7. Have you ever laughed at a dirty joke?   YES NO

they respond to a particular state of affairs. Sociable people, for example, are motivated to seek out socially challenging situations, shy people to avoid them; neurotic people might become anxious in stressful situations and hence tend to avoid them, more laid back people might cope better in such situations. From an evolutionary point of view we might think of personality as a behavioural strategy; a tendency to respond in specific ways to particular circumstances. Personality tests usually measure 'traits' (or sometimes 'factors' – see later) – that is, enduring facets of a personality such as how 'outgoing' or 'liberal' a person is rather than states (Schultz and Schultz, 2005).

How many personality traits are there?

In the 1930s psychologist Gordon Allport (Allport and Odbert, 1936) determined that the English dictionary contained no fewer than 17,953 different words for personality traits, but this does not necessarily mean that there are this many different personality traits. Many of the words are close synonyms (e.g. outgoing, gregarious, sociable, extravert) whereas some are antonyms (e.g. outgoing vs. shy, assertive vs. passive, anxious vs. calm). So it is certainly possible to reduce the thousands of words to substantially fewer (perhaps a hundred or so) personality traits. But this is still too many to be useful. One way of reducing them still further is to look for latent patterns in the still-large set of words. For example 'gregariousness' and 'assertiveness' might not be synonymous but they might be somewhat related to each other in the sense that someone who tended to be gregarious might also tend towards being assertive, i.e. the two traits were positively correlated.

The technical method of reducing a vast number of potential traits to a manageable few is known as factor analysis. A detailed explanation of how this works is beyond the scope of this book, but here is an overview of the process. We begin by presenting a group of participants with a large number of questions relating to personality (such as those above). We then look for intercorrelations between the responses to these questions. Any answers to questions that are highly correlated with each other can be collapsed together to form a more inclusive personality trait (e.g. shyness, aggressiveness, gregariousness, impulsivity). We could simply stop there, but we can also carry on by factor analysing these inclusive traits to find still higher-order personality clusters. To do this we look for correlations between the traits; again if the correlation is sufficiently high we can collapse the correlated traits together to form a personality **factor**. We might find, for example, that gregariousness and shyness are (negatively) correlated, so these would be collapsed into a factor that we might call extraversion. We could presumably keep going until there was only one factor but this is never done, presumably because a single factor isn't a very meaningful way of explaining human personality.

'Lumpers' and 'splitters'

Personality theorists tend to fall into two camps: lumpers and splitters. Lumpers tend to produce a small number of personality factors, whereas splitters tend to produce larger numbers. The ultimate lumper was Hans Eysenck (see Eysenck, 1990) who reduced all of the variation in personality to just three factors, which are the famous extraversion vs. introversion, neuroticism vs. stability and psychoticism

Figure 13.1 Like father like son. Psychologist and personality theorist Hans Jürgen Eysenck with his son Michael William who is also a psychologist

vs. socialised. Extraversion is most often thought of as being concerned with how socially outgoing a person is. A person high on extraversion will frequently be outgoing and sociable, whereas a person low on extraversion (or high on intro-version) will generally be more reserved. Neuroticism is generally concerned with how psychologically stable a person is. People scoring high on neuroticism are quite highly strung and tend towards anxiousness, people lower on this dimen-sion being quite laid back and unruffled. Finally psychoticism is associated with 'niceness' (or its polar opposite – 'nastiness'), people scoring high on this factor tend towards cruelty and can be quite manipulative, lower scorers being kinder and more considerate.

Each factor is a continuum rather than a type. A person is not simply assigned to the category of, for example, extravert or introvert, but rather is given a score on this dimension. Each dimension is also **orthogonal** to the others, which means that the score on one factor is not correlated with the score on any other factor when sampled across a large number of individuals. Therefore, a person's extraversion score cannot be used to predict his or her score on any of the other factors.

Table 13.1 **The Big Five personality factors with typical characteristics of high and low scorers on these factors**

Factor	High scorer	Low scorer
Openness to experience (also known as intellect)	Tendency to be adventurous, curious	Tendency to be conservative and closed-minded
Conscientiousness	Tendency to be self-disciplined and goal-directed	Tendency to be impulsive, driven more by the situation
Extraversion (also known as surgency)	Tendency to seek stimulation including social stimulation	Tendency to avoid stimulating situations, reserved
Agreeableness	Tendency to be compassionate, cooperative and sympathetic towards others	Tendency to be antagonistic and distrustful of others
Neuroticism	Prone to negative emotions such as anxiety, depression, anger	Calmer, less prone to these emotions

Other lumpers are those researchers who produced the so-called Big Five personality factors (McCrae and Costa, 1996). The Big Five personality factors are openness to experience, conscientiousness, extraversion, agreeableness and neuroticism (as a mnemonic they spell the word OCEAN). Table 13.1 lists the key features of these personality factors.

In table 13.1 conscientiousness and agreeableness are essentially subfactors of Eysenck's psychoticism factor, kept separate here as it is believed they can explain behavioural characteristics better individually than they can when lumped together as one generic factor. Openness to experience is, in Eysenck's scheme, incorporated into extraversion. The Big Five separates out the sociable aspects of behaviour – which it calls extraversion – from openness to experience, again because it is believed that these factors account for behaviour better when kept separate.

Today most psychologists interested in individual differences subscribe to the Big Five view of personality factors (Schultz and Schultz, 2005). One evolutionary psychologist who has a special interest in personality, David Buss (Buss, 1991; Larsen and Buss, 2009), has argued that the Big Five factors represent a more evolutionarily plausible way of carving up human personality than the other methods such as that of Eysenck and another well-known typology developed by Raymond Cattell (1965). Cattell was a splitter and his typology uses sixteen non-orthogonal factors – the non-orthogonality means that some of the factors are correlated with some others. What Buss means by evolutionarily plausible is that each personality type represents a motivational force that is likely to benefit an organism living in the kind of social and physical environment that humans do (or at least did during the EEA). For example, Eysenck's extraversion pushes together traits concerned with sociability with those concerned with curiosity and imaginativeness. This according to Buss is unsatisfactory, because curiosity is likely to have fitness implications that are entirely different from sociability, and they are therefore better separated as in the Big Five.

Two other points are worth mentioning about the personality factors discussed above if personality theory is to be properly understood. First, it is rather too easy to think of scoring highly on some factor as being essentially positive and low as being negative. For example, being agreeable – where a person is trusting, and cooperative – seems a good thing to be, whereas being disagreeable, with its associated traits of cynicism and uncooperativeness, seems inherently negative. This, however, is a prejudice that we must shake off. If we adopt an evolutionary point of view calling a trait or factor 'positive' or 'negative' only makes sense to the extent that they have beneficial or detrimental effects on inclusive fitness. Traits or factors that seem negative in some moral sense might well have positive effects on fitness. As an example, one can imagine agreeable people, due to their trusting nature, being more easily exploited by others, whereas cynical people might be more likely to withdraw cooperation in the face of freeriding (see chapters 2 and 8) and hence avoid the potentially disastrous consequences of exploitation. In this way the environment may act as a trigger to help mould or 'release' certain personality traits.

The second point is that an individual's personality (including how they might behave in a given situation) is only captured adequately by knowing his or her score on all of the relevant factors. Exactly how a person high in extraversion will behave will also depend, for example, on whether they are open to experience or narrow minded, neurotic or stable.

Personality and evolutionary theory

Nature, nurture and personality

Research from the behavioural genetics tradition (see chapter 6), which conducts studies on the personalities of twins (monozygotic and dizygotic, reared together and apart) and on adopted individuals, has estimated that the Big Five personality factors show heritability coefficients of between 0.3 and 0.5 (Tellegan *et al.*, 1998; Plomin *et al.*, 2008). This means that between 30 and 50 per cent of the variation among people in personality is accounted for by genetic factors. This therefore means that between 50 and 70 per cent of the variation is down to the non-genetic factors,

> ## Box 13.2 **The consistency of behaviour across situations**
>
> Trait approaches to personality, such as those discussed above, hang on the assumption that our behaviour is relatively consistent over time. For example, people scoring high on extraversion should behave in an extravert manner over a variety of different situations. One of the first psychologists to question this assumption was Walter Mischel. After reviewing the evidence in 1968 he found that when behaviour relevant to personality was investigated (e.g. outgoingness, honesty) people behaved somewhat differently across different situations. In other words, a person who acts gregariously in one situation might act less so in a different situation. The resultant debate, often referred to as the **person–situation debate**, is concerned with whether the primary determiner of behaviour is a person's personality or the specifics of the situation. The debate has continued over the years (see Mischel, 1992; Ross and Nisbett, 1991) but it is important that it is properly understood: no one doubts that there is *some* level of consistency across situations – there are always some effects of personality – the key question is to what extent personality matters in guiding behaviour. This debate is unlikely to be resolved as there is no a priori generally agreed upon number above which, say, one could decide that personality is more important, below which it becomes the situation. Finding a correlation of 0.4 across situations might be sufficient for both sides to claim victory.
>
> The evolutionary perspective sees behaviour as part of an evolutionary strategy that maximises inclusive fitness. Stable differences in personality represent different life strategies: some people, for example, gain access to resources by dominating others, whereas others do it by being deferential. At the same time behaviour should also be situationally contingent; it would be a poor behavioural strategy, in an inclusive fitness sense, for us to ride roughshod over the demands of the immediate situation or our own long- and short-term goals. For example, a person who generally seeks to dominate others might show deference in the presence of someone of high prestige who might be able to offer valuable information and material resources (see Henrich and Gil-White, 2001). A person who is generally deferential might, on the other hand, become more dominant when in the presence of individuals of lower status.
>
> The evolutionary viewpoint would ask a different question of the person–situation debate. Rather than asking what the most important determiner of behaviour is, it would ask how stability and variability in behaviour can be seen as part of a strategy that maximises inclusive fitness (or would have done so in the EEA).

which is usually thought of as being due to the environment. But remember that the environment is a very broad category that encompasses everything that is not genetic (or correlated with the effects of the genes – see later). The environment might include the following:

- How your parents, peers, siblings or teachers treated you as a child.
- Toxins, drugs, radiation or diseases that make their way into the uterus during pregnancy and disrupt foetal development. Technically such substances are known as teratogens and include alcohol, thalidomide, the rubella (German measles) virus and cosmic rays.
- Aspects of the mother's diet or lifestyle during pregnancy or perhaps even before. For example, there is evidence that a woman's diet during pregnancy can affect the development of her children and perhaps also her grandchildren (Barker, 1998).
- Birth trauma such as oxygen starvation and other obstetric complications.
- Diseases and toxins encountered during childhood.
- Any other experiences, good or bad, physical or psychological, that might have occurred at any point during the life span (including the time spent *in utero*).

Some points need clarification. In the case of identical twins, in order for any of the above to appear as effects of the environment in behavioural genetic studies they need to affect one twin and not the other. One of the quirks of behavioural genetic studies is that if, for example, a teratogen affected each identical twin in the same way it would appear as an effect of the genes. In order for an effect to appear as environmental (or not genetic) it has to drive identical twins in different directions. Later we shall see that even in this case labelling such a finding an environmental effect might be misleading. In some cases the environment might merely serve as a trigger that leads to phenotypic change under the control of evolved mechanisms.

The search for an evolutionary theory for variation in personality – what needs to be explained?

Let us remind ourselves of what an evolutionary theory of personality needs to explain, and what a theory might look like. First of all we need to explain why the observation that at least 30 per cent of variation among individuals in most personality factors (e.g. the Big Five) is accounted for by genes. We therefore need to explain why particular personality traits are, to some extent, passed down the generations. Evolutionary theory, and the rest of this book, teaches us that heritable traits (physical or psychological) are usually passed on for a reason; if they have negative fitness consequences they usually die out over the generations. Second, we know that something like 50–70 per cent of the variation among people is not down to genes (or, at least, not directly due to genes) and this variation is usually thought of as being down to the environment. If there are real benefits in passing on personality traits (as we might assume from the first of these points) then why is so much seemingly left to chance? We therefore have yet another paradox. If we try to explain heritable variation by assuming that the traits are fitness enhancing (in some, as yet unspecified, way) we are left with the question as to why personality is

Table 13.2 **Summary of the different accounts of individual variation depending on its source (heritable versus environmental) and its effect (adaptive, non-adaptive, maladaptive)**

		Source of individual variation	
		Heritable variation	Non-heritable variation
Proposed effect of the individual variation	Adaptive	• Frequency dependent adaptive strategies (e.g. Mealey's primary psychopathy) • Genetically based niche filling.	• Early environmental calibration 'weather forecasting' (e.g. the Belsky/Chisholm view of attachment) • Strategic niche specialisation (e.g. frequency dependent strategies such as Mealey's secondary psychopathy)
	Non-adaptive	• Variation because of changing environments • Differential susceptibility to rearing influence (Belsky, 2005) • Variation due to fitness trade-offs (e.g. survival, reproduction, childrearing) • Phenotypic variation because of sexual recombination • By-product of an adaptation (e.g. homosexuality in men might be a side effect of genes which when in females increase their fertility)	• Environmentally based niche filling e.g. peer socialisation (Harris), birth order effects (Sulloway) • None yet proposed • Chance variation due to incomplete specification of phenotype (see Pinker, 2002) • Social learning (e.g. Social Learning Theory)
	Maladaptive	• Genetic abnormalities (e.g. Huntington's chorea)	• Environmental trauma (e.g. foetal alcohol syndrome), physical or psychological trauma

not completely inherited. An evolutionary theory of personality differences therefore should account for both of these features of personality: heritable and non-heritable (or environmental).

There are three general categories of evolutionary explanation for these two types of variation. Adaptive theories suggest that there is some benefit in terms of inclusive fitness in having these types of variation; non-adaptive theories suggest that in some ways the differences might be due to noise, or knock-on effects of other adaptations; and maladaptive accounts would suggest that variation might have deleterious effects on inclusive fitness, such as might be found in some psychopathologies (see chapter 12). These accounts are not mutually exclusive: some accounts might work for some phenomena and other accounts might work for different phenomena. Table 13.2 is adapted from the work of David Buss (Buss and Greiling, 1999) and tries to explain the heritable and non-heritable variation in personality by virtue of whether the variation may be adaptive (is beneficial for fitness), non-adaptive (has no effect on fitness) or maladaptive (has negative fitness consequences). This table summarises the various positions that we discuss over the next few sections.

Explaining the heritable component of individual difference

Non-adaptive variation due to sexual recombination and mutation

As we discussed in chapters 2 and 3, the shuffling of genes that occurs during sexual recombination means that each offspring has a unique combination of their parents' genes. Genes have various effects on each other; some genes switch other genes off or on at different points in development for example. Moreover, each of us has on average around 100 mutated genes. The net result could be that a large degree of variation that is genetic occurs as a result of an epiphenomenon – that is, as a side effect of the process of recombination, sex and mutations, rather than as a direct result of natural selection. Hence some individual differences might merely be due to the side effect of sexual reproduction and the interactions among genes.

Adaptive variation as a result of changing environments

As all of us are doubtless aware, environments change over time. During the time of the dinosaurs, the earth's climate was known as 'greenhouse earth' as there was no permanent ice; the North and South Poles enjoyed tropical conditions. Some time later the earth was plunged into several ice ages with ice-sheets over a large proportion of the planet; a situation that, for the time being at least, exists today as the poles are still frozen. Environments change on a smaller scale too; there might be periods in which food is scarce, followed by periods of comparative plenty. One possible account for the genetic variation among individuals leading to individual differences in personality is that some phenotypes might profit in certain conditions and others in quite different conditions (this may even be the reason that sex exists – see the Red Queen hypothesis in chapter 3). For example, speculatively, hard times might favour individuals who are likely to cooperate – there is a powerful need to work together to eke out a living from a hostile environment – whereas good times might favour individuals who are somewhat more selfish – since there is plenty for all, individuals can more easily lead a productive life on their own. If we imagine that the environment favours cooperators, then this phenotype will profit at the expense of more selfish individuals. If such conditions were to obtain for a long period of time then selfish individuals would probably die out, but if the environment fluctuates back and forth comparatively rapidly (over a cycle of, say, 100 years or so) then under different conditions the selfish individuals might find themselves at a fitness advantage and their numbers would increase at the expense of cooperators.

When we discuss 'personality' in non-human animals later in this chapter we point out some instances in which the environment changes somewhat more rapidly than discussed above (e.g. every year or few years) and how this seems to lead to the existence of multiple personalities in a population.

Variation in personality as a non-adaptive side effect

Above we discussed that variation in offspring might be beneficial in an uncertain world but it is possible that heritable variation in personality is merely a side effect of some other factors that are beneficial. Many genes, as we have discussed, are pleiotropic, meaning that they have a variety of phenotypic effects (see chapters 2 and 12). For example, there is some evidence that it pays to have offspring whose immune systems vary from one another to prevent the parents putting all their genetic eggs in one basket. It is possible that other sources of variation give rise, as an epiphenomenon, to differences in personality. If the environment becomes more predictable there will be a strong selection pressure on the most beneficial of these characteristics leading to them becoming the population norm. Although this argument might sound somewhat tortuous, there is some evidence to support the general point, if not the specifics. For example, we know that on average women live longer than men and due to this sex difference we might construct an argument that this is an adaptation that has affected only females. However, we know that a shorter life in males is partly due to the effect of testosterone that leads to men developing broader chests and greater upper body strength in early adulthood. Thus, there may be no benefit for females living longer – this is simply a side effect of the fact that they have less testosterone than men. Putting it another way, the genes that control testosterone in men also shorten their lives. Hence these genes are pleiotropic.

We can clearly see that the genes have been sexually selected in the ancestral past in order both to impress women and to compete with other men. Thus such genes are kept in the population despite their negative non-adaptive side effect of causing men to die younger (Nesse and Williams, 1995; Nesse and Dawkins, 2010; see also chapter 12).

Adaptive variation due to the existence of different ecological niches and frequency dependency

As we discussed above, one reason for individual differences might be that there is no one universally optimal human nature, just as there is no one universally optimal design of car. In evolutionary personality theory this might mean that having a different personality from other members of the group may even be beneficial because there is the possibility that you can occupy a behavioural niche with less competition from others of similar personality. Across species such niche fitting is commonplace, but it might also occur within species, in particular species with a high degree of sociality such as humans. Put simply, there is more than one way to win at the game of life where winning means, in evolutionary terms, leaving behind surviving offspring (and other kin). Therefore people high in psychoticism might profit from their ability to manipulate others, whereas people low in psychoticism might profit from their ability to gain the trust of others and hence engage with them in reciprocal exchange. In extreme cases this may help to explain why psychopaths remain in the population (see chapter 12 and below).

Further, the successfulness of a 'personality type' will, up to a point, be dependent on the strategies adopted by other members of the population. Driving to work early in order to miss the rush is only an effective strategy so long as few people do it. If large numbers of people adopt the same strategy then it becomes increasingly less effective.

When the effectiveness of an inherited strategy depends upon the number of individuals adopting the same strategy it can lead to frequency dependent selection. For example, Linda Mealey's claims that psychopathy might be a frequency dependent behavioural strategy (Mealey, 1995). Psychopathy is characterised by manipulativeness, sensation seeking, and a lack of consideration for the feelings of other people (see chapter 12). These characteristics can often lead the psychopath into a life of crime and thus it is usually considered to be a pathological condition. Mealey argues that there are two sub-groups of psychopathy: primary psychopathy and secondary psychopathy. Primary psychopaths, she suggests are born not made, whereas secondary psychopathy is produced by an interaction between a genetic predisposition and specific environmental factors (we shall discuss secondary psychopathy later, when we discuss the non-heritable component of personality).

Focusing, for the moment, on primary psychopaths, Mealey argues the psychopathic personality is, in fact, an adaptive strategy: psychopaths might use their manipulative tendencies in order to exploit others, gaining resources including sex (recall from chapter 12 that the majority of psychopaths are male). If all of this seems rather far-fetched, the pre-eminent researcher in psychopathy Robert Hare (see Hare 1980; 1993; 2006) has argued that many of the character traits exhibited by psychopaths (manipulativeness, charm, tough-mindedness) are just the sort of traits that lead to success in high-level business executives. The crucial point, however, is that the effectiveness of the psychopathic strategy depends on how many psychopaths there are. So long as there are comparatively few psychopaths their victims will tend to be trusting and hence easily exploited (you might recall from chapter 12 that the frequency of psychopaths in the population is estimated to be between 1 and 3 per cent). If, however, the number of psychopaths increases due to it being an effective strategy, potential victims will become more wary and hence less easily exploited (imagine if 20 per cent of the population were psychopathic, then we would meet them almost every day and be in a constant state of vigilance). As a result of this psychopathy becomes a victim of its own success and psychopaths leave behind fewer offspring leading to a reduction in numbers over the generations. At some point psychopaths will become sufficiently rare for the strategy to become effective again and numbers will rise. We can see, therefore, that frequency dependent selection keeps the number of psychopaths relatively small.

Before discussing explanations for the non-heritable component of personality, we first look at research that attempts to identify the genetic basis for individual differences in some of the personality factors described above.

Differential susceptibility to rearing influence

We discussed Belsky's recent theory of child development in chapter 6 (Belsky, 2005). To recap, Belsky's argument is that children might be genetically 'programmed' to respond differently to parental influence. Some children are strongly influenced by parental input (including, perhaps, their parent's personality), whereas others are less responsive. Belsky's argument is that this state of affairs might have been adaptive if the environment were unpredictable (periods of comparatively little change punctuated by periods of rapid change). Those children that learn from their parents might be at an advantage during periods of stasis, whereas children who are less influenced by parents might be at an advantage during periods of rapid change when creativity is at a premium (it's worth mentioning at this point that Judith Harris has also argued that children may differ in the extent to which they respond to parental influence – see Harris, 2006).

Figure 13.2 Some researchers have argued that psychopathic tendencies might be adaptive in the business world

Variation as a result of cost–benefit trade-offs

A final explanation for individual differences in personality derives from the fact that for any one environment there are multiple strategies for ensuring that genes survive into future generations. One strategic choice is discussed later in this chapter and in previous chapters (chapters 3 and 6): the C–F (or related r–K) continuum. Recall that the C–F continuum describes whether an individual opts to maximise its current fitness (having a lot of children but investing comparatively little in them) or future fitness (having few children but investing a great deal in them). Recall, also, that we discussed the effectiveness of choosing current fitness over future fitness is dependent on how much environmental risk is present (Chisholm, 1996; Belsky, 1997, see later). However there may also be alternative strategies that are equally workable within a single environment. Nettle (2005) discusses the case of extraversion. As we saw above, extraverts tend to be more socially outgoing and more prone to risk taking compared to introverts. Nettle argues that such a difference could have consequences for fitness, with extraverts tending to maximise current reproductive success and introverts tending to maximise future reproductive success. Consistent with these predictions it was found that in a study of 545 adults extraversion was positively correlated with the number of sexual partners throughout the lifetime, and the number of children borne by other partners and the number of extramarital relationships.

On the negative side, extraversion was also positively correlated with the number of hospitalisations, and extraverts were more likely to have visited the doctor four or more times in the past two years. Nettle therefore argues that extraverts are acting to maximise the number of children they have at the expense of their ability to care for their children as a result of premature death or serious disability. Thus, it is claimed that although extraversion has its benefits in terms of fitness – more sex with more people so presumably more copies of genes in the next generation, this is offset by an increased likelihood that parents may die or become disabled due to their risky behaviour, and therefore less likely to be able to care for their children and foster these genes into the next generation. Swings and roundabouts.

These data are still preliminary and not without their problems. First, although some of the predictions were supported by the data there was no evidence that extraverts had more children, or that they were more likely to die as a result of their own actions. There was also no evidence that extraverts spent less time caring for their children than introverts. On a different line, even if future data more unambiguously support this hypothesis, it does not explain why such individual differences arose – other than some version of the 'noise' explanation given above – only how they are maintained due to there being no net benefit of introversion or extraversion overall.

The search for the genetic underpinnings of personality

If individual differences are, in part, the product of evolution then we must as a species have a genetic foundation for these differences. As we saw in chapters 2 and 6, behavioural geneticists generally attempt to understand the genetic contribution to differences in personality. Up until the mid-1990s their methods were indirect, such as comparing twins and other relatives on personality scales. Recently, however, behaviour geneticists have begun to identify specific genes implicated in personality. Where a gene (allele) is implicated in having a causal role in differences in personality (or intelligence) between people it is known as a **candidate** gene (note – some experts restrict the term 'candidate' to cases where the gene is implicated in disease or mental health issues).

Hunting for genes

There are two ways in which a candidate gene can be identified – through linkage or **association**. Linkage analysis involves studying the entire genome by making use of common variations in the DNA and combining this with knowledge of family genealogies. Linkage refers to the tendency for **genetic markers** that are close to each other on a chromosome to be inherited together. A genetic marker is a DNA segment that is in a known physical location. It is broader than a single gene and may or may not have a known function. The point is that specific genes that may be involved in facets of personality (such as sensation-seeking) or disorders (such as schizophrenia) are passed on to offspring along with the known genetic markers due to their proximity to the markers. In linkage studies geneticists examine large families, some of which will have the trait and some won't. They then determine the genotype of each person and in particular the genetic markers (maybe 300). Next they establish which marker alleles are shared by members of the family with the trait but not by those without the trait. In this way they can then determine whether an individual has a specific candidate gene.

Association studies, rather than focusing on members of the same family, make use of two samples from the population – one sample that has the trait and one that does not. Individuals from the two groups are then genotyped to establish differences in allele frequencies between the groups. In this way association studies are able to localise a genomic region (and possibly a specific gene) involved in differences between people for a particular trait. So far linkage and association studies have largely been confined to genetic disorders since they are expensive and time-consuming. But they have also been used for facets of personality such as novelty-seeking and proneness to anxiety.

Linkage and association studies have led to the identification of a number of candidate genes some of which are implicated in differences between people in personality traits. During the early years of these new technological developments a number of candidate genes were identified that were considered to be involved in differences in personality between people by producing variations in the receptor sites for neurotransmitters or by affecting the release or re-uptake of neurotransmitters. People appear to be polymorphic for the genes that code for these structures (i.e. there are a number of different genes that can potentially occur in the same position on the chromosome – see chapter 2). Two genes in particular were implicated in personality differences among people.

D4DR and the dopaminergic system. On the long arm of chromosome 11 there is a gene that has been labelled D4DR. This gene codes for the production of a protein that protrudes from the membrane of various neurones in the brain and receives the neurotransmitter molecule dopamine. This protein is called the D4 receptor (i.e. it was the fourth type of dopamine receptor to be discovered). This dopamine receptor picks up dopamine molecules and, should sufficient numbers of these be trapped by these receptors, then the neurone will discharge an electrical signal (i.e. it will 'fire'). Of course, individual neurones work in combination with others to form bundles or pathways. Dopamine pathways are very much involved in motivation and arousal. It is now known that the D4DR gene varies between individuals in its length and that this length affects how well the dopamine receptor it codes for works. The longer the D4DR portion of the chromosome the less responsive to dopamine an individual's neurones are. People who inherit a longer D4DR gene do not appear to feel the effects of dopamine as much as those with a shorter D4DR.

When assessed on a sensation-seeking scale, the longer the gene the greater the craving for new and exciting experiences (Ebstein *et al.*, 1996; Eichhammer *et al.*, 2005). Putting it crudely, it is suggested that those individuals with a long D4DR gene, being unable to feel the full effects of their dopamine pathways, are the sensation seekers – constantly trying to turn up their levels of this arousal-enhancing chemical. This means that a single gene that naturally occurs in different forms appears to have a profound effect on personality, making a person more likely to act in an extravert manner.

5-HTT and serotonin activity. A second gene that has been implicated in differences between people in personality factors codes for a protein that affects serotonin activity. The 5-HTT gene exists in two forms – known as the 'long' and 'short' forms (L and S alleles). Which form you inherit determines how well serotonin is transported (i.e. how well serotonin that has been released into the synaptic gap is then transported back into the nerve cell to be reused). This, in turn, is believed to affect how shy a person is. The gene is on chromosome 17 and a portion of it is known as the 'serotonin transporter promoter regulatory region' or 5-HTTLPR (5-HT is the abbreviation that is traditionally used for serotonin). Some researchers are now claiming that alleles of this gene may be involved in a number of disorders such as obsessive–compulsive disorder, bulimia, alcoholism and even autism. A number of studies suggested that the long form (or the heterozygous form SL) is related to shyness, anxiety and even eating disorders (Benjamin *et al.*, 2002; Monteleone *et al.*, 2006). Such studies might suggest that there is a relationship between the combination of the alleles you inherit and your level of shyness.

Such findings sound like a breakthrough for areas such as evolutionary psychology that rely in some sense on a genetic foundation for behaviour and internal states. In recent years, however, the picture of single gene effects has become less positive. First, each time a study is published that reports a significant relationship between a candidate gene and a personality score, another study appears to follow that disputes this finding (Flint *et al.*, 2010). Second, a number of meta-analyses (reviews that combine the findings from a large number of previous studies to reanalyse a large body of data) suggest that these single gene effects either do not stand up to scrutiny or that the amount of variation they account for between people is really very small (Munafò *et al.*, 2008; Mathieson *et al.*, 2012; Webb *et al.*, 2012). Why might this be the case? One reason is that each of these single gene effects is likely to interact with other single gene effects. It is known for example that dopamine and serotonin interact in complex ways, with the former being regulated by the latter (Toates, 2011). Hence variations of the 5-HTT and D4DR genes are likely to interact in their phenotypic effects on personality. These two genes are also likely to interact with other genes – so disentangling the effects of the various genes involved in personality is going to be a very complex business. We also have to factor in the fact that many aspects of personality are likely to be polygenic (i.e. they depend on a number of genes – Heck *et al.*, 2009). Finally, having these genes may predispose people to a type of personality profile but that the predisposition may not be that strong. Returning to the sources of variation outlined in table 13.1, in a sense the activity of these genes may be context dependent – that is, dependent on the early environment (see earlier). A particular early environment might lessen the effects of these alleles or even reverse them. It is also worth mentioning at this point that the twin studies suggest that even for anxiety-related personality traits heritability is between 40 and 60 per cent. And this is one of the highest heritability findings in the field of behaviour genetics. In contrast, the degree of heritability of other personality dispositions, such as 'agreeableness' and 'extraversion', is a little lower – around 30–50 per cent (see Plomin *et al.*, 2008).

Finally, when considering the effect of genes on personality, it is important to recall, as discussed earlier, that many genes are pleiotropic – that is, they code for more than one phenotypic effect. Hence genes that affect personality might have originally been selected for other phenotypic effects (see also chapter 2).

Explaining the non-heritable component of individual difference

Non-adaptive differences due to social learning

B. F. Skinner's behaviourism has already been examined in some detail when we discussed language in chapter 10. His claims for language apply equally to personality. Personality, in Skinner's view, is just a set of behaviours that are learned by the various processes of reward and punishment: children who are rewarded for their gregariousness and punished for being withdrawn become extraverts, those for whom the opposite applies become introverts. This idea was modified somewhat by Albert Bandura who proposed that children could learn their personalities by observing other people, via a process of social learning. The heritability estimates shown above contradict the strongest version of social learning theory, but the substantial non-heritable component to personality suggests that the environment is likely to play an important role.

Non-adaptive variation due to chance

The brain is a hugely complex organ containing approximately one hundred thousand million neurones each of which interfaces with many other neurones. Such is the interconnectivity of the brain, that it has been estimated that the mature adult brain has 150 million million synaptic connections (Pakkenberg and Gundersen, 1997). It is therefore almost impossible that such a complex wiring diagram could be specified by a genome that contains, at current estimates, around 20,300 genes (see chapter 2), approximately one-third of which are expressed primarily in the brain (the highest proportion of genes expressed in any part of the body – National Institutes of Health, 2010).

It is therefore not surprising that although monozygotic twins are genetically identical, their brains appear to be different from birth, even at the fairly gross level of the size of particular brain regions. Given these facts it seems reasonable to assume that the behavioural traits of monozygotic twins should be different, up to a point, which is indeed what we find. The correlations between pairs of identical twins on personality measures are usually between 0.6 and 0.7 (which leads to the variances of 0.3–0.5 presented above, variance being the square of the correlation coefficient); the correlations for intelligence usually being slightly higher (see box 13.4). Steven Pinker speculates that these differences might be due to blind chance:

One twin lies one way in the womb and stakes out her share of the placenta, the other has to squeeze around her. A cosmic ray mutates a stretch of DNA, a neurotransmitter zigs instead of zags, the growth cone of an axon goes left instead of right, and one identical twin's brain might gel into a slightly different configuration than the other's. (2002, p. 396)

Because the genes cannot specify the wiring of the brain in its entirety (nor the rest of the body for that matter), some of the brain's structure is left to the whims of the environment. In support of this, Pinker cites evidence that a range of organisms such as mice, fruit flies and roundworms raised in carefully controlled laboratory conditions still show variations in a number of areas between genetically identical individuals. For example, differences in the number of bristles in the case of fruit flies, or life expectancy in the case of roundworms (Austad, 2000). This account for the non-heritable component is therefore non-adaptive – variation arises simply as a result of the impossibility in specifying an entire organism (including, most crucially for the discussion here, the brain) with only a limited amount of information provided by the genes.

Adaptive variation due to early environmental calibration or 'weather forecasting'

In addition to explaining the heritable component of traits, changing environments have also been used to explain variations in personality that are not, on the face of it, the result of genes. According to the theory of early environmental calibration, a capricious environment means that natural selection cannot specify entirely a successful phenotype. One reason, therefore, why personality might only be partly genetically specified is that in an uncertain world there is a risk of producing sub-optimal phenotypes that offer a poor fit to the environment. Therefore, rather than specifying a complete personality, they specify psychological mechanisms that are capable of tuning or calibrating a personality that better fits the environment in which an individual develops as one might calibrate a scientific instrument, or set a watch, by attending to local conditions (some others also refer to this phenomenon as demonstrating that traits are 'facultative').

An example will help to illustrate this principle. Certain species of grasshopper have the handy knack of blending in with their surroundings (Rowell and Cannis, 1972; see also Bateson and Martin, 1999). A juvenile grasshopper that is placed into a dark coloured environment will, when it next sheds its skin, itself become dark. (Grasshoppers, like all organisms with an exoskeleton, have to shed it in order to grow, with growth occurring in the period immediately following the moult while the new skin is still soft.) If one then places the now-dark grasshopper into a light-coloured environment then following the next moult (technically: ecdysis), it develops a light colouration. This variation is apparently completely due to the environment and has seemingly nothing to do with the genes, as two genetically identical grasshoppers reared in different coloured environments would turn out to be different colours as above. In behavioural genetics terms, genes therefore account for none of the variation, and the environment 100 per cent of it. Does this therefore mean that the environment 'causes' the colour change? It depends on what is meant by 'cause'. Forest fires are, it turns out, a commonplace in the environment inhabited by these particular insects, blackening the previously light coloured landscape. Against a backdrop of charred plants a pale coloured grasshopper would be easy pickings for any predators. Therefore any mutation that enabled the simple colour switch would be favoured by natural selection, which is what seems to have happened. So the environment is really only a trigger for a set of genetically specified processes that lead to the switch. The key environmental variable being the amount of light reflected from the ground, its intensity being positively related to the lightness of colour of the grasshopper. This ability of organisms to change their characteristics according to environmental signals is technically known as **phenotype switching**, because the organism can literally change its physical characteristics on the basis of environmental information.

To return to humans, it has been claimed that some of the variation among individuals is due to a similar mechanism. As we saw above, if the environment is predictably unpredictable (meaning that there is a fixed set of environments but it is not clear from the outset which you will be born into) then, as with grasshoppers, humans might be born with mechanisms designed to sample key features of the environment which lead to a set of processes that affect the direction of the developmental trajectory. We have already discussed two versions of this theory at length in chapter 6. As we saw, Belsky (1997) and Chisholm (1996) both argued that early experiences might lead to different reproductive strategies. Parental cues that signal high-investment childrearing practices might lead to children themselves starting on a pathway of high-investment parenting (for example, higher age of first sexual encounter, fewer sexual partners, stable relationships and fewer offspring). Conversely, cues that signal that the child's parents are low investors might lead them to develop along a low-investment pathway (such as lower age of first sexual encounter, more sexual partners). There is evidence that parental behaviour can affect children's development (see, again, chapter 6), most of which has been conducted under the strictures of 'attachment theory'. The modifications by Belsky and Chisholm suggest that parental cues in childhood might signal what is likely to happen in the future (Are parents likely to still be around when I'm a teenager? Will they still be caring for me?) and evolved mechanisms possessed by the children use these cues as a 'weather forecast' (Bateson and Martin, 1999) and act accordingly, changing personality and other factors.

Secondary psychopathy as a gene–environment interaction

In addition to primary psychopaths, discussed above, whose cheating behaviour is specified by their genes, Mealey has proposed that so-called secondary psychopaths inherit a predisposition to adopt the cheating strategy – whether they become psychopaths depends upon the environment in which they grow up. Individuals with this predisposition might need certain environmental triggers such as growing up in an environment that has few opportunities for gaining resources by cooperating, a dense population (so that there are many opportunities for cheating) and the potential for comparatively anonymous interactions (so that your cheating is less likely to be found out). In a sense, unlike the primary psychopaths (see above) that are maintained in the population due to frequency dependent selection, secondary psychopaths are more flexible and their behavioural repertoire is 'calibrated' to their early environment.

The notion of early environmental calibration is a relatively new area and also an exciting one. Exciting because it suggests that some of this 50–70 per cent environmental variation in personality discussed by behavioural geneticists might be at least partly the result of evolved, environmentally contingent cognitive and emotional mechanisms that sample the world and affect the phenotype based upon a best-guess prediction of the future. Incidentally, this perspective provides further artillery against the view that evolutionary thinking is necessarily determinist (see chapter 1). In this case the environment makes an important difference but, at least in some cases, it doesn't pound us into shape – instead development can be seen as a process where a phenotype is selected from a battery of alternatives.

Adaptive niche filling

Two otherwise quite different theories claim that some of the non-heritable variation in personality might be the result of a person occupying a particular niche as it becomes available. We discussed Harris's group socialisation theory in some depth in chapter 6. Part of this theory suggests that children's personalities might be affected by the availability of particular niches in their group. For example, a group might have space for only one leader, so if that position is already occupied a child will either compete for leadership with the present incumbent or occupy a different 'ecological niche' (e.g. as a joker, a pragmatist or some other role). One researcher who has been influenced by evolutionary theory and has used the notion of 'fulfilling different ecological niches' is Berkeley academic Frank Sulloway. Sulloway has developed a radical theory to account for some of the differences in personality that occur between siblings. Sulloway's theory is rather different from Harris's, as it is squarely based within the family. Frequently firstborn children will act as surrogate parents, helping to bring up the younger siblings and, Sulloway argues, to help them achieve this end they are equipped with an appropriate personality (genes that help other copies of themselves, recall, will tend to propagate). Firstborns therefore usually adopt what Sulloway terms the 'responsible achiever' strategy, being dominant, conscientious and somewhat conservative in their approach to life. Laterborns, on the other hand, are born into an environment where there is at least one older child than them, and that older sibling will usually be physically stronger and more experienced in gaining parental attention. Rather than attempting to compete directly using the responsible achiever strategy – which is unlikely to succeed given their older sibling's advantages – they tend towards a rather different strategy. Laterborns, according to Sulloway, win parental attention by being more sociable and more creative and less respectful of the status quo (Sulloway, 1996; 2011, see box 13.3).

Evaluation of evolution and personality

Above we have presented an evolutionary explanation for the variation in personality that accounts for both the heritable and non-heritable components. Identical twins are similar in personality whether they are reared together or apart. This alone suggests that genes are involved in the differences between people in personality. That personality is somewhat heritable suggests that there might be inclusive fitness advantages for having a population that has some degree of diversity. It is easy to get drawn into thinking that this might be of benefit to the group as a whole, but such a group selectionist point of view is unnecessary. A soccer team has a number of different roles (striker, defender, goal keeper and so on) and of course it benefits the team that there is this variety: think of a soccer team made entirely of goalkeepers. But this variation also benefits the individuals in it. Each individual in that team benefits from winning matches in terms of status, financial reward and so forth, so it is of benefit to a striker that there is a goalkeeper who is in turn helped by the presence of defenders. In this way it is not necessary to resort to group selectionism to explain the benefit of variety, it also makes sense at the individual (or gene) level of selection.

Box 13.3 **Birth order and personality**

Frank Sulloway is a historian of science but is perhaps most widely known for his 1996 book *Born to Rebel* in which he argued that birth order has a significant effect on personality. As a historian it is perhaps natural that he looked to the past to find some of his most interesting data. He noticed that many of the most iconoclastic and creative people in history tended to be laterborns, including Lenin, Thomas Jefferson, Fidel Castro, Charles Darwin, Bill Gates and Rousseau. In fact of 6,556 'revolutionary' historical figures, more were laterborns than would be expected by chance. He also conducted a meta-analysis of 196 personality studies of which 72 supported his predictions, 14 contradicted them and 110 showed no effect either way (Sulloway, 1995).

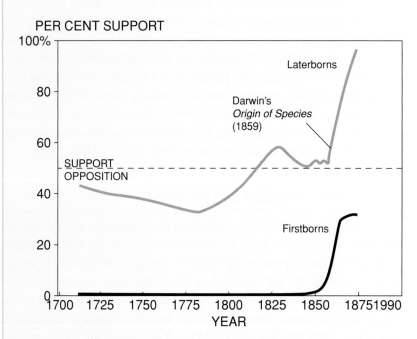

The reception of evolutionary theory from 1700 to 1875 by birth order (N = 433). During the long period of debate preceding publication of Darwin's *Origin of Species* (1859), individual laterborns were 9.7 times more likely than individual firstborns to endorse evolution. These group differences are corrected for the greater frequency of laterborns in the population. The likelihood of these birth-order differences arising by chance is less than one in a billion. Note that firstborn conversions to Darwinism peaked soon after publication of the *Origin*. Those firstborns capable of being converted to Darwin's theories were converted quickly, leaving fewer open-minded firstborns to be converted later on.

Sulloway (1999, 2001) conducted a study in which he asked participants to rate their own personalities and that of another sibling using questions related to the Big Five personality factors. Firstborns rated themselves and a younger sibling; laterborns themselves and an older sibling. The correlation of each of these scores with birth order is shown below. All five of the correlations between trait variation and birth order are in the predicted direction and statistically significant. Firstborns are usually more conscientious and neurotic (less stable) but less agreeable, less open to experience, less extravert (in the sense of gregarious).

Partial correlations of the Big Five personality factors with birth order (adapted from Sulloway, 2001)

Personality factor (and predicted effect of birth order)	Partial correlation with birth order	Significance level, $p <$
CONSCIENTIOUSNESS Firstborns are more deliberate, dutiful, effective, energetic, hard-working, organised, self-disciplined and under control.	−.18	.001
AGREEABLENESS Laterborns are more acquiescent, cooperative, easygoing, modest, straightforward, unassertive/submissive, tender-minded and trusting.	.10	.001
OPENNESS TO EXPERIENCE Laterborns are more aesthetically inclined, prone to fantasy, attentive to inner feelings, untraditional, attracted by novelty and drawn to ideas.	.08	.001
EXTRAVERSION Laterborns are more affectionate, excitement-seeking, fun-loving and gregarious.	.14	.001
NEUROTICISM Firstborns are more anxious, as well as more prone to depression. Laterborns are *more self-conscious*	−.04	.01

You might have noticed that although significant, the correlations are rather small. Correlations, recall, vary between −1 and +1 – a correlation of .8 (or −.8) is usually considered to be strong whereas .3 is weak. Some of the correlations presented above are very weak indeed. Thus although the correlations are significant (unlikely to be a fluke effect), birth order, at least in this study, accounts for very little of the variation in personality. You can find out what percentage of the variance of one variable is explained by another by squaring the correlation and multiplying by 100. A correlation of .1, as above, means that 1 per cent of the variance in agreeableness is explained by birth order. Sulloway addresses this point (see Sulloway, 2001) first by arguing that using variance is misguided and might underestimate the importance of a factor such as birth order. While he may have a point, most psychologists would still consider the correlations above to be remarkably small. Second, he suggests that many factors (e.g. sex, age, social class) can affect personality and although small (in conventional statistical terms) birth order is still important. There might be something in his argument, as a fitness advantage of even 1 per cent might be enough for one genotype to win out over its competitors in the long run.

Some have criticised Sulloway's interpretation of the data, perhaps most prominently Judith Harris who, among other things, takes issue with his low effect sizes. Others have argued that his theory is incompatible with evolutionary theory itself. For example, Steven Pinker (2002) suggests that strategies that work within the family are unlikely to work outside the family: your parents will usually give you resources (including love) no matter how poorly behaved you are, but non-kin are unlikely to be so kind. Evolution should have provided us with strategies for dealing with kin, and strategies for dealing with non-kin.

The observation that personality is not 100 per cent heritable (identical twins do not have the same personalities) has an adaptive explanation too. Perhaps variation in the environment and the availability of different niches leads the individuals to adopt a partial 'wait and see' strategy by constructing the best behavioural phenotype it can based on the environment (early environmental calibration and niche fitting). Whether this is an evolved strategy, as some of the life history researchers have claimed (Belsky, Chisholm, Mealey), or is simply the result of the inability of the genome to specify each and every synaptic connection in the central nervous system, is an empirical question.

The variability we see in personality between people may have led some to consider that it is free of evolutionary processes. Evolutionists, however, have argued that this malleability or **developmental plasticity** is an adaptation in itself, which allows us to alter our strategies in order to exploit the circumstances in which we grow up. In addition to personality factors people also vary in how clever they appear to be. If evolutionary psychology is to make a contribution to individual differences, then it will also have to help explain this variation.

Do non-human animals differ in personality?

Recent research has demonstrated that it is not only humans that have individual differences. In one sense, this has been known for centuries. Any pet owner will tell you how no two dogs are the same or that their cats are like chalk and cheese. What is different is that the recent evidence shows that some differences are, as for humans, heritable. For example, O'Steen *et al.* (2002), have shown that guppies that live in fast-flowing water are bolder than those living in calmer environments, the reason seemingly being that fast-flowing water is less likely to contain predators such as pike. In the absence of such predators it pays guppies to be bold as this opens up more opportunities for obtaining food and for mating, the presence of pike mean that excess boldness can be a disadvantage as it increases the chances of predation. These are not learned behaviours. If offspring of guppies from populations from fast-flowing waters are placed in pike-infested territory, they show the same boldness, and catastrophic insouciance when they eventually meet their nemesis. Put simply, timidity is an anti-predator adaptation.

Similar findings were obtained in research on the great tit (*Parus major*) with an interesting sex-related twist. It has been found that great tits vary in their degree of what is called exploration; high scorers are bold, inquisitive and show high aggression, low scorers being more reserved (Dingemanse *et al.*, 2002). As with guppies this trait is heritable (heritability estimates range from .3 to .6). Again as with guppies, it seems that there are fitness consequences of this trait. For females, being high in exploration benefits them when food supplies are scarce as such individuals are more likely to search and find food supplies. When food is plentiful, however, the extra risk of predation of moving farther afield and reduced inter-species conflict tends favour those low in exploration. For males the opposite is true. When food supplies are poor, mortality through starvation means that there are comparatively few other males to compete with so males scoring low in exploration tend to do well, plentiful food means plentiful males and increased competition for mates and resources which favours aggressive males high in exploration (Dingemanse *et al.*, 2004).

There are many other examples of such heritable individual differences in non-human animals (see Nettle, 2006) but the question is, are these the same kind of thing that we see in humans? Should we even refer to such consistent differences as personality? There are a number of objections, many of which are familiar to researchers on human personality (see Katsnelson, 2010). Are these behaviours consistent over time, or just 'random noise' (see box 13.2 on the person–situation debate); are these traits the actual cause of enhanced or decreased fitness or are they merely correlated with some other behaviour that is causally related? For example, aggressive male great tits might be larger and it may be their increased size not aggression that leads to success in competition. All of these questions are scientifically answerable by the usual means of removing confounding variables and using controlled experimentation. Others, such as Giraldeau (cited in Katsnelson, 2010) suggest that researchers into non-human animal personality have not produced a convincing explanation for how such differences might have evolved. But, as we can see from this chapter, the same applies to human work.

In addition to various scientific objections there are those who are queasy about use of the word 'personality' when applied to non-human animals (see, again, Katsnelson, 2010). To be sure, personality has all sorts of non-technical connotations relating to a person's character such as when we say that someone has a 'larger-than-life personality' or 'no discernible personality'. However, when used technically in the way that personality theorists use it, it is hard to see what – beyond anthropocentric chauvinism – people are objecting to. If by personality we mean relatively stable differences in measurable traits that affect behaviour (which is what we mean when we talk about humans) then, with the important proviso that the above research is correct, animals surely have personality. Alternatively, we could join in with those nay-sayers, but stipulate that if we cannot describe non-human animals as having a personality, then we should refrain from applying this word, in its technical sense, to humans. One of the important contributions of evolutionary psychology is that it retains barriers between species only when it is theoretically meaningful to do so but removes those that are based merely on prejudice. As Richard Dawkins (1976/2006) points out, we are all survival machines and although different species are likely to have evolved different solutions to survival, it is also likely that similar strategies might be used. Having differences in personality might be one of them.

Intelligence

What is intelligence and how is it measured?

Intelligence is a difficult concept to define. Even among psychologists there is much debate. In 1986 twenty-four of the world's leading experts on intelligence met up to produce a definition of intelligence. They failed. Or, in a sense, they succeeded rather too well – inasmuch as they came up with many (Sternberg and Kaufman, 2002). Despite this failure what did emerge from the debate was that there were clearly 'overlapping themes' which suggests that, despite differences of opinion, there is some degree of consensus. Interestingly for our purpose, the most common theme to emerge was 'adaptation to the environment'. This might suggest that experts on intelligence have been influenced by evolutionary theory. For the most part this is not strictly true because, while this 'adapting to the environment' sounds superficially Darwinian, the adapting is generally ontogenic (development of the individual) rather than phylogenic (development of the species). In fact few psychometricians (people who measure psychological abilities) have considered the role of evolution in the development of human intelligence. A typical modern-day definition of intelligence that we feel most psychologists would broadly accept is provided by Passer and Smith (2007):

Intelligence is the ability to acquire knowledge, to think and reason effectively, and to deal adaptively with the environment.

History of intelligence testing

The measurement of intellectual ability has had a long history dating back to tests that were devised by the Chinese civil service around 2000 BC (Cooper, 2012). Hence it is likely that ever since our ancestors developed the notion of division of labour we have tried to use some form of assessment to rank and select people (Ridley, 1996). In the history of psychology, the first intelligence test was devised by the French psychologists Alfred Binet and Theodore Simon in 1905 and become known as the Binet–Simon intelligence scale. Binet and Simon initially produced this first intelligence test in order to identify schoolchildren who needed special attention, but later versions of it were used to test and rank mainstream school pupils. Binet and Simon realised that problem-solving abilities increase with age during childhood. They therefore created a series of tasks which drew on memory, judgement and comprehension and which ranged from simple to complex. How well a child did on these tasks determined their **mental age** – that is, where they were in comparison to an average child at each age. In this way a 'bright' 6-year-old whose performance on the Binet-Simon test is at the typical level of an 8-year-old would have a mental age of 8. Binet and Simon's early intelligence test was later further developed by Lewis Terman working at Stanford University in 1916 and hence this become known as the Stanford–Binet IQ test. IQ stands for 'intelligence quotient', 'quotient' being the mathematical term for the process of dividing one number by another. In the case of IQ mental age is divided by chronological age, thus the average person's mental age should be the same as their chronological age which would give a quotient of 1, whereas a person whose mental age was lower than their chronological age would have a quotient of less than 1. For reasons of convenience IQ scores are derived by multiplying the quotient by 100, so that average IQ is always 100. This means a child with a mental age of 12 and a chronological age of 10 would have an above-average IQ of 120 (12 divided by 10 multiplied by 100), whereas a child with a mental age of 5 but a chronological age of 10 would have a below-average IQ of 50. Since this form of IQ is based on the ratio of mental age to chronological age it became known as ratio IQ. Ratio IQ has subsequently been superseded by deviation IQ which is a measurement of how far an individual deviates from the norm of 100. Norms are derived from a large number of people and a person's score is derived mathematically by looking at how much they deviate (above or below) from the middle of a normal distribution – or, if you like, a bell-shaped curve (Cooper, 2012).

One intelligence or many? – The search for 'g'

When we think of intelligence we usually consider it to be a unitary phenomenon, as being something that an individual has more or less 'of', and many psychological theories of intelligence have conceptualised intelligence in a similar way. The search for this **general intelligence** or 'g' began with British psychologist Charles Spearman

(1923) who observed that children tended to score at a similar level on a number of different sub-tests of Binet and Simon's original test such as arithmetic and vocabulary. Although Spearman had uncovered a high level of positive correlations between these test items, American psychologist Louis Thurstone (1938) later pointed out that these were far from perfect. Thurstone's own research suggested that, rather than a single general intelligence, there are seven primary mental abilities or factors:

- Space (i.e. reasoning about visual scenes)
- Verbal comprehension (i.e. understanding verbal statements)
- Word fluency (i.e. producing verbal statements)
- Number fluency (i.e. dealing with numbers)
- Perceptual speed (i.e. recognising visual patterns)
- Rote memory (i.e. memorisation)
- Reasoning (i.e. dealing with novel problems)

Thurstone's view of seven different primary mental abilities stimulated a debate within psychology that continues to this day. This 'g' versus separate abilities debate has been further explored by those interested in the relationship between evolution and intelligence (see below).

Intelligence and evolution

While few twentieth-century theorists placed evolutionary processes at the centre of their theories of intelligence, two exceptions have done so independently – Robert Sternberg and Howard Gardner. Sternberg (1985; 1998) was one of the first psychometricians to argue for a broader, more naturalistic concept of intelligence. By the mid-1980s Sternberg had become convinced that conventional IQ tests were really measuring 'being successful in twentieth-century America' (Cooper, 2012). He suggested that we should incorporate more of what people of a particular culture saw as 'smart' into them. To Sternberg this meant we need to be aware of the context in which the 'smart' behaviour occurs – i.e. most of the clever things that we do that help us to get on (and certainly in the case of our ancestors), such as planning and building a bridge over a river, are done outside the classroom. Many such activities would necessitate the ability to work with others successfully. Hence Sternberg's expansion of intelligence involved a social dimension that traditional IQ tests don't measure. In this way we can see that Sternberg redefined intelligence as the ability to succeed in a more naturalistic way.

If Sternberg's work on intelligence has considered adaptive aspects in a Darwinian manner, then Harvard-based Gardner has explicitly incorporated evolutionary theory into his view of multiple intelligences (MI). Gardner has attempted to broaden out our concept of intelligence to cover abilities that are adaptations (in the Darwinian sense). In one sense we can think of Gardner's model as re-kindling Thurstone's argument for

Figure 13.3 Cristiano Ronaldo in action for Portugal

distinct abilities. But in another sense his view is quite distinct as the eight varieties of intelligence that he currently proposes go well beyond traditional definitions of intelligence. In its current formulation Gardner (2000; 2003; 2010) considers there to be eight forms of intelligence:

- Linguistic (ability to use language)
- Logical–mathematical (ability to reason mathematically)
- Visuospatial (ability to manipulate objects in space and mental visualisation)
- Musical (perception of and ability to produce music)
- Bodily-kinesthetic (ability to control body movements)
- Interpersonal (ability to understand others)
- Intrapersonal (ability to understand oneself)
- Naturalistic (ability to understand and read the natural world)

We can see that the first three overlap with traditional views of intelligence. The last five clearly do not.

Gardner's model incorporates a broader, more ultimate, perspective on intelligence(s). For example, bodily-kinesthetic ability is not one that is normally measured in the classroom – but clearly this would have been an asset during the EEA. A world-class soccer player today might have advanced bodily-kinesthetic abilities that may have been equivalent to hunting or tracking skills during the EEA. This means that under Gardner's conception of IQ Portuguese striker Cristiano Ronaldo, for example, would be rated as having a very high level of this form of intelligence.

According to Gardner's theory, these abilities are quite independent of each other; a view that has led to a fair share of criticism from within mainstream personality psychology. Cooper (2012), for example, has suggested that currently Gardner's hypotheses are unsupported by empirical evidence. Evolutionary psychologists have generally been more positive, however. As Gaulin and McBurney have pointed out:

Because modern intelligence tests were developed to predict success in school, an evolutionarily novel setting, we should not be surprised if they neglect many abilities that are obviously intelligent. (2001, p. 183)

If Gardner's model of intelligence is to receive support it will be necessary to demonstrate through factor analysis that abilities such as 'relating well to others' and 'understanding natural phenomena' are quite independent facets of human abilities. Such abilities are likely to be difficult to quantify. Quantifying them and demonstrating that they are relatively independent would not of course prove Gardner's model to be correct, but would at least lend support to it.

Evolutionarily speaking, Gardner's scheme makes some sense. Interpersonal intelligence is strongly related to theory of mind as discussed in chapter 5. Others, however (for example, developmentalists such as Susan Carey and Frank Keil), might wish to divide naturalistic intelligence into physical intelligence (understanding the behaviour of objects) and biological (understanding the behaviour of natural systems).

Why do we vary in levels of intelligence?

Like personality researchers, intelligence researchers can be categorised into lumpers and splitters. In this case, those who view intelligence as a unitary phenomenon – advocates of g – can be seen as lumpers, whereas multiple intelligence theorists such as Gardner represent the splitters. Out of the two, the multiple intelligences approach is seen as the more relevant to evolutionary psychology and especially the Santa Barbara school of Tooby, Cosmides and their co-workers. Like advocates of MI, the Santa Barbara approach emphasises the role of domain-specific mental modules in psychological functioning. We might think of each form of intelligence as being the result of a mental module (e.g. one for interpersonal behaviour, one for visual-spatial ability and so on) with a person's ability in a particular domain being the result of differences in processing power of the underlying mental module.

Although evolutionarily attractive, one of the problems with multiple intelligence theory is that there really does seem to be something akin to general intelligence. One of the assumptions of, for example, Gardner's model of MI is that the eight intelligences are independent of one another, so someone can have good verbal skills and poor spatial skills. This might well be the case in some individuals, but across the population four of Gardner's eight intelligences (verbal, logical-mathematical, spatial and musical) are correlated with one another, and all correlate with measures of general intelligence (Jensen, 1998).

So do the findings of Scarr and Weinberg (see box 13.4) suggest that differences between individuals are all down to environmental input after all? No, their findings suggest that differences in IQ scores between people of different ethnicities are better explained by environmental differences. Individual differences within an ethnic grouping, however, are still likely to be due in large part to genetic differences between those individuals (there was a fair degree of individual variation in Scarr and Weinberg's sample). Put simply, the fact that genetic differences between individuals may well be related to differences in intelligence should not be taken as evidence that a difference between 'racial groups' is also due to genetic differences.

Others have argued for a combination of specific and general intelligences (see Anderson, 1992). Such researchers think that, although something akin to multiple intelligences exists, this still does not rule out the existence of *g*. Chiappe and MacDonald (2005) argue that there could well be an evolutionary advantage for general intelligence in addition to the advantages provided by separate multiple intelligences. They claim that the EEA may well have involved a great deal of rapid change including a number of ice ages which would have placed a premium on the ability to adapt creatively to this changing environment. This meant that individuals who were generally good at solving novel problems (e.g. finding new ways of obtaining and preparing foods, ways of keeping warm or new hunting techniques) tended to be more successful and passed these abilities on to their offspring (recall that general intelligence has a high degree of heritability). Chiappe and MacDonald argue that the potential advantages of general intelligence are so great that it warrants an evolutionary explanation.

If our level of intelligence did arise from selection pressures during the ancestral past then we might ask why it is that today we vary so much in intelligence. How could it possibly have been of benefit for some of our ancestors to have had a relatively low level of intelligence? Two reasons are relatively straightforward as they deal with the environmental effects on intelligence. First, as we argued above, for personality factors sex and recombination lead to variation around the mean in traits that are polygenic (i.e. contributed by a number of genes). If intelligence is due to a number of genes then, as with other polygenic traits, new combinations due to sex mean that intelligence will vary around the optimum. A second reason is that variability in environmental input both intrauterine and following birth are likely to affect the developing brain and have a knock-on effect on intelligence (examples include diet, parental feedback and teratogens – see earlier).

More problematical is trying to explain why some of this variation is heritable. One possible reason is that what we perceive as intelligence (i.e. the ability to score well on IQ tests) may have been of less importance to our ancestors. Being able

Box 13.4 **Use and abuse of IQ – heritability, race and IQ**

Few debates within psychology (and indeed within the social sciences) have polarised researchers and commentators as much as the nature/nurture debate for IQ. This debate has been rumbling on ever since Binet and Simon developed the first test of intelligence over 100 years ago. The pendulum of academic (and public) opinion has swung back and forth several times in the last century. Initially, following the early development of IQ tests, there was a widespread belief that intelligence was largely hereditary and governments began to show concern that less intelligent people were out-breeding brighter people. By the 1920s in some states of the USA and in some European countries many 'mentally defective individuals' (known at the time as 'morons') were forcibly sterilised (i.e. 'negative eugenics' as discussed in chapter 1; see also Gould, 1981; Ridley, 2003). Following the atrocities of the Second World War such practices fell into disrepute. By the 1960s with the rise of cultural relativism the pendulum had swung back so severely to the nurture/blank slate side of the argument that even voicing the opinion that intelligence might be inherited became politically suspect. When Arthur Jensen published an article in 1969 suggesting that IQ shows a high level of heritability he was vilified for what was an empirical not a moral argument.

During the 1980s a series of studies considered the correlation on IQ tests between twins and other relatives. The surprisingly strong correlations between close family members (even when reared apart) suggested that intelligence has quite a high degree of heritability. Plomin, for example (1988; see also Plomin *et al.*, 2008) brought together a large number of twin, family and adoption studies and concluded that IQ has a heritability of 0.68. We should bear in mind that although this is higher than the degree of heritability for personality factors it still leaves room for a fair degree of environmental input.

So it appears that while the early adherents of IQ testing overestimated the heritability of intelligence, the 'blank-slaters' clearly underestimated the impact of genes on intellectual abilities – at least as measured by IQ tests. Despite this broad resolution to the determinants of IQ, its use remains controversial with regard to 'race' or ethnicity. When Richard Herrnstein and Charles Murray published *The Bell Curve* (1994), which argued that racial differences in performance on IQ tests are largely determined by genetic factors, it once again sparked a row within academia. Herrnstein and Murray suggested that the fact that white Americans tended to outperform black Americans on IQ tests was due to genetic differences between these two 'racial groupings'. You don't need to be a moral philosopher to predict that many would be upset by this suggestion. *The Bell Curve* was criticised from many angles, and in particular by those who found the suggestion morally outrageous. While this reaction is understandable, the question is an empirical one – 'does it stand up to scientific scrutiny?' – rather than a moralistic one relating to how we would like things to be (recall mixing up 'is' and 'ought' arguments commits the naturalistic fallacy). In fact Herrnstein and Murray's thesis does not appear to stand up very well to scientific scrutiny. The difference appears to be explained by socio-economic differences between the groups leading to differences in educational opportunity, rather than to differences in ethnicity (i.e. more Afro-Caribbean Americans find themselves in poverty than white Anglo-Saxon Americans). In fact Sandra Scarr and Richard Weinberg had already presented strong evidence in favour of the socio-economic explanation some twenty years earlier. Scarr and Weinberg demonstrated that when African American children were adopted from poor black households into well-to-do white households, their scores on IQ tests rose up to the average score of white middle-class Americans (Scarr and Weinberg, 1976).

Figure 13.4 Intelligence theorists have often underplayed the importance of practical intelligence. Here an African bushman teaches a boy how to track prey

to find your way back to camp or to hurl rocks at predators may not necessarily correlate well with all of the tasks that modern-day IQ tests assess (as we saw earlier with Sternberg's comment on IQ tests measuring what makes someone successful in twentieth-century America). Likewise, and arguably more importantly, being socially adept may well have been of greater importance but is not really measured by standard IQ tests (note this is the sort of ability that Gardner feels we should be measuring under his multiple intelligences model). We might even see why variation in multiple intelligences might be favoured by natural selection. Recall that when we discussed personality we considered the notion that variation within a population can benefit the individual (as in the analogy that it benefits a goalkeeper to have a defender on his team). A similar argument can be advanced for variation in multiple intelligences; an individual who has high visuospatial intelligence but low kinaesthetic intelligence can make up for his deficit by entering into alliances with a different person whose psychological profile is the opposite of theirs (and the other person likewise benefits). This is a version of the niche-fitting approach outlined above for personality. (Note, again, that this is *not* a group selectionist theory as the benefit is for the individual's genes, not the group as a whole.)

This explanation does not work if, like Chiappe and MacDonald, we wish to explain the evolutionary benefit of variations in general intelligence or *g*. From a unitary perspective people are either smart or less smart and it is difficult to think of an evolutionary advantage for being less smart if, like Chiappe and MacDonald, you want to argue for the evolutionary function of general intelligence. One possible explanation is that not being smart is not disadvantageous; it simply doesn't make any difference. The explanation hangs on the assumption that the variability that we see as being quite large is in reality rather small. This notion is supported by a longitudinal study of a cohort of men of low IQ. Ross *et al.* (1985) followed up a group of men who had been classified as 'retarded' in school (their average IQ score was 67) into adulthood. Although as a group their average income was a little lower than the national average, most were holding down reasonable jobs including a fair proportion having skilled jobs (29 per cent of the sample compared with 32 per cent of a control group). Although this group of men did not enter professional or management-level jobs, Ross *et al.*'s main conclusion was that, as a group, they were 'holding their own' and able to blend in with the rest of the population. Ross *et al.*'s main conclusion was that an IQ between the range of 60 and 70 is not a major drawback. In fact compared to a chimp even a person with an IQ in the range of 60–70 is a veritable genius (and people who score in this range account for less than 1 per cent of the population).

Bringing these last two points together in a sense we might argue that in the ancestral environment (but not in post-industrial societies) there was a minimal ability beyond which it didn't matter if your *g* score was higher or lower (e.g. the kind of abstract reasoning tasks that IQ tests measure might not have mattered so much for hunter-gatherers). Hence what we see as great variation only appears as such since we invented schools and colleges during the last few millennia. Clearly abstract thinking is part and parcel of human nature – but perhaps not always of the type tapped into by traditional IQ tests (Sternberg and Kaufman, 2002).

Evaluation of evolution and intelligence

The above discussion shows that there are two ways in which intelligence can be considered. One way is captured by the MI approach. This is compatible with the prominent Santa Barbara school of evolutionary psychology in that it suggests that we evolved separate faculties for dealing with problems we encountered in the EEA (understanding people, understanding the natural world and so on). As we saw, we can understand variations in these kinds of intelligence by adopting a niche-fitting approach. The other conceptualisation of intelligence, and the one most commonly used and researched, sees intelligence as a general ability that an individual can have more or less of. Explanations for the existence of general intelligence suggest that it enabled humans to respond flexibly to a rapidly changing world by producing novel solutions to novel problems (see Chiappe and MacDonald, 2005 and Causey and Bjorklund, 2011). However, trying to explain the heritable variation in this form of intelligence is more difficult than it is for the MI approach. Perhaps we will have a clearer explanation when we understand more fully the genetic underpinnings of intelligence.

The nature and nurture of individual differences

When it comes to both personality and intelligence the reasons why people vary so greatly are complicated and still controversial to many. Even today many personality theorists and psychometricians shy away from evolutionary explanations (Schultz and Schultz, 2005). And yet individual differences may prove to be a fruitful area for exploring the interactive nature of genes and environment (Workman, 2007). The explanations that we have discussed in this chapter demonstrate well the complex nature of the interaction between genes and the environment. But judging from the new research that is currently being reported on the relationship between specific genes and measures of personality, perhaps the most exciting discoveries are just around the corner.

We began this chapter by questioning whether an evolutionary approach might help us to understand individual differences. Throughout this chapter we have seen that evolutionary psychology might well help us to understand not only the innate mental structures of our species but also why they vary so much between individuals.

In the final chapter we turn our attention to the question of why it is that cultures also vary greatly.

Summary

- Individual differences researchers investigate many kinds of psychological variation, but the most widely studied of these are personality and intelligence.
- Personality is defined in many ways, but one way of thinking of it is as a form of motivational system which predisposes people to seek out particular situations and respond in particular ways.
- Personality is measured in a number of ways, most frequently by using a self-report questionnaire. These questionnaires usually describe a personality on a number of dimensions of factors (e.g. extraversion, neuroticism, psychoticism).
- Research using twin and adoption studies suggests that personality is moderately heritable (e.g. 30–50 per cent on most factors).
- Theories developed to explain variation in personality have to account for both heritable and non-heritable components. It is necessary not only to understand why personality might be passed on through the genes, but also why so much of the variation in personality appears to be due to the environment. Various theories were advanced attempting to explain both of these aspects of personality.
- Research on the genetic underpinning of personality is in its infancy, but a number of possible 'candidate' alleles have been identified, for example, D4DR and 5-HTT. The role of these genes has, however, been disputed.
- In intelligence research there is a long-standing debate as to whether there is a single underlying general intelligence (g), several multiple intelligences or some combination of both of these.
- Evolutionary psychologists, particularly those of the Santa Barbara school, have tended towards adopting a multiple intelligences perspective (containing modules such as theory of mind, naïve physics, language and so on). Despite this, other evolutionists have attempted to explain how a single general intelligence evolved.
- Like personality, some of the variation in intelligence can be accounted for by genes, although the heritability estimates are higher, some research putting it as high as 0.7.
- For those who adhere to the multiple intelligences view, variation in intelligence can be explained by 'niche fitting'. Some people might be good at spatial tasks, others good at linguistic tasks or understanding people. For those who adhere to g, trying to explain why some people are less intelligent than others is more problematical although attempts have been made based on the fact that intelligence is one of many traits that aid survival and reproduction (physical strength or dexterity might be others).

Questions

1. What are the possible benefits (in terms of inclusive fitness) of being narrow-minded, unconscientious, disagreeable, introverted and neurotic?
2. A gene associated with variability in levels of intelligence was discovered at the end of the last century – IGF2R. This gene was said to account for around four points in IQ. What would happen to our view of the relationship between genes and intelligence if a further twenty genes were found that were related to intelligence?
3. It might be argued that the reason people vary is because evolution requires variation in order to operate. Can you outline the problems with this argument?
4. Howard Gardner has suggested we may have eight forms of intelligence including the abilities 'bodily-kinesthetic' (control of body movements) and 'interpersonal abilities' (understanding others). Can you devise a method of measuring these two abilities?

FURTHER READING

Buss, D. M. and Hawley, P. (eds.) (2011). *The Evolution of Personality and Individual Differences*. Oxford: Oxford University Press. High-powered, multi-authored text that draws on diverse fields such as evolutionary genetics, life history theory and personality psychology in order to examine the relationship between evolution and personality.

Harris, J. R. (2006). *No Two Alike: Human Nature and Human Individuality*. New York: Norton. A follow-up to her provocative book *The Nurture Assumption* of 1998. Harris proposes that children are born with a number of separate social development systems that are best understood by understanding the conditions of the Paleolithic.

Ridley, M. (2003). *Nature via Nurture: Genes, Experience and What Makes us Human*. London: HarperCollins. Accessible yet ambitious and insightful account of the relationship between genes and the environment in our species.

14 Evolutionary psychology and culture

KEY CONCEPTS

superorganic • cultural transmission • evoked culture • transmitted culture • dual inheritance theory • gene-culture co-evolution • culturegens • memes and memetics • imitation

The study of culture is usually the preserve of social anthropologists, sociologists and cultural theorists who have developed sophisticated theories to describe and explain cultural phenomena. Recently, there has been much interest in an evolutionary approach to culture. In contrast to many earlier theories these evolutionary theories attempt to provide ultimate rather than proximate explanations of culture. One of the biggest ultimate questions about culture is why do we have culture at all? From this perspective, the phenomenon of culture is not something that 'just happened'; there is good evidence that human culture needs a particular sort of brain in order to sustain it. Therefore, there is a distinct possibility that the emergence of culture conferred some advantage to our ancestors in terms of their inclusive fitness (see chapters 2 and 7). In addition to ultimate questions, evolutionists have also asked proximate questions. What, for example, are the cognitive processes that are necessary to enable the transmission of culture, what psychological factors can lead to changes in cultural practices and what is the relationship between culture and genes? The following chapter addresses these and other questions in exploring the relationship between evolution and culture.

The importance of culture

Human beings have come a long way in a remarkably short time. In a mere 10,000 years or so – the blink of an eye by evolutionary standards – we have gone from living in small hunter-gatherer communities with primitive artefacts to vast liberal democracies with intensive agriculture, writing, mass education and Twitter. Ten thousand years is generally regarded as too short a time for our brains to have changed significantly, so the difference between us and our ancestors is unlikely to be a result of changes in our mental hardware (the brain). Rather it seems that these differences are due to continual changes in software – the knowledge that we have acquired and the practices that this knowledge informs. These repeated software upgrades come courtesy of other people through the process of cultural transmission.

That culture has had such a large influence can mislead us into thinking that culture has nothing to do with evolution or our biological inheritance. It is easy to imagine evolution and biology as entirely separate forces that mould us into our current shape, and that an understanding of biology cannot help us to understand the nature of culture. Both of these arguments have been contested by recent cultural theorists. First, as we shall see, some theorists argue that cultural practices – variable though they might seem – are not completely arbitrary; rather they are influenced by a human nature shaped by natural selection. Second, the very process of cultural transmission – our ability and desire to imitate others – is underpinned by specialised neural mechanisms that were likely to have been produced by evolution. As we shall see, although imitation is often considered crude, it is a much more complex skill than first meets the eye.

Before presenting evolutionary theories of culture, we begin by discussing some of the earlier ideas about culture, in particular the notion that culture, far from being constrained by human nature, is an autonomous force that shapes the way we behave.

Culture as 'superorganism'

The majority of research studying culture has tended to focus on trying to explain cultural differences, and this was something that certainly preoccupied the thoughts of the Victorians. Why, they asked, do we in the West have agriculture, steel tools and democracy whereas people in other parts of the world live a hunter-gatherer existence, with stone tools and lack organised politics? To the eyes of many Victorians the difference was clearly the result of innate differences between the people who inhabited these societies. Many considered the so-called savages to be incapable of logical thought and some regarded them as a separate species altogether. The zoologist Ernst Haeckel (1834–1919), for example, proposed that 'natural men are closer to the higher vertebrates than to highly civilised Europeans'.

This way of thinking was turned on its head by anthropologist Franz Boas (1852–1942). Instead of explaining cultural variation in terms of psychological differences between people, Boas proposed that people's behaviour needed to be understood in terms of their culture. It was culture that caused the psychological differences, not the other way round. Nowadays this is an uncontroversial claim and one with which the overwhelming majority of psychologists (including evolutionary psychologists) concur. There is no evidence that cultural differences are reducible to genetic differences; as we saw in chapter 6, children easily adopt the culture of the environment in which they grow up irrespective of their genetic origins.

Figure 14.1 Margaret Mead between two Samoan girls, c.1926

Once culture had been identified as a force that can shape human behaviour, some followers of Boas set about presenting it as the only significant influence of human behaviour. One of Boas's students, anthropologist Alfred Kroeber, argued that culture was **superorganic**; that it existed as an autonomous force free from human influence. Sociologist Ellsworth Faris summed up this position when he wrote in 1927 that:

Instincts do not create customs; customs create instincts, for the putative instincts of human beings are always learned, never native. (Quoted in Degler, 1991, p. 161)

In the early part of the twentieth century Margaret Mead, another of Boas's students, wrote a number of influential books taken as demonstrating the flexibility of human culture. In *Coming of Age in Samoa* (1928) she describes how the attitudes of adolescent girls to sex and marriage were very different from those of girls in contemporary Western society. In particular she claimed that unmarried Samoan adolescents had a much more liberal attitude towards sex than their counterparts in 1920s Europe and America. In other works, she described the Tchambuli tribe (whose name has subsequently been standardised as the Chambri, which we use here) where the sex roles were apparently reversed. Chambri women were the breadwinners whereas the men seemed to spend their time engaged in what were seen as traditional female roles such as painting and dancing. Partly inspired by Mead, anthropological research exploded, with globetrotting researchers unearthing cultures that were seemingly diametrically opposed to what was considered the norm by Westerners. By the 1950s it seemed that no practices were culturally universal; it appeared that any cultural practice that we might imagine could be found to exist – so long as we looked in the right place.

These and other examples of the variety of human culture seem to support the notion that culture is indeed superorganic. As Mead argued:

We are forced to conclude that human nature is almost unbelievably malleable, responding accurately and contrastingly to contrasting cultural conditions. (1935, p. 280)

The notion of culture as a superorganic force that shapes human behaviour is part of what Tooby and Cosmides call the Standard Social Sciences Model (SSSM) or alternatively cultural relativism and was adopted by many social scientists from Mead's time to the present day (see Pinker, 2002, for a review of the prevalence of this style of thinking). Recently the superorganic view of culture has come under attack on a number of fronts. First, some of the evidence supporting this view has been challenged (see box 14.1) and second, evidence has been presented that, far from culture being autonomous and infinitely variable, there are a number of 'cultural universals'.

Cultural universals – the 'universal people'

Anthropologist Donald Brown (1991) describes a number of cultural norms and practices that seem to exist in all cultures studied. Brown describes the origins of his enterprise as the result of a discussion with evolutionary psychologist and anthropologist Donald Symons, who argued for the universality of certain sex differences. As an anthropologist from the cultural relativist school, Brown did not believe in cultural universals and bet Symons that he could find a culture in which each of Symons's proposed universal sex differences was reversed. He didn't win the bet. In fact he completely revised his opinions. After studying a large number of cultures Brown discovered that there were over 200 characteristics common to all cultures including characteristics as diverse as burial rituals, logical operators, sex role differentiation, incest taboos, rituals surrounding food, dance, metaphorical speech, tool making, wariness of snakes, classification of colour and thumb sucking.

This work suggests that rather than being infinitely variable human cultures are in fact strikingly similar when viewed from a suitably abstract level. Universality is not, however, in itself conclusive evidence for innateness; good ideas tend to spread from culture to culture (known as **idea diffusion**). Pottery and agriculture, for example, appear in the overwhelming majority of societies, but no one would argue that there are innate mental modules for throwing pots or tilling the soil. But universals might be the starting point for research on innate aspects of culture, especially when such practices seem unlikely to have arisen by idea diffusion (by virtue of their isolation many of the cultures studied by Brown had no opportunities to acquire traits from other cultures).

Box 14.1 Re-evaluating Margaret Mead

Margaret Mead's work was one of the cornerstones of the superorganic view of culture and has recently been the subject of a great deal of criticism. Anthropologist Derek Freeman (see Freeman, 1983) has written several excoriating critiques of her work. Freeman argues that Mead was opposed to biological and evolutionary approaches to the study of human behaviour and culture, and that she interpreted her data in order to repudiate such an approach. He also claims that some of Mead's data were questionable, that she was at best misled by some of the subjects of her research and at worst culpable of exaggeration and fabrication. Freeman argues that Mead's Samoan adolescents enjoyed making up stories about their sexual liberation, and Mead, perhaps because she wanted to believe them, failed to seek corroborative evidence for their stories.

However, in Mead's defence, anthropologist Paul Shankman (1998) proposes that, far from being an anti-evolutionist, Margaret Mead saw human behaviour as being both culturally and biologically determined. He argues that in the early years of her academic life, Mead did indeed embrace a form of cultural malleability and even cultural determinism, but her views matured to embrace a more multi-factorial view of human behaviour. For instance, in 1961 she expressed concern that the influence of genetics research on anthropology was principally in the sub-discipline of physical anthropology and urged her fellow social anthropologists to investigate their role in social behaviour. More generally she spoke of 'the opportunity provided by the new upsurge of interest in the whole field of evolution, in which human evolution is one part and cultural evolution a smaller one' (1961, p. 481). Mead was involved in the sociobiology controversy (see chapter 1); in his autobiography E. O. Wilson (1994) recounts how at a meeting of the American Anthropological Association in 1976 Mead protested against an attempt to officially censure sociobiology. Intriguingly, in her own autobiography Mead intimates that at least one of the reasons for her extreme cultural relativism was political.

> We knew how politically loaded discussions of inborn differences could become . . . [I]t seemed clear to us that [their] further study . . . would have to wait upon less troubled times.

Mead was certainly not an evolutionist, but it seems that in her later writings she recognised the importance of evolution as a motivating force in the shaping of human behaviour. Of course, as is the case with many great figures, it is her earlier rather than her later work with which she has become most closely associated.

Evolutionary theories of culture

Evoked versus transmitted culture

Above we described the existence of cultural universals as suggesting that certain aspects of culture might be constrained by human nature. However, according to Cosmides and Tooby (1994), finding cultural variability among cultural elements should not be taken as suggesting that human nature plays no role in their existence. They coined the term **evoked culture** to describe cultural practices that might arise as a result of mental modules that are environmentally contingent (they contrast this with **transmitted culture** which are the result of factors such as imitation, modelling and idea diffusion). For example, the life history theory of attachment presented in chapter 6 suggests that high-risk environments might lead individuals to adopt strategies that maximise current reproductive gain, whereas low-risk environment might lead to strategies that maximise future reproductive gain. The variability here might be seen as the result of parameter setting in an evolved module which is sensitive to specific environmental cues such as parental investment. This is analogous to Chomsky's claim that the language module sets parameters (such as whether a language is Subject, Verb, Object or Verb, Subject, Object) based on the child's minimal experience of the linguistic environment. Thus a **contingent universal** exists only if some other condition (or conditions) is present in the environment and might thus give rise to variability (we discussed this idea in chapter 13). Currently research into these contingent universals is sparse and some researchers (including Boyd and Richerson, whom we discuss next) are sceptical as to their utility in explaining human behaviour. However, contingent universals and evoked cultures are important areas for future research and may add to the already large number of universals that we presented above.

Dual inheritance theory and the evolution of culture

Biologist Robert Boyd and anthropologist Peter Richerson (Boyd and Richerson, 1985; Richerson and Boyd, 2001; Boyd, Richerson and Henrich, 2011) propose that in humans, and perhaps some other animals, the mind (and thus behaviour) is produced by two interacting modes of inheritance: genes and culture. Their theory enables researchers to model the effects of genes on culture (the reductionist approach despised by many psychologists and anthropologists) but also the effects that culture has on genes (see Tomasello, 1999, and later in this chapter).

Biological evolution is slow. It takes a human between twelve and sixteen years to reach sexual maturity, which sets an upper limit of between six and eight generations every hundred years. By comparison some viruses and bacteria can produce offspring at a rate that is measured in minutes. Of course, and as we saw in chapter 3, humans have the advantage of sexual rather than asexual reproduction to produce greater variability in offspring and thus speed evolution along but, even taking this into account, biological evolution is a painfully slow process. As we pointed out above, biologically speaking, the bodies of twenty-first century humans seem to have changed little in the past 100,000 years or so (Mourre and Henshilwood, 2010) – a period in which human culture has, for most people, changed beyond recognition. Culture, therefore, doesn't just benefit us by providing us with specific practices, skills and artefacts; it benefits us by enabling us to change our behaviour extremely rapidly to fit environmental conditions. Boyd and Richerson argue that this potential for rapid adaptation is one reason why the mind evolved an ability to generate and sustain culture.

Imagine that the temperature dropped dramatically in some part of the world. Many organisms, ill equipped by natural selection to cope with the cooler temperatures, might freeze to death unless cold-resistant mutations arise. Humans, with their second mode of inheritance, can develop new ways of combating the cold such as by wearing animal skins, and pass such technologies on to their offspring, enabling them too to survive. This process of 'technological inheritance' is crucial. In many mammalian species individuals will learn new ways of coping with the environment (usually by trial and error or by lucky accident), but without the ability to pass these on to their offspring the innovations will die with their creator.

Culture therefore enables humans to 'evolve' (adapt to the environment) at a faster rate than would be possible if we relied simply on biological evolution, but cultural transmission works as an adaptive strategy only under certain conditions. Mathematical models suggest that in order for cultural transmission to be beneficial the environment must have changed at a particular rate. If the environment changed too rapidly, then knowledge held by one generation would be of little use to the next generation. Under such conditions it would be futile for parents to pass their knowledge on to their children and it would make more sense for each generation to learn for themselves. If, on the other hand, the environment changed too slowly then genetic change could keep up and there would have been no need for the metabolically costly brains that are required to maintain culture.

It seems that the time that modern human beings started to appear coincides with the environmental conditions that Boyd and Richerson claim are optimal for cultural transmission to be adaptive. During the Pleistocene period there was a significant degree of environmental change. There were several ice ages lasting tens of thousands of years, and there were also more local changes with temperatures varying dramatically over periods of a few thousand years. These temperature changes would have had direct and indirect effects on our ancestors. The direct effects would have included the effects of extreme cold on the human body, necessitating different forms of clothing, shelter and dietary requirements. The indirect effects would have been the changes in vegetation and animal populations that could inhabit the particular regions, which would have required different hunting and gathering techniques. Both of these effects would have meant that the ability to pass on new technologies and practices via cultural transmission would have been advantageous to those capable of doing so. This is, however, circumstantial, as Boyd and Richerson freely admit, and does not count as conclusive evidence for their theory of why the ability to acquire culture evolved.

Boyd and Richerson also speculate on the evolution of the specifics of culture – the particular practices and values adopted by a group of individuals. They propose that cultural practices can evolve by a process akin to group selection (but only cultural practices, they are adamant that biological processes are not shaped by group selection – see chapter 2). In their view, different cultures can be seen in competition with the successful culture being the one whose practices are passed on to the next 'generation'. For example, one tribe might destroy another as a result of war (perhaps because their war-making cultural technologies are more effective – see Diamond's research discussed later). Alternatively the 'weaker' tribe might not be killed outright but might be captured and have the dominant culture forced upon them (language, practices, religions, etc.). Or the 'weaker' tribe might simply adopt the cultural practices of another perhaps because the people recognise that they are superior to their own (Richerson and Boyd, 2005). Thus although the ability to acquire culture (and perhaps some of the universals described above) might be the result of an evolved human nature, evolutionary processes might also account for the spread of 'learned culture' albeit by a process of group selection.

Gene-culture co-evolution

Above we discussed arguments concerning 'universal people' and evoked culture which suggests that genes might directly or indirectly affect cultural practices. A consequence of dual inheritance theory is that cultural practices can affect genetic evolution. Sociobiologists Charles Lumsden and E. O. Wilson (Lumsden and Wilson, 1981) have developed a theory known as **gene-culture co-evolution** in which genes and culture are seen as intimately entwined and co-dependent. They argue that humans have innate learning capacities which make some cultural elements easier to learn than others, with the result that they are more likely to become established in the culture (Lumsden and Wilson, 1981). The close relationship between culture and biology espoused by Lumsden and Wilson was best summed up by Wilson when he stated that

The genes hold culture on a leash. The leash is very long but inevitably values will be constrained in accordance with their effects on the human gene pool. (Wilson, 1978, p. 167)

Lumsden and Wilson focus on the process of **epigenesis**, the interaction between genes and the environment that occurs during development. They proposed that

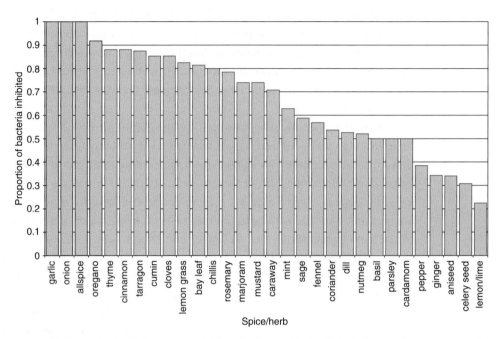

Figure 14.2 The antimicrobial properties of different spices and herbs. Note that some of the more powerful ones (e.g. garlic, allspice, chillies) are those that tend to be eaten in hot countries

epigenetic rules embody certain biological imperatives (behaviours or dispositions that enhance the survival of an organism), and that these rules influence the set of cultural entities that are likely to exist. Because these epigenetic rules are themselves shaped by genes Lumsden and Wilson suggest that genes indirectly influence culture. But culture influences genes as well. Different cultural opportunities can lead to shifts in the sorts of epigenetic rules that are useful, and consequently to changes in the successfulness of particular genes in a given population.

Lumsden and Wilson (1981) also introduced the concept of **culturegens**, which are the patterns of culture that are transmitted between individuals (this is closely related to the notion of a meme, see later). They further argue that many culturegens serve to increase the inclusive fitness of those humans who acquire the particular aspects of a culture. Thus, culturegens such as incest taboos (one of Brown's cultural universals) can aid human genetic fitness by deterring people from mating with their close genetic relatives, thereby avoiding the fitness-reducing consequences of inbreeding (see chapter 3). Food taboos such as viewing certain animals as unclean and unfit for consumption might have arisen because – in the ancestral environment – such animals were the hosts to a variety of dangerous pathogens (see chapters 3 and 4). Culturally specific methods for the preparation of food, on the other hand, might have rendered certain foodstuffs safe to eat. In particular, the observation that food from hot parts of the world such as Africa, South Asia and the Mediterranean tends to be highly spiced, whereas food from cold countries such as Scandinavia, Britain and the Polar regions is traditionally more bland, can be at least partly explained by the antibiotic properties of spices such as garlic, and chilli (see figure 14.2). Food left out in hotter climates becomes infested by potentially life-threatening bacteria and other parasites much more rapidly than it does in cooler regions.

But culture also has effects on genetic evolution. You may know that some people are unable to digest lactose, a sugar found in milk and hence have to avoid milk and its products in their diet. Lactose intolerance, however, is no mystery: milk is a food designed to feed babies and most mammals lose the ability to digest it once they become adults by turning off the gene that produces the digestive enzyme lactase. What needs to be explained, therefore, is not lactose intolerance but lactose *tolerance*. The answer, it seems, is culture. Those people whose ancestors habitually herded cows, sheep or goats have a genetic mutation that supports lactase production in adulthood, those whose ancestors did not, tend to turn off lactase production following weaning (Bloom and Sherman, 2005). Thus cultural practices can cause selective pressures that, over generations, affect biological evolution. A similar story can be told for alcohol tolerance. Alcohol is a poison unless it is metabolised by the enzyme alcohol dehydrogenase (ADH). ADH, and hence alcohol tolerance, is higher among Europeans than South Asians possibly because alcohol was discovered by Europeans as a way of purifying water (most people in Europe, even children, drank a weak ale) whereas South Asians used antimicrobial herbs in the form of tea for the same purpose (Osier *et al.*, 2002). Thus in Europe people possessing genes for low levels of ADH were less able to avail themselves of the purifying effects of alcohol were more likely to die and therefore less likely to pass their genes on to the next generation. Some people, it seems, are designed for beer.

Gene-culture co-evolutionary theories emphasise the two-way relationship between genes and culture. Genes have an effect on the kinds of cultures that are possible, but culture itself, once established, become part of the selective environment (Richerson *et al.*, 2010).

The future of culture-gene theories

All three theories outlined above are still in their infancy as theoretical accounts of the development of the interaction between genes and the environment. Each of them, however, seems promising as a way of explaining the evolution of culture. There are some differences between them. For instance, Tooby and Cosmides and Lumsden and Wilson place more emphasis on the biological basis of specific cultural practices, whereas Richerson and Boyd focus more on transmitted elements of culture. This is, however, largely a difference of emphasis as surely both are important factors in a

Box 14.2 Is cultural evolution always progressive?

Are cultural practices arbitrary, or can they be seen as adaptations to the environment? Some evidence that shows how cultural practices adapt to the prevailing environmental conditions can be seen in a natural experiment in Polynesia (see Diamond, 1998). The Maori is a group of people descended from Polynesian farmers who colonised New Zealand around the eleventh century. Not long after (probably by the thirteenth or fourteenth century) a group of Maori – most probably from the West coast of New Zealand's North Island – colonised a neighbouring island which the new inhabitants named Rekohu some 500 miles to the east (the official name for Rekohu is now the Chatham islands). Initially the two groups would have been culturally similar, but over time their trajectories diverged.

By the 1830s the Maori had reached an advanced stage of cultural evolution, engaging in intensive agriculture. This method of exploiting the land meant that they produced food in such abundance that their society could afford to support non-food producing specialists such as craftsmen, bureaucrats, hereditary chiefs who did no manual work and – because many of the societies were continually at war – part-time soldiers.

At the same time, the colonists on Rekohu, now known as the Moriori, seemed to have 'regressed'. Instead of engaging in intensive farming and supporting specialist craftsmen, soldiers and a sophisticated political system, the Moriori had reverted to being hunter gatherers with little cultural specialisation and were more peaceable than the warlike Maori who – true to form – invaded in 1835 and took over the island. What had happened? Does this not show that cultural practices are not adaptive? In fact, it shows the opposite. One of the great misconceptions about culture is that there is an inevitable progress towards more complex forms of agriculture, technological innovation, specialisation and social organisation. (There is a similar misconception that biological evolution will always produce organisms that are bigger, faster and stronger.) In many situations, such a trajectory is unsustainable. Rekohu was much colder than North Island New Zealand (the name Rekohu describes the mist that clings to the island); this meant that the seed crops originally taken when the islands were colonised failed. Additionally, Rekohu had an abundance of naturally occurring food such as fish, seals, sea birds, small mammals, seafood and edible vegetation. So in this case it made sense to move from agriculture to hunting and gathering. Because foraging is unable to produce the surplus of food that intensive agriculture produces, the Moriori were unable to support specialist craftsmen, so the sophistication of artefacts decreased. They were also unable to fund a governing class so the political organisation became simpler – just a hereditary chief and a small number of aides. Because they were on an island with no other tribes around them, there was no need to fund soldiers, even if they could have afforded them. Thus the hunter-gatherer lifestyle was actually more adaptive in the case of the Moriori. There were also some innovations. The tribespeople realised that naturally occurring food was abundant only so long as the population didn't increase beyond a certain point, otherwise the stocks would rapidly deplete, so they engaged in population control by castrating a percentage of their male offspring. As a result of this population management, and other measures, the Moriori managed to preserve their food resources throughout their history. Their seal colonies, for example, were managed by killing only older male seals and remained virtually unchanged in number until Europeans arrived in the late eighteenth century. The Moriori are not alone in abandoning 'progressive' practices such as agriculture, and in nearly all cases where this has happened it has been due to sound practical reasons.

complete understanding of culture. So far, all the theories discussed have assumed that the individual (or rather his or her genes) are the beneficiaries of cultural practices – next we present an account that questions that this is necessarily the case.

Cultural information as replicator: the meme's-eye view

Many of the examples of cultural phenomena given above are obviously advantageous. Most would agree that pottery, fire, incest taboos and ways of purifying food and water have a positive effect on fitness, but it is not always so easy to see the fitness-enhancing property of a cultural practice. Clothing is undoubtedly useful, but what about fashion? What are the consequences – in terms of fitness – of whether you wear your baseball cap with the peak up, down or round the back of your head. Some cultural practices seem to have no obvious direct benefit to fitness, inclusive or otherwise. This observation leads to a radical hypothesis: maybe cultural information is not for our benefit at all; maybe it is just for its own benefit.

In *The Selfish Gene* (1976/2006) Richard Dawkins argues that to understand genes fully, we need to adopt the 'gene's eye view' (see chapter 2). Successful genes (i.e. ones that are prevalent in the gene pool) need not be beneficial to the individual organism in which they reside, all that matters is that they do not harm their chances of being passed on to the next generation. We often think that genes are there for the benefit of the individual but this is not always the case as there is only one player who always benefits: the gene itself (again see chapter 2). As examples you might consider the self-sacrificial behaviour of the male redback widow spider who offers himself to his partner as a post-copulatory snack, or bees that kill themselves in defence of their hive – these behaviours evolved not because they benefited the individual, but because they benefited the genes for that behaviour. Likewise many cultural phenomena such as music and chastity might have no benefit to the individual, all that matters is that they replicate. Like viruses, units or conglomerations of units of cultural inheritance spread by capitalising on the nature of the human mind. Dawkins labelled these units of cultural inheritance **memes** by analogy to genes, the units of biological inheritance.

What are memes?

The definition of a meme varies depending on the particular author that one consults; this is not necessarily a great problem; memetics (the study of memes) is a relatively young discipline and it is therefore unsurprising that people think of memes in different ways. Dawkins (1982) proposes that a meme is 'a unit of cultural inheritance... naturally selected by virtue of its "phenotypic" consequences on its own survival and replication' (p. 109). Dawkins (1976) gives examples of memes: they are 'tunes, catch-phrases, clothes fashions, ways of making pots or building arches' (p. 206). Importantly, according to Dawkins, the meme is *not* the tune, the catch phrase or the arch; these are merely the physical manifestations of the meme. The meme is the *idea* of the arch, or more formally the underlying mental representation of 'archness'. In explaining memes, Dawkins makes a distinction analogous to that between genotype and phenotype. The colour of a human iris, for example, is the phenotypic expression of the underlying genotype. Likewise, an arch is the phenotypic expression of the underlying meme for an arch. A similar distinction was made by Cloak (1975) who distinguished between m-culture (culture that is 'out there' in the real world) and i-culture (culture that exists in people's heads).

This point relates to a question often raised by people new to the idea of memetics: what are memes made from? Genes, as most people know, exist in a physical form as sections of DNA. When an individual inherits a gene from one of his or her parents, we can 'see' a copy of the gene at the same locus in both parent and offspring. If we examine the genes of someone with blue eyes, we can see genetic similarities with other blue-eyed people precisely because genes have an underlying physical basis. Many have pointed to this as being a failure in the analogy between genes and memes: genes have a physical basis whereas memes do not. Unfortunately for the critics, this is wrong. When a person learns something, such as how to make an arch, or how to whistle a popular tune, physical changes occur in the brain. When someone learns to whistle 'Yankee Doodle' their brain is physically different from the way it was before they knew the tune. This fact is not the result of some obscure brain scanning experiment; it has to be the case otherwise we could not have the behavioural difference. This is a consequence of having a materialist theory of mental life: every change in behaviour, every nuance in the way you think, has to be accompanied by (more correctly it is caused by) a physical change in the brain.

We must be careful of applying distinctions such as that of genotype and phenotype too closely to memes – we can find that it soon starts to become confusing. If the idea of an arch is a meme, then how would you classify a set of instructions on how to build an arch? Is that also a meme? If you wrote down the music for Yankee Doodle, would that be a meme? Susan Blackmore (1999; 2010) proposes that the written form also constitutes a meme but sensibly cautions that one should not expect to use the language of genes to apply to memes too closely. After all, memes are not genes: they are a different kind of replicator and therefore obey their own rules. Another example of this is in deciding what a meme is. Critics (e.g. Wimsatt, 1999) have questioned how one identifies an individual meme. In certain cases, such as a joke or a short tune, the meme is easily identified, but in other cases such as a religion is the religion itself a meme or is it many memes, and if the latter, where are the boundaries between individual memes? The problem with this criticism is that exactly the same criticism could be levelled at genes (Haig, 2006). The generally accepted way of defining a gene (and the one we discussed in chapter 2) is as a unit of DNA that codes for a polypeptide or RNA string, but there are other ways of defining them. In the *Selfish Gene* Dawkins uses George C. Williams's (1966) definition of a gene as 'any portion of chromosomal material that potentially lasts for enough generations to serve as a unit of natural selection' (1976/2006, p. 28). While this might seem a vague definition, from the point of view of selection it is the definition that matters. Genes are not selected directly, but are selected by virtue of the effect that they have on the phenotype (they cause us to be lactose tolerant, or to have colour vision); they are not selected because they code for this polypeptide or that RNA sequence. So the definition of a gene depends upon what is useful: if we are biochemists, then the first one is more useful; if we are evolutionary psychologists, behavioural ecologists or evolutionary biologists, then the latter is more useful. If we are interested in the behavioural consequences of memes, then we can follow Dawkins's definition of a gene and simply define it as 'that which is copied'.

Notwithstanding this debate, we can see that a meme does have a physical basis, although it is unlikely that it is as simple as the way that genes are manifested in DNA (and that is hardly trivial). Maybe, when brain scanning technologies have developed beyond those currently available, we might be able to see how particular ideas are manifested in the brain, we might even be able to tell whether or not a person has the meme for arch. But we need not wait until then to study memes. Recall from chapters 1 and 2 that Gregor Mendel never saw a gene – he inferred their existence and nature from observing the results of his experiments on pea plants which allowed him to formulate his laws of genetics. Likewise it is possible to study the nature and transmission of memes without detailed knowledge of their physical basis, so despite the critics the difference between memes and genes is not as great as it might at first seem.

Memes and cultural evolution

One difference between memes and genes is that the mutation of genes is assumed to be random, whereas the mutations that occur as cultural entities change over time are generally non-random. Many changes are the result of deliberate human effort and creativity, such as new songs, improvements to cars, or new techniques for making pottery. Another difference is that genes and viruses are transmitted directly from body to body whereas memes generate behaviour that is observed by someone else who then infers the underlying representation that allows them to replicate that behaviour (Sperber, 1996 – see later). This process of observation and inference can lead to further variation, either intentional or accidental. Even completely unintentional mutations are frequently non-random. Chinese whispers – the game where a person whispers a short phrase to the person next to them who then whispers it to the next and so on – often gives rise to mutations (in fact the game would be dull if it didn't). But these are not merely random mishearings as they typically use real words, are grammatical and make some sort of sense (even if it is absurd).

British psychologist Frederick Bartlett (1932, see chapter 9) studied such misre-memberings in the 1930s. Bartlett was interested in how memory becomes distorted over time and constant retellings, in his experiment he presented his participants with an Inuit folk tale called *The War of the Ghosts*. The war of the ghosts is a tale laden with culturally specific meaning; and describes the soul leaving the body of a man following his death. To his, almost certainly, middle and upper-class British participants the story doubtless sounded strange, and this very fact was ascertained when participants were asked to retell the story after a variety of time delays. The retellings regularised the story so that it became more consistent with their own particular culture. For example, the original tale describes how some men went hunting for seals, but this was often misremembered as going fishing, presumably because it made more cultural sense to the experimental participants.

So there are certainly differences between the mutation of genes and the mutation of memes in that the latter 'mutate' in a much less random way than the former. Then maybe the difference between memes and genes is not so great. As we have seen, a meme in the human mind exists in an environment of other memes, and the nature of this environment (whether it is hostile or benign) will determine the memes' success. As Dawkins points out, an individual gene exists within an environment of other genes which will likewise have an impact on the gene's success (Dawkins, 1982).

The relationship between memes and genes

Memes, therefore, can influence memes and some memeticists have argued that this fact is of paramount importance in understanding cultural variation, perhaps more important than genes. Dennett (1999), for instance, objects to Wilson's argument that genes hold culture 'on a leash':

Consider the huge space of *imaginable* cultural entities, practices, values. Is there any point in that vast space that is utterly unreachable? Not that I can see. The constraints Wilson speaks of can be so co-opted, exploited, and blunted in a recursive cascade of cultural products and meta-products that there may well be traversable paths to every point in that space of imaginable possibilities. I am suggesting, that is, that cultural possibility is less constrained than genetic possibility...To combat Wilson's metaphor with one of my own: the genes provide not a leash but a launching pad, from which you can get almost anywhere, by one devious route or another. It is precisely in order to explain the patterns in cultural evolution that are *not* strongly constrained by genetic forces that we need the memetic approach.

Dennett argues, therefore, that much of culture is unexplainable by appealing to genes, and we need to explain the existence of culture in terms of other cultural entities (or memes in terms of memes). Educational psychologists have argued that the single most important variable that determines success in learning is what the person already knows: the same information can be informative to one person, incomprehensible to a second, and redundant to a third. In the language of memetics, the meme-complexes that inhabit the minds of particular individuals will influence what other memes will inhabit that mind.

Intriguingly, the implications of Dennett's argument are strikingly similar to those of cultural relativists such as Margaret Mead and Franz Boas, that culture is largely unconstrained by human nature, albeit influenced by biology in the first instance. The crucial difference between Dennett's perspective and that of the cultural relativists is that Dennett considers that genes can explain *some* aspects of culture, those that are the most directly linked to human inclusive fitness (e.g. incest taboos, sexual preferences, food choice). Other aspects of culture that have no effects on fitness might better be explained by interactions between memes.

One critic of memes is anthropologist Dan Sperber (1996). He suggests that the fidelity of cultural replication is not reliable enough to explain how practices persist in a culture. In only a short time errors and other changes when copying would soon lead to practices being very different. His alternative, known as the *epidemiology of representations* proposes that ideas and practices tend to converge around 'cultural attractors',

[C]onsider your views on President Clinton. They are likely to be very similar to the views of many, and to have been influenced by the views of some. However, it is unlikely that you formed your own views simply by copying, or by averaging other people's views. Rather, you used your own background knowledge and preferences to put into perspective information you were given about Clinton, and to arrive by a mixture of affective reactions and inferences at your present view. (1996, p. 106)

Box 14.3 Myths, mind viruses and the Internet

One curious type of cultural entity that spreads from person to person is the urban myth. These take the form of true stories, but are often expressed as happening to a person only distantly known to the teller: usually 'a friend of a friend'. The stories are often funny (the friend of a friend who came downstairs naked to be greeted by his friends and family who had organised a surprise party in his house), and sometimes contain warnings (sewer-living alligators in the United States, rats found in hamburgers, aliens masquerading as family members). From a replicator's point of view, urban myths are tailor-made to infect human minds. Human beings like telling stories, particularly if they invoke emotional reactions in their audience such as mirth, shock or incredulity. The advent of the Internet drastically increased the ability of these 'mind viruses' (Dawkins, 1995) to replicate. Now we don't even need to remember the joke, story or idea, in order to transmit it to our friends and acquaintances. The ready availability of Internet access, coupled with the ease with which individuals can copy or forward messages, greatly facilitates the proliferation of cultural information. In the 1980s and early 1990s, for example, millions of email users received the following message:

> A little boy (his name varies), dying of an incurable disease (the disease varies), wants to make it in the Guinness Book of Records for 'the most get-well cards'. Well-meaning computer users ask you to send a card so the little boy gets his dying wish.

The boy has now been identified as Craig Shergold and as a result of the media coverage he came to the attention of American billionaire John Kluge who arranged for Craig to undergo a new form of treatment at the University of Virginia Medical Center in 1991. The operation was a success but still the cards kept coming, forcing the family to move to a new home which was given its own postal code. By 2007 it was estimated that he had received around 350 million cards. He has requested that people stop. There are many examples like this and although they seem harmless, it has been estimated that they cost businesses billions of dollars a year in terms of lost productivity. (Compare this to many living parasites which, although fairly harmless, can 'jam up' the human body to such an extent that they can become life-threatening when food becomes scarce for the unfortunate host.)

Perhaps even more pernicious are emails that warn of bogus computer viruses. When told that they may have a virus, most people's response is to panic. As we were writing this book, one of us received the following message from a close friend via email (the chevrons denote that it was copied multiple times when forwarding).

> > > PLEASE MAKE SURE YOU FOLLOW THE INSTRUCTIONS THAT FOLLOW AS THE VIRUS IS

> > > SPREAD THROUGH AN ADDRESS BOOK AND, THEREFORE, WILL NOW BE IN YOURS!

> >>THE VIRUS LIES DORMANT FOR 14 DAYS, THEN KILLS YOUR HARD DRIVE. PLEASE
>
> >>FORWARD THESE DIRECTIONS ON HOW TO REMOVE IT TO EVERYONE IN YOUR
>
> >>ADDRESS BOOK

The message then contained detailed instructions on how to delete the offending file, called 'sulfnbk.exe'.

Given that the author knew the person, and given that the person from whom she had received the message was a priest, it seems reasonable to assume that it was valid. But sulfnbk.exe is in fact a part of the Microsoft Windows operating system. Deleting it only means that you have to reinstall it at a later date (which takes time, effort and – usually – numerous phone calls to the computer-support department). The message, therefore, was a hoax, albeit sent with the best intentions. Hoax virus warnings cause panic and invoke in most people the impulse to warn their friends and loved ones; this is one of the reasons they replicate so quickly and in such numbers.

So the fact that ideas tend to spread through a population unaltered, is not due to high-fidelity copying, but rather due to the fact that people have similar brains (partly due to innate biases). Rather than simply copying, therefore, Sperber argues for a process of 'triggered production' whereby 'information provided by the stimulus is complemented information already in the system' (in terms of attitudes, beliefs and so on that are already present in the mind, Sperber, 2000).

Although there are clear differences between Sperber's epidemiology of representations and the notion of memes – the pre-eminent one being the former's emphasis on the constraining effect of the mind – both share the view that culture can be seen as being constituted of discrete entities that spread from mind to mind. It is not yet clear whether the constraining effect of the mind advocated by Sperber constitutes an entirely different approach to the study of culture compared to that of memes, or just a difference in emphasis – is Sperber's theory just a different form of meme theory?

How useful is memetics?

There is something attractive about the idea of memes, something that has made the idea spread, infect the minds of renowned philosophers, scientists and the public alike. The meme meme has been greatly aided by the fact that many of its advocates are wonderful wordsmiths and storytellers (principally Dawkins and Dennett). Many of the critics of memetics have pointed to various disanalogies between genes and memes (Midgley, 2000; Wimsatt, 1999): for example the difficulties in isolating individual memes and differences in mutations discussed above. However the biggest problem with memetics is probably less conceptual and more functional: what can you actually *do* with it? Adopting the gene-centred view of evolution (see chapter 2) was genuinely revolutionary in biology, enabling us to explain behaviours that were previously mysterious such as altruism among kin, self-sacrificial behaviour, sibling rivalry and parent–offspring conflict to name but a few (see chapter 7); while the meme-centred view of cultural evolution is doubtless fascinating, it has failed to explain any phenomena that aren't explainable by traditional concepts such as conformity, obedience, compliance and memorability (Haney *et al.*, 1973; Milgram, 1963; Asch, 1956; Centola *et al.*, 2005; Bartlett, 1932).

The psychological mechanisms of cultural transmission

As we saw in our discussion of memes, one of the mechanisms of cultural transmission is imitation. We will often learn how to tie our shoes, how to behave at a religious ceremony and how to cook a meal by imitating our parents and peers. Human beings are very good at imitation, as is revealed by the work of psychologists Winthrop and Luella Kellogg (Kellogg and Kellogg, 1933), who conducted an experiment in which they reared an infant chimpanzee named Gua alongside their similar aged son Donald. They were interested in whether the chimp would become more human if reared in a similar manner to a human child. Gua was made to wear clothes and shoes, was allowed to run free round the house, was bathed, potty trained and generally treated just like a normal infant (see figure 14.3).

Gua and Donald got on very well playing together just like two siblings of similar age. Gua was also ahead of Donald in a variety of developmental tests that Winthrop Kellogg devised. She was able to feed herself with a spoon earlier and was better able than her human counterpart to use a chair to reach a biscuit that had been suspended from the ceiling. But, at least in the early years before Donald acquired language, there was one thing that Donald beat Gua at hands down: he was the better imitator. Rather worryingly for his parents, Donald would imitate Gua's chimpanzee food bark and it was Gua, rather than Donald, who usually took the lead in finding new things to do, Donald generally just copied her. What this story reveals is just how good humans – even infant humans – are at imitating the behaviour of others, even when those others might not be the best role models.

Why are humans such good imitators?

On the face of it, imitation does not seem to be a particularly intelligent act and indeed many of the words we use to describe imitation are pejorative, we talk of doing things

Figure 14.3 Gua and Donald Kellogg (above); Winthrop Kellogg with Gua (below)

'parrot fashion', of 'verbatim regurgitation', 'plagiarism' and of one person 'aping' another. Interestingly, although we use the verb 'ape' to describe mindless copying, the Kelloggs' research suggests that humans are somewhat better at aping than are apes! Recently, many researchers have come to see the importance of imitation in human development and as an essential component of the development of culture.

There is considerable debate, however, as to what imitation is. Psychologist E. L. Thorndike's definition as 'learning to do an act from seeing it done' (Thorndike, 1898, p. 50) is a good enough definition but this includes a variety of behaviours that vary in complexity. For example many simple forms of apparent imitation can be explained by a process known as **stimulus enhancement** (see Byrne and Russon, 1998). Stimulus enhancement is simply the tendency of an animal to pay attention to an object or area as a result of seeing some other animal achieve some success with that object or in that area. An animal that goes to a food patch after seeing another animal successfully exploit it might be explained by stimulus enhancement. But this seems quite different from an animal deliberately imitating the *actions* of another (such as potato washing in Japanese Macaques, Kawai, 1965 – see box 14.4). There is now evidence that a number of animals including budgerigars (Galef *et al.*, 1986), rats (Heyes and Dawson, 1990), chimpanzees (Whiten *et al.*, 1999) as well as human newborns (Meltzoff and Moore, 1977; 1983) can copy the actions of conspecifics. Comparative research by Nagell *et al.* (1993) indicates that, although adult chimpanzees are able to imitate a human in using a rake to retrieve an out-of-reach object, they are only able to do this to the level of a 2-year-old child. Even the positive examples of cultural transmission in non-human primates – such as food washing in Japanese macaques – spread quite slowly through a population of a few tens of individuals. In a human population of equal size the innovation would have spread like wildfire.

Tomasello argues that one reason humans have such complex culture is that they are better than other animals at identifying with their conspecifics. Primates seem to be alone in the animal kingdom in being able to represent the mental states of their conspecifics; when they observe actions they are able to infer what the animal's intentions are behind the action. This is important in imitation since it gives meaning to the actions; without being able to figure out why someone is doing what they are doing the actions will seem meaningless. According to Tomasello, an important reason humans are better at imitating than other primates such as chimps is that they are better able to represent the goals and intentions of other people; they have a more sophisticated **theory of mind** (see chapter 5). To see why this is important, imagine that an animal observes a conspecific poking a stick into the ground. If that animal has a sophisticated theory of mind it can use it to infer that the individual goal in using the stick is to obtain food – termites. Armed with this knowledge the animal can then decide whether or not to imitate this action and, crucially, to apply it only in situations where there are known to be termites. Without this ability to

Box 14.4 **Do non-human animals have culture?**

The debate as to whether other animals possess culture is strongly reminiscent of other debates such as whether animals have language, or whether other animals use tools. On the one side, given that we humans so obviously have culture (or language), it seems likely other animals – particularly our close relatives the apes – must have it too. Such a line of reasoning is not necessarily correct. There are many instances in the natural world where one species has a unique adaptation. The classic example is the elephant's trunk. No other animal has an organ anything like as sophisticated as this flexible, delicate and at the same time immensely strong organ. This is not because the trunk evolved in some massive leap of evolution, it is because all of the elephant's close relatives have died out. Likewise, there is no reason to rule out the notion that we might be alone in the natural world in having a culture.

Of course, as with all such debates (see chapter 10) it depends on how we define culture. Clearly, no other animal has the breadth of technological innovation that is present in human cultures, but what about a more modest definition of culture as a system of transmitted behaviours; is there any evidence that non-human animals have culture in these terms? Some have observed innovations spreading through populations of primates. In 1952 (Kawai, 1965) on Koshima island a group of scientists studying the social behaviour of Japanese macaques (an old-world primate) attracted the primates towards them by throwing sweet potatoes on the ground. Initially the macaques wiped the dust and sand off the potatoes by wiping them with their hands, then one day a juvenile female known as Imo took her potatoes to the water's edge and washed them clean. This washing behaviour spread through the population so that by 1958 fourteen of the fifteen juveniles and two of the eleven adults washed potatoes. Other examples where novel behaviours are apparently transmitted through a population are the use of twigs to catch termites in chimpanzees (Goodall, 1964), birdsong (Jenkins, 1978) and fear of snakes in rhesus monkeys (Mineka and Cook, 1988). Furthermore, research on the common chimpanzee (*Pan troglodytes* – see chapter 4) reveals that there is substantial variation across the different groups that is reminiscent of the human cultural variation (Whiten *et al.*, 1999). The authors describe 39 variations in behaviours including grooming, tool use and courtship. The distribution of these behaviours suggests that they are transmitted culturally rather than genetically. For example, nut-cracking behaviour terminates at the boundary of the Sassandra-N'Zo river, even though the chimps on either side are close genetic relatives. Field data suggest that chimpanzees imitate each other (particularly more senior chimps and parents) in the use of tools and the execution of behaviours. A group of chimps known as Taï chimps use a rock as an anvil and a stone or wooden 'hammer' in order to crack nuts, a behaviour that young chimps seem to learn from adults. A different group, the Gombe chimps, are unable to crack nuts, even though they are in plentiful supply. The observation that behaviours vary when the environment does not (in this case the presence of nuts) tends to rule out the claims that variation is simply due to variation in environmental opportunity. The observations that chimps learn by imitation are supported by experimental research, demonstrating that chimps imitate each other when opening novel artificial 'fruits' (Whiten, 1998).

Not everyone believes that animals have culture. Many claim that the research outlined above is the result of genetic variation in behavioural traits, or the results of environmental pressures forcing animals to adapt one or other strategy. Others protest that although chimps (and other animals) might be able to learn new behaviours from each other and pass these on to their offspring, this does not constitute culture. Nagell *et al.* (1993) present evidence that while human children are able to imitate the method by which a particular goal was achieved (in this case reaching an object with a rake) chimpanzees arrive at the same goal by many means, irrespective of the behaviour shown to them. Nagell *et al.* refer to this as learning by **emulation** rather than imitation. Imitation requires the individual to mentally represent the intention of the actor and thereby see the method as a means of achieving this goal. In emulation, on the other hand, the intention isn't as salient, so the method is imprecisely executed.

infer intention all that is seen is the poking action with no knowledge of why it is being done. In this case there is no reason why the animal should imitate and even if it did, it is likely that the poking action would be deployed in a random way because the animal has no knowledge of its purpose.

Other forms of cultural learning

Humans do not only have an imperative to acquire culture, they are also disposed to transmit culture through teaching and other means. Language obviously plays an important role in this form of cultural transmission. Unlike other animals, humans can describe to their children what the best tasting fruits look like, how to prepare food properly, or how to turn animal skins into clothing. According to Tomasello *et al.* (1993) this **instructed learning** is of particular importance for children because instructions are internalised and used to regulate their subsequent cognitions and actions. Not only do young children acquire specific skills through instruction, they also learn more general skills such as self-monitoring.

Learning by instruction greatly extends the range of things that we are able to learn. As we have seen, it is possible for an animal such as a Macaque to learn how to wash potatoes by imitating others, but this requires them to see the value in potato washing. With language we don't have to leave this to chance, we can explain the value of an activity, thereby vastly improving the process of transmission. We can say 'I'm cooking this food to stop it from causing illness', 'I'm praying to save my spirit from damnation', or 'Don't eat the fruit of that tree because it will make you ill'. Language not only facilitates the spread of culture, it greatly increases the sorts of cultural entities that can be spread.

Why is there such a difference in cultural wealth?

Why do different areas of the world have such differences in wealth and technology? Why, for instance, is Europe rich and sub-Saharan Africa poor? Why was it Europe that colonised the Americas rather than the other way round? Answers to this question are various. Some have suggested that Europeans – especially Northern Europeans – are biologically superior: that they are innately more intelligent or more suited to leadership. It perhaps goes without saying that there is no evidence for such explanations. Others have pointed out that the reason Europe (or more correctly Eurasia – the landmass that incorporates Europe and Asia) dominated the other continents of the world (North and South America, Australia and Africa) was due to Europeans' discovery and use of steel weapons, their success at domesticating animals (including horses) and their sophisticated political organisation. While there is truth in this assertion, biologist Jared Diamond (1997) felt such an explanation incomplete as it begs further questions as to why the Eurasians were the ones with the steel weapons, the domesticated animals and the political organisation. In short, he sought ultimate explanations for the way things are, not simply proximate explanations.

Figure 14.4 shows a schematic representation of Diamond's framework. At the bottom of the diagram are the proximate causes of the Eurasian domination of recent history: domesticated animals such as horses for pulling ploughs and using in war, technologies that enable travel and efficient killing, the organisational capacities to manage colonies and large armies, and finally, epidemic diseases. This last category often surprises people; how did epidemic diseases enable Eurasians to colonise the rest of the world? During many sorties abroad, Eurasian soldiers often found they didn't need to engage with the natives; the diseases that the soldiers carried with them did their work for them. For example, the Spanish colonisation of South America was made much easier because the population had been decimated by smallpox brought over from Europe. But why did the Spaniards have smallpox rather than the South Americans? It turns out that most epidemic diseases are the product of agriculture. The main killers of the past few hundred years – smallpox, influenza, cholera, tuberculosis, bubonic plague, malaria and measles – all derived from animals, often domesticated animals. South Americans having few if any domesticated animals simply did not have the opportunity to benefit from this early (and unintentional) form of biological warfare.

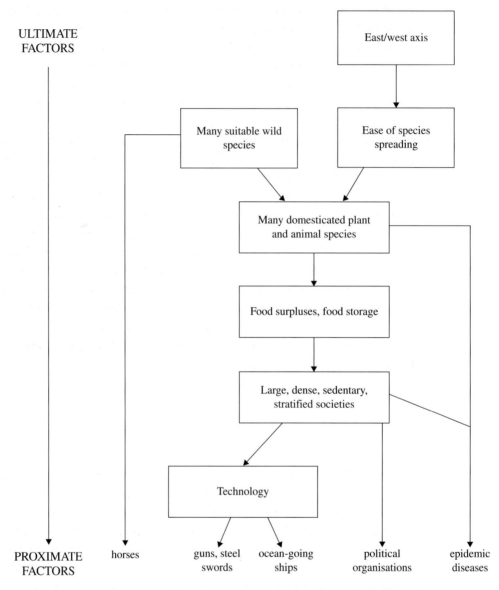

Figure 14.4 A schematic diagram of the causal factors (proximate and ultimate) that led to the development of advanced civilisation

Ultimately, Diamond suggests, Eurasians were at an advantage because the continent extends a vast distance in an east–west direction whereas the other continents do not. This east–west axis means that animals and plants domesticated in one part of Eurasia can be imported to another part with relative ease – something which is not true where the axis is primarily north–south as it is in Africa and South America. Moving north or south will lead to significant changes in climate – something that is potentially harmful for the crops or livestock. Eurasia also had the largest number of animals suitable for domestication. In fact, of the fourteen large, domesticated animals, Eurasia had thirteen, South America one (the ancestor of the llama) and Australia, North America and sub-Saharan Africa none at all.

Domestication of plants and animals made agriculture possible and the resultant food surplus meant that many more mouths could be fed than by hunting and gathering. The explosion in population had two consequences. First it meant that there was a need for some form of centralised political organisation, and second it meant that the people in these societies could specialise, which led to the development of the aforementioned technologies.

So where did civilisation begin? The evidence suggests it began in a region known as the Fertile Crescent which spans the area that now includes Syria, Lebanon and Iraq. This area appears to be the birthplace not just of agriculture but also the alphabet and is the area which was the birthplace of the Indo-European language family (see chapter 10) that now includes most European languages (e.g. English, Italian, Norwegian and Russian), the languages of the Indian sub-continent (e.g. Hindi, Urdu, Punjabi) and some Middle Eastern Languages (e.g. Persian and Pashto).

Diamond's theory shows that the unequal distribution of wealth is largely the result of historical accident, Eurasians had the raw materials of civilisation, whereas those living on other continents did not.

The importance of specialisation in culture

One of the benefits of moving to agriculture is that it enabled cultural specialisation. Matt Ridley (2010) gives the following example. Imagine that there are two people Adam and Oz. Adam takes four hours to make a spear and three hours to make an axe (total time seven hours). Oz, on the other hand, takes one hour to make a spear and two hours to make an axe (total time three hours). Oz is better at both spears and axes so does Oz need Adam?

Superficially you might think that the answer is no, Oz is more efficient at making both spears and axes than Adam so why would he need his help? In fact if Oz specialised in making spears he could make two spears in two hours (a saving of one hour if he made both spears and axes), and if Adam specialised in making axes he could make two axes in six hours (again with a saving of one hour). And of course now that Oz is focused solely on spears and Adam on axes the extra practice will make them even more efficient than if they were generalists. The moral is that it is always better to offload a task that you are not so good at even if the person to whom you offload it is even less efficient than you are. Of course a person only needs so many spears or axes so this system only works where there is a system of trade either by a system of favours – Oz gives Adam a spear when Adam needs a spear, Adam gives Oz an axe when Oz needs an axe – some kind of barter system – one spear is worth two axes – or some kind of token economy, such as money. The biologist Mark Pagel (2012) argues that the evolution of language was an essential component in enabling trade to happen. Chimpanzee culture, he argues, is restricted by their inability to do the deals necessary for specialisation to occur. Likewise it seems that although Neanderthals had sophisticated cultural artefacts there is little evidence that they traded. Neanderthal artefacts were always made of local materials whereas the artefacts of contemporary ancestral humans were often made from non-local materials, suggesting that these were obtained through trade (Gamble, 1999). Research by Horan *et al.* (2005) suggests that the reason why Neanderthals became extinct is because they were outcompeted by our ancestors who were able to develop better technologies as a result of trade.

There are many consequences of trade. First, goods and services become cheaper and therefore more plentiful so that everyone, not just the privileged few, can afford a spear, clothes or protection by way of a professional army. As an example of this Ridley cites the work of economist William D. Nordhaus (Nordhaus, 1996) who attempts to estimate how many hours the average person would have to work to purchase 1,000 lumens of light for a single hour (lumens are the SI unit of how much visible light is emitted by source, 1,000 lumens is about the brightness of an average household light bulb). In 1992 the average person would have had to work for half a second to obtain an hour's worth of light; in 1960 about 3.5 seconds; in 1940, 20 seconds; in 1900, about 15 minutes and in 1800, when candles were used, between 5 and 12 hours, depending on the quality of the candle. The high price of candles in 1800 meant that they were unavailable to most and, when it went dark, people either sat by the fire or went to bed (see Ekirch, 2006, for a fascinating history of life before the electric light).

Second, increasing specialisation leads to innovation as experts find increasingly better ways of working with materials or providing services such as cooking or medicine. A final consequence is that we are no longer self-sufficient. Given enough time and suitable materials most of us – just like our ancestors – could manufacture a crude hand axe, but how many of us could make something as apparently simple as a pencil? In 1958 economist Leonard Read transcribed the biography of a pencil:

I have a profound lesson to teach. And I can teach this lesson better than can an automobile or an airplane or a mechanical dishwasher because – well, because I am seemingly so simple.

Simple? Yet, *not a single person on the face of this earth knows how to make me.*

The pencil's point (as told to Leonard) is that its construction required the efforts of thousands if not millions of people: graphite miners, foresters, lumberjacks, paint manufacturers and so on and not one person has the expertise to acquire, process and assemble the materials to produce the final product. Lack of self-sufficiency is the price we pay for advanced culture. And before you consider that to be a bad thing Robert Wright (2001; 2007) makes the point that one of the many reasons he doesn't want to declare war on Japan is the fact that they made his car. His joke is intended to point out that specialisation has reached such a point that we are increasingly dependent on each other and that this is one of the factors that is leading to increased peace throughout the world (see Pinker, 2011).

The importance of culture in the development of culture

Imitation, instruction and powerful minds are essential to the development of culture, but there is another factor: culture itself. Agriculture means that not everyone has to be involved in food production (as we saw with the Maori). Freeing up people leads to a division of labour so that some can work on other things, perhaps developing better farming tools or techniques. Moreover, this benefits farmers who are able to produce more food per hectare, which frees up even more people.

Other technologies such as development of writing also had a profound effect on the development of culture. The earliest known form of writing is Sumerian cuneiform from Mesopotamia dating from before 3000 BC. Later writing systems developed independently, in Mexico before 600 BC and possibly in Ancient Egypt and China, but all other types of writing appear to derive from these four (or two) sources. Writing enables us to share expertise with people we have never met; it also enables us to learn from people who died many years ago. Writing also means that cultural entities can be copied with far greater fidelity than if they were passed along only by the spoken word, and ultimately enables the development of mathematics and science. More recently developments in communications technology from the printing press to the Internet have had profound effects on the way that we live our lives.

The importance of horizontal transmission

As we have seen, the transmission of genetic information is always vertically downwards, in that children inherit their genes from their parents. Cultural transmission, on the other hand, can occur in any direction. The most frequently discussed form of transmission is that which is passed vertically downward, as happens when a human child (or perhaps chimp) learns from an adult. It can, however, also be transmitted vertically upwards, such as when a parent assumes an interest first adopted by his children, and it can be transmitted in a horizontal fashion such as when people trade ideas as discussed above. Interestingly, while a great deal of research has focused

Table 14.1 **The peak ages at which individuals from a variety of disciplines were at their most productive**

Discipline	Peak age in years
Astronomers	24–9
Poets	25–35
Chemists	30–4
Writers of great books	30–4
Philosophers	35–9
Psychologists	35–9
Writers of best-sellers	40–4
Metaphysicians	40–9
Mean	32.5–37.9
Peak age	35

Source: Lehman (1953)

on the transmission of culture from parent to offspring, rather less effort has been placed on the horizontal forms of transmission, especially those that occur in child-hood. This is curious, since it could be argued that horizontal transmission is of paramount importance if culture is to evolve (Harris, 1998 – see chapter 6).

The physicist Max Planck suggested that new theories triumph over old not because adherents of the old theory have embraced the new one, but rather because the adherents to the old theory have died out and been replaced by open-minded younger scientists. Whether or not this is universally true (see Hull, 2000), there is certainly some truth in the notion that the great cultural and scientific innovators tend to be young rather than old. Historical examples are manifest. For example Einstein was twenty-eight when he published his theory of general relativity and Darwin was twenty-nine when he formulated the idea of evolution by natural selection. A study conducted by Lehman (1953) looked at the ages at which individuals from a variety of disciplines did their best work (see table 14.1). This research suggests that for most disciplines the peak age is between the late twenties and mid thirties (see Over, 1988 for a critique of this work).

More mundanely, it is the young who most readily adopt new technology (itself usually produced by younger rather than older people) and practices. The first macaque to wash sweet potatoes in the Koshima island group was a juvenile (see box 14.4) and the younger macaques took up this innovation more readily than the older members of the group. The young are therefore the engines of cultural evolution.

In chapter 6 we outlined Judith Rich Harris's group socialisation theory (Harris, 1998) which proposed that – in stark contrast to the prevailing vertically down notion of cultural transmission – the peer-to-peer horizontal form of transmission might be more important in the enculturation of individuals. We may now be able to see a reason why group socialisation might be an evolutionarily sensible strategy. Societies that faithfully transmit ideas vertically downwards would tend to be rather static; they would be able to say how this thing or that thing had been done in exactly the same way for thousands of years, and they would be right. If this culture lived in a vacuum this would be fine, but we live in an uncertain world that often changes rapidly. The history of humanity is one of competition; humans compete not only with the physical environment, but also with other people in different groups. In such a situation, it would pay a society to adapt quickly to develop new means of keeping themselves warm, new ways of hunting or farming food, to develop new weapons and battle tactics. For this to happen, we need not only innovators (who, as we have argued will tend to be young) but also a group of willing disciples ready to take up and employ the new ideas. Thus, the desire of the young to learn from each other might be an essential component in rapid cultural evolution.

Striking a balance between horizontal and vertical transmission

Would it not make evolutionary sense for older people to adopt new ideas with the enthusiasm of the young? Perhaps it would, but there may be barriers to this happening. Perhaps it is just a side effect of the way that the mind works that older people find it difficult to take on new ideas (as stated in the famous proverb that you can't teach an old dog new tricks). Once a person has acquired a particular way of doing things it might be difficult to learn new ones. But these are proximate explanations; is there any reason why the brain might not have evolved to make new ideas easier to adopt? Maybe the correct mutations have simply not arisen to enable older people rapidly to adopt new ideas, or maybe they did arise but had unfortunate costs that rendered them unsustainable.

There may also be a way in which it might be adaptive for older people to be comparatively unreceptive to new ideas and practices. As well as it being disadvantageous for culture to evolve too slowly, it can also be damaging for it to evolve too quickly. Imagine what it would be like to have innovations proposed and taken up apace without any real consideration as to how beneficial such ideas might actually be. Such a society could end up destroying itself as rival camps battle for their own favourite way of doing things, or being destroyed by their adopting an unworkable practice. Perhaps older people act as brakes on cultural evolution; by being scornful

Box 14.5 **Evolution and religion**

Religion is a cultural universal, which is to say that religious belief exists in all cultures. Given that religion often leads people to behave in apparently un-Darwinian ways, it warrants explanation. For example religious people will sometimes take vows of celibacy, will sacrifice themselves, or will give up a substantial portion of their resources for their religion – all behaviours which hardly seem designed to maximise inclusive fitness. Is religion, therefore maladaptive? Or might there be some adaptive explanation for religion? David Sloan Wilson (Wilson, 2002) suggests that we can consider religion as a kind of superorganism which promotes the survival and reproduction of the group rather than the individual members of the group. Thus the fact that some people might reduce their fitness through self-sacrifice is irrelevant, what matters is that the group as a whole benefits. Successful religions (ones that have many adherents) are those where the group as a whole performs better than groups which have different religions, or no religions at all. What matters, therefore is the reproductive fitness of the religion itself which is linked to, but not dependent upon, the fitness of the individual adherents to that religion. Wilson's theory therefore invokes group- rather than gene- (or individual) selection to explain religion, although unlike early group selectionists (see chapter 2) Wilson doesn't rule out the existence of individual selection.

An alternative is provided by anthropologist Scott Atran (2002) who attempts to explain religion using more conventional processes operating at the level of the individual. According to Atran, religion is not an adaptation, rather it emerges as a by-product (or 'spandrel', see chapter 1) of other processes which are adaptive. The first is people's predisposition to perceive agency. For example in a famous study by Fritz Heider and Mary-Ann Simmel participants were shown a film depicting two triangles and a circle moving in and out of a box. When asked to describe what was happening participants attributed agency and mental states to the shapes. For example the larger triangle was described as an aggressor. The second of Atran's processes is causal attribution. When two events happen close together in time and space people often assume that one is causing the other even if no mechanism can be seen linking the two events. This can give rise to superstitious behaviour. For instance, if a person happens to be wearing a particular item of clothing when their favourite team wins, they might continue to wear it on subsequent occasions in the hope that it will bring them luck. A third process is theory of mind. As we saw in chapter 5 we attribute mental states not just to genuine intentional agents, but to all manner of things including inanimate objects such as cars, and computers. These three mechanisms play a role in helping us to predict and understand the world, but – as the above examples demonstrate – can be misapplied so that we see agency, causality and intentionality where there is none. This can, according to Atran, lead to the perception that there are intelligent agents (gods) who can intervene in the world.

A number of other theories have been proposed to explain religion. In his famous (some would say notorious) work *The God Delusion* (Dawkins, 2006) Richard Dawkins argues that a different mechanism might underlie the transmission of religious beliefs. He argues that children need to acquire skills and knowledge from adults in order to negotiate the world; children's blind acceptance of cultural mores can be seen as part of an adaptive 'culture acquisition device'. This makes them susceptible to all kinds of information, including acquisition of religious information. Religion can therefore be thought of as a kind of meme (or system of memes – a memeplex – see Blackmore, 1999) that children acquire uncritically. From this perspective, religion needn't be beneficial to the individual, all that matters is the 'fitness' of the meme – religion itself. A similar line is taken up by Daniel Dennett in his book *Breaking the Spell* (2006).

of the new, they might ensure that new ideas generated and championed by the young are properly tested out before they are applied, with potentially disastrous consequences.

Finally, we should sound a warning about the interpretation of the benefits of culture. It is all too easy to think of culture as benefiting a society or being for 'the good of the group'. In strict evolutionary terms this is not the case. As we saw in chapter 2, there is little evidence that selection occurs at the level of the group. Instead most modern evolutionists adopt a 'gene-centred' perspective in which the benefits of culture somehow increase inclusive fitness of the members of that group (or rather the genes of its members).

Conclusions

Many consider culture to be something that has nothing to do with biology and evolution; this is likely to be wrong on two counts. First, some cultural practices (e.g. incest taboos) might in some way have a genetic basis (Lumsden and Wilson, 1981). Brown's accounts of cultural universals have been used as evidence that this might be the case. Second, it appears that the fact that we have culture at all might be down to evolution. If Boyd and Richerson are correct, culture evolved as a second mode of inheritance as a way of enabling human beings to deal with a changing environment. Certainly, it seems that from a young age human beings are engaging in a process of enculturation, and that the cognitive capacities necessary for acquiring culture seem to be uniquely human.

Understanding culture surely represents one of the most difficult tasks for evolutionists, and we hope we have shown that the attempts so far raise more questions than it answers. To what extent are cultural universals the result of human nature? What headway might be made in the exploration of contingent universals? Why did culture evolve? Is it meaningful to treat cultural information as a selfish replicator? What specific psychological mechanisms are required for cultural transmission and so on? Perhaps more than any other area addressed in this book, the application of evolutionary theory to the understanding of culture reveals how adopting a Darwinian framework can not only help answer existing questions, but can unearth new and interesting questions to set a research agenda for the twenty-first century.

We've come a long way culturally in 10,000 years but evolutionary psychologists would argue that if we are to understand the human mind then we would do well to realise that that mind is the same one that scanned the plains of equatorial Africa in the days of our Pleistocene ancestors.

Summary

- Early theories of culture (described by Tooby and Cosmides as adopting the Standard Social Sciences Model or SSSM otherwise known as cultural relativism) tended to reject the importance of biology in explaining cultural phenomena. Instead culture was seen as a superorganism unaffected by human nature.
- In contrast to the view of the cultural relativists, Donald Brown argues that there are many cultural universals, and some of these might be the product of a comparatively fixed underlying human nature. Tooby and Cosmides propose that evoked culture might give rise to contingent universals, practices that are the result of mental models being sensitive to certain environmental conditions.
- Many evolutionists such as Lumsden and Wilson and Tooby and Cosmides argue that many cultural practices are constrained by genes; culture exists to improve our inclusive fitness. Richerson and Boyd are more concerned with how our ability to acquire and learn culture evolved, what factors led to the 'cultural revolution'. They argue that culture provides us with a second mode of inheritance that evolved as a way of adapting to an environment that changed faster than could be addressed by biological evolution.
- Memetics is the treatment of information as replicator (memes), it suggests that in many situations, cultural practices and behaviours need not have any benefit to the host. Rather, cultural information is seen as a selfish replicator or mind virus that takes advantage of human beings' ability to imitate and copy each other.
- Although many animals appear to change their behaviour by imitating others, none appear to do it quite as much or as efficiently as humans. This has led some researchers to suggest that the ability to imitate might represent an adaptation that enables us to acquire culture (as in Boyd and Richerson's theory).

- Specialisation (probably facilitated by the development of agriculture) and trade has led to the incredible advancement of human culture over the cultures of non-human animals which are transmitted vertically.
- Although we typically think of cultural information as being passed on vertically (like biological information), there is reason to believe that a lot of information is passed horizontally between peers; this might be particularly important in childhood.

Questions

1. Make a list of examples of cultural practices from around the world (it might be easier to consider some from your own culture first). Consider to what extent each of these practices might be (1) adaptive (2) maladaptive (3) neutral with regards to inclusive fitness. To what extent might the theories mentioned above (innate, cultural learning, memetic, gene-culture co-evolution) account for the existence of these practices? Are there any that no theory can account for?
2. Technology has a role to play in cultural practices and modern technologies such as mobile phones, computer games, television and the Internet have changed the way we do things to some extent. But have they changed our practices fundamentally? Or do we simply do the same kinds of things we did before but in a different way? How does this relate to the notion of an evolved human nature?
3. Being self-sufficient is often portrayed as a good thing, both at the individual level and at the national level. To what extent might a lack of self-sufficiency lead to interdependence among people and nations and therefore lead to greater cooperation and peace?
4. To what extent does culture exist in non-human animals? In what ways do the proposed cultures of such animals differ from human culture?

FURTHER READING

Aunger, R. A. (2000). *Darwinizing Culture. The Status of Memetics as a Science.* Oxford: Oxford University Press. Good exposition and critique of current thinking in the memes debate.

Brown, D. E. (1991). *Human Universals.* New York, McGraw Hill. Landmark book that describes some possible universals of human culture.

Diamond, J. (1998). *Guns, Germs and Steel: A Short History of Everybody for the Last 13,000 Years.* London: Vintage. A wonderfully scholarly work that tries to provide ultimate explanations for why the world is as it is today.

Pagel, M. (2012). *Wired for Culture: Origins of the Human Social Mind.* London: W. W. Norton. Readable account of the origins of culture and sociality and the importance of language in its evolution.

Richerson, P. and Boyd, R. (2005). *Not by Genes Alone*. Chicago: University of Chicago Press. Introduces their notion of dual inheritance theory and the 'multileveled' selection of cultural units.

Tomasello, M. (1999). *The Cultural Origins of Human Cognition*. Cambridge, MA: Harvard University Press. Quite a technical book that attempts to explain the many differences between humans and non-humans in terms of cognition and culture.

Glossary

abiotic Non-living (or at least non-biological) features of an environment.

adaptation A trait (physical or behaviour) that has been selected by virtue of its positive effects on survival or reproduction (including care of offspring). Some (e.g. Theodosius Dobzhansky) argue that 'adaptation' is a process rather than a thing and prefer the phrase 'adaptive trait'.

adaptive memory approach The notion that memory has evolved not only to be an efficient mechanism for supporting decisions but is particularly sensitive to content that would have been important to the lives of our ancestors (e.g. in the EEA).

adrenalin (epinephrine) A hormone and a neurotransmitter that prepares the body for 'fight or flight'.

affective disorders Psychiatric disorders that involve problems of mood and emotion.

allele An abbreviation for allelomorph. Each **gene** occupies a specific position on a chromosome, i.e. its **locus**. At any specific locus different forms of a gene may occur. Such genes are alleles for that locus.

altruism Self-sacrificing behaviour. To an evolutionary psychologist true altruism involves behaviour that promotes the inclusive fitness of another at a cost to oneself.

amenorrhea Cessation of the menstrual cycle (often associated with the eating disorder **anorexia nervosa**).

amino acid The building blocks of proteins.

amygdala An almond-shaped structure in the forebrain that is involved in processing emotion. A part of the **limbic system**.

androgens Sex hormones, such as testosterone, responsible for male sexual maturation and involved in aggressive and sexual responses.

anorexia nervosa An eating disorder characterised by measures to control weight at a level at least 15 per cent below the healthy norm through dieting, use of laxatives and excessive exercise to burn off calories.

antisocial personality disorder A serious personality disorder (this term is used by DSM-5) whereby the individual lacks guilt, shame and empathy. They may also demonstrate a callous disregard for others. Related to 'psychopathy'.

arbitrary culture theory The theory that the variation seen in customs and practices between cultures may be traced back to arbitrary events rather than being related to human adaptations (see **superorganic theory of culture, SSSM**).

Ardipithecus ramidus A human-like ape (**hominid or hominin**) living in Africa around 4.4 million years ago. Believed to be an early ancestor of humans. Sometimes referred to colloquially as 'Ardi'.

arms race The phenomenon of a change or improvement on one side of a competition leading to change or improvement in the other. Applied particularly, but not exclusively, to predator/prey and host/parasite relationships.

Asperger's syndrome (or Asperger syndrome) A condition like **autism** but sufferers are usually less intellectually impaired. Technically Asperger's syndrome differs from autism in that sufferers from Asperger's syndrome do not suffer impaired language or language delay.

attachment A theory first proposed by Bowlby and later modified by Ainsworth which investigates the effects of early experiences between the child and caregiver on subsequent development.

Australopithecus A genus consisting of a number of species that evolved in Africa around 4.2 million years ago. One of these species is believed to be an early ancestor of humans.

autism A developmental disorder that describes a broad spectrum of symptoms including language delay and usually mental retardation. In particular it has been suggested that people with autism have difficulty understanding the mental states of others, i.e. they have an impaired **theory of mind**.

balancing theory The proposal that selection pressures from the social environment lead to different levels of a trait being observed.

base rate neglect A phrase used to describe the way that we ignore prior probabilities when making judgements of likelihood.

behavioural genetics A discipline that investigates the effect of genes and the environment on individual differences (e.g. personality, intelligence, etc.)

biophobia Fear and suspicion of biological explanations.

biotic Living/biological features of the environment.

bipedalism Walking upright on two legs.

bipolar depression The clinical condition whereby a person oscillates between periods of mania and depression. In most cases there may also be periods of normal mood. Also called bipolar affective disorder.

BSD theory A theory that proposes that individuals can follow different developmental trajectories to maximise reproductive success based on current conditions. The abbreviation comes from original research by Belsky, Steinberg and Draper (1991).

cerebral cortex The outer covering of the forebrain, involved in emotion, perception, thought and planning.

cerebral hemispheres The two halves of the forebrain. The left hemisphere is specialised for language and logical and sequential responses; the right hemisphere is specialised for visuo-spatial abilities, and emotional processing.

C–F continuum Related to **K-** and **r-selection** the C–F continuum specifies whether an organism invests in current fitness (C) or future fitness (F).

chromosome A string of genes found in a cell's nucleus.

Cinderella effect The notion that step-parents invest less in their stepchildren than in their own biological children. Has been used by Daly and Wilson to help understand the mistreatment of children within an evolutionary framework.

codon A triplet of nucleotides (DNA units) codifying an amino acid.

co-efficient of relatedness (r) The proportion of genes shared between two relatives, measured on a scale of 0–1.

computational theory of mind The belief that the mind can be described as a type of computation produced by the brain.

conditional reasoning Type of reasoning which solves problems of the form IF X THEN Y (see **denotic task, indicative task**).

conjunction fallacy The false assumption that a specific condition is more likely than a general one of which it is a subset (see the bank teller problem in chapter 9)

consequentialist ethics An ethical system based on the outcomes or consequences of an action rather than the means (see **deontological ethics, utilitarian ethics**).

Consilience A term used by E. O. Wilson to describe a coming together of different scientific traditions to produce a unified whole.

conspecifics Members of one's own species.

constructivism A position held by Piaget which proposes that development occurs as a result of an interaction between innate principles and experience (see **nativism** and **empiricism**).

contingent shift theory The proposal that all individuals may have the propensity to develop psychopathy given the (in)appropriate circumstances.

Coolidge effect The observation that male animals (including humans), following mating, demonstrate renewed sexual potency when a novel receptive female appears.

corpus callosum The large bundle of nerve fibres joining the two cerebral hemispheres.

cortical plasticity The capacity of the cortex to organise itself during development and in particular reorganise itself following brain damage.

corticosteroids Cortisol and other related stress hormones.

cortisol A hormone produced in the cortex of the adrenal glands that helps the body deal with stress.

critical period A developmental period within which certain experiences must be had in order for them to be learned. There is evidence to suggest that in the development of the visual system, for example, certain inputs have to be experienced before a certain age in order for vision to develop normally (see **sensitive period**).

crossing over The exchange of genes between two homologous **chromosomes** prior to **gamete** formation.

cryptic oestrus The idea that human females, in contrast to other mammals, conceal their period of oestrus.

cultural relativism The philosophical position whereby what is considered correct (both morally and empirically) is determined by your culture, and that the views of all cultures should be treated as equally valid – sometimes called the **Standard Social Sciences Model (SSSM)**.

culturegens E. O. Wilson's term for a unit of culture inheritance (see **memes**).

Darwinian medicine Applying Darwinian principles to understanding and improving health-related problems.

deontic task Logical task based on rights, duties and obligations.

deontological ethics Set of ethical principles based on the rights of the individual.

derivational morphology In language this is the way in which words are modified by the addition of **morphemes** to make new words. For example the recent coinage 'microwaveable' is made up of three morphemes, 'micro', 'wave' and 'able'.

developmental plasticity The theory that malleability is built into development as an adaptation.

diploid An organism is diploid if it has two pairs of **chromosomes** in each cell. In a species that reproduces sexually one of each pair of chromosomes comes from each parent.

direct fitness A measure of the proportion of an individual's genes that are passed on to the next generation directly via their offspring.

display rules The unwritten rules that determine the extent to which emotions may be exhibited publicly in a given society.

DNA (deoxyribonucleic acid) The chemical of which genes are composed. Physically it is a giant double helix molecule.

dopamine A neurotransmitter known to be involved in emotional responses.

dual inheritance theory A theory proposed by Boyd and Richerson, who argue that humans have two sources of inheritance, via the genes and via culture. In their theory culture evolved as a way of enabling humans to change more rapidly in an uncertain world.

Dualism A philosophical position that proposes that there are two different kinds of something. The most familiar form of dualism is Descartes' substance dualism in which the mind and body (including the brain) are seen as being made from two fundamentally different substances.

EEA See Environment of Evolutionary Adaptedness (EEA).

empiricism A philosophical position that holds that the mind is initially a blank slate and all knowledge is the result of learning (see **nativism** and **constructivism**).

Environment of Evolutionary Adaptedness (or Adaptation) (EEA) A combination of the time, place and ecological pressures faced by our species during its evolution.

epigenesis The developmental process that leads from genotype to phenotype within a given environment. The process of epigenesis can lead to some genes being expressed and others not depending on the nature of the environment.

episodic memory A memory that is responsible for storing particular experiences in our lives, e.g. a holiday in Paris. Episodic memories usually contain perceptions (sights, smells, tastes) as well as other facts (see **semantic memory**).

ethnocentrism Perceiving one's own culture as the norm and different cultures as in some way odd or inferior.

eugenics A practice whereby humans are 'selectively bred' for the good of humanity. So-called positive eugenics attempts to mate people with positive characteristics (e.g. people who are industrious or intelligent), negative eugenics, on the other hand, seeks to prevent people deemed unfit from breeding.

evoked culture Tooby and Cosmides suggest that certain cultural phenomena might be innate and are triggered by the environment; these are known as evoked cultural phenomena (see **transmitted culture**).

evolutionarily stable strategy A strategy that is successful in a population where that strategy is most common.

evolutionary medicine A new branch of medicine that makes use of modern Darwinism to help understand and treat both physical and mental health problems (also known as 'Darwinian Medicine').

female choice The theory that females should be more selective than males when it comes to choosing a sexual partner because they invest more heavily in offspring.

fission–fusion society Social group formation in primates whereby a large group frequently divides up into a number of smaller groups while foraging and then recombines when a large food source is discovered.

fitness A measure of the number of offspring produced, or, in the view of some evolutionists, the proportion of genes passed on to future generations.

foramen magnum The hole in the skull through which the spinal cord passes.

FOXP2 A gene that is associated with language.

frequency dependent selection The process whereby the success of a phenotype (in terms of fitness) depends on the frequency of other phenotypes in a population.

frugivorous Fruit eating.

gambler's fallacy, the Incorrect notion that after a run of bad luck some good luck is due.

game theory A method of examining strategic moves based on mathematics.

gamete A sperm or egg cell.

gavagai problem A thought experiment created by philosopher W. V. O. Quine which attempts to show that word learning is impossible via **ostensive communication** unless we make certain assumptions.

gene The fundamental unit of heredity; a section of DNA that codes for one polypeptide. Since proteins are made up of polypeptides then we can say that genes code for proteins.

gene flow The transfer of specific genes from one population to another.

gene selection The notion that natural selection occurs at the level of the gene.

gene-culture co-evolution E. O. Wilson's suggestion of how genes and culture interact. Culture, he argues, is constrained by the genes.

genetic drift The process of changes in gene frequencies in a population due to chance.

genetic marker A DNA segment that is in a known physical location on a chromosome. A genetic marker is broader than a single gene and may or may not have a known function.

genome All of the genes that an organism possesses.

genotype The genetic constitution of an organism encoded in the nucleus of each cell of the body.

Great Chain of Being, the (*scala naturae*) A false theory of evolution which sees some creatures as more highly evolved than others. This view would see humans as being a more evolved version of a chimp, rather than the correct view which sees each descending from a common ancestor.

greedy reductionism A term coined by Daniel Dennett to describe the attempt to explain everything at its most basic level ignoring the complexity of what is to be explained.

group selection The notion that natural selection occurs at the level of the group.

group socialisation theory A theory proposed by Judith Harris which suggests that peer groups have a greater impact on a child's socialisation and personality development than the parental environment.

habituation Following a period of exposure to a novel stimulus an animal learns not to respond to it.

handicap hypothesis The theory that males develop an impediment such as elaborate tail feathers in order to demonstrate to potential mates their ability to survive despite having such a handicap. First proposed by Amotz Zahavi in 1975.

haploid An organism is said to be haploid if it has a single set of **chromosomes** in each cell. Sex cells (i.e. sperm and ova) are also in sexually reproducing **diploid** species.

heritability The extent to which variation in a trait is due to genetic rather than environmental components.

heterozygous Having different **alleles** at the same **locus** on each of the paired **chromosomes** in a cell's nucleus.

heuristic A 'rule of thumb' used for achieving some end such as solving a problem. Heuristics are normally fast and computationally inexpensive even though they might not always work. They are usually contrasted with algorithms, which guarantee the correct solution if there is one but are often costly and time consuming to use.

histrionic personality disorder A personality disorder where the individual tends to be attention-seeking, self-centred and overly dramatic. They may also engage in fantasy.

hominin Modern humans and all of their immediate ancestors.

Homo erectus An early ancestor of humans living around 1.8 million to less than 100,000 years ago.

Homo habilis An early ancestor of humans living around two million years ago.

Homo sapiens The species to which we belong. Evolved less than 400,000 years ago.

homozygous Having identical **alleles** at the same **locus** on each of the paired **chromosomes** in a cell's nucleus.

honest signallers Individuals that provide signals that neither over- or underplay their qualities or needs.

hormones Chemical messengers secreted by a number of glands to regulate the activity of various parts of the body. Hormones play a role in growth and sexual development and activity as well as helping to regulate metabolism.

Human Proteome Project A project launched in 2011 to identify at least one protein for each of the exons (protein-producing genes).

hypothalamus A structure deep within the brain that is involved in regulating a number of activities including metabolism and motivational/emotional states.

imprinting A mechanism explored by Konrad Lorenz whereby chicks rapidly acquire a representation of their 'mother' and are thus able to identify her.

inclusive fitness A measure of the proportion of an individual's genes passing on to future generations directly via offspring and indirectly via other relatives.

indicative task A logical task based upon the truth value of a particular state of affairs e.g. *If* it is raining *then* I will use an umbrella.

indirect fitness A measure of the proportion of an individual's genes that are passed on to the next generation indirectly via relatives other than their offspring.

individual selection The notion that **natural selection** occurs at the level of the individual.

inflectional morphology In language this is the way that words change to convey properties such as tense, agreement and aspect. English has a sparse inflectional system compared with languages such as Latin and French.

inheritance of acquired characteristics, the A theory which proposed that characteristics acquired through experience could be passed on to offspring through the genes. Famously proposed by Lamarck and now generally held not to be true.

intelligent design The notion that living things show signs of having been designed by a higher intelligence. Suggests that the complexity of life cannot be accounted for by Darwinism.

intersexual selection Competition to attract members of the opposite sex for the purposes of mating.

intrasexual selection Competition between members of one sex for sexual access to members of the other sex.

James–Lange theory The theory that we feel emotions because of the physical reactions of the body to emotional events rather than vice versa.

just-so story A phrase coined by Stephen Jay Gould to describe a set of historical circumstances that could have led to some trait being adaptive with little or no substantiating evidence. The term is used pejoratively.

kin altruism Apparent self-sacrificing behaviour aimed at relatives.

K-selection A population or species in which individuals produce relatively small numbers of offspring which are well developed at birth (or at point of hatching) and in which there is high parental investment.

lateralisation The term used to describe the differential functioning of the left and right **cerebral hemispheres.**

learnability argument Also known as 'the argument from the poverty of the stimulus'. Chomsky argued that the linguistic information that children encounter is so sparse and unsystematic that language learning is impossible unless it is supported by innate knowledge.

life history theory A theory that investigates the way that organisms allocate time and resources to different activities (e.g. feeding, reproduction, learning) throughout the lifespan.

limbic system A series of brain structures including the hippocampus, **amygdala** and septum involved in the regulation of emotion and memory.

locus The position of a gene on a **chromosome.**

Machiavellian intelligence A term coined by Whiten and Byrne, Machiavellian intelligence relates to the ability of animals to manipulate conspecifics by deception, etc.

mania A state of excessive excitement where mood is extremely elevated. The polar opposite of a depressed state in **bipolar depression**.

manipulation When one individual, such as a dominant conspecific, coerces another into providing aid.

Materialism A philosophical position that sees mental events are fundamentally reducible to physical events in the brain. Materialism is a form of **monism** and is contrasted with forms of **dualism**.

matrilineal society A society where social relationships are based around the mature females.

meat-for-sex hypothesis The contentious notion that in some primate species the giving of meat to fertile females increases a male's chances of mating with her.

meiosis The process of producing cells that have half the number of **chromosomes** of the mother cell (i.e. they are **haploid**). Meiosis leads to **gamete** formation.

meme The term coined by Richard Dawkins for a unit of cultural inheritance. Analogous to a gene as the unit of biological inheritance.

memetics The scientific study of **memes**.

mental age An estimation of a child's level of intelligence expressed in terms of what would be expected for a given age (e.g. a child of ten that scores at the level of a typical 5-year-old would have a mental age of 5).

mismatch hypothesis The notion that humans have developed a lifestyle that did not exist in our ancestral past too rapidly for selection pressures to have led to appropriate changes.

mitosis The process of producing cells that have the same number of **chromosomes** as the mother cell (i.e. they are **diploid**). Mitosis leads to the formation of new body cells.

modularity The claim that the mind contains innate faculties each designed for a particular purpose (such as language, face processing, etc.). Most famously advocated by philosopher Jerry Fodor but modified by Tooby and Cosmides and other evolutionary psychologists to give it a Darwinian twist.

molecular genetics The study of genes at the molecular level.

monism A philosophical position which proposes that there is only one kind of thing (see **materialism**), it is usually contrasted with **dualism**.

monogamy A mating system where individuals mate with only one partner.

moral illusion Something that people respond to as if it is a moral transgression but which they find difficult to justify based on moral or ethical principles.

morphemes Minimal units of meaning in a language. The word 'talk' is a morpheme as it cannot be broken down further without destroying the meaning. Not all morphemes, however, are words. The suffix 'ing' is also a morpheme and can be added to words to make new words, e.g. 'talking'.

Muller's ratchet The notion that, in an asexual population, due to mutations over a number of generations, deleterious genes will build up (i.e. due to a lack of sex it is difficult to remove such genes from a population – rather like a ratchet that only allows a cog to turn in one direction).

multilevel selection theory The hypothesis that natural selection acts at the level of the group in addition to acting at the level of the gene/individual. Associated with David Sloan Wilson and Elliot Sober.

multi-regional hypothesis The hypothesis that anatomically modern *Homo sapiens* evolved independently at a number of locations during our evolution.

mutation A random inherited change in genetic material.

mutualism When two (or more) individuals benefit from a cooperative act at the time of the act (such as cooperative hunting). In contrast to reciprocation where there is an initial cost–benefit asymmetry that is later repaid.

nativism A philosophical position that holds that certain psychological abilities are inborn and therefore not learned. More recent interpretations of nativism postulate innate mechanisms for acquiring certain abilities such as language (see **empiricism** and **constructivism**).

natural selection The prime mover of evolutionary change. The name given by Darwin to what is today considered to be differential gene replication. May more loosely be described as differential reproductive success of different **phenotypes**.

naturalistic fallacy The false assumption that because something is found in nature it is necessarily good or desirable in some kind of moral sense.

Neanderthal A sub-species of early *Homo sapiens* – *Homo sapiens neanderthalensis* (some experts consider them to constitute a separate species – *Homo neanderthalensis*).

Neanderthal Genome Project A project to sequence the genome for the Neanderthals.

neocortex The most recently evolved part of the mammalian brain. A six-cell thick outer covering of much of the cerebral hemispheres. Not found in non-mammalian species.

neuroconstructivism The notion that while module-like structures exist in the adult mind, they are formed through experience rather than being innate.

neurodevelopment Development of the brain.

neuroimaging The collective term for various techniques that allow a scientist to study the structure and/or functioning of the brain. Includes CT, PET and fMRI.

neurotransmitter A chemical released by neurons to relay information between neurones.

niche fitting The notion that individuals alter to exploit a particular 'niche' (place within an environment). Has been applied to explain some aspects of personality development.

non-zero-sum game A game played by two or more people in which win–lose is not the only outcome (as it is for **zero-sum games**). In this form of game it is possible for everyone to win, everyone to lose or any other combination of outcomes. Many real-life situations are non-zero-sum. For example it is possible for two people to cooperate, together achieving far more than either could alone.

obsessive–compulsive disorder A disorder where the sufferer has two related problems – obsessions such as recurrent thoughts and urges that cause anxiety, and compulsions to carry out repetitive acts that they consider will reduce the obsessions.

orbitofrontal cortex A portion of the cortex that lies just above the eyes and is involved in processing socially appropriate responses.

ostensive communication Communicating by referring to things in the environment, e.g. pointing at objects.

out-of-Africa The hypothesis that anatomically modern *Homo sapiens* evolved in Africa around 100,000 years ago and that a group from this species left Africa around 60,000 years ago eventually populating the rest of the world.

parameter setting In Chomsky's theory the **Universal Grammar** is innate knowledge of the abstract structure common to all languages. Parameter setting is where the specifics of a given language are 'learned'. E.g. whether the particular language in a child's environment is subject, verb, object (like English) or verb, subject, object (like Gaelic).

parental investment The time, effort and resources expended by a parent on one offspring that might otherwise be expended on other offspring.

parental manipulation hypothesis The proposal that parents might manipulate the behaviour of their offspring in order to boost the **inclusive fitness** of the parents.

parthenogenesis 'Virgin birth'. The process of producing offspring from unfertilised eggs.

perineum The area around the vagina and anus which becomes swollen and reddened in female primates during oestrus.

person–situation debate The debate as to whether the primary determiner of behaviour is a person's personality or the specifics of the situation.

phenotype Individual characteristics resulting from environmental interaction of an organism's **genotype**.

phonemes Minimal units of sound in a language. In the alphabetic system of writing used in English and other languages, phonemes often correspond to an individual letter (but not always).

pleiotropy The phenomenon of one gene having more than one **phenotypic** effect.

polyandry A form of **polygamy** where individual females mate with more than one male.

polygamy Mating with more than one individual.

polygenic The phenomenon of a trait being coded for by more than one gene.

polygyny A form of polygamy where individual males mate with more than one female.

pragmatics A branch of linguistics which studies the intended and interpreted meaning of an utterance.

preparedness theory The hypothesis that we (and other species) are born with propensities to develop certain responses. Most frequently applied to phobias.

prisoner's dilemma A non-zero-sum game in which each of two players has to decide whether to cooperate or defect. Used in game theory.

proband Term used in genetics to denote the individual being studied (as opposed to control groups and/or relatives).

prototype A generalisation made about something in the world, e.g. that birds fly. Prototypes are thought to be useful because they enable rapid mental processing, even if they are not always entirely correct (as in the previous example).

provisioning hypothesis The notion that the male–female pair bond arose, in part, out of the fact that males provided meat for their female partners.

proximate level of explanation A style of explanation that explains the immediate cause of a particular trait (see **ultimate level of explanation**).

reciprocal altruism The process of reciprocating acts of self-sacrificing behaviour between two individuals such that both ultimately gain because the benefits outweigh the costs for each (often termed 'direct reciprocation' simply 'reciprocation' today). First proposed by Robert Trivers in 1971.

recombination The process by which genetic material (usually a DNA molecule) is broken and then joined to other genetic material.

reductionism A philosophical approach which explains nature by reducing it to the interaction of simpler elements. For example, heat is explained by the oscillation of atoms and molecules. Reductionism is central to modern science and should not be treated as an insult (see **greedy reductionism**).

Red Queen hypothesis The notion that evolutionary 'improvements' to members of a species counteracting changes in members of other species, which may for example be parasites of that species, lead members of the first species back to where they started.

replication The process of forming a new DNA molecule from an existing molecule of DNA.

reproduction suppression hypothesis The proposal that females suffering from **anorexia nervosa** reduce their weight in order to avoid becoming pregnant.

reproductive effort The amount of effort an organism puts into reproduction such as producing offspring and rearing offspring (as opposed to **somatic effort**).

reproductive value A theoretical measurement of the potential for future offspring production. In practice very difficult to quantify.

resource extraction Extracting resources from another individual (particularly associated with female primates in a pair-bonded relationship).

RNA (ribonucleic acid) A polynucleotide molecule consisting of a long chain of nucleotides which are used as the template for protein production.

r-selection A population or species in which individuals produce relatively large numbers of offspring and in which there is low parental investment.

runaway selection The hypothesis proposed by R. A. Fisher that a trait may become elaborated purely on the basis of its attraction to the opposite sex. An example of this might be the elaborate tail feathers of a peacock.

Santa Barbara school (of evolutionary psychology) A term we use to describe the type of evolutionary psychology proposed by Tooby and Cosmides. This posits that we evolve domain-specific mental modules in the EEA.

schizophrenia A serious psychological disorder where a person may have periods of delusional behaviour, hallucinations, disordered thought and in some cases paranoia.

semantic memory A memory that is responsible for storing general knowledge about the world, e.g. that Paris is the capital of France (see **episodic memory**).

sensitive period Like a **critical period** but less hard and fast. During a sensitive period certain skills are acquired more rapidly than at other times.

sexual competition hypothesis The proposal that eating disorders are driven by high levels of female–female competition for the attention of potential partners.

sexual dimorphism The degree to which the males and females of a population differ (both physically and in terms of behaviour).

sexual selection Darwin's second mechanism of evolutionary change. Sexual selection 'selects for' characteristics that help an individual gain access to mates. May be divided into **intersexual** and **intrasexual** selection.

Signalling theory or costly signalling theory A theory in biology which proposes that animal signals are kept 'honest' by virtue of their cost. Only those animals that can afford the cost of the signal can display the signal. See also **honest signallers** and **handicap hypothesis.**

smoke detector principle The hypothesis that we are likely to demonstrate higher levels of anxiety than is strictly necessary since, like a smoke detector, the cost of reacting to a false alarm is much lower than the cost of not responding to a real alarm.

social competition hypothesis The theory that high levels of depression in today's society are related to finding ourselves in apparent competition with large numbers of people, many of whom appear to be more successful than ourselves.

social contract hypothesis A theory that proposes that language evolved in order to make promises and other forms of social contract.

social grooming hypothesis A hypothesis put forward by Robin Dunbar to explain the origins of language. He argued that as group sizes increase ancestral humans needed to maintain social cohesion that was obtained in other primates by grooming. Language fulfilled this role, he argues.

sociobiology A framework that attempts to explain social phenomena in terms of biology including genes. There is debate as to whether or not sociobiology is the same thing as evolutionary psychology.

somatic effort The effort an organism puts into growth and maturation through feeding, avoiding predation and learning (as opposed to **reproductive effort**).

Spandrel A word used to describe a trait that is the side effect of an adaptation rather than an adaptation itself. The term was coined by Gould and Lewontin (1979) in their article 'The spandrels of San Marco'.

specific action tendencies The hypothesis that specific emotional states lead to states of mind and these, in turn, are likely to lead to adaptive responses.

specific language impairment A developmental language disorder that appears to affect **inflectional morphology.**

Standard Social Science Model (SSSM) The set of assumptions considered by many evolutionary psychologists to be held by the majority of social scientists and which place environmental/cultural factors as pre-eminent in understanding human behaviour.

substrate neutrality The assumption made in the cognitive sciences that the nature of mental processes is independent of the hardware that 'runs' them. This assumption makes it possible for cognitive scientists to model human thought processes on a digital computer.

superorganic theory of culture A theory proposed by sociologists and anthropologists that sees culture as above and beyond biology – a 'superorganism'. This sees culture as being an autonomous force that shapes human behaviour.

s-value A term used in the **adaptive memory** approach to describe the survival value of an item or situation. Things with a high s-value are more memorable.

theory of mind The ability to understand the mental states of others. Also called mind reading or naive psychology.

trait A characteristic (physical or behavioural) that is a fundamental unit of the **phenotype**.

transcription The process of converting a genetic code from DNA to RNA.

transmitted culture Unlike **evoked culture,** transmitted cultural phenomena that have no innate basis.

ultimate level of explanation A style of explanation which attempts to answer the function that a particular trait has in terms of fitness (see **proximate** level of explanation).

unimale group Social organisation based around one male and several females (particularly associated with silverback gorillas).

Universal Grammar Part of Chomsky's theory of language acquisition. According to Chomsky we are born with knowledge of the abstract structure that underlies all languages; this is called the universal grammar.

utilitarian ethics An ethical system based upon the consequences of an action rather than the means, the consequences are usually for the greater good (see **consequentialist ethics**).

Williams syndrome A developmental disorder caused by damage to chromosome 7. In particular Williams syndrome sufferers have low IQ but their language and theory of mind are spared. Some have argued that Williams syndrome is the mirror image of **autism.**

xenophobia A fear or dislike of strangers.

zero-sum-game A game played by two or more people in which the outcomes of the participants of the game sum to zero. For example in a game such as chess one person wins and the other loses so the win is cancelled out by the loss. Rather less technically it is applied to games where it is impossible for all players to win (see **non-zero-sum game**).

zygote A cell that is formed from the fusion of two **gametes** (i.e. a fertilised egg).

References

Abed, R., Mehta, S., Figueredo, A. J., Aldridge, S., Balson, H., Meyer, C. and Palmer, R. (2012). Eating disorders and intrasexual competition: Testing an evolutionary hypothesis among young women. *Scientific World Journal*. Published online 1 April 2012. doi: 10.1100/2012/290813

Adams, D. *et al.* (1986). Seville statement on violence. *American Psychologist* (publication date 1990), 45(10), 167–8.

Adelson, E. H. (1993). Perceptual organization and the judgment of brightness. *Science*. 262, 2042–4.

Aiello, L. C. (1993). The fossil evidence for modern human origins in Africa: A revised view. *American Anthropologist*. 95, 73–96.

Ainsworth, M. (1967). *Infancy in Uganda: Infant Care and the Growth of Love*. Baltimore: Johns Hopkins University Press.

Aitchison, J. (1989). *The Articulate Mammal* (4th edn). London: Routledge.

Akhtar, N. and Tomasello, M. (1997). Young children's productivity with word order and verb morphology. *Developmental Psychology*. 33, 952–65.

Alcock, J. (2001). *The Triumph of Sociobiology*. New York: Oxford University Press.

(2005). *Animal Behavior: An Evolutionary Approach* (8th edn). Sunderland, MA: Sinauer.

(2009). *Animal Behavior: An Evolutionary Approach* (9th edn). Sunderland, MA: Sinauer.

Alexander, R. D. (1974). The evolution of social behaviour. *Annual Review of Ecology and Systematics*. 5, 325–83.

(1980). *Darwinism and Human Affairs*. Seattle: University of Washington Press.

(1987). *The Biology of Moral Systems*. New York: Aldine de Gruyter.

Alexander, R. D. and Noonan, K. M. (1979). Concealment of ovulation, parental care and human social evolution. In N. A. Chagnon and W. Irons (eds.). *Evolutionary Biology and Human Social Behaviour* (402–35). North Scituate, MA: Duxbury Press.

Alexander, R. D., Hoodland, J. L., Howard, R. D., Noonan, K. M. and Sherman, P. W. (1979). Sexual dimorphisms and breeding systems in pinnepeds, ungulates, primates and humans. In N. A. Chagnon and W. Irons (eds.). *Evolutionary Biology and Human Social Behaviour* (436–53). North Scituate, MA: Duxbury Press.

Allen, E. *et al.* (1975). Against 'sociobiology'. *New York Times Review of Books*. 22(18), 13 November.

Allport, G. W. and Odbert, H. S. (1936). Trait names: A psycho-lexical study. *Psychological Monographs*. 47 (whole no. 211).

Anderson, C. M. (1992). Male investment under changing conditions among chacma baboons at Suikerbosrand. *American Journal of Physical Anthropology*. 87, 479–96.

Anderson, J. R. (1983). *The Architecture Of Cognition*. Mahwah, NJ: Erlbaum.
 (1990). *The Adaptive Character of Thought*. Hillsdale, NJ: Lawrence Erlbaum.
Anderson, J. R. and Milson, R. (1989). Human memory: An adaptive perspective. *Psychological Review*. 96(4), 703–19.
Anderson, K. G. (1999). Paternal care by genetic fathers and stepfathers I: Reports from Albuquerque men. *Evolution and Human Behaviour*. 20, 405–31.
Anderson, M. (1992). *Intelligence and Development: A Cognitive Theory*. Oxford: Blackwell.
Andersson, M. (1982). Female choice selects for extreme tail length in a widow bird. *Nature*. 299, 818–20.
 (1986). Evolution of condition-dependent sex ornaments and mating preferences: Sexual selection based on viability differences. *Evolution*. 40. 804–16.
Andrew, R. J. (1963a). The origins and evolution of the calls and facial expressions of the primates. *Behaviour*. 20, 1–109.
 (1963b). Evolution of facial expressions. *Science*. 142, 1034–41.
Andrews, P. W. and Thomson, Jr., J. A. (2009). The bright side of being blue: Depression as an adaptation for analyzing complex problems. *Psychological Review*. 116, 620–54.
Andrews, P. W., Thomson, Jr., J. A., Amstadter, A. and Neale, M. C. (2012). *Primum non nocere*: An evolutionary analysis of whether antidepressants do more harm than good. *Frontiers in Psychology*. 3, 117.
Angier, N. (1999). Men, women, sex and Darwin. *New York Times*, 21 February.
Angrist, B., Lee, H. K. and Gershon, S. (1974). The antagonism of amphetamine-induced symptomology by a neuroleptic. *American Journal of Psychiatry*. 131, 817–19.
Archer, J. (1996). Evolutionary social psychology. In M. Hewstone, S. Wolfgang and G. M. Stephenson (eds.). *Introduction to Social Psychology* (24–45). Oxford: Blackwell.
 (2001). Evolving theories of behaviour. *The Psychologist*. 14, 414–19.
Ardrey, R. (1961). *African Genesis: A Personal Investigation into the Animal Origins and Nature of Man*. New York: Dell.
Asch, S. E. (1956). Studies of independence and conformity. A minority of one against a unanimous majority. *Psychological Monographs*. 70(9), 1–70.
Atkinson, A. P. (2007). Face processing and empathy. In T. F. D. Farrow and P. W. R. Woodruff (eds.). *Empathy in Mental Illness* (360–85). Cambridge: Cambridge University Press.
Atran, S. (1990). *The Cognitive Foundations of Natural History: Towards an Anthropology of Science*. New York: Cambridge University Press.
 (1994). Core domains versus scientific theories: Evidence from systematics and Itza Maya folkbiology. In L. A. Hirschfeld and S. A. Gelman (eds.). *Mapping the Mind: Domain Specificity in Cognition and Culture*. Cambridge: Cambridge University Press.
 (2002). *In Gods We Trust: The Evolutionary Landscape of Religion*. Oxford: Oxford University Press.
Aunger, R. A. (2000). *Darwinizing Culture: The Status of Memetics as a Science*. Oxford: Oxford University Press.

Austad, S. (2000). Varied fates from similar states. *Science.* 290, 944.

Averill, J. R. (1980). On the paucity of positive emotions. In K. R. Blankstein, P. Pliner and J. Polivy (eds.). *Advances in the Study of Communication and Affect. Vol. 6, Assessment and Modification of Emotional Behaviour* (7–45). New York: Plenum.

Axelrod, R. (1984). *The Evolution of Co-operation.* New York: Basic Books.

Axelrod, R. and Hamilton, W. D. (1981). The evolution of co-operation. *Science.* 211, 1390–6.

Badcock, C. (1991). *Evolution and Individual Behaviour: An Introduction to Human Sociobiology.* Oxford: Blackwell.

(2000). *Evolutionary Psychology: A Critical Introduction.* Malden, MA: Blackwell.

Baillargeon, R. (1986). Representing the existence and the location of hidden objects: Object permanence in six- and eight-month-old infants. *Cognition.* 23, 21–41.

(1987). Object permanence in 3½- and 4½-month-old infants. *Developmental Psychology.* 23, 655–64.

(1991). Reasoning about the height and location of a hidden object in 4.5- and 6.5-month-old infants. *Cognition.* 38, 13–42.

Baker, R. R. (2006). *Sperm Wars: Infidelity, Sexual Conflict, and Other Bedroom Battles.* New York: Basic Books.

Baker, R. R. and Bellis, M. A. (1989). Number of sperm in human ejaculates varies in accordance with sperm competition. *Animal Behaviour.* 37, 867–9.

(1995). *Human Sperm Competition.* London: Chapman and Hall.

Baldwin, D. A., Markman, E. M., Bill, B., Desjardins, R. N., Irwin, J. and Tidball, G. (1996). Infants' reliance on a social criterion for establishing word–object relations. *Child Development.* 67, 3135–53.

Banku, M. and Abalaka, M. (2012). Recent advances in medicine using molecular genetics. *Innovative Journal of Medical and Health Science.* 2, 17–24.

Barker, D. J. P. (1998). *Mothers, Babies and Health in Later Life.* London: Churchill Livingstone.

Barkow, J. H., Cosmides, L. and Tooby, J. (eds.) (1992). *The Adapted Mind: Evolutionary Psychology and the Generation of Culture.* Oxford/New York: Oxford University Press.

Baron-Cohen, S. (1989). The autistic child's theory of mind: A case of specific developmental delay. *Journal of Child Psychology and Psychiatry.* 30, 285–97.

(1995). *Mindblindness: Essays in Autism and Theory of Mind.* Cambridge, MA: MIT Press.

(1997). *The Maladapted Mind: Classic Readings in Evolutionary Psychopathology.* London: Psychology Press.

(2002). The extreme male brain theory of autism. *Trends in Cognitive Sciences.* 6(6), 248–54.

(2004). *The Essential Difference.* London: Penguin.

Baron-Cohen, S. and Wheelwright, S. (1999). Obsessions in children with autism or Asperger syndrome: A content analysis in terms of core domains of cognition. *British Journal of Psychiatry.* 175, 484–90.

Baron-Cohen, S., Jolliffe, T., Mortimore, C. and Robertson, M. M. (1997). Another advanced test of theory of mind: Evidence from very high functioning adults with autism or Asperger syndrome. *Journal of Child Psychology and Psychiatry.* 37, 813–22.

Baron-Cohen, S., Leslie, A. M. and Frith, U. (1985). Does the autistic child have a 'theory of mind'? *Cognition.* 21, 37–46.

Baron-Cohen, S., Wheelwright, S., Scahill, V. *et al.* (2001). Are intuitive physics and intuitive psychology independent? A test with children with Asperger Syndrome. *Journal of Developmental Learning Disorders.* 5, 47–78.

Barrett, L. and Dunbar, R. I. M. (1994). Not now dear, I'm busy. *New Scientist.* 142, 30–4.

Barrett, L., Dunbar, R. I. M. and Lycett, J. (2002). *Human Evolutionary Psychology.* New York: Palgrave.

Barsegyan, A., Mackenzie, S., Kurose, B. D., McGaugh, J. L. and Roozendaal, B. (2010). Glucocorticoids in the prefrontal cortex enhance memory consolidation and impair working memory by a common neural mechanism. *Proceedings, National Academy of Sciences, USA.* 107, 16655–60.

Bartlett, F. (1932). *Remembering.* New York: Cambridge University Press.

Basolo, A. L. (1990). Female preference predates the evolution of the sword in sword-tail fish. *Science.* 250, 808–10.

(1995). Phylogenetic evidence for the role of a pre-existing bias in sexual selection. *Proceedings of the Royal Society of London.* B. 265, 2223–8.

Bates, E. (1994). Modularity, domain specificity and the development of language. In D. C. Gajdusek, G. M. McKhann and C. L. Bolis (eds.), Evolution and neurology of language. *Discussions in Neuroscience.* 10(1–2), 136–49.

Bateson, M., Brilot, B. and Nettle, D. (2011). Anxiety: An evolutionary approach. *Canadian Journal of Psychiatry.* 56: 707–15.

Bateson, P. (2000). Taking the stink out of instinct. In H. Rose and S. Rose (eds.). *Alas Poor Darwin: Arguments Against Evolutionary Psychology* (157–73). London: Jonathan Cape.

Bateson, P. and Hinde, R. A. (1987). Developmental changes in sensitivity to experience. In M. H. Bornstein (ed.). *Sensitive Periods in Development* (19–34). Hillsdale, NJ: Lawrence Erlbaum.

Bateson, P. P. G. and Martin, P. (1999). *Design for a Life: How Behaviour Develops,* London: Jonathan Cape.

Bateson, P., Mendl, M. and Feaver, J. (1990). Play in the domestic cat is enhanced by rationing of the mother during lactation. *Animal Behaviour.* 40, 514–25.

Bell, G. (1982). *The Masterpiece of Nature.* London: Croom Helm.

Bellugi, U., Bihrle, A., Jernigan, T., Trauner, D. and Doherty, S. (1990). Neuropsychological, neurological, and neuroanatomical profile of Williams syndrome. *American Journal of Medical Genetics Supplement.* 6, 115–25.

Belsky, J. (1997). Attachment, mating, and parenting: An evolutionary interpretation. *Human Nature.* 8, 361–81.

(2005). Differential susceptibility to rearing influence: An evolutionary hypothesis and some evidence. In B. Ellis and D. Bjorklund (eds.), *Origins of the Social Mind: Evolutionary Psychology and Child Development* (139–63). New York: Guildford.

Belsky, J., Houts, R. M. and Fearon, R. M. P. (2010). Infant attachment security and timing of puberty: Testing an evolutionary hypothesis. *Psychological Science.* 21, 1195–1201.

Belsky, J., Steinberg, L. and Draper, P. (1991). Childhood experience, interpersonal development and reproductive strategy: An evolutionary theory of socialization. *Child Development.* 62(4), 647–70.

Belsky, J., Steinberg, L., Houts, Renate M., Halpern-Felsherd, Bonnie L. and the NICHD Early Child Care Research Network (2010). The development of reproductive strategy in females: early maternal harshness → earlier menarche → increased sexual risk taking. *Developmental Psychology.* 46 (1), 120–8.

Benjamin, J., Osher, Y., Kotler, M., Gritsenko, I., Nemanov, L., Belmaker, R. H. and Ebstein, R. P. (2002). Association between tridimensional personality questionnaire (TPQ) traits and three functional polymorphisms: Dopamine receptor D4 (DRD4), serotonin transporter promoter region (5-HTTLPR) and catechol O-methyltransferase (COMT). *Molecular Psychiatry.* 5, 96–100.

Bentall, R. (2003) *Madness Explained: Psychosis and Human Nature.* London: Allen Lane.

Benton, T. (2000). Social causes and natural relations. In H. Rose and S. Rose (eds.). *Alas Poor Darwin: Arguments Against Evolutionary Psychology* (206–24). London: Jonathan Cape.

Bergman, T. J., Beehner, J. C., Cheney, D. L. and Seyfarth, R. M. (2003). Hierarchical classification by rank and kinship in baboons. *Science.* 302, 1234–6.

Berko, J. (1958). The child's learning of English morphology. *Word.* 14(2–3), 150–77.

Berle, D. and Phillips, E. (2006). Disgust and obsessive–compulsive disorder: An update. *Psychiatry.* 69, 228–38.

Berndt, T. J. (1986). Children's comments about their friendships. In M. Perlmutter (ed.). *Minnesota Symposia in Child Development. Vol. 18, Cognitive Perspectives on Children's Social and Behavioral Development* (189–212). Hillsdale, NJ: Lawrence Erlbaum.

Beroldi, G. (1994). Critique of the Seville statement on violence. *American Psychologist.* 49, 847–8.

Betzig, L. (1997). *Human Nature: A Critical Reader.* New York: Oxford University Press.

Bickerton, D. (2007). Language evolution: A brief guide for linguists. *Lingua.* 510–26.

Bierhoff, H. M. and Rohmann, E. (2004). Altruistic personality in the context of the empathy–altruism hypothesis. *European Journal of Personality.* 18. 351–65.

Bierhoff, H. W. (1996). Heterosexual partnerships: Initiation, maintenance and disengagement. In A. E. Auhagen and M.V. Salisch (eds.). *The Diversity of Human Relationships* (173–96). Cambridge: Cambridge University Press.

Birkhead, T. (2000). *Promiscuity: An Evolutionary History of Sperm Competition and Sexual Conflict.* London: Faber and Faber.

Bishop, D.V. (2002). Motor immaturity and specific speech and language impairment: Evidence for a common genetic basis. *American Journal of Medical Genetics.* 114, 56–63.

Bishop, D. V. M., North, T. and Donlan, C. (1995). Genetic basis of specific language impairment. *Developmental Medicine and Child Neurology.* 37, 56–71.

Bisson, T. (1991). They're made out of meat. *Bears Discover Fire and Other Stories.* Electricstory.com.

Blackmore, S. J. (1999). *The Meme Machine.* Oxford: Oxford University Press.

(2010). Dangerous memes; or, what the Pandorans let loose. In S. Dick and M. Lupisella (eds.). *Cosmos and Culture: Cultural Evolution in a Cosmic Context.* Washington, DC: NASA Press.

Blair, R. J., Morris, J. S., Frith, C. D., Perrett, D. S. and Dolan, R. J. (1999). Dissociable neural responses to facial expressions of sadness and anger. *Brain.* 122, 883–93.

Block, N. (1995). How heritability misleads about race. *Cognition.* 56, 99–128.

Bloom, G. and Sherman, P. W. (2005). Dairying barriers affect the distribution of lactose malabsorption. *Evolution and Human Behavior,* 26(4), 301–12.

Boden, M. A. (1994). *Piaget.* London: Fontana.

Bower, T. G. R. (1974). *Development in Infancy.* San Francisco: Freeman.

Bowlby, J. (1951). *Maternal Care and Mental Health.* Geneva: WHO.

(1969). *Attachment and Loss. Vol. 1, Attachment.* New York: Basic Books.

Boyd, R. and Richerson, P. J. (1985). *Culture and the Evolutionary Process.* Chicago: Chicago University Press.

Boyd, R., Richerson, P. J. and Henrich, J. (2011). The cultural niche: Why social learning is essential for human adaptation. *Proceedings of the National Academy of Sciences.* 108(Supplement 2), 10918–25.

Boyd, R. and Silk, J. B. (2000). *How Humans Evolved.* New York: Norton.

Brasil-Neto, J. P., Pascual-Leone, A., Valls-Sole, J., Cohen, L. G. and Hallett, M. (1992). Focal transcranial magnetic stimulation and response bias in a forced-choice task. *Journal of Neurology, Neurosurgery and Psychiatry.* 55, 964–6.

Breland, K. and Breland, M. (1961). The misbehavior of organisms. *American Psychologist.* 16, 681–4.

Brennan, K. A., Shaver, P. and Tobey, A. E. (1991). Attachment styles, gender, and parental problem drinking. *Journal of Social and Personal Relationships.* 8, 451–66.

Brennan, P. (2010). Sexual selection. *Nature Education Knowledge.* 1, 24.

Brewer, M. B. and Crano, W. D. (1994). *Social Psychology.* New York: West Publishing Co.

Brown, D. E. (1991). *Human Universals.* New York: McGraw-Hill.

Brown, R. (1973). *A First Language: The Early Stages.* Cambridge, MA: MIT Press.

Brüne, M. (2004). Schizophrenia – An evolutionary enigma? *Neuroscience and Biobehavioral Reviews.* 28, 41–53.

Buck, R. (1988). *Human Motivation and Emotion* (2nd edn). New York: Wiley.

Buller, D. (2005a). *Adapting Minds: Evolutionary Psychology and the Persistent Quest for Human Nature.* Cambridge, MA: MIT Press.

(2005b). Evolutionary psychology: The emperor's new paradigm. *Trends in Cognitive Sciences.* 9, 277–83.

Burns, J. (2007). *The Descent of Madness: Evolutionary Origins of Psychosis and the Social Brain.* New York: Routledge.

Burnstein, E., Crandell, C. and Kitayama, S. (1994). Some neo-Darwinian decision rules for altruism: Weighing cues for inclusive fitness as a function of the biological importance of the decision. *Journal of Personality and Social Psychology.* 67, 773–89.

Bushnell, I. W. R., Sai, F. and Mullin, J. T. (1989). Neonatal recognition of the mother's face. *British Journal of Developmental Psychology.* 7, 3–15.

Buss, D. M. (1989). Sex differences in human mate preferences: evolutionary hypotheses tested in 37 cultures. *Behavioral and Brain Sciences.* 12, 1–49.

(1991). Evolutionary personality psychology. *Annual Review of Psychology.* 42, 459–91.

(1995). *The Evolution of Desire.* New York: Basic Books.

(1997). The emergence of evolutionary social psychology. In J. A. Simpson and D. T. Kenrick (eds.). *Evolutionary Social Psychology* (21–48). Hillsdale, NJ: Lawrence Erlbaum.

(1999). *Evolutionary Psychology: The New Science of the Mind* (1st edn). Boston: Allyn and Bacon.

(2003). *The Evolution of Desire: Strategies of Human Mating.* New York: Basic Books.

(2007). The evolution of human mating. *Acta Psychologica Sinica.* 39, 502–12.

(2009). How can evolutionary psychology successfully explain personality and individual differences? *Perspectives on Psychological Science.* 4, 359–66.

(2011). *Evolutionary Psychology: The New Science of the Mind* (4th edn). Boston: Allyn and Bacon.

Buss, D. M. and Greiling, H. (1999). Adaptive individual differences. *Journal of Personality.* 67, 209–43.

Buss, D. M. and Hawley, P. (eds.) (2011). *The Evolution of Personality and Individual Differences.* Oxford: Oxford University Press.

Buss, D. M. and Schmitt, D. P. (1993). Sexual strategies theory: An evolutionary perspective on human mating. *Psychological Review.* 100, 204–32.

Buss, D. M. *et al.* (1990). International preferences in selecting mates: A study of 37 cultures. *Journal of Cross-Cultural Psychology.* 21, 5–47.

Byrne, R. W. (1995). *The Thinking Ape: Evolutionary Origins of Intelligence.* Oxford: Oxford University Press.

Byrne, R. W. and Russon, A. E. (1998). Learning by imitation: A hierarchical approach. *Behavioral and Brain Sciences.* 21(5), 667–84.

Calder, A. J., Young, A. W., Perret, D. I., Etcoff, N. L. and Rowland, D. (1996). Categorical perception of morphed facial expressions. *Visual Cognition.* 3, 81–117.

Callender, L. A. (1988). Gregor Mendel: An opponent of descent with modification. *History of Science.* 26, 41–75.

Campbell, A. (2002). *A Mind of her Own: The Evolutionary Psychology of Women.* Oxford: Oxford University Press.

(2006). Sex differences in direct aggression: What are the psychological mediators? *Aggression and Violent Behavior.* 11, 237–64.

(2008). The morning after the night before: Affective reactions to one-night stands among mated and unmated women and men. *Human Nature.* 19, 157–73.

Caporael, L. R. and Baron, R. M. (1997). Groups as the mind's natural environment. In J. A. Simpson and D. T. Kenrick (eds.). *Evolutionary Social Psychology* (21–48). Mahwah, NJ: Lawrence Erlbaum.

Carey, S. and Spelke, E. S. (1994). Domain-specific knowledge and conceptual change. In L. Hirschfeld and S. Gelman (eds.). *Mapping the Mind: Domain Specificity in Cognition and Culture* (169–200). Cambridge: Cambridge University Press.

Carlson, N. R. (2002). *Foundations of Physiological Psychology.* Boston: Allyn and Bacon. (2012). *Physiology of Behavior* (11th edn). Boston: Pearson.

Carlson, N. R., Buskist, W. and Martin, G. N. (2000). *Psychology: The Science of Behaviour.* London: Allyn and Bacon.

Cashdan, E. (1996). Women's mating strategies. *Evolutionary Anthropology.* 5, 134–43.

Caspi, A., McClay, J., Moffitt, T., Mill, J., Martin, J., Craig, I., Taylor, A. and Poulton, R. (2002). Role of genotype in the cycle of violence in maltreated children. *Science.* 297, 851–4.

Casscells, W., Schoenberger, A. and Grayboys, T. (1978). Interpretation by physicians of clinical laboratory results. *New England Journal of Medicine.* 299, 999–1000.

Cattell, R. B. (1965). *The Scientific Analysis of Personality.* Chicago: Aldine.

Causey, B. C. and Bjorklund, D. F. (2011). The evolution of cognition. In V. Swami (ed.). *Evolutionary Psychology: A Critical Introduction.* (31–71). Chichester: Wiley-Blackwell.

Cavalli-Sforza, L. L. (1991). Genes, peoples and languages. *Scientific American.* 265(5), 72–8.

Centola, D., Willer, R. and Macy, M. (2005). The emperor's dilemma: A computational model of self-enforcing norms. *American Journal of Sociology.* 110(4), 1009–40.

Chagnon, N. A. (1983). *Yanomamo: The Fierce People* (3rd edn). New York: Holt, Rinehart and Winston.

(1988). *Yanomamo: The Fierce People* (4th edn). New York: Holt, Rinehart and Winston.

(1992). *Yanomamo: The Fierce People* (5th edn). New York: Holt, Rinehart and Winston.

(1997). *Yanomamö* (6th edn). New York: Holt, Rinehart and Winston.

(2012). *Yanomamö: Case Studies in Cultural Anthropology* (6th edn). Belmont, CA: Wadsworth.

Charlesworth, W. and Dzur, C. (1987). Gender comparisons of preschoolers' behavior and resource utilization in group problem solving. *Child Development.* 58, 191–200.

Chater, N. and Oaksford, M. (1999). Ten years of the rational analysis of cognition. *Trends in Cognitive Sciences.* 3, 57–65.

Cheney, D. L. and Seyfarth, R. M. (1982). How vervet monkeys perceive their grunts: Field playback experiments. *Animal Behaviour.* 30, 739–51.

(2007): *Baboon Metaphysics: The Evolution of a Social Mind.* Chicago: Chicago Press.

Chernin, K. (1994). *The Hungry Self: Women, Eating, and Identity.* New York: Harper Perennial.

Chiappe, D. and MacDonald, K. B. (2005). The evolution of domain-general mechanisms in intelligence and learning. *Journal of General Psychology.* 132(1), 5–40.

Chisholm, J. S. (1996). The evolutionary ecology of attachment organization. *Human Native*. 7, 1–38.

    (1999). *Death, Hope and Sex: Steps to an Evolutionary Ecology of Mind*. Cambridge: Cambridge University Press.

Chomsky, N. (1957). *Syntactic Structures*. The Hague: Mouton.

    (1959). A review of B. F. Skinner's 'Verbal Behaviour'. *Language*. 35, 26–58.

Chua, S. E. and McKenna, P. J. (1995). Schizophrenia – a brain disease? A critical review of abnormalities of structural and functional cerebral abnormality in the disorder. *British Journal of Psychiatry*. 166, 563–82.

Clamp, A. (2001). *Evolutionary Psychology*. London: Hodder Headline.

Clark, R. and Hatfield, E. (1989). Gender differences in receptivity to sexual offers. *Journal of Psychology and Human Sexuality*. 2, 39–55.

Cloak, F. T. (1975). Is a cultural ethology possible? *Human Ecology*. 3, 161–82.

Clutton-Brock, T. (2009). Cooperation between non-kin in animal societies. *Nature*. 462, 51–7. doi:10.1038/nature08366

Clutton-Brock, T. H. and Harvey, P. (1977). Primate ecological social organization. *Journal of Zoology*. 183, 1–39.

Clutton-Brock, T. H., Guinness, F. E. and Albon, S. D. (1982). *Red Deer: Behaviour and Ecology of Two Sexes*. Chicago: University of Chicago Press.

Collins, D. W. and Kimura, D. (1997). A large sex difference on a two-dimensional mental rotation task. *Behavioural Neuroscience*. 111, 845–9.

Confer, J. C., Easton, J. A., Fleischman, D. S. *et al.* (2010). Evolutionary psychology: Controversies, questions, prospects, and limitations. *American Psychologist*. 65(2), 110–26.

Connellan, J., Baron-Cohen, S., Wheelwright, S., Ba'tki, A. and Ahluwalia, J. (2001). Sex differences in human neonatal social perception. *Infant Behavior and Development*. 23, 113–18.

Coop, G., Bullaughey, K., Luca, F. and Przeworski, M. (2008). The timing of selection at the human FOXP2 gene. *Molecular Biology and Evolution*. 25(7), 1257–9.

Cooper, C. (2012). *Individual Differences and Personality* (3rd edn). London: Hodder Arnold.

Corballis, M. C. (2009). The evolution and genetics of cerebral asymmetry. *Philosophical Transactions of the Royal Society London B Biological Sciences*. 364: 867–79.

Coryell, W. A. (1980). A blind family history study of Briquet's syndrome. *Archives of General Psychiatry*. 37, 1266–9.

Cosmides, L. (1989). The logic of social exchange: Has natural selection shaped how humans reason? Studies from the Wason selection task. *Cognition*. 31, 187–276.

Cosmides, L. and Tooby, J. (1992). Cognitive adaptations for social exchange. In J. Barkow, L. Cosmides and J. Tooby (eds.). *The Adapted Mind* (163–228). New York: Oxford University Press.

    (1994). Origins of domain specificity: The evolution of functional organization. In L. A. Hirschfeld and S. A. Gelman (eds.). *Mapping the Mind: Domain Specificity in Cognition and Culture* (85–116). Cambridge: Cambridge University Press.

(1996). Are humans rational thinkers after all? Rethinking some conclusions from the literature on judgement under uncertainty. *Cognition.* 58, 1–73.

Cosmides, L., Barrett, H. C. and Tooby, J. (2010). Adaptive specializations, social exchange, and the evolution of human intelligence. *Proceedings of the National Academy of Sciences,* 107, 9007–14.

Cosmides, L., Tooby, J., Fiddick, L. and Bryant, G. (2005). Detecting cheaters. *Trends in Cognitive Sciences.* 9(11), 505–6.

Costa, P. T. and McCrae, R. R. (1990). Personality disorders and the five factor model of personality. *Journal of Personality Disorders.* 4, 362–371.

(1992). Four ways five factors are basic. *Personality and Individual Differences.* 13, 653–65.

Cox, C. R. and Le Boeuf, B. J. (1977). Female incitation of male competition: A mechanism of mate selection. *American Naturalist.* 111, 317–35.

Crago, M. B. and Gopnik, M. (1994). From families to phenotypes: Theoretical and clinical implications of research into the genetic basis of specific language impairment. In R. Watkins and M. Rice (eds.). *Specific Language Impairments in Children* (35–51). Baltimore: Paul H. Brookes.

Crain, S. and Nakayama, M. (1986). Structure dependence in children's language. *Language.* 62, 522–43.

Crawford, C., Smith, M. and Krebs, D. (1987). *Sociobiology and Psychology: Ideas, Issues and Applications.* London: Lawrence Erlbaum.

Crespi, B., Summers, K. and Dorus, S. (2007). Adaptive evolution of genes underlying schizophrenia. *Proceedings of the Royal Society.* B 2801–10.

Crews, D. (1994). Animal sexuality. *Scientific American.* 270, 108–14.

Cronin, H. (1991). *The Ant and the Peacock: Altruism and Sexual Selection from Darwin to Today.* Cambridge: Cambridge University Press.

Crooks, R. L. and Baur, K. (2013). *Our Sexuality* (12th edn). Belmont, CA: Wadsworth.

Cross, J. E. and Cross, J. (1971). Age, sex, race and the perception of facial beauty. *Developmental Psychology.* 5, 433–9.

Crow, T. J. (1995). A Darwinian approach to the origins of psychosis. *British Journal of Psychiatry.* 167, 12–25.

(2005). Who forgot Paul Broca? The origin of language as test case for speciation theory. *Journal of Linguistics.* 41, 133–56.

Crowell, J. A. and Feldman, S. S. (1988). The effects of mothers' internal models of relationships and children's behavioral and developmental status on mother–child interaction. *Child Development.* 59, 1273–85.

(1991). Mothers' working models of relationships and child behavior during separation and reunion. *Developmental Psychology.* 27, 597–605.

Cummins, D. D. and Cummins, R. (1999). Biological preparedness and evolutionary explanation. *Cognition.* 73, 37–53.

Cunningham, M. R., Roberts, A. R., Barbee, A. P. *et al.* (1995). Their ideas of beauty are, on the whole, the same as ours: Consistency and variability in the cross-cultural perception of female physical attractiveness. *Journal of Personality and Social Psychology.* 68, 261–79.

Daly, M. and Wilson, M. (1983). *Sex, Evolution and Behaviour* (2nd edn). Belmont, CA: Wadsworth.

(1984). A sociobiological analysis of human infanticide. In G. Hausfater and S. B. Hardy (eds.). *Infanticide: Comparative and Evolutionary Perspectives* (487–502). New York: Aldine.

(1985). Child abuse and other risks of not living with both parents. *Ethology and Sociobiology.* 6, 197–210.

(1988). *Homicide.* New York: Aldine de Gruyter.

(1994). Evolutionary psychology of male violence. In J. Archer (ed.). *Male Violence* (253–88). London: Routledge.

(1998). *The Truth about Cinderella: A Darwinian View of Parental Love.* New Haven: Yale University Press.

(2005). The 'Cinderella effect' is no fairy tale. *Trends in Cognitive Sciences.* 9, 507–8.

(2007). Is the 'Cinderella effect' controversial? In C. Crawford and D. L. Krebs (eds.). *Foundations of Evolutionary Psychology* (383–400). Mahwah, NJ: Lawrence Erlbaum.

Damasio, A. R. (2003). *Looking for Spinoza: Joy, Sorrow and the Feeling Brain.* Fort Worth: Harcourt Brace College Publishers.

Damasio, H., Grabowski, T., Frank, R., Galaburda, A. M. and Damasio, A. R. (1994). The return of Phineas Gage: Clues about the brain from the skull of a famous patient. *Science.* 264, 1102–5.

Darwin, C. (1859). *On the Origin of Species by Natural Selection.* London: Murray.

(1871). *The Descent of Man, and Selection in Relation to Sex.* London: Murray.

(1872). *The Expression of the Emotions in Man and Animals.* London: HarperCollins.

(1877). A biographical sketch of an infant. *Mind.* 2, 285–94.

(1998). *The Expression of the Emotions in Man and Animals* (3rd edn, with Introduction and Afterword by Paul Ekman). London: HarperCollins (originally published in 1872).

Darwin, L. (1925). Race deterioration and practical politics. *Eugenics Review.* 141–3.

Davidson, R. J. and Sutton, S. K. (1995). Affective neuroscience: The emergence of a discipline. *Special Cognitive Neuroscience issue for Current Opinions in Neurobiology.* 5, 217–24.

Dawkins, R. (1976). *The Selfish Gene* (1st edn). Oxford: Oxford University Press.

(1979a). Twelve misunderstandings of kin selection. *Zeitschrift für Tier -psychologie.* 51, 184–200.

(1979b). In defence of selfish genes. *Philosophy.* 56, 556–73.

(1982). *The Extended Phenotype.* Oxford: Oxford University Press.

(1986). *The Blind Watchmaker.* Harlow: Longman.

(1989). *The Selfish Gene* (2nd edn). Oxford: Oxford University Press.

(1994). Burying the vehicle. *Behavioural and Brain Sciences.* 17, 617.

(1995). *River Out of Eden.* New York: Basic Books.

(2003). *A Devil's Chaplain: Reflections on Hope, Lies, Science, and Love.* London: Weidenfeld and Nicolson.

(2004). *The Ancestor's Tale: A Pilgrimage to the Dawn of Life*. Weidenfeld Nicolson Illustrated, London.

(2006). *The God Delusion*. London: Bantam Press.

(2012). The descent of Edward Wilson. *Prospect*. 24 May.

Dawson, A. and Tylee, A. (2001). *Depression: Social and Economic Timebomb*. London: BMJ Books.

Deacon, T. W. (1997). *The Symbolic Species: The Co-Evolution of Language and the Brain*. London: Penguin.

Deaux, K. and Wrightsman, L. (1983). *Social Psychology* (4th edn). Pacific Grove, CA: Brooks/Cole.

Degler, C. (1991). *In Search of Human Nature: The Decline and Revival of Darwinism in American Social Thought*. New York: Oxford University Press.

Dennett, D. C. (1994). E Pluribus Unum? *Behavioural and Brain Sciences*. 17, 617–18.

(1995). *Darwin's Dangerous Idea: Evolution and the Meanings of Life*. New York: Simon and Schuster.

(1996). *Kinds of Minds: Towards an Understanding of Consciousness*. London: Weidenfeld and Nicolson.

(1999). The evolution of culture. *The Edge*. Retrieved from www.edge.org/3rdculture/dennett/dennettp1.htmlon28/08/03.

(2006). *Breaking the Spell: Religion as a Natural Phenomenon*. London: Allen Lane.

Derryberry, D. and Tucker, D. M. (1994). Motivating the focus of attention. In P. M. Neidenthale and S. Kitayama (eds.). *The Heart's Eye: Emotional Influences in Perception and Attention* (167–96). San Diego: Academic Press.

Dessalles, J.-L. (1998). Altruism, status and the origin of relevance. In J. R. Hurford, M. Studdert-Kennedy and C. Knight (eds.). *Approaches to the Evolution of Language: Social and Cognitive Bases* (130–47). Cambridge: Cambridge University Press.

Diamond, J. (1992). *The Third Chimpanzee*. New York: HarperCollins.

(1997). *Why is Sex Fun?* New York: Basic Books.

(1998). *Guns, Germs and Steel: A Short History of Everybody for the Last 13,000 Years*. London: Vintage.

Dickins, T. E. (2011). Evolutionary approaches to behaviour. In V. Swami (ed.). *Evolutionary psychology: A Critical Introduction* (1–30). Chichester: Wiley-Blackwell.

Dingemanse, N. J., Both, C., Drent, P. J. and Tinbergen, J. M. (2002). Repeatability and heritability of exploratory behaviour in great tits from the wild. *Animal Behaviour*. 64, 929–38.

Dingemanse, N. J., Both, C., Drent, P. J., Van Oers, K. and Van Noordwijk, A. J. (2004). Fitness consequences of avian personalities in a fluctuating environment. Proceedings of the Royal Society of London, Series B: *Biological Sciences*. 271, 847–52.

Dion, K. K. (1972). Physical attractiveness and evaluation of children's transgressions. *Journal of Personality and Social Psychology*. 24, 207–13.

Dobzhansky, T. (1970). *Genetics of the Evolutionary Process*. New York: Columbia.

Draper, P. and Belsky, J. (1990). Personality development in evolutionary perspective. *Journal of Personality*. 58, 141–57.

Draper, P. and Harpending, H. (1982). Father absence and reproductive strategy: An evolutionary perspective. *Journal of Anthropological Research*. 38(3), 255–73.

Drickamer, L. C. and Vessey, S. H. (1992). *Animal Behaviour: Mechanisms, Ecology and Evolution* (3rd edn). Dubuque: Wm C. Brown.

(1996). *Animal Behaviour: Mechanisms, Ecology and Evolution* (4th edn). Dubuque: Wm C. Brown.

Drickamer, L. C., Vessey, S. H. and Jakob, E. M. (2002). *Animal Behavior: Mechanisms, Ecology, and Evolution*. (5th edn). New York: McGraw-Hill.

Dudai, Y. (2002). *Memory – from A to Z: Keywords, Concepts, and Beyond*. Oxford: Oxford University Press.

Dunbar, R. I. M. (1988). *Primate Social Systems*. London: Croom Helm.

(1993). Coevolution of neocortical size, group size and language in humans. *Behavioral and Brain Science*. 16, 681–735.

(1995). *The Trouble with Science*. London: Faber and Faber.

(1996). *Grooming, Gossip, and the Evolution of Language*. Cambridge, MA: Harvard University Press.

(2004). *The Human Story: A New History of Mankind's Evolution*. London: Faber and Faber.

Dunbar, R. I. M., Duncan, N. and Nettle, D. (1995). Size and structure of freely forming conversational groups. *Human Nature*. 6, 67–78.

Dunn, M. J. and Searle, R. (2010). Effect of manipulated prestige-car ownership on both sex attractiveness ratings. *British Journal of Psychology*. 101, 69–80.

Dutton, D. (2009). *The Art Instinct: Beauty, Pleasure, and Human Evolution*. Oxford: Oxford University Press.

Eagly, A. H. and Steffan, V. J. (1986). Gender and aggressive behavior: A meta-analytic review of the social psychological literature. *Psychological Bulletin*. 100, 283–308.

Eagly, A. H. and Wood, W. (1999). The origins of sex differences in human behavior: Evolved dispositions versus social roles. *American Psychologist*. 54, 408–23.

(2011). Feminism and the evolution of sex differences and similarities. *Sex Roles*. 64, 758–67.

Ebstein, R., Novick, O., Umansky, R., Priel, B., Osher, Y., Blaine, D., Bennett, E. R., Nemanov, L., Katz, M. and Belmaker, R. H. (1996). D4DR exon polymorphism associated with the personality trait of novelty seeking in normal human volunteers. *Nature Genetics*. 12, 78–80.

Eibl-Eibesfeldt, I. (1984). *Human Ethology*. New York: Aldine de Gruyter.

Eichenbaum, H. and Cohen, N. J. (1991). *From Conditioning to Conscious Recollection: Memory Systems of the Brain*. New York: Oxford University Press.

Eichhammer, P., Sand, P. G., Stoertebecker, P. *et al*. (2005). Variation at the DRD4 promoter modulates extraversion in Caucasians. *Molecular Psychiatry*. 10, 520–2.

Ekirch, A. R. (2006). *At Day's Close: Night in Times Past*. London: Norton.

Ekman, P. (1980). *The Face of Man: Expressions of Universal Emotions in a New Guinea Village*. New York: Garland STPM Press.

(1992). An argument for basic emotions. *Cognition and Emotion*. 6, 169–200.

(1994). Are there basic emotions? In P. Ekman and R. Davidson (eds.). *The Nature of Emotions: Functional Questions* (15–19). Oxford: Oxford University Press.

(1998). *Charles Darwin: The Expression of the Emotions in Man and Animals* (3rd edn, with Introduction, Afterwords and Commentaries by Paul Ekman). London: HarperCollins.

Ekman, P. and Friesen, W. V. (1967). Hand and body cues in the judgement of emotion: A reformulation. *Perceptual and Motor Skills*. 24, 711–24.

(1969). The repertoire of nonverbal behaviour: Categories, origins, usage and coding. *Semiotics*. 1, 49–98.

(1971). Constants across cultures in the face and emotion. *Journal of Personality and Social Psychology*. 17, 124–9.

Ekman, P., Friesen, W. V. and Ellsworth, P. C. (1972). *Emotions in the Human Face: Guidelines for Research and an Integration of Findings*. New York: Pergamon Press.

Elder, G.H. (1969). Appearance and education in marriage mobility. *American Sociological Review*. 34, 519–33.

Eldridge, N. and Gould, S. (1972). Punctuated equilibria: An alternative to phyletic gradualism. In J. M. Schopf (ed.). *Models in Paleobiology* (82–115). San Francisco: Freeman.

Ellis, B. J., McFadyen-Ketchum, S., Dodge, K. A., Pettit, G. S. and Bates, J. E. (1999). Quality of early family relationships and individual differences in the timing of pubertal maturation in girls. *Journal of Personality and Social Psychology*, 77, 387–401.

Ellis, L. (1996). A discipline in peril: Sociology's future hinges on curing its biophobia. *American Sociologist*. 27, 21–41.

Ellsberg, D. (1961). Risk, ambiguity, and the Savage axioms. *Quarterly Journal of Economics*. 75, 643–69.

Elman, A. (1996), *Sexual Subordination and State Intervention. Comparing Sweden and the United States*. Providence, RI: Berghahn Books.

Enard, W., Przeworski, M., Fisher, S. E. *et al.* (2002). Molecular evolution of *FOXP2*, a gene involved in speech and language. *Nature*. 418, 869–72.

Estioko-Griffin, A. and Griffin, P. B. (1981). Woman the hunter: The Agta. In F. Dahlberg (ed.). *Woman the Gatherer* (121–51). New Haven: Yale University Press.

Evans, D. and Cruse, P. (eds.) (2004). *Emotion, Evolution and Rationality*. Oxford: Oxford University Press.

Evans, J. St. B. T., Handley, S. H., Perham, N., Over, D. E. and Thompson, V. A. (2000). Frequency versus probability formats in statistical word problems. *Cognition*. 77, 197–213.

Evans, J. St. B. T. and Over, D. (1996). *Rationality and Reasoning*. Hove: Psychology Press.

Ewald, P. W. (1994). *Evolution of Infectious Disease*. New York: Oxford University Press.

(2002). *Plague Time: The New Germ Theory of Disease*. New York: Random House.

Ewing, K. and Pratt, M. W. (1995). The role of adult romantic attachment in marital communication and parenting stress. Poster presented at the Society for Research in Child Development Meetings, Indianapolis, March.

Eysenck, H. J. (1990). Biological dimensions of personality. In L. A. Pervin (ed.). *Handbook of Personality: Theory and Research* (244–76). New York: Guildford Press.

(1991). Dimensions of personality: 16, 5, or 3? – Criteria for a taxonomic paradigm. *Personality and Individual Differences*. 12, 773–90.

Fagen, R. (1981). *Animal Play Behaviour*. New York: Oxford University Press.

Fantz, R. L. (1961). The origin of form perception. *Scientific American*. 204, 66–72.

Farah, M. J., Rabinowitz, C., Quinn, G. E. and Liu, G. T. (2000). Early commitment of neural substrates for face recognition. *Cognitive Neuropsychology*. 17, 117–24.

Faris, E. (1921). Are instincts data or hypotheses? *American Journal of Sociology*. 27, 184–98.

Feeney, J. A. and Noller, P. (1992). Attachment style and romantic love: Relationship dissolution. *Australian Journal of Psychology*. 44(2), 69–74.

Fehr, E. and Gächter, S. (2000). Cooperation and punishment in public goods experiments. *American Economic Review*. 90, 980–94.

(2002). Altruistic punishment in humans. *Nature*. 415. 137–40.

Fehr, E. and Schmidt, K. M. (1999). A theory of fairness, competition, and cooperation. *Quarterly Journal of Economics*. 114, 817–68.

Finger, E. C., Marsh, A. A., Mitchell, D. G., Reid, M. E., Sims, C., Budhani, S. *et al.* (2008). Abnormal ventromedial prefrontal cortex function in children with psychopathic traits during reversal learning. *Archives of General Psychiatry*. 65, 586–94.

Fisher, R. A. (1930). *The Genetical Theory of Natural Selection*. Oxford: Clarendon Press.

(1958). *The Genetical Theory of Natural Selection* (2nd edn). New York: Dover.

Fisher, S. E., Vargha-Khadem, F., Watkins, K. E., Monaco, A. P. and Pembrey, M. E. (1998). Localisation of a gene implicated in a severe speech and language disorder. *Nature Genetics*. 18, 168–70.

Flaxman, S. M. and Sherman, P. W. (2008). Morning sickness: Adaptive cause or nonadaptive consequence of embryo viability? *American Naturalist*. 172, 54–62.

Flinn, M. V. (1989). Household composition and female strategies in a Trinidadian village. In A. E. Rasa, C. Vogel and E. Voland (eds.). *The Sociobiology of Sexual and Reproductive Strategies* (206–33). New York: Chapman and Hall.

(2011). Evolutionary anthropology of the human family. In C. Salmon and T. Shackleford (eds.). *Oxford Handbook of Evolutionary Family Psychology*. (12–32). Oxford: Oxford University Press.

Flint, J., Greenspan, R. J. and Kendler, K. S. (2010). *How Genes Influence Behavior*. Oxford: Oxford University Press.

Fodor, J. (1983). *The Modularity of Mind*. Cambridge, MA: MIT Press.

(2000). *The Mind Doesn't Work That Way: The Scope and Limits of Computational Psychology*. Cambridge, MA: MIT Press.

Fodor, J., Bever, T. and Garrett, M. (1974). *The Psychology of Language*. New York: McGraw-Hill.

Foley, R. (1995). The adaptive legacy of human evolution: A search for the environment of evolutionary adaptedness. *Evolutionary Anthropology: Issues, News, and Reviews.* 4(6), 194–203.

Ford, C. S. and Beach, F. A. (1951). *Patterns of Sexual Behaviour.* New York: Harper and Row.

Fouts, R. S., Fouts, D. H. and Schoenfeld, D. (1984). Sign language conversational interactions between chimpanzees. *Sign Language Studies.* 42, 1–12.

Fox, R. (1988). On the Seville statement on violence. *Human Ethology Newsletter.* 5(5), 4.

Frangiskakis, J. M., Ewart, A., Morris, C. A., Mervis, C. B., Bertrand, J., Robinson, B. F. *et al.* (1996). LIM-kinase1 hemizygosity implicated in impaired visuospatial constructive cognition. *Cell.* 86, 59–69.

Fredrickson, B. L. (1998). What good are positive emotions? *Review of General Psychology.* 2, 300–19.

(2006). Unpacking positive emotions: Investigating the seeds of human flourishing. *Journal of Positive Psychology.* 1, 57–60.

(In press 2013). Positive emotions broaden and build. In E. Ashby Plant and P. G. Devine (eds.). *Advances on Experimental Social Psychology*, vol. 47.

Freeman, D. G. (1983). *Margaret Mead and Samoa: The Making and Unmaking of an Anthropological Myth.* Cambridge, MA: Harvard University Press.

(1999). *The Fateful Hoaxing of Margaret Mead: A Historical Analysis of Her Samoan Research.* Boulder, CO: Westview Press.

Freud, S. (1914). *On Narcissism: An Introduction.* Standard edition 14: 73–102.

Fridlund, A. J. (1992). Darwin's anti-Darwinism and the expression of the emotions in man and animals. In K. T. Strongman (ed.). *International Review of Emotion.* Vol. 2 (117–37). New York: Wiley.

Frijda, N. H. (1986). *The Emotions.* Cambridge: Cambridge University Press.

Galef, B. J., Jr, Manzig, L. A. and Field, R. M. (1986). Imitation learning in budgerigars: Dawson and Foss (1965) revisited. *Behavioral Processes.* 13, 191–202.

Galton, F. (1864). Hereditary talent and character. *MacMillan's Magazine.* 11, 157–66.

(1908). *Memories of My Life.* London: Methuen.

Gamble, C. (1999). *The Paleolithic Societies of Europe.* Cambridge: Cambridge University Press.

Gangestad, S. W. and Buss, D. M. (1993). Pathogen prevalences and human mate preferences. *Ethology and Sociobiology.* 14, 89–96.

Gangestad, S. W. and Simpson, J. A. (1990). Toward an evolutionary history of females' sociosexual variation. *Journal of Personality.* 58, 69–96.

Gao, Y., Raine, A., Venables, P. H., Dawson, M. E. and Mednick, S. A. (2010). Early maternal and paternal bonding, childhood physical abuse, and adult psychopathic personality. *Psychological Medicine*, 40, 1007–16.

Gardner, H. (2000). The case against spiritual intelligence [Response to R. Emmons. The psychology of ultimate concern: Personality, spirituality, and intelligence]. *International Journal for the Psychology of Religion.* 10, 27–34.

(2003). Multiple intelligences after twenty years. Paper presented at the American Educational Research Association, Chicago, Illinois, 21 April.

(2010). A debate on 'multiple intelligences'. In J. Traub (ed.). *Cerebrum: Forging Ideas in Brain Science* (34–61). Washington, DC: Dana Press.

Gardner, M. (2000). Kilroy was here. Review of *The Meme Machine* by Susan J. Blackmore. *Los Angeles Times*, 5 March.

Gaulin, S. J. C. and McBurney, D. H. (2001). *Psychology: An Evolutionary Approach*. Upper Saddle River, NJ: Prentice-Hall.

Ge, X., Conger, R. D., Cadoret, R. J., Neiderhiser, J. M., Yates, W. *et al.* (1996). The developmental interface between nature and nurture: A mutual influence model of child antisocial behaviour and parent behaviours. *Developmental Psychology*. 32, 574–89.

Geary, D. C. (1998). *Male, Female*. Washington, DC: American Psychological Association.

(n.d.). Commentary on the extreme male brain theory of autism. *The Edge*. www.edge. org/3rd_culture/baron-cohen05/baron-cohen05_index.html. Accessed 25/4/07.

Gigerenzer, G. (1991). How to make cognitive illusions disappear: Beyond heuristics and biases. In W. Stroebe and M. Hewstone (eds.). *European Review of Social Psychology*. Vol. 2 (83–115). Chichester, UK: Wiley.

(1997). The modularity of social intelligence. In A. Whiten and R. W. Byrne (eds.). *Machiavellian Intelligence II* (264–88). Cambridge: Cambridge University Press.

Gigerenzer, G. and Hug, K. (1992). Domain-specific reasoning: Social contracts, cheating, and perspective change. *Cognition*. 43, 127–71.

Gilby, I. C., Emery Thompson, M., Ruane, J. D. and Wrangham, R. W. (2010). No evidence of short term exchange of meat for sex among chimpanzees. *Journal of Human Evolution*. 59, 44–53.

Ginsburg, H. J. and Miller, S. M. (1982). Sex differences and children's risk taking behavior. *Child Development*. 53, 426–28.

Glass, S. P. and Wright, T. L. (1992). Justifications for extramarital relationships: The association between attitudes, behaviours and gender. *Journal of Sex Research*. 29, 361–87.

Glenn, A. L., Kurzban, R. and Raine, A. (2011). Evolutionary theory and psychopathy. *Aggression and Violent Behavior*. 16, 371–80.

Gluckman, P., Beedle, A. and Hanson, M. (2009). *Principles of Evolutionary Medicine*. Oxford: Oxford University Press.

Gluckman, P. and Hanson, M. (2008). *Mismatch: The Lifestyle Diseases Timebomb*. Oxford: Oxford University Press.

Goldsmith, T. H. and Zimmerman, W. F. (2001). *Biology, Evolution and Human Nature*. New York: Wiley.

Gomes, C. M. and Boesch, C. (2009). Wild chimpanzees exchange meat for sex on a long-term basis. *PLoS ONE*. 4(4): e5116 doi: 10.1371/journal.pone.0005116

Goodall, J. (1964). Tool-using and aimed throwing in a community of free-living chimpanzees. *Nature*. 201, 1264–6.

(1986). *The Chimpanzees of Gombe*. Cambridge, MA: Belknap.

Goodman, M., Waters, S. F. and Thompson, R. A. (2012). Parent–offspring conflict. In V. S. Ramachandran. (ed.). *Encyclopedia of Human Behavior* (2nd edn). (28–33).

Gopnik, A. and Astington, J. W. (1988). Children's understanding of representational change, and its relation to the understanding of false belief and the appearance–reality distinction. *Child Development*. 59, 26–37.

Gopnik, A., Meltzoff, A. N. and Kuhl, P. K. (1999). *How Babies Think*. London: Weidenfeld and Nicolson.

Gopnik, M. (1994). Impairments of tense in a familial language disorder. *Journal of Neurolinguistics*. 8, 109–33.

(1997). Language deficits and genetic factors. *Trends in Cognitive Science*. 1(1), 5–9.

Gopnik, M. and Crago, M. (1991). Familial aggregation of a developmental language disorder. *Cognition*. 39, 1–50.

Gordon, P. (1985). Level ordering in lexical development. *Cognition*. 21, 73–93.

Gorelik, G. and Shackelford, T. K. (2012). Spheres of sexual conflict. In T. K. Shackelford and A. T. Goetz (eds.). *Oxford Handbook of Sexual Conflict in Humans* (331–46). New York: Oxford University Press.

Gottesman, I. I., McGuffin, P. and Farmer, A. E. (1987). Clinical genetics as clues to the 'real' genetics of schizophrenia. *Schizophrenia Bulletin*. 13, 23–47.

Gould, J. L. and Gould, G. C. (1989; 1997). *Sexual Selection: Mate Choice and Courtship in Nature*. New York: W. H. Freeman and Co.

Gould, S. J. (1977). *Ontogeny and Phylogeny*. Cambridge, MA: Harvard University Press.

(1981). *The Mismeasure of Man*. New York: Norton.

Gould, S. J. and Lewontin, R. C. (1979). The spandrels of San Marco and the panglossian paradigm: A critique of the adaptationist programme. *Proceedings of the Royal Society of London*. 205, 281–8.

Grafen, A. (1990). Biological signals as handicaps. *Journal of Theoretical Biology*. 144, 517–46.

Grandin, T. (2005). *Animals in Translation*. London: Bloomsbury.

Graves, H. B., Hable, C. P. and Jenkins, T. H. (1985). Sexual selection in *Gallus*. Effects of morphology and dominance on female spatial behaviour. *Behavioural Processes*. 11, 189–97.

Green, R. E., Krause, J., Briggs, A. W., Maricic, T., Udo, S. *et al.* (2010). A Draft Sequence of the Neandertal Genome. *Science*. 328, 710–22.

Greenberg, J. H. (1987). *Language in the Americas*. Stanford, CA: Stanford University Press.

Greene, J. D. and Haidt, J. (2002). How (and where) does moral judgment work? *Trends in Cognitive Science*. 6, 517–23.

Greene, J. D., Nystrom, L. E., Engell, A. D. *et al.* (2004). The neural bases of cognitive conflict and control in moral judgment. *Neuron*. 44, 389–400.

Greene, J. D., Sommerville, R. B., Nystrom, L. E., Darley, J. M. and Cohen, J. D. (2001). An fMRI investigation of emotional engagement in moral judgment. *Science*. 293, 2105–8.

Griggs, R. A. and Cox, J. R. (1982). The elusive thematics material effect in Wason's selection task. *British Journal of Psychology*. 73, 407–20.

Gurven, M., Hill, K. and Kaplan, H. (2002). From forest to reservation: Transitions in food sharing behavior among the Ache of Paraguay. *Journal of Anthropological Research*. 58, 91–118.

Haeckel, E. (1969). *The History of Creation, Vol. 1* (trans. E. Ray Lankester). London: Kegan Paul.

Haidt, J. and Joseph, C. (2004). Intuitive ethics: How innately prepared intuitions generate culturally variable virtues. *Daedalus*. Fall (special issue on human nature). 55–66.

Haidt, J., Koller, S. H. and Dias, M. G. (1993). Affect, culture, and morality, or, is it wrong to eat your dog? *Journal of Personality and Social Psychology*. 65(4), 613–28.

Haig, D. (1993). Genetic conflicts in human pregnancy. *Quarterly Review of Biology*. 68, 495–523.

   (1998). Genetic conflicts of pregnancy and childhood. In S. C. Stearns (ed.). *Evolution in Health and Disease* (77–90). Oxford: Oxford University Press.

   (2002). *Genomic Imprinting and Kinship*. New Brunswick, NJ: Rutgers University Press.

   (2006). The gene meme. In A. Grafen and M. Ridley (eds.). *Richard Dawkins: How a Scientist Changed the Way We Think*. Oxford: Oxford University Press.

Haines, S. and Gould, J. (1994). Female platys prefer long tails. *Nature*. 370, 512.

Haldane, J. B. S. (1955). Population genetics. *New Biology*. 18, 34–51.

Hall, J. A. (1978). Gender effects in decoding nonverbal cues. *Psychological Bulletin*. 85, 845–58.

Halliday, T. R. (1994). Sex and Evolution. In P. J. B. Slater and T. R. Halliday. *Behaviour and Evolution* (150–92). Cambridge: Cambridge University Press.

Hamer, D. and Copeland, P. (1998). *Living with Our Genes: Why They Matter More Than You Think*. New York: Doubleday.

Hamilton, W. D. (1964a and b). The genetical evolution of social behaviour (vols I and II). *Journal of Theoretical Biology*. 7, 1–52.

Hamilton, W. D. and Zuk, M. (1982). Heritable true fitness and bright birds: A role for parasites? *Science*. 218, 384–7.

Hammerstein, P. (2003). Why is reciprocity so rare in social animals? A protestant appeal. In P. Hammerstein (ed.). *Genetic and Cultural Evolution of Cooperation. Dahlem Workshop Report* (83–93). Cambridge, MA: MIT Press.

Haney, C., Banks, W. C. and Zimbardo, P. G. (1973). A study of prisoners and guards in a simulated prison. *Naval Research Review*. 30, 4–17.

Hare, R. D. (1980) A research scale for the assessment of psychopathy in criminal populations. *Personality and Individual Differences*. 1, 111–19.

   (1993) *Without Conscience: The Disturbing World of the Psychopaths among Us*. London: Guilford Press.

   (2006). Psychopathy: A clinical and forensic overview. *Psychiatric Clinics of North America*. 29, 709–24.

Harlow, J. M. (1848). Passage of an iron rod through the head. *Boston Medical and Surgical Journal*. 39, 389–93.

Harré, R. (1986). *The Social Construction of Emotions*. Oxford: Basil Blackwell.

Harris, J. R. (1995). Where is the child's environment? A group-socialization theory of development. *Psychological Review.* 102(3), 458–89.

(1998). *The Nurture Assumption: Why Children Turn Out the Way They Do.* New York: Simon and Schuster.

(2006). *No Two Alike: Human Nature and Human Individuality.* New York: Norton and Co.

Harris, M. (1979). *Cultural Materialism: The Struggle for a Science of Culture.* New York: Random House.

(1985). *Good to Eat: Riddles of Food and Culture.* New York: Simon and Schuster.

Hartle, D. L. and Orel, V. (1992). What did Mendel think he discovered? *Genetics.* 131, 245–53.

Hassett, J. M., Siebert, E. R. and Wallen, K. (2008). Sex differences in rhesus monkey toy preferences parallel those of children. *Hormones and Behavior.* 54(3), 359–64.

Hauser, M. D. (2006). *Moral Minds.* New York: Springer.

Hauser, M. D. and Carey, S. (1998). Building a cognitive creature from a set of primitives: Evolutionary and developmental insights. In D. Cummins and C. Allen (eds.). *The Evolution of Mind* (51–106). Oxford: Oxford University Press.

Hauser, M. D., Chomsky, N. and Fitch, W. T. (2002). The faculty of language: What is it, who has it, and how did it evolve? *Science.* 298, 1569–79.

Hauser, M. D., Cushman, F., Young, L., Kang-Xing, K. and Mikhail, J. (2007). A dissociation between moral judgments and justifications. *Mind & Language.* 22 (1), 1–21.

Hauser, M. D., Young, L. and Cushman, F. A. (in press). Reviving Rawls' linguistic analogy. In W. Sinnott-Armstrong (ed.). *Moral Psychology and Biology.* New York: Oxford University Press.

Haviland, J. M. and Malatesta, C. (1981). A description of the development of sex differences in nonverbal signals: Fantasies, fallacies, and facts. In C. Mayo and N. Henley (eds.). *Gender and Nonverbal Behaviors* (183–208). New York: Springer-Verlag.

Hayes, N. (1995). *Access to Psychology.* London: Hodder and Stoughton.

Hazan, C. and Shaver, P. (1987). Romantic love conceptualized as an attachment process. *Journal of Personality and Social Psychology.* 52(3), 511–24.

Hazarika, Manji (2007). Homo erectus/ergaster and out of Africa: Recent developments in paleoanthropology and prehistoric archaeology. 1st Summer School of the European Anthropological Association 16–30 June 2007, Prague, Czech Republic *EAA Summer School eBook* 1: 35–41.

Heck, A., Lieb, R., Ellgas, A. *et al.* (2009). Investigation of 17 candidate genes for personality traits confirms effects of the HTR2A gene on novelty seeking. *Genes Brain and Behavior.* 8, 464–72.

Heider, F. and Simmel, M. (1944). An experimental study of apparent behavior. *American Journal of Psychology.* 57, 243–9.

Henrich, J. and Gil-White, F. J. (2001). The evolution of prestige: Freely conferred deterrence as a mechanism for enhancing the benefits of cultural transmission. *Evolution and Human Behavior.* 22, 165–96.

Herrnstein, R. and Murray, C. (1994) *The Bell Curve: Intelligence and Class Struggle in American Life*. New York: The Free Press.

Hewstone, M. W., Stroebe, W. and Jonas, K. (eds.) (2012). *Introduction to Social Psychology: A European Perspective* (5th edn). Oxford: Blackwell.

Hewstone, M. W., Stroebe, W. and Stephenson, G. M. (eds.) (1996). *Introduction to Social Psychology*. Oxford: Blackwell.

Heyes, C. M. and Dawson, G. R. (1990). A demonstration of observational learning using a bidirectional control. *Quarterly Journal of Experimental Psychology*. 42, 59–71.

Hidaka, B. H. (2012). Depression as a disease of modernity: Explanations for increasing prevalence. *Journal of Affective Disorders*. 140, 205–14.

Hill, K. (2002). Altruistic cooperation during foraging by the Ache, and the evolved predisposition to cooperate. *Human Nature*. 13, 105–28.

Hill, K. and Hurtado, A. M. (1996). *Ache Life History: The Ecology and Demography of a Foraging People*. Foundations of Human Behavior. Hawthorne, NY: Aldine de Gruyter.

   (1999). The Ache of Paraguay. In R. Lee and R. Daly (eds.). *The Cambridge Encyclopedia of Hunters and Gatherers* (92–6). Cambridge: Cambridge University Press.

Hill, K. and Kaplan, H. (1988). Trade-offs in male and female reproductive strategies among the Ache. In L. Batzig, M. Borgerhof Mulder and P. Turke (eds.). *Human Reproductive Behaviour* (277–305). Cambridge: Cambridge University Press.

Hinde, R. A. (1977). Mother–infant separation and the nature of inter-individual relationships: Experiments with rhesus monkeys. *Proceedings of the Royal Society of London* B. 196, 29–50.

Hirschfeld, L. A. and Gelman, S. A. (eds.) (1994). *Mapping the Mind: Domain Specificity in Cognition and Culture*. New York: Cambridge University Press.

Hirsh-Pasek, K. and Golinkoff, R. M. (1991). Language comprehension: A new look at some old themes. In N. Krasnegor, D. Rumbaugh, M. Studdert-Kennedy and R. Schiefelbusch (eds.). *Biological and Behavioral Determinants of Language Development* (301–20). Hillsdale, NJ: Lawrence Erlbaum.

Hite, S. (1987). *Women and Love: A Cultural Revolution in Progress*. New York: Knopf.

Hockett, C. F. and Altmann, S. (1968). A note on design features. In Thomas A. Sebeok (ed.). *Animal Communication: Techniques of Study and Results of Research* (61–72). Bloomington, IN: Indiana University Press.

Hoffman, M. L. (1977). Empathy, its development and prosocial implications. In C. B. Keasey (ed.). *Nebraska Symposium on Motivation*. Vol. 25 (169–208). Lincoln: University of Nebraska Press.

   (1978). Psychological and biological perspectives on altruism. *International Journal of Behavioral Development*. 1, 323–39.

   (1982). Development of prosocial motivation: Empathy and guilt. In N. Eisenberg (ed.). *The Development of Prosocial Behavior* (281–313). New York: Academic Press.

Horan, R. D., Bulte, E. and Shogren, J. F. (2005). How trade saved humanity from biological exclusion: An economic theory of Neanderthal extinction. *Journal of Economic Behavior and Organization*. 58(1), 1–29.

Horwitz, A. and Wakefield, J. C. (2007). *The Loss of Sadness: How Psychiatry Transformed Normal Sorrow Into Depressive Disorder.* Oxford: Oxford University Press.

Hsiao, J. H. and Man Lam, S. (2013). The modulation of visual and task characteristics of a writing system on hemispheric lateralization in visual word recognition – A computational exploration. *Cognitive Science.* 37(5), 861–90.

Hull, D. (2000). Taking memetics seriously: Memetics will be what we make it. In R. Aunger (ed.). *Darwinizing Culture: The Status of Memetics as a Science* (43–67). Oxford/New York: Oxford University Press.

Hunt, M. (1974). *Sexual Behaviour in the 70s.* Chicago: Playboy Press.

Ilardi, S. S. (2010). *The Depression Cure: The 6-Step Program to Beat Depression without Drugs.* Cambridge, MA: Da Capo Press.

Ilardi, S. S., Jacobson, J. D., Lehman, K. A. *et al.* (2007). Therapeutic lifestyle change for depression: Results from a randomized controlled trial. Paper presented at the annual meeting of the Association for Behavioral and Cognitive Therapy, Philadelphia, PA.

Izard, C. E. (1977). *Human Emotions.* New York: Plenum.

(1992). Basic emotions, relations among emotions and emotion–cognition relations. *Psychological Review.* 99, 561–5.

(1994). Innate and universal facial expressions: Evidence from developmental and cross-cultural research. *Psychological Bulletin.* 115, 288–99.

(2009). Emotion theory and research: Highlights, unanswered questions, and emerging issues. *Annual Review of Psychology.* 60, 1–25.

Jablensky, H., Sartorius, N., Ernberg, G. *et al.* (1992). *Schizophrenia: Manifestations, Incidence and Course in Different Cultures: A WHO, Ten Country Study. Psychological Medicine.* Monograph Supplement 20. Cambridge: Cambridge University Press.

Jackendoff, R. (2007). Linguistics in cognitive science: The state of the art. *Linguistic Review.* 24(4), 347.

Jackendoff, R. and Pinker, S. (2005). The nature of the language faculty and its implications for evolution of language (Reply to Fitch, Hauser and Chomsky). *Cognition.* 97(2), 211–25.

Jackson, D. J. and Huston, T. L. (1975). Physical attractiveness and assertiveness. *Journal of Social Psychology.* 96, 79–84.

James, O. (2002). *They F*** You Up: How to Survive Family Life.* London: Bloomsbury.

James, W. (1884). What is an emotion? *Mind.* 9, 188–205.

(1890). *Principles of Psychology.* New York: Holt.

James, W. H. (1981). The honeymoon effect on marital coitus. *Journal of Sex Research.* 17, 114–23.

Jamison, K. R. (1989). Mood disorders and patterns of creativity in British writers and artists. *Psychiatry: Journal for the Study of Interpersonal Processes.* 52, 125–34.

(1993). *Touched with Fire: Manic-Depressive Illness and the Artistic Temperament.* New York: The Free Press.

(1995). Manic-depressive illness and creativity. *Scientific American.* 272, 62–7.

(2011). Great wits and madness: More near allied? *British Journal of Psychiatry.* 199, 351–2.

Jankowiak, W. and Fischer, C. R. (1992). A cross-cultural perspective on romantic love. *Ethology.* 31, 149–55.

Jenkins, P. F. (1978). Cultural transmission of song patterns and dialect development in a free-living bird population. *Animal Behaviour.* 25, 50–78.

Jennings, K. D. (1977). People versus object orientation in preschool children: Do sex differences really occur? *Journal of Genetic Psychology.* 131, 65–73.

Jensen, A. R. (1998). *The g Factor: The Science of Mental Ability.* Westport, CT: Praeger.

Johanson, D. C., White, T. D. and Coppens, V. (1978). A new species of the genus Australopithecus (Primate: Hominidae) from the Pliocene of eastern Africa. *Kirtlandia.* 28, 1–14.

Johnson, K. J., Waugh, C. E. and Fredrickson, B. L. (2010). Smile to see the forest: Facially expressed positive emotions broaden cognition. *Cognition and Emotion.* 24, 299–321.

Johnson, M. H. and Bolhuis, J. J. (1991). Imprinting, predispositions and filial preference in the chick. In R. J. Andrew (ed.). *Neural and Behavioural Plasticity* (133–56). Oxford: Oxford University Press.

Johnson, M. H. and Morton, J. (1991). *Biology and Cognitive Development: The Case of Face Recognition.* Oxford: Blackwell.

Johnson-Laird, P. N. and Oatley, K. (1992). Basic emotions, rationality and folk theory. *Cognition and Emotion.* 6, 201–23.

Johnson-Laird, P. N. and Wason, P. C. (1970). Insight into a logical relation. *Quarterly Journal of Experimental Psychology.* 22, 49–61.

Johnston, V. S. and Franklin, M. (1993). Is beauty in the eye of the beholder? *Ethology and Sociobiology.* 14, 183–99.

Jolliffe, T. and Baron-Cohen, S. (1997). Are people with autism or Asperger's syndrome faster than normal on the Embedded Figures Task? *Journal of Child Psychology and Psychiatry.* 38, 527–34.

Jordan, L. A. and Brooks, R. C. (2010). The lifetime costs of increased male reproductive effort: courtship, copulation and the Coolidge effect. *Journal of Evolutionary Biology.* 23, 2403–9.

Jordania, J. (2009). Times to fight and times to relax: Singing and humming at the beginning of human evolutionary history. *Kadmos.* 1, 272–7.

Kagan, J. (1998). A parent's influence is peerless. *Boston Globe.* 13 September, 3.

Kahneman, D. and Tversky, A. (1982). On the study of statistical intuitions. *Cognition.* 11, 123–41.

Kaminski, J., Call, J. and Fischer, J. (2004). Word learning in a domestic dog: Evidence for fast mapping. *Science.* 304, 1682–3.

Kanazawa, S. and Kovar, J. L. (2004). Why beautiful people are more intelligent. *Intelligence.* 32, 227–43.

Kant, I. (1798/1996). *Anthropology from a Pragmatic Point of View.* Carbondale, IL: Southern Illinois University Press.

Kardum, I., Gračanin, A. and Hudek-Knežević, J. (2008). Evolutionary explanations of eating disorders. *Psychological Topics*. 17, 247–63.

Karmiloff-Smith, A. (1992). *Beyond Modularity: A Developmental Perspective on Cognitive Science*. Cambridge, MA: MIT Press.

(1997). Crucial differences between developmental cognitive neuroscience and adult neuropsychology. *Developmental Neuropsychology*. 13(4), 513–24.

(2000). Why babies' brains are not Swiss-army knives. In S. Rose and H. Rose (eds.). *Alas Poor Darwin: Arguments Against Evolutionary Psychology* (129–43). London: Jonathan Cape.

Karmiloff-Smith, A., Klima, E., Bellugi, U., Grant, J. and Baron-Cohen, S. (1995). Is there a social module? Language, face processing and theory of mind in subjects with Williams syndrome. *Journal of Cognitive Neuroscience*. 7(2), 196–208.

Karmiloff-Smith, A., Tyler, L. K., Voice, K., Sims, K., Udwin, O., Davies, M. and Howlin, P. (1998). Linguistic dissociations in Williams syndrome: Evaluating receptive syntax in on-line and off-line tasks. *Neuropsychologia*. 36(4), 342–51.

Katsnelson, A. (2010). Do fish have personalities? *The Scientist*, 1 March. Retrieved from www.the-scientist.com/?articles.view/articleNo/28820/title/Odd-Man-Out

Kawai, M. (1965). Newly-acquired pre-cultural behavior of the natural troop of Japanese monkeys on Koshima Islet. *Primates*. 6, 1–31.

Keeley, L. H. (1996). *War Before Civilization*. New York: Oxford University Press.

Kellogg, W. N. and Kellogg, L. A. (1933). *The Ape and the Child*. New York: McGraw-Hill.

Kenrick, D. T. and Keefe, R. C. (1992). Age preferences in mates reflects sex differences in reproductive strategies. *Behavioural and Brain Sciences*. 15, 75–133.

Kenrick, D. T. and Simpson, J. A. (1997). Why social psychology and evolutionary psychology need one another. In J. A. Simpson and D. T. Kenrick (eds.). *Evolutionary Social Psychology* (1–20). Mahwah, NJ: Lawrence Erlbaum.

Kimura, D. (1999). *Sex and Cognition*. Boston: MIT Press.

King-Hele, D. (1968). *The Essential Writings of Erasmus Darwin*. London: MacGibbon and Kee.

Kinsey, A. C., Pomeroy, W. E. and Martin, C. E. (1953). *Sexual Behaviour in the Human Female*. Philadelphia: Saunders.

Kirkpatrick, L. A. and Hazan, C. (1994). Attachment styles and close relationships: A four-year prospective study. *Personal Relationships*. 1, 123–42.

Klein, S. B., Cosmides, L., Tooby, J. and Chance, S. (2002). Decisions and the evolution of memory: Multiple systems, multiple functions. *Psychological Review*. 109, 306–29.

Klein, S. B., Loftus, J. and Kihlstrom, J. F. (1996). Self-knowledge of an amnesic patient: Toward a neuropsychology of personality and social psychology. *Journal of Experimental Psychology: General*. 13, 501–18.

Kleinginna, P. R. and Kleinginna, A. M. (1981a). A categorized list of emotion definitions with suggestions for a consensual definition. *Motivation and Emotion*. 5, 263–91.

(1981b). A categorized list of emotion definitions with suggestions for a consensual definition. *Motivation and Emotion*. 5, 345–79.

Koenigs, M., Kruepke, M., Zeier, J. *et al.* (2012). Utilitarian moral judgment in psychopathy. *Social, Cognitive, and Affective Neuroscience*. 7, 708–14.

Koenigs, M., Young, L., Adolphs, R. *et al.* (2007). Damage to the prefrontal cortex increases utilitarian moral judgements. *Nature.* 446(7138), 908–11.

Koss, M. (n.d.). Rape and the criminal justice system. Online article http://vip.msu.edu/theCAT/CAT_Author/MPK/justicecritique.html accessed 2 May 2007.

Krause, J., Lalueza-Fox, C., Orlando, L. *et al.* (2007). The derived FOXP2 variant of modern humans was shared with Neanderthals. *Current Biology.* 17(21), 1908–12.

(in press). Evolutionary models of why men rape: Acknowledging the complexities. *Trauma, Violence and Abuse: A Review Journal.*

Krebs, D. L. and Denton, K. (1997). Social illusions and self-deception: The evolution of biases in person perception. In J. A. Simpson and D. T. Kendrick (eds.). *Evolutionary Social Psychology* (21–48). Hillsdale, NJ: Lawrence Erlbaum.

Krebs, J. R. and Dawkins, R. (1984). Animal signals: Mind-reading and manipulation. In J. R. Krebs and N. B. Davies (eds.). *Behavioural Ecology: An Evolutionary Approach* (380–402). Oxford: Blackwell.

Krebs, J. R. and Davies, N. B. (1978). *Behavioural Ecology.* Sunderland, MA: Sinauer Assoc.

(1981). *An Introduction to Behavioural Ecology.* Oxford: Blackwell Scientific Publications.

Kring, A. M., Davison, G. C., Neale, J. M. *et al.* (2007). *Abnormal Psychology.* Chichester, UK: Wiley.

Kring, A. M., Johnson, S. L., Davison, G. *et al.* (2010). *Abnormal Psychology* (11th edn). Chichester, UK: Wiley.

Kringelbach, M. L. and Rolls, E. T. (2004). The functional neuroanatomy of the human orbitofrontal cortex: evidence from neuroimaging and neuropsychology. *Progress in Neurobiology.* 72, 341–72.

Kuhl, P., Williams, K. A., Lacerda, F., Stevens, K. N. and Lindblom, B. (1992). Linguistic experience alters phonetic perception in infants by six months of age. *Science.* 255, 606–8.

Kunce, L. J. and Shaver, P. R. (1994). An attachment-theoretical approach to care-giving in romantic relationships. In K. Bartholomew and D. Perlman (eds.). *Advances in Personal Relationships.* Vol. 5 (205–37). London: Kingsley.

Kuroda, S. (1984). Interaction over food among pygmy chimpanzees. In: R. Sussman (ed.). *The Pygmy Chimpanzee: Evolutionary Biology and Behavior.* (301–24). New York: Plenum.

Kurzban, R. and Haselton, M. G. (2006). Making hay out of straw? Real and imagined controversies in evolutionary psychology. In J. H. Barkow (ed.). *Missing the Revolution: Darwinism for Social Scientists* (149–61). Oxford: Oxford University Press.

Lahr, M. M. and Foley, R. (1994). Multiple dispersals and modern human origins. *Evolutionary Anthropology.* 3, 48–60.

Lai, C. S. L., Fisher, S. E., Hurst, J. A., Vargha-Khadem, F. and Monaco, A. P. (2001). A forkhead-domain gene is mutated in a severe speech and language disorder. *Nature.* 413, 519–23.

Laland, K. N. and Brown, G. R. (2011). *Sense and Nonsense: Evolutionary Perspectives on Human Behaviour.* Oxford: Oxford University Press.

Landy, D. and Aronson, E. (1969). The influence of the character of the criminal and his victim on the decisions of simulated jurors. *Journal of Experimental Social Psychology*. 5, 141–52.

Lange, C. G. (1885/1912). The emotions: A psychophysiological study, trans. I.A. Haupt. In C. G. Lange and W. James (eds.). *Psychology Classica*. Vol. 1. Baltimore, MD: Wilkins.

Larsen, R. J. and Buss, D. M. (2009). *Personality Psychology: Domains of Knowledge about Human Nature* (4th edn). New York: McGraw-Hill.

Lazarus, R. S. (1991). *Emotion and Adaptation*. New York: Oxford University Press.

Leakey, R. and Lewin, R. (1992). *Origins Reconsidered: In Search of What Makes us Human*. London: Little, Brown.

(1996). *The Sixth Extinction: Biodiversity and its Survival*. London: Phoenix.

LeDoux, J. E. (1996). *The Emotional Brain: The Mysterious Underpinnings of Emotional Life*. New York: Simon and Schuster.

Lee, R. B. (1972). The !Kung Bushmen of Botswana. In M. C. Bicchieri (ed.). *Hunters and Gatherers Today*. New York: Holt Rinehart Winston.

(1979). *The !Kung San. Men, Women and Work in Foraging Society*. Cambridge: Cambridge University Press.

Lee, Y. T., Jussim, L. J. and McCauley, C. R. (eds.) (1995). *Stereotyped Accuracy: Toward Appreciating Group Differences*. Washington, DC: American Psychological Association Press.

Lehman, H. C. (1953). *Age and Achievement*. Princeton: Princeton University Press.

Leonard, L. (1992). Specific language impairments in three languages: Some cross-linguistic evidence. In P. Fletcher and D. Hall (eds.). *Specific Speech and Language Disorder in Children* (119–26). London: Whurr.

(1998). *Children with Specific Language Impairment*. Cambridge, MA: MIT Press.

Leslie, A. M. (1994). ToMM, ToBy, and agency: Core architecture and domain specificity in cognition and culture. In L. A. Hirschfeld and S. A. Gelman (eds.). *Mapping the Mind: Domain Specificity in Cognition and Culture* (119–48). New York: Cambridge University Press.

Levy, J., Heller, W., Banich, M. and Burton, L. (1983). Asymmetry of perception in free viewing of chimeric faces. *Brain and Cognition*. 2, 404–19.

Lewin, R. (1998). *Principles of Human Evolution*. Oxford: Blackwell Science.

Lewontin, R. C. (2001). *It Ain't Necessarily So: The Dream of the Human Genome and other Confusions*. New York: Granta.

Lewontin, R. C., Rose, S. and Kamin, L. J. (1984). *Not in Our Genes: Biology, Ideology, and Human Nature*. New York: Pantheon.

Libet, B. (1985). Unconscious cerebral initiative and the role of conscious will in voluntary action. *Behavioral and Brain Sciences*. 8, 529–66.

Liddle, J. R., Shackelford, T. K. and Weekes-Shackelford, V. A. (2012). Evolutionary perspectives on violence, homicide, and war. In T. K. Shackelford and V. A. Weekes-Shackelford (eds.). *Oxford Handbook of Evolutionary Perspectives on Violence, Homicide, and War* (3–22). New York: Oxford University Press.

Lieberman, P. (1984). *The Biology and Evolution of Language*. Cambridge, MA: Harvard University Press.

Ligon, J. P. and Ligon, S. H. (1978). Communal breeding in green woodhoopoes as a case for reciprocity. *Nature.* 276, 496–8.

Lively, C. (1987). Evidence from a New Zealand snail for the maintenance of sex by parasitism. *Nature.* 328, 519–21.

Lively, C., Craddock, C. and Vrijenhoek, R. C. (1990). Red Queen hypothesis supported by parasitism in sexual and clonal fish. *Nature.* 344, 864–6.

Locke, J. L. and Bogin, B. (2006) Language and life history: A new perspective on the development and evolution of human language. *Behavioral and Brain Sciences.* 29, 259–80.

Loehlin, J. C., McCrae, R. R., Costa, P. T., Jr and John, O. P. (1998). Heritabilities of common and measure-specific components of the Big Five personality factors. *Journal of Research in Personality.* 32, 431–53.

Loftus, E. F. and Palmer, J. C. (1974). Reconstruction of auto-mobile destruction: An example of the interaction between language and memory. *Journal of Verbal Learning and Verbal Behaviour.* 13, 585–9.

Lovejoy, C. O. (1981a). The origin of man. *Science.* 211, 341–50.

  (1981b). Models of human evolution. *Science.* 217, 304–6.

  (1988). Evolution of human walking. *Scientific American.* 259, 118–25.

  (2009). Re-examining human origins in light of *Ardipithecus ramidus. Science* 326:74e1–74e8.

Low, B. S. and Heinen, J. T. (1993). Population, resources and environment: Implications of human behavioural ecology for conservation. *Population and Environment.* 15, 7–41.

Lozano, G. L. (2008). Obesity and sexually selected anorexia nervosa. *Medical Hypotheses.* 71, 933–40.

Ludwig, A. M. (1992). Creative achievement and psychopathology: Achievement across professions. *American Journal of Psychotherapy.* 46, 330–54.

Lumsden, C. J. and Wilson, E. O. (1981). *Genes, Mind, and Culture: The Coevolutionary Process.* Cambridge, MA: Harvard University Press.

Luria, A. (1968). *The Mind of a Mnemonist.* New York: Basic Books.

Lutchmaya, S., Baron-Cohen, S. and Raggett, P. (2002). Foetal testosterone and eye contact at 12 months. *Infant Behavior and Development.* 25, 327–35.

Lyons, M. J., True, W. R., Eisen, S. A., Goldberg, J., Meyer, J. M., Farone, S. V. *et al.* (1995). Differential heritability of adult and juvenile antisocial traits. *Archives of General Psychiatry.* 52, 906–15.

McCloskey, M. (1983). Naive theories of motion. In D. Gentner and A. L. Stevens (eds.). *Mental Models* (299–324). Hillsdale, NJ: Lawrence Erlbaum.

Maccoby, E. E. (1990). Gender and relationships: A developmental account. *American Psychologist.* 45, 513–20.

McCrae, R. R. and Costa, P. T. (1996). Toward a new generation of personality theories: Theoretical contexts for the five-factor model. In J. S. Wiggins (ed.). *The Five-Factor Model of Personality: Theoretical Perspectives* (51–87). New York: Guilford.

MacDonald, K. B. (1998). Evolution and development. In A. Campbell and S. Muncer (eds.). *Social Development* (21–49). London: UCL Press.

McFarland, D. (1999). *Animal Behaviour: Psychobiology, Ethology and Evolution* (3rd edn). Harlow: Addison Wesley Longman.

McGaugh, J. L. (1992). Neuromodulatory regulation of memory: Role of the amygdaloid complex. *International Journal of Psychology*. 27, 403.

(2004). The amygdala modulates the consolidation of memories of emotionally arousing experiences. *Annual Review of Neuroscience*. 27, 1–28.

McGuire, M., Marks, I., Nesse, R. M. and Troisi, A. (1992). Evolutionary biology: A basic science for psychiatry? *Acta Psychiatrica Scandinavica*. 86, 89–96.

McGuire, M. and Troisi, A. (1998). *Darwinian Psychiatry*. Oxford: Oxford University Press.

McGuire, M., Troisi, A. and Raleigh, M. M. (1997). Depression in an evolutionary context. In S. Baron-Cohen (ed.). *The Maladapted Mind* (255–82). Hove: Psychology Press.

McHenry, H. M. (1991). Sexual dimorphism in *Australopithecus afarensis*. *Journal of Human Evolution*. 20, 21–32.

(2009). *Human Evolution*. In M. Ruse and J. Travis (eds.). *Evolution: The First Four Billion Years*. (261–5). Cambridge, MA: Harvard University Press.

MacLarnon, A. and Hewitt, G. P. (1999). The evolution of human speech: The role of enhanced breathing control. *American Journal of Physical Anthropology*. 10(3), 341–3.

McMillan, G. (2000). Ache residential grouping and social foraging. Ph.D. dissertation, Department of Anthropology, University of New Mexico.

Madsen, D. (1985). A biochemical property relating to power seeking in humans. *American Political Science Review*. 79, 448–57.

Madsen, D. and McGuire, M. (1984). Rapid communication, whole blood serotonin and the type A behavior pattern. *Psychosomatic Medicine*. 46, 546–8.

Maestripieri, D. (2004). Genetic aspects of mother–offspring conflict in rhesus macaques. *Behavioral Ecology and Sociobiology*. 55, 381–7.

Malinowski, B. (1929). *The Sexual Life of Savages in North Western Melanesia*. London: Routledge.

Manktelow, K. I. and Evans, J. St. B. T. (1979). Facilitation of reasoning by realism: Effect or non-effect? *British Journal of Psychology*. 70, 477–88.

Manktelow, K. I. and Over, D. E. (1990). Deontic thought and the selection task. In K. I. Gilhooly, M. Keane, R. H. Logie and G. Erdos (eds.). *Lines of Thinking: Reflections on the Psychology of Thought*. Vol. 1 (153–64). Chichester, UK: Wiley.

Manning, A. and Stamp-Dawkins, M. (1998). *An Introduction to Animal Behaviour*. Cambridge: Cambridge University Press.

Markman, E. (1989). *Categorization and Naming in Children: Problems of Induction*. Cambridge, MA: MIT Press.

Marks, I. M. and Nesse, R. M. (1994). Fear and fitness: An evolutionary analysis of anxiety disorders. *Ethology and Sociobiology*. 15, 247–61.

Marlowe, F. (2007). Hunting and gathering: The human sexual division of foraging labor. *Cross-Cultural Research*. 41, 170–95.

Marr, D. (1982). *Vision*. San Francisco: Freeman.

Martin, C. H. and Johnsen, S. (2007). A field test of the Hamilton–Zuk hypothesis in the Trinidadian guppy (*Poecilia reticulata*). *Behavioral Ecology and Sociobiology.* 61, 1897–1909.

Martin, P. (1997) *The Sickening Mind: Brain, Behaviour, Immunity and Disease.* London: HarperCollins.

Martin, R. D. (1983). *Human Brain Evolution in an Ecological Context.* New York: American Museum of Natural History.

Mason, P. H. and Short, R. V. (2011). Neanderthal–human Hybrids. *Hypothesis.* 9(1), e1.

Mathieson, I., Munafò, M. R. and Flint, J. (2012). Meta-analysis indicates that common variants at the DISC1 locus are not associated with schizophrenia. *Molecular Psychiatry.* 17, 634–41.

Maynard Smith, J. (1964). Group selection and kin selection. *Nature.* 201, 1145–7.

(1971). What is sex? *Journal of Theoretical Biology.* 30, 319–35.

(1974). The theory of games and the evolution of animal conflicts. *Journal of Theoretical Biology.* 47, 209–21.

(1978). *The Evolution of Sex.* Cambridge: Cambridge University Press.

(1993). *The Theory of Evolution.* Cambridge: Cambridge University Press.

Mead, M. (1928). *Coming of Age in Samoa.* New York: William Morrow.

(1935). *Sex and Temperament in Three Primitive Societies.* New York: William Morrow.

(1949). *Male and Female.* New York: William Morrow.

(1961). Anthropology among the sciences. *American Anthropologist.* 63, 475–82.

Mealey, L. (1995). The sociobiology of sociopathy: An integrated evolutionary model. *Behavioral and Brain Sciences.* 18, 523–99.

(2005). Evolutionary psychopathology and abnormal development. In R. L. Burgess and K. MacDonald (eds.). *Evolutionary Perspectives on Human Development* (2nd edn) (381–406). Thousand Oaks, CA: Sage.

Meltzoff, A. N. and Moore, M. K. (1977). Imitation of facial and manual gestures by human neonates. *Science.* 198, 75–8.

(1983). Newborn infants imitate adult facial gestures. *Child Development.* 54, 702–9.

Mendle, J., Turkheimer, E., D'Onofrio, B. M., Lynch, S. K., Emery, R. E., Slutske, W. S. *et al.* (2006). Family structure and age at menarche: A children-of-twins approach. *Developmental Psychology.* 42, 533–42.

Meredith, M. (2011). *Born in Africa: The Quest for the Origins of Human Life.* New York: Public Affairs.

Meston, C. M. and Buss, D. M. (2009). *Why Women Have Sex: Understanding Sexual Motivations from Adventure to Revenge.* New York: Times Books.

Midgley, M. (1979). *Beast and Man.* Ithaca, NY: Cornell University Press.

(2000). Why memes? In H. Rose and S. Rose (eds.). *Alas, Poor Darwin* (67–84). London: Cape.

Milan, E. L. (2010). *Looking for a Few Good Males: Female Choice in Evolutionary Biology.* Baltimore: Johns Hopkins University Press.

Milgram, S. (1963). Behavioral study of obedience. *Journal of Abnormal and Social Psychology.* 67(4), 371.

Miller, G. F. (2000). *The Mating Mind: How Sexual Choice Shaped the Evolution of Human Nature*. London: Heinemann/Doubleday.

(2009). *Spent: Sex, Evolution, and Consumer Behavior*. New York: Viking.

Miller, W. B., and Pasta, D. J. (2000). Early family environment, reproductive strategy and contraceptive behaviour. In J. L. Rodgers, D. C. Rowe and W. B. Miller (eds.). *Genetic Influences on Human Fertility and Sexuality* (183–230). Boston, MA: Kluwer Academic.

Mineka, S. and Cook, M. (1988). Social learning and the acquisition of snake fear in monkeys. In T. Zentall and B. G. Galef (eds.). *Social Learning: Psychological and Biological Perspectives* (51–73). Hillsdale, NJ: Lawrence Erlbaum.

Minton, C., Kagan, J. and Levine, J. (1971). Maternal control and obedience in the two-year-old. *Child Development*. 42, 1873–94.

Mischel, W. (1992). Convergences and challenges in the search for consistency. *American Psychologist*. 39, 351–64.

Mitani, J. C. and Watts, D. P. (2001). Why do chimpanzees hunt and share meat? *Animal Behaviour*. 51, 915–24.

Mitchell, P. (1996). *Acquiring a Concept of Mind: A Review of Psychological Research and Theory*. Hove: Psychology Press.

Moffitt, T., Caspi, A., Belsky, J. and Silva, P. (1992). Childhood experience and the onset of menarche: A test of a sociobiological model. *Child Development*. 63, 47–58.

Moller, A. P. (1988). Female choice selects for male tail ornaments in the monogamous swallow. *Nature*. 332, 640–2.

(1990). Effects of a haematophagous mite on secondary sexual tail ornaments in the barn swallow: A test of the Hamilton and Zuk hypothesis. *Evolution*. 44, 771–84.

Monteleone, M. R., Clark, T. G., Moore, L. R. *et al.* (2006). Genetic polymorphisms and personality in healthy adults: A systematic review and meta-analysis. *Molecular Psychiatry*. 8, 471–84.

Morran, L. T., Schmidt, O. G., Gelarden, I. A., Parrish, R. C. and Lively, C. M. (2011). Running with the Red Queen: Host–parasite coevolution selects for biparental sex. *Science* 333 (6039): 216–18.

Morris, J. S., Friston, K. J., Beuchel, C., Frith, C. D., Young, A. W., Calder, A. J. *et al.* (1998). A neuromodularity role for the human amygdala in processing emotional facial expressions. *Brain*. 121, 47–57.

Morton, J. and Johnson, M. H. (1991). CONSPEC and CONLERN: A two-process theory of infant face recognition. *Psychological Review*. 98, 164–81.

Mourre, V. P. and Henshilwood, C. S. (2010). Early use of pressure flaking on lithic artifacts at Blombos Cave, South Africa. *Science*. 330, 659–62.

Muller, H. J. (1964). The relation of recombination to mutational advance. *Mutation Research*. 1, 2–9.

Munafò, M. R., Yalcin, B., Willis-Owen, S. A. and Flint, J. (2008). Association of the dopamine D4 receptor (DRD4) gene and approach-related personality traits: Meta-analysis and new data. *Biological Psychiatry*. 63, 197–206.

Myers Thompson, J. A. (2002). Bonobos of the Lukuru wildlife research project. In C. Boesch, G. Hohmann and L. F. Marchant (eds.). *Behavioral Diversity in Chimpanzees and Bonobos* (61–70). Cambridge: Cambridge University Press.

Mykletun, A., Bjerkeset, O., Overland, S. *et al.* (2009). Levels of anxiety and depression as predictors of mortality: the HUNT study. *British Journal of Psychiatry.* 195, 118–25.

Nagell, K., Olguin, K. and Tomasello, M. (1993). Processes of social learning in the tool use of chimpanzees (Pan troglodytes) and human children (Homo sapiens). *Journal of Comparative Psychology.* 107, 174–86.

Nagy, W. E. and Anderson, R. C. (1984). How many words are there in printed English? *Reading Research Quarterly.* 19, 304–30.

Nairne, J. S. and Pandeirada, J. N. S. (2008). Adaptive memory: Remembering with a stone-age brain. *Current Directions in Psychology.* 17(4), 239–43.

Nairne, J. S., Thompson, S. R. and Pandeirada, J. N. S. (2007). Adaptive memory: Survival processing enhances retention. *Journal of Experimental Psychology: Learning, Memory and Cognition.* 33(2), 263–73.

National Institutes of Health. (2010). *Genes at Work in the Brain.* Bethesda, MD: Maryland Publication No. 10–5475. braininfo@ninds.nih.gov

Nesse, R. M. (1990). Evolutionary explanations of emotions. *Human Nature.* 1, 261–89.

(2004). Natural selection and the elusiveness of happiness. *Philosophical Transactions of the Royal Society of London Series B, Biological Sciences.* 359, 1341.

(2005). Natural selection and the regulation of defenses: A signal detection analysis of the smoke detector principle. *Evolution and Human Behavior.* 26, 88–105.

(2009). Evolutionary origins and functions of emotions. In K. Scherer and D. Sander (eds.) *The Oxford Companion to Emotion and Affective Sciences.* Oxford: Oxford University Press.

(2011). Why has natural selection left us so vulnerable to anxiety and mood disorders? *Canadian Journal of Psychiatry.* 56, 705–6.

(2012). Evolution: A basic science for medicine. In A. Poiani (ed.). *Pragmatic Evolution: Applications of Evolutionary Theory* (107–14). Cambridge: Cambridge University Press.

Nesse, R. M. and Williams, G. C. (1995). *Evolution and Healing: The New Science of Darwinian Medicine.* London: Weidenfeld and Nicolson.

(1996). *Why We Get Sick.* New York: Vintage.

Nesse, R. M. and Dawkins, R. (2010). Evolution: Medicine's most basic science. In D. A. Warrell, T. M. Cox, J. D. Firth and E. J. J. Benz (eds.). *Oxford Textbook of Medicine* (5th edn) (12–15). Oxford: Oxford University Press.

Nettle, D. (2004). Evolutionary origins of depression: A review and reformulation. *Journal of Affective Disorders.* 81, 91–102.

(2005). An evolutionary perspective on the extraversion continuum. *Evolution and Human Behavior.* 26, 363–73.

(2006). The evolution of personality variation in humans and other animals. *American Psychologist.* 61, 622–31.

Nettle, D. and Bateson, M. (2012). Evolutionary origins of mood and its disorders. *Current Biology.* 22, 712–21.

Nettle, D., Coall, D. A. and Dickins, T. E. (2011). Early-life conditions and age at first pregnancy in British women. *Proceedings of the Royal Society.* B278: 1721–7.

Neuberg, S. L., Kenrick, D.T. and Schaller, M. (2010). Evolutionary social psychology. In S. T. Fiske, D. T. Gilbert and G. Lindzey (eds.). *Handbook of Social Psychology* (5th edn) (761–6). New York: John Wiley and Sons.

Neville, H., Coffey, S., Holcomb, P. and Tallal, P. (1993). The neurobiology of sensory and language processing in language impaired children. *Journal of Cognitive Neuroscience.* 5, 235–53.

Nishida, T. and Hiraiwa-Hasegawa, M. (1987). Chimpanzees and Bonobos: Cooperative Relationships among Males. In B. B. Smuts, D. L. Cheney, R. M. Seyfarth, R. W. Wrangham and T. T. Struhsaker (eds.). *Primate Societies* (165–77). Chicago: University of Chicago Press.

Nolan-Hoeksema, S. (2007). *Abnormal Psychology.* Boston: McGraw-Hill.

Norberg, R. Å. (1994). Swallow tail streamer is a mechanical device for self-deflection of tail leading edge, enhancing aerodynamic efficiency and flight manoeuvrability. *Proceedings of the Royal Society of London, B.* 257, 227–33.

Nordhaus, W. D. (1996). Do real-output and real-wage measures capture reality? The history of lighting suggests not. In T. F. Bresnahan and R. J. Gordon (eds.). *The Economics of New Goods* (27–70). Chicago: University of Chicago Press.

Nowak, M. A., Tarnita, C. E. and Wilson, E. O. (2010). The evolution of eusociality. *Nature,* 466 (7310): 1057 DOI: 10.1038/nature09205

Oaksford, M. and Chater, N. (1994). A rational analysis of the selection task as optimal data selection. *Psychological Review.* 101, 608–31.

  (1999). Ten years of the rational analysis of cognition. *Trends in Cognitive Sciences.* 3(2), 57–65.

Ohman, A. and Mineka, S. (2001). Fears, phobias, and preparedness. Toward an evolved module of fear and fear learning. *Psychological Review.* 108, 483–522.

Oppenheimer, S. (2004). *The Real Eve: Modern Man's Journey Out of Africa.* New York: Carroll & Graf.

Ortony, A. and Turner, T. J. (1990). What's basic about emotions? *Psychological Review.* 97, 315–31.

Osier, M. V., Pakstis, A. J., Soodyall, H., Comas, D., Goldman, D. and Odunsi, A. (2002). A global perspective on genetic variation at the ADH genes reveals unusual patterns of linkage disequilibrium and diversity. *American Journal of Human Genetics.* 71(1), 84–99.

O'Steen, S., Cullum, A. J. and Bennett, A. F. (2002). Rapid evolution of escape ability in Trinidadian guppies (*Poecilia reticulata*). *Evolution.* 56, 776–84.

Ostrom, E. (1990). *Governing the Commons: The Evolution of Institutions for Collective Action, the Political Economy of Institutions and Decisions.* Cambridge: Cambridge University Press.

Over, R. (1988). Does scholarly impact decline with age? *Scientometrics.* 13, 215–23.

Packer, C. (1977). Reciprocal altruism in *Papio anubis. Nature.* 265, 441–3.

Pagel, M. (2012). Wired for Culture: Origins of the Human Social Mind. London: W. W. Norton.

Pakkenberg, B. and Gundersen, H. J. G. (1997). Neocortical neuron number in humans: Effect of sex and age. *Journal of Comparative Neurology.* 384, 312–20.

Panksepp, J. and Panksepp, J. B. (2000). The seven sins of evolutionary psychology. *Evolution and Cognition*. 6(2), 108–31.

Park, J. H. and Schaller, M. (2009). Parasites, minds and cultures: Could the most human of qualities owe their existence to tiny, mindless organisms? *The Psychologist*. 22, 942–5.

Parker, H. M. and McDaniel, C. D. (2009). Parthenogenesis in unfertilized eggs of *Coturnix chinensis*, the Chinese painted quail, and the effect of egg clutch position on embryonic development. *Poultry Science*. 88, 784–90.

Pascalis, O., de Haan, M. and Nelson, C. A. (2002). Is face processing species-specific during the first year of life? *Science*. 296, 1321–3.

Pascalis, O., Scott, L. S., Kelly, D. J., Shannon, R. W., Nicholson, E. and Coleman, M. (2005). Plasticity of face processing in infancy. *Proceedings of the National Academy of Sciences*. 102, 5297–5300.

Passer, M. W. and Smith, R. E. (2007). *Psychology: The Science of Mind and Behaviour*. Boston: McGraw-Hill.

Pawlowski, B. and Dunbar, R. I. M. (1999). Impact of market value on human mate choice decisions. *Proceedings of the Royal Society of London, B*. 266, 281–5.

Perner, J., Leekam, S. and Wimmer, H. (1987). Three-year-olds' difficulty with false belief: The case for a conceptual deficit. *British Journal of Developmental Psychology*. 5, 125–37.

Petrie, M., Halliday, T. and Sanders, C. (1991). Peahens prefer peacocks with elaborate trains. *Animal Behaviour*. 41, 323–31.

Piattelli-Palmarini, M. (1994a). Ever since language and learning: Afterthoughts on the Piaget-Chomsky debate. *Cognition*. 50, 315–46.

(1994b). *Inevitable Illusions: How the Mistakes of Reason Rule Our Minds*. Somerset, NJ: John Wiley and Sons.

Pilleri, G. and Knuckey, J. (1969). Behaviour patterns of some Delphinidae observed in the western Mediterranean. *Zeitschrift für Tierpsychologie*. 26, 48–72.

Pinker, S. (1994). *The Language Instinct: How the Mind Creates Language*. London: Penguin.

(1997). *How the Mind Works*. London: Allen Lane.

(2002). *The Blank Slate: The Modern Denial of Human Nature*. London: Allen Lane.

(2005). So how *does* the mind work? *Mind and Language*. 20(1), 1–24.

(2011). *The Better Angels of Our Nature: The Decline of Violence in History and Its Causes*. London: Penguin.

Pinker, S. and Bloom, P. (1990). Natural language and natural selection. *Behavioral and Brain Sciences*. 13(4), 707–84.

Pirolli, P. and Card, S. K. (1999). Information foraging. *Psychological Review*. 105(1), 58–82.

Plomin, R. (1988). The nature and nurture of cognitive abilities. In R. Sternberg (ed.). *Advances in the psychology of human intelligence* (vol. 4, 1–33). Hillsdale, NJ: Lawrence Erlbaum.

(2011). Commentary: Why are children in the same family so different? Non-shared environment three decades later. *International Journal of Epidemiology*. 40, 582–92.

Plomin, R., Chipuer, H. M. and Neiderhiser, J. M. (1994). Behavior genetic evidence for the importance of nonshared environment. In E. M. Hetherington, D. Reiss and R. Plomin (eds.). *Separate Social Worlds of Siblings: The Impact of Nonshared Environment on Development* (1–31). Hillsdale, NJ: Lawrence Erlbaum.

Plomin, R. and Daniels, D. (1987). Why are children in the same family so different from one another? *Behavioral and Brain Sciences.* 10, 1–60.

Plomin, R., DeFries, J. C., McGuffin, P. and McClearn, G. E. (2008). *Behavioral Genetics* (5th edn). New York: Worth Publishers.

Pollard, P. and Evans, J. St. B. T. (1987). Content and context effects in reasoning. *American Journal of Psychology.* 100, 41–60.

Popper, K. (1959). *The Logic of Scientific Discovery.* London: Hutchinson.

Posner, R. A. (1992). *Sex and Reason.* Cambridge, MA: Harvard University Press.

Potts, R. (1996). *Humanity's Descent: The Consequences of an Ecological Instability.* New York: William Morrow.

Pratto, F. and John, O. P. (1991). Automatic vigilance: The attention-grabbing power of negative social information. *Journal of Personality and Social Psychology.* 61, 380–91.

Premack, A. J. and Premack, D. (1972). Teaching language to an ape. *Scientific American.* 227(4), 92–9.

Price, J. S. (1967). Hypothesis: The dominance hierarchy and the evolution of mental illness. *Lancet.* 2, 243–6.

Price, J. S., Sloman, L., Gardner, R., Gilbert, P. and Rohde, P. (1994). The social competition hypothesis of depression. *British Journal of Psychiatry.* 164, 309–35.

Price, M. E., Cosmides, L. and Tooby, J. (2002). Punitive sentiment as an anti-free rider psychological device. *Evolution and Human Behavior.* 23, 203–31.

Profit, M. (1992). Pregnancy sickness as an adaptation: A deterrent to maternal ingestion of teratogens. In J. Barkow, L. Cosmides and J. Tooby (eds.). *The Adapted Mind* (327–65). New York: Oxford University Press.

Prüfer, K., Munch, K., Hellmann, I. *et al.* (2012). The bonobo genome compared with the chimpanzee and human genomes. *Nature.* 486, 527–31.

Quine, W. V. O. (1960). *Word and Object.* Cambridge, MA: MIT Press.

Quinlan, R. J., Quinlan, M. B. and Flinn, M. V. (2003). Parental investment & age at weaning in a Caribbean village. *Evolution and Human Behavior.* 24, 1–17.

Rabbie, J. M. (1992) The effects of intragroup cooperation and intergroup competition on in-group cohesion and out-group hostility. In A. H. Harcourt and F. B. M. de Waal (eds.). *Coalitions and Alliances in Humans and Other Animals* (175–205). New York: Oxford University Press.

Radke-Yarrow, M. and Zahn-Waxler, C. (1986) The role of familial factors in the development of prosocial behavior: Research findings and questions. In D. Olweus, J. Block and M. Radke-Yarrow (eds.). *Development of Antisocial and Prosocial Behavior: Research, Theories, and Issues* (207–33). New York: Academic Press.

Raleigh, M. and McGuire, M. (1991). Serotonin in vervet monkeys. *Brain Research.* 559, 181–90.

Rapoport, A. and Chummah, A. M. (1965). *Prisoner's Dilemma*. Ann Arbor: University of Michigan Press.

Read, L. (1958). *I, Pencil: My Family Tree as Told to Leonard E. Read*. Irvington-on-Hudson: Foundation for Economic Education.

Reader, W. R. and Payne, S. J. (2002). Browsing multiple texts under time pressure. 24th Meeting of the Cognitive Science Society, George Mason University. Washington, DC.

(2007). Allocating time across multiple texts: Sampling and satisficing. *Human Computer Interaction*. 22(3), 263–98.

Real, L. A. (1991). Animal choice behavior and the evolution of cognitive architecture. *Science*. 253, 980–6.

Reilly, P. (1991). *The Surgical Solution: A History of Involuntary Sterilization in the United States*. Baltimore: Johns Hopkins University Press.

Reiss, D., Neiderhiser, J. M., Hetherington, E. M. and Plomin, R. (2000). *The Relationship Code: Deciphering Genetic and Social Patterns in Adolescent Development*. Cambridge, MA: Harvard University Press.

Renfrew, C. (1987). *Archaeology and Language*. New York: Penguin.

Reno, P. L., Meindl, R. S., McCollum, M. A. and Lovejoy, C. O. (2003). Sexual dimorphism in Australopithecus afarensis was similar to that of modern humans. *Proceedings of the National Academy of Science, USA*. 100, 9404–9. Epub, 23 July.

Resnick, P. J. (1970). Murder of the newborn: A psychiatric review of neonaticide. *American Journal of Psychiatry*. 126, 58–64.

Reuter-Lorenz, P. and Davidson, R. (1981). Differential contributions of the two cerebral hemispheres to the perception of happy and sad faces. *Neuropsychologia*. 19, 609–13.

Richell, R. A., Mitchell, D. G. V., Newman, C., Leonard, A., Baron-Cohen, S., and Blair, R. J. R. (2002). Theory of mind and psychopathy: Can psychopathic individuals read 'the language of the eyes'? *Neuropsychologia*. 41, 523–6.

Richerson, P. J. and Boyd, R. (2001). Culture is part of human biology: Why the superorganic concept serves the human sciences badly. In S. Maasen and M. Winterhager (eds.). *Science Studies: Probing the Dynamics of Scientific Knowledge* (147–77). New York: Transcript Verlag.

(2005). *Not by Genes Alone*. Chicago: University of Chicago Press.

Richerson, P. J., Boyd, R. and Henrich, J. (2010). Gene-culture coevolution in the age of genomics. *Proceedings of the National Academy of Sciences*. 107(Supplement 2). 8985–92.

Ridley, M. (1993). *The Red Queen: Sex and the Evolution of Human Nature*. London: Penguin.

(1996). *The Origins of Virtue*. London: Viking.

(1999). *Genome: The Autobiography of a Species in 23 Chapters*. New York: HarperCollins.

(2003). *Nature via Nurture: Genes, Experience and What Makes Us Human*. London: HarperCollins.

(July, 2010). Matt Ridley: When ideas have sex [video file]. Retrieved from www.ted. com/talks/matt_ridley_when_ideas_have_sex.html

Roberts, S. G. B. and Dunbar, R. I. M. (2011). The costs of family and friends: An 18-month longitudinal study of relationship maintenance and decay. *Evolution and Human Behavior*. 32, 186–97.

Rode, C., Cosmides, L., Hell, W. and Tooby, J. (1999). When and why do people avoid unknown probabilities in decisions under uncertainty? Testing some predictions from optimal foraging theory. *Cognition*. 72, 269–304.

Roediger, H. L. and McDermott, K. B. (1995). Creating false memories: Remembering words not presented in lists. *Journal of Experimental Psychology: Learning, Memory, and Cognition*. 21, 803–14.

Rood, J. P. (1986). Ecology and social evolution in the mongooses. In D. I. Rubenstein and R. W. Wrangham (eds.). *Ecological Aspects of Social Evolution. Birds and Mammals* (131–52). Princeton: Princeton University Press.

Rosch, E. (1973). On the internal structure of perceptual and semantic categories. In T. M. Moore (ed.). *Cognitive Development and the Acquisition of Language* (111–44). New York: Academic Press.

Rosch, E., Mervis, C. B., Gray, W. D., Johnson, D. M. and Boyes-Braem, P. (1976). Basic objects in natural categories. *Cognitive Psychology*. 8, 382–439.

Rose, H. and Rose, S. (2000). *Alas Poor Darwin: Arguments against Evolutionary Psychology*. London: Jonathan Cape.

(2001). Much ado about very little. *The Psychologist*. 14, 428–9.

Rose, S., Kamin, L. J. and Lewontin, R. C. (1984). *Not in Our Genes*. London: Pelican.

Ross, L. and Nisbett, R. E. (1991). *The Person and the Situation*. New York: McGraw-Hill.

Ross, R., Begab, M., Dondis, E., Giampiccolo, J. and Myers, C. (1985). *Lives of the Mentally Retarded: A Forty-year Follow-up Study*. Stanford: Stanford University Press.

Rothbart, M. K. (1989). Temperament and development. In G. Kohnstamm, J. Bates and M. K. Rothbart (eds.). *Temperament in Childhood* (187–248). Chichester, UK: Wiley.

Rowe, D. C. (1994). *The Limits of Family Influence: Genes, Experience, and Behavior*. New York: Guilford Press.

Rowell, C. H. and Cannis, T. L. (1972). Environmental factors affecting the green/brown polymorphism in the Cyrtacanthacridine grasshopper *Schistocerca vaga*. *Acrida*. 1, 69–77.

Rozin, P., Lowery, L., Imada, S. and Haidt, J. (1999) The moral–emotion triad hypothesis: A mapping between three moral emotions (contempt, anger, disgust) and three moral ethics (community, autonomy, divinity). *Journal of Personality and Social Psychology*. 76, 574–86.

Ruffman, T., Perner, J., Naito, M., Parkin, L. and Clements, W. (1998). Older (but not younger) siblings facilitate false belief understanding. *Developmental Psychology*. 34, 161–74.

Ruse, M. (1987). Sociobiology and knowledge: Is evolutionary epistemology a viable option? In C. Crawford, M. Smith and D. Krebs (eds.). *Sociobiology and Psychology: Ideas, Issues and Applications* (61–79). London: Lawrence Erlbaum.

Rutherford, M. J., Cacciola, J. S. and Alterman, A. I. (1999). Antisocial personality disorder and psychopathy in cocaine-dependent women. *American Journal of Psychiatry*. 156, 849–56.

Ryle, G. (1949). *The Concept of Mind*. London: Hutchinson.

Sahlins, M. (1976). *The Use and Abuse of Biology: An Anthropological Critique of Sociobiology*. Ann Arbor: University of Michigan Press.

Samuels, R., Stich, S. and Bishop, M. (2002). Ending the rationality wars: How to make disputes about human rationality disappear. In R. Elio (ed.). *Common Sense, Reasoning and Rationality* (236–68). New York: Oxford University Press.

Sandstrom, P. E. (1994). An optimal foraging approach to information seeking and use. *Library Quarterly*. 64, 414–49.

Sanvito, S., Galimberti, F. and Miller, E. (2007). Vocal signalling of male southern elephant seals is honest but imprecise. *Animal Behaviour*. 73, 287–99.

Savage-Rumbaugh, E. S., Murphy, J., Sevick, R. A., Brakke, K. E., Williams, S. L. and Rumbaugh, D. (1993). *Language Comprehension in Ape and Child*. Monographs of the Society for Research in Child Development, 233. Chicago: University of Chicago Press.

Scally, A. *et al.* (2012). *Nature*. Insights into hominid evolution from the gorilla genome sequence. 483 (7388): 169 doi: 10.1038/nature10842

Scarr, S. and Weinberg, R. A. (1976). IQ test performance of black children adopted by white families. *American Psychologist*. 31, 726–39.

Schacter, D. (2001). *The Seven Sins of Memory: How the Mind Forgets and Remembers*. New York: Houghton Mifflin.

Schaller, G. B. (1972). *The Serengeti Lion*. Chicago: University of Chicago Press.

Schaller, M., Simpson, J. A. and Kenrick, D. T. (2006). *Evolution and Social Psychology (Frontiers of Social Psychology)*. New York: Psychology Press.

Schultz, D. P. and Schultz, S. E. (2005). *Theories of Personality*. Belmont, CA: Thomson-Wadsworth.

Seligman, M. E. P. (1970). On the generality of the laws of learning. *Psychology Review*. 77, 406–18.

Seyfarth, R. M. and Cheney, D. L. (1984). Grooming, alliances and reciprocal altruism in vervet monkeys. *Nature*. 308, 541–3.

Shackelford, T. K., Pound, N. and Goetz, A. T. (2005). Psychological and physiological adaptation to human sperm competition. *Review of General Psychology*. 9, 228–48.

Shankman, P. (1998). Margaret Mead, Derek Freeman, and the issue of evolution. *Skeptical Inquirer*. 22, 35–9.

Shavit, V., Fischer, C. S. and Koresh, Y. (1994). Kin and non-kin under collective threat: Israeli networks during the Gulf War. *Social Forces*. 72, 1197–215.

Shepard, R. (1990). *Mind Sights*. New York: W. H. Freeman.

Sherif, M. (1956). *In Common Predicament: Social Psychology of Intergroup Conflict and Cooperation*. New York: Houghton Mifflin.

Sherman, P. W. and Flaxman, S. M. (2002). Nausea and vomiting of pregnancy in an evolutionary perspective. *American Journal of Obstetrics and Gynecology*. 186(suppl.). S190–S197.

Sherman, P. W., Jarvis, J. U. M. and Alexander, R. D. (1991). *The Biology of the Naked Mole-Rat.* Princeton: Princeton University Press.

Short, R. V. (1979). Sexual selection and its component parts, somatic and genital selection, as illustrated by man and the Great Apes. *Advances in the Study of Behaviour.* 9, 131–58.

Shu, W., Cho, J. Y., Jiang, Y., Zhang, M., Weisz, D., Elder, G. A., Schmeidler, J., De Gasperi, R., Gama Sosa, M. A., Rabidou, D., Santucci, A. C., Perl, D., Morrisey, E. and Buxbaum, J. D. (2005). Altered ultrasonic vocalization in mice with a disruption in the Foxp 2 gene. *Proceedings of the National Academy of Science.* 102, 9643–8.

Shweder, R. A., Much, N. C., Mahapatra, M. and Park, L. (1997). The 'big three' of morality (autonomy, community and divinity) and the 'big three' explanations of suffering. In A. Brand and P. Rozin (eds.). *Morality and Health.* New York: Routledge.

Sigmund, K. and Hauert, C. (2002). Altruism. *Current Biology.* 12, 270–2.

Silk, J. B. (1980). Adoption and kinship in Oceania. *American Anthropologist.* 82, 799–820.

(1990). Human adoption in evolutionary perspective. *Human Nature.* 1, 25–52.

Simner, M. L. (1971). Newborn's response to the crying of another infant. *Developmental Psychology.* 5, 136–50.

Simpson, J. A. and Kenrick, D. T. (1997). *Evolutionary Social Psychology.* Mahwah, NJ: Lawrence Erlbaum.

Simpson, J. A., Gangestad, S. W. and Biek, M. (1993). Personality and nonverbal behaviour: An ethological perspective of relationship initiation. *Journal of Experimental Social Psychology.* 29, 434–61.

Singer, P. (1981). *The Expanding Circle: Ethics and Sociobiology.* New York: Farrar, Straus and Giroux.

Singh, D. (1993). Adaptive significance of female physical attractiveness: Role of waist-to-hip ratio. *Journal of Personality and Social Psychology.* 65, 293–307.

Singh, D. and Luis, S. (1995). Ethic and gender consensus for the effect of waist-to-hip ratio on judgement of women's attractiveness. *Human Nature.* 6, 51–65.

Singh, D. and Singh, D. (2011). Shape and significance of feminine beauty: An evolutionary perspective. *Sex Roles.* 64, 723–31.

Skinner, B. F. (1957). *Verbal Behaviour.* New York: Appleton-Century-Crofts.

Slater, P. J. B. (1994). Kinship and altruism. In J. S. B. Slater and T. R. Halliday (eds.). *Behaviour and Evolution* (193–222). Cambridge: Cambridge University Press.

Slater, P. J. B. and Halliday, T. R. (1994). *Behaviour and Evolution.* Cambridge: Cambridge University Press.

Slobodchikoff, C. N. (2002). Cognition and communication in prairie dogs. In M. Bekoff, C. Allen and G. Burghardt (eds.). *The Cognitive Animal* (257–64). Cambridge, MA: MIT Press.

Slobodchikoff, C. N., Paseka, A. and Verdolin, J. L. (2009). Prairie dog alarm calls encode labels about predator colors. *Animal Cognition.* 12(3), 435–9.

Sloman, S. A., Over, D., Slovak, L. and Stibel, J. M. (2003). Frequency illusions and other fallacies. *Organizational Behavior and Human Decision Processes.* 91, 296–309.

Slotta, J. D., Chi, M. T. H. and Joram, E. (1995). Assessing students' misclassification of physics concepts: An ontological basis for conceptual change. *Cognition and Instruction.* 13, 373–400.

Smith, E. A. (2004). Why do good hunters have higher reproductive success? *Human Nature.* 15, 343–6.

(2007). Reconstructing the evolution of the human mind. *Evolution of Mind: Fundamental Questions and Controversies.* 53.

Smith, M. S. (1987). Evolution and developmental psychology: Towards a sociobiology of human development. In C. Crawford, M. Smith and D. Krebs (eds.). *Sociobiology and Psychology: Ideas, Issues, and Applications* (225–52). Hillsdale, NJ: Lawrence Erlbaum.

Smith, R. L. (1984). Human sperm competition. In R. L. Smith (ed.). *Sperm Competition and the Evolution of Mating Systems* (601–59). New York: Academic Press.

Sober, E. and Wilson, D. S. (1999) *Unto Others: The Evolution and Psychology of Unselfish Behavior.* Cambridge, MA: Harvard University Press.

Sociobiology Study Group (1975). *New York Review of Books,* 13 November.

Sokal, A. (1996). Transgressing the boundaries: Towards a transformative hermeneutics of quantum gravity. *Social Text.* 46/47, 217–52.

Soldz, S. and Vaillant, G. E. (1999). The big five personality traits and the life course: A 45-year longitudinal study. *Journal of Research in Personality.* 33, 208–32.

Spearman, C. (1923). *The Nature of Intelligence and Principles of Cognition.* London: Macmillan.

Spelke, E. S., Breinlinger, K., Macomber, J. and Jacobson, K. (1992). Origins of knowledge. *Psychological Review.* 99(4), 605–32.

Spencer, H. (1864). *Principles of Biology.* London: Williams and Norgate.

Sperber, D. (1994). The modularity of thought and the epidemiology of representations. In L. A. Hirschfeld and S. A. Gelman (eds.). *Mapping the Mind: Domain Specificity in Cognition and Culture* (39–67). New York: Cambridge University Press.

(1996). *Explaining Culture: A Naturalistic Approach.* Oxford: Blackwell.

(2000). An objection to the memetic approach to culture. In R. Aunger (ed.). *Darwinizing Culture: The State of Memetics as a Science* (163–74). Oxford: Oxford University Press.

(2002). In defense of massive modularity. In E. Dupoux (ed.). *Language, Brain and Cognitive Development: Essays in Honor of Jacques Mehler* (47–57). Cambridge, MA: MIT Press.

(2005). Modularity and relevance: How can a massively modular mind be flexible and context-sensitive? In P. Carruthers, S. Laurence and S. Stich (eds.). *The Innate Mind: Structure and Contents* (53–68). New York: Oxford University Press.

Springer, S. P. and Deutsch, G. (1998). *Left Brain, Right Brain: Perspectives from Cognitive Neurosciences.* New York: Freeman and Co.

Stanford, C. B. (1995). Chimpanzee hunting behaviour. *American Scientist.* 83, 256–61.

(1998). *Chimpanzee and Red Colobus.* Cambridge, MA: Harvard University Press.

(1999). *The Hunting Apes: Meat Eating and the Origins of Human Behavior.* Princeton, NJ: Princeton University Press.

Steiger, H., Bruce, K. and Israel, M. (2003). Eating disorders. In G. Stricker, T. A. Widiger and I. B. Weiner (eds.). *Handbook of Psychology, Vol. 8, Clinical psychology* (173–94). New York: John Wiley.

Stephens, D. W. and Krebs, J. R. (1986). *Foraging Theory.* Princeton: Princeton University Press.

Sternberg, R. J. (1985). *Beyond IQ: A Triarchic Theory of Human Intelligence.* Cambridge: Cambridge University Press.

(1998). Principles of teaching for successful intelligence. *Educational Psychologist.* 33(2–3), 65–72.

Sternberg, R. J. and Kaufman, R. J. (2002). *The Evolution of Intelligence.* Mahwah, NJ: Lawrence Erlbaum.

Stevens, A. and Price, J. (2000). *Evolutionary Psychiatry.* London: Routledge.

Stewart, K. and Harcourt, A. (1987). Gorillas: Variation in female relationships. In B. B. Smuts, D. L. Cheney, R. M. Seyfarth *et al.* (eds.). *Primate Societies* (155–64). Chicago: University of Chicago Press.

Stewart-Williams, S. (2007). Altruism among kin vs. non-kin: Effects of cost of help and reciprocal exchange. *Evolution and Human Behavior.* 28, 193–8.

Stopher, K. V., Nussey, D. H., Clutton-Brock, T. H., Guinness, F. E., Morris, A. and Pemberton, J. M. (2011). The red deer rut revisited: female excursions but no evidence females move to mate with preferred males. *Behavioral Ecology* doe: 10.1093/beheco/arr052.

Straus, M. A. (1971). Some social antecedents of physical punishment: A linkage theory interpretation. *Journal of Marriage and the Family.* 33, 658–63.

Straus, M. A., Gelles, R. J. and Steinmetz, S. K. (1980). *Behind Closed Doors: Violence in American Families.* New York: Doubleday.

Strauss, E., Gaddes, W. H. and Wada, J. (1987). Performance on a free-recall verbal dichotic listening task and cerebral dominance determined by carotid amytal test. *Neuropsychologia.* 25, 747–53.

Strier, K. B. (2011). *Primate Behavioral Ecology* (4th edn). Boston: Pearson.

Strum, S. C. (1981). Processes and products of change: Baboon predatory behaviour at Gilgil, Kenya. In R. Harding and G. Teleki (eds.). *Omnivorous Primates* (255–302). New York: Columbia University Press.

(1987). *Almost Human.* New York: W. W. Norton.

Strum, S. C. and Mitchell, W. (1987). Baboon models and muddles. In W. G. Kinzey (ed.). *The Evolution of Human Behavior: Primate Models* (87–104). Albany: State University of New York Press.

Stumpf, R. M., Emery Thompson, M. and Knott, C. D. (2008). A comparison of female mating strategies in Pan troglodytes and Pongo spp. *International Journal of Primatology.* 29, 865–84.

Sugiyama, L. S. (2005). Physical Attractiveness in Adaptationist Perspective. In D. M. Buss (ed.). *Evolutionary Psychology Handbook.* (292–343). New York: Wiley.

Sulloway, F. J. (1995). Birth order and evolutionary psychology: A meta-analytic overview (commentary on target article by Buss). *Psychological Inquiry.* 6, 75–80.

(1996). *Born to Rebel: Birth Order, Family Dynamics, and Creative Lives.* New York: Pantheon.

(1999). Birth order. In M. A. Runco and S. R. Pritzker (eds.). *Encyclopedia of Creativity* (vol. 1, 189–202). San Diego, CA: Academic Press.

(2001). Birth order, sibling competition, and human behavior. In P. S. Davies and H. R. Holcomb (eds.). *Conceptual Challenges in Evolutionary Psychology: Innovative Research Strategies* (39–83). Dordrecht and Boston: Kluwer Academic Publishers.

(2011). Why siblings are like Darwin's finches: Birth order, sibling competition, and adaptive divergence within the family. In D. M. Buss and P. H. Hawley (eds.). *The Evolution of Personality and Individual Differences* (86–119). Oxford: Oxford University Press.

Sumner, W. G. (1906). *Folkways: A Study of the Sociological Importance of Usages, Manners, Customs, Mores and Morals.* Boston: Ginn.

Surbeck, M. and Hohmann, G. (2008). Primate hunting by bonobos at LuiKotale, Salonga National Park. *Current Biology.* 18: R906–7. doi: 10.1016/j.cub.2008.08.040.

Surbeck, M., Mundry, R. and Hohmann, G. (2010). Mothers matter! Maternal support, dominance status, and mating success in male bonobos (Pan paniscus). *Proceedings of the Royal Society B: Biological Sciences.* 22, 590–98.

Sussman, R. L. (1987). Pygmy chimpanzees and common chimpanzees: Models for the behavioural ecology of the earliest hominids. In W. G. Kinzey (ed.). *The Evolution of Human Behavior: Primate Models* (87–104). Albany: State University of New York Press.

Swami, V. (2011). *Evolutionary Psychology: A Critical Introduction.* (ed.). Chichester: Wiley-Blackwell.

Swami, V. and Salem, N. (2011). The evolutionary psychology of human beauty. In V. Swami (ed.). *Evolutionary psychology: A critical introduction* (131–82). Chichester: Wiley-Blackwell.

Symons, D. (1979). *The Evolution of Human Sexuality.* New York: Oxford University Press.

(1989). The psychology of human mate preferences. *Behavioral and Brain Sciences.* 12, 34–5.

Tager-Flusberg, H. and Sullivan, K. (2000). A componential view of theory of mind: Evidence from Williams syndrome. *Cognition.* 76(1), 59–89.

Tager-Flusberg, H., Boshart, J. and Baron-Cohen, S. (1998). Reading the windows to the soul: Evidence of domain-specific sparing in Williams syndrome. *Journal of Cognitive Neuroscience.* 10(5), 631–9.

Tajfel, H. L. (1970). Experiments in intergroup discrimination. *Scientific American.* 223, 96–102.

Tajfel, H. L., Billig, M., Bundy, R. and Flament, C. (1971). Social categorization and intergroup behaviour. *European Journal of Social Psychology.* 1, 149–78.

Tallal, P., Stark, R. E. and Mellitts, E. D. (1985). Identification of language-impaired children on the basis of rapid perception and production skills. *Brain and Language*. 25, 314–22.

Tanner, N. M. (1981). *On Becoming Human*. Cambridge: Cambridge University Press.

Tanner, N. M. and Zihlman, A. (1976). Women in evolution part 1: Innovation and selection in human origins. *Signs: Women, Culture and Society*. 1, 585–608.

Tattersall, I. and Matternes, J. H. (2000). Once we were not alone. *Scientific American*. 282, 56–62.

Taylor, C. P. A. and Glenn, N. D. (1976). The utility of education and attractiveness for females' status attainment through marriage. *American Sociological Review*. 41, 484–98.

Taylor, S., Workman, L. and Yeomans, H. (2012). Abnormal patterns of cerebral lateralisation as revealed by the universal chimeric faces task in individuals with autistic disorder. *Laterality: Asymmetries of Body, Brain and Cognition*.17, 428–37.

Tellegan, A., Lykken, D. T., Bouchard, T. J., Wilcox, K. J., Segal, N. L. and Rich, S. (1998). Personality similarity in twins reared apart and together. *Journal of Personality and Social Psychology*. 54, 1031–9.

Thomas, E. M. (1959). *The Harmless People*. New York: Alfred Knopf.

Thorndike, E. L. (1898). Animal intelligence: An experimental study of the associative processes in animals. *Psychological Review, Monograph Supplements* No. 8. New York: Macmillan.

Thornhill, R. and Palmer, C. T. (2000). *A Natural History of Rape: Biological Bases of Sexual Coercion*. Cambridge, MA: MIT Press.

Thurstone, L. L. (1938). Primary mental abilities. *Psychometric Monographs: Vol. 1*. Chicago: Chicago University Press.

Tinbergen, N. (1951). *The Study of Instinct*. Oxford: Oxford University Press.

Tither, J. M. and Ellis, B. J. (2008). Impact of fathers on daughters' age of menarche: A genetically and environmentally controlled sibling study. *Developmental Psychology*. 44, 1409–20.

Toates, F. (2011). *Biological Psychology: An Integrative Approach* (3rd edn). Harlow: Pearson Education.

Tomasello, M. (1999). *The Cultural Origins of Human Cognition*. Cambridge, MA: Harvard University Press.

(2005). Beyond formalities: The case of language acquisition. *Linguistic Review*. 22(2/4), 183.

Tomasello, M., Kruger, A. C. and Ratner, H. H. (1993). Cultural learning. *Behavioral and Brain Sciences*. 16, 495–552.

Tomlin, R. S. (1986). *Basic Word Order: Functional Principles*. London: Croom Helm.

Tooby, J. and Cosmides, L. (1990a). On the universality of human nature and the uniqueness of the individual: The role of genetics and adaptation. *Journal of Personality*. 58, 17–67.

(1990b). The past explains the present – Emotional adaptations and the structure of ancestral environments. *Ethology and Sociobiology*. 11(4–5), 375–424.

(1992). The psychological foundations of culture. In J. H. Barkow, L. Cosmides and J. Tooby (eds.). *The Adapted Mind: Evolutionary Psychology and the Generation of Culture* (19–136). New York: Oxford University Press.

(1997). Evolutionary psychology: A primer. www.psych.ucsb.edu/research/cep/primer.html. Accessed 11 February 2004.

Tooby, J. and DeVore, I. (1987). The reconstruction of hominid behavioural evolution through strategic modelling. In W. G. Kinzey (ed.). *The Evolution of Human Behaviour: Primate Models* (183–237). Albany: State University of New York Press.

Tooby, J., Cosmides, L. and Price, M. (2006). Cognitive adaptations for n-person exchange: The evolutionary roots of organizational behavior. *Managerial and Decision Economics.* 27, 103–29.

Tooley, G. A., Karakis, M., Stokes, M. and Ozannesmith, J. (2006). Generalising the Cinderella Effect to unintentional childhood fatalities. *Evolution and Human Behavior.* 27, 224–30.

Trask, R. L. (1999). *Language: The Basics.* London: Routledge.

Trivers, R. L. (1971). The evolution of reciprocal altruism. *Quarterly Review of Biology.* 46, 35–57.

(1972). Parental investment and sexual selection. In B. Campbell (ed.). *Sexual Selection and the Descent of Man* (139–79). Chicago: Aldine.

(1974). Parent–offspring conflict. *American Zoologist.* 14, 249–64.

(1976). Foreword. In R. Dawkins, *The Selfish Gene.* London: Oxford University Press.

(1985). *Social Evolution.* Menlo Park, CA: Benjamin/Cummings.

Troisi, A. and McGuire, M. T. (2000). Psychotherapy in the context of Darwin psychiatry. In P. Gilbert and K. G. Bailey (eds.). (28–41). *Genes on the Couch: Explorations in Evolutionary Psychotherapy.* London: Routledge.

Tudge, C. (1995). *The Day before Yesterday: Five Million Years of Human History.* London: Jonathan Cape.

Tulving, E. (1972). Episodic and semantic memory. In E. Tulving and W. Donaldson (eds.). *Organization of Memory* (381–403). New York: Academic Press.

Turkheimer, E. (2000). Three laws of behavior genetics and what they mean. *Current Directions in Psychological Science.* 9, 160–4.

Turkheimer, E., Haley, A., Waldron, M., D'Onofrio, B. and Gottesman, I. I. (2003). Socioeconomic status modifies heritability of IQ in young children. *Psychological Science.* 14(6), 623–28.

Turner, A. K. (1994). Genetic and hormonal influences on male violence. In J. Archer (ed.). *Male Violence* (233–52). New York and London: Routledge.

Turner, P. E. and Chao, L. (1999). Prisoner's dilemma in an RNA virus. *Nature.* 398, 441–3.

Tversky, A. and Kahneman, D. (1973). Availability: A heuristic for judging frequency and probability. *Cognitive Psychology.* 5, 207–32.

(1982). Judgments of and by representativeness. In D. Kahneman, P. Slovic and A. Tversky (eds.). *Judgment Under Uncertainty: Heuristics and Biases* (84–100). Cambridge: Cambridge University Press.

Ullman, M. (2001a). The declarative/procedural model of lexicon and grammar. *Journal of Psycholinguistic Research*. 30, 37–69.

  (2001b). The neural basis of lexicon and grammar in first and second language: The declarative/procedural model. *Bilingualism: Language and Cognition*. 4, 105–22.

  (2004). Contributions of memory circuits to language: The declarative/procedural model. *Cognition*. 92, 231–70.

Ullman, M. and Pierpont, R. (2005). Specific language impairment is not specific to language: The procedural deficit hypothesis. *Cortex*. 41, 399–433.

Ustun, T. B. and Chatterji, S. (2001). Global burden of depressive disorders and future projections. In A. Dawson and A. Tylee (eds.). *Depression: Social and Economic Time Bomb* (31–43). London: BMJ Books.

Van der Lely, H. and Ullman, M. (2001). Past tense morphology in specifically language impaired and normally developing children. *Language and Cognitive Processes*. 16, 177–217.

Van Hooff, J. A. R. A. M. (1967). Facial displays of catarrhine monkeys and apes. In D. Morris (ed.). *Primate Ethology* (7–68). London: Weidenfeld and Nicolson.

  (1972). A comparative approach to the phylogeny of laughter and smile. In R. A. Hinde (ed.). *Non-Verbal Communication* (209–41). Cambridge: Cambridge University Press.

Van Valen, L. (1973). A new evolutionary law. *Evolutionary Theory*. 1, 1–30.

Vandell, D. L. (2000). Parents, peer groups, and other socializing influences. *Developmental Psychology*. 36(6), 600–710.

Videan, E. N. and McGrew, W. C. (2002). Bipedality in chimpanzee (Pan troglodytes) and bonobo (Pan paniscus): Testing hypotheses on the evolution of bipedalism. *American Journal of Physical Anthropology*. 118, 184–90.

Voland, E. and Voland, R. (1989). Evolutionary biology and psychiatry: the case for anorexia nervosa. *Ethology and Sociobiology*. 10, 223–40.

Von Frisch, K. (1954). *The Dancing Bees: An Account of the Life and Senses of the Honeybee* (trans. Dora Ilse). London: Methuen.

  (1967). Honeybees: Do they use direction and distance information provided by their dances? *Science*. 158, 1072–6.

Vranas, P. (2000). Gigerenzer's normative critique of Kahneman and Tversky. *Cognition*. 76(3), 179–93.

Waal, F. B. M. de (2001). *Tree of Origin*. Cambridge, MA: Harvard University Press.

Waddington, C. (1975). *The Evolution of an Evolutionist*. Edinburgh: Edinburgh University Press.

Waguespack, N. M. (2005). The organization of male and female labor in foraging societies: Implications for early Paleoindian archaeology. *American Anthropologist*. 107, 666–76.

Wallace, A. R. (1864). The development of human races under the law of natural selection. Reprinted in A. R. Wallace (ed.). *Contributions to the Theory of Natural Selection* (303–31). London: Macmillan (1875).

Wallace, B. (2010). *Getting Darwin wrong: Why Evolutionary Psychology Won't Work*. Exeter: Imprint Academic.

Walsh, A. (1993). Love styles, masculinity/feminity, physical attractiveness and sexual behaviour: A test of evolutionary theory. *Ethology and Sociobiology.* 14, 25–38.

Walton, G., Bower, N. and Bower, T. (1992). Recognition of familiar faces by newborns. *Infant Behaviour and Development.* 15, 265–9.

Ward, T. and Durrant, R. (2011). Evolutionary behavioural science and crime: Aetiological and intervention implications. *Legal and Criminological Psychology.* 16, 193–210.

Washburn, S. L. (1968). *The Study of Human Evolution.* Eugene: Oregon State System of Higher Education.

Washburn, S. L. and Lancaster, J. S. (1968). The evolution of hunting. In R. B. Lee and I. De Vore (eds.). *Man the Hunter* (293–303). Chicago: Aldine.

Wason, P. C. (1966). Reasoning. In B. M. Foss (ed.). *New Horizons in Psychology* (135–51). Harmondsworth: Penguin.

Watling, D., Workman, L. and Bourne, V. (2012). The development of lateralized emotion processing: A review. *Laterality: Asymmetries of Body, Brain and Cognition.* 17, 389–411.

Watson, J. B. (1925). *Behaviorism.* New York: W. W. Norton.

Watson, P. J. and Andrews, P. W. (2002). Toward a revised evolutionary adaptationist analysis of depression: The social navigation hypothesis. *Journal of Affective Disorders.* 72, 1–14.

Waynforth, D. and Dunbar, R. I. M. (1995). Conditional mate choice strategies in humans: evidence from 'lonely hearts' advertisements. *Behaviour.* 132, 755–79.

Waynforth, D., Hurtado, A. M. and Hill, K. (1998). Environmentally contingent reproductive strategies in Ache and Mayan men. *Evolution and Human Behavior.* 19, 369–85.

Webb, B. T., Guo, A.-Y., Maher, B. S., Zhao, Z., van den Oord, E. J., Kendler, K. S. *et al.* (2012). Meta-analyses of genome-wide linkage scans of anxiety-related phenotypes. *European Journal of Human Genetics.* 20, 1078–84.

Wegner, D. (2003). *The Illusion of Conscious Will.* Cambridge, MA: MIT Press.

Weinstein, Y., Bugg, J. M. and Roediger, H. L., III (2008). Can the survival recall advantage be explained by basic memory processes? *Memory and Cognition.* 36, 913–19.

Weissman, M. M. (1985). The epidemiology of anxiety disorders: Rates, risks and familial patters. In H. A. Tuma and J. Masser (eds.). *Anxiety and the Anxiety Disorders* (275–96). Hillsdale, NJ: Lawrence Erlbaum.

Weizembaum, J. (1976). *Computer Power and Human Reason: From Judgment to Calculation.* San Francisco: W. H. Freeman.

Wellman, H. M. (1988). First steps in the child's theorizing about the mind. In J. Astington, P. Harris and D. Olson (eds.). *Developing Theories of Mind* (64–92). Cambridge: Cambridge University Press.

Wells, S. (2003). *The Journey of Man: A Genetic Odyssey.* Princeton, NJ: Princeton University Press.

White, T. D., Suwa, G. and Lovejoy, O. C. (2010). Response to Comment on the Paleobiology and Classification of Ardipithecus ramidus. Science [Internet]. 328:1105-c+. Available from: http://dx.doi.org/10.1126/science.1185462

Whiten, A. (1998). Imitation of the sequential structure of actions by chimpanzees (*Pan troglodytes*). *Journal of Comparative Psychology*. 112, 270–81.

Whiten, A. and Byrne, R. (eds.). (1988). *Machiavellian Intelligence: Social Expertise and the Evolution of Intellect in Monkeys, Apes and Humans*. Oxford: Clarendon Press.

Whiten, A., Goodall, J., McGrew, W. C., Nishida, T., Reynolds, V., Sugiyama, Y. *et al.* (1999). Cultures in chimpanzees. *Nature*. 399, 682–5.

Whiting, B. B. (1965). Sex identity conflict and physical violence: A comparative study. *American Anthropologist*. 67, 123–40.

WHO (2008). *The Global Burden of Disease. 2004 Update*. (Geneva: World Health Organization).

(2012). *WHO Depression Factsheet October 2012*. (Geneva: World Health Organization).

Wildlife Conservation Society (2007, December 11). World's Most Endangered Gorilla Fights Back. *ScienceDaily*. Retrieved 5 September.

Wilkinson, G. S. (1984). Reciprocal food sharing in the vampire bat. *Nature*. 308, 181–4.

Williams, G. C. (1966). *Adaptation and Natural Selection: A Critique of Some Current Evolutionary Thought*. Princeton, NJ: Princeton University Press.

(1975). *Sex and Evolution* (Monographs in Population Biology). Princeton, NJ: Princeton University Press.

Willis, C. and Poulin, R. (2000). Preference of female rats for the odours of non-parasitized males: The smell of good genes. *Folia Parasitol*. 47: 6–10.

Wilson, D. S. (2002). *Darwin's Cathedral: Evolution, Religion and the Nature of Society*. Chicago: University of Chicago Press.

Wilson, D. S. and Sober, E. (1994). Reintroducing group selection to the human behavioral sciences. *Behavioural and Brain Sciences*. 17, 585–654.

Wilson, E. O. (1975). *Sociobiology: The New Synthesis*. Cambridge, MA: Harvard University Press.

(1978). *On Human Nature*. Cambridge, MA: Harvard University Press.

(1994). *Naturalist*. Washington, DC: Island Press.

(1998). *Consilience: The Unity of Knowledge*. New York: Vintage.

(2005). Kin selection as the key to altruism: Its rise and fall. *Social Research*. 72(1), 159–66.

(2012). *The Social Conquest of Earth*. New York: Norton.

Wilson, E. O. and Holldobler, B. (2005). Eusociality: Origin and consequences. *Proceedings of the National Academy of Sciences of the USA*. 102, 13367–71.

Wimmer, H. and Hartl, M. (1991). Against the Cartesian view on mind: Young children's difficulty with own false belief. *British Journal of Developmental Psychology*. 9, 125–38.

Wimmer, H. and Perner, J. (1983). Beliefs about beliefs: Representation and constraining function of wrong beliefs in young children's understanding of deception. *Cognition*. 13, 103–28.

Wimsatt, W. (1999). Genes, memes, and cultural heredity. *Biology and Philosophy*. 14, 279–310.

Wittiger, L. and Sunderland-Groves, J. (2007). Tool use during display behavior in wild cross river gorillas. *American Journal of Primatology*. 69, 1307.

Woolfenden, G. E. and Fitzpatrick, J. W. (1984). *The Florida Scrub Jay: Demography of a Cooperative-Breeding Bird*. Princeton, NJ: Princeton University Press.

Workman, L. (2007) Why aren't we all the same? The evolutionary psychology of individual differences. *Psychology Review*. 13(1), 7–10.

(2014). *Charles Darwin: Shaper of Evolutionary Thinking*. Basingstoke: Palgrave Macmillan.

Workman, L., Adam, J. and Andrew, R. J. (2000). Opportunities for visual experience which might allow imprinting in chicks raised by broody hens. *Behaviour*. 137, 221–31.

Workman, L., Chilvers, L., Yeomans, H. and Taylor, S. (2006). Development of cerebral lateralization for emotional processing of chimeric faces in children aged 5 to 11. *Laterality*. 11, 493–507.

Workman, L., Peters, S. and Taylor, S. (2000). Lateralisation of perceptual processing of pro- and anti-social emotions displayed in chimeric faces. *Laterality*. 5, 237–49.

Wrangham, R. W. (1987). Evolution of social structure. In B. B. Smuts, D. L. Cheney, R. M. Seyfarth, R. W. Wrangham and T. T. Struhsaker (eds.). *Primate Societies* (282–98). Chicago: University of Chicago Press.

(1993). The evolution of sexuality in chimpanzees and bonobos. *Human Nature*. 4, 47–79.

(2009). *Catching Fire: How Cooking Made Us Human*. New York: Basic Books.

Wrangham, R. and Carmody, R. N. (2010). Human adaptation to the control of fire. *Evolutionary Anthropology: Issues, News and Reviews*. 19, 187–99.

Wright, R. (1994). *The Moral Animal*. London: Abacus.

(2001). *Nonzero: History, Evolution & Human Cooperation*. London: Abacus.

(January, 2007). Robert Wright: The logic of non-zero-sum progress. [video file]. Retrieved from www.ted.com/talks/robert_wright_on_optimism.html

Wynn, K. (1993). An evolved capacity for number. In D. Cummins and C. Allen (eds.). *The Evolution of Mind* (51–106). Oxford: Oxford University Press.

Wynn, T. (1998). Did *Homo erectus* speak? *Cambridge Archaeological Journal*. 8(1), 78–81.

Wynne-Edwards, V. C. (1962). *Animal Dispersion in Relation to Social Behaviour*. Edinburgh: Oliver and Boyd.

Yotova, V., Lefebvre, J. F., Moreau, C., Gbeha, E., Hovhannesyan, K., Bourgeois, S. *et al.* (2011). An X-linked haplotype of Neanderthal origin is present among all non-African populations. *Molecular Biology and Evolution*. 28(7), 1957–62.

Yuill, N. (1984). Young children's coordination of motive and outcome in judgements of satisfaction and morality. *British Journal of Developmental Psychology*. 2, 73–81.

Zahavi, A. (1975). Mate selection: A selection for a handicap. *Journal of Theoretical Biology*. 53, 205–14.

(2003). Indirect selection and individual selection in socio-biology: My personal views on theories of social behaviour. *Animal Behaviour*. 65, 859–63.

Zahn-Waxler, C. and Radke-Yarrow, M. (1982). The development of altruism: Alternative research strategies. In N. Eisenberg (ed.). *The Development of Prosocial Behavior* (109–37). New York: Academic Press.

Zahn-Waxler, C., Radke-Yarrow, M., Wagner, E. and Chapman, M. (1992). Development of concern for others. *Developmental Psychology*. 28, 126–36.

Zuk, M. (1992). The role of parasites in sexual selection: Current evidence and future directions. *Advances in the Study of Behavior*. 21, 39–68.

Index

Note: page numbers in bold indicate items in boxes, page numbers in italics indicate illustrations and tables

Evolutionary Psychology

THIRD EDITION

Written for undergraduate psychology students, and assuming little knowledge of evolutionary science, the third edition of this classic textbook provides an essential introduction to evolutionary psychology. Fully updated with the latest research and new learning features, it provides a thought-provoking overview of evolution and illuminates the evolutionary foundation of many of the broader topics taught in psychology departments. The text retains its balanced and critical evaluation of hypotheses and full coverage of the fundamental topics required for undergraduates. This new edition includes more material on the social and reproductive behaviour of non-human primates, morality, cognition, development and culture as well as new photos, illustrations, text boxes and thought questions to support student learning. Nearly 300 online multiple choice questions complete the student questioning package. This new material complements the classic features of this text, which include suggestions for further reading, chapter summaries, a glossary and two-colour figures throughout.

Lance Workman is Honorary Visiting Professor of Psychology at the University of South Wales.

Will Reader is a Senior Lecturer in Psychology at Sheffield Hallam University.